Introduction to e-Business Systems

Enterprise and e-Business Systems

Electronic Commerce Systems

Decision Support Systems

Continued on back endsheet

MANAGEMENT INFORMATION SYSTEMS

Managing Information Technology in the Business Enterprise

InformationTechnology

At **McGraw-Hill Higher Education**, we publish instructional materials targeted at the higher education market. In an effort to expand the tools of higher learning, we publish texts, lab manuals, study guides, testing materials, software, and multimedia products.

At **McGraw-Hill/Irwin** (a division of McGraw-Hill Higher Education), we realize technology will continue to create new mediums for professors and students to manage resources and communicate information with one another. We strive to provide the most flexible and complete teaching and learning tools available and offer solutions to the changing world of teaching and learning.

McGraw-Hill/Irwin is dedicated to providing the tools necessary for today's instructors and students to navigate the world of Information Technology successfully.

Seminar Series—McGraw-Hill/Irwin's Technology Connection seminar series, offered across the country every year, demonstrates the latest technology products and encourages collaboration among teaching professionals.

Osborne/McGraw-Hill—A division of the McGraw-Hill Companies known for its best-selling Internet titles, *Harley Hahn's Internet & Web Yellow Pages* and the *Internet Complete Reference*, offers an additional resource for certification and has strategic publishing relationships with corporations such as Oracle Corporation, Corel Corporation, and America Online. For more information, visit Osborne at www.osborne.com.

Digital Solutions—McGraw-Hill/Irwin is committed to publishing Digital Solutions. Taking your course online doesn't have to be a solitary venture. Nor does it have to be a difficult one. We offer several solutions, which will let you enjoy all the benefits of having course material online. For more information, visit www.mhhe.com/digital_solutions.

Packaging Options—For more about our discount options, contact your local McGraw-Hill/Irwin sales representative at 1-800-338-3987, or visit our website at www.mhhe.com/it.

MANAGEMENT INFORMATION SYSTEMS

Managing Information Technology in the Business Enterprise

Sixth Edition

James A. O'Brien

College of Business Administration
Northern Arizona University

Boston   Burr Ridge, IL   Dubuque, IA   Madison, WI   New York   San Francisco   St. Louis
Bangkok   Bogotá   Caracas   Kuala Lumpur   Lisbon   London   Madrid   Mexico City
Milan   Montreal   New Delhi   Santiago   Seoul   Singapore   Sydney   Taipei   Toronto

MANAGEMENT INFORMATION SYSTEMS:
MANAGING INFORMATION TECHNOLOGY IN THE BUSINESS ENTERPRISE
Published by McGraw-Hill/Irwin, a business unit of The McGraw-Hill Companies, Inc., 1221
Avenue of the Americas, New York, NY 10020. Copyright © 2004, 2002, 1999, 1996, 1993, 1990
by The McGraw-Hill Companies, Inc. All rights reserved. No part of this publication may be
reproduced or distributed in any form or by any means, or stored in a database or retrieval
system, without the prior written consent of The McGraw-Hill Companies, Inc., including, but
not limited to, in any network or other electronic storage or transmission, or broadcast for
distance learning.

Some ancillaries, including electronic and print components, may not be available to customers
outside the United States.

This book is printed on acid-free paper.

domestic   1 2 3 4 5 6 7 8 9 0 DOW/DOW 0 9 8 7 6 5 4 3
international   1 2 3 4 5 6 7 8 9 0 DOW/DOW 0 9 8 7 6 5 4 3

ISBN 0-07-282311-9

Publisher: *George Werthman*
Senior sponsoring editor: *Paul Duchan*
Developmental editor: *Kelly L. Delso*
Manager, Marketing and Sales: *Paul Murphy*
Media producer: *Greg Bates*
Project manager: *Caterine R. Schultz*
Senior production supervisor: *Rose Hepburn*
Coordinator freelance design: *Mary L. Christianson*
Photo research coordinator: *Judy Kausal*
Photo researcher: *Judy Mason*
Senior supplement producer: *Rose M. Range*
Senior digital content specialist: *Brian Nacik*
Cover design: *©GettyImages/Stephen Hunt*
Typeface: *10/12 Janson Text*
Compositor: *The GTS Companies*
Printer: *R. R. Donnelley*

Library of Congress Cataloging-in-Publication Data

O'Brien, James A.
    Management information systems : managing information technology in the business
enterprise / James A. O'Brien—6th ed.
        p. cm.
    Includes bibliographical references and index.
    ISBN 0-07-282311-9 (alk. paper) — ISBN 0-07-121498-4 (international : alk. paper)
    1. Electronic commerce. 2. Information technology—Management. 3. Management
information systems. 4. Business—Data processing. I. Title.
HF5548.32.O27 2004
658.4'038—dc21

                                                                    2002045535

INTERNATIONAL EDITION ISBN 0-07-121498-4
Copyright © 2004. Exclusive rights by The McGraw-Hill Companies, Inc. for manufacture and
export. This book cannot be re-exported from the country to which it is sold by McGraw-Hill.
The International Edition is not available in North America.

www.mhhe.com

To your love, happiness, and success

James A. O'Brien is an adjunct professor of Computer Information Systems in the College of Business Administration at Northern Arizona University. He completed his undergraduate studies at the University of Hawaii and Gonzaga University and earned an M.S. and Ph.D. in Business Administration from the University of Oregon. He has been professor and coordinator of the CIS area at Northern Arizona University, professor of Finance and Management Information Systems and chairman of the Department of Management at Eastern Washington University, and a visiting professor at the University of Alberta, the University of Hawaii, and Central Washington University.

Dr. O'Brien's business experience includes working in the Marketing Management Program of the IBM Corporation, as well as serving as a financial analyst for the General Electric Company. He is a graduate of General Electric's Financial Management Program. He has also served as an information systems consultant to several banks and computer services firms.

Jim's research interests lie in developing and testing basic conceptual frameworks used in information systems development and management. He has written eight books, including several that have been published in multiple editions, as well as in Chinese, Dutch, French, Japanese, or Spanish translations. He has also contributed to the field of information systems through the publication of many articles in business and academic journals, as well as through his participation in academic and industry associations in the field of information systems.

Preface

A Business and Managerial Perspective

This new Sixth Edition is designed for business students who are or who will soon become business professionals in the fast changing business world of today. The goal of this text is to help business students learn how to use and manage information technologies to revitalize business processes, improve business decision making, and gain competitive advantage. Thus it places a major emphasis on up-to-date coverage of the essential role of Internet technologies in providing a platform for business, commerce, and collaboration processes among all business stakeholders in today's networked enterprises and global markets.

This is the business and managerial perspective that this text brings to the study of information systems. Of course, as in all my texts, this edition:

- Loads the text with real world cases, examples, and exercises about real people and companies in the business world.
- Organizes the text around a simple five-area framework that emphasizes the IS knowledge a business professional needs to know.
- Places a major emphasis on the strategic role of information technology in providing business professionals with tools and resources for managing business operations, supporting decision making, enabling enterprise collaboration, and gaining competitive advantage.

Audience

This text is designed for use in undergraduate or introductory MBA courses in Management Information Systems that are required in many Business Administration or Management programs as part of the common body of knowledge for all business majors. Thus, this edition treats the subject area known as Information Systems (IS), Management Information Systems (MIS), or Computer Information Systems (CIS) as a major functional area of business that is as important to management education as are the areas of accounting, finance, operations management, marketing, and human resource management.

Key Features

The new Sixth Edition has been updated with many new topics and real world examples and reorganized to provide students and instructors with a superb teaching-learning resource about the business uses and managerial challenges of information technology.

All New Real World Cases and Examples

This text provides all new up-to-date real world case studies. These are not fictional stories, but actual situations faced by business firms and other organizations as reported in current business and IS periodicals. This includes five real world case studies in each chapter that apply specifically to that chapter's contents.

In addition, each chapter contains several application exercises, including two hands-on spreadsheet or database software assignments and new Internet-based real world assignments in most chapters. Also, many new highlighted in-text real world examples have been added to illustrate concepts in every chapter. The purpose of this variety of learning and assignment options is to give instructors and students many opportunities to apply each chapter's material to real world situations.

All New! Real World Cases are provided for every chapter. These cases relate concepts in the book to real companies.

---

182 ● Module III / Business Applications

SECTION I Customer Relationship Management: The Business Focus

Introduction

Today, customers are in charge. It is easier than ever for customers to comparison shop and, with a click of the mouse, to switch companies. As a result, customer relationships have become a company's most valued asset. These relationships are worth more than the company's products, stores, factories, web addresses, and even employees. Every company's strategy should address how to find and retain the most profitable customers possible [8].

The primary business value of customer relationships today is indisputable. That's why we emphasized in Chapter 2 that becoming a *customer-focused business* was one of the top business strategies that can be supported by information technology. Thus, many companies are implementing **customer relationship management** (CRM) business initiatives and information systems as part of a customer-focused or *customer-centric* strategy to improve their chances for success in today's competitive business environment. In this section, we will explore basic CRM concepts and technologies, as well as examples of the benefits and challenges faced by companies that have implemented CRM systems as part of their customer-focused business strategy. Let's start with a real world example.

Analyzing Mitsubishi Motor Sales

Read the Real World Case on Mitsubishi Motor Sales on the next page. We can learn a lot about the many ways companies are implementing customer relationship management systems. See Figure 6.1.

Mitsubishi Motor Sales realized their business lacked a customer focus and decided to change that through a customer relationship management initiative. The CRM project involved acquiring and installing the hardware, software, network, and

FIGURE 6.1
Greg O'Neill is executive vice president and general manager of Mitsubishi Motor Sales of America and led the implementation of their customer relationship management initiative.

Source: Mark Robert Halper.

Chapter 6 / Enterprise e-Business Systems ● 183

REAL WORLD CASE 1 Mitsubishi Motor Sales: Implementing Customer Relationship Management Systems

Until the late 1990s, Mitsubishi Motor Sales of America Inc. (www.mitsucars.com) was only about cars, and its approach to retail customer service reflected that. There were more than 18 toll-free customer service numbers that callers had to navigate to find information on topics ranging from financing to sales to repairs. "We were fragmented in our approach, and we clearly lacked a customer focus," says Greg O'Neill, executive vice president and general manager.

Mitsubishi decided to change that. In the spring of 1999, as part of a companywide shift to an increased focus on customers, executives challenged the call center to provide "one voice and one set of ears for the customer," says CIO Tony Romero. That was the beginning of a continuing drive toward improved customer service through a customer relationship management (CRM) initiative that would eventually engage multiple departments and 18 vendors.

Today, Mitsubishi has one call center and an outsourced service provider that handles the most basic calls. The cost per call has decreased by about two-thirds, and that savings alone paid for the system in 18 months, according to Rich Donnelson, director of customer relations. The system saves agents time and uncertainty and enabled the call center to handle 38 percent more call volume in 2001 than in 2000, with an even staffing level. Meanwhile, the company's customer satisfaction rate rose by 8 percent, according to a survey by J. D. Power and Associates.

Mitsubishi's call center project team included members from its sales, marketing, finance, and IT departments, all of which contributed resources as needed. Early on, the team members established some rules of the road. First, they would selectively choose best-of-breed CRM software components, not the integrated CRM suites that seemed intent on force-fitting Mitsubishi's needs into fixed product offerings. But that required a constant struggle to keep 18 vendors heading in the same direction.

The team members also decided to implement changes slowly, adding a technology only when all employees were using the last one implemented. This approach allowed call center agents to get comfortable with the new technology over time. To accommodate the deliberate, modular approach, all products had to pass the "three S" test: Is it simple? Does it satisfy? Is it scalable? "If we couldn't answer yes to all three, we didn't do it," says Greg Stahl, Mitsubishi's director of advertising.

The journey began in earnest in June 1999, when Mitsubishi chose to outsource its most basic level of customer calls to Baltimore-based Sitel Corp. Within two months, Mitsubishi's 18 toll-free customer numbers and the multiple call centers behind them were consolidated, and call center software from Siebel Systems was implemented. Also, as part of the companywide customer focus, a new customer-centric database was consolidated in-house the next year. The database

became the engine powering the call center, but unfortunately, dirty data were a major stumbling block. The project stalled for months as the data were cleansed and updated.

In early 2001, a digital phone switch from Avaya Inc. was installed that allowed flexible skills-based call routing. Callers to the single toll-free number were routed based on menu choices. About half the callers got the information they needed from an interactive voice response unit, which can answer fairly sophisticated queries without live contact. Simple calls went to Sitel, and the rest were routed to call center agents with the appropriate skills. In March 2001, graphical user interface upgrades put 11 screens' worth of customer information on one screen of call center agents. And Smart Scripts workflow software from Siebel provided agents with decision-tree scripts and automated customer correspondence.

In May 2001, Mitsubishi managers began listening to outsourced service calls, and they could see agents' screens with Avaya IP Agent software. The next month, the company started using workforce management software from Blue Pumpkin Software to hourly forecast call center coverage. Then NiceLog software from Nice Systems was installed to record agents' voice and screen activity for quality assurance and training.

Aside from happier customers, the benefits to call center employees include career growth and higher pay. Previously, agents in separate call centers handled specific areas: accounts, vehicles, titles, or retailer queries. Now the silos are gone and agents can learn new skills in multiple areas, greatly increasing call center flexibility. The workforce management software schedules training time during lags, and agents who learn multiple skills earn more money. Call center turnover, which has traditionally been more than 20 percent, was about 7 percent last year.

O'Neill says the executive team members regularly listen in on service calls to get a feel for customer concerns, and they act on what they hear. "That bubble up of information has driven more early marketing decisions and made us more effective earlier on than I could have ever thought," O'Neill says. "That's been a huge dividend."

Case Study Questions

1. What are the key application components of Mitsubishi's CRM system? What is the business purpose of each of them?

2. What are the benefits to a business and its customers of a CRM system like Mitsubishi's?

3. Do you approve of Mitsubishi's approach to acquiring and installing its CRM system? Why or why not?

Source: Adapted from "Driven to Better Service," *Computerworld*, July 8, 2002, pp. 40–41. Reprinted with permission from *Computerworld*.

Key Features

Coverage of e-Business and e-Commerce

Recently coined, yet already clichéd, the expression "e-business is business" speaks the truth . . .

Contrary to popular opinion, e-business is not synonymous with e-commerce. E-business is much broader in scope, going beyond transactions to signify use of the Net, in combination with other network technologies and forms of electronic communication, to enable any type of business activity [1].

Today, businesses of all sizes and types are using Internet technologies to enable all kinds of business activities. That's what e-business really is. The new Sixth Edition recognizes that Internet-enabled business processes are becoming so fundamentally pervasive in business that the term "e-business" is becoming redundant in many instances. Therefore this edition has significantly reduced its use of that term, while concentrating the e-business coverage that today's business students need into two chapters on e-business applications and one chapter on e-commerce.

This edition refocuses its coverage of e-business and e-commerce applications and issues with a restructured introductory chapter on functional and cross-functional e-business systems (Chapter 5), a new chapter on enterprise e-business systems (Chapter 6), and a highly praised introductory chapter on electronic commerce (Chapter 7). The text material and real world cases and examples in these chapters provide students with a solid e-business foundation for their studies and work in business.

Strategic, International, and Ethical Coverage

This edition also contains substantial text material and real world cases and examples reflecting strategic issues and uses of information technology for competitive advantage (Chapter 2), ethical and security issues and challenges (Chapter 11), and international and global business issues and practices (Chapter 12). These chapters demonstrate the strategic and ethical challenges of managing information technology for competitive advantage in today's dynamic global business markets.

The book profiles companies like Cisco Systems to emphasize the continued importance of the Internet on business strategy.

Cisco Systems: e-Business and e-Commerce Leader

Top telecom manufacturer Cisco Systems uses 36 manufacturing plants, of which it owns but two. One of them is downstairs from the San Jose office of Randy Pond, Senior Vice President for Operations. The rest belong to top contract manufacturers like Jabil Circuit and Solectron. It's "virtual manufacturing," Pond says, made possible by a "suite of Internet-based tools and processes that lets me manage an extended enterprise I don't own as if I do own it."

The key, says Pond, is "real-time data on a real-time basis so my partners know what goes on in my business every single day." As much as possible, Cisco and a partner work with the same stream of e-business information, doubling its value. Every day Cisco compiles its inventory, forecast for each model, order backlog, and thirteen weeks of daily data about parts and subassemblies; every day its partner compiles data on in-process inventory, cycle time by process step, optimal lot size, and yield; every night computers combine the Internet data streams into a river of information; every morning everyone knows what to build that day.

Cisco works the other end of the process—e-commerce—the same way. Eighty-seven percent of Cisco's sales are entered directly from the Net and available instantaneously. Except for commodity parts, Cisco's e-business supply chain is as visible and as live as a televised football game. Validation and testing are also Internet-based. Autotest, a homemade tool, tests machines as they are built and won't print a packing label for a machine unless every test has been done and passed. Another tool checks a customer's order as he enters it, to make sure that he hasn't asked for incompatible gear.

The benefits of real-time e-business add up to about $400 million a year, by Pond's reckoning, plus up to a $1 billion saving in capital costs—from equipment Cisco doesn't carry on its books, improved utilization by suppliers, and minimal inventory [18].

Key Features

An Information Systems Framework

O'Brien uses a five-arch IS framework to reduce the complexity of MIS. On each chapter opener the appropriate area is highlighted depending on what is being covered in that chapter.

This text reduces the complexity of a course in management information systems by using a conceptual framework that organizes the knowledge needed by business students into five major areas (see Figure 1):

- Foundation Concepts. Fundamental business information systems concepts including trends, components, and roles of information systems (Chapter 1) and competitive advantage concepts and applications (Chapter 2). Other behavioral, managerial, and technical concepts are presented where appropriate in selected chapters.
- Information Technologies. Includes major concepts, developments, and managerial issues involved in telecommunications network and data resource management technologies (Chapters 3 and 4). A review of computer hardware (Chapter 13) and computer software (Chapter 14) technologies is provided in Module VI. Other technologies used in business information systems are discussed where appropriate in selected chapters.
- Business Applications. How businesses use Internet and other information technologies to support their business processes, e-business and e-commerce initiatives, and business decision making (Chapters 5, 6, 7, and 8).
- Development Processes. Developing and implementing business/IT strategies and systems using several strategic planning and application development approaches (Chapters 9 and 10).
- Management Challenges. The challenges of business/IT technologies and strategies, including security and ethical challenges and global IT management (discussed in many chapters, but emphasized in Chapters 11 and 12).

Modular Structure of the Text

The text is organized into modules that reflect the five major areas of the framework for information systems knowledge mentioned earlier. See Figure 2. Also, each chapter is organized into two distinct sections. This is done to avoid proliferation of chapters, as well as to provide better conceptual organization of the text and each chapter. This organization increases instructor flexibility in assigning course material since it structures the text into modular levels (i.e., modules, chapters, and sections) while reducing the number of chapters that need to be covered.

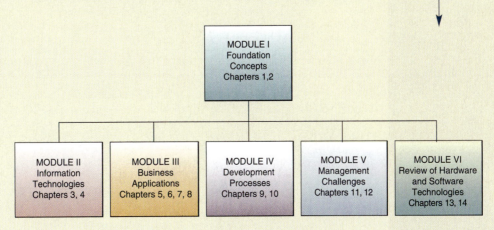

Key Features

FIGURE 5.26
The QuickBooks Solutions Marketplace provides online application software services from Intuit and their many business partners.

Source: Courtesy of Intuit.

a. Check out the QuickBooks Solutions Marketplace at www.marketplace.intuit.com. What is the business value of the software and services they offer?

b. Link to the websites of several of the other online application service providers in the QuickBooks Marketplace. Evaluate the business value of two of these more specialized ASPs.

c. Would you use or recommend any of the online application services to a small business? Why or why not?

2. eWork Exchange and eLance.com: Online Job Matching and Auctions

Web Many opportunities await those who troll the big job boards, the free-agent sites, the auction services where applicants bid for projects, and the niche sites for specialized jobs and skills. Examples of top job matching and auction sites are eWork Exchange and eLance.com.

eWork Exchange (www.eworkexchange.com). No more sifting through irrelevant search results: Fill out a list of your skills and let eWork Exchange's proprietary technology find the most suitable projects for you—no bidding required.

eLance.com (www.elance.com). This global auction marketplace covers more than just IT jobs; it runs the gamut from astrology and medicine to corporate work and cooking projects. Register a description of your services or go straight to browsing

the listings of open projects—and then start bidding. A feedback section lets both employers and freelancers rate one another.

a. Check out eWork Exchange and eLance, and other online job sites on the Web.

b. Evaluate several sites based on their ease of use and their value to job seekers and employers.

c. Which website was your favorite? Why?

3. Job Search Database

DB Visit websites like Monster.com and others mentioned in the chapter to gather information about available jobs. Look up and record the relevant data for at least 10 current job openings that are of interest to you or that meet criteria provided by your instructor.

a. Create a database table to store key characteristics of jobs. Include all of the job characteristics shown in the list that follows as fields in your table, but feel free to add additional fields of interest to you. If data are not available for some fields (such as, salary range) for a particular job, leave that field blank.

b. Write queries that will enable you to retrieve (a) just those jobs in a specified location, and (b) just those jobs in a specified job category.

c. Create a report that groups jobs by Location and sorts jobs within each group by Job category.

Each chapter starts with Chapter Highlights and Learning Objectives and ends with a Summary, Key Terms and Concepts, a Review Quiz tied directly to the Key Terms and Concepts, Discussion Questions, and Application Exercises. Real World Cases are placed at the beginning of the two sections of each chapter (with a brief analysis), and at the end of each chapter, to help students understand the chapter material in the context of examples from the real world of business.

Application Exercises

Each chapter contains application exercises in the end-of-chapter material. These exercises allow students to use Access in order to acquire some hands-on database experience. Data files are provided for these exercises.

Changes to This Edition

Besides providing all new Real World Cases, the Sixth Edition adds a new chapter on Enterprise e-Business Systems and makes other major changes to the Fifth Edition's coverage, many of them suggested by a review panel of 22 professors, that update, reorganize, and refocus its content. Highlights of changes in this edition include:

- Introductory coverage of managerial challenges in Chapter 1 and competitive strategy issues in Chapter 2 has been simplified by reducing the number of topics covered in these early foundation chapters.

- At the suggestion of reviewers, coverage of data resource management (Chapter 3) and telecommunications and networks (Chapter 4) has been significantly restructured and revised and included earlier in the text, so that they provide a technology foundations module that precedes the chapters in the business applications module that follows.

- The former chapter on the internetworked e-business enterprise has been dropped, and its coverage of the Internet, intranets, and extranets revised and moved to the chapter on telecommunications and networks. Coverage of enterprise collaboration systems has been significantly condensed and moved to the introductory chapter on e-business applications.

- Coverage of e-business applications has been revised, restructured, and expanded into two chapters at the suggestion of reviewers. Thus, Chapter 5, Introduction to e-Business Systems, introduces the functional foundations of e-business applications in Section I, followed by introductory coverage of cross-functional enterprise applications in Section II. Chapter 6, Enterprise e-Business Systems, is a new chapter that provides greater coverage of the business value, challenges, and trends in customer relationship management, enterprise resource planning, and supply chain management needed by business students today.

- Coverage of computer hardware (Chapter 13) and computer software (Chapter 14) remains in a final optional review module on hardware and software technologies that can be assigned at the option of the instructor.

- All other chapters have been updated with new text material, and most in-text real world examples that illustrate major topics throughout the text have been replaced with more current examples. In addition, most of the photos and software screen shots in the text have been replaced with updated content.

A **presentation manager Instructor CD-ROM** is available to adopters and offers the following resources for course presentation and management:

- An Instructor's Resource Manual, authored by Margaret Trenholm-Edmunds of Mount Allison University, contains suggestions for using the book in courses of varying lengths, detailed chapter outlines with teaching suggestions for use in lectures, and answers to all end-of-chapter questions, application exercises, and problems and case study questions.
- A Test Bank, authored by Queen Booker of the University of Arizona, contains true-false, multiple choice, fill-in-the-blank, and short essay questions.
- Computerized/Network Testing with Brownstone Diploma software is fully networkable for LAN test administration; tests also can be printed for standard paper delivery or posted to a website for student access.
- Slide shows in Microsoft PowerPoint, authored by Lanny Wilke of Montana State University, are available for each chapter to support classroom discussion of chapter concepts and real world cases.
- Data/solutions files, authored by James N. Morgan of Northern Arizona University, for the database and spreadsheet application exercises in the text are included.
- Video clips are available that highlight how specific companies apply and use information technology.

The McGraw-Hill/Irwin Information Systems Video Library contains 2002 and 2003 video updates on numerous companies demonstrating use of a variety of IT areas like intranets, multimedia, or computer-based training systems, and concepts like client/server computing and business process reengineering. This library is available free to adopters. For further information, visit www.mhhe.com/business/mis/videos or contact your local McGraw-Hill/Irwin sales representative. A video guide for all updates is available on the O'Brien, 6/e website at www.mhhe.com/obrien.

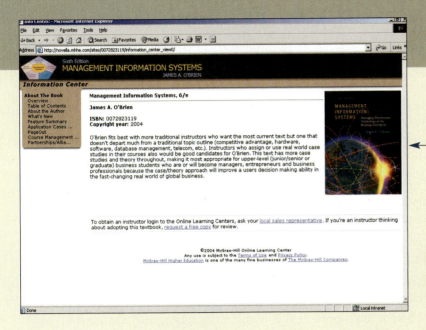

Digital Solutions— Website/OLC

The book's website at http://www.mhhe.com/obrien provides resources for instructors and students using the text. The Online Learning Center (OLC) builds on the book's pedagogy and features with self-assessment quizzes, extra material not found in the text, Web links, and other resources for students and instructors.

Digital Solutions—PageOut

Our Course Website Development Center, PageOut, offers a syllabus page, website address, Online Learning Center content, online quizzing, gradebook, discussion forum, and student Web page creation.

Create a custom course website with **PageOut**, free to instructors using a McGraw-Hill textbook.

To learn more, contact your McGraw-Hill publisher's representative or visit www.mhhe.com/solutions.

Packaging Options

The McGraw-Hill/Irwin *Advantage*, O'Leary, and Laudon Interactive computing series are collections of software application manuals and interactive computer-based training products for Microsoft Office. In addition, we offer several paperback Internet literacy books or CDs, perfect for introducing the World Wide Web, e-mail, and Web page design to students. These texts and CDs are available for discounted packaging options with any McGraw-Hill/Irwin title. For more about our discount options, contact your local McGraw-Hill/Irwin sales representative or visit our website at www.mhhe.com/it.

SimNet MIS

Animate the concepts you cover with SimNet MIS. This computer-based training program reinforces concepts using a variety of methods.

- Teach Me mode introduces the skill using text, graphics, and interactivity.
- Show Me mode uses narration and animation to illustrate how the skill is used.
- Let Me Try mode gets students involved with practice in a non-threatening simulated environment.

Concepts covered include:

Types of Information Systems
Using IS for Competitive/Strategic Advantage (with focus on the Value Chain)
Data Warehousing
Data Mining (please note this topic will be written for the SimNet Computer Concepts program, and there is no added cost for this task)
Decision Support Systems
Artificial Intelligence and Expert Systems (please note this topic will be written for the SimNet Computer concepts program, and there is no added cost for this task)
Online Transaction Processing
Types of E-commerce
The Systems Development Life Cycle: Overview (version 1)
The Systems Development Life Cycle: Overview (version 2)
The Systems Development Life Cycle: Overview (version 3)
The Systems Development Life Cycle: Planning
The Systems Development Life Cycle: Scoping
The Systems Development Life Cycle: Analysis
The Systems Development Life Cycle: Alternatives
The Systems Development Life Cycle: Selection
The Systems Development Life Cycle: Design
The Systems Development Life Cycle: Implementation
The Systems Development Life Cycle: Maintenance
Excel
Access

In addition, a software casebook—*Application Cases in MIS: Using Spreadsheet and Database Software and the Internet*, fourth edition, by James N. Morgan of Northern Arizona University—is available to supplement the hands-on exercises in this edition. This optional casebook contains an extensive number of hands-on cases, many of which include a suggested approach for solving each case with the Internet, spreadsheet, or database management software packages to develop solutions for realistic business problems.

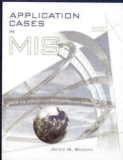

In addition to application exercises, the Morgan *Application Cases* book can be packaged with the O'Brien text. Jim Morgan also authors the application exercises in the end-of-chapter material, so his casebook complements the text nicely and offers more in-depth coverage of how databases work.

Acknowledgments

I wish to acknowledge the assistance of the following 22 professors whose constructive criticism and suggestions helped invaluably in shaping the form and content of the Sixth Edition:

Joseph Aguirre, *University of Phoenix*
Noushnin Ashrafi, *University of Massachusetts–Boston*
David Bell, *Central Washington University*
Warren Boe, *University of Iowa*
Gurpreet Dhillon, *University of Nevada–Las Vegas*
Sean B. Eom, *Southeast Missouri State University*
Dale Foster, *Memorial University of Newfoundland*
Robert Fulkerth, *Golden Gate University*
Ronald J. Kizior, *Loyola University–Chicago*
Andrew G. Kotulic, *Kent State University*
Elizabeth E. Little, *University of Central Oklahoma*
Stephen L. Loy, *Eastern Kentucky University*

Joan B. Lumpkin, *Wright State University*
Daniel McUsic, MBA Program, *Jones International University*
Pam Milstead, *Louisiana Tech University*
George Nezlek, *Loyola University–Chicago*
Leonard Presby, *William Paterson University*
Young Ryu, *University of Texas–Dallas*
Ronald D. Schwartz, *Florida Atlantic University*
Judith Symonds, *The Open Polytechnic of New Zealand*
Len Turi, *New York University*
Jennifer J. Williams, *University of Southern Indiana*

I would also like to thank the following professors for their contributions to previous editions of this text:

Harry C. Benham, *Montana State University*
Karen E. Bland-Collins, *Morgan State University*
Ranjit Bose, *University of New Mexico–Albuquerque*
Doris Duncan, *California State University–Hayward*
Yvonne A. Greenwood, *Penn. State University–Berks-Lehigh Valley*
Babita Gupta, *California State University–Monterey*
Philip Johnson, *College of William and Mary*
Michelle L. Kaarst-Brown, *University of Richmond*
Douglas M. Kline, *Sam Houston State University*
Martha Leva, *Penn. State University–Abington*
Randy Maule, *California State University–Monterey*
Murli Nagasundaram, *Boise State University*

Margaret H. Neumann, *Governors State University*
Rene F. Reitsma, *St. Francis Xavier University*
Erik Rolland, *University of California–Riverside*
Dolly Samson, *Weber State University*
Tod Sedbrooke, *University of Northern Colorado*
Richard S. Segall, *Arkansas State University*
Gerhard Steinke, *Seattle Pacific University*
Dana V. Tesone, *University of Hawaii and Nova Southeastern University*
E. Lamar Traylor, *Our Lady of the Lake in Houston*
Craig VanLengen, *Northern Arizona University*
H. Joseph Wen, *New Jersey Institute of Technology*
Karen L. Williams, *University of Texas–San Antonio*

My thanks also go to James N. Morgan of Northern Arizona University, who is the author of the software casebook that can be used with this text and who developed most of the hands-on Application Exercises in the text, as well as the data/solutions files on the Instructor CD-ROM. I am also grateful to Margaret Trenholm-Edmunds of Mount Allison University, the author of the Instructor's Resource Manual, for her revision of this valuable teaching resource.

Much credit should go to several individuals who played significant roles in this project. Thus, special thanks go to the editorial and production team at Irwin/ McGraw-Hill, especially Rick Williamson, senior sponsoring editor; Paul Ducham, senior sponsoring editor; Kelly Delso, developmental editor; Paul Murphy, senior marketing manager; Cathy Schultz, project manager; and Mary Christianson, designer. Their ideas and hard work were invaluable contributions to the successful completion of the project. Thanks also to Kay Pinto, whose word processing skills helped me meet my manuscript deadlines. The contributions of many authors, publishers, and firms in the computer industry that contributed case material, ideas, illustrations, and photographs used in this text are also thankfully acknowledged.

Acknowledging the Real World of Business

The unique contribution of the hundreds of business firms and other computer-using organizations that are the subject of the real world cases, exercises, and examples in this text is gratefully acknowledged. The real-life situations faced by these firms and organizations provide the readers of this text with a valuable demonstration of the benefits and limitations of using the Internet and other information technologies to enable electronic business and commerce, and enterprise communications and collaboration in support of the business processes, managerial decision making, and strategic advantage of the e-business enterprise.

James A. O'Brien

BRIEF CONTENTS

MODULE IV Development Processes

MODULE V Management Challenges

MODULE VI Review of Hardware and Software Technologies

CONTENTS

MODULE I Foundation Concepts

MODULE II Information Technologies

CHAPTER 3

Data Resource Management   69

CHAPTER 4

Telecommunications and Networks   101

MODULE III   Business Applications

CHAPTER 5

Introduction to e-Business Systems   143

CHAPTER 6

Enterprise e-Business
Systems   181

CHAPTER 7

Electronic Commerce
Systems   217

CHAPTER 8

Decision Support Systems   257

MODULE IV   Development Processes

CHAPTER 9

Developing Business/IT Strategies   309

CHAPTER 10

Developing Business/IT Solutions   341

MODULE V   Management Challenges

CHAPTER 11

Security and Ethical Challenges   379

CHAPTER 12

Enterprise and Global Management of Information Technology   421

MODULE VI   Review of Hardware and Software Technologies

MANAGEMENT INFORMATION SYSTEMS

Managing Information Technology in the Business Enterprise

MODULE I

FOUNDATION CONCEPTS

Why study information systems? Why do businesses need information technology? What do you need to know about the use and management of information technologies in business? The introductory chapters of Module I are designed to answer these fundamental questions about the role of information systems in business.

- **Chapter 1: Foundations of Information Systems in Business** presents an overview of the five basic areas of information systems knowledge needed by business professionals, including the conceptual system components and major types of information systems.

- **Chapter 2: Competing with Information Technology** introduces fundamental concepts of competitive advantage through information technology, and illustrates major strategic applications of information systems.

After completing these chapters, you can move on to study chapters on information technologies (Module II), business applications (Module III), development processes (Module IV), and the management challenges of information systems (Module V). An optional review of hardware and software technologies (Module VI) is also provided.

CHAPTER 1

FOUNDATIONS OF INFORMATION SYSTEMS IN BUSINESS

Chapter Highlights

Section I
Foundation Concepts: Information Systems and Technologies

Why Information Systems Are Important

The Real World of Information Systems

Real World Case: BellSouth Corporation: The Business Payback of Information Technology

What You Need to Know

An IS Framework for Business Professionals

System Concepts: A Foundation

Components of an Information System

Information System Resources

Information System Activities

Recognizing Information Systems

Section II
Foundation Concepts: Business Applications, Development, and Management

The Fundamental Roles of IS Applications in Business

Real World Case: Royal Caribbean International: Renewing and Realigning IT with Business

e-Business in Business

Trends in Information Systems

Types of Information Systems

Managerial Challenges of Information Technology

Success and Failure with IT

Developing IS Solutions

Challenges of Ethics and IT

Challenges of IT Careers

Learning Objectives

After reading and studying this chapter, you should be able to:

1. Explain why knowledge of information systems is important for business professionals and identify five areas of information systems knowledge they need.

2. Give examples to illustrate how the business applications of information systems can support a firm's business processes, managerial decision making, and strategies for competitive advantage.

3. Provide examples of the components of real world information systems. Illustrate that in an information system, people use hardware, software, data, and networks as resources to perform input, processing, output, storage, and control activities that transform data resources into information products.

4. Provide examples of several major types of information systems from your experiences with business organizations in the real world.

5. Identify several challenges that a business manager might face in managing the successful and ethical development and use of information technology in a business.

SECTION I

Foundation Concepts: Information Systems and Technologies

Why Information Systems Are Important

The blending of Internet technologies and traditional business concerns is impacting all industries and is really the latest phase in the ongoing evolution of business. All companies need to update their business infrastructures and change the way they work to respond more immediately to customer needs [12].

Why study information systems and information technology? That's the same as asking why anyone should study accounting, finance, operations management, marketing, human resource management, or any other major business function. Information systems and technologies (including e-business and e-commerce technologies and applications) have become a vital component of successful businesses and organizations. They thus constitute an essential field of study in business administration and management. That's why most business majors must take a course in information systems. Since you probably intend to be a manager, entrepreneur, or business professional, it is just as important to have a basic understanding of information systems as it is to understand any other functional area in business.

The Real World of Information Systems

Let's take a moment to bring the real world into our discussion of the importance of information systems (IS) and information technology (IT). Read the Real World Case on BellSouth Corporation on the next page. Then let's analyze it together. See Figure 1.1.

Analyzing BellSouth Corp.

We can learn a lot about the importance of information technology and information systems from the Real World Case of BellSouth Corp.

This case dramatizes just one of the countless examples of the business challenges and opportunities created by the growth of the Internet and the World Wide Web.

BellSouth has moved many customer-facing business processes to the Web to help support its strategic business goals. In this case, top management approved the

FIGURE 1.1
CIO Fran Dramis says IT investments have to directly support BellSouth's business goals.

Source: Ann States/Corbis Saba

BellSouth Corporation: The Business Payback of Information Technology

Ask 10 IT leaders how they measure payback on their companies' technology investments, and you're likely to get back at least 10 different answers. But there's also a good chance you'll hear a common theme in all of their replies. Regardless of how they measure payback or the financial formulas they might apply, they are under excruciating pressure to show bigger and better returns faster. Many are responding to the demand for a return on investment by homing in on one or two critical IT projects that directly support and add value to their companies' primary business goals. In other words, they're following the money.

"At the corporate level, our revenue strategy is to broadband-enable customers in the wireline business and get into long distance in the nine states we service, so our IT prioritizations are subject to those two things," says Fran Dramis, CIO and chief e-commerce officer at BellSouth Corp. (www.bellsouthcorp.com) in Atlanta, a $28 billion telecommunications company serving nine states in the Southeast.

BellSouth measures the return on its technology projects strictly by the value they add to those business goals. For example, a recent success story is its new broadband ordering system, which significantly cut the overall business operations budget by lowering per-subscriber ordering costs by more than 50 percent.

In February of 2001, BellSouth had a choice: hobble forward on their traditional customer ordering system or invest in a new one that would better support thousands of new broadband subscribers—a key customer segment in the company's revenue strategy. It may sound like a no-brainer, but given the post-dot-com capital constraints plaguing the entire telecommunications industry, it was anything but an easy decision. But Dramis convinced the executive team to invest in the new project and buy into his strategic business vision for IT. "What Fran really does is set the strategic direction," says Lori Groves, the project leader on the ADSL ordering system project.

It took nine months to implement a customized version of Oracle Corporation's customer relationship management software, which was integrated with proprietary ordering features in other BellSouth systems. This gave new subscribers the ability to use BellSouth's website to order and even self-install the software they would need to get up and running on the new ADSL (Asymmetric Digital Subscriber Line) "FastAccess" high-speed Internet service.

The result: By year's end, BellSouth's broadband customer base had grown from 200,000 to 660,000, with 90 percent of customers using the self-service option. The effort has also resulted in a 50 percent decrease in per-subscriber ordering costs because the new system supports more customers at a lower cost than the previous one and captures more customer information. That, in turn, works to reduce the number of help desk calls that have to be fielded and helps to identify new services and capabilities that customers want. For example, one new service that the new system helped identify is a telecommuting billing option, which lets companies aggregate billing for ADSL services they provide to remote workers.

"All of this allowed us to increase customers at fairly negligible systems costs," says Dramis. "And these are all things that help the growth activities of the business." For proof, Dramis points out that just a few years ago, the company's annual ADSL revenue generated no more than "a couple of million dollars." This year, Bell South's FastAccess Internet Service is a half-billion-dollar business and was ranked first in the 2002 J.D. Power and Associates residential Internet customer satisfaction study of high-speed Internet service providers.

Dramis says a key first step to implementing this follow-the-money ROI approach for IT was creating the concept of a "technology transformation road map" for BellSouth. Developed by business unit presidents, the road map identifies and prioritizes "leverageable" systems—defined as those that the businesses need to run and enhance their revenue generating operations, and therefore of highest priority for IT development. "Nonleverageable" systems, by contrast, are more traditional "legacy" systems earmarked for retirement in the near future.

Previously, decisions regarding technology investments had generally been pushed down to a level too low in the company to have a direct impact on strategic business goals. "I'm turning the pyramid upside down," he says. Now, for example, investments in legacy or nonleverageable systems must be approved at the most senior management level by Dramis and two other group presidents. "What I'm trying to do is raise IT up to a senior level so we can understand the business impact of our technologies," Dramis explains.

Case Study Questions

1. How well is IT supporting the business goals of BellSouth? Explain.
2. Is BellSouth's technology transfer map a good way to determine IT investment priorities? Why or why not?
3. What else could BellSouth do to guarantee the strategic business value of potential IT investment projects? Visit their website for ideas. Defend your proposals.

Source: Adapted from Julia King, "ROI: Make It Bigger, Better, Faster," *Computerworld*, January 1, 2002, p. 20; and "What Have You Done for Me Lately?" *Computerworld*, March 4, 2002, p. 29. Reprinted with permission of *Computerworld*.

development of a new web-based customer ordering system for ADSL Internet service proposed by CIO Fran Dramis to support their goal of significantly increasing revenues by a major expansion of broadband services among their customers. The new ordering system for BellSouth's award-winning FastAccess Internet Service has helped fuel a 330 percent increase in broadband customers. The new system is also credited with significantly lowering ordering costs, capturing more customer information, reducing customer help-desk requests, and identifying potential new services. Dramis also credits the identification of this successful project to the technology road map developed by senior business unit presidents for evaluating and identifying IT projects that directly support BellSouth's business goals.

Thus, information technologies, including Internet-based information systems, are playing a vital and expanding role in business. Information technology can help all kinds of businesses improve the efficiency and effectiveness of their business processes, managerial decision making, and workgroup collaboration and thus strengthen their competitive positions in a rapidly changing marketplace. This is true whether information technology is used to support product development teams, customer support processes, interactive electronic commerce transactions, or any other business activity. Internet-based information technologies and systems are fast becoming a necessary ingredient for business success in today's dynamic global environment.

What You Need to Know

There is no longer any distinction between an IT project and a business initiative. IT at Marriott is a key component of the products and services that we provide to our customers and guests at our properties. As such, there's very little that goes on within the company that either I personally or one of my top executives is not involved in [13].

Those are the words of Carl Wilson, executive vice-president and CIO of Marriott International. So even top executives and managers must learn how to apply information systems and technologies to their unique business situations. In fact, business firms depend on all of their managers and employees to help them manage their use of information technologies. So the important question for any business professional or manager is: What do you need to know in order to help manage the hardware, software, data, and network resources of your business, so they are used for the strategic success of your company?

An IS Framework for Business Professionals

The field of information systems encompasses many complex technologies, abstract behavioral concepts, and specialized applications in countless business and nonbusiness areas. As a manager or business professional you do not have to absorb all of this knowledge. Figure 1.2 illustrates a useful conceptual framework that organizes the knowledge presented in this text and outlines what you need to know about information systems. It emphasizes that you should concentrate your efforts in five areas of knowledge:

- **Foundation Concepts.** Fundamental behavioral, technical, business, and managerial concepts about the components and roles of information systems. Examples include basic information system concepts derived from general systems theory, or competitive strategy concepts used to develop business applications of information technology for competitive advantage. Chapters 1 and 2 and other chapters of the text support this area of knowledge.

- **Information Technologies.** Major concepts, developments, and management issues in information technology—that is, hardware, software, networks, data resource management, and many Internet-based technologies. Chapters 3 and 4 provide coverage of data resource management and communications network topics, while Chapters 13 and 14 provide an optional review of hardware and software technologies.

FIGURE 1.2

This framework outlines the major areas of information systems knowledge needed by business professionals.

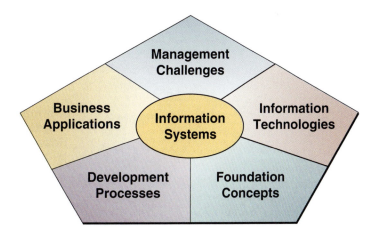

- **Business Applications.** The major uses of information systems for the operations, management, and competitive advantage of a business, including electronic business, commerce, collaboration and decision making using the Internet, intranets, and extranets are covered in Chapters 5 through 8.

- **Development Processes.** How business professionals and information specialists plan, develop, and implement information systems to meet business opportunities using several application development approaches. Chapters 9 and 10 help you gain such knowledge as well as an appreciation of the business issues involved.

- **Management Challenges.** The challenges of effectively and ethically managing information technologies, strategies, and security at the end user, enterprise, and global levels of a business. Chapters 11 and 12 specifically cover these topics, but all of the chapters in the text emphasize the managerial challenges of information technology in today's global business environment.

In this chapter, we will discuss some of the foundation concepts of information systems and introduce other topics that give you an overview of the five areas of IS knowledge covered in this text.

What Is an Information System?

Let's begin with a simple definition of an information system, which we will expand in the next few pages. An **information system** can be any organized combination of people, hardware, software, communications networks, and data resources that collects, transforms, and disseminates information in an organization. See Figure 1.3. People have relied on information systems to communicate with each other using a variety of physical devices *(hardware)*, information processing instructions and procedures *(software)*, communications channels *(networks)*, and stored data *(data resources)* since the dawn of civilization.

Information Technologies

Business professionals rely on many types of information systems that use a variety of **information technologies.** For example, some information systems use simple manual (paper-and-pencil) hardware devices and informal (word-of-mouth) communications channels. However, in this text, we will concentrate on *computer-based information systems* that use computer hardware and software, the Internet and other telecommunications networks, computer-based data resource management techniques, and many other computer-based information technologies to transform data resources into an endless variety of information products for consumers and business professionals. Now let's look at some of the basic foundation concepts of information systems and technologies.

FIGURE 1.3

Information systems rely on people, and a variety of hardware, software, data, and communications network technologies as resources to collect, transform, and disseminate information in an organization.

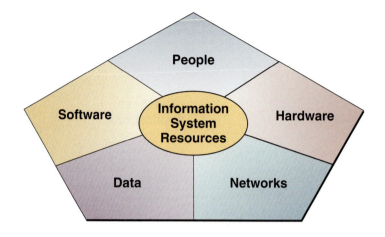

System Concepts: A Foundation

System concepts underlie the field of information systems. That's why we need to discuss how generic system concepts apply to business firms and the components and activities of information systems. Understanding system concepts will help you understand many other concepts in the technology, applications, development, and management of information systems that we will cover in this text. For example, system concepts help you understand:

- **Technology.** That computer networks are systems of information processing components that use a variety of hardware, software, data management, and telecommunications network technologies.
- **Applications.** That electronic business and commerce applications involve interconnected business information systems.
- **Development.** That developing ways to use information technology in business includes designing the basic components of information systems.
- **Management.** That managing information technology emphasizes the quality, strategic business value, and security of an organization's information systems.

What Is a System?

What is a *system*? A system can be most simply defined as a group of interrelated or interacting elements forming a unified whole. Many examples of systems can be found in the physical and biological sciences, in modern technology, and in human society. Thus, we can talk of the physical system of the sun and its planets, the biological system of the human body, the technological system of an oil refinery, and the socioeconomic system of a business organization.

However, the following generic system concept provides a more appropriate foundation concept for the field of information systems: a **system** is a group of interrelated components working together toward a common goal by accepting inputs and producing outputs in an organized transformation process.

Such a system (sometimes called a *dynamic* system) has three basic interacting components or functions:

- **Input** involves capturing and assembling elements that enter the system to be processed. For example, raw materials, energy, data, and human effort must be secured and organized for processing.
- **Processing** involves transformation processes that convert input into output. Examples are a manufacturing process, the human breathing process, or mathematical calculations.
- **Output** involves transferring elements that have been produced by a transformation process to their ultimate destination. For example, finished

products, human services, and management information must be transmitted to their human users.

Example. A manufacturing system accepts raw materials as input and produces finished goods as output. An information system is a system that accepts resources (data) as input and processes them into products (information) as output. A business organization is a system where economic resources are transformed by various business processes into goods and services.

Feedback and Control

The system concept becomes even more useful by including two additional components: feedback and control. A system with feedback and control components is sometimes called a *cybernetic* system, that is, a self-monitoring, self-regulating system.

- **Feedback** is data about the performance of a system. For example, data about sales performance is feedback to a sales manager.

- **Control** involves monitoring and evaluating feedback to determine whether a system is moving toward the achievement of its goal. The control function then makes necessary adjustments to a system's input and processing components to ensure that it produces proper output. For example, a sales manager exercises control when reassigning salespersons to new sales territories after evaluating feedback about their sales performance.

Example. A familiar example of a self-monitoring, self-regulating system is the thermostat-controlled heating system found in many homes; it automatically monitors and regulates itself to maintain a desired temperature. Another example is the human body, which can be regarded as a cybernetic system that automatically monitors and adjusts many of its functions, such as temperature, heartbeat, and breathing. A business also has many control activities. For example, computers may monitor and control manufacturing processes, accounting procedures help control financial systems, data entry displays provide control of data entry activities, and sales quotas and sales bonuses attempt to control sales performance.

Other System Characteristics

Figure 1.4 uses a business organization to illustrate the fundamental components of a system, as well as several other system characteristics. Note that a system does not exist in a vacuum, rather, it exists and functions in an *environment* containing other systems. If a system is one of the components of a larger system, it is a *subsystem*, and the larger system is its environment.

Several systems may share the same environment. Some of these systems may be connected to one another by means of a shared boundary, or *interface*. Figure 1.4 also illustrates the concept of an *open system*; that is, a system that interacts with other systems in its environment. In this diagram, the system exchanges inputs and outputs with its environment. Thus, we could say that it is connected to its environment by input and output interfaces. Finally, a system that has the ability to change itself or its environment in order to survive is an *adaptive system*.

Example. Organizations such as businesses and government agencies are good examples of the systems in society, which is their environment. Society contains a multitude of such systems, including individuals and their social, political, and economic institutions. Organizations themselves consist of many subsystems, such as departments, divisions, process teams, and other workgroups. Organizations are examples of open systems because they interface and interact with other systems in their environment. Finally, organizations are examples of adaptive systems, since they can modify themselves to meet the demands of a changing environment.

FIGURE 1.4

A business is an example of an organizational system where economic resources (input) are transformed by various business processes (processing) into goods and services (output). Information systems provide information (feedback) on the operations of the system to management for the direction and maintenance of the system (control) as it exchanges inputs and outputs with its environment.

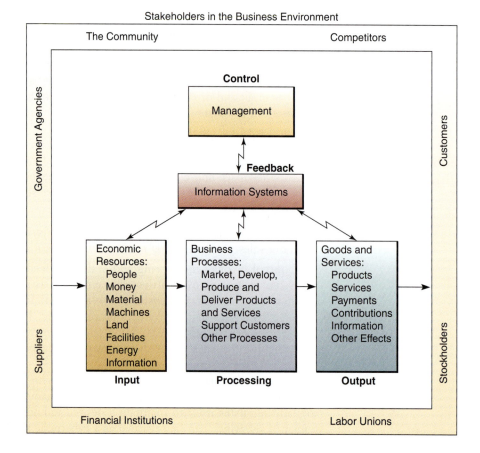

Components of an Information System

We are now ready to apply the system concepts we have learned to help us better understand how an information system works. For example, we have said that an information system is a system that accepts data resources as input and processes them into information products as output. How does an information system accomplish this? What system components and activities are involved?

Figure 1.5 illustrates an **information system model** that expresses a fundamental conceptual framework for the major components and activities of information systems. An information system depends on the resources of people (end users and IS specialists), hardware (machines and media), software (programs and procedures), data (data and knowledge bases), and networks (communications media and network support) to perform input, processing, output, storage, and control activities that convert data resources into information products.

This information system model highlights the relationships among the components and activities of information systems. It provides a framework that emphasizes four major concepts that can be applied to all types of information systems:

- People, hardware, software, data, and networks are the five basic resources of information systems.

- People resources include end users and IS specialists, hardware resources consist of machines and media, software resources include both programs and procedures, data resources can include data and knowledge bases, and network resources include communications media and networks.

- Data resources are transformed by information processing activities into a variety of information products for end users.

- Information processing consists of the system activities of input, processing, output, storage, and control.

FIGURE 1.5

The components of an information system. All information systems use people, hardware, software, data, and network resources to perform input, processing, output, storage, and control activities that transform data resources into information products.

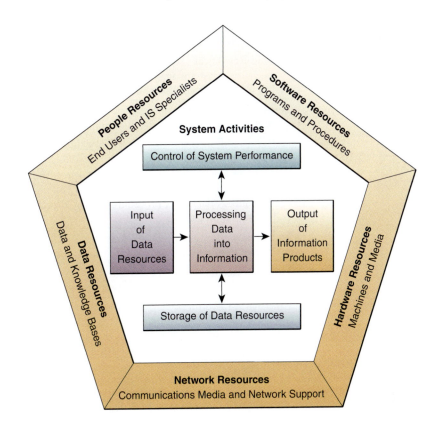

Information System Resources

Our basic IS model shows that an information system consists of five major resources: people, hardware, software, data, and networks. Let's briefly discuss several basic concepts and examples of the roles these resources play as the fundamental components of information systems. You should be able to recognize these five components at work in any type of information system you encounter in the real world. Figure 1.6 outlines several examples of typical information system resources and products.

People Resources

People are required for the operation of all information systems. These people resources include end users and IS specialists.

- **End users** (also called users or clients) are people who use an information system or the information it produces. They can be customers, salespersons, engineers, clerks, accountants, or managers. Most of us are information system end users. And most end users in business are **knowledge workers,** that is, people who spend most of their time communicating and collaborating in teams and workgroups and creating, using, and distributing information.

- **IS specialists** are people who develop and operate information systems. They include systems analysts, software developers, system operators, and other managerial, technical, and clerical IS personnel. Briefly, systems analysts design information systems based on the information requirements of end users, software developers create computer programs based on the specifications of systems analysts, and system operators help to monitor and operate large computer systems and networks.

Hardware Resources

The concept of **hardware resources** includes all physical devices and materials used in information processing. Specifically, it includes not only **machines,** such as computers and other equipment, but also all data **media,** that is, tangible objects on which data are recorded, from sheets of paper to magnetic or optical disks. Examples of hardware in computer-based information systems are:

FIGURE 1.6

Examples of information system resources and products.

Information Systems Resources and Products
People Resources   Specialists—systems analysts, software developers, system operators.   End Users—anyone else who uses information systems.
Hardware Resources   Machines—computers, video monitors, magnetic disk drives, printers, optical scanners.   Media—floppy disks, magnetic tape, optical disks, plastic cards, paper forms.
Software Resources   Programs—operating system programs, spreadsheet programs, word processing programs, payroll programs.   Procedures—data entry procedures, error correction procedures, paycheck distribution procedures.
Data Resources   Product descriptions, customer records, employee files, inventory databases.
Network Resources   Communications media, communications processors, network access and control software.
Information Products   Management reports and business documents using text and graphics displays, audio responses, and paper forms.

- **Computer systems,** which consist of central processing units containing microprocessors, and a variety of interconnected peripheral devices. Examples are hand-held, laptop, or desktop microcomputer systems, midrange computer systems, and large mainframe computer systems.

- **Computer peripherals,** which are devices such as a keyboard or electronic mouse for input of data and commands, a video screen or printer for output of information, and magnetic or optical disks for storage of data resources.

Software Resources

The concept of **software resources** includes all sets of information processing instructions. This generic concept of software includes not only the sets of operating instructions called **programs,** which direct and control computer hardware, but also the sets of information processing instructions called **procedures** that people need.

It is important to understand that even information systems that don't use computers have a software resource component. This is true even for the information systems of ancient times, or the manual and machine-supported information systems still used in the world today. They all require software resources in the form of information processing instructions and procedures in order to properly capture, process, and disseminate information to their users.

The following are examples of software resources:

- **System software,** such as an operating system program, which controls and supports the operations of a computer system.

- **Application software,** which are programs that direct processing for a particular use of computers by end users. Examples are a sales analysis program, a payroll program, and a word processing program.

- **Procedures,** which are operating instructions for the people who will use an information system. Examples are instructions for filling out a paper form or using a software package.

Data Resources

Data are more than the raw material of information systems. The concept of data resources has been broadened by managers and information systems professionals. They realize that data constitute valuable organizational resources. Thus, you should view data as **data resources** that must be managed effectively to benefit all end users in an organization.

Data can take many forms, including traditional alphanumeric data, composed of numbers and alphabetical and other characters that describe business transactions and other events and entities. Text data, consisting of sentences and paragraphs used in written communications; image data, such as graphic shapes and figures; and audio data, the human voice and other sounds, are also important forms of data.

The data resources of information systems are typically organized, stored, and accessed by a variety of data resource management technologies into:

- Databases that hold processed and organized data.
- Knowledge bases that hold knowledge in a variety of forms such as facts, rules, and case examples about successful business practices.

For example, data about sales transactions may be accumulated, processed, and stored in a web-enabled sales database that can be accessed for sales analysis reports by managers and marketing professionals. Knowledge bases are used by knowledge management systems and expert systems to share knowledge or give expert advice on specific subjects. We will explore these concepts further in later chapters.

Data versus Information. The word **data** is the plural of *datum*, though data commonly represents both singular and plural forms. Data are raw facts or observations, typically about physical phenomena or business transactions. For example, a spacecraft launch or the sale of an automobile would generate a lot of data describing those events. More specifically, data are objective measurements of the *attributes* (the characteristics) of *entities* (such as people, places, things, and events).

Example. Business transactions such as buying a car or an airline ticket can produce a lot of data. Just think of the hundreds of facts needed to describe the characteristics of the car you want and its financing, or the details for even the simplest airline reservation.

People often use the terms *data* and *information* interchangeably. However, it is better to view data as raw material resources that are processed into finished information products. Then we can define **information** as data that have been converted into a meaningful and useful context for specific end users. Thus, data are usually subjected to a value-added process (we call *data processing* or *information processing*) where (1) its form is aggregated, manipulated, and organized; (2) its content is analyzed and evaluated; and (3) it is placed in a proper context for a human user. So you should view information as processed data placed in a context that gives it value for specific end users.

Example. Names, quantities, and dollar amounts recorded on sales forms represent data about sales transactions. However, a sales manager may not regard these as information. Only after such facts are properly organized and manipulated can meaningful sales information be furnished, specifying, for example, the amount of sales by product type, sales territory, or salesperson.

Network Resources

Telecommunications technologies and networks like the Internet, intranets, and extranets have become essential to the successful electronic business and commerce operations of all types of organizations and their computer-based information systems. Telecommunications networks consist of computers, communications processors, and other devices interconnected by communications media and controlled by communications software. The concept of **network resources** emphasizes that communications technologies and networks are a fundamental resource component of all information systems. Network resources include:

- **Communications media.** Examples include twisted-pair wire, coaxial cable, and fiber-optic cable; and microwave, cellular, and satellite wireless technologies.
- **Network support.** This generic category emphasizes that many hardware, software, and data technologies are needed to support the operation and use of a communications network. Examples include communications processors such as modems and internetwork processors, and communications control software such as network operating systems and Internet browser packages.

Information System Activities

Let's take a closer look now at each of the basic **information processing** (or **data processing**) activities that occur in information systems. You should be able to recognize input, processing, output, storage, and control activities taking place in any information system you are studying. Figure 1.7 lists business examples that illustrate each of these information system activities.

Input of Data Resources

Data about business transactions and other events must be captured and prepared for processing by the **input** activity. Input typically takes the form of *data entry* activities such as recording and editing. End users typically enter data directly into a computer system, or record data about transactions on some type of physical medium such as a paper form. This usually includes a variety of editing activities to ensure that they have recorded data correctly. Once entered, data may be transferred onto a machine-readable medium such as a magnetic disk until needed for processing.

For example, data about sales transactions can be recorded on source documents such as paper sales order forms. (A **source document** is the original formal record of a transaction.) Alternately, salespersons can capture sales data using computer keyboards or optical scanning devices; they are visually prompted to enter data correctly by video displays. This provides them with a more convenient and efficient **user interface,** that is, methods of end user input and output with a computer system. Methods such as optical scanning and displays of menus, prompts, and fill-in-the-blanks formats make it easier for end users to enter data correctly into an information system.

Processing of Data into Information

Data are typically subjected to **processing** activities such as calculating, comparing, sorting, classifying, and summarizing. These activities organize, analyze, and manipulate data, thus converting them into information for end users. The quality of any data stored in an information system must also be maintained by a continual process of correcting and updating activities.

FIGURE 1.7

Business examples of the basic activities of information systems.

Information System Activities
● **Input.** Optical scanning of bar-coded tags on merchandise.
● **Processing.** Calculating employee pay, taxes, and other payroll deductions.
● **Output.** Producing reports and displays about sales performance.
● **Storage.** Maintaining records on customers, employees, and products.
● **Control.** Generating audible signals to indicate proper entry of sales data.

Example. Data received about a purchase can be (1) *added* to a running total of sales results, (2) *compared* to a standard to determine eligibility for a sales discount, (3) *sorted* in numerical order based on product identification numbers, (4) *classified* into product categories (such as food and nonfood items), (5) *summarized* to provide a sales manager with information about various product categories, and, finally, (6) used to *update* sales records.

Output of Information Products

Information in various forms is transmitted to end users and made available to them in the **output** activity. The goal of information systems is the production of appropriate **information products** for end users. Common information products include messages, reports, forms, and graphic images, which may be provided by video displays, audio responses, paper products, and multimedia. We routinely use the information provided by these products as we work in organizations and live in society. For example, a sales manager may view a video display to check on the performance of a salesperson, accept a computer-produced voice message by telephone, and receive a printout of monthly sales results.

Storage of Data Resources

Storage is a basic system component of information systems. Storage is the information system activity in which data and information are retained in an organized manner for later use. For example, just as written text material is organized into words, sentences, paragraphs, and documents, stored data are commonly organized into a variety of data elements and databases. This facilitates its later use in processing or its retrieval as output when needed by users of a system. Such data elements and databases are discussed further in Chapter 3 on data resource management.

Control of System Performance

An important information system activity is the **control** of its performance. An information system should produce feedback about its input, processing, output, and storage activities. This feedback must be monitored and evaluated to determine if the system is meeting established performance standards. Then appropriate system activities must be adjusted so that proper information products are produced for end users.

For example, a manager may discover that subtotals of sales amounts in a sales report do not add up to total sales. This might mean that data entry or processing procedures need to be corrected. Then changes would have to be made to ensure that all sales transactions would be properly captured and processed by a sales information system.

Recognizing Information Systems

As a business professional, you should be able to recognize the fundamental components of information systems you encounter in the real world. This means that you should be able to identify:

- The people, hardware, software, data, and network resources they use.
- The types of information products they produce.
- The way they perform input, processing, output, storage, and control activities.

This kind of understanding will help you be a better user, developer, and manager of information systems. And that, as we have pointed out in this chapter, is important to your future success as a manager, entrepreneur, or professional in business.

Analyzing BellSouth's Information Systems

Refer back to the Real World Case on BellSouth Corp. on page 5. Now let's try to recognize or visualize the resources used, activities performed, and information products produced by some of their information systems.

IS Resources. People resources include end users like BellSouth's online customers and employees, and IS specialists like CIO Fran Dramis and project leader Lori

Groves. Hardware resources include the thousands of PCs, servers, and other computers that BellSouth and its customers must be using. Software resources include everything from web browsers, operating systems, and e-commerce website software to Oracle's customer relationship management system and other proprietary Bell-South business software. You can just visualize all of the communications media and network support components that are part of the network resources that BellSouth would need to support the e-business and e-commerce activities of such a large telecommunications company. Finally, BellSouth undoubtedly has vast data resources in the form of computer-accessible databases of data about their customers, employees, services, and other necessary business information.

Information Products. The information products we can most easily visualize are the displays on customer and employee networked PCs that provide information about and support the provision of BellSouth's services, such as you can find by visiting their websites at www.bellsouth.com and www.bellsouthcorp.com.

IS Activities. Some of the input activities we can visualize are the input of website navigation clicks, e-commerce and e-business data entries and selections, and online collaboration queries and responses made by customers, suppliers, and employees. Processing activities are accomplished whenever any of BellSouth's computers executes the programs that are part of their e-business and e-commerce software resources. Output activities primarily involve the display or printing of the information products we identified earlier. Storage activities take place whenever business data is stored and managed in the files and databases on the disk drives and other storage media of BellSouth's computer systems. Finally, we can visualize several control activities, including the use of passwords and other security codes by customers, suppliers, and employees for entry into BellSouth's e-business and e-commerce websites, and access of their databases and knowledge bases.

So you see, analyzing an information system to identify its basic components is not a difficult task. Just identify the resources that the information system uses, the information processing activities it performs, and the information products it produces. Then you will be better able to identify ways to improve these components, and thus the performance of the information system itself. That's a goal that every business professional should strive to attain.

SECTION II Foundation Concepts: Business Applications, Development, and Management

The Fundamental Roles of IS Applications in Business

There are three fundamental reasons for all business applications of information technology. They are found in the three vital roles that information systems can perform for a business enterprise.

- Support of its business processes and operations.
- Support of decision making by its employees and managers.
- Support of its strategies for competitive advantage.

We will introduce these roles and applications in this chapter, and cover them in more detail later. The strategic applications of information systems for competitive advantage will be covered in Chapter 2. Business applications of information technology for electronic business operations, electronic commerce, enterprise collaboration, and decision making will be discussed in Chapters 5, 6, 7, and 8.

Analyzing Royal Caribbean International

Read the Real World Case on Royal Caribbean International on the next page. We can learn a lot about the challenges of revitalizing and redirecting information technology in a company from this example. See Figure 1.8.

The IT group at Royal Caribbean was disorganized and ineffective in supporting the needs of the business, and had thus lost the respect of the rest of the company. New CIO Tom Murphy has revitalized the IT group by stressing and demonstrating integrity, respect, thorough communication, accountability, teamwork, and a service- and customer-oriented focus. Murphy broke up special-interest IT factions by requiring cross-teams of specialists on development projects and improved performance by establishing specific performance measures for managers, whom he freed from other chores to concentrate on managing their people. Murphy also personally sold the board of directors on a $180 million project to overhaul the entire

FIGURE 1.8

CIO Tom Murphy (center) turned around a failing IT operation at Royal Caribbean and realigned it to support the business needs and goals of the company.

Source: Jennie Zeiner

Royal Caribbean International: Renewing and Realigning IT with Business

When CIO Tom Murphy came to Royal Caribbean International (www.royalcaribbean.com) in April 1999, the company's IT workforce was as diverse as they come. Employees hailed from more than 40 countries, and nearly half of them were minorities or women. But IT management was foundering. "I want to be honest with you," President and Chief Operating Officer Jack Williams told Murphy. "IT is screwed up."

"It was a very traditional IT organization: command and control. Everything was locked down; everything was about not spending money," Murphy recalls. It was a traditional '70s data processing shop," Murphy says. Cost-cutting was the mantra. Voice mail was new, and the cruise operator was only dabbling with e-mail. There was no IT strategy for the future and no respect from the business side for IT.

Adam Goldstein, senior vice president of total guest satisfaction, was "vitriolic in his disdain for all things IT," Murphy recalls, and he wasn't alone. "To a person, the business had absolutely lost confidence" in the company's IT department, he says. "No matter what we did, it was never right," recalls IT Director Percy Lopez.

Internally, the IT group was made up of factions, and morale was terrible. Word around the department was that two opposing "mafias"—Cuban and African American—controlled the data center and the networking group. "Each department in IT did its thing and didn't want any involvement with the others," says IT manager Dennis Wright. "It was an emotionless, beaten-down group," says Murphy, who had come from well-oiled, homogeneous IT machines at Marriott International and Omni Hotels.

Almost three years later, everything has changed. "Silos," or special-interest technical fiefdoms, and their resulting resentments have disappeared, and the IT group has become phenomenally successful. Murphy personally sold the board of directors on a $180 million effort called Project Leapfrog aimed at pulling Royal Caribbean into the 21st century. Since then, the firm's IT group has been overhauling the entire IT infrastructure. This effort includes a PeopleSoft enterprise resource planning implementation, a revamped public website, and additional automation to facilitate shipboard and shore excursion activities.

These days, the IT department is respected by the business and proud. "I never doubted that he would transform the organization," Williams says. "But Murphy did it quicker than I thought he would."

Murphy, 39, insists that there's no magic formula for getting a diverse group to pull together. "All I do is try to create the atmosphere and the environment that allows people to be successful," he says. Murphy acknowledges that there's one more thing that contributes to harmony in a heterogeneous workplace. "Integrity establishes a foundation for everything that you do," he says. "If you don't have that, you have nothing."

The folks at Royal Caribbean watch this play out at work every day. Here's their account of how Murphy manages diversity.

Communication. "He communicates all the time, everything to everybody, and that prevents silos," says Leigh Baker, manager of shipboard applications delivery. "Silos still arise around projects or products, but as long as he's communicating the same message and the same goals to everyone evenly, then no one can use information as a weapon."

Silo-busting. "Before Tom, there was more 'us versus them' in IT," Baker recalls. She notes, for example, that shipboard and onshore IT people didn't mix. "But now we're forced to work in cross-teams to bring out products for the business, and the result is to break down the silos," she says.

Metrics and Time. Murphy has established very specific performance measures to let his managers know exactly what's expected of them. He's also centralized administrative responsibilities to give managers more time for their people. "We used to spend a lot of time with vendors and make arrangements for training and travel," says IT manager Illeyana Gonzalez. "All that was removed so that we could focus more on our people."

Respect. "The change has been profound," says Goldstein, no longer vitriolic. "I give Tom tremendous credit for turning around the organization and making it extremely service- and customer-oriented. Instead of being seen as an obstacle, it's seen as an assist to business." This new respect makes the IT team proud of itself. "We have a great working relationship with the business now," Lopez says. "They respect us, they look to us, and that raises morale of the staff."

Case Study Questions

1. Why did the IT group at Royal Caribbean have such poor performance and business status in the company?

2. What are the top three factors in Tom Murphy's turnaround of the IT function at Royal Caribbean? Explain the reasons for your choices.

3. Visit the website of Royal Caribbean. Evaluate the effectiveness of the website and the services being offered to attract and serve the travel needs of customers and prospective customers. What could be improved? Outline the business impact of your idea.

Source: Adapted from Kathleen Melymuka, "All Hands on Deck," *Computerworld*, March 4, 2002, pp. 30–31. Reprinted with permission of *Computerworld*.

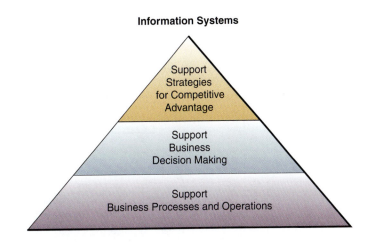

FIGURE 1.9

The three major roles of the business applications of information systems. Information systems provide an organization with support for business processes and operations, decision making, and competitive advantage.

IT infrastructure. The morale of the IT group is high, and they have earned the respect of the rest of the company by creating IT solutions that support the needs and goals of the business.

The Major Roles of IS: Examples

Figure 1.9 illustrates the three major roles of the business applications of information systems. Let's look at a retail store as a good example of how these three fundamental roles can be implemented by a business.

Support Business Processes. As a consumer, you have to deal regularly with the information systems that support the business processes and operations at the many retail stores where you shop. For example, most retail stores now use computer-based information systems to help them record customer purchases, keep track of inventory, pay employees, buy new merchandise, and evaluate sales trends. Store operations would grind to a halt without the support of such information systems.

Support Decision Making. Information systems also help store managers and other business professionals make better decisions and attempt to gain a competitive advantage. For example, decisions on what lines of merchandise need to be added or discontinued, or on what kind of investment they require, are typically made after an analysis provided by computer-based information systems. This not only supports the decision making of store managers, buyers, and others, but also helps them look for ways to gain an advantage over other retailers in the competition for customers.

Support Competitive Advantage. Gaining a strategic advantage over competitors requires innovative use of information technology. For example, store management might make a decision to install touch-screen kiosks in all of their stores, with links to their e-commerce website for online shopping. This might attract new customers and build customer loyalty because of the ease of shopping and buying merchandise provided by such information systems. Thus, strategic information systems can help provide products and services that give a business a comparative advantage over its competitors.

e-Business in Business

The explosive growth of the Internet and related technologies and applications is revolutionizing the way businesses are operated and people work, and how information systems support business processes, decision making, and competitive advantage. Thus, many businesses today are using Internet technologies to web-enable business processes and create innovative *e-business* applications.

FIGURE 1.10
Businesses today depend on the Internet, intranets, and extranets to implement and manage electronic business operations, electronic commerce, and enterprise collaboration.

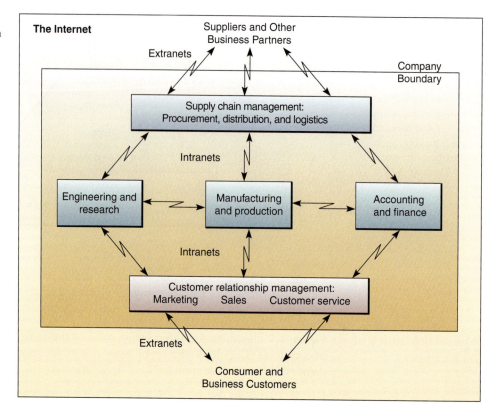

In this text, we define **e-business** as the use of Internet technologies to inter-network and empower business processes, electronic commerce, and enterprise communication and collaboration within a company and with its customers, suppliers, and other business stakeholders. The Internet and Internet-like networks—inside the enterprise **(intranets),** and between an enterprise and its trading partners **(extranets)**—have become the primary information technology infrastructure that supports the e-business applications of many companies. These companies rely on e-business applications to (1) reengineer internal business processes, (2) implement electronic commerce systems with their customers and suppliers, and (3) promote enterprise collaboration among business teams and workgroups. Figure 1.10 illustrates how businesses depend on Internet technologies to implement and manage e-business operations and electronic commerce and collaboration.

Enterprise collaboration systems involve the use of software tools to support communication, coordination, and collaboration among the members of networked teams and workgroups. A business may use intranets, the Internet, extranets, and other networks to implement such systems. For example, employees and external consultants may form a *virtual team* that uses a corporate intranet and the Internet for electronic mail, videoconferencing, electronic discussion groups, and Web pages of work-in-progress information to collaborate on business projects.

Electronic commerce is the buying and selling, and marketing and servicing of products, services, and information over a variety of computer networks. Many businesses now use the Internet, intranets, extranets, and other networks to support every step of the commercial process. This might include everything from advertising, sales, and customer support on the World Wide Web, to Internet security and payment mechanisms that ensure completion of delivery and payment processes. For example, electronic commerce systems include Internet websites for online sales, extranet access of inventory databases by large customers, and the use of corporate intranets by sales reps to access customer records for customer relationship management. Now let's look in more detail at how one company is using the Internet for electronic business and commerce.

**Cisco Systems:
e-Business and
e-Commerce
Leader**

Top telecom manufacturer Cisco Systems uses 36 manufacturing plants, of which it owns but two. One of them is downstairs from the San Jose office of Randy Pond, Senior Vice President for Operations. The rest belong to top contract manufacturers like Jabil Circuit and Solectron. It's "virtual manufacturing," Pond says, made possible by a "suite of Internet-based tools and processes that lets me manage an extended enterprise I don't own as if I do own it."

The key, says Pond, is "real-time data on a real-time basis so my partners know what goes on in my business every single day." As much as possible, Cisco and a partner work with the same stream of e-business information, doubling its value. Every day Cisco compiles its inventory, forecast for each model, order backlog, and thirteen weeks of daily data about parts and subassemblies; every day its partner compiles data on in-process inventory, cycle time by process step, optimal lot size, and yield; every night computers combine the Internet data streams into a river of information; every morning everyone knows what to build that day.

Cisco works the other end of the process—e-commerce—the same way. Eighty-seven percent of Cisco's sales are entered directly from the Net and available instantaneously. Except for commodity parts, Cisco's e-business supply chain is as visible and as live as a televised football game. Validation and testing are also Internet-based. Autotest, a homemade tool, tests machines as they are built and won't print a packing label for a machine unless every test has been done and passed. Another tool checks a customer's order as he enters it, to make sure that he hasn't asked for incompatible gear.

The benefits of real-time e-business add up to about $400 million a year, by Pond's reckoning, plus up to a $1 billion saving in capital costs—from equipment Cisco doesn't carry on its books, improved utilization by suppliers, and minimal inventory [18].

Trends in Information Systems

The business applications of information systems have expanded significantly over the years. Figure 1.11 summarizes these changes.

Until the 1960s, the role of most information systems was simple: transaction processing, record-keeping, accounting, and other *electronic data processing* (EDP) applications. Then another role was added, as the concept of *management information systems* (MIS) was conceived. This new role focused on developing business applications that provided managerial end users with predefined management reports that would give managers the information they needed for decision-making purposes.

By the 1970s, it was evident that the prespecified information products produced by such management information systems were not adequately meeting many of the decision-making needs of management. So the concept of *decision support systems* (DSS) was born. The new role for information systems was to provide managerial end users with ad hoc and interactive support of their decision-making processes. This support would be tailored to the unique decision-making styles of managers as they confronted specific types of problems in the real world.

In the 1980s, several new roles for information systems appeared. First, the rapid development of microcomputer processing power, application software packages, and telecommunications networks gave birth to the phenomenon of *end user computing*. Now, end users could use their own computing resources to support their job requirements instead of waiting for the indirect support of corporate information services departments.

Second, it became evident that most top corporate executives did not directly use either the reports of management information systems or the analytical modeling capabilities of decision support systems, so the concept of *executive information systems* (EIS) was developed. These information systems were created to give top executives an easy way to get the critical information they want, when they want it, tailored to the formats they prefer.

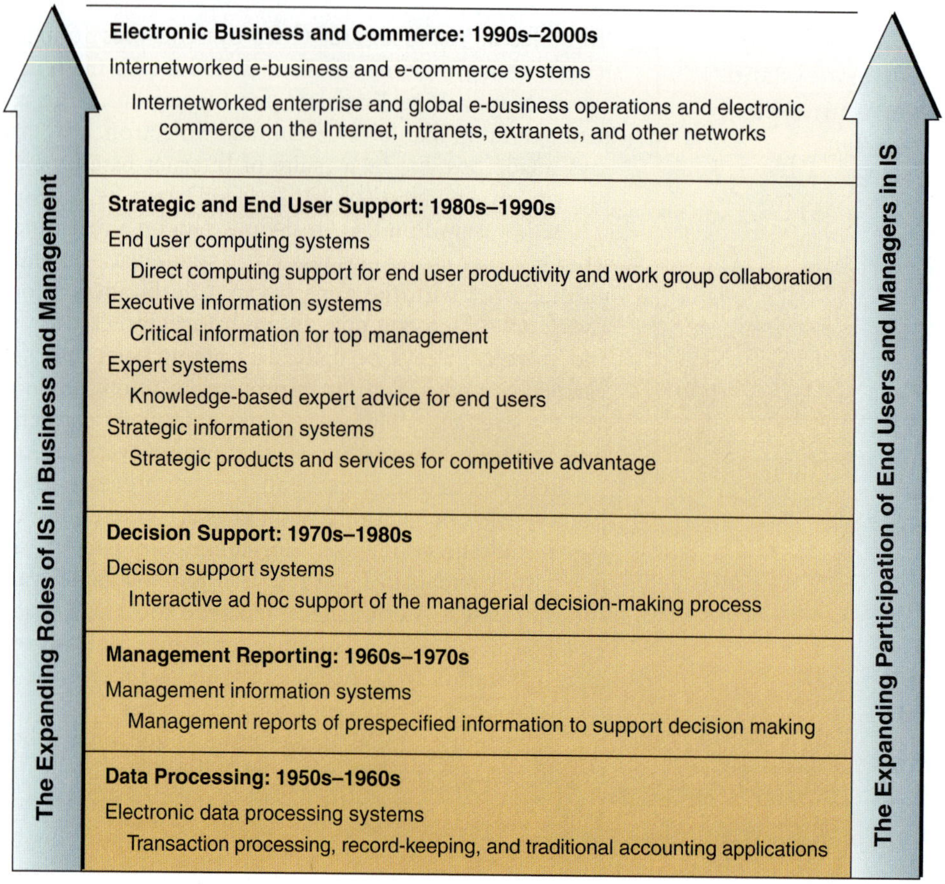

FIGURE 1.11

The expanding roles of the business applications of information systems. Note how the roles of computer-based information systems have expanded over time. Also, note the impact of these changes on the end users and managers of an organization.

The Expanding Roles of IS in Business and Management

The Expanding Participation of End Users and Managers in IS

Electronic Business and Commerce: 1990s–2000s

Internetworked e-business and e-commerce systems

Internetworked enterprise and global e-business operations and electronic commerce on the Internet, intranets, extranets, and other networks

Strategic and End User Support: 1980s–1990s

End user computing systems

Direct computing support for end user productivity and work group collaboration

Executive information systems

Critical information for top management

Expert systems

Knowledge-based expert advice for end users

Strategic information systems

Strategic products and services for competitive advantage

Decision Support: 1970s–1980s

Decison support systems

Interactive ad hoc support of the managerial decision-making process

Management Reporting: 1960s–1970s

Management information systems

Management reports of prespecified information to support decision making

Data Processing: 1950s–1960s

Electronic data processing systems

Transaction processing, record-keeping, and traditional accounting applications

Third, breakthroughs occurred in the development and application of artificial intelligence (AI) techniques to business information systems. *Expert systems* (ES) and other *knowledge-based systems* forged a new role for information systems. Today, expert systems can serve as consultants to users by providing expert advice in limited subject areas.

An important new role for information systems appeared in the 1980s and continued through the 1990s. This is the concept of a strategic role for information systems, sometimes called *strategic information systems* (SIS). In this concept, information technology becomes an integral component of business processes, products, and services that help a company gain a competitive advantage in the global marketplace.

Finally, the rapid growth of the Internet, intranets, extranets, and other interconnected global networks of the 1990s has dramatically changed the capabilities of information systems in business at the beginning of the twenty-first century. Internetworked enterprise and global electronic business and commerce systems are revolutionizing the operations and management of today's business enterprises.

Types of Information Systems

Conceptually, the applications of information systems that are implemented in today's business world can be classified in several different ways. For example, several types of information systems can be classified as either operations or management information systems. Figure 1.12 illustrates this conceptual classification of information systems applications. Information systems are categorized this way to spotlight the major roles each plays in the operations and management of a business. Let's look briefly at some examples of such information systems categories.

Operations Support Systems

Information systems have always been needed to process data generated by, and used in, business operations. Such **operations support systems** produce a variety of information products for internal and external use. However, they do not empha-

FIGURE 1.12

Operations and management classifications of information systems. Note how this conceptual overview emphasizes the main purposes of information systems that support business operations and managerial decision making.

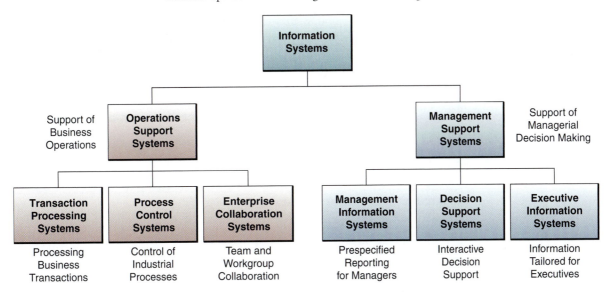

size producing the specific information products that can best be used by managers. Further processing by management information systems is usually required. The role of a business firm's operations support systems is to efficiently process business transactions, control industrial processes, support enterprise communications and collaboration, and update corporate databases. See Figure 1.13.

Transaction processing systems are an important example of operations support systems that record and process data resulting from business transactions. They process transactions in two basic ways. In *batch processing*, transactions data are accumulated over a period of time and processed periodically. In *real-time* (or online) processing, data are processed immediately after a transaction occurs. For example, point-of-sale (POS) systems at many retail stores use electronic cash register terminals to electronically capture and transmit sales data over telecommunications links to regional computer centers for immediate (real-time) or nightly (batch) processing. See Figure 1.14.

Process control systems monitor and control physical processes. For example, a petroleum refinery uses electronic sensors linked to computers to continually monitor chemical processes and make instant (real-time) adjustments that control the refinery process. **Enterprise collaboration systems** enhance team and workgroup communications and productivity, and are sometimes called *office automation systems*. For example, knowledge workers in a project team may use electronic mail

FIGURE 1.13

A summary of operations support systems with examples.

Operations Support Systems
● **Transaction processing systems.** Process data resulting from business transactions, update operational databases, and produce business documents. Examples: sales and inventory processing and accounting systems.
● **Process control systems.** Monitor and control industrial processes. Examples: petroleum refining, power generation, and steel production systems.
● **Enterprise collaboration systems.** Support team, workgroup, and enterprise communications and collaboration. Examples: e-mail, chat, and videoconferencing groupware systems.

FIGURE 1.14

QuickBooks is a popular accounting package that automates small business accounting transaction processing while providing business owners with management reports.

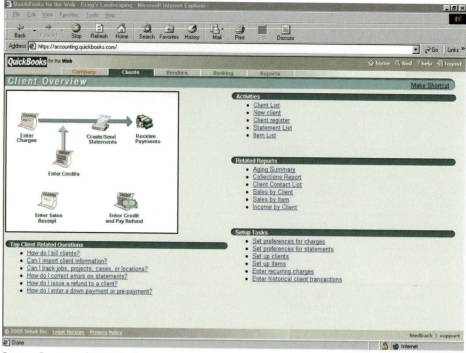

Source: Courtesy of QuickBooks.

to send and receive electronic messages, and videoconferencing to hold electronic meetings to coordinate their activities.

Management Support Systems

When information system applications focus on providing information and support for effective decision making by managers, they are called **management support systems.** Providing information and support for decision making by all types of managers and business professionals is a complex task. Conceptually, several major types of information systems support a variety of decision-making responsibilities: (1) management information systems, (2) decision support systems, and (3) executive information systems. See Figure 1.15.

Management information systems provide information in the form of reports and displays to managers and many business professionals. For example, sales managers may use their networked computers and Web browsers to get instantaneous displays about the sales results of their products and to access their corporate intranet for daily sales analysis reports that evaluate sales made by each salesperson. **Decision support systems** give direct computer support to managers during the decision-

FIGURE 1.15   A summary of management support systems with examples.

Management Support Systems
• **Management information systems.** Provide information in the form of prespecified reports and displays to support business decision making. Examples: sales analysis, production performance, and cost trend reporting systems.
• **Decision support systems.** Provide interactive ad hoc support for the decision-making processes of managers and other business professionals. Examples: product pricing, profitability forecasting, and risk analysis systems.
• **Executive information systems.** Provide critical information from many sources tailored to the information needs of executives. Examples: systems for easy access to analyses of business performance, actions of competitors, and economic developments to support strategic planning.

FIGURE 1.16

Management information systems provide information to business professionals in a variety of easy-to-use formats.

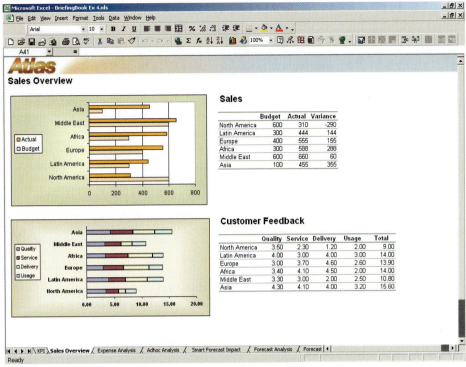

Source: Courtesy of Comshare

making process. For example, advertising managers may use an electronic spreadsheet program to do what-if analysis as they test the impact of alternative advertising budgets on the forecasted sales of new products. **Executive information systems** provide critical information from a wide variety of internal and external sources in easy-to-use displays to executives and managers. For example, top executives may use touchscreen terminals to instantly view text and graphics displays that highlight key areas of organizational and competitive performance. See Figure 1.16.

Other Classifications of Information Systems

Several other categories of information systems can support either operations or management applications. For example, **expert systems** can provide expert advice for operational chores like equipment diagnostics, or managerial decisions such as loan portfolio management. **Knowledge management systems** are knowledge-based information systems that support the creation, organization, and dissemination of business knowledge to employees and managers throughout a company. Information systems that focus on operational and managerial applications in support of basic business functions such as accounting or marketing are known as **functional business systems.** Finally, **strategic information systems** apply information technology to a firm's products, services, or business processes to help it gain a strategic advantage over its competitors.

It is also important to realize that business applications of information systems in the real world are typically integrated combinations of the several types of information systems we have just mentioned. That's because conceptual classifications of information systems are designed to emphasize the many different roles of information systems. In practice, these roles are combined into integrated or **cross-functional informational systems** that provide a variety of functions. Thus, most information systems are designed to produce information and support decision making for various levels of management and business functions, as well as do record-keeping and transaction processing chores. So whenever you analyze an information system, you will probably see that it provides information for a variety of managerial levels and business functions.

FIGURE 1.17 A summary of other categories of information systems with examples.

> **Other Categories of Information Systems**
>
> - **Expert systems.** Knowledge-based systems that provide expert advice and act as expert consultants to users. Examples: credit application advisor, process monitor, and diagnostic maintenance systems.
> - **Knowledge management systems.** Knowledge-based systems that support the creation, organization, and dissemination of business knowledge within the enterprise. Examples: intranet access to best business practices, sales proposal strategies, and customer problem resolution systems.
> - **Strategic information systems.** Support operations or management processes that provide a firm with strategic products, services, and capabilities for competitive advantage. Examples: online stock trading, shipment tracking, and e-commerce Web systems.
> - **Functional business systems.** Support a variety of operational and managerial applications of the basic business functions of a company. Examples: information systems that support applications in accouting, finance, marketing, operations management, and human resource management.

Figure 1.17 summarizes these categories of information system applications. We will explore many examples of the use of information systems in business in Chapters 5, 6, 7, and 8.

Managerial Challenges of Information Technology

Prospective managers and business professionals like you should become aware of the problems and opportunities presented by the use of information technology and learn how to effectively confront such managerial challenges. Today's internetworked information systems play a vital role in the business success of an enterprise. For example, the Internet, intranets, and extranets can provide much of the IT infrastructure a business needs for e-business operations, effective management, and competitive advantage.

Success and Failure with IT

However, Figure 1.18 emphasizes that information systems and their technologies must be managed to support the business strategies, business processes, and organizational structures and culture of a business enterprise. That's because computer-

FIGURE 1.18
Internetworked information systems and technologies must be managed to support business strategies, processes, and organizational structures and culture to increase the customer and business value of a business enterprise.

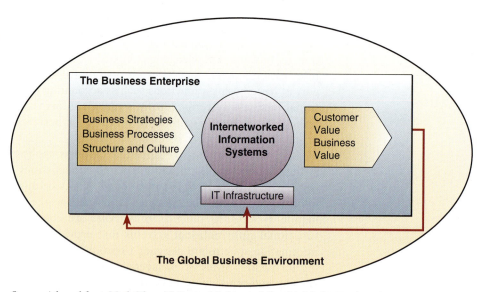

Source: Adapted from Mark Silver, M. Lynne Markus, and Cynthia Mathis Beath, "The Information Technology Interaction Model: A Foundation for the MBA Core Course," *MIS Quarterly*, September 1995, p. 366, and Allen Lee, "Inaugural Editor's Comments," *MIS Quarterly*, March 1999, pp. v–vi. Reprinted with permission from the *MIS Quarterly*.

FIGURE 1.19   Turning business failure into business success with information technology.

From Failure to Success with IT	
The Boeing Company	**Thomson Consumer Electronics**
Business Failure Costly delays ($1.6 billion in 1997) in obtaining 6 million parts to build each aircraft with unintegrated IT systems.	**Business Failure** Retailers not getting quick replenishment of core products with old inventory systems.
New IT Solution Integrate entire supply chain into internal production systems.	**New IT Solution** Demand collaboration system with top retailers that link directly into internal production and logistics systems.
Business Success Output capacity up 100% in 4 years. Aircraft lead times reduced by 60%.	**Business Success** Out-of-stock scenarios reduced to 1% with forecast accuracy now above 95%.

Source: Adapted from Peter Fingar, Harsha Kumar, and Tarun Sharma, *Enterprise e-Commerce* (Tampa, FL: Meghan-Kiffer Press, 2000), p. 176.

based information systems, though heavily dependent on information technologies, are designed, operated, and used by people in a variety of organizational settings and business environments. The goal of such companies is to increase their customer and business value in today's global business environment.

Therefore, the success of an information system should not be measured only by its *efficiency* in terms of minimizing costs, time, and the use of information resources. Success should also be measured by the *effectiveness* of information technology in supporting an organization's business strategies, enabling its business processes, enhancing its organizational structures and culture, and increasing the customer and business value of the enterprise.

However, it is important that you realize that information technology and information systems can be mismanaged and misapplied so that IS performance problems create both technological and business failure. For example, Figure 1.19 outlines two dramatic examples of how information technology contributed to business failure and success at two major corporations.

Developing IS Solutions

Developing successful information system solutions to business problems is a major challenge for business managers and professionals today. As a business professional, you will be responsible for proposing or developing new or improved uses of information technologies for your company. As a business manager, you will also frequently manage the development efforts of information systems specialists and other business end users.

Most computer-based information systems are conceived, designed, and implemented using some form of systematic development process. Figure 1.20 shows that several major activities must be accomplished and managed in a complete IS development cycle. In this development process, end users and information specialists *design* information system applications based on an *analysis* of the business requirements of an organization. Examples of other activities include *investigating* the economic or technical feasibility of a proposed application, acquiring and learning how to use the software required to *implement* the new system, and making improvements to *maintain* the business value of a system.

We will discuss the details of the information systems development process in Chapter 10. Many of the business and managerial challenges that arise in developing and implementing new uses of information technology will be explored in Chapters 11 and 12. Now let's look at an example of the challenges faced and overcome by a company that developed and installed a major new information system application. This example emphasizes how important good systems development practices are to a business.

FIGURE 1.20

Developing information systems solutions to business problems can be implemented and managed as a multistep process or cycle.

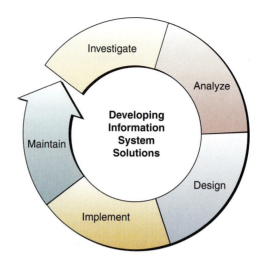

After turning on Baan Co.'s enterprise resource planning (ERP) suite of business software, A-DEC expected it to automate much of their manufacturing, distribution, and financial information processing. But they soon fell behind on processing orders, building products, and then shipping the goods to dealers. "We lost a lot of business," said CIO Keith Bearden, who was brought in to manage A-DEC's information systems three months into the rollout. To get by, the Newberg, Oregon, dental equipment maker even had to fill some orders outside the system "because workers didn't understand it, and the performance was so bad," he said. At A-DEC, business changes initially were fought, Bearden said. End-user training also fell short at first, he said, and the IT department underestimated the processing power that Baan's software required.

After Bearden was hired, he pulled together a stabilization team from all parts of the company. It took about six months of systems development work to fix the performance issues by changing databases and upgrading A-DEC's servers and network. Another six months were spent redesigning business processes and training users. All that work basically doubled the cost of the project, Bearden said. "We spent a lot of money just cleaning up problems," he said. Even now, 50-plus key users spend 20 percent of their work time looking for ways to improve A-DEC's use of the software.

But the company now is getting some of the benefits it expected, Bearden said. For example, inventory levels have been cut by about 30 percent since the new system was put into use. And one of A-DEC's four product lines has been switched to a fast turnaround modular manufacturing approach that wasn't feasible before [17].

Challenges of Ethics and IT

As a prospective manager, business professional, and knowledge worker, you will be challenged by the **ethical responsibilities** generated by the use of information technology. For example, what uses of information technology might be considered improper, irresponsible, or harmful to other individuals or to society? What is the proper business use of the Internet and an organization's IT resources? What does it take to be a **responsible end user** of information technology? How can you protect yourself from computer crime and other risks of information technology? These are some of the questions that outline the ethical dimensions of information systems that we will discuss and illustrate with Real World Cases in Chapter 11 and other chapters of this text. Figure 1.21 outlines some of the ethical risks that may arise in the use of several major applications of information technology. The following example illustrates some of the ethical challenges in the use of business resources to access the Internet.

FIGURE 1.21 Examples of some of the ethical challenges that must be faced by business managers who implement major applications of information technology.

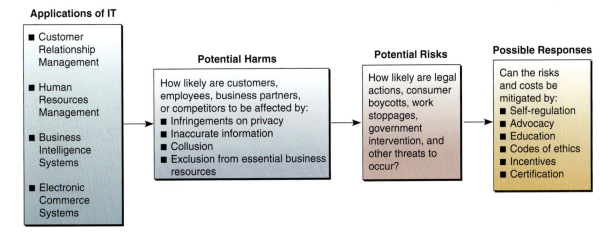

| 3M Corp. and Others: Internet Ethics | Faced with international controversies over pornography and hate speech on the Internet, employers are setting policies to limit Internet usage to business purposes. They also are penalizing employees who send out abusive electronic mail, "flame" people on newsgroups, or visit inappropriate sites on the World Wide Web.

For most companies, an Internet usage policy is straightforward. It generally informs employees that their Internet access is a company resource that should be used only for their jobs. "3M's policy is simply put: that the Web must be used for business purposes. If people get on and abuse it, then you've got a problem with that individual and need to handle it," said Luke Crofoot, a marketing services supervisor at 3M in St. Paul, Minnesota.

Firms that want more control over their employees develop detailed Internet usage policies. Companies that have detailed usage policies include the Chase Manhattan Bank NA; Johnson Controls, Inc.; Pioneer Hi-Bred International Inc.; and Monsanto Co. But some attorneys take a tougher stance. Says Neal J. Friedman, a Washington attorney who specializes in online law, "Employees need to know they have no right of privacy and no right of free speech using company resources" [19]. |

Challenges of IT Careers

Information technology and its uses in information systems have created interesting, highly paid, and challenging career opportunities for millions of men and women. So learning more about information technology may help you decide if you want to pursue an IT-related career. Employment opportunities in the field of information systems are excellent, as organizations continue to expand their use of information technology. However, this poses a resource management challenge to many companies, since employment surveys continually forecast shortages of qualified information systems personnel in a variety of job categories. Also, job requirements in information systems are continually changing due to dynamic developments in business and information technology.

One major recruiter is the IT industry itself. Thousands of companies develop, manufacture, market, and service computer hardware, software, data and network products and services, or provide e-business and commerce applications and services, end user training, or business systems consulting. However, the biggest need for qualified people comes from the millions of businesses, government agencies, and other organizations that use information technology. They need many types of IS professionals to help them support the work activities and supply the information needs of their employees, managers, customers, suppliers, and other business partners. Let's take a look at IT career challenges at a leading e-commerce company.

Amazon.com: IT Career Challenges

John Vlastelca is the technical recruiting manager of Amazon.com Inc. in Seattle. He says: "We have a huge demand for people who have experience building relationships with customers online—people who bring together a retailing background and some IT background. We hire smart folks, and they are working their butts off. There is a heavy dose of informality. People aren't title-centric; the best idea wins and the career path is often a vertical crossover to management or content areas.

"The one thing that drives us is an obsession with the customer. What helps us make our selection decision is the question, 'Is this a technical person who views technology as a means to an end, where the end is the customer? Or does this person define him or herself as just a Java programmer?'

"But the bar is incredibly high here. It is really hard for my team to find the combination of skills—the software engineer who really understands the customer and the business. So half don't make it because they are not strong enough technically. Other reasons have to do with soft skills—being open to ideas, just raw smarts and not being passionate enough. The problem space we operate in is unexplored territory" [10].

The IS Function

In summary, successful management of information systems and technologies presents major challenges to business managers and professionals. Thus, the information systems function represents:

- A major functional area of business that is as important to business success as the functions of accounting, finance, operations management, marketing, and human resources management.
- An important contributor to operational efficiency, employee productivity and morale, and customer service and satisfaction.
- A major source of information and support needed to promote effective decision making by managers and business professionals.
- A vital ingredient in developing competitive products and services that give an organization a strategic advantage in the global marketplace.
- A dynamic, rewarding, and challenging career opportunity for millions of men and women.
- A key component of the resources, infrastructure, and capabilities of today's business enterprises.

Summary

- **Why Information Systems Are Important.** An understanding of the effective and responsible use and management of information systems and technologies is important for managers, business professionals, and other knowledge workers in today's internetworked enterprises. Information systems play a vital role in the e-business and e-commerce operations, enterprise collaboration and management, and strategic success of businesses that must operate in an internetworked global environment. Thus, the field of information systems has become a major functional area of business administration.

- **An IS Framework for Business Professionals.** The IS knowledge that a business manager or professional needs to know is illustrated in Figure 1.2 and covered in this chapter and text. This includes (1) *foundation concepts:* fundamental behavioral, technical, business, and managerial concepts like system components and functions, or competitive strategies; (2) *information technologies:* concepts, developments, or management issues regarding hardware, software, data management, networks, and other technologies; (3) *business applications:* major uses of IT for business processes, operations, decision making, and strategic/competitive advantage; (4) *development processes:* how end users and IS specialists develop and implement business/IT solutions to problems and opportunities arising in business; and (5) *management challenges:* how to effectively and ethically manage the IS function and IT resources to achieve top performance and business value in support of the business strategies of the enterprise.

- **System Concepts.** A system is a group of interrelated components working toward the attainment of a common goal by accepting inputs and producing outputs in an organized transformation process. Feedback is data about the performance of a system. Control is the component that monitors and evaluates feedback and makes any necessary adjustments to the input and processing components to ensure that proper output is produced.

- **An Information System Model.** An information system uses the resources of people, hardware, software, data, and networks to perform input, processing, output, storage, and control activities that convert data resources into information products. Data are first collected and converted to a form that is suitable for processing (input). Then the data are manipulated and converted into information (processing), stored for future use (storage), or communicated to their ultimate user (output) according to correct processing procedures (control).

- **IS Resources and Products.** Hardware resources include machines and media used in information processing. Software resources include computerized instructions (programs) and instructions for people (procedures). People resources include information systems specialists and users. Data resources include alphanumeric, text, image, video, audio, and other forms of data. Network resources include communications media and network support. Information products produced by an information system can take a variety of forms, including paper reports, visual displays, multimedia documents, electronic messages, graphics images, and audio responses.

- **Business Applications of Information Systems.** Information systems perform three vital roles in business firms. Business applications of IS support an organization's business processes and operations, business decision making, and strategic competitive advantage. Major application categories of information systems include operations support systems, such as transaction processing systems, process control systems, and enterprise collaboration systems, and management support systems, such as management information systems, decision support systems, and executive information systems. Other major categories are expert systems, knowledge management systems, strategic information systems, and functional business systems. However, in the real world most application categories are combined into cross-functional information systems that provide information and support for decision making and also perform operational information processing activities. Refer to Figures 1.13, 1.15, and 1.17 for summaries of the major application categories of information systems.

Key Terms and Concepts

These are the key terms and concepts of this chapter. The page number of their first explanation is in parentheses.

1. Computer-based information system (7)
2. Control (9)
3. Data (13)
4. Data or information processing (14)
5. Data resources (13)
6. Developing business/IT solutions (26)
7. E-business (20)
8. E-business in business (19)
9. Electronic commerce (20)
10. End user (28)
11. Enterprise collaboration systems (20)
12. Extranet (20)

13. Feedback (9)

14. Hardware resources (11)

   a. Machines (11)

   b. Media (11)

15. Information (13)

   a. Products (16)

   b. Quality (16)

16. Information system (7)

17. Information system activities (8)

   a. Input (8)

   b. Processing (8)

   c. Output (8)

   d. Storage (15)

   e. Control (15)

18. Information system model (10)

19. Information technology (IT) (7)

20. Intranet (20)

21. IS knowledge needed by business professionals (6)

22. Knowledge workers (11)

23. Management challenges of IS (26)

   a. Ethics and IT (28)

   b. IT career challenges (29)

   c. IT success and failure (26)

24. Network resources (13)

25. People resources (11)

   a. IS specialists (11)

   b. End users (11)

26. Roles of IS applications in business (17)

   a. Support of business processes and operations (19)

   b. Support of business decision making (19)

   c. Support of strategies for competitive advantage (19)

27. Software resources (12)

   a. Programs (12)

   b. Procedures (12)

28. System (8)

29. Trends in information systems (21)

30. Types of information systems (22)

   a. Cross-functional systems (25)

   b. Management support systems (24)

   c. Operations support systems (22)

Review Quiz

Match one of the previous key terms and concepts with one of the following brief examples or definitions. Look for the best fit for answers that seem to fit more than one key term or concept. Defend your choices.

____ 1. You should know some fundamental concepts about information systems and their technologies, development processes, business applications, and management challenges.

____ 2. People who spend most of their workday creating, using, and distributing information.

____ 3. Computer hardware and software, networks, data management, and other technologies.

____ 4. Information systems support an organization's business processes, operations, decision making, and strategies for competitive advantage.

____ 5. Using IT to reengineer business processes to support e-business operations.

____ 6. Using Web-based decision support systems to support sales managers.

____ 7. Using information technology for electronic commerce to gain a strategic advantage over competitors.

____ 8. A system that uses people, hardware, software, and network resources to collect, transform, and disseminate information within an organization.

____ 9. An information system that uses computers and their hardware and software.

____ 10. Anyone who uses an information system or the information it produces.

____ 11. Businesses today are using the Internet, corporate intranets, and interorganizational extranets for electronic business operations, e-commerce, and enterprise collaboration.

____ 12. The buying, selling, marketing, and servicing of products over the Internet and other networks.

____ 13. The use of groupware tools to support collaboration among networked teams.

____ 14. A group of interrelated components working together toward the attainment of a common goal.

____ 15. Data about a system's performance.

____ 16. Making adjustments to a system's components so that it operates properly.

____ 17. Facts or observations.

____ 18. Data that have been placed into a meaningful context for an end user.

____ 19. The act of converting data into information.

____ 20. An information system uses people, hardware, software, network, and data resources to perform input, processing, output, storage, and control activities that transform data resources into information products.

____ 21. Machines and media.

____ 22. Computers, disk drives, video monitors, and printers are examples.

____ 23. Magnetic disks, optical disks, and paper forms are examples.

____ 24. Programs and procedures.

____ 25. A set of instructions for a computer.

____ 26. A set of instructions for people.

____ 27. End users and information systems professionals.

____ 28. Using the keyboard of a computer to enter data.

____ 29. Computing loan payments.

____ 30. Printing a letter you wrote using a computer.

____ 31. Saving a copy of the letter on a magnetic disk.

____ 32. Having a sales receipt as proof of a purchase.

____ 33. Information systems can be classified into operations, management, and other categories.

____ 34. Includes transaction processing, process control, and end user collaboration systems.

____ 35. Includes management information, decision support, and executive information systems.

____ 36. Information systems that perform transaction processing and provide information to managers across the boundaries of functional business areas.

____ 37. Information systems have evolved from a data processing orientation to the support of strategic decision making, end user collaboration, and electronic business and commerce.

____ 38. Internet-like networks and websites inside a company.

____ 39. Interorganizational Internet-like networks among trading partners.

____ 40. You need to be a responsible end user of IT resources in your company.

____ 41. Managing the IT resources of a company effectively and ethically to improve its business performance and value.

____ 42. Using the Internet, intranets, and extranets to empower internal business operations, electronic commerce, and enterprise collaboration.

Discussion Questions

1. How can information technology support a company's business processes and decision making, and give it a competitive advantage? Give examples to illustrate your answer.

2. How does the use of the Internet, intranets, and extranets by a business enterprise support their e-commerce activities?

3. Refer to the Real World Case on BellSouth in the chapter. Is there any sound business reason why companies sometimes invest in IT projects that do not "directly add value and support their primary business goals"?

4. Why do big companies still fail in their use of information technology? What should they be doing differently?

5. How can a manager demonstrate that he or she is a responsible end user of information systems? Give several examples.

6. Refer to the Real World Case on Royal Caribbean in the chapter. Are business managers or IT executives responsible for successfully aligning an IT organization with the business needs and goals of a company?

7. What are some of the toughest management challenges in developing IT solutions to solve business problems and meet new business opportunities?

8. Why are there so many conceptual classifications of information systems? Why are they typically integrated in the information systems found in the real world?

9. In what major ways have the roles of information systems applications in business expanded during the last 40 years? What is one major change you think will happen in the next 10 years?

10. Can the business use of Internet technologies help a company gain a competitive advantage? Give an example to illustrate your answer.

Application Exercises

Complete the following exercises as individual or group projects that apply chapter concepts to real world business situations.

1. **Using the Internet for Business Research**

    Web Search the Internet for additional information and business examples about some of the topics or companies in this chapter. For example, use search engines like Google or Fast Search to research the latest developments in e-business, e-commerce, IT ethics and security, or IT careers. Or find and visit the websites of companies in the Real World Cases in this chapter. Look for examples of the business use of information technology in your search.

    a. Prepare a one- or two-page summary of some of your findings and the sources you used.

    b. End your paper with a few sentences describing one thing you have learned from your research that might help you in your future career in business.

2. **Using PowerWeb Resources**

    Web Visit the McGraw-Hill PowerWeb website for Management Information Systems, which is available for users of this text. See Figure 1.22. (Consult

FIGURE 1.22

The McGraw-Hill PowerWeb home page for management information systems.

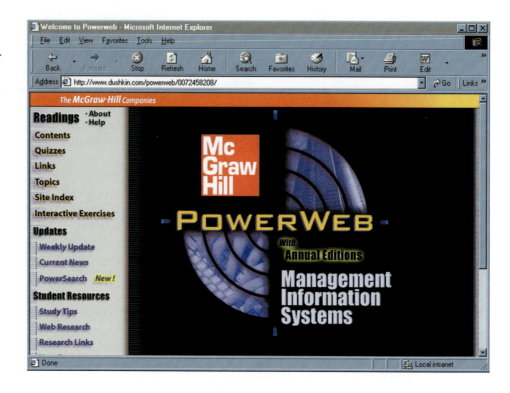

your instructor for details on how to register for PowerWeb if you did not receive a card with your text with an access code that enables you to register for the site.)

As you will see, PowerWeb is a great online resource for self-study resources on MIS topics covered in this text, Web research tips and links, MIS periodicals, and current news on information technology topics. For example, click on the *Current News* link and search for and read a few current news articles on an MIS topic you are interested in, such as cyber crime or e-commerce.

a. Prepare a one- or two-page summary describing the *Current News* articles you found most interesting and relevant as a business end user.

b. End your paper with a few sentences describing one thing you have learned from your research that might help you in your future career in business.

3. Jefferson State University: Recognizing IS Components

Students in the College of Business Administration of Jefferson State University use their desktop and laptop microcomputers for a variety of assignments. For example, a student may use a word processing program stored on the microcomputer system's hard disk drive and proceed to type a case study analysis. When the analysis is typed, edited, and properly formatted to an instructor's specifications, the student may save it on a floppy disk, e-mail a copy to the instructor via the Internet, and print out a copy on the system's printer. If the student tries to save the case study analysis using

a file name he or she has already used for saving another document, the program will display a warning message and wait until it receives an additional command.

Make an outline to identify the information system components in the preceding example.

a. Identify the people, hardware, software, network, and data resources and the information products of this information system.

b. Identify the input, processing, output, storage, and control activities that occurred.

4. Office Products Corporation: Recognizing IS Components

Office Products Corporation receives more than 10,000 customer orders a month, drawing on a combined inventory of over 1,000 office products stocked at the company's warehouse. About 60 PCs are installed at the Office Products headquarters and connected in a local area network to several IBM Netfinity servers. Orders are received by phone or mail and entered into the system by customer representatives at network computers, or they are entered directly by customers who have shopped at the electronic commerce website developed by Office Products. Entry of orders is assisted by formatted screens that help users follow data entry procedures to enter required information into the system, where it is stored on the magnetic disks of the Netfinity servers.

As the order is entered, a server checks the availability of the parts, allocates the stock, and updates customer and part databases stored on its magnetic disks. It then sends the order pick list to the warehouse printer, where it is used by warehouse personnel to fill the order. The company president has a networked PC workstation in her office, as do the controller, sales manager, inventory manager, and other executives. They use simple database management inquiry commands to get responses and reports concerning sales orders, customers, and inventory, and to review product demand and service trends.

Make an outline that identifies the information system components in Office Products' order processing system.

a. Identify the people, hardware, software, data, and network resources and the information products of this information system.

b. Identify the input, processing, output, storage, and control activities that occurred.

5. Western Chemical Corporation: Recognizing the Types and Roles of Information Systems

Western Chemical uses the Internet and an electronic commerce website to connect to its customers and suppliers, and to capture data and share information about sales orders and purchases. Sales and order data are processed immediately, and inventory and other databases are updated. Videoconferencing and electronic mail services are also provided. Data generated by a chemical refinery process are captured by sensors and processed by a computer that also suggests answers to a complex refinery problem posed by an engineer. Managers and business professionals access reports on a periodic, exception, and demand basis, and use computers to interactively assess the possible results of alternative decisions. Finally, top management can access text summaries and graphics displays that identify key elements of organizational performance and compare them to industry and competitor performance.

Western Chemical Corporation has started forming business alliances and using intranets, extranets, and the Internet to build a global electronic commerce website to offer their customers worldwide products and services. Western Chemical is in the midst of making fundamental changes to their computer-based systems to increase the efficiency of their e-business operations and their managers' ability to react quickly to changing business conditions.

Make an outline that identifies:

a. How information systems support (1) business operations, (2) business decision making, (3) strategic advantage, (4) an e-business enterprise, and (5) electronic commerce at Western Chemical.

b. There are many different types of information systems at Western Chemical. Identify as many as you can in the preceding scenario. Refer to Figure 1.13, 1.15, and 1.17 to help you. Explain the reasons for your choices.

Clariant International: Developing e-Business Systems That Pay Off

Forget about major e-commerce build-outs or fancy IT infrastructure projects. The big IT spending of the past few years—projects such as Y2K remediation, fancy e-business applications, and new e-commerce projects—is history. The economic climate and previous investments in IT applications have many IT leaders focusing on finding creative ways to optimize and integrate the e-business systems that are already in place.

Yes, these are dog days for technology. Stocks have been hammered. Programmers are out of work. Many companies have disappeared, and those still around have been humbled. In the flush of Internet mania, most businesses overspent wildly on all sorts of disparate software and systems. A lot of it still doesn't work properly. At almost every big company, applications that any idiot knows should be linked—for instance, the sales system and the one that tracks inventory—remain unconnected and autonomous islands of data. Employees were told this stuff would change their lives. Instead they're screaming in frustration.

For the next several years, corporate managers will be focused on reining in IT budgets and only funding IT projects that demonstrate a hard payoff. They'll look for technologies that address business problems directly, provide a near-term return on investment, and improve customer acquisition and retention, cost cutting, revenue, or profits. The word from the top is clear: Make this stuff work. Said American Express CEO Ken Chenault at the 2002 World Economic Forum in New York City: "We have not backed off on our efforts to integrate offline and online. We see its value in our numbers." Or listen to Mike Volpi, who runs Cisco Systems' biggest product line—data switches—and sells to just about every Fortune 500 company: "In the last four years the trend was faster and bigger. Now its about smarter."

Mike Smith, director of e-business at Clariant International Ltd. (www.clariant.com), a Muttenz, Switzerland–based global company with specialty chemicals manufacturing plants in 90 countries, acknowledges that his team got temporarily caught up in the hype aspects of e-business. But two years ago, when it looked closely at the online tools available for simplifying business processes and moving them to the Web, the team realized there were no cost-cutting guarantees in web-enabling their processes. "Don't assume, like people did in the middle of the e-hype, that you have to do it because it's going to save you money," Smith says. "If you don't get into the detail, you can't change your business processes to get the cost out."

For example, by examining purchasing records, Smith and his team found that Clariant bought a high volume of lower-cost equipment and supplies, such as notebook PCs, printer cartridges, and laboratory equipment, from catalogs. They also discovered that Clariant's paper-based procurement process added between $50 and $100 to each transaction. Storing and maintaining backup supplies of machinery parts boosted each product's cost by 30 to 50 percent. Smith and his team figured that online procurement might reduce overhead costs as well as simplify workers' jobs and free up their time so that chemists, for instance, could spend more time doing lab work and less time on administrative tasks.

That's when the real work began, says Smith. Clariant formed three teams. The first group cut the company's multiple maintenance, repair, and operations suppliers down to a few key vendors based on factors such as high-volume discounts and reliable service (overnight in many cases, which reduced the need to store most supplies). The second team, consisting of accounting, operations, and purchasing staffers, analyzed the number of annual purchases that could be made from an electronic catalog and looked at the procurement chain to see which steps could be cut or streamlined. The third team, the IT workers, weighed the "e-readiness" of suppliers and selected the most cost-effective technology. All three teams worked hand in hand under one project manager, says Smith.

The final step was conducted by a steering committee of senior managers who guided the implementation of the project and the job of demonstrating to workers the value and simplicity of the new system. "It had to be real easy," says Smith. "Easier than thumbing through a catalog." If any details were skipped, the $2 million project might not have met its targeted 30 to 40 percent internal rate of return, says Smith. Based on the demonstrated savings payoff in Germany, where the pilot implementation took place, the online procurement process is starting a worldwide rollout, beginning with Brazil, France, Switzerland, and the U.K. this year, he adds.

Case Study Questions

1. How has the focus of business managers toward IT projects changed according to this case? Do you agree? Why or why not?

2. Are web-enabling business processes a cost effective strategy? Why or why not?

3. Give an example of an IT system that you experience that doesn't work properly. How could it be fixed in a cost-effective way by the organization responsible for the system? Defend your proposal.

REAL WORLD CASE 4

Hershey Foods Corp.: Failure and Success with Information Technology

Hershey Foods Corp. (www.hersheys.com) ran into major problems when it deployed SAP AG's R/3 software and other business applications in 1999. But the candy maker had better luck with a major upgrade to the Web-enabled version of R/3 completed in 2002.

A $112 million ERP project blew up in the face of Hershey back then, while it struggled to fix order-processing problems that hampered its ability to ship candy and other products to retailers. Analysts and sources in the industry said the Hershey, Pennsylvania, manufacturer appeared to have lost a gamble when it installed a wide swath of SAP AG's R/3 enterprise resource planning applications, plus companion packages from two other vendors, simultaneously during one of its busiest shipping seasons. Hershey squeezed what was originally envisioned as a four-year project into just 30 months before going live with the full ERP system in July of 1999. That's when retailers begin ordering large amounts of candy for back-to-school and Halloween sales.

Hershey wouldn't specify whether the problems stemmed from its configuration of the system or the software itself, which also included planning and scheduling applications developed by Manugistics Group, and a pricing promotions package from Siebel Systems. Manugistics said it's working with Hershey and the other vendors on "business process improvements." A spokesman for IBM, the lead consultant on the project, said the new system required "enormous" changes in the way Hershey's workers do their jobs. Siebel officials weren't available for comment.

Hershey turned on some of SAP's finance applications, plus its purchasing, materials management, and warehousing modules, in January 1999. The order processing and billing portions of R/3 were added along with the Manugistics and Siebel packages in July. Jim Shepherd, an analyst at AMR Research, said most companies install ERP systems in a more staged manner, especially when applications from multiple vendors are involved. "These systems tie together in very intricate ways, and things that work fine in testing can turn out to be a disaster when you go live," Shepherd said. He added that the software Hershey turned on all at once in July was "a huge bite to take, given that processing orders is the lifeblood of their business."

On the other hand, Hershey says the recent upgrade of its enterprise resource planning (ERP) system to R/3 version 4.6 was completed 20 percent under budget and without any of the order processing and product-shipment disruptions that marred the initial $112 million rollout in 1999. The upgrade began in July 2001 and was finished in May 2002, the Hershey, Pennsylvania–based company said.

Hershey said it was able to make more than 30 improvements to its core business processes within 60 days of going live with R/3 4.6, which is part of SAP's mySAP.com product line. The company cited enhancements such as the automation of pick-list processing and materials management invoice verification, plus credit processing for distributors to military customers.

Those improvements have helped reduce costs and speed up processing times, Hershey said in a statement. The company added that it has also "achieved a near-zero-defect production environment" with R/3 4.6 and is using SAP's business analysis tools to measure the impact of sales and marketing programs as they happen. In the statement, Joe Zakutney, director of the SAP upgrade program, said Hershey's IT staff was able to exceed its delivery commitments for the project because of "strong program management and executive leadership, diligent planning and . . . an extensive testing and training plan."

Joshua Greenbaum, an analyst at Enterprise Applications Consulting in Daly City, California, said Hershey's experiences illustrate the fact that most troubled ERP rollouts are caused by project management issues, not faulty software. Despite the initial problems, Hershey stuck with R/3 because it recognized that it could get a lot of business value from the technology "if they bothered to do it right," Greenbaum said.

In fall 2000, Hershey said that it had fixed most of the problems with their initial ERP system. For the upgrade, the company enlisted the help of SAP and Accenture Ltd. An SAP spokesman acknowledged that there was "some pain involved" in Hershey's initial installation. "This has often been a case that's cited for past troubles . . . which is why we're particularly pleased" about the upgrade process, he said.

Case Study Questions

1. How could Hershey have avoided the failure of its first implementation of a major new IT system? Defend your proposals.

2. Why did Hershey's major upgrade of that system succeed? Explain your reasoning.

3. Why do failures in major business/IT projects continue to occur to large companies with so much IT expertise and financial resources?

Source: Adapted from Craig Steadman, "Failed ERP Gamble Haunts Hershey," *Computerworld*, November 1, 1999, pp. 1, 67; and Todd Weiss, "Hershey Upgrades R/3 ERP System without Hitches," *Computerworld*, September 9, 2002, p. 25. Reprinted with permission from *Computerworld*.

WH Smith PLC: Supporting Retail Management with Information Technology

Customer relationship management (CRM) systems are usually billed as tools to help companies better understand their customers. But in the case of WH Smith PLC (www.whsmith.com), CRM helped the international bookseller better understand itself and how it turns a profit.

WH Smith wanted to get a grasp on customers' buying patterns, anticipate trends, and more carefully align inventory to maximize profits in its 1,200 U.K.-based stores. So Trevor Dukes, the company's head of information strategy, last fall worked with a team that included store managers and central office executives to install a Web intelligence CRM system from McLean, Virginia–based MicroStrategy Inc. The goal was to cut the amount of paper shuttling back and forth between stores and the corporate headquarters in Swindon, England, and give store managers greater insight into what is happening in their own stores and throughout the WH Smith network.

"We had only been able to monitor sales and stock at the central office, and store managers were sending us tons of paperwork about their stores," Dukes recalls. The communications process was grinding to a halt, and information was out of date once it was organized and put into reports. In addition, while directives from headquarters about promotions or incentives did make their way to each retail outlet, there was no integration or insight about the most profitable items among the more than 60,000 CDs, books, games, stationery, and gifts the stores offer.

At WH Smith, with sales last year of $3.9 billion and profits of $188 million, this meant a rethinking of responsibilities and roles for store managers vis-à-vis the central office executives. "What shores up success for managers in the field is if they are clearly profit-focused and have tools to get visibility and confidence about making merchandise and stock decisions," notes Ian Rowley, a 22-year veteran and area manager for 20 stores. But the issue, according to Dukes, was how to share information about what was profitable in one store with managers in other stores. Before the new system was implemented, there was no way to share this information.

The new web-based CRM system begins generating reports in template form from the time a customer makes a purchase in a store. Sales and inventory data are sent from cash retail locations to a central data warehouse that store managers can access via an intranet. The software tools available to managers include report templates and wizards so managers can get customized views of inventory based on criteria such as highest-margin items ranked by sales.

Barrie Stewart, manager of the WH Smith store in Dunbartonshire, Scotland, says he can now see which specific products in the store are selling well, badly, or according to

expected trends, allowing him to take appropriate action. "It allows me to ask several questions, such as, Is the performance down due to poor display standards, poor stock availability or incorrect location?" Stewart says. Other questions he can ask include, Is the product right for this store? Does it provide enough profit from space allocated, or could another product's space be enlarged or a new product brought in to provide better profit for the space?

Stewart says he gives key information to store employees about which specific products sell the most and which are the most profitable. This ensures that the staff will display best-selling products in key areas with high display standards and well-maintained stock levels. "They are aware of higher profit margin products which can be sold as add-ons or displayed adjacent to best sellers or in fast-flow areas," Stewart explains. Store personnel can also feed back information or ideas to managers, such as out-of-trend sellers or local opportunities that can generate more sales and profit.

"It is all about maximizing your store's layout," says Rowley, adding that because he's armed with data from the CRM system, he can see how sales are being produced and whether those sales are actually generating profits. "Our stores tended to be very sales-driven, as many retail environments are, but the store personnel didn't know what products were driving the profits," he says. Now Rowley says, the stores' staffers know that displaying high-margin products such as branded stationery or books will produce a better yield on the store's overall inventory.

"We can track specific items, and if we see that a high-margin book is selling particularly well in, say, a tourist location, we can add a display at a shop that has high tourist traffic to try and take advantage of that information," he notes. The CRM system is also able to match actual buying information about customers at the point of sale, giving greater depth to information in the customer data warehouse. "The marketing people can really see trends from individual customers," Rowley says.

Case Study Questions

1. Why did WH Smith need a new retail management system?

2. How well does WH Smith's new CRM system support its business goals? Explain.

3. In what other ways could IT help WH Smith support its retail managers, marketers, and customers? Defend your proposals.

Source: Adapted from Pimm Fox, "Insights Turn into Profits," *Computerworld*, February 18, 2002, pp. 36–38. Reprinted with permission from *Computerworld*.

CHAPTER 2

COMPETING WITH INFORMATION TECHNOLOGY

Chapter Highlights

Learning Objectives

After reading and studying this chapter, you should be able to:

1. Identify several basic competitive strategies and explain how they can use information technologies to confront the competitive forces faced by a business.

2. Identify several strategic uses of information technologies for electronic business and commerce, and give examples of how they give competitive advantages to a business.

3. Give examples of how business process reengineering frequently involves the strategic use of Internet technologies.

4. Identify the business value of using Internet technologies for total quality management, to become an agile competitor, or to form a virtual company.

5. Explain how knowledge management systems can help a business gain strategic advantages.

Fundamentals of Strategic Advantage

Strategic IT

Technology is no longer an afterthought in forming business strategy, but the actual cause and driver [23].

This chapter will show you that it is important that you view information systems as more than a set of technologies that support efficient business operations, workgroup and enterprise collaboration, or effective business decision making. Information technology can change the way businesses compete. So you should also view information systems strategically, that is, as vital competitive networks, as a means of organizational renewal, and as a necessary investment in technologies that help a company adopt strategies and business processes that enable it to reengineer or reinvent itself in order to survive and succeed in today's dynamic business environment.

Section I of this chapter introduces fundamental competitive strategy concepts that underlie the strategic use of information systems. Section II then discusses several major strategic applications of information technology used by many companies today.

Analyzing WESCO International

Read the Real World Case on WESCO International on the next page. We can learn a lot about the strategic business uses of information technologies from this case. See Figure 2.1.

WESCO sales reps were spending 40 percent of their time gathering information from their suppliers to support the sales to their customers of nonstocked items that accounted for only 20 percent of total sales. So WESCO developed a new e-procurement system to connect their customer ordering system and inventory systems to the inventory systems of their suppliers. Now sales reps can connect to the inventory systems of major suppliers in a one-button process to determine if an item is in stock, and communicate this information to customers in only a few seconds. The new system has increased sales of nonstock items, reduced phone costs, and saved sales reps an enormous amount of time. E-commerce director Russ Lambert

FIGURE 2.1

Russ Lambert is director of e-commerce for WESCO International, which developed a new e-procurement system that connects to the inventory systems of its suppliers.

Source: Larry Ripple

REAL WORLD CASE 1

WESCO International, Inc.: Strategic Links in the Supply Chain

WESCO International, Inc. (www.wescodist. com), a $3.9 billion Pittsburgh-based company, through its WESCO Distribution subsidiary, is one of the largest distributors of electrical products and other MRO (maintenance, repair, and operating) supplies to large companies. WESCO has over 6,000 employees working out of five distribution centers in the U.S. and Canada, and about 360 branches mainly in the U.S., and also in Canada, Mexico, Nigeria, Singapore, the U.K., and Venezuela to serve over 100,000 global customers. Major markets served by WESCO include commercial and industrial construction, industrial processes and discrete manufacturers, large OEMs (original equipment manufacturers), data communications and electric utilities, institutions, and government agencies. WESCO's major competitors include Arrow Electronics, Graybar Electric, and W.W. Grainger.

WESCO also includes Bruckner Supply (www. brucknersupply.com), a division that provides a range of online and on-the-ground procurement and materials management outsourcing services to many companies. WESCO Distribution stocks more than 140,000 items from hundreds of manufacturers and offers its customers almost a million other maintenance, repair, and operating products that the company itself doesn't stock but distributes for over 20,000 suppliers.

Until recently, when WESCO sales representatives received orders for nonstocked items, they had to call the manufacturers directly or check their websites for pricing and availability. That information was then relayed back to the customer in a separate phone call. Although orders for nonstocked items account for only 20 percent of WESCO's business, gathering information on those purchases for customers took 40 percent of the sales force's time, says Russ Lambert, WESCO's director of e-commerce.

To address the problem, the company decided to develop a new e-procurement system to connect its customer ordering system and inventory systems to the inventory systems of its major suppliers. But WESCO had to find a standard way to query and pull information from heterogeneous supplier systems over the Web and into its own 20-year-old proprietary, mainframe "legacy" systems. That was the most difficult part of the project, Lambert says.

The company built an Internet gateway with a common set of network doorways that created inbound and outbound pathways to the legacy system. New custom software was written both to pull data into WESCO's legacy system and to integrate supplier systems with the gateway. WESCO used Vignette's content management software and BEA Systems' WebLogic application server as its core technologies for the project.

Since the new system went live in June, WESCO's 1,000 salespeople in 400 locations have been able to directly access the finished goods inventory systems of major suppliers. Now, while a customer requesting nonstocked items is still on the line, a salesperson can send a query over the Web to the supplier's inventory system with a one-button application, receive an answer in about 30 seconds, and communicate that to the customer.

WESCO's e-procurement system has resulted in increased sales of nonstock items and cut phone costs by reducing the duration of each call by at least six minutes. It has also saved an enormous amount of time for salespeople, Lambert says. He estimates that the company could save nearly $12 million annually if the new system saves 1,000 salespeople just three hours per week (at $75 per hour).

Considering that it has cost about $400,000 to implement the system, demonstrating return on investment has been a "slam dunk," says Lambert. The e-procurement system is also bound to have a major positive impact on customer perceptions of WESCO and future sales results, and strengthen the ties between WESCO and its suppliers, he says. Because of WESCO's new system, customers know when they call that they're making a real-time order against instock supplies, Lambert says. "It has been a great proof-of-concept about the power of direct linkage in the supply chain," he says.

"More and more, distributors are moving away from stocking inventory to becoming supplier reps," says Andy Chatha, an analyst at ABC Advisory Group in Dedham, Massachusetts. And e-business applications like WESCO's new system provide the visibility into supplier inventory systems that enables distributors like WESCO to carry less inventory and thereby cut costs, he adds.

Case Study Questions

1. What are the business benefits to WESCO and its suppliers of its new e-procurement system?

2. Is WESCO's new system a strategic use of information technology? Why or why not? Does it give the company a competitive advantage? Explain.

3. What other strategic moves could WESCO implement to gain competitive advantages? Visit the websites of WESCO and its competitors to help you answer.

Source: Adapted from Jaikumar Vijayan, "E-Procurement Talks Back," *Premiere 100 Best in Class* supplement, *Computerworld*, March 11, 2002, p. 17. Reprinted with permission from *Computerworld*.

also believes the new system will have a major positive impact on customer perceptions of WESCO and future sales results, and strengthen the ties between WESCO and its suppliers.

Competitive Strategy Concepts

In Chapter I, we emphasized that a major role of information systems applications in business was to provide effective support of a company's strategies for gaining competitive advantage. This strategic role of information systems involves using information technology to develop products, services, and capabilities that give a company major advantages over the competitive forces it faces in the global marketplace.

This creates **strategic information systems,** information systems that support or shape the competitive position and strategies of a business enterprise. So a strategic information system can be any kind of information system (TPS, MIS, DSS, etc.) that uses information technology to help an organization gain a competitive advantage, reduce a competitive disadvantage, or meet other strategic enterprise objectives [31]. Let's look at several basic concepts that define the role of such strategic information systems.

How should a business professional think about competitive strategies? How can competitive strategies be applied to the use of information systems by a business? Figure 2.2 illustrates an important conceptual framework for understanding and applying competitive strategies.

A company can survive and succeed in the long run only if it successfully develops strategies to confront five **competitive forces** that shape the structure of competition in its industry. In Michael Porter's classic model of competitive strategy, any business that wants to survive and succeed must develop and implement strategies to effectively counter (1) the rivalry of competitors within its industry, (2) the threat of new entrants, (3) the threat of substitutes, (4) the bargaining power of customers, and (5) the bargaining power of suppliers [34].

Figure 2.2 also illustrates that businesses can counter the threats of competitive forces that they face by implementing five basic **competitive strategies** [31].

FIGURE 2.2

Businesses can develop competitive strategies to counter the actions of the competitive forces they confront in the marketplace.

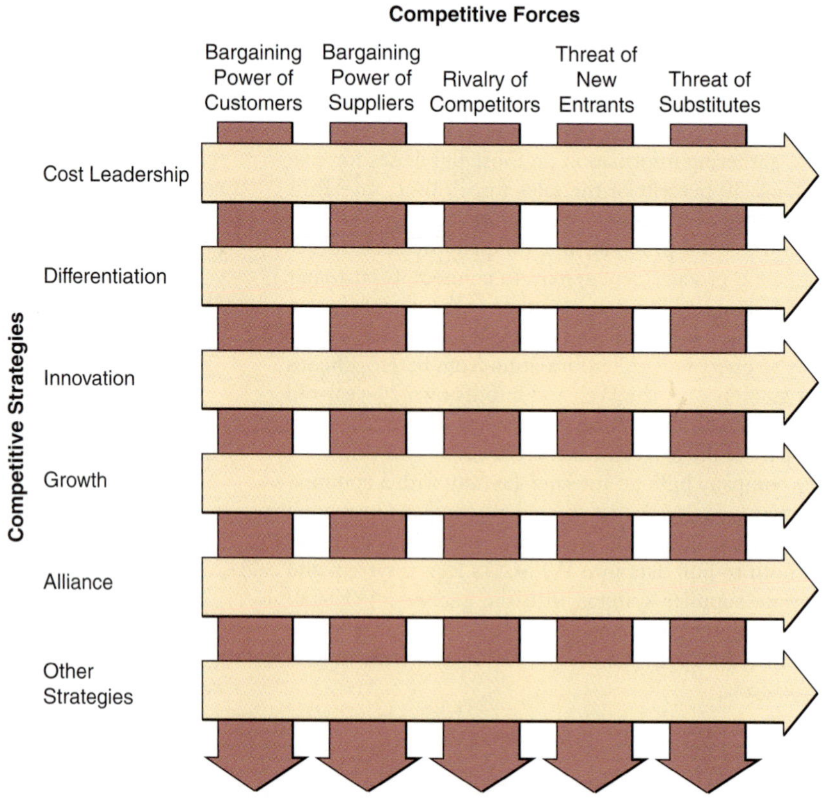

FIGURE 2.3

A summary of how information technology can be used to implement the five basic competitive strategies. Many companies are using Internet technologies as the foundation for such strategies.

Basic Strategies in the Business Use of Information Technology
Lower Costs   • Use IT to substantially reduce the cost of business processes.   • Use IT to lower the costs of customers or suppliers.
Differentiate   • Develop new IT features to differentiate products and services.   • Use IT features to reduce the differentiation advantages of competitors.   • Use IT features to focus products and services at selected market niches.
Innovate   • Create new products and services that include IT components.   • Develop unique new markets or market niches with the help of IT.   • Make radical changes to business processes with IT that dramatically cut costs, improve quality, efficiency, or customer service, or shorten time to market.
Promote Growth   • Use IT to manage regional and global business expansion.   • Use IT to diversify and integrate into other products and services.
Develop Alliances   • Use IT to create virtual organizations of business partners.   • Develop interenterprise information systems linked by the Internet and extranets that support strategic business relationships with customers, suppliers, subcontractors, and others.

- **Cost Leadership Strategy.** Becoming a low-cost producer of products and services in the industry. Also, a firm can find ways to help its suppliers or customers reduce their costs or to increase the costs of their competitors.

- **Differentiation Strategy.** Developing ways to differentiate a firm's products and services from its competitors' or reduce the differentiation advantages of competitors. This may allow a firm to focus its products or services to give it an advantage in particular segments or niches of a market.

- **Innovation Strategy.** Finding new ways of doing business. This may involve the development of unique products and services, or entry into unique markets or market niches. It may also involve making radical changes to the business processes for producing or distributing products and services that are so different from the way a business has been conducted that they alter the fundamental structure of an industry.

- **Growth Strategies.** Significantly expanding a company's capacity to produce goods and services, expanding into global markets, diversifying into new products and services, or integrating into related products and services.

- **Alliance Strategies.** Establishing new business linkages and alliances with customers, suppliers, competitors, consultants, and other companies. These linkages may include mergers, acquisitions, joint ventures, forming of "virtual companies," or other marketing, manufacturing, or distribution agreements between a business and its trading partners.

Strategic Uses of Information Technology

How can business managers use investments in information technology to directly support a firm's competitive strategies? Figure 2.3 answers that question with a summary of the many ways that information technology can help a business implement the five basic competitive strategies. Figure 2.4 provides examples of how specific companies have used strategic information systems to implement each of these five

FIGURE 2.4   Examples of how companies used information technology to implement five competitive strategies for strategic advantage. Note the use of Internet technologies for electronic business and commerce applications.

Strategy	Company	Strategic Information System	Business Benefit
Cost Leadership	Buy.com Priceline.com EBay.com	Online price adjustment Online seller bidding Online auctions	Lowest price guarantee Buyer-set pricing Auction-set prices
Differentiation	AVNET Marshall Ross Operating Valves Consolidated Freightways	Customer/supplier e-commerce Online customer design Customer online shipment tracking	Increase in market share Increase in market share Increase in market share
Innovation	Charles Schwab & Co. Federal Express Amazon.com	Online discount stock trading Online package tracking and flight management Online full service customer systems	Market leadership Market leadership Market leadership
Growth	Citicorp Wal-Mart Toys 'Я' Us Inc.	Global intranet Merchandise ordering by global satellite network POS inventory tracking	Increase in global market Market leadership Market leadership
Alliance	Wal-Mart/Procter & Gamble Cisco Systems Airborne Express/ Rentrak Corp.	Automatic inventory replenishment by supplier Virtual manufacturing alliances Online inventory management/ shipment tracking	Reduced inventory cost/increased sales Agile market leadership Increase in market share

basic strategies for competitive advantage. Note the major use of Internet technologies for electronic business and commerce applications. In the rest of this chapter, we will discuss and provide examples of many strategic uses of information technology.

Other Competitive Strategies

There are many other competitive strategies in addition to the five basic strategies of cost leadership, differentiation, innovation, growth, and alliance. Let's look at several key strategies that are also implemented with information technology. They are: locking in customers or suppliers, building switching costs, raising barriers to entry, and leveraging investment in information technology.

Investments in information technology can allow a business to **lock in customers and suppliers** (and lock out competitors) by building valuable new relationships with them. This can deter both customers and suppliers from abandoning a firm for its competitors or intimidating a firm into accepting less-profitable relationships. Early attempts to use information systems technology in these relationships focused on significantly improving the quality of service to customers and suppliers in a firm's distribution, marketing, sales, and service activities. Then businesses moved to more innovative uses of information technology.

Wal-Mart and Others

For example, Wal-Mart built an elaborate satellite network linking the point-of-sale terminals in all of its stores. The network was designed to provide managers, buyers, and sales associates with up-to-date sales and inventory status information to improve product buying, inventories, and store management. Then Wal-Mart began to use the operational efficiency of such information systems to offer lower cost, better-quality products and services, and differentiate itself from its competitors.

Companies like Wal-Mart began to extend their networks to their customers and suppliers in order to build innovative continuous inventory replenishment systems that would lock in their business. This creates **interenterprise information systems** in which the Internet, extranets, and other networks electronically link the computers of businesses with their customers and suppliers, resulting in new business alliances and partnerships. Extranets between businesses and their suppliers are prime examples of such strategic linkages. An even stronger e-business link is formed by *stockless* inventory replenishment systems such as those between Wal-Mart and Procter & Gamble. In that system, Procter & Gamble automatically replenishes Wal-Mart's stock of Procter & Gamble products [6, 27].

A major emphasis in strategic information systems has been to find ways to build **switching costs** into the relationships between a firm and its customers or suppliers. That is, investments in information systems technology, such as those mentioned in the Wal-Mart example, can make customers or suppliers dependent on the continued use of innovative, mutually beneficial interenterprise information systems. Then, they become reluctant to pay the costs in time, money, effort, and inconvenience that it would take to change to a company's competitors.

By making investments in information technology to improve its operations or promote innovation, a firm could also erect **barriers to entry** that would discourage or delay other companies from entering a market. Typically, this happens by increasing the amount of investment or the complexity of the technology required to compete in an industry or a market segment. Such actions would tend to discourage firms already in the industry and deter external firms from entering the industry.

Investing in information technology enables a firm to build strategic IT capabilities that allow it to take advantage of strategic opportunities when they arise. In many cases, this results when a company invests in advanced computer-based information systems to improve the efficiency of its own business processes. Then, armed with this strategic technology platform, the firm can **leverage investment in information technology** by developing new products and services that would not be possible without a strong IT capability. An important current example is the development of corporate intranets and extranets by many companies, which enables them to leverage their previous investments in Internet browsers, PCs, servers, and client/server networks. Figure 2.5 summarizes the additional strategic uses of IT we have just discussed.

FIGURE 2.5   Additional ways that information technology can be used to implement competitive strategies.

Other Strategic Uses of Information Technology
• Develop interenterprise information systems whose convenience and efficiency create switching costs that lock in customers or suppliers.
• Make major investments in advanced IT applications that build barriers to entry against industry competitors or outsiders.
• Include IT components in products and services to make substitution of competing products or services more difficult.
• Leverage investment in IS people, hardware, software, databases, and networks from operational uses into strategic applications.

Merrill Lynch and Charles Schwab

Merrill Lynch is a classic example of the use of several competitive strategies. By making large investments in information technology, along with a groundbreaking alliance with BancOne, they became the first securities brokers to offer a credit line, checking account, Visa credit card, and automatic investment in a money market fund, all in one account. This gave them a major competitive advantage for several years before their rivals could develop the IT capability to offer similar services on their own [31].

However, Merrill is now playing catch-up in online discount securities trading with Charles Schwab, e-Trade, and others. Schwab is now the leading online securities company with millions of online customers, far surpassing Merrill's online statistics. Thus, large investments in IT can make the stakes too high for some present or prospective players in an industry, but can evaporate over time as new technologies are employed by competitors [28].

The Value Chain and Strategic IS

Let's look at another important concept that can help you identify opportunities for strategic information systems. The value chain concept was developed by Michael Porter [34] and is illustrated in Figure 2.6. It views a firm as a series, chain, or network of basic activities that add value to its products and services, and thus add a margin of value to the firm. In the value chain conceptual framework, some business activities are primary processes; others are support processes. This framework can highlight where competitive strategies can best be applied in a business. That is, managers and business professionals should try to develop a variety of strategic uses of Internet and other technologies for those basic processes that add the most value to a company's products or services, and thus to the overall business value of the company.

Value Chain Examples

Figure 2.6 provides examples of how and where information technologies can be applied to basic business processes using the value chain framework. For example, Figure 2.6 emphasizes that collaborative workflow intranet-based systems can increase the communications and collaboration needed to dramatically improve administrative coordination and support services. A career development intranet can

FIGURE 2.6   The value chain of a firm. Note the examples of the variety of strategic information systems that can be applied to a firm's basic business processes for competitive advantage.

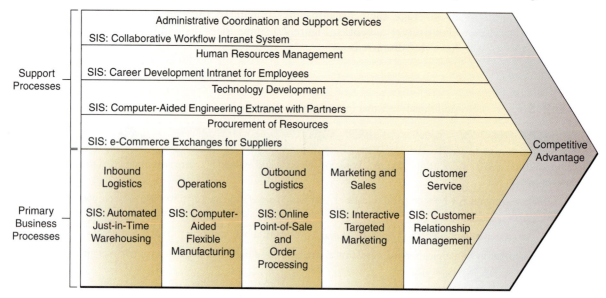

help the human resources management function provide employees with professional development training programs. Computer-aided engineering and design extranets enable a company and its business partners to jointly design products and processes. Finally, e-commerce auctions and exchanges can dramatically improve procurement of resources by providing an online marketplace for a firm's suppliers.

Other examples of strategic applications of information systems technology to primary business processes are identified by the value chain model in Figure 2.6. These include automated just-in-time warehousing systems to support inbound logistic processes involving storage of inventory, computer-aided flexible manufacturing (CAM) systems for manufacturing operations, and online point-of-sale and order processing systems to improve out-bound logistics processes that process customer orders. Information systems can also support marketing and sales processes by developing an interactive targeted marketing capability on the Internet and its World Wide Web. Finally, customer service can be dramatically improved by a coordinated and integrated customer relationship management system.

Thus, the value chain concept can help you decide where and how to apply the strategic capabilities of information technology. It shows how various types of information technologies might be applied to specific business processes to help a firm gain competitive advantages in the marketplace.

SECTION II   Using Information Technology for Strategic Advantage

Strategic Uses of IT

There are many ways that organizations may view and use information technology. For example, companies may choose to use information systems strategically, or they may be content to use IT to support efficient everyday operations. But if a company emphasized strategic business uses of information technology, its management would view IT as a major competitive differentiator. It would then devise business strategies that would use IT to develop products, services, and capabilities that would give the company major advantages in the markets in which it competes. In this section, we will provide many examples of such strategic business applications of information technology.

Analyzing Staples Inc.

Read the Real World Case on Staples Inc. on the next page. We can learn a lot about electronic business and commerce strategies from this example. See Figure 2.7.

Under the leadership of Michael Ragunas, chief technology officer of Staples. com, Staples developed a Web-based procurement system which uses the Staples business website as the interface between Staples procurement system and the procurement systems of large corporate customers. The new Web-based system has earned the loyalty of existing clients and attracted new corporate clients who wanted the same capability. Another innovation led by Ragunas was a multichannel sales system for Staples in-store customers. Now, customers can purchase and pay for items in the store or bought on the Staples website through online kiosks in the stores, as well as configure and buy PCs online through the kiosks or on the Staples.com website. These new clicks and bricks capabilities have resulted in increased online and in-store sales, reduced PC inventory costs, freed space for other products, and increased the sales per customer of customers who shop in Staples stores and on the Web.

FIGURE 2.7

Michael J. Ragunas is chief technology officer at Staples.com and led the development of a new Web-based procurement system for large business clients, and multichannel sales systems for Staples in-store customers.

Source: Christopher Harting

REAL WORLD CASE 2

Staples Inc.: Innovation in Business and Consumer e-Commerce

Sometimes real innovation lies in what's tried and true: hiring top-notch people, building a solid team, and listening to what they have to say. "'Eureka' ideas sometimes work, but I get more ideas—and better ones—by involving my team," says Michael J. Ragunas, chief technology officer at Staples.com in Framingham, Massachusetts. "Innovation is not something that comes down from the mountain, but from making sure the whole organization is able to come up with ideas and get them heard."

In his 15-year tenure at Staples Inc. (www.staples.com), Ragunas has transformed the office supplies retailer's stores with a complete systems overhaul, built dot-com revenue to nearly $1 billion when other dot-coms were dropping like flies, and took a flier on building a Web-based integration platform for their major corporate clients.

Ragunas, 37, says he doesn't have any magic formula for producing the kinds of ideas that have branded him as an innovator among IT leaders; he just follows good, sound management principles. "We push the envelope, but in a way that best serves shareholders and customers and that generates more revenue for the business," he says. "If you have the right team in place and provide them with food for thought, challenge them with forward-looking ideas, they will collectively generate more innovative ideas than you will as an individual."

To harvest the best ideas of his staff, Ragunas regularly schedules roundtables with 10 or 12 people. He also comes up with ideas on his own, such as Staples' web-based procurement project, which he calls the riskiest business decision he ever made.

Staples had several large corporate customers that wanted to connect their internal procurement systems via the Internet to StaplesLink.com, the company's business-to-business site. The big technology challenge for Staples was the decision to use XML (Extensible Markup Language) technology to build the software interface between the website and external procurement systems. Although XML was generating a lot of buzz as the web-interface language of the future, few companies had committed to it as a Web system integration standard. But Ragunas wanted to build a system that would be flexible enough to adapt to future needs.

"It wasn't a super hard sale," Ragunas says. "We could see the future of the technology and it was a pretty good wager that it would be around for a while and be more useful over time." So Staples developed an XML-based interface and first hooked its own procurement system up to the site. Not only has the web-based procurement system won the loyalty of existing partners, but it has also won the company new corporate accounts seeking the same capability.

Another innovation powered by Ragunas and his team was a clicks and bricks multichannel sales capability for Staples' in-store customers. Through in-store kiosks, Staples had already given shoppers at its stores the option of ordering merchandise from its Staples.com website and paying for it with their credit cards. The in-store access point project involved making system changes to let those customers consolidate their Staples.com and in-store purchases into one transaction and pay with cash, check, or credit card at the cash register. As part of the project, Staples also built a custom-configuration system that customers can use to design their own PCs at the in-store kiosks and on the Staples.com website.

Now when customers walk into any of Staples' more than 1,100 retail stores, they have access not only to the 7,000 to 8,000 stocked items but also to the 50,000 offered through Staples.com. "We are offering a much broader assortment to customers in the stores," says Ragunas. "The fact that you can consolidate your purchases and choose multiple ways to make purchases in the store puts them a level ahead of competitors like OfficeMax at this point," said Geri Spieler, an analyst at Stamford, Connecticut–based Gartner Inc.

Staples has logged close to $4 million in sales per week on the kiosks and eliminated its inventory of PCs in more than 200 stores, Ragunas says. With the custom-configuration system, customers get exactly what they want and Staples has reduced its PC inventory costs and freed space for other products, he adds. And customers using Staples.com in stores are more likely to also order merchandise through the website from their homes or offices. "We know that customers who shop with us in multiple channels spend more with us overall—2.5 times if two channels, 4.5 times if three," says Ragunas, emphasizing the business value of Staples' new multichannel capabilities.

Case Study Questions

1. What is the strategic business value to Staples and their large business clients of the new web-based procurement system?

2. What is the strategic business value to Staples and the value proposition to their consumer customers of Staples new clicks and bricks capabilities?

3. What other e-business or e-commerce strategy would you recommend to Staples to help them gain a competitive advantage in their industry? Visit their website and those of some of their competitors to gain ideas. Defend your proposal.

Source: Adapted from Leslie Goff, "The Innovators: What Makes Them Tick," *Computerworld*, January 1, 2002, p. 44; and Carol Sliwa, "Transaction Tool Ties Sales Channels," *Premiere 100 Best in Class* supplement to *Computerworld*, March 11, 2002, pp. 6–7. Reprinted with permission from *Computerworld*.

Building a Customer-Focused Business

The driving force behind world economic growth has changed from manufacturing volume to improving customer value. As a result, the key success factor for many firms is maximizing customer value [9].

For many companies, the chief business value of becoming a **customer-focused business** lies in its ability to help them keep customers loyal, anticipate their future needs, respond to customer concerns, and provide top-quality customer service. This strategic focus on **customer value** recognizes that quality, rather than prices, has become the primary determinant in a customer's perception of value. From a customer's point of view, companies that consistently offer the best value are able to keep track of their customers' individual preferences, keep up with market trends, supply products, services, and information anytime, anywhere, and provide customer services tailored to individual needs [9]. And so electronic commerce has become a strategic opportunity for companies, large and small, to offer fast, responsive, high-quality products and services tailored to individual customer preferences.

Internet technologies can make customers the focal point of all e-business and e-commerce applications. Internet, intranet, and extranet websites create new chan-

FIGURE 2.8
How a customer-focused business builds customer value and loyalty in electronic commerce.

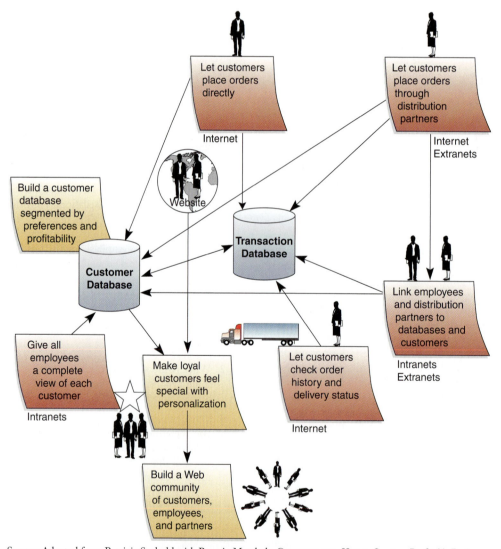

Source: Adapted from Patricia Seybold with Ronnie Marshak, *Customers.com: How to Create a Profitable Business Strategy for the Internet and Beyond* (New York: Times Books, 1998), p. 32.

nels for interactive communications within a company, with customers, and with the suppliers, business partners, and others in the external environment. This enables continual interaction with customers by most business functions and encourages cross-functional collaboration with customers in product development, marketing, delivery, service, and technical support [9].

Typically, e-commerce customers use the Internet to ask questions, air complaints, evaluate products, request support, and make and report their purchases. Using the Internet and corporate intranets, specialists in business functions throughout the enterprise can contribute to an effective response. This encourages the creation of cross-functional discussion groups and problem-solving teams dedicated to customer involvement, service, and support. Even the Internet and extranet links to suppliers and business partners can be used to enlist them in a way of doing business that ensures prompt delivery of quality components and services to meet a company's commitments to its customers [20]. This is how a business demonstrates its focus on customer value.

Figure 2.8 illustrates the interrelationships in a customer-focused business. Intranets, extranets, e-commerce websites, and web-enabled internal business processes form the invisible IT platform that supports this e-business model. This enables the business to focus on targeting the kinds of customers it really wants, and "owning" the customer's total business experience with the company. A successful business streamlines all business processes that impact their customers, and provides its employees with a complete view of each customer, so they can offer their customers top-quality personalized service. A customer-focused business helps their e-commerce customers to help themselves, while also helping them do their jobs. Finally, a successful business nurtures an online community of customers, employees, and business partners that builds great customer loyalty, while fostering cooperation to provide an outstanding customer experience [37]. Let's review a real world example.

Hilton Hotels: Customer-Focused e-Business Systems	Hilton Hotels, via Hilton.com, has one of the fastest reservation services in the world: The average time to complete a reservation is less than two minutes. Frequent guests have services automatically tailored to their last visit, and meeting planners access the website for group reservations and floor plans of venues. Bruce Rosenberg, Hilton's vice president of market distribution, says, "The Web opened up people's eyes about how we can and should do business. We looked at all the business models—every customer segment from the business traveller, the tourist, the meeting planner, the travel agent—and identified an e-business way of doing business with them."

Hilton's e-business initiative required information from multiple business units, interactivity among the customer, Hilton.com, and Hilton's existing back-end reservation systems, and a high level of personalization. "We want profiles on the customers, their history with us and what they like and don't like, accessible no matter where they touch us in the world," Rosenberg says. Hilton has very good profiles of members of HHonors (the Hilton frequent-customer loyalty program), but not so good profiles, Rosenberg notes, for the tens of millions of customers that only occasionally stay with Hilton. "The new systems we are building will allow us to have a larger number of profiles and a finer segmentation of our customer base. The Web will enable us to reach them cost effectively and develop a deeper personal relationship. We just couldn't do this before by mailing material to them. The budgets weren't there to support it."

Hilton is implementing a direct-to-customer business model via the Web channel, targeting the frequent-traveller segment and providing a single point of contact. All customer segments can use the Web channel, including both individuals |

and travel agents—with some travel agents bypassed when individuals contact Hilton directly. To implement this e-business initiative, Hilton integrates work-flows, reservation systems, call centers, and business processes with the common goal of obtaining more finely segmented customer data. The initiative required a strong vision to evolve to an e-business, many negotiations across business units within Hilton, alliances with other firms, investment in IT infrastructure, and integration of Internet-based application with a large database of segmented customer profiles and various existing reservation systems [40].

Reengineering Business Processes

One of the most important implementations of competitive strategies today is **business process reengineering** (BPR), most often simply called reengineering. Reengineering is a fundamental rethinking and radical redesign of business processes to achieve dramatic improvements in cost, quality, speed, and service. So BPR combines a strategy of promoting business innovation with a strategy of making major improvements to business processes so that a company can become a much stronger and more successful competitor in the marketplace.

However, Figure 2.9 points out that while the potential payback of reengineering is high, so is its risk of failure and level of disruption to the organizational environment [16]. Making radical changes to business processes to dramatically improve efficiency and effectiveness is not an easy task. For example, many companies have used cross-functional enterprise resource planning (ERP) software to reengineer, automate, and integrate their manufacturing, distribution, finance, and human resource business processes. While many companies have reported impressive gains with such ERP reengineering projects, many others have failed to achieve the improvements they sought (as we saw in the real world example of A-DEC in Chapter 1).

That's why *organizational redesign* approaches are an important enabler of reengineering, along with the use of information technology. For example, one common approach is the use of self-directed cross-functional or multidisciplinary *process teams*. Employees from several departments or specialties including engineering, marketing, customer service, and manufacturing may work as a team on the product development process. Another example is the use of *case managers*, who handle almost all tasks in a business process, instead of splitting tasks among many different specialists.

FIGURE 2.9
How business process reengineering differs from business improvement.

	Business Improvement	Business Reengineering
Definition	Incrementally improving existing processes	Radically redesigning business processes
Target	Any process	Strategic business processes
Primary Enablers	IT and work simplification	IT and organizational redesign
Potential Payback	10%–50% improvements	10-fold improvements
What Changes?	Same jobs, just more efficient	Big job cuts; new jobs; major job redesign
Risk of Failure and Level of Disruption	Low	

FIGURE 2.10   The order management process consists of several business processes and crosses the boundaries of traditional business functions.

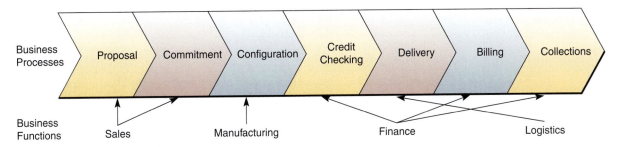

The Role of Information Technology

Information technology plays a major role in reengineering most business processes. The speed, information processing capabilities, and connectivity of computers and Internet technologies can substantially increase the efficiency of business processes, as well as communications and collaboration among the people responsible for their operation and management. For example, the order management process illustrated in Figure 2.10 is vital to the success of most companies [10]. Many of them are reengineering this process with enterprise resource planning software and Web-enabled electronic business and commerce systems. See Figure 2.11. Now, let's take a look at an example from Ford Motor Company.

Ford Motor Company: Driving e-Engineering

Ford believes the Internet is ushering in an even bigger wave of business transformation than reengineering. Call it e-engineering. Ford realizes it's not enough to put up simple websites for customers, employees, and partners. To take full advantage of the Net, they've got to reinvent the way they do business—changing how they design, manufacture, and distribute goods, collaborate inside and outside the company, and deal with suppliers.

Ford is using Web technologies to reengineer its internal business processes as well as those between the company and its dealers, suppliers, and customers. For example, Ford's global intranet connects thousands of designers in the United States and Europe so they can collaborate on design projects. Also, extranet links enable suppliers from all over the world to collaborate on the design, manufacture, and assembly of automotive components. All of these e-engineering initiatives are designed to slash costs, reduce time to market, and lower inventory and workforce levels, while improving the sales, quality, and consistency of Ford's products. Ford's global intranet brings 4,500 engineers from labs in the United States, Germany, and England together in cyberspace to collaborate on automobile design projects. The idea is to break down the barriers between regional operations so basic auto components are designed once and used everywhere. When design plans conflict, the software automatically sends out e-mail alerts to members of design teams. When all of the pieces are in place, the company hopes to transform the way it designs and produces cars, so it can quickly build them to order [21, 40].

FIGURE 2.11
Examples of information technologies that support reengineering the sales and order management processes.

Reengineering Order Management
• Customer relationship management systems using corporate intranets and the Internet.
• Supplier managed inventory systems using the Internet and extranets.
• Cross-functional ERP software for integrating manufacturing, distribution, finance, and human resource processes.
• Customer-accessible e-commerce websites for order entry, status checking, payment, and service.
• Customer, product, and order status databases accessed via intranets and extranets by employees and suppliers.

Improving Business Quality

Information technology can be used strategically to improve business performance in many ways other than in supporting reengineering initiatives. One important strategic thrust is continuous quality improvement, popularly called **total quality management** (TQM). Previous to TQM, quality was defined as meeting established standards or specifications for a product or service. Statistical *quality control* programs were used to measure and correct any deviations from standards [10].

Total Quality Management

Total quality management is a much more strategic approach to business improvement. Quality is emphasized from the customer's viewpoint, rather than the producer's. Thus, quality is defined as meeting or exceeding the requirements and expectations of customers for a product or service. This may involve many features and attributes, such as performance, reliability, durability, responsiveness, and aesthetics, to name a few [33].

TQM may use a variety of tools and methods to seek continuous improvement of quality, productivity, flexibility, timeliness, and customer responsiveness. According to quality expert Richard Schonberger, companies that use TQM are committed to:

1. Even better, more appealing, less-variable quality of the product or service.
2. Even quicker, less-variable response—from design and development through supplier and sales channels, offices, and plants all the way to the final user.
3. Even greater flexibility in adjusting to customers' shifting volume and mix requirement.
4. Even lower cost through quality improvement, rework reduction, and non-value-adding waste elimination [33].

FIGURE 2.12
The results of GE's Six Sigma total quality management program in its Superabrasives division.

GE Superabrasives Business Process Results
• Operating margins rose from 9.8% to 25.5%.
• Variable manufacturing costs fell 50%.
• The number of carats per manufacturing run rose 500%.
• On-time deliveries improved 85%.
• Product quality improved 87%.
• Late deliveries to customers declined 85%.
• Billing mistakes fell 87%.
• Capital expenditures decreased 40%.

Source: Adapted from Kathleen Melymuka, "GE's Quality Gamble," *Computerworld,* June 8, 1998, p. 64.

GE's Six Sigma Quality Initiative

Six Sigma is one of the most fundamental and far-reaching strategic initiatives ever undertaken by General Electric (GE) to optimize its competitiveness.

Six Sigma is the mother of all quality efforts. To achieve it, GE will have to eliminate 9,999.5 of every 10,000 defects in its processes or only 3.4 defects per million opportunities. That's a tall order, but it's one that would add $8 billion to $12 billion to the bottom line.

GE's Superabrasives business, which produces industrial diamonds, has virtually completed the implementation of Six Sigma, giving a glimpse of what might be expected companywide in a few years. Figure 2.12 outlines the improvements that occurred.

The Six Sigma mantra for approaching any process is "define, measure, analyze, improve, control," and information technology enables many of those activities. GE uses IT to collect baseline quality data, model defect-free Six Sigma processes, automate those processes to lock in improvements, and monitor them to assure they remain defect-free.

For example, a foundation of Six Sigma is that customers define a defect. GE developed an extranet website called the "customer dashboard" that invites more than 1,000 key customers to identify the most critical-to-quality (CTQ) aspects of GE products and services that define a good performance and a defect. For example, if a customer chose speedy product delivery as a CTQ aspect, it would then define a good performance—say, five days. Anything slower is a defect.

Having defined the CTQ aspects, customers use the dashboard to provide regular, precise, quantitative feedback on how GE's processes measure up, giving a snapshot of its performance at a given moment and a trend line over time.

GE also developed an intranet website that helps all employees focus on the Six Sigma process. It provides information and status reports on every project and shares best practices among 6,000 "black belt" Six Sigma experts, who work full-time on the effort, and 30,000 "green belts," who integrate Six Sigma projects into their regular workloads [29].

Becoming an Agile Company

We are changing from a competitive environment in which mass-market products and services were standardized, long-lived, information-poor, and exchanged in one-time transactions, to an environment in which companies compete globally with niche market products and services that are individualized, short-lived, information-rich, and exchanged on an ongoing basis with customers [19].

Agility in business performance is the ability of a company to prosper in rapidly changing, continually fragmenting global markets for high-quality, high-performance, customer-configured products and services. An **agile company** can make a profit in markets with broad product ranges and short model lifetimes, and can produce orders in arbitrary lot sizes. It supports *mass customization* by offering individualized products while maintaining high volumes of production. Agile companies depend heavily on Internet technologies to integrate and manage business processes, while providing the information processing power to treat masses of customers as individuals.

To be an agile company, a business must implement four basic strategies. First, customers of an agile company perceive products or services as solutions to their individual problems. Thus, products can be priced based on their value as solutions, not on their cost to produce. Second, an agile company cooperates with customers, suppliers, and other companies, even *competition* with competitors. This allows a business to bring products to market as rapidly and cost-effectively as possible, no matter where resources are located and who owns them. Third, an agile company organizes so that it thrives on change and uncertainty. It uses flexible organizational structures keyed to the requirements of different and constantly changing customer opportunities. Finally, an agile company leverages the impact of its people and the knowledge they possess. By nurturing an entrepreneurial spirit, an agile company provides powerful incentives for employee responsibility, adaptability, and innovation [19]. Now let's take another look at AVNET Marshall, which is a great example of an agile company.

AVNET Marshall: Agile for the Customer

Marshall realized that customers, if given a choice, wanted everything: products and services at the lowest possible cost, highest possible quality, greatest possible customization, and fastest possible delivery time. At the limit, this translates to the impossible goals of "Free.Perfect.Now" [13].

Figure 2.13 reveals the components of the Free.Perfect.Now business model that inspired the company then known as Marshall Industries to be an agile, customer-focused company. AVNET Marshall developed the model as a clear, simple, and powerful tool to focus its employees and its information technology platform on serving its customers in the most agile and responsive ways.

The Free dimension emphasizes that most customers want the lowest cost for value received, but are willing to pay more for a value-added services such as inventory management. The Perfect dimension stresses that AVNET Marshall's products and services should not only be defect-free, but that their quality can be enhanced by added features, customization, and anticipation of the future needs of the customer. Finally, the Now dimension of this business model emphasizes that customers want 24/7 accessibility to products and services, short delivery times, and consideration of the time-to-market for their own products [13].

AVNET Marshall's extensive use of Internet technologies for innovative Internet, intranet, and extranet e-commerce websites and services for its customers, suppliers, and employees is a cornerstone of their IT and e-business strategies. Such technologies are essential to the agility and customer responsiveness that have made them a successful e-business pioneer.

FIGURE 2.13   The Free.Perfect.Now business model developed by AVNET Marshall to guide its transformation into an agile, customer-focused company.

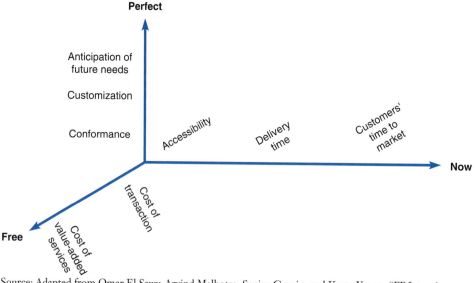

Source: Adapted from Omar El Sawy, Arvind Malhotra, Sanjay Gosain, and Kerry Young, "IT Intensive Value Innovation in the Electronic Economy: Insights from Marshall Industries," *MIS Quarterly*, September 1999, p. 311. Reprinted with permission from the *MIS Quarterly*.

FIGURE 2.14   A virtual company uses the Internet, intranets, and extranets to form virtual workgroups and support alliances with business partners.

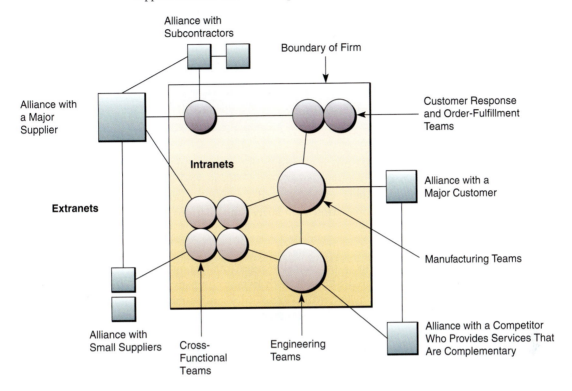

Creating a Virtual Company

These days, thousands of companies, large and small, are setting up virtual corporations that enable executives, engineers, scientists, writers, researchers, and other professionals from around the world to collaborate on new products and services without ever meeting face to face. Once the exclusive domain of Fortune 500 companies with banks of powerful computers and dedicated wide area networks, remote networking is now available to any company with a phone, a fax, and e-mail access to the Internet [36].

In today's dynamic global business environment, forming a **virtual company** can be one of the most important strategic uses of information technology. A virtual company (also called a *virtual corporation* or *virtual organization*) is an organization that uses information technology to link people, assets, and ideas.

Figure 2.14 illustrates that virtual companies typically form virtual workgroups and alliances with business partners that are interlinked by the Internet, intranets, and extranets. Notice that this company has organized internally into clusters of process and cross-functional teams linked by intranets. It has also developed alliances and extranet links that form **interenterprise information systems** with suppliers, customers, subcontractors, and competitors. Thus, virtual companies create flexible and adaptable virtual workgroups and alliances keyed to exploit fast-changing business opportunities [4].

Virtual Company Strategies

Why are people forming virtual companies? Several major reasons stand out and are summarized in Figure 2.15. People and corporations are forming virtual companies as the best way to implement key business strategies and alliances that promise to ensure success in today's turbulent business climate.

For example, in order to exploit a diverse and fast-changing market opportunity, a business may not have the time or resources to develop the manufacturing and distribution infrastructure, people competencies, and information technologies needed. Only by quickly forming a virtual company through a strategic alliance of

FIGURE 2.15

The basic business strategies of virtual companies.

Strategies of Virtual Companies
● Share infrastructure and risk with alliance partners.
● Link complementary core competencies.
● Reduce concept-to-cash time through sharing.
● Increase facilities and market coverage.
● Gain access to new markets and share market or customer loyalty.
● Migrate from selling products to selling solutions.

all-star partners can it assemble the components it needs to provide a world-class solution for customers and capture the market opportunity. Of course, today, the Internet, intranets, extranets, and a variety of other Internet technologies are vital components in creating such successful solutions.

Cisco Systems: Virtual Manufacturing Alliances

Cisco Systems is the world's largest manufacturer of telecommunications products. Jabil Circuit is the fourth largest company in the electronics contract manufacturing industry, with annual sales approaching $1 billion. Cisco has a *virtual manufacturing company* arrangement with Jabil and Hamilton Corporation, a major electronics parts supplier. Let's look at an example of how these three companies are involved in a typical business transaction.

An order placed for a Cisco 1600 series router (an internetwork processor used to connect small offices to networks) arrives simultaneously at Cisco in San Jose, California, and Jabil in St. Petersburg, Florida. Jabil immediately starts to build the router by drawing parts from three on-site inventories: Jabil's, one belonging to Cisco, and one owned and controlled by Hamilton. When completed, the router is tested and checked against the order in St. Petersburg by computers in San Jose, then shipped directly to the customer by Jabil. That triggers a Cisco invoice to the customer and electronic billings from Jabil and Hamilton to Cisco in San Jose. Thus, Cisco's virtual manufacturing company alliance with Jabil and Hamilton gives them an agile, build-to-order capability in the fiercely competitive telecommunications equipment industry [39].

Building a Knowledge-Creating Company

In an economy where the only certainty is uncertainty, the one sure source of lasting competitive advantage is knowledge. When markets shift, technologies proliferate, competitors multiply, and products become obsolete almost overnight, successful companies are those that consistently create new knowledge, disseminate it widely throughout the organization, and quickly embody it in new technologies and products. These activities define the "knowledge-creating" company, whose sole business is continuous innovation [32].

To many companies today, lasting competitive advantage can only be theirs if they become **knowledge-creating companies** or *learning organizations*. That means consistently creating new business knowledge, disseminating it widely throughout the company, and quickly building the new knowledge into their products and services.

Knowledge-creating companies exploit two kinds of knowledge. One is *explicit knowledge*—data, documents, things written down or stored on computers. The other kind is tacit knowledge—the "how-tos" of knowledge, which reside in workers. As illustrated in Figure 2.16, successful **knowledge management** creates techniques, technologies, systems, and rewards for getting employees to share what they know and to make better use of accumulated workplace and enterprise knowledge.

FIGURE 2.16

Knowledge management can be viewed as three levels of techniques, technologies, and systems that promote the collection, organization, access, sharing, and use of workplace and enterprise knowledge.

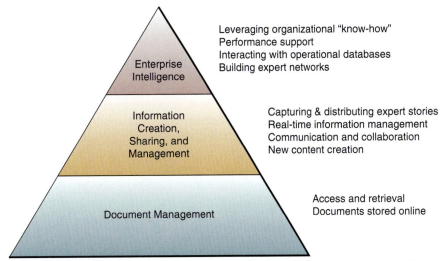

Source: Adapted from Marc Rosenberg, *e-Learning: Strategies for Delivering Knowledge in the Digital Age* (New York, McGraw-Hill, 2001), p. 70.

In that way, employees of a company are leveraging knowledge as they do their jobs [32].

Knowledge Management Systems

Making personal knowledge available to others is the central activity of the knowledge-creating company. It takes place continuously and at all levels of the organization [32]

Knowledge management has thus become one of the major strategic uses of information technology. Many companies are building **knowledge management systems** (KMS) to manage organizational learning and business know-how. The goal of such systems is to help knowledge workers create, organize, and make available important business knowledge, wherever and whenever it's needed in an organization. This includes processes, procedures, patents, reference works, formulas, "best practices," forecasts, and fixes. As you will see in Chapter 8, Internet and intranet websites, groupware, data mining, knowledge bases, and online discussion groups are some of the key technologies that may be used by a KMS.

Knowledge management systems facilitate organizational learning and knowledge creation. They are designed to provide rapid feedback to knowledge workers, encourage behavior changes by employees, and significantly improve business performance. As the organizational learning process continues and its knowledge base expands, the knowledge-creating company works to integrate its knowledge into its business processes, products, and services. This helps the company become a more innovative and agile provider of high-quality products and customer services, and a formidable competitor in the marketplace [35]. Now let's close this chapter with an example of knowledge management strategies from the real world.

Siemens AG: Global Knowledge Management System

Joachim Doring is a Siemens vice president in charge of creating a high-tech solution to the age-old problem of getting employees to stop hoarding their know-how. His grand plan: Use the Internet to spread the knowledge of 461,000 co-workers around the globe so that people could build off one another's expertise. At the heart of his vision is a website called ShareNet. The site combines elements of a chat room, a database, and a search engine. An online entry form lets employees store information they think might be useful to colleagues—anything from a description of a successful project to a PowerPoint presentation. Other Siemens workers can search or browse by topic, then contact the authors via e-mail for more information.

So far, the payoff has been a dandy: Since its inception in April 1999, ShareNet has been put to the test by nearly 12,000 salespeople in Siemens' $10.5 billion Information & Communications Networks Groups, which provides telecom equipment and services. The tool, which cost only $7.8 million, has added $122 million in sales. For example, it was crucial to landing a $3 million contract to build a pilot broadband network for Telecom Malaysia. The local salespeople did not have enough expertise to put together a proposal, but through ShareNet they discovered a team in Denmark that had done a nearly identical project. Using the Denmark group's expertise, the Malaysia team won the job.

Better yet, the system lets staffers post an alert when they need help fast. In Switzerland, Siemens won a $460,000 contract to build a telecommunications network for two hospitals even though its bid was 30 percent higher than a competitor's. The clincher: Via ShareNet, colleagues in the Netherlands provided technical data to help the sales rep prove that Siemens' system would be substantially more reliable [15].

Summary

- **Strategic Uses of Information Technology.** Information technologies can support many competitive strategies. They can help a business cut costs, differentiate and innovate in its products and services, promote growth, develop alliances, lock in customers and suppliers, create switching costs, raise barriers to entry, and leverage its investment in IT resources. Thus, information technology can help a business gain a competitive advantage in its relationships with customers, suppliers, competitors, new entrants, and producers of substitute products. Refer to Figures 2.3 and 2.5 for summaries of the uses of information technology for strategic advantage.

- **Building a Customer-Focused Business.** A key strategic use of Internet technologies is to build a company that develops its business value by making customer value its strategic focus. Customer-focused companies use Internet, intranet, and extranet e-commerce websites and services to keep track of their customers' preferences; supply products, services, and information anytime, anywhere; and provide services tailored to the individual needs of their customers.

- **Reengineering Business Processes.** Information technology is a key ingredient in reengineering business operations by enabling radical changes to business processes that dramatically improve their efficiency and effectiveness. Internet technologies can play a major role in supporting innovative changes in the design of work flows, job requirements, and organizational structures in a company.

- **Improving Business Quality.** Information technology can be used to strategically improve the quality of business performance. In a total quality management

approach, IT can support programs of continual improvement in meeting or exceeding customer requirements and expectations about the quality of products, services, customer responsiveness, and other features.

- **Becoming an Agile Company.** A business can use information technology to help it become an agile company. Then it can prosper in rapidly changing markets with broad product ranges and short model lifetimes in which it must process orders in arbitrary lot sizes, and can offer its customers customized products while maintaining high volumes of production. An agile company depends heavily on Internet technologies to help it be responsive to its customers with customized solutions to their needs and cooperate with its customers, suppliers, and other businesses to bring products to market as rapidly and cost-effectively as possible.

- **Creating a Virtual Company.** Forming virtual companies has become an important competitive strategy in today's dynamic global markets. Internet and other information technologies play an important role in providing computing and telecommunications resources to support the communications, coordination, and information flows needed. Managers of a virtual company depend on IT to help them manage a network of people, knowledge, financial, and physical resources provided by many business partners to quickly take advantage of rapidly changing market opportunities.

- **Building a Knowledge-Creating Company.** Lasting competitive advantage today can only come from innovative use and management of organizational knowledge by knowledge-creating companies and learning organizations. Internet technologies are widely used in knowledge management systems to support the

creation and dissemination of business knowledge and its integration into new products, services, and business processes.

Key Terms and Concepts

These are the key terms and concepts of this chapter. The page number of their first explanation is in parentheses.

1. Agile company (55)
2. Business process reengineering (52)
3. Competitive forces (42)
4. Competitive strategies (42)
5. Creating switching costs (44)
6. Customer-focused business (50)
7. Interenterprise information systems (57)
8. Knowledge-creating company (58)
9. Knowledge management system (59)
10. Leveraging investment in IT (45)
11. Locking in customers and suppliers (44)
12. Raising barriers to entry (45)
13. Strategic information systems (42)
14. Strategic uses of information technology (43)
15. Strategic uses of Internet technologies (51)
16. Total quality management (54)
17. Value chain (46)
18. Virtual company (57)

Review Quiz

Match one of the key terms and concepts listed previously with one of the brief examples or definitions that follow. Try to find the best fit for answers that seem to fit more than one term or concept. Defend your choices.

_____ 1. A business must deal with customers, suppliers, competitors, new entrants, and substitutes.

_____ 2. Cost leadership, differentiation of products, and new product innovation are examples.

_____ 3. Using investment in technology to keep firms out of an industry.

_____ 4. Making it unattractive for a firm's customers or suppliers to switch to its competitors.

_____ 5. Time, money, and effort needed for customers or suppliers to change to a firm's competitors.

_____ 6. Information systems that reengineer business processes or promote business innovation are examples.

_____ 7. Internet technologies enable a company to emphasize customer value as its strategic focus.

_____ 8. Highlights how strategic information systems can be applied to a firm's business processes and support activities for competitive advantage.

_____ 9. A business can find strategic uses for the computing and telecommunications capabilities it has developed to run its operations.

_____ 10. A business can use information systems to build barriers to entry, promote innovation, create switching costs, and so on.

_____ 11. Information technology can help a business make radical improvements in business processes.

_____ 12. Programs of continual improvement in meeting or exceeding customer requirements or expectations.

_____ 13. A business can prosper in rapidly changing markets while offering its customers individualized solutions to their needs.

_____ 14. A network of business partners formed to take advantage of rapidly changing market opportunities.

_____ 15. Many companies use the Internet, intranets, and extranets to achieve strategic gains in their competitive position.

_____ 16. Learning organizations that focus on creating, disseminating, and managing business knowledge.

_____ 17. Information systems that manage the creation and dissemination of organizational knowledge.

_____ 18. Using the Internet and extranets to link a company's information systems to those of its customers and suppliers.

Discussion Questions

1. Suppose you are a manager being asked to develop e-business and e-commerce applications to gain a competitive advantage in an important market for your company. What reservations might you have about doing so? Why?

2. How could a business use information technology to increase switching costs and lock in its customers and suppliers? Use business examples to support your answers.

3. How could a business leverage its investment in information technology to build strategic IT capabilities that serve as a barrier to entry by new entrants into its markets?

4. Refer to the Real World Case on Staples Inc. in the chapter. Is an integrated clicks and bricks strategy, like that chosen by Staples, the Internet strategy that most businesses, large and small, should adopt? Defend your position.

5. What strategic role can information play in business process reengineering and total quality management?

6. How can Internet technologies help a business form strategic alliances with its customers, suppliers, and others?

7. How could a business use Internet technologies to form a virtual company or become an agile competitor?

8. Refer to the Real World Case on Enron Corp. and Others at the end of the chapter. "Is it time to go back to the days when IT supported the business rather than became the business?" Explain your position on this question from the case.

9. Information technology can't really give a company a strategic advantage, because most competitive advantages don't last more than a few years and soon become strategic necessities that just raise the stakes of the game. Discuss.

10. MIS author and consultant Peter Keen says: "We have learned that it is not technology that creates a competitive edge, but the management process that exploits technology." What does he mean? Do you agree or disagree? Why?

Application Exercises

Complete the following exercises as individual or group projects that apply chapter concepts to real world business situations.

1. **AVNET Marshall and Hilton Hotels: Customer-Focused Businesses**

   Web Visit the top-rated websites of AVNET Marshall (www.avnetmarshall.com) and Hilton Hotels (www.hilton.com), which are highlighted in the chapter as examples of customer-focused companies. Check out many of their website features and e-commerce services.

   a. Which site provided you with the best quality of service as a prospective customer? Explain.

   b. How could these companies improve their website design and marketing to offer even better services to their customers and prospective customers?

2. **Sabre's Travelocity and American Airlines: Competing for e-Travel Services**

   Web Visit the top-rated websites of Travelocity (www.travelocity.com), which is 70 percent owned by Sabre, and American Airlines (www.aa.com), the former corporate owner of Sabre. Check out their website features and e-commerce services.

   a. How do their e-commerce websites and business models seem to differ?

   b. Refer to the summaries of strategic uses of IT in Figures 2.3 and 2.5. Which strategies can you see each company using? Explain.

   c. How could each company improve their competitive position in travel services e-commerce?

3. **Assessing Strategy and Business Performance**

    SS Recent annual figures for eBay.com's net revenue, stock price, and earnings per share at the time of publication of this book are shown in Table 2.1. eBay™ is one of the firms identified in Figure 2.4 as following a cost leadership strategy. Update the data for eBay™ if more recent annual figures are available and get comparable data for at least one other firm from the set of firms listed in Figure 2.4. (You can get financial data about most companies by looking on their website for a link called investor relations or about the company. If necessary search the index or site map.)

    a. Create a spreadsheet based on these data. Your spreadsheet should include measures of percentage change in revenues, earnings per share and stock price. You should also compute the price earnings (PE) ratio, that is stock price divided by earnings per share. (Note that some companies may have no earning for a particular year so that the PE ratio cannot be computed for that year.)

    b. Create appropriate graphs highlighting trends in the performance of each company.

    c. Write a brief (one page) report addressing how successful each company appears to be in maintaining strategic advantage? How important were general market conditions in affecting the financial performance of your companies?

TABLE 2.1
eBay's financial performance.

Year	Net Revenue (in millions)	Earnings per Share	Stock Price (at Year End)
1998	$186.129	$0.05	$40.21
1999	224.724	0.08	62.59
2000	431.424	0.17	33.00

4. **Just-in-Time Inventory Systems for Pinnacle Manufacturing**

    SS Pinnacle Manufacturing is evaluating a proposal for the development of a new inventory management system that will allow it to use just-in-time techniques to manage the inventories of key raw materials. It is estimated that the new system will allow Pinnacle to operate with inventory levels for gadgets, widgets, and sprockets equaling 10 days of production and with inventories equaling only 5 days of production for cams and gizmos. In order to estimate the inventory cost savings from this system, you have been asked to gather information about current inventory levels at all of Pinnacle's production facilities. You have received estimates of the current inventory level of each raw material, the amount of each raw material used in a typical production day, and the average dollar value of a unit of each raw material. These estimates are shown in Table 2.2.

    a. Create a spreadsheet based on estimates below. Your spreadsheet should include a column showing the number of days of inventory of each raw material currently held (inventory value divided by inventory used per production day). It should also include columns showing the inventory needed under the new system (inventory used per day times 10 or 5) and the reduction in inventory under the new system for each raw material. Finally you should include columns showing the dollar value of existing inventories, the dollar value of inventories under the new system, and the reduction in dollar value of the inventories held.

    b. Assume that the annual cost of holding inventory is 10 percent times the level of inventory held. Add a summary showing the overall annual savings from the new system.

TABLE 2.2
Pinnacle's inventory estimates.

Item	Inventory (units)	Units Used per Day	Cost per Unit
Gadget	2,437,250	97,645	$2.25
Widget	3,687,450	105,530	0.85
Sprocket	1,287,230	29,632	3.25
Cam	2,850,963	92,732	1.28
Gizmo	6,490,325	242,318	2.60

Enron Corp. and Others: Lessons in the Strategic Business Use of IT

Even great ideas have their limits. Following the debut of Enron Corp.'s web-based power and gas trading platform, revenue at the Houston-based energy company jumped from $40.1 billion in 1999 to $100.8 billion the following year. But after striking gold by combining its energy industry experience with a world-class trading system, Enron (www.enron.com) kept digging into new markets, convinced that its IT infrastructure had the Midas touch. In 2000, Enron suffered a $60 million loss in its broadband business. It struggled in more than a dozen unfamiliar industries and crashed within a year.

Questionable partnerships, overaggressive investments, and shady accounting practices top a long list of factors in Enron's downfall. But as they look for lessons from history's biggest bankruptcy, executives in all industries are questioning whether they, like Enron, spent so much time turning IT into a profit center that they lost sight of their organizations' core missions.

Is it time to go back to the days when IT supported the business rather than became the business? "I think Enron's bankruptcy is going to have a very sobering effect on boardrooms across the country," said Dick Hudson, former CIO of Houston-based oil drilling company Global Marine Inc. and now president of Hudson & Associates, an executive IT consulting firm in Katy, Texas. "You can almost see a bunker mentality taking hold in the senior suites." Hudson said he has heard from CEOs who have been reviewing their risky IT ventures, such as application service provider spin-offs or extraneous e-commerce services, to make sure they don't have any investments that will blow up in their face. If they find any such ventures, he added, "they will probably retrench. It's a bottomless pit."

Charlie Lacefield, who retired from his position as CIO at Midland, Michigan–based Dow Corning Corp. three years ago, warned that although IT innovation is critical for companies to thrive in a global economy, those that stray too far from their core business strategies could see their plans backfire on them, as it did with Enron. "If IT is not the core competency of the organization, then why throw away the core business competency in favor of IT?" asked Lacefield, who now lives in North Carolina. "Why would you want to do that with so many IT companies out there . . . that already have a running start on you?"

Hudson said he thinks Enron started with a good business strategy and that if it hadn't pushed the envelope, it could well have been a successful Fortune 1,000 firm. But its sights were set on the Fortune 10, so it got into markets such as broadband, which is a tough nut to crack even for the industry's leaders, he added. "Those good old boys in Houston, they had to walk with the big dogs," said Hudson. "They are a textbook case of greed and mismanagement." Enron officials couldn't be reached for comment.

"What the 90s showed us was how much IT can do," said Charlie Feld, CEO of Irving, Texas-based IT management firm the Feld Group. "I think the next decade is going to be about businesses finding ways to harness all that creativity and use it, rather than chasing it because it's there." As a CIO for hire at companies like Delta Air Lines Inc. in Atlanta and Frito-Lay Inc. in Plano Texas, Feld's jobs have often been about simplifying IT infrastructures that grew complex because companies chased so many new opportunities that they lost focus. "Companies fall in love with different technologies or business plans, and suddenly they find their infrastructure's been built in stovepipes," said Feld. "IT should make life simpler."

Companies poured cash into customer relationship management, enterprise resource planning, and web-based systems during the 1990s, said Lacefield, and many are now realizing that they never saw returns from them. At the time, he said, "it was nothing to talk about tens of millions of dollars of expense." The problem, said Bill Schiano, an e-commerce professor at Bentley College in Waltham, Massachusetts, is that companies were developing e-commerce IT strategies. "What they really needed was . . . a business strategy with e-commerce at its center," he said.

Another mistake companies made was pursuing complex business-to-business processes when they couldn't even integrate their internal data, added Mark Evans, CIO at Tesoro Petroleum Corp. in San Antonio. Industrial-strength application integration tools that unlock legacy data and break down traditional IT silos are only now hitting the market, he said. "Truth is, you can save more money improving internal processes than you can with any B2B project," Evans said.

Companies are done with the pipe dream prospectuses of the 1990s, and they're back to the fundamentals: using IT to deliver ever-increasing quality to customers at ever lower costs, said Jim Prevno, CIO at Waterbury, Vermont–based Green Mountain Coffee Inc. "I think the whole world went nuts," he said. "But somehow, the truth has a way of winning in the end."

Case Study Questions

1. Did mistakes in the use or management of IT play a part in the failure of Enron? Why or why not?

2. What are several major lessons for the future use of information technology in business that you gained from this case?

3. How would you apply one of these lessons in your present job situation or future business career? Give a specific example to illustrate your proposal.

Source: Adapted from Melissa Solomon and Michael Meehan, "Enron Lesson: Tech Is for Support," *Computerworld*, February 18, 2002, pp. 1, 61. Reprinted with permission from *Computerworld*.

REAL WORLD CASE 4

Delta Technology and FirstHealth Group: Evaluating the ROI of Strategic IT

Delta Technology Inc. (www.deltadt.com), the IT arm of $16 billion Atlanta-based Delta Air Lines Inc. (www.delta.com), has bumped up technology investment decisions to a higher level in the corporate chain. "We have been carefully reviewing every project and every spend with approvals at the senior vice president level. Before, we delegated decisions to a lower level," says Curtis Robb, senior vice president and chief technology officer. "Finance is also much more actively involved in business cases that are developed for IT projects."

Delta is also focusing on its IT infrastructure, in which it has invested more than $1 billion in the past three years, according to Robb. "Now, we're reviewing all projects we do in infrastructure to make sure they're absolutely necessary in terms of either lowering our operating costs or supporting new business functions going forward," Robb says. For example, among the projects to take a back seat is an upgrade from Windows NT to Windows XP.

Delta has also significantly tightened up accountability for the business payback of IT projects. "Now when we start a project, we're booking the promised savings out of the beneficiary business unit's budget," according to Robb. "You can't just say it's going to save you money. You actually get signed up for the savings."

One recent example is the IT group's investment in systems management tools, which, among other benefits, will enable the automatic electronic distribution of software and upgrades. "The business case for the project literally shows a reduction in effort to manage desktops that equates to a specific head-count reduction in the operating budget," Robb explains. "Before, there were lots of promises of cost savings and other benefits but not as hard a look at ensuring that they actually occurred.

"Companies can get a little bit sloppy in how they account for the results of investment," Robb acknowledges. "We're certainly homing in on that and will make it a real checkpoint. We're not doing a project unless the business unit involved is signed up for the results."

FirstHealth Group FirstHealth Group Corp. (www.firsthealth.com), a national group health insurance company headquartered in Downers Grove, Illinois, has grown from a $25 million company to a $700 million company in the past decade by steadily acquiring other health care benefits companies. Another reason for its growth: FirstHealth emphasizes an electronic paperless health claims process for its clients, which makes it very attractive to participating businesses and other organizations, and the health professionals and hospitals that belong to its national FirstHealth Network.

Thus, FirstHealth invests 12 percent of its top-line revenue in IT annually, and its IT department comprises 10 percent of its work force. At FirstHealth, business results from technology projects, notably systems integration projects, are measured mainly in terms of the company's ability to attract new customers and enter new niche markets. "Every investment is signed to gain us opportunity," says Ron Boeving, vice president of information systems. "We don't do traditional ROI, but we do analyze return on opportunity." Moreover, since the health insurer is a "pure information company, every one of our products and services is underpinned by the IT infrastructure," Boeving notes.

FirstHealth's business strategy is to steadily expand by acquiring other companies, which necessarily involves a lot of systems integration work. Boeving says the company has come up with a formula for measuring return on these integration projects based on how much they contribute to increasing customer service, which, in turn, brings in new business. "One of our main strategies is bringing world-class service to health care," he explains. "For us, that means when you talk to a customer service person, they will be able to answer all of your questions in one call."

Behind the scenes, what makes this possible is a system called OneSource that links 15 systems and databases and gives customer service representatives access to medical management, pharmacy, case management, and any other customer information on file, all on a single computer screen. "This integration is really part of our sales story," says Boeving. He also points out that potential corporate clients are given a tour of FirstHealth's IT facility and a firsthand demonstration of its integrated IT capabilities and how they translate into fast and accurate customer service. "We bring them in and show them how our infrastructure works, and it's very convincing," he says.

Case Study Questions

1. What are Delta Technology's new requirements for IT investments? What is their business value to Delta?

2. Is FirstHealth's "return on opportunity" guideline for IT investments a good way to evaluate investments in IT? Why or why not?

3. Are the IT investment guidelines of Delta and FirstHealth applicable to other companies, including small businesses? Explain.

Source: Adapted from Julia King, "ROI: Make It Bigger, Better, Faster," *Computerworld*, January 1, 2002, pp. 20–21. Reprinted with permission from *Computerworld*.

Ford, Dow Chemical, IBM, and Others: Success and Failure with Six Sigma

Six Sigma is back, and it is bigger than ever—maybe too big, critics say. Seemingly destined for oblivion several years ago, this approach to reducing defects in corporations has made a stunning resurgence thanks to highly publicized successes, such as the claim by corporate icon General Electric that Six Sigma cut $1.5 billion from its costs last year. By some estimates, more than a quarter of the Fortune 200 roster of big companies have Six Sigma projects under way.

Daniel Laux, president of the Six Sigma Academy (www.6-sigma.com), the consulting firm founded by the inventor of the practice, says it is the methodology's success that has led practitioners to greatly expand how it is used. While Six Sigma initially was applied primarily to manufacturing and logistics, Laux says it now can be applied to "all industries and all functions." Six Sigma can even be used in research and development to find innovative products, Laux says. This method for minimizing mistakes has become so all encompassing that, according to Laux, "some companies view it as an enterprisewide business strategy."

Others aren't so sure. While acknowledging that Six Sigma is great in some uses, they say the system assumes that what exists is fundamentally sound and merely needs refinement. As a result, critics charge, Six Sigma is ill-suited for developing innovative products, finding fundamentally new internal processes, or setting overall corporate strategy.

For sure, Six Sigma savings can add up at a company such as Ford Motor Company (www.ford.com), whose processes mostly carry over from year to year. Ford, whose Six Sigma projects each shoot for at least $250,000 in annual savings and at least a 70 percent reduction in defects in the area being targeted, has applied the methodology so widely that the corporation says it saved $325 million in costs last year. Phong Vu, the corporate deployment director of what Ford calls Consumer Driven 6-Sigma, adds that "in the first two months of this year we saved more than during all of last year."

Similarly, Dow Chemical Co. (www.dow.com) helped a supplier save an estimated $20 million a year because a Six Sigma team sorted through the complex series of reasons that caused some injection-molding equipment to operate at a whopping 28 percent rejection rate. Tom Gurd, Dow Chemical's vice president of quality and business excellence, says the chemical concern's three-year-old Six Sigma program is more than halfway to its goal of saving at least $1.5 billion by 2005.

Six Sigma's proponents acknowledge that problems can arise, but they say the problems relate to bad implementation rather than to the methodology itself. Critics say those acknowledgements gloss over the fundamental limits of the methodology. "Despite the extravagant claims, Six Sigma success is not synonymous with business success," reengineering guru Michael Hammer says. "Some of its early

adopters—Eastman Kodak Co., Xerox Corp., and Polaroid Corp., among others—have experienced significant business reversals recently. Even Motorola has seen its performance fall and rise and fall again, despite its continuing practice of Six Sigma."

International Business Machines Corp. (www.ibm.com) serves as a textbook example of what can go wrong. Six Sigma was almost a religion there in the early 1990s and was improving product quality across the board. The company won a Malcolm Baldrige Quality Award at the facility in Rochester, Minnesota, that makes the AS/400 line of minicomputers. The use of Six Sigma didn't, however, help the company spot a glaring problem: IBM was, in many cases, building the wrong products.

While IBM was focused on reducing the defects in its networking equipment, Cisco Systems was innovating with a new type of networking equipment, known as routers. While IBM was making incremental improvements to its disk drives, EMC Corp. was pioneering a wholly new approach, known as RAID, for redundant arrays of inexpensive disks. Cisco and EMC tapped into explosive growth and took the leading position in their markets away from IBM.

The use of Six Sigma also failed to help IBM spot a strategic fiasco in its personal computer business. The business was using the Six Sigma methodology to improve its forecasts for consumer demand—when the right approach would have been to do away with the forecasts. As rival computer maker Dell Computer has shown, it is far more efficient to wait until a consumer orders before building the computer. Because IBM just made incremental changes to the wrong approach, it posted losses of as much as $1 billion a year in the PC business in the 1990s and ultimately abandoned the consumer part of the market.

IBM's great turnaround since 1993 was accomplished without Six Sigma. "We were encountering a whole set of problems and issues that went beyond the elimination and reduction of defects," explains Fred DeWald, an IBM vice president. "So we shifted our focus to business process re-engineering."

Case Study Questions

1. Is Six Sigma "an enterprise-wide business strategy"? Why or why not?

2. What role does information technology play in Six Sigma business initiatives?

3. What are the benefits and limitations of Six Sigma as a business strategy?

MODULE II

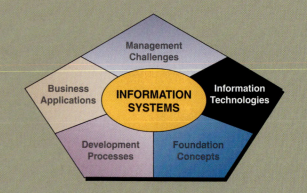

Management
Challenges

Business
Applications

INFORMATION
SYSTEMS

Information
Technologies

Development
Processes

Foundation
Concepts

INFORMATION TECHNOLOGIES

What challenges do information system technologies pose for business professionals? What basic knowledge should you possess about information technology? The two chapters of this module give you an overview of the data resource management and telecommunications network technologies used in information systems and their implications for business managers and professionals.

- **Chapter 3: Data Resource Management,** emphasizes management of the data resources of computer-using organizations. This chapter reviews key database management concepts and applications in business information systems.

- **Chapter 4: Telecommunications and Networks,** presents an overview of the Internet and other telecommunications networks, business applications, and trends, and reviews technical telecommunications alternatives.

Technical Note: At the option of your instructor, you may be assigned some of the topics in **Module VI: Review of Hardware and Software Technologies,** as well as the chapters in this module. Module VI contains material on computer hardware (Chapter 13) and computer software (Chapter 14), some of which you may have previously covered in other computer courses, but may be asked to review to refresh your knowledge of these important aspects of information technology.

CHAPTER 3

DATA RESOURCE MANAGEMENT

Chapter Highlights

Section I
Managing Data Resources

Data Resource Management

Real World Case: IBM versus Oracle: Playing Catch-Up in Database Management

Foundation Data Concepts

Types of Databases

Data Warehouses and Data Mining

The Database Management Approach

Implementing Data Resource Management

Section II
Technical Foundations of Database Management

Database Management

Real World Case: Experian Automotive: The Business Value of Data Resource Management

Database Structures

Accessing Databases

Database Development

Learning Objectives

After reading and studying this chapter, you should be able to:

1. Explain the importance of implementing data resource management processes and technologies in an organization.

2. Outline the advantages of a database management approach to managing the data resources of a business.

3. Explain how database management software helps business professionals and supports the operations and management of a business.

4. Provide examples to illustrate each of the following concepts:

   a. Major types of databases.

   b. Data warehouses and data mining.

   c. Logical data elements.

   d. Fundamental database structures.

   e. Database access methods.

   f. Database development.

<table>
<tr><td>SECTION I</td><td></td></tr>
</table>

SECTION I   Managing Data Resources

Data Resource Management

Data are a vital organizational resource that need to be managed like other important business assets. Today's e-business enterprises cannot survive or succeed without quality data about their internal operations and external environment.

> *With each online mouse click, either a fresh bit of data is created or already-stored data are retrieved from all those business websites. All that's on top of the heavy demand for industrial-strength data storage already in use by scores of big corporations. What's driving the growth is a crushing imperative for corporations to analyze every bit of information they can extract from their huge data warehouses for competitive advantage. That has turned the data storage and management function into a key strategic role of the information age [9].*

That's why organizations and their managers need to practice **data resource management,** a managerial activity that applies information systems technologies like *database management, data warehousing,* and other data management tools to the task of managing an organization's data resources to meet the information needs of their business stakeholders. This chapter will show you the managerial implications of using data resource management technologies and methods to manage an organization's data assets to meet business information requirements.

Analyzing IBM versus Oracle

Read the Real World Case on IBM versus Oracle on the next page. We can learn a lot from this case about the major choices companies face in selecting database management software. See Figure 3.1.

Oracle Corporation's database management system has dominated the enterprise database software market for almost 20 years. IBM fell way behind Oracle and others by offering only mainframe database software until Janet Perna and her colleagues finally began developing and marketing DB2, a competing database product. After

FIGURE 3.1

Janet Perna is head of IBM's database software division and directed the development and marketing of its DB2 Universal database management product.

Source: Brad Hines

REAL WORLD
CASE 1

IBM versus Oracle: Playing Catch-Up in Database Management

Janet Perna was just 26 and an ex–high school math teacher when she joined the IBM Corporation (www.ibm.com). Now 53, she is one of Big Blue's most senior female executives and runs its worldwide database business. That division earned nearly $3 billion last year and by some measures has recently inched past perennial market leader Oracle Corporation (www.oracle.com) as the industry's top seller. The only reason IBM is even in the running with Oracle is that 11 years ago, Perna rescued the division from its obsession with mainframe computers and helped lead it into the modern era of servers and PCs.

Every business needs a system for storing what it knows and retrieving the information when needed. That essentially is all a database management system does. But what companies can do today with the information—everything from analyzing customers' buying patterns to predicting how many machinery parts they'll need to order next quarter—makes databases and their software indispensable.

Larry Ellison realized this more than 20 years ago, when he started Oracle and began selling database software that ran on Unix, the operating system of choice for minicomputers and servers that were becoming a popular alternative to IBM mainframes. IBM executives at the time, afraid that a Unix product would jeopardize their dominance in the mainframe market, continued to make databases only for their own hardware.

It was not until late 1991, as database sales at Oracle, Sybase, and other companies boomed, that Perna got her second life-changing assignment: Steve Mills, now boss of IBM's $13 billion software group, asked her to build a Unix database product that would go head-to-head with Oracle and others. Naturally, IBM wanted the new software ready in a year.

It certainly couldn't be done the cautious IBM way. Perna first broke IBM's protocol for product development by pairing up her researchers and programmers rather than keeping them sequestered, as per company tradition. "We had to speed things up," Perna says. "We couldn't afford handoffs." Next, she insisted that the database, called DB2, be made for other non-IBM platforms such as Sun's and Hewlett-Packard's. IBM released DB2 for Unix in 1993, on schedule, and in 1995 began delivering other versions tuned specifically for Sun and HP servers.

Building the new product was one thing, selling it was another. IBM had just a few hundred software salespeople, (compared with about 10,000 at Oracle), none of them specifically selling DB2. So when then IBM Chairman Lou Gerstner asked Perna at a strategy session in 1997 why DB2 sales were lagging, Perna rolled the dice. She asked Gerstner for the money to build a DB2 sales team of more than 2,000 people. Gerstner, to Perna's great surprise, agreed—and handed her a $1 billion budget to get it done.

Perna next began tying salaries of her salespeople to customer-satisfaction surveys as well as sales goals—another IBM first—and often invited customers to the research labs for troubleshooting sessions. The attention Perna lavished on customers helped offset the drawbacks of a product then still considered technologically inferior to Oracle's. By 2000, however, IBM's nonmainframe database sales had reached $2 billion, and its share of the Unix market, just 5 percent five years ago, is up to nearly 25 percent today.

Next, thanks to the budget that Gerstner approved, she significantly underpriced her competition. DB2's enterprise edition costs $20,000 per server; Oracle used to charge more than three times that amount for its comparable database, and it only recently got that base price down to $40,000 per server.

More important than pricing was the marketing strategy that Perna helped to formulate, which aligned IBM with most of Oracle's biggest competitors in the applications market, where Oracle had been a powerhouse for years. Oracle's strategy is to tie its database platform to its E-Business Suite of powerful business application programs that plug into it—for human resources, supply chain management, and other services. Perna and Mills, however, decided not to compete in the applications market. Instead they designed DB2 as an open-ended platform that would work easily alongside customer-relationship management software from Siebel Systems, for example, or supply chain programs from SAP AG.

As DB2 began to take off in the Unix world, so did concurrent sales through Siebel and other software companies, whose customers were increasingly persuaded to use DB2 as the database platform for their applications. Since 1998, installations of Siebel's CRM software alone have generated more than $750 million in DB2 sales for IBM, and now 44 percent of Perna's $3 billion in revenue comes through her software partners.

Most customers, analysts, and clients now agree that Oracle's and IBM's database platforms are similar. Both can mine data at comparable speeds and offer self-managing features that reduce the need to hire database administrators. Database software has become more of a commodity, a means of getting at what companies really want, which are the applications that run a business. Which is why success for Perna these days depends less on pushing her developers and more on the success of how applications companies who depend on DB2, like PeopleSoft, SAP, and Siebel, compete with Oracle.

Case Study Questions

1. What key business strategies did Janet Perna implement to help IBM catch up to Oracle in the database management software market?

2. What is the business case for both IBM's and Oracle's product strategy for their database software?

3. Which approach would you recommend to a company seeking a database system today? Why?

Source: Adapted from Stephanie Clifford, "Big Blue's Unlikely Revolutionary," *Business 2.0*, October 2002, pp. 73–75. © 2002 Time Inc. All rights reserved.

ten years, IBM's DB2 and other database software products have finally caught up with Oracle. Perna used a combination of innovative development, a large DB2 sales team, a customer satisfaction focus, and lowball pricing to close the gap. But now the two companies are fighting it out with two opposing marketing and product strategies. Oracle is tying its database sales to its E-Business Suite of business application software in one integrated package that it is marketing to all enterprise software users. IBM is not developing its own application software, but partnering with Oracle's competitors like Siebel Systems, SAP AG, and PeopleSoft to include DB2 as the database foundation for business applications like customer relationship management and enterprise resource planning. Only time will tell which strategy will prevail.

Foundation Data Concepts

Before we go any further, let's review some fundamental concepts about how data are organized in information systems. A conceptual framework of several levels of data has been devised that differentiates between different groupings, or elements, of data. Thus, data may be logically organized into characters, fields, records, files, and databases, just as writing can be organized in letters, words, sentences, paragraphs, and documents. Examples of these logical data elements are shown in Figure 3.2.

Character

The most basic logical data element is the **character,** which consists of a single alphabetic, numeric, or other symbol. One might argue that the bit or byte is a more elementary data element, but remember that those terms refer to the physical storage elements provided by the computer hardware, discussed in Chapter 13. From a user's point of view (that is, from a *logical* as opposed to a physical or hardware view of data), a character is the most basic element of data that can be observed and manipulated.

Field

The next higher level of data is the **field,** or data item. A field consists of a grouping of characters. For example, the grouping of alphabetic characters in a person's name forms a name field, and the grouping of numbers in a sales amount forms a sales amount field. Specifically, a data field represents an **attribute** (a characteristic or quality) of some **entity** (object, person, place, or event). For example, an employee's salary is an attribute that is a typical data field used to describe an entity who is an employee of a business.

FIGURE 3.2

Examples of the logical data elements in information systems. Note especially the examples of how data fields, records, files, and databases are related.

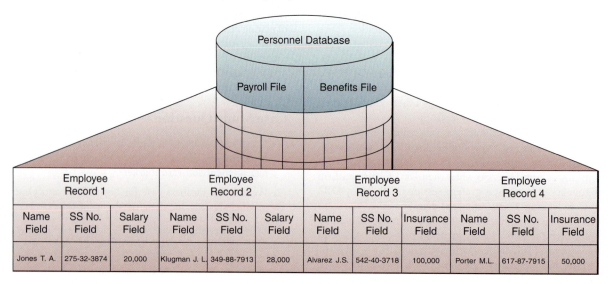

FIGURE 3.3

Some of the entities and relationships in a simplified electric utility database. Note a few of the business applications that access the data in the database.

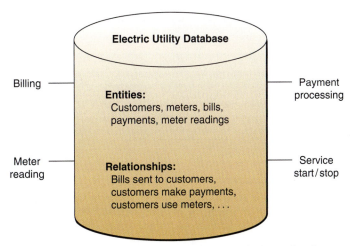

Source: Adapted from Michael V. Mannino, *Database Application Development and Design* (Burr Ridge, IL: McGraw-Hill/Irwin, 2001), p. 6.

Record

Related fields of data are grouped to form a **record.** Thus, a record represents a collection of *attributes* that describe an *entity.* An example is the payroll record for a person, which consists of data fields describing attributes such as the person's name, Social Security number, and rate of pay. *Fixed-length* records contain a fixed number of fixed-length data fields. *Variable-length* records contain a variable number of fields and field lengths.

File

A group of related records is a data **file,** or *table.* Thus, an employee file would contain the records of the employees of a firm. Files are frequently classified by the application for which they are primarily used, such as a *payroll file* or an *inventory file*, or the type of data they contain, such as a *document file* or a *graphical image file*. Files are also classified by their permanence, for example, a payroll *master file* versus a payroll weekly *transaction file*. A transaction file, therefore, would contain records of all transactions occurring during a period and might be used periodically to update the permanent records contained in a master file. A *history file* is an obsolete transaction or master file retained for backup purposes or for long-term historical storage called *archival storage*.

Database

A **database** is an integrated collection of logically related data elements. A database consolidates records previously stored in separate files into a common pool of data elements that provides data for many applications. The data stored in a database are independent of the application programs using them and of the type of storage devices on which they are stored.

Thus, databases contain data elements describing entities and relationships among entities. For example, Figure 3.3 outlines some of the entities and relationships in a database for an electric utility. Also shown are some of the business applications (billing, payment processing) that depend on access to the data elements in the database.

Types of Databases

Continuing developments in information technology and its business applications have resulted in the evolution of several major types of databases. Figure 3.4 illustrates several major conceptual categories of databases that may be found in many organizations. Let's take a brief look at some of them now.

Operational Databases

Operational databases store detailed data needed to support the business processes and operations of a company. They are also called *subject area databases* (SADB), *transaction databases*, and *production databases*. Examples are a customer database, human resource database, inventory database, and other databases containing data

FIGURE 3.4   Examples of some of the major types of databases used by organizations and end users.

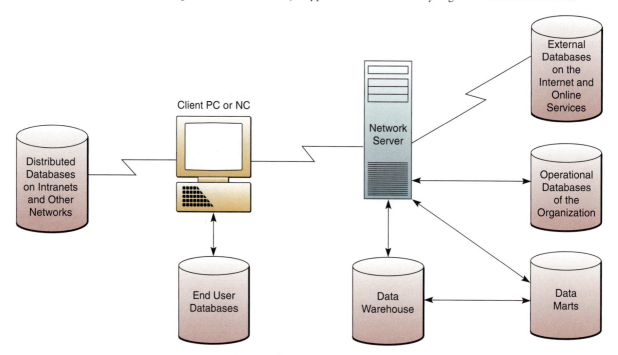

generated by business operations. This includes databases of Internet and electronic commerce activity, such as *click stream data* describing the online behavior of customers or visitors to a company's website. Figure 3.5 illustrates some of the common operational databases that can be created and managed for a small business using Microsoft Access database management software.

Distributed Databases

Many organizations replicate and distribute copies or parts of databases to network servers at a variety of sites. These distributed databases can reside on network servers on the World Wide Web, on corporate intranets or extranets, or on other company

FIGURE 3.5

Examples of operational databases that can be created and managed for a small business by microcomputer database management software like Microsoft Access.

FIGURE 3.6   The components of a Web-based information system include Web browsers, servers, and hypermedia databases.

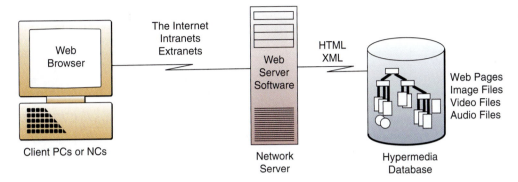

networks. Distributed databases may be copies of operational or analytical databases, hypermedia or discussion databases, or any other type of database. Replication and distribution of databases is done to improve database performance and security. Ensuring that all of the data in an organization's distributed databases are consistently and concurrently updated is a major challenge of distributed database management.

External Databases

Access to a wealth of information from external databases is available for a fee from commercial online services, and with or without charge from many sources on the Internet, especially the World Wide Web. Websites provide an endless variety of hyperlinked pages of multimedia documents in *hypermedia databases* for you to access. Data are available in the form of statistics on economic and demographic activity from *statistical* data banks. Or you can view or download abstracts or complete copies of hundreds of newspapers, magazines, newsletters, research papers, and other published material and other periodicals from *bibliographic* and *full text* databases.

Hypermedia Databases

The rapid growth of websites on the Internet and corporate intranets and extranets has dramatically increased the use of databases of hypertext and hypermedia documents. A website stores such information in a **hypermedia database** consisting of hyperlinked pages of multimedia (text, graphic, and photographic images, video clips, audio segments, and so on). That is, from a database management point of view, the set of interconnected multimedia pages at a website is a database of interrelated hypermedia page elements, rather than interrelated data records [3].

Figure 3.6 shows how you might use a Web browser on your client PC to connect with a Web network server. This server runs Web server software to access and transfer the Web pages you request. The website illustrated in Figure 3.6 uses a hypermedia database consisting of Web page content described by HTML (Hypertext Markup Language) code or XML (Extended Markup Language) labels, image files, video files, and audio. The Web server software acts as a database management system to manage the transfer of hypermedia files for downloading by the multimedia plug-ins of your Web browser.

Data Warehouses and Data Mining

A **data warehouse** stores data that have been extracted from the various operational, external, and other databases of an organization. It is a central source of the data that have been cleaned, transformed, and cataloged so they can be used by managers and other business professionals for data mining, online analytical processing, and other forms of business analysis, market research, and decision support. Data warehouses may be subdivided into **data marts,** which hold subsets of data from the warehouse that focus on specific aspects of a company, such as a department or a business process.

FIGURE 3.7   The components of a complete data warehouse system.

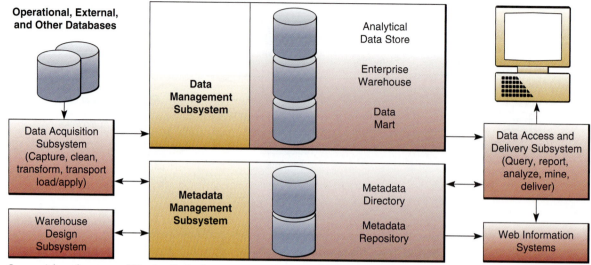

Source: Adapted courtesy of Hewlett-Packard.

Figure 3.7 illustrates the components of a complete data warehouse system. Notice how data from various operational and external databases are captured, cleaned, and transformed into data that can be better used for analysis. This acquisition process might include activities like consolidating data from several sources, filtering out unwanted data, correcting incorrect data, converting data to new data elements, and aggregating data into new data subsets.

This data is then stored in the enterprise data warehouse, from where it can be moved into data marts or to an *analytical data store* that holds data in a more useful form for certain types of analysis. *Metadata* (data that defines the data in the data warehouse) is stored in a metadata repository and cataloged by a metadata directory. Finally, a variety of analytical software tools can be provided to query, report, mine, and analyze the data for delivery via Internet and intranet Web systems to business end users.

Trimac Corp: Building a Data Warehouse

It wasn't always easy for Trimac Corp.'s internal users to access critical data for their reporting need. Although Trimac kept data about its day-to-day operations, it didn't have a database that could consolidate all of the business information from various sources within the company and provide a multidimensional view of that data so employees could analyze business conditions.

The problem affected users' ability to perform key analyses such as trip standards and analysis, which examine factors like profitability based on equipment or a particular customer by reviewing variables such as load time, loaded miles traveled, and gross vehicle weight. Financial reporting in areas such as accounts payable and accounts receivable was also fragmented.

So Trimac, a bulk hauling and trucking firm based in Calgary, Alberta, Canada, decided to improve access to corporate data from across the organization. "We initiated our Business Intelligence Project," says Len Mori, project manager for infrastructure at Trimac. "One of the tasks was to build a data warehouse. We didn't have the tools to do that, so we started looking around for a solution."

That's where data warehousing and access software tools come in. "This technology facilitates the implementation of data marts used for trip analysis, haul analysis, and profitability, either by customer or equipment," says Martin Zardecki, business intelligence manager at Trimac.

Genio Suite is a data extract, transform, and load (ETL) software tool that pulls data from its original database, converts the data into the right format for analysis and loads it into a central repository, or target database. Trimac implemented Genio Suite to populate its data warehouse with clean, accurate data from various financial and human resources applications.

The tool lets Trimac's IT department cost-effectively and easily design, deploy, and maintain data transformation and exchange processes, according to Mori. This dramatically simplified Trimac's internal systems and ensured the consistency of data.

The company uses PeopleSoft financial and human resources applications accessing an Oracle database. Business intelligence tools from Cognos deliver querying, reporting, and online analytical processing capabilities to users. Using Genio, Trimac is able to extract data from its various applications and populate the data warehouse. Several data marts were also created for use with the Cognos tools for multidimensional analysis of data such as account information, products, customers, and schedules [15].

Data Mining

Data mining is a major use of data warehouse databases. In data mining, the data in a data warehouse are analyzed to reveal hidden patterns and trends in historical business activity. This can be used to help managers make decisions about strategic changes in business operations to gain competitive advantages in the marketplace. See Figure 3.8.

Data mining can discover new correlations, patterns, and trends in vast amounts of business data (frequently several terabytes of data), stored in data warehouses. Data mining software uses advanced pattern recognition algorithms, as well as a variety of mathematical and statistical techniques to sift through mountains of data to extract previously unknown strategic business information. We discuss data mining, online analytical processing (OLAP), and other technologies that analyze the data in databases and data warehouses to provide vital support for business decisions in Chapter 8. Let's look at a real world example.

Bank of America: Benefits of Data Mining

The Bank of America (BofA) is using a data warehouse and data mining software to develop more accuracy in marketing and pricing financial products, such as home equity loans. BofA's data warehouse is so large—for some customers, there are 300 data points—that traditional analytic approaches are overwhelmed. For each market, BofA can offer a variety of tailored product packages by adjusting fees, interest rates, and features. The result is a staggering number of potential strategies for reaching profitable customers. Sifting through the vast number of combinations requires the ability to identify very fine opportunity segments.

Data extracted from the data warehouse were analyzed by data mining software to discover hidden patterns. For example, data mining discovered that a certain set of customers were 15 times more likely to purchase a high-margin lending product. The bank also wanted to determine the sequence of events leading to purchasing. They fed the parameters to the Discovery data mining software from HYPERparallel and built a model for finding other customers. This model proved to be so accurate that it discovered people already in the process of applying and being approved for the lending product. Using this profile, a final list of quality prospects for solicitation was prepared. The resulting direct marketing response rates have dramatically exceeded past results [14].

FIGURE 3.8
How data mining extracts
business knowledge from a
data warehouse.

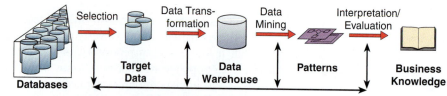

Source: Adapted from Usama Fayyad, Gregory Piatetsky-Shapiro, and Padhraic Smith, "The KDD
Process for Extracting Useful Knowledge from Volumes of Data," *Communications of the ACM,*
November 1996, p. 29. Copyright © 1996, Association of Computing Machinery. Used by permission.

The Database Management Approach

The development of databases and database management software is the foundation
of modern methods of managing organizational data. The **database management
approach** consolidates data records and objects into databases that can be accessed
by many different application programs. In addition, a *database management system*
(DBMS) serves as a software interface between users and databases. This helps users
easily access the data in a database. Thus, database management involves the use of
database management software to control how databases are created, interrogated,
and maintained to provide information needed by end users and their organizations.

For example, customer records and other common types of data are needed for
several different applications in banking, such as check processing, automated teller
systems, bank credit cards, savings accounts, and installment loan accounting. These
data can be consolidated into a common *customer database*, rather than being kept in
separate files for each of those applications. See Figure 3.9.

FIGURE 3.9

An example of a database
management approach in a
banking information
system. Note how the
savings, checking, and
installment loan programs
use a database management
system to share a customer
database. Note also that the
DBMS allows a user to
make a direct, ad hoc
interrogation of the
database without using
application programs.

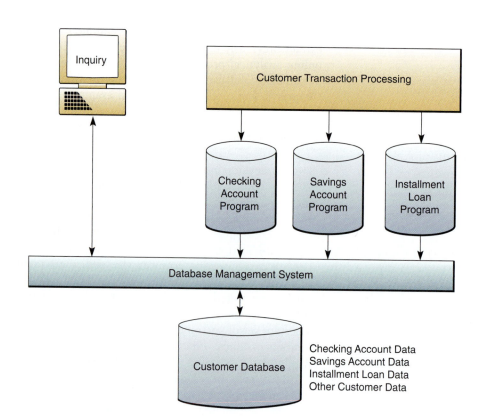

Alberta Central: Converting to Database Management

Alberta Central is the administrative services organization for thirty-eight credit unions with more than half a million customers in Alberta, Canada. Alberta Central recently moved to a database management approach to support their banking system's vision to provide credit union analysts and managers with more meaningful and timely information to analyze and manage their credit union's performance and risk. The primary business driver for the project was feedback from the credit unions, which wanted more detailed customer demographics, account and product analysis, and profitability forecasting.

Alberta Central's new DB2 Universal Database software from IBM manages a database that stores demographic information as well as account and product information such as the type and amount of loan or investment products and interest rate yields. Users at each credit union access the database via a corporate intranet using the Business Objects query and reporting software tool.

According to Bill Gnenz, Alberta Central's project manager of Retail Banking and Corporate Systems, the new database management approach has delivered dramatic reductions in response times for queries and generation of reports. The system's new user interface, ease of use, and flexibility have also boosted the business creativity and productivity of credit union staff. And Gnenz expects the cost of the project to achieve full payback soon [8].

Database Management Software

A **database management system** (DBMS) is a software tool that controls the creation, maintenance, and use of the databases of an organization and its end users. Database management packages are needed to create, manage, and use the databases of an organization. The three major uses of a DBMS are illustrated in Figure 3.10; common DBMS software components and functions are summarized in Figure 3.11. We will discuss database development in Section II of this chapter.

Database Interrogation

A database interrogation capability is a major benefit of the database management approach. End users can use a DBMS by asking for information from a database using a *query* feature or a *report generator*. They can receive an immediate response in the form of video displays or printed reports. No difficult programming is required. The **query** feature lets you easily obtain immediate responses to ad hoc data requests: You merely key in a few short inquiries. The **report generator** feature allows you to quickly specify a report format for information you want presented as a report. Figure 3.12 illustrates the use of a DBMS report generator.

FIGURE 3.10

The three major uses of DBMS software are to create, manage, and use the databases of an organization.

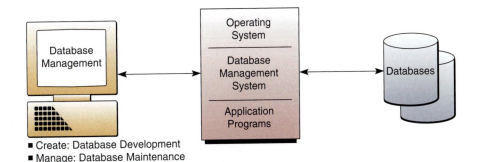

■ Create: Database Development
■ Manage: Database Maintenance
■ Use: Database Interrogation, Application Development

FIGURE 3.11   Common software components and functions of a database management system.

Common DBMS Software Components	
● **Database definition**	Language and graphical tools to define entities, relationships, integrity constraints, and authorization rights
● **Nonprocedural access**	Language and graphical tools to access data without complicated coding
● **Application development**	Graphical tools to develop menus, data entry forms, and reports
● **Procedural language interface**	Language that combines nonprocedural access with full capabilities of a programming language
● **Transaction processing**	Control mechanisms to prevent interference from simultaneous users and recover lost data after a failure
● **Database tuning**	Tools to monitor and improve database performance

Source: Adapted from Michael V. Mannino, *Database Application Development and Design* (Burr Ridge, IL: McGraw-Hill/Irwin, 2001), p. 7.

SQL Queries. SQL, or Structured Query Language, is a query language found in many database management packages. The basic form of an SQL query is:

SELECT . . . FROM . . . WHERE . . .

After SELECT you list the data fields you want retrieved. After FROM you list the files or tables from which the data must be retrieved. After WHERE you specify conditions that limit the search to only those data records in which you are interested. Figure 3.13 compares an SQL query to a natural language query for information on customer orders.

Graphical and Natural Queries. Many end users (and IS professionals) have difficulty correctly phrasing SQL and other database language queries. So most end user database management packages offer GUI (graphical user interface) point-and-click methods, which are easier to use and are translated by the software into SQL commands. See Figure 3.14. Other packages are available that use *natural language* query statements similar to conversational English (or other languages), as is illustrated in Figure 3.13.

Database Maintenance

The **database maintenance** process is accomplished by *transaction processing systems* and other end user applications, with the support of the DBMS. End users and information specialists can also employ various utilities provided by a DBMS for database maintenance. The databases of an organization need to be updated continually

FIGURE 3.12

Using the report generator of Microsoft Access to create an employee report.

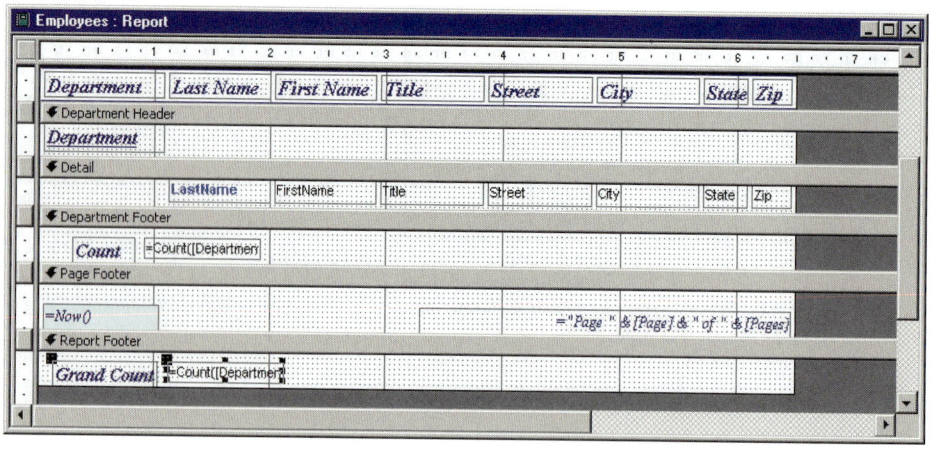

FIGURE 3.13

Comparing a natural language query with an SQL query.

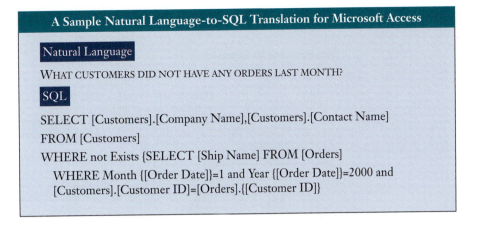

A Sample Natural Language-to-SQL Translation for Microsoft Access

Natural Language

WHAT CUSTOMERS DID NOT HAVE ANY ORDERS LAST MONTH?

SQL

SELECT [Customers].[Company Name],[Customers].[Contact Name]

FROM [Customers]

WHERE not Exists {SELECT [Ship Name] FROM [Orders]

    WHERE Month {[Order Date]}=1 and Year {[Order Date]}=2000 and [Customers].[Customer ID]=[Orders].{[Customer ID]}

to reflect new business transactions and other events. Other miscellaneous changes must also be made to update and correct data, to ensure accuracy of the data in the databases. We introduced transaction processing systems in Chapter 1 and will discuss them in more detail in Chapter 5.

Application Development

DBMS packages play a major role in **application development.** End users, systems analysts, and other application developers can use the internal 4GL programming language and built-in software development tools provided by many DBMS packages to develop custom application programs. For example, you can use a DBMS to easily develop the data entry screens, forms, reports, or Web pages of a business application. A DBMS also makes the job of application software developers easier, since they do not have to develop detailed data-handling procedures using conventional programming languages every time they write a program. Instead, they can include features such as *data manipulation language* (DML) statements in their software that call on the DBMS to perform necessary data-handling activities.

Implementing Data Resource Management

Propelled by the Internet, intranets, a flood of multimedia information, and applications such as data warehousing and data mining, data storage at most companies is growing faster than ever. That has information technology managers in the most information-intensive industries wondering if technology can keep up with the surging tide—and, if it can, whether they can manage it [2].

Managers and business professionals need to view data as an important resource that they must manage properly to ensure the success and survival of their organizations. But this is easier said than done. For example, database management is an important application of information technologies to the management of a firm's

FIGURE 3.14

Using the Query Wizard of the Microsoft Access database management package to develop a query about employee health plan choices.

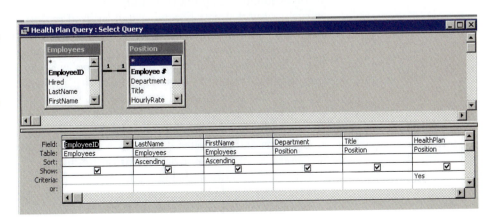

FIGURE 3.15   Data resource management includes database administration, data planning, and data administration activities.

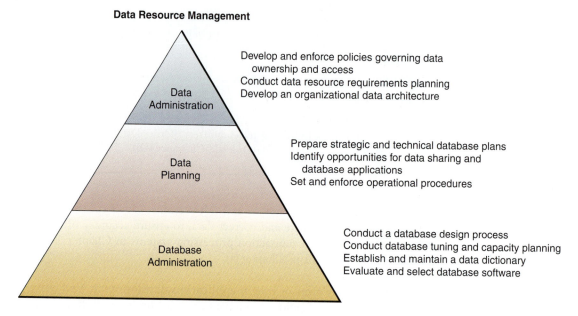

Data Resource Management

Data Administration
- Develop and enforce policies governing data ownership and access
- Conduct data resource requirements planning
- Develop an organizational data architecture

Data Planning
- Prepare strategic and technical database plans
- Identify opportunities for data sharing and database applications
- Set and enforce operational procedures

Database Administration
- Conduct a database design process
- Conduct database tuning and capacity planning
- Establish and maintain a data dictionary
- Evaluate and select database software

data resources. However, other major data resource management efforts are needed in order to supplement the solutions provided by a database management approach. Those are (1) database administration, (2) data planning, and (3) data administration. See Figure 3.15.

Database administration is an important data resource management function responsible for the proper use of database management technology. Database administration includes responsibility for developing and maintaining the organization's data dictionary, designing and monitoring the performance of databases, and enforcing standards for database use and security. Database administrators and analysts work with systems developers and end users to provide their expertise to major systems development projects.

Data planning is a corporate planning and analysis function that focuses on data resource management. It includes the responsibility for developing an overall data architecture for the firm's data resources that ties in with the firm's strategic mission and plans, and the objectives and processes of its business units. Data planning is done by organizations that have made a formal commitment to long-range planning for the strategic use and management of their data resources.

Data administration is another vital data resource management function. It involves administering the collection, storage, and dissemination of all types of data in such a way that data become a standardized resource available to all end users in the organization. The focus of data administration is the support of an organization's business processes and strategic business objectives. Data administration may also include responsibility for developing policies and setting standards for corporate database design, processing, and security arrangements.

Challenges of Data Resource Management

The data resource management approach provides business managers and professionals with several important benefits. Database management reduces the duplication of data and integrates data so that they can be accessed by multiple programs and users. Software is not dependent on the format of the data or the type of secondary storage hardware being used. Business professionals can use inquiry/response and reporting capabilities to easily obtain information they need from databases, data warehouses, or data marts, without complex programming. Software development is simplified, because programs are not dependent on either the logical format of the data or their physical storage location. Finally, the integrity and security of data are increased, since access to data and modification of data are controlled by data management software, data dictionaries, and a data administration function.

The challenge of data resource management arises from its technological complexity and the vast amounts of business data that need to be managed. Developing large databases of complex data types and installing data warehouses can be difficult and expensive. More hardware capability is required, since storage requirements for the organization's data, overhead control data, and the database management or data warehouse software are greater. Finally, if an organization relies on centralized databases, its vulnerability to errors, fraud, and failures is increased. Yet problems of inconsistency of data can arise if a distributed database approach is used. Therefore, supporting the security and integrity of their databases and data warehouses is a major objective of data resource management.

Aetna Inc.: Challenges of Data Resource Management	How does an enterprise deal gracefully and effectively with unwieldy mountains of information? For Aetna Inc., data are a significant corporate asset resulting from huge investments of time and effort. The data are also the source of many trials and tribulations for the employees who keep vigilant watch over it.

On a daily basis, Renee Zaugg, operations manager in the operational services central support area at Aetna, is responsible for 174.6 terabytes (TB) of data. She says 119.2TB reside on mainframe-connected disk drives, while the remaining 55.4TB sit on disks attached to midrange computers running Unix by IBM or Sun. Almost all of these data are located in the company's headquarters in Hartford, Connecticut. Most of the information is in relational databases, handled by IBM's DB2 Universal Database, Oracle8, or Sybase. To make matters even more interesting, Zaugg adds, outside customers have access to about 20TB of the information. Four interconnected data centers contain 14 mainframes and more than 4,100 direct-access storage devices to hold Aetna's key databases.

Nancy Tillberg, head of strategic data planning, says: "Data integrity, backup, security, and availability are our biggest concerns." So Zaugg says that her data handling software tools, procedures, and operations schedules have to stay ahead of not only the normal growth that results from the activities of the sales, underwriting, and claims departments but also growth from corporate acquisitions and mergers.

She adds that Aetna has a server consolidation effort under way to reduce the effort necessary to manage data on the midrange machines. For its Web servers, Aetna uses load balancing software to distribute Web data traffic to the nearest available server that's least busy. Tillberg also says the company is increasing its use of storage-area networks to centralize and streamline the management of that data. And she says that Aetna uses performance monitor software to monitor the network, distribute files, and track database usage [14].

SECTION II   Technical Foundations of Database Management

Database Management

Just imagine how difficult it would be to get any information from an information system if data were stored in an unorganized way, or if there was no systematic way to retrieve it. Therefore, in all information systems, data resources must be organized and structured in some logical manner so that they can be accessed easily, processed efficiently, retrieved quickly, and managed effectively. Thus, data structures and access methods ranging from simple to complex have been devised to efficiently organize and access data stored by information systems. In this section, we will explore these concepts, as well as more technical concepts of database management.

Analyzing Experian Automotive

Read the Real World Case on Experian Automotive on the next page. We can learn a lot from this case about using business databases to create profitable information products through effective data resource management. See Figure 3.16.

Experian, one of the largest U.S. credit reporting agencies, wanted to expand its automotive-related business beyond credit checks for auto loans. So it used a data extraction and transformation software tool and database management system to create an automotive database extracted from thousands of data files from state department of motor vehicle systems. Then it added other credit- and vehicle-related information of its own and from other sources to create a huge automotive database that is maintained by just three IT professionals with the help of database management software. This has enabled its Experian Automotive division to create and market many new profitable services and information products.

Database Structures

The relationships among the many individual data elements stored in databases are based on one of several logical data structures, or models. Database management system packages are designed to use a specific data structure to provide end users with quick, easy access to information stored in databases. Five fundamental database structures are the hierarchical, network, relational, object-oriented, and multi-dimensional models. Simplified illustrations of the first three database structures are shown in Figure 3.17.

FIGURE 3.16
Ken Kauppila is vice president of IT at Experian Automotive, which has developed profitable information products from a new automotive database.

Source: Marc Berlow

REAL WORLD CASE 2

Experian Automotive: The Business Value of Data Resource Management

Many companies say they want to create new, breakthrough business opportunities from their valuable data resources. Experian Inc. (www.experian.com) is one of a growing number of companies that are actually doing it.

Experian, a unit of London-based GUS PLC, runs one of the largest credit reporting agencies in the United States. But Experian wanted to expand its business beyond credit checks for automobile loans. If it could collect vehicle data from the nation's various motor-vehicle departments and blend that with other data, such as change-of-address records, then its Experian Automotive division could sell the enhanced data to a variety of customers. For example, car dealers could use the data to make sure their inventory matches local buying preferences. And toll collectors could match license plates to addresses to find motorists who sail past toll booths without paying.

But to offer new services, Experian first needed a way to extract, transfer, and load data from the 50 different U.S. state department of motor vehicles (DMV) systems (plus Puerto Rico) into a single database. That was a big challenge. "Unlike the credit industry that writes to a common format, the DMVs do not," says Ken Kauppila, vice president of IT at Experian Automotive in Costa Mesa, California. Of course, Experian didn't want to replicate the hodge-podge of file formats it inherited when the project began in January 1999—175 formats among 18,000 files. So Kauppila decided to transform and map the data to a common relational database format.

Fortunately, off-the-shelf software tools for extracting, transforming, and loading data (called ETL tools) make it economical to combine very large data repositories. Software vendors offering ETL tools include Evolutionary Technologies, Informatica, Oracle, and Sybase. Using ETL Extract from Evolutionary Technologies, Experian created a database that can incorporate vehicle information within 48 hours of its entry into any of the nation's DMV computers.

This is one of the areas in which data management software tools can excel, says Guy Creese, analyst at Aberdeen Group in Boston. "It can simplify the mechanics of multiple data feeds, and it can add to data quality, making fixes possible before errors are propagated to data warehouses," he says.

Using the ETL extraction and transformation tools along with IBM's DB2 database system, Experian Automotive created a database that processes 175 million transactions per month and has created a variety of new revenue streams. Now, for $10.99 per query, Experian can make available via the Web the ownership history for any vehicle bought or sold in the United States. For example, car dealerships are a big market for Experian's database because they'll pay for data about vehicle ownership preferences in particular geographic areas. Each 17-digit vehicle identification number in the database contains references to model, make, and color. Armed with this data, dealers can determine what kind of vehicle inventory mix might sell best in different regions.

The new automotive database—which has raised the hackles of privacy advocates—includes Experian's own corporate records, data from 30,000 credit granters, and address-change information licensed from the U.S. Postal Service. Plus, Experian is expanding the database to include accident and emission reports, as well as information about vehicle auctions. The result: Experian offers more comprehensive information than that maintained by state DMVs and auto manufacturers.

This gold mine of information could, for example, help ensure that automakers and auto parts companies are able to contact the majority of vehicle owners affected by recalls—even owners who have moved—and thereby help save lives and avert vehicular and auto parts–related injuries. Previously, recalls were initiated using dealer service and sales records. In addition, Experian's data assets can uncover patterns useful to manufacturers and retailers in creating brand loyalty campaigns and in launching new auto models. Retailers can use the data to speed the process of providing credit to potential buyers. Auto auction companies can check the histories of millions of cars.

Experian's automotive database is the 10th largest database in the world—now, with up to 16 billion rows of data. But the company says the relational database is managed by just three IT professionals. Experian says this demonstrates how efficiently database software like DB2 and the ETL tools can work with a large database to handle vast amounts of data quickly.

Case Study Questions

1. How do the database software tools discussed in this case help companies exploit their data resources?

2. What is the business value of the automotive database created by Experian?

3. What other business opportunities could you recommend to Experian that would capitalize on their automotive database? Visit their website and the links to Business Services/Data/Automotive Information to help you answer.

Source: Adapted from Pimm Fox, "Extracting Dollars from Data," *Computerworld*, April 15, 2002, p. 42. Reprinted with permission from *Computerworld*.

Hierarchical Structure

Early mainframe DBMS packages used the **hierarchical structure,** in which the relationships between records form a hierarchy or treelike structure. In the traditional hierarchical model, all records are dependent and arranged in multilevel structures, consisting of one *root* record and any number of subordinate levels. Thus, all of the relationships among records are *one-to-many*, since each data element is related to only one element above it. The data element or record at the highest level of the hierarchy (the department data element in this illustration) is called the root element. Any data element can be accessed by moving progressively downward from a root and along the branches of the tree until the desired record (for example, the employee data element) is located.

FIGURE 3.17

Example of three fundamental database structures. They represent three basic ways to develop and express the relationships among the data elements in a database.

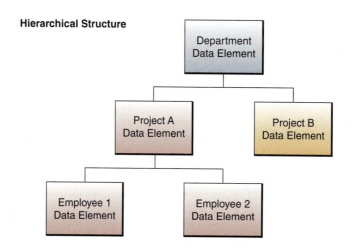

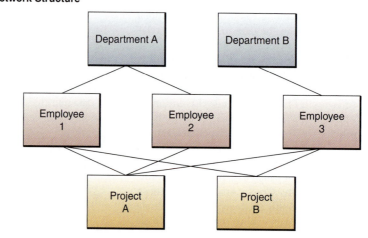

Relational Structure

Department Table

Deptno	Dname	Dloc	Dmgr
Dept A			
Dept B			
Dept C			

Employee Table

Empno	Ename	Etitle	Esalary	Deptno
Emp 1				Dept A
Emp 2				Dept A
Emp 3				Dept B
Emp 4				Dept B
Emp 5				Dept C
Emp 6				Dept B

Network Structure

The **network structure** can represent more complex logical relationships, and is still used by some mainframe DBMS packages. It allows *many-to-many* relationships among records; that is, the network model can access a data element by following one of several paths, because any data element or record can be related to any number of other data elements. For example, in Figure 3.17, departmental records can be related to more than one employee record, and employee records can be related to more than one project record. Thus, one could locate all employee records for a particular department, or all project records related to a particular employee.

Relational Structure

The **relational model** has become the most popular of the three database structures. It is used by most microcomputer DBMS packages, as well as by most midrange and mainframe systems. In the relational model, all data elements within the database are viewed as being stored in the form of simple **tables.** Figure 3.17 illustrates the relational database model with two tables representing some of the relationships among departmental and employee records. Other tables, or **relations,** for this organization's database might represent the data element relationships among projects, divisions, product lines, and so on. Database management system packages based on the relational model can link data elements from various tables to provide information to users. For example, a DBMS package could retrieve and display an employee's name and salary from the employee table in Figure 3.17, and the name of the employee's department from the department table, by using their common department number field (Deptno) to link or join the two tables.

Multidimensional Structure

The multidimensional database structure is a variation of the relational model that uses multidimensional structures to organize data and express the relationships between data. You can visualize multidimensional structures as cubes of data and cubes within cubes of data. Each side of the cube is considered a dimension of the data. Figure 3.18 is an example that shows that each dimension can represent a different category, such as product type, region, sales channel, and time [7].

Each cell within a multidimensional structure contains aggregated data related to elements along each of its dimensions. For example, a single cell may contain the total sales for a product in a region for a specific sales channel in a single month. A major benefit of multidimensional databases is that they are a compact and easy-to-understand way to visualize and manipulate data elements that have many interrelationships. So multidimensional databases have become the most popular database structure for the analytical databases that support *online analytical processing* (OLAP) applications, in which fast answers to complex business queries are expected. We discuss OLAP applications in Chapter 8.

Object-Oriented Structure

The **object-oriented** database model is considered to be one of the key technologies of a new generation of multimedia web-based applications. As Figure 3.19 illustrates, an **object** consists of data values describing the attributes of an entity, plus the operations that can be performed upon the data. This *encapsulation* capability allows the object-oriented model to better handle more complex types of data (graphics, pictures, voice, text) than other database structures.

The object-oriented model also supports *inheritance*; that is, new objects can be automatically created by replicating some or all of the characteristics of one or more *parent* objects. Thus, in Figure 3.19, the checking and savings account objects can both inherit the common attributes and operations of the parent bank account object. Such capabilities have made *object-oriented database management systems* (OODBMS) popular in computer-aided design (CAD) and in a growing number of applications. For example, object technology allows designers to develop product designs, store them as objects in an object-oriented database, and replicate and modify them to create new product designs. In addition, multimedia web-based applications for the Internet and corporate intranets and extranets have become a major application area for object technology, as we will discuss shortly.

FIGURE 3.18 An example of the different dimensions of a multidimensional database.

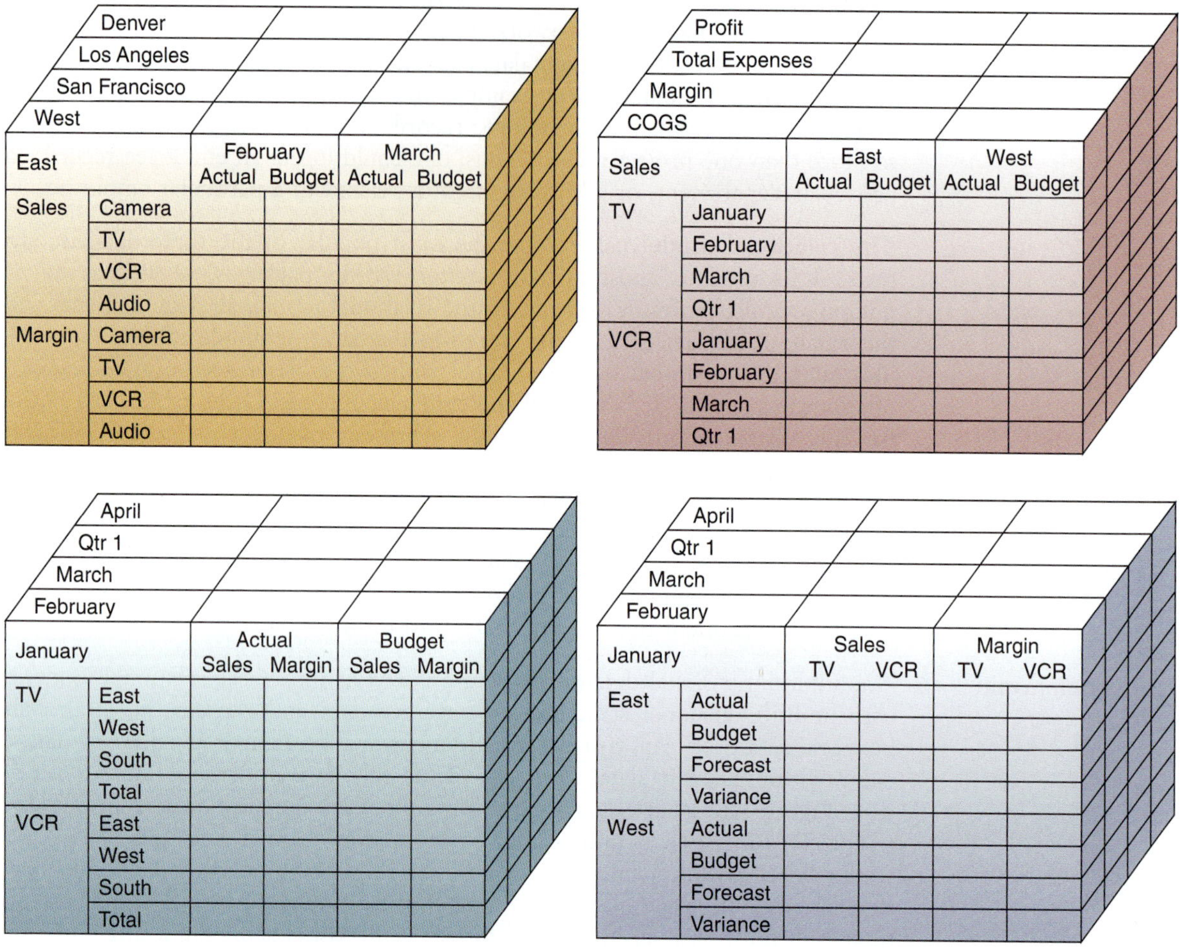

Object Technology and the Web

Object-oriented database software is finding increasing use in managing the hypermedia databases and Java applets on the World Wide Web and corporate intranets and extranets. Industry proponents predict that object-oriented database management systems will become the key software component that manages the hyperlinked multimedia pages and other types of data that support corporate websites. That's because an OODBMS can easily manage the access and storage of objects such as document and graphic images, video clips, audio segments, and other subsets of Web pages.

Object technology proponents argue that an object-oriented DBMS can work with such *complex data types* and the Java applets that use them much more efficiently than relational database management systems. However, major relational DBMS vendors have countered by adding object-oriented modules to their relational software. Examples include multimedia object extensions to IBM's DB2, and Oracle's object-based "cartridges" for Oracle 9i. See Figure 3.20.

Evaluation of Database Structures

The hierarchical data structure was a natural model for the databases used for the structured, routine types of transaction processing that was a characteristic of many business operations. Data for these operations can easily be represented by groups of records in a hierarchical relationship. However, there are many cases where information is needed about records that do not have hierarchical relationships. For example, it is obvious that, in some organizations, employees from more than one department can work on more than one project (refer back to Figure 3.17). A network data structure could easily handle this many-to-many relationship. It is thus

FIGURE 3.19

The checking and savings account objects can inherit common attributes and operations from the bank account object.

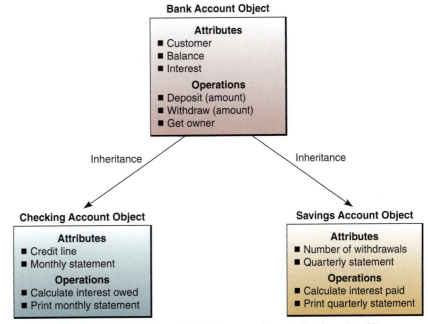

Source: Adapted from Ivar Jacobsen, Maria Ericsson, and Ageneta Jacobsen, *The Object Advantage: Business Process Reengineering with Object Technology* (New York: ACM Press, 1995), p. 65. Copyright © 1995, Association for Computing Machinery. By permission.

more flexible than the hierarchical structure in support of databases for many types of business operations. However, like the hierarchical structure, because its relationships must be specified in advance, the network model cannot easily handle ad hoc requests for information.

Relational databases, on the other hand, allow an end user to easily receive information in response to ad hoc requests. That's because not all of the relationships between the data elements in a relationally organized database need to be specified when the database is created. Database management software (such as Oracle 9i, DB2, Access, and Approach) creates new tables of data relationships using parts of the data from several tables. Thus, relational databases are easier for programmers to work with and easier to maintain than the hierarchical and network models.

FIGURE 3.20

This claims analysis graphics display provided by the CleverPath enterprise portal is powered by the Jasmine ii object-oriented database management system of Computer Associates.

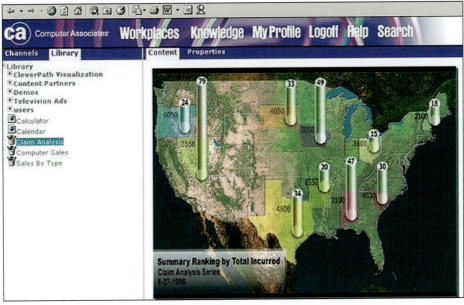

Source: Courtesy of Computer Associates

The major limitation of the relational model is that relational database management systems cannot process large amounts of business transactions as quickly and efficiently as those based on the hierarchical and network models, or complex, high-volume applications as well as the object-oriented model. This performance gap has narrowed with the development of advanced relational DBMS software with object-oriented extensions. The use of database management software based on the object-oriented and multidimensional models is growing steadily, as these technologies are playing a greater role for OLAP and web-based applications.

Accessing Databases

Efficient access to data is important. In database maintenance, records or objects have to be continually added, deleted, or updated to reflect business transactions. Data must also be accessed rapidly so information can be produced in response to end user requests.

Key Fields

That's why all data records usually contain one or more identification fields, or keys, that identify the record so it can be located. For example, the Social Security number of a person is often used as a *primary* **key field** that uniquely identifies the data records of individuals in student, employee, and customer files and databases. Other methods also identify and link data records stored in several different database files. For example, hierarchical and network databases may use *pointer fields*. These are fields within a record that indicate (point to) the location of another record that is related to it in the same file, or in another file. Hierarchical and network database management systems use this method to link records so they can retrieve information from several different database files.

Relational database management packages use primary keys to link records. Each table (file) in a relational database must contain a primary key. This field (or fields) uniquely identifies each record in a file and must also be found in other related files. For example, in Figure 3.17, department number (Deptno) is the primary key in the Department table and is also a field in the Employee table. As we mentioned earlier, a relational database management package could easily provide you with information from both tables by joining the tables and retrieving the information you want. See Figure 3.21.

Sequential Access

One of the original and basic ways to access data is by **sequential access.** This method uses a *sequential organization*, in which records are physically stored in a specified order according to a key field in each record. For example, payroll records could be placed in a payroll file in a numerical order based on employee Social Security numbers. Sequential access is fast and efficient when dealing with large volumes of data that need to be processed periodically. However, it requires that all new transactions be sorted into the proper sequence for sequential access processing. Also, most of the database or file may have to be searched to locate, store, or modify even a small number of data records. Thus, this method is too slow to handle applications requiring immediate updating or responses.

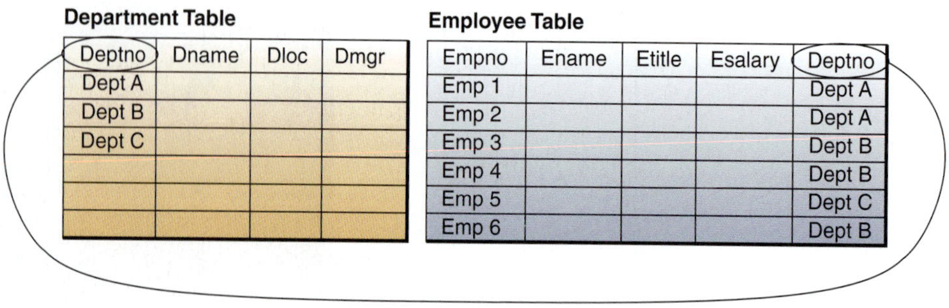

FIGURE 3.21

Joining the Employee and Department tables in a relational database enables you to selectively access data in both tables at the same time.

Department Table

Deptno	Dname	Dloc	Dmgr
Dept A			
Dept B			
Dept C			

Employee Table

Empno	Ename	Etitle	Esalary	Deptno
Emp 1				Dept A
Emp 2				Dept A
Emp 3				Dept B
Emp 4				Dept B
Emp 5				Dept C
Emp 6				Dept B

Direct Access

When using direct access methods, records do not have to be arranged in any particular sequence on storage media. However, the computer must keep track of the storage location of each record using a variety of direct organization methods so that data can be retrieved when needed. New transactions data do not have to be sorted, and processing that requires immediate responses or updating is easily handled. There are a number of ways to directly access records in the direct organization method. Let's take a brief look at three widely used methods to accomplish such direct access processing.

One common technique of direct access is **key transformation.** This method performs an arithmetic computation on a key field of record (such as a product number or Social Security number) and uses the number that results from that calculation as an address to store and access that record. Thus, the process is called key transformation because an arithmetic operation is applied to a key field to transform it into the storage location address of a record. Another direct access method used to store and locate records involves the use of an **index** of record keys and related storage addresses. A new data record is stored at the next available location, and its key and address are placed in an index. The computer uses this index whenever it must access a record.

In the **indexed sequential access method** (ISAM), records are stored in a sequential order on a magnetic disk or other direct access storage device based on the key field of each record. In addition, each database contains an index that references one or more key fields of each data record to its storage location address. Thus, an individual record can be directly located by using its key fields to search and locate its address in the database index, just as you can locate key topics in this book by looking them up in its index. As a result, if a few records must be processed quickly, the index is used to directly access the record needed. However, when large numbers of records must be processed periodically, the sequential organization provided by this method is used. For example, processing the weekly payroll for employees or producing monthly statements for customers could be done using sequential access processing of the records in the database.

Database Development

Database management packages like Microsoft Access or Lotus Approach allow end users to easily develop the databases they need. See Figure 3.22. However, large organizations usually place control of enterprisewide database development in the hands of **database administrators** (DBAs) and other database specialists. This improves the integrity and security of organizational databases. Database developers use the *data definition language* (DDL) in database management systems like Oracle 11i or IBM's DB2 to develop and specify the data contents, relationships, and structure of each database, and to modify these database specifications when necessary. Such information is cataloged and stored in a database of data definitions and specifications called a *data dictionary*, or *metadata respository*, which is managed by the database management software and maintained by the DBA.

A **data dictionary** is a database management catalog or directory containing **metadata,** that is, data about data. A data dictionary relies on a DBMS software component to manage a database of data definitions, that is, metadata about the structure, data elements, and other characteristics of an organization's databases. For example, it contains the names and descriptions of all types of data records and their interrelationships, as well as information outlining requirements for end users' access and use of application programs, and database maintenance and security.

Data dictionaries can be queried by the database administrator to report the status of any aspect of a firm's metadata. The administrator can then make changes to the definitions of selected data elements. Some *active* (versus *passive*) data dictionaries automatically enforce standard data element definitions whenever end users and application programs use a DBMS to access an organization's databases. For example, an

FIGURE 3.22

Creating a database table using the Table Wizard of Microsoft Access.

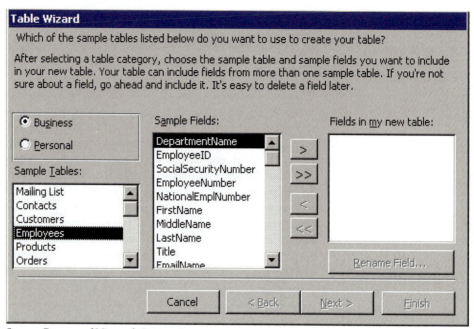

Source: Courtesy of Microsoft Corporation

active data dictionary would not allow a data entry program to use a nonstandard definition of a customer record, nor would it allow an employee to enter a name of a customer that exceeded the defined size of that data element.

Developing a large database of complex data types can be a complex task. Database administrators and database design analysts work with end users and systems analysts to model business processes and the data they require. Then they determine (1) what data definitions should be included in the database and (2) what structure or relationships should exist among the data elements.

Data Planning and Database Design

As Figure 3.23 illustrates, database development may start with a top-down **data planning process.** Database administrators and designers work with corporate and end user management to develop an *enterprise model* that defines the basic business process of the enterprise. Then they define the information needs of end users in a business process, such as the purchasing/receiving process that all businesses have [18].

Next, end users must identify the key data elements that are needed to perform their specific business activities. This frequently involves developing *entity relationship diagrams* (ERDs) that model the relationships among the many entities involved in business processes. For example, Figure 3.24 illustrates some of the relationships in a purchasing/receiving process. End users and database designers could use database management or business modeling software to help them develop ERD models for the purchasing/receiving process. This would help identify what supplier and product data are required to automate their purchasing/receiving and other business processes using enterprise resource management (ERP) or supply chain management (SCM) software.

Such user views are a major part of a **data modeling** process where the relationships between data elements are identified. Each data model defines the logical relationships among the data elements needed to support a basic business process. For example, can a supplier provide more than one type of product to us? Can a customer have more than one type of account with us? Can an employee have several pay rates or be assigned to several project workgroups?

Answering such questions will identify data relationships that have to be represented in a data model that supports a business process. These data models then serve as logical frameworks (called *schemas and subschemas)* on which to base the *physical design* of databases and the development of application programs to support

FIGURE 3.23

Database development involves data planning and database design activities. Data models that support business processes are used to develop databases that meet the information needs of users.

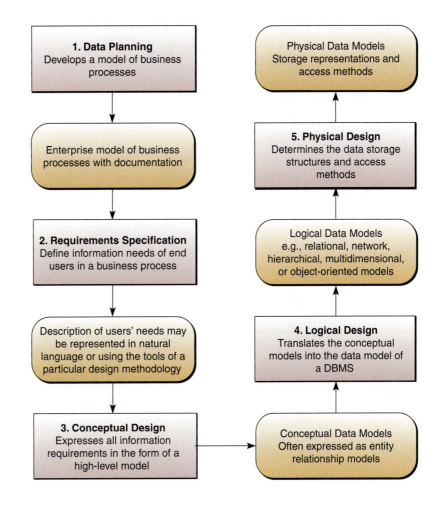

the business processes of the organization. A schema is an overall logical view of the relationships among the data elements in a database, while the subschema is a logical view of the data relationships needed to support specific end user application programs that will access that database.

Remember that data models represent *logical views* of the data and relationships of the database. Physical database design takes a *physical view* of the data (also called the internal view) that describes how data are to be physically stored and accessed on the storage devices of a computer system. For example, Figure 3.25 illustrates these different database views and the software interface of a bank database processing system. In this example, checking, savings, and installment lending are the business processes whose data models are part of a banking services data model that serves as a logical data framework for all bank services.

FIGURE 3.24

This entity relationship diagram illustrates some of the relationships among the entities (product, supplier, warehouse, etc.) in a purchasing/receiving business process.

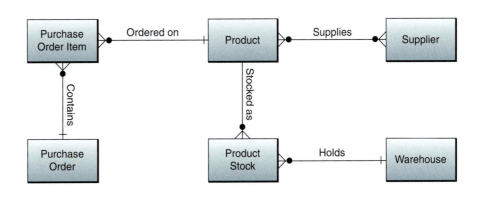

FIGURE 3.25   Example of the logical and physical database views and the software interface of a banking services information system.

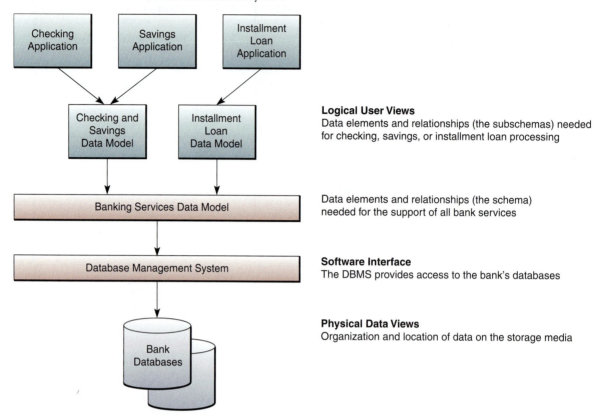

Logical User Views
Data elements and relationships (the subschemas) needed for checking, savings, or installment loan processing

Software Interface
The DBMS provides access to the bank's databases

Data elements and relationships (the schema) needed for the support of all bank services

Physical Data Views
Organization and location of data on the storage media

Aetna and Shop at Home Network: Development Solutions

Database administrators maintain the more than 15,000 database table definitions with the ERWin data modeling tool, according to Michael Mathias, an information systems data storage expert at Aetna Inc. Mathias sees the importance of viewing the maintenance of large amounts of data from a logical perspective. While the physical management of large data stores is certainly a nontrivial effort, Mathias says that failing to keep the data organized leads inexorably to user workflow problems, devaluation of the data as a corporate asset and, eventually, customer complaints [14].

Shop At Home Network has created a team of three senior developers for its Oracle database management system. One team member is responsible for creating the data models that define the entities and relationships that represent the end user's view into the data. Another is a business analyst and project lead who finds out what types of queries are needed by business end users and how users want to see information summarized to create the best system design. The third, a database administrator, is responsible for the physical structure of the warehouse itself and making sure it gets loaded correctly so users get the right information at the right time [14].

Summary

- **Data Resource Management.** Data resource management is a managerial activity that applies information systems technology and management tools to the task of managing an organization's data resources. It includes the database administration function that focuses on developing and maintaining standards and controls for an organization's databases. Data administration, however, focuses on the planning and control of data to support business functions and strategic organizational objectives. This includes a data planning effort that focuses on developing an overall data architecture for a firm's data resources.

- **Database Management.** The database management approach affects the storage and processing of data. The data needed by different applications are consolidated and integrated into several common databases, instead of being stored in many independent data files. Also, the database management approach emphasizes updating and maintaining common databases, having users' application programs share the data in the database, and providing a reporting and an inquiry/response capability so end users can easily receive reports and quick responses to requests for information.

- **Database Software.** Database management systems are software packages that simplify the creation, use, and maintenance of databases. They provide software tools so end users, programmers, and database administrators can create and modify databases, interrogate a database, generate reports, do application development, and perform database maintenance.

- **Types of Databases.** Several types of databases are used by business organizations, including operational, distributed, and external databases. Data warehouses are a central source of data from other databases that have been cleaned, transformed and cataloged for business analysis and decision support applications. That includes data mining, which attempts to find hidden patterns and trends in the warehouse data. Hypermedia databases on the World Wide Web and corporate intranets and extranets store hyperlinked multimedia pages at a website. Web server software can manage such databases for quick access and maintenance of the Web database.

- **Database Development.** The development of databases can be easily accomplished using microcomputer database management packages for small end user applications. However, the development of large corporate databases requires a top-down data planning effort. This may involve developing enterprise and entity relationship models, subject area databases, and data models that reflect the logical data elements and relationships needed to support the operation and management of the basic business processes of the organization.

- **Data Access.** Data must be organized in some logical manner on physical storage devices so that they can be efficiently processed. For this reason, data are commonly organized into logical data elements such as characters, fields, records, files, and databases. Database structures, such as the hierarchical, network, relational, and object-oriented models, are used to organize the relationships among the data records stored in databases. Databases and files can be organized in either a sequential or direct manner and can be accessed and maintained by either sequential access or direct access processing methods.

Key Terms and Concepts

These are the key terms and concepts of this chapter. The page number of their first explanation is in parentheses.

1. Data dictionary (91)
2. Data mining (77)
3. Data modeling (92)
4. Data planning (82)
5. Data resource management (70)
6. Database access (90)
   - *a.* Direct (91)
   - *b.* Sequential (90)
7. Database administration (82)
8. Database administrator (91)
9. Database management approach (78)
10. Database management system (79)
11. Database structures (84)
    - *a.* Hierarchical (86)
    - *b.* Multidimensional (87)
    - *c.* Network (87)
    - *d.* Object-oriented (87)
    - *e.* Relational (87)
12. DBMS uses (79)
    - *a.* Application development (81)
    - *b.* Database development (91)
    - *c.* Database interrogation (79)
    - *d.* Database maintenance (80)
13. Key field (72)
14. Logical data elements (72)
    - *a.* Character (72)
    - *b.* Field (72)
    - *c.* Record (73)
    - *d.* File (73)
    - *e.* Database (73)
15. Metadata (76)
16. Query language (79)
17. Report generator (79)
18. Types of databases (73)
    - *a.* Data warehouse (75)
    - *b.* Distributed (74)
    - *c.* External (75)
    - *d.* Hypermedia (75)
    - *e.* Operational (73)

Review Quiz

Match one of the key terms and concepts listed previously with one of the brief examples or definitions that follow. Try to find the best fit for answers that seem to fit more than one term or concept. Defend your choices.

_____ 1. The use of integrated collections of data records and files for data storage and processing.

_____ 2. A DBMS allows you to create, interrogate, and maintain a database, create reports, and develop application programs.

_____ 3. A specialist in charge of the databases of an organization.

_____ 4. This DBMS feature allows users to easily interrogate a database.

_____ 5. Defines and catalogs the data elements and data relationships in an organization's database.

_____ 6. Helps you specify and produce reports from a database.

_____ 7. The main software package that supports a database management approach.

_____ 8. Databases are dispersed to the Internet and corporate intranets and extranets.

_____ 9. Databases that organize and store data as objects.

_____ 10. Databases of hyperlinked multimedia documents on the Web.

_____ 11. The management of all the data resources of an organization.

_____ 12. Developing databases and maintaining standards and controls for an organization's databases.

_____ 13. Processing data in a data warehouse to discover key business factors and trends.

_____ 14. Enterprise planning that ties database development to the support of basic business processes.

_____ 15. Developing conceptual views of the relationships among data in a database.

_____ 16. A customer's name.

_____ 17. A customer's name, address, and account balance.

_____ 18. The names, addresses, and account balances of all of your customers.

_____ 19. An integrated collection of all of the data about your customers.

_____ 20. An identification field in a record.

_____ 21. A treelike structure of records in a database.

_____ 22. A tabular structure of records in a database.

_____ 23. Records are organized as cubes within cubes in a database.

_____ 24. Transactions are sorted in ascending order by Social Security number before processing.

_____ 25. Unsorted transactions can be used to immediately update a database.

_____ 26. Databases that support the major business processes of an organization.

_____ 27. A centralized and integrated database of current and historical data about an organization.

_____ 28. Databases available on the Internet or provided by commercial information services.

Discussion Questions

1. How should an e-business enterprise store, access, and distribute data and information about their internal operations and external environment?

2. What roles do database management, data administration, and data planning play in managing data as a business resource?

3. What are the advantages of a database management approach to organizing, accessing, and managing an organization's data resources? Give examples to illustrate your answer.

4. Refer to the Real World Case on IBM and Oracle in the chapter. The case states that "database software has become more of a commodity." Do you agree? Why or why not?

5. What is the role of a database management system in an e-business information system?

6. Databases of information about a firm's internal operations were formerly the only databases that were

considered to be important to a business. What other kinds of databases are important for a business today?

7. Refer to the Real World Case on Experian Automotive in the chapter. The case states that Experian's automotive database "has raised the hackles of privacy advocates." What legitimate privacy concerns and safeguard suggestions might be raised about this database and its use?

8. What are the benefits and limitations of the relational database model for business applications today?

9. Why is the object-oriented database model gaining acceptance for developing applications and managing the hypermedia databases at business websites?

10. How have the Internet, intranets, extranets, and the World Wide Web affected the types and uses of data resources available to business end users?

Application Exercises

Complete the following exercises as individual or group projects that apply chapter concepts to real world business

1. Tracking Employee Software Training

DB You have the responsibility for managing software training for Sales, Accounting, and Operations Department workers in your organization. The data below present summary information about training sessions held in the last quarter. You want to record this information in a database table and use that table to record information about all future training sessions as they occur.

a. Create a database table to store this information and enter the ten records shown below. Session ID can serve as the primary key. Print out a listing of your table.

b. Create and print the results of queries showing: **a.** Average attendance at Database Fundamentals Classes, **b.** the total number of hours of spreadsheet, SS, class attendance by workers in each department, and **c.** the average attendance for each course (Title).

c. Generate a report Grouped by Category and showing the number of sessions, average attendance, and total hours of training provided for each course title. Your report should include subtotal and grand total figures as well.

d. If the number of hours and category for a particular course title are always the same, e.g., the Spreadsheet Fundamentals class is always 16 hours long and in the SS Category, can you see any problems caused by recording the hours and category as an attribute of this table?

2. Calculating Training Costs

DB Database systems typically involve multiple tables that are related to each other and can be combined on the basis of their logical relationship.

The data that follows describe a set of training classes that are available to workers in the Sales, Accounting, and Operations departments. For each course there is a title which can be used to identify it (Title), the duration of the class in hours (Hours), the fixed costs of an instructor and room for the class (Fixed Cost) and a per student cost for materials (Unit Cost).

Title	Category	Hours	Fixed Cost	Unit Cost
Advanced Database Features	DB	16	$3,250.00	$120.00
Advanced Spreadsheet	SS	16	$3,000.00	$90.00
Database Fundamentals	SS	24	$4,000.00	$100.00
Enliven Your Presentations	PR	8	$1,000.00	$30.00
Spreadsheet Fundamentals	SS	16	$2,500.00	$65.00
Using Presentation Graphics	PR	12	$1,500.00	$40.00

a. If you have not completed the previous Application Exercise, complete part a of that exercise now. For this exercise, we will delete the Hours and Category columns from the existing table because they are characteristics of the course and not a particular session, so delete those columns now. Next create a course table with the structure and data shown in the example above. Make sure that the Title column in this new table has exactly the same data type and length that you used for the Title column on the previous table. Create and print a listing of a query that joins the two tables based on the common Title column and displays all columns of both tables.

b. Create a report that could be used to bill the costs of each session to the appropriate departments. Each department will be billed only for Unit Costs, so join the tables and multiply unit cost by the number of attendees from each department to get the billing for that department. Include a total to be billed to each department across all training sessions that have been held.

c. Create a report grouped by Course and Category that shows the total cost of each session (fixed cost + unit cost * total attendees) and cost per attendee (the above divided by total attendees).

Session ID	Hours	Title	Category	Sales Attendees	Accounting Attendees	Operations Attendees
100	16	Spreadsheet Fundamentals	SS	5	3	8
101	24	Database Fundamentals	DB	4	6	4
102	12	Using Presentation Graphics	PR	9	2	3
103	16	Advanced Spreadsheet	SS	1	9	6
104	24	Database Fundamentals	DB	3	8	4
105	12	Using Presentation Graphics	PR	10	1	3
106	16	Advanced Database Features	DB	0	8	4
107	8	Enliven Your Presentations	PR	9	0	2
108	16	Spreadsheet Fundamentals	SS	2	7	7
109	16	Advanced Spreadsheet	SS	1	6	4

Shell Exploration and Others: Using Data Warehouses for Data Resource Management

Redundant data, wrong data, missing data, miscoded data. Every company has some of each, probably residing in IT nooks that don't communicate much. It's not a new problem, but these days the jumble becomes very apparent during high-profile projects, such as installing enterprise resource planning (ERP) or supply chain management (SCM) software. That's when companies often focus on the business processes and not on the form and congruity of the resulting data, says John Hagerty, an analyst at AMR Research Inc. in Boston. When a company does that, its IT department has to step back to cleanse, reconcile, and integrate data from various data silos around the company into a data warehouse.

Shell Exploration and Production is in the throes of such a project. Early last year, the fuel company wanted to combine data from its ERP financial applications with data from its mishmash of volumetric systems, which process information on how much gas and oil the company finds and collects. "Every different system has its own internal sets of codes," explains Steve Mutch, data warehouse team leader at Shell Exploration in Aberdeen, Scotland. "Going back and cleansing and integrating the data in those host systems wasn't an option." It would have taken too much time and been too expensive, he says. Instead, Mutch found a tool from Kalido Ltd. in London that analyzes and maps the data from various systems and then combines it into one warehouse. After nearly seven months of data analysis and mapping work, 27 data sources now come together in one 450GB warehouse, Mutch says.

Corporate politics weren't too bad because no single business unit lost control of its data, he says. And now they all contribute to a greater understanding of the information for the company as a whole. "Once the concept was proved, we had pressure from the top executives to integrate other applications as well," he says. "They could see [for] themselves what information they could now get and how powerful it is."

Even if a company decides to replace different applications with one new one as a way to address data chaos, it probably won't be easy. Many of the top customer relationship management (CRM) and ERP vendors, for example, offer suites comprised of their own applications plus others they have acquired. The products in the suites, therefore, weren't built together and may not pass data back and forth smoothly, says Jon Dell'Antonia, vice president of MIS at OshKosh B'Gosh, Inc., a clothing maker in Oshkosh, Wisconsin. "You immediately find out it's not seamless."

ERP vendors are trying to address the issue by providing data models and data warehouses with their suites. But Dell'Antonia has avoided data warehouses from ERP suites. His approach to data warehousing was to create a homegrown IBM DB2 warehouse that unifies data from different applications. For example, in one of OshKosh B'Gosh's transaction-processing applications, the term "sales" is used.

But on the user interface, it's called "customer sales." A software tool from DataMirror Corp. in Toronto, Canada, uploads sales data to DB2 once a day. And the data warehouse recognizes the differently named items as the same because OshKosh B'Gosh programmers created tags that reconcile incoming data elements.

Cost-justifying data warehouse projects isn't all that hard, users say. "Once you start putting all your data in one spot, all the past sins are clearly visible," says Cathy Witt, the CIO at computer retailer CompUSA Inc., which is based in Dallas. The first data integration project should be inside a business unit that produces a lot of revenue for the company, says Witt. It's sometimes easier, you might think, to start with a small business unit, but you won't get the cost justification that leads to buy-in from upper management, she says.

The logic to use when broaching the subject with business unit managers is simple, she says: "You tell them, 'Data make us what we are. If I can give you good clean data, as opposed to your only being able to use a portion of it, you will make better decisions,'" That's how Witt convinced CompUSA's retail stores, and later, the product warranty unit, to fund a data cleanup for a data warehouse last year.

To help CompUSA sell more warranties on its consumer computer products, the IT department now retrieves sale data from its Siebel Systems CRM applications. The data are then sent through a cleansing tool from Trillium Software. The Trillium tool searches for duplicate and incomplete information. It also helps fill in missing information by, for instance, matching ZIP codes against its own ZIP code database. The data are then put in a data warehouse to be analyzed and mined by sales agents for leads on good prospects for CompUSA warranties and other products.

Although third-party data cleaning companies could have been hired to do the same work, Witt didn't want to farm out the job. "We have the skills," she says, "and we care about the quality of our data more than anyone else does."

Case Study Questions

1. Why do companies still have problems with the quality of the data resources stored in their business information systems?

2. How do data warehouse approaches help companies like Shell and OshKosh meet their data resource management challenges?

3. What business benefits can companies derive from a data warehouse approach? Use CompUSA as an example.

Source: Adapted from Kim Nash, "Merging Data Silos," *Computerworld*, April 15, 2002, pp. 30–32. Reprinted with permission from *Computerworld*.

BlueCross BlueShield and Warner Bros.: The ROI of Storage Area Networks

BlueCross BlueShield of Tennessee Inc. has spent between $3 million and $3.5 million over the past three years on a storage-area network (SAN) that includes 40TB of disk and tape storage. That may seem like a hefty capital investment, especially in storage, which is increasingly considered a commodity item. But you must also consider the savings, says Bob Venable, enterprise systems manager at the Chattanooga-based health insurer. They amount to more than $1.5 million per year and come largely from reductions in the time and labor costs related to identifying and solving storage-related problems.

BlueCross BlueShield's return on investment is impressive, but it's also far from typical. In fact, experts say there's no such thing as typical when it comes to cost savings from SANs, since there's no single formula for calculating their cost. Instead, the cost of implementing and running a SAN can vary tremendously, depending on a company's existing equipment, storage needs, and planned acquisitions. The same variables also affect a company's ROI.

Storage area networks are high-speed local area networks dedicated to providing high-performance data storage for many companies today. SANs cut data storage costs by connecting servers, storage systems, and backup devices to allow centralized storage management and real-time reallocation of data storage. "This is a data center management team's nirvana," says David Cyganski, a professor of electrical and computer engineering at Worcester Polytechnic Institute in Worcester, Massachusetts.

But comparing the costs of implementing and running a SAN with those for other storage systems, such as direct-attached storage or network-attached storage (NAS), is tricky. The initial costs associated with a SAN are significantly higher, but the long-term payoffs are much greater, experts say. "If I compare the storage costs of buying servers and managing them on a server-by-server basis and the costs of buying a SAN and managing it from a centralized place, the purchase cost is maybe four times higher with a SAN, but the total cost of ownership is about half," says Bob Passmore, an analyst at Gartner Inc., in Stamford, Connecticut.

Don Cawthorne is a user-turned-vendor who was working at Northern Trust Bank in Chicago five years ago when it decided to build a SAN infrastructure. SANs were still in their infancy at the time. Cawthorne budgeted $1.7 million for about a half-dozen servers. But technological advancements have resulted in a huge drop in SAN costs and a big increase in SAN performance. Today, a SAN for six servers would cost only a fraction of the amount he paid, says Cawthorne, who is now director of SAN architecture at SANcastle Technologies Inc. in San Jose.

Still, what goes into a SAN now depends on factors such as how large a network is and the class of equipment to be used. "Cost is driven very much by the complexity of the situation," Passmore says. However, users often find that the cost savings they accrue are well worth the price. They also report intangible benefits, such as having more floor space available in the data center after converting to a SAN.

Anthony Lloyd, vice president of computer operations at motion picture company Warner Bros., recovered about 35 percent of his data center's floor space when he installed four storage area networks. This will allow for better planning as he brings in more hardware, he says. Although it's nice to have extra floor space, users, analysts, and vendors say the real advantage of SANs comes from better management of storage.

Before implementing SANs at New York-based Warner Bros., Lloyd had problems projecting what his storage needs and costs would be. "We were immediately able to fix that in the SAN environment," he says. What's more, he estimates that a total investment of about $1.3 million has already yielded about $700,000 in savings over the past year as a result of less downtime and more efficient use of resources.

Now Warner Bros. procures new storage every quarter instead of almost every week. And Lloyd says that because he buys in bulk, he gets better discounts. He also can now generate reports for Warner's business departments to show them how much storage they have available, how much they've used, and how much the additional storage will cost them.

"The cost reductions come in terms of storage management and higher availability," says Arun Tancja, an analyst at The Enterprise Storage Group Inc. in Milford, Massachusetts. "Your data's available all the time: it's not crashing. There's easier storage management, easier implementation of storage applications. Any costs you invest in SANS are oftentimes recovered in a matter of months, not years."

Case Study Questions

1. What is a storage area network? Why are many companies installing SANs?

2. What are the reasons for the quick payback on SAN investments?

3. What are the challenges and alternatives to SANs as a data storage technology?

Source: Adapted from Mary K. Pratt, "Saving with SANs," *Computerworld*, July 1, 2002, p. 38. Reprinted with permission from *Computerworld*.

Sherwin-Williams and Krispy Kreme: Managing External Data Sources

Once a week, Jim Revak, IT manager at The Sherwin-Williams Co. in Cleveland, faces the daunting task of collecting business intelligence from 15,000 third-party retailers that sell the company's paint products, and downloading that information into a data warehouse. Customer demographics and data on 4,000 products arrive from Sherwin-Williams' major retailers in disparate formats. Add to that the handful of external data the company collects from other sources, and you've got a data warehousing nightmare. "The good news is, you have a lot more information on how your products are doing out there with your customers. But the bad news is, it's so overwhelming. We don't have enough arms and legs" to analyze all the information, Revak says. Welcome to the world of external data overload.

External information in corporate data warehouses has increased during the past few years because of the wealth of information available, the desire to work more closely with third parties and business partners, and the Internet, says Warren Thornthwaite of data warehousing consultancy InfoDynamics LLC in Menlo Park, California.

Don't be fooled by the abundance of "reliable" data for sale or the deceptive simplicity of integrating it, industry observers caution. Not only does the additional data consume disk space and go largely unanalyzed, but the amount of "pick-and-shovel work" required to clean up all of those files also increases exponentially for the IT department, says Revak. The key is getting the data from trusted sources and creating a full design and development life cycle.

Krispy Kreme Doughnuts Inc. in Winston-Salem, North Carolina, sells more than 2 billion pastries annually at 128 franchises and at thousands of grocery-store bakery cases across the country. But keeping track of its sales at myriad stores became a challenge. So Krispy Kreme acquired external data from Deerfield, Illinois-based Efficient Marketing Services Inc., which takes checkout scanner data from grocery stores, refines them into codes compatible with Krispy Kreme's data warehouse, and transmits them to Krispy Kreme each Friday morning. That information helps the company speed up its billing cycle and understand how its pastries get lost or stolen. It also helps Krispy Kreme reach more customers and markets, says Frank Hood, the doughnut maker's vice president of information services.

Each grocery store could have been asked to send its scanned data directly to Krispy Kreme in return for information on how that store is doing compared to its competitors. But Krispy Kreme's IT executives preferred a faster integration method purchased by subscription from a third party. "Using an external group to help you manage that process allows a more consistent data stream," says Hood. Plus, the third-party provider has contingency plans in place in case data are unavailable, he adds.

Other companies, like Sherwin-Williams, prefer to get their data straight from the source. Its major retail partners, including Wal-Mart Stores Inc., Kmart Corp., Target Corp., Lowes Co., and The Home Depot Inc., "have IT departments big enough to consolidate point-of-sale data, with departments to break it down," Revak says. For Sherwin-Williams, "It all ties into the relationship sales and marketing people have with their customers," he says.

In either case, Thornthwaite advises that companies find a trusted resource to work as partners on consistency, formatting reliability, and contingency plans. For example, timing is critical in Krispy Kreme's electronic billing cycle, so if data don't arrive, its sales analysis application will identify them as missing and kick out any exceptions. But no matter how well planned the process, observers say there's no substitute for customer contact and having tactical detail behind census data or external information. "Data, unless you control it and generate it, may not be correct," says Hood.

Tips for Managing External Data

- *Do* purchase external data from a reliable source that will do most of the refining for you and will work with you on contingency plans.
- *Do* run a test load first. A load of test data can pave the way for accurate production loads.
- *Don't* collect data until business and IT staff have agreed on the amount, frequency, format, and content of the data you need.
- *Don't* acquire more data or use more data sources than you really need.
- *Don't* mingle external and homegrown data without adding unique identifiers to each record, in case you need to pull it out.
- *Don't* overestimate the data's integrity. Nothing beats direct customer contact and tactical details behind the data.

Case Study Questions

1. What challenges in acquiring and using data from external sources are identified in this case?

2. Do you prefer the Sherwin-Williams or Krispy Kreme approach to acquiring external data? Why?

3. What other sources of external data might a business use to gain valuable marketing and competitive intelligence?

Source: Adapted from Stacy Collett, "Incoming!" *Computerworld*, April 15, 2002, p. 34. Reprinted with permission from *Computerworld*.

CHAPTER 4

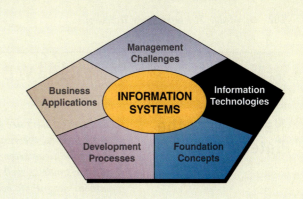

TELECOMMUNICATIONS AND NETWORKS

Chapter Highlights

Learning Objectives

After reading and studying this chapter; you should be able to:

1. Identify several major developments and trends in the industries, technologies, and business applications of telecommunications and Internet technologies.

2. Provide examples of the business value of Internet, intranet, and extranet applications.

3. Identify the basic components, functions, and types of telecommunications networks used in business.

4. Explain the functions of major types of telecommunications network hardware, software, media, and services.

The Networked Enterprise

Networking the Enterprise

When computers are networked, two industries—computing and communications—converge, and the result is vastly more than the sum of the parts. Suddenly, computing applications become available for business-to-business coordination and commerce, and for small as well as large organizations. The global Internet creates a public place without geographic boundaries—cyberspace—where ordinary citizens can interact, publish their ideas, and engage in the purchase of goods and services. In short, the impact of both computing and communications on our society and organizational structures is greatly magnified [15].

Thus, telecommunications and network technologies are internetworking and revolutionizing business and society. Businesses have become **networked enterprises.** The Internet, the Web, and intranets and extranets are networking business processes and employees together, and connecting them to their customers, suppliers, and other business stakeholders. Companies and workgroups can thus collaborate more creatively, manage their business operations and resources more effectively, and compete successfully in today's fast-changing global economy. This chapter presents the telecommunications and network foundations for these developments.

Analyzing FedEx versus UPS

Read the Real World Case on FedEx versus UPS on the next page. We can learn a lot about the role that telecommunications technologies can play in creating competitive advantages in business. See Figure 4.1.

FedEx founder Fred Smith rightly foresaw the strategic business value of the electronic communication of information about packages in the express delivery business. Thus, FedEx has been a pioneer in developing hardware, software, and networking solutions that use wireless telecommunications to coordinate the pickup and delivery of packages and track their progress, both within the FedEx system and with their customers. UPS has had to play catch-up in the use of wireless

FIGURE 4.1

Laurie A. Tucker is senior vice president of global marketing for FedEx and a champion of its innovative use of information technology.

Source: Courtesy of Federal Express Corporation

REAL WORLD CASE 1

FedEx versus UPS: Playing Catch-Up in Telecommunications Innovation

"Information about the package will soon be just as important as the delivery of that package." On any list of insightful statements about the impact of technology during the past 35 years, that one belongs near the top. FedEx Corp. (www.fedex.com) founder and CEO Frederick W. Smith made that statement in 1979, succinctly predicting the next quarter-century of IT innovation. The statement has become so totemic that it's repeated—in generic form, to be sure, with no credit given to its original source—in the corporate literature of rival United Parcel Service (www.ups.com).

The telecommunications innovations really began in 1980, when FedEx launched a proprietary and then-revolutionary wireless data network called Digitally Assisted Dispatch System (DADS). The system increased efficiency by eliminating radio chatter; dispatchers were now able to use text messages to change drivers' routes and pickup requests. DADS, which is still in use, led to a 30 percent increase in couriers' productivity—the first day it was used.

In 1986, the company adopted its present generation of wireless handhelds, called SuperTrackers. These devices capture package data via a bar-code scan. When couriers return to their trucks, they insert the SuperTracker in their DADS unit, and the information is downloaded to the company's proprietary package-tracking system, the Customer Oriented Service and Management Operating System, or COSMOS.

Urged on by Smith, FedEx has been an early adopter—and, in many cases, a pioneer—of technologies such as videoconferencing, wireless connectivity, and bar codes. But companies that value innovation must put up with its cousin: failure. Laurie A. Tucker has been at FedEx since 1979 in a host of positions and is now senior vice president of global marketing. She recalls a 1996 effort that never took off; a Web publishing operation. It was intended to help enterprises set up websites using FedEx-designed templates. It didn't have a prayer. "People wondered what this transportation company was doing in the publishing business," Tucker says. "But nobody got fired for that. We don't punish people for taking risks."

United Parcel Service Because of FedEx's impressive and well-published record on IT innovation, it's tempting to think of 94-year-old UPS as a plodder that tries hard but always lags by a step. Even UPS CIO Ken Lacy concedes that the company's approach to IT is "very methodical," in keeping with its button-down management style. "That's just how we approach governance," he says. However, analysts say UPS has played an excellent game of catch-up and pulled even with its rival, which is no mean feat.

In contrast with FedEx's freewheeling, let's-give-it-a-shot style, UPS has four standing IT committees devoted to finance, governance, strategy, and new technologies. The committees are composed of business executives as well as technologists who report to Lacy and steer UPS's efforts. That may seem unwieldy, but analysts say the system has

allowed UPS to spend not just massively—"We've invested $14 billion-plus since the mid-1980s to build integrated global networks," Lacy says—but also wisely, never decoupling its IT spending from business goals.

In 1990, UPS introduced its own handheld, called the Delivery Information Acquisition Device (DIAD). The devices are still in use, having been upgraded several times. In its present incarnation, the DIAD both captures and transmits delivery data in real time (UPS is happy to point out that it beat FedEx to the punch on this feature), serves as a cell phone, and has a host of new ease-of-use and maintainability features. Today's DIAD runs on PSOS, an embedded operating system; however, the next-generation devices will be based on Windows CE.

UPS also offers an innovative set of application programming interfaces that let companies create their own hooks into online UPS functions such as package and signature tracking. Called UPS OnLine tools, this initiative enables business customers to connect their own e-commerce applications to UPS, while simultaneously offering selected UPS services to their end users' Web browsers. Analysts say the platform-independent tools offer customers convenience, as well as a virtual lock-in to UPS services.

The Future And what of the future? FedEx CIO Robert B. Carter becomes animated when discussing his company's upcoming wireless tool, called PowerPad. Carter says the company's other IT focus for the near future is "better integrating systems across divisions." In addition to its trademark FedEx Express service, the company is a large player in ground, palletized-freight, and international shipping. Carter's goal is to funnel package data from all these operations into one transparent system.

UPS, too, is upgrading its handhelds. The company is also focusing on automating processes at its sorting facilities in an effort to reduce training costs. And like its competitor, UPS is leveraging its IT expertise to become a logistics outsourcer. With both FedEx and UPS consistently hailed as innovation leaders, that evolution seems like a natural.

Case Study Questions

1. Why does telecommunications play such a key role in the competition between FedEx and UPS?

2. Why does "information about the package" have such a strategic business value in the express delivery business?

3. What telecommunications products or services would you recommend that FedEx or UPS use to improve their competitive position in the overnight delivery and shipping business? Defend your recommendations.

Source: Adapted from Steve Ulfelder, "Signed, Sealed, and Delivered," *Computerworld*, September 30, 2002, pp. 50–52. Reprinted with permission from *Computerworld*.

technologies, but has done an innovative job of using information technology to provide application interfaces and network links to business customers for offering UPS services on their websites. This innovative competition is expected to continue in the future as both companies move further into global shipping and complete logistics services.

Trends in Telecommunications

Telecommunications is the exchange of information in any form (voice, data, text, images, audio, video) over computer-based networks. Major trends occurring in the field of telecommunications have a significant impact on management decisions in this area. You should thus be aware of major trends in telecommunications industries, technologies, and applications that significantly increase the decision alternatives confronting business managers and professionals. See Figure 4.2.

Industry Trends

The competitive arena for telecommunications service has changed dramatically in many countries in recent years. The telecommunications industry has changed from government-regulated monopolies to a deregulated market with fiercely competitive suppliers of telecommunications services. Numerous companies now offer businesses and consumers a choice of everything from local and global telephone services to communications satellite channels, mobile radio, cable TV, cellular phone services, and Internet access. See Figure 4.3.

The explosive growth of the Internet and the World Wide Web has spawned a host of new telecommunications products, services, and providers. Driving and responding to this growth, business firms have dramatically increased their use of the Internet and the Web for electronic commerce and collaboration. Thus, the service and vendor options available to meet a company's telecommunications needs have increased significantly, as have a business manager's decision-making alternatives.

Technology Trends

Open systems with unrestricted connectivity, using **Internet networking technologies** as their technology platform, are today's primary telecommunications technology drivers. Web browser suites, HTML Web page editors, Internet and intranet servers and network management software, TCP/IP Internet networking products, and network security fire walls are just a few examples. These technologies

FIGURE 4.2

Major trends in business telecommunications.

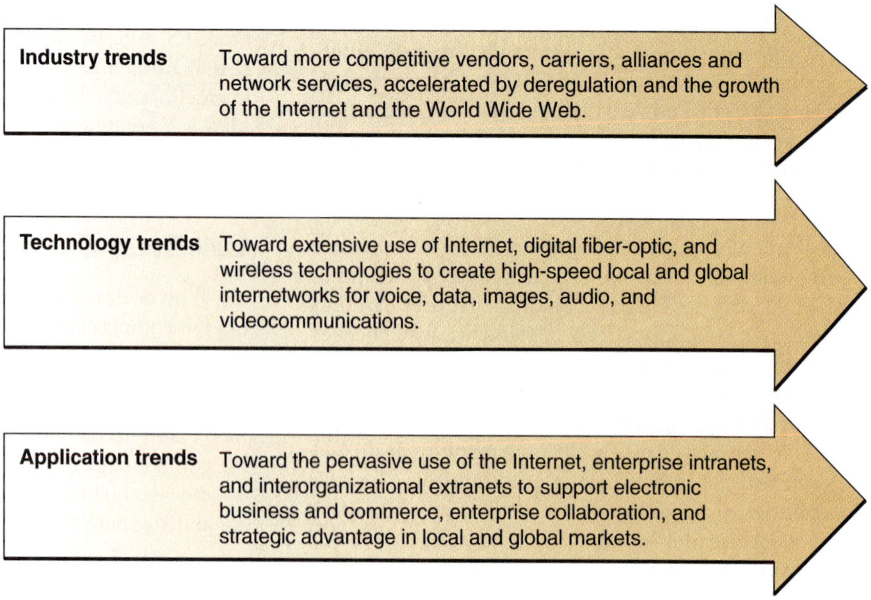

Industry trends — Toward more competitive vendors, carriers, alliances and network services, accelerated by deregulation and the growth of the Internet and the World Wide Web.

Technology trends — Toward extensive use of Internet, digital fiber-optic, and wireless technologies to create high-speed local and global internetworks for voice, data, images, audio, and videocommunications.

Application trends — Toward the pervasive use of the Internet, enterprise intranets, and interorganizational extranets to support electronic business and commerce, enterprise collaboration, and strategic advantage in local and global markets.

FIGURE 4.3

The spectrum of telecommunications-based services available today.

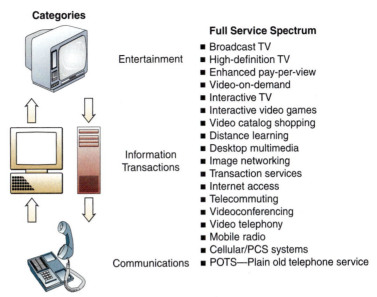

Categories

Entertainment

Information Transactions

Communications

Full Service Spectrum
- Broadcast TV
- High-definition TV
- Enhanced pay-per-view
- Video-on-demand
- Interactive TV
- Interactive video games
- Video catalog shopping
- Distance learning
- Desktop multimedia
- Image networking
- Transaction services
- Internet access
- Telecommuting
- Videoconferencing
- Video telephony
- Mobile radio
- Cellular/PCS systems
- POTS—Plain old telephone service

Source: Adapted from Samir Chatterjee, "Requirements for Success in Gigabit Networking," *Communications of the ACM*, July 1997, p. 64. Copyright © 1997, Association of Computing Machinery. By permission.

are being applied in Internet, intranet, and extranet applications, especially those for electronic commerce and collaboration. This trend has reinforced previous industry and technical moves toward building client/server networks based on an open systems architecture.

Open systems are information systems that use common standards for hardware, software, applications, and networking. Open systems, like the Internet and corporate intranets and extranets, create a computing environment that is open to easy access by end users and their networked computer systems. Open systems provide greater **connectivity,** that is, the ability of networked computers and other devices to easily access and communicate with each other and share information. Any open systems architecture also provides a high degree of network **interoperability.** That is, open systems enable the many different applications of end users to be accomplished using the different varieties of computer systems, software packages, and databases provided by a variety of interconnected networks. Frequently, software known as *middleware* may be used to help diverse systems work together.

Telecommunications is also being revolutionized by the rapid change from analog to **digital network technologies.** Telecommunication systems have always depended on voice-oriented analog transmission systems designed to transmit the variable electrical frequencies generated by the sound waves of the human voice. However, local and global telecommunications networks are rapidly converting to digital transmission technologies that transmit information in the form of discrete pulses, as computers do. This provides (1) significantly higher transmission speeds, (2) the movement of larger amounts of information, (3) greater economy, and (4) much lower error rates than analog systems. In addition, digital technologies allow telecommunications networks to carry multiple types of communications (data, voice, video) on the same circuits.

Another major trend in telecommunications technology is a change from reliance on copper wire-based media and land-based microwave relay systems to fiber-optic lines and cellular, PCS, communications satellite, and other **wireless technologies.** Fiber-optic transmission, which uses pulses of laser-generated light, offers significant advantages in terms of reduced size and installation effort, vastly greater communication capacity, much faster transmission speeds, and freedom from electrical interference. Satellite transmission offers significant advantages for organizations that need to transmit massive quantities of data, audio, and video over global networks, especially to isolated areas. Cellular, PCS, mobile radio, and other wireless systems are connecting cellular and PCS phones, PDAs, and other wireless appliances to the Internet and corporate networks.

Business Application Trends

The changes in telecommunications industries and technologies just mentioned are causing a significant change in the business use of telecommunications. The trend toward more vendors, services, Internet technologies, and open systems, and the rapid growth of the Internet, the World Wide Web, and corporate intranets and extranets dramatically increase the number of feasible telecommunications applications. Thus, telecommunications networks are now playing vital and pervasive roles in electronic commerce, enterprise collaboration, and other e-business applications that support the operations, management, and strategic objectives of both large and small business enterprises.

An organization's local and global computer networks can dramatically cut costs, shorten business lead times and response times, support electronic commerce, improve the collaboration of workgroups, develop online operational processes, share resources, lock in customers and suppliers, and develop new products and services. This makes telecommunications a more complex and important decision area for businesses that must increasingly find new ways to compete in both domestic and global markets.

The Business Value of Telecommunications Networks

What *business value* is created by the trends in business applications of telecommunications we have identified? A good way to summarize the answer to this question is shown in Figure 4.4. Information technology, especially in telecommunications-based business applications, helps a company overcome geographic, time, cost, and structural barriers to business success. Figure 4.4 outlines examples of the business value of these four strategic capabilities of telecommunications networks. This figure emphasizes how several e-business applications can help a firm capture and provide information quickly to end users at remote geographic locations at reduced costs, as well as supporting its strategic organizational objectives.

FIGURE 4.4   Examples of the business value of e-business applications of telecommunications networks.

Strategic Capabilities	e-Business Examples	Business Value
Overcome geographic barriers: Capture information about business transactions from remote locations	Use the Internet and extranets to transmit customer orders from traveling salespeople to a corporate data center for order processing and inventory control	Provides better customer service by reducing delay in filling orders and improves cash flow by speeding up the billing of customers
Overcome time barriers: Provide information to remote locations immediately after it is requested	Credit authorization at the point of sale using online POS networks	Credit inquiries can be made and answered in seconds
Overcome cost barriers: Reduce the cost of more traditional means of communication	Desktop videoconferencing between a company and its business partners using the Internet, intranets, and extranets	Reduces expensive business trips; allows customers, suppliers, and employees to collaborate, thus improving the quality of decisions reached
Overcome structural barriers: Support linkages for competitive advantage	Business-to-business electronic commerce websites for transactions with suppliers and customers using the Internet and extranets	Fast, convenient services lock in customers and suppliers

For example, traveling salespeople and those at regional sales offices can use the Internet, extranets, and other networks to transmit customer orders from their laptop or desktop PCs, thus breaking geographic barriers. Point-of-sale terminals and an online sales transaction processing network can break time barriers by supporting immediate credit authorization and sales processing. Teleconferencing can be used to cut costs by reducing the need for expensive business trips since it allows customers, suppliers, and employees to participate in meetings and collaborate on joint projects. Finally, business-to-business electronic commerce websites are used by the business to establish strategic relationships with their customers and suppliers by making business transactions fast, convenient, and tailored to the needs of the business partners involved.

The Internet Revolution

The explosive growth of the **Internet** is a revolutionary phenomenon in computing and telecommunications. The Internet has become the largest and most important network of networks today, and has evolved into a global *information superhighway*. The Internet is constantly expanding, as more and more businesses and other organizations and their users, computers, and networks join its global web. Thousands of business, educational, and research networks now connect millions of computer systems and users in more than 200 countries to each other. The Internet has also become a key platform for a rapidly expanding list of information and entertainment services and business applications, including enterprise collaboration and electronic commerce systems.

The Net doesn't have a central computer system or telecommunications center. Instead, each message sent has a unique address code so any Internet server in the network can forward it to its destination. Also, the Internet does not have a headquarters or governing body. International standards groups of individual and corporate members (such as the World Wide Web Consortium), promote use of the Internet and the development of new communications standards. These common standards are the key to the free flow of messages among the widely different computers and networks of the many organizations and *Internet service providers* (ISPs) in the system.

Internet Applications

The most popular Internet applications are e-mail, instant messaging, browsing the sites on the World Wide Web, and participating in *newsgroups* and *chat rooms*. Internet e-mail messages usually arrive in seconds or a few minutes anywhere in the world, and can take the form of data, text, fax, and video files. Internet browser software like Netscape Navigator and Microsoft Explorer enables millions of users to surf the World Wide Web by clicking their way to the multimedia information resources stored on the hyperlinked pages of businesses, government, and other websites. Websites offer information and entertainment, and are the launch sites for electronic commerce transactions between businesses and their suppliers and customers. As we will discuss in Chapter 7, e-commerce websites offer all manner of products and services via online retailers, wholesalers, service providers, and online auctions. See Figure 4.5.

The Internet provides electronic discussion forums and bulletin board systems formed and managed by thousands of special-interest newsgroups. You can participate in discussions or post messages on thousands of topics for other users with the same interests to read and respond to. Other popular applications include downloading software and information files and accessing databases provided by thousands of business, government, and other organizations. You can make online searches for information at websites in a variety of ways, using search sites and search engines such as Yahoo!, Google, and Fast Search. Logging on to other computers on the Internet and holding real-time conversations with other Internet users in *chat rooms* are also popular uses of the Internet.

FIGURE 4.5
Popular uses of the
Internet.

● **Surf.** Point and click your way to thousands of hyperlinked websites and resources for multimedia information, entertainment, or electronic commerce.
● **e-Mail.** Use e-mail and instant messaging to exchange electronic messages with colleagues, friends, and other Internet users.
● **Discuss.** Participate in discussion forums or post messages on bulletin board systems formed by thousands of special-interest newsgroups.
● **Chat.** Hold real-time text conversations in website chat rooms with Internet users around the world.
● **Buy and Sell.** You can buy and sell practically anything via e-commerce retailers, wholesalers, service providers, and online auctions.
● **Download.** Transfer data files, software, reports, articles, pictures, music, videos, and other types of files to your computer system.
● **Compute.** Log on to and use thousands of Internet computer systems around the world.
● **Other Uses:** Make long-distance phone calls, hold desktop videoconferences, listen to radio programs, watch television, play video games, explore virtual worlds, etc.

Business Use of the Internet

As Figure 4.6. illustrates, business use of the Internet has expanded from an electronic information exchange to a broad platform for strategic business applications. Notice how applications like collaboration among business partners, providing customer and vendor support, and electronic commerce have become major business uses of the Internet. Companies are also using Internet technologies for marketing, sales, and customer relationship management applications, as well as cross-functional business applications, and applications in engineering, manufacturing, human resources, and accounting. Let's look at a real world example.

GE Power Systems: Using the Internet

General Electric Co. (GE) provides a fascinating glimpse of how the Net changes things. At GE Power Systems, customers and designers can use intranets, extranets, the Internet, and project collaboration technology to help construct a power plant from the ground up on the Web, says Jose A. Lopez, the subsidiary's general manager of e-business.

GE and customer engineers can now hold virtual meetings in which blueprints can be exchanged and manipulated in real time. Then customers can use the Web to watch from anywhere in the world as a turbine is built and moves down the production line, ordering last-minute changes as needed. Because the turbines cost an average of $35 million each and contain about 18,000 parts, catching changes—and errors—early is priceless. And after the turbine is delivered, a new Net-powered system called the Turbine Optimizer lets both customers and GE compare the performances of the turbines with other GE turbines around the world.

While GE's new systems should give the company a 20 percent to 30 percent reduction in the time it takes to build a turbine and could improve the annual output of each turbine by 1 percent to 2 percent, that's just the beginning. "Sure, there are productivity gains for us, but this is mainly a competetive advantage," says Lopez. "If customers find this helps them, they'll come back." So far, so good: Sales at GE Power Systems increased to about $13 billion in 2000, up 30 percent from 1999 [21].

FIGURE 4.6   Examples of how a company can use the Internet for business.

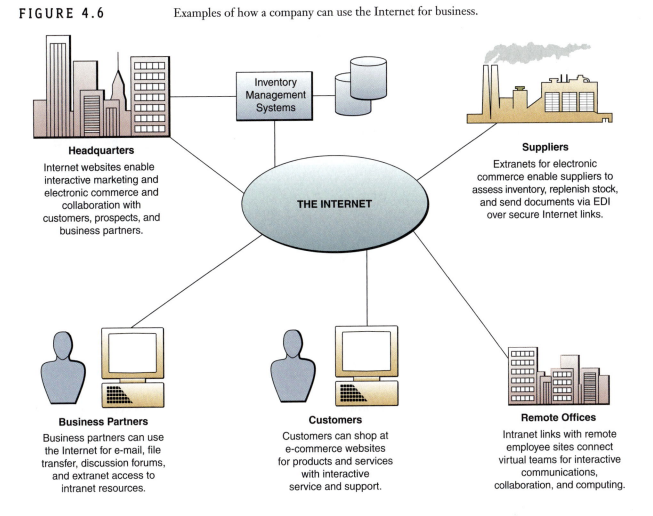

Headquarters
Internet websites enable interactive marketing and electronic commerce and collaboration with customers, prospects, and business partners.

Suppliers
Extranets for electronic commerce enable suppliers to assess inventory, replenish stock, and send documents via EDI over secure Internet links.

Business Partners
Business partners can use the Internet for e-mail, file transfer, discussion forums, and extranet access to intranet resources.

Customers
Customers can shop at e-commerce websites for products and services with interactive service and support.

Remote Offices
Intranet links with remote employee sites connect virtual teams for interactive communications, collaboration, and computing.

The Business Value of the Internet

The Internet provides a synthesis of computing and communication capabilities that adds value to every part of the business cycle [5].

What business value do companies derive from their business applications on the Internet? Figure 4.7 summarizes how many companies perceive the business value of the Internet for electronic commerce. Substantial cost savings can arise because applications that use the Internet and Internet-based technologies (like intranets and extranets) are typically less expensive to develop, operate, and maintain than traditional systems. For example, American Airlines saves money every time customers use their website instead of their customer support telephone system.

Other primary reasons for business value include attracting new customers with innovative marketing and products, and retaining present customers with improved customer service and support. Of course, generating revenue through electronic commerce applications is a major source of business value, which we will discuss in Chapter 7. To summarize, most companies are building e-business and e-commerce websites to achieve six major business values:

● Generate new revenue from online sales.

● Reduce costs through online sales and customer support.

● Attract new customers via Web marketing and advertising and online sales.

FIGURE 4.7
How companies are
deriving business value from
their e-business and
e-commerce applications.

- Increase the loyalty of existing customers via improved Web customer service and support.
- Develop new Web-based markets and distribution channels for existing products.
- Develop new information-based products accessible on the Web [11].

The Role of Intranets

Many companies have sophisticated and widespread intranets, offering detailed data retrieval, collaboration tools, personalized customer profiles, and links to the Internet. Investing in the intranet, they feel, is as fundamental as supplying employees with a telephone [18].

Before we get any further, let's redefine the concept of an intranet, to specifically emphasize how intranets are related to the Internet and extranets. An **intranet** is a network inside an organization that uses Internet technologies (such as Web browsers and servers, TCP/IP network protocols, HTML hypermedia document publishing and databases, and so on) to provide an Internet-like environment within the enterprise for information sharing, communications, collaboration, and the support of business processes. An intranet is protected by security measures such as passwords, encryption, and fire walls, and thus can be accessed by authorized users through the Internet. A company's intranet can also be accessed through the intranets of customers, suppliers, and other business partners via *extranet* links.

The Business Value of Intranets

Organizations of all kinds are implementing a broad range of intranet uses. One way that companies organize intranet applications is to group them conceptually into a few user services categories that reflect the basic services that intranets offer to their users. These services are provided by the intranet's portal, browser, and server software, as well as by other system and application software and groupware that are part of a company's intranet software environment. Figure 4.8 illustrates how intranets provide an *enterprise information portal* that supports communication and collaboration, Web publishing, business operations and management, and intranet portal management. Notice also how these applications can be integrated with existing IS resources and applications, and extended to customers, suppliers, and business partners via the Internet and extranets.

FIGURE 4.8

Intranets can provide an enterprise information portal for applications in communication and collaboration, business operations and management, Web publishing, and intranet portal management.

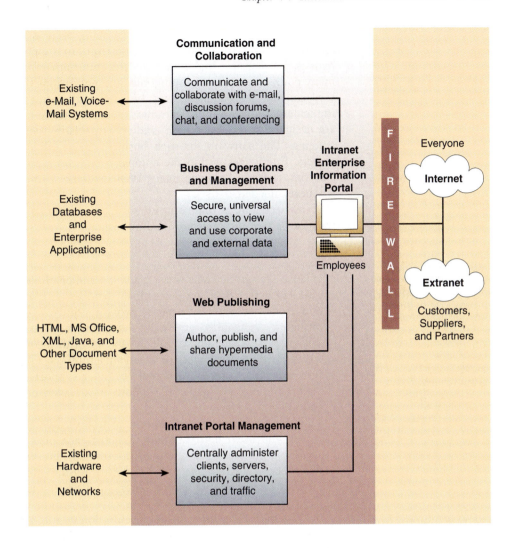

Communications and Collaboration. Intranets can significantly improve communications and collaboration within an enterprise. For example, you can use your intranet browser and your PC or NC workstation to send and receive e-mail, voice-mail, paging, and faxes to communicate with others within your organization, and externally through the Internet and extranets. You can also use intranet groupware features to improve team and project collaboration with services such as discussion groups, chat rooms, and audio- and videoconferencing.

Web Publishing. The advantages of developing and publishing hyperlinked multimedia documents to hypermedia databases accessible on World Wide Web servers has moved to corporate intranets. The comparative ease, attractiveness, and lower cost of publishing and accessing multimedia business information internally via intranet websites have been the primary reasons for the explosive growth in the use of intranets in business. For example, information products as varied as company newsletters, technical drawings, and product catalogs can be published in a variety of ways, including hypermedia Web pages, e-mail, and net broadcasting, and as part of in-house business applications. Intranet software browsers, servers, and search engines can help you easily navigate and locate the business information you need.

Business Operations and Management. Intranets have moved beyond merely making hypermedia information available on Web servers, or pushing it to users via net broadcasting. Intranets are also being used as the platform for developing and deploying critical business applications to support business operations and managerial decision making across the internetworked enterprise. For example, many companies are developing custom applications like order processing, inventory control, sales management, and enterprise information portals that can be implemented on intranets, extranets, and the Internet. Many of these applications are designed to interface with, and access, existing company databases and legacy systems. The software for such business uses is then installed on intranet Web servers. Employees within the company, or external business partners, can access and run such applications using Web browsers from anywhere on the network whenever needed.

Now let's look at one company's use of an intranet in more detail to get a better idea of how intranets are used in business.

Cadence OnTrack: Business Value of an Intranet

Cadence Design Systems is the leading supplier of electronic design automation (EDA) software tools and professional services for managing the design of semiconductors, computer systems, networking and telecommunications equipment, consumer electronics, and other electronics-based products. The company employs more than 3,000 people in offices worldwide to support the requirements of the world's leading electronics manufacturers. Cadence developed an intranet for 500 managers, sales reps, and customer support staff. Called OnTrack, the intranet project provides sales support for a Cadence product line of over 1,000 products and services.

The OnTrack system uses a home page with links to other pages, information sources, and other applications to support each phase of the sales process with supporting materials and reference information. For example, at any point in the sales process, such as one called "Identify Business Issues," a sales rep can find customer presentations, sample letters, and the internal forms needed to move effectively through this step.

With OnTrack, sales reps now use the intranet as a single enterprise information portal that provides all of the information and data needed to go through the sales process, from prospecting, to closing a deal, to account management. In addition, global account teams have their own home page where they can collaborate and share information. Information on customers or competitors is now available instantly through access to an outside provider of custom news. The sales rep simply searches using a company name to get everything from financial information to recent news articles and press releases about the customer or competitor [4].

The Role of Extranets

As businesses continue to use open Internet technologies [extranets] to improve communication with customers and partners, they can gain many competitive advantages along the way—in product development, cost savings, marketing, distribution, and leveraging their partnerships [2].

As we have explained earlier, **extranets** are network links that use Internet technologies to interconnect the intranet of a business with the intranets of its customers, suppliers, or other business partners. Companies can establish direct private network links between themselves, or create private secure Internet links between them called *virtual private networks*. Or a company can use the unsecured Internet as the extranet link between its intranet and consumers and others, but rely on encryption of sensitive data and its own fire wall systems to provide adequate security. Thus, extranets enable customers, suppliers, consultants, subcontractors, business prospects, and others to access selected intranet websites and other company databases. See Figure 4.9.

FIGURE 4.9   Extranets connect the internetworked enterprise to consumers, business customers, suppliers, and other business partners.

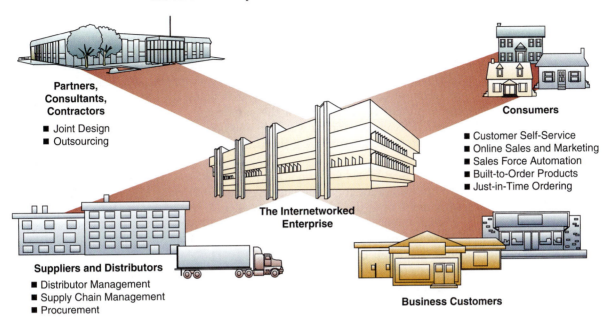

Partners, Consultants, Contractors
■ Joint Design
■ Outsourcing

The Internetworked Enterprise

Consumers
■ Customer Self-Service
■ Online Sales and Marketing
■ Sales Force Automation
■ Built-to-Order Products
■ Just-in-Time Ordering

Suppliers and Distributors
■ Distributor Management
■ Supply Chain Management
■ Procurement

Business Customers

Business Value of Extranets

The business value of extranets is derived from several factors. First, the Web browser technology of extranets makes customer and supplier access of intranet resources a lot easier and faster than previous business methods. Second, as you will see in two upcoming examples, extranets enable a company to offer new kinds of interactive Web-enabled services to their business partners. Thus, extranets are another way that a business can build and strengthen strategic relationships with its customers and suppliers. Also, extranets can enable and improve collaboration by a business with its customers and other business partners. Extranets facilitate an online, interactive product development, marketing, and customer-focused process that can bring better-designed products to market faster.

Countrywide and Snap-on: Extranet Examples

Countrywide Home Loans has created an extranet called Platinum Lender Access for its lending partners and brokers. About 500 banks and mortgage brokers can access Countrywide's intranet and selected financial databases. The extranet gives them access to their account and transaction information, status of loans, and company announcements. Each lender or broker is automatically identified by the extranet and provided with customized information on premium rates, discounts, and any special business arrangements they have negotiated with Countrywide [1].

Snap-on Incorporated spent $300,000 to create an extranet link to their intranet called the Franchise Information Network. The extranet lets Snap-on's 4,000 independent franchises for automotive tools access a secured intranet website for customized information and interactive communications with Snap-on employees and other franchisees. Franchisers can get information on sales plus marketing updates. Tips and training programs about managing a franchise operation and discussion forums for employees and franchisees to share ideas and best practices are also provided by the extranet. Finally, the Franchise Information Network provides interactive news and information on car racing and other special events sponsored by Snap-on, as well as corporate stock prices, business strategies, and other financial information [19].

SECTION II Telecommunications Network Alternatives

Telecom-munications Alternatives

Telecommunications is a highly technical, rapidly changing field of information systems technology. Most business professionals do not need a detailed knowledge of its technical characteristics. However, it is necessary that you understand some of the important characteristics of the basic components of telecommunications networks. This understanding will help you participate effectively in decision making regarding telecommunications alternatives.

Analyzing Nielsen Media Research and Others

Read the Real World Case on Nielsen Media Research and Others on the next page. We can learn a lot about the business impact of managing telecommunications network usage from this case. See Figure 4.10.

Many companies are managing their use of network bandwidth to cut costs and provide more telecommunications capacity for their high priority business applications, and avoid buying more bandwidth. The companies in this case use network management software to monitor the use of network bandwidth, and enforce policies for allowed usage by notifying users or blocking improper use. Other companies concentrate on streamlining and fine-tuning their networks, and testing proposed business unit applications for bandwidth use to establish their business priority before allowing them on the company network.

FIGURE 4.10
Kim Ross is CIO of Nielsen Media Research and manages the use of the company's telecommunications network resources.

Source: Red Morgan

REAL WORLD CASE 2

Nielsen Media Research and Others: Network Bandwidth Management Challenges

Let's admit it—we were all made a little drunk by the booming economy. When applications with a deep thirst for bandwidth bellied up to the network bar, the call was to just buy more bandwidth. Cheap bandwidth gushed from the taps as though the party would never stop. "Bandwidth hasn't been so expensive that you couldn't afford to just get more to stay ahead of demand," says Kim Ross, CIO at Nielsen Media Research (www.nielsenmedia.com) in Dunedin, Florida.

"The real driver here is money," agrees Corey Ferengul, an analyst at Meta Group Inc. in Stamford, Connecticut. "The solution used to be JBM: Just Buy More. Today, I don't know any company that has excess money to buy bandwidth."

In any case, buying more bandwidth may not be the solution, Ross says. "In the old days, you had one main application, one pipe, one concern," he says. "But with Internet applications, more resources are shared. If you add more capacity to a shared pool without a clear idea of why or where it's needed, you're unlikely to get the result you want. And the tools just haven't been there to help you manage networks, to isolate problem cases." That has left enterprise network managers seeking new ways to slake their networks' bandwidth thirst. Let's look at four of them.

Monitoring and Enforcing "The way we deal with it is we watch bandwidth utilization day by day, week by week and watch for spikes in utilization," Ross says. "Usually it's someone trying something new, but nine times out of 10, it's not something that's business-critical. We'll do the detective work to find out where it's coming from, but it takes way more than it should." Ross adds, "One aspect of our control policy is to be sure our IT governance system communicates guidelines to our users. Clear, well-understood policies can help you prevent some problems from even coming up."

Online gaming and peer-to-peer networking services that allow downloading of audio files, software, and movies, such as those offered at the Morpheus, Kazaa, and Grokster websites, can quickly gobble up bandwidth. "We have had a Morpheus problem and we handled it by blocking it at the firewall so it can't connect," says David Leuck, technical services manager for the Culver City, California, municipal government. Part of tuning the network at investment management services firm Ark Asset Management Co. (www.the-ark.com) in New York was "toughening up on users," says Danny Shpak, manager of Ark's IT group. "That means no gaming, for one thing."

Streamlining Networks Ark uses Eye of the Storm from New York–based Entuity Ltd. to monitor its network and locate and ease the pain points. Streaming stock quotes constitute the single greatest use of bandwidth, says Shpak, but "no one thing really put us over the top." Monitoring helped him identify bottlenecks such as those resulting from misconfigured connections between clients and servers. Sometimes the fix was as simple as moving an application server closer to those workers who used it most. In other cases, he had to invest in larger routers or switches or more bandwidth. "Tuning was most important," Shpak says. "I'm interested in solving problems, not measuring bandwidth. For me, the more important issue is to have my network run cleanly."

Centralizing Operations Centralizing some network functions can trim bandwidth use while addressing some security goals, says Tom Revak, domain architect at Glaxo-SmithKline (www.corp.gsk.com), a pharmaceutical company based in Research Triangle Park, North Carolina. "If you centralize data center functions, you cut down on the amount of replication and synchronization of data," Revak says. "It also helps maintain data integrity, if only because there aren't so many copies to synchronize and replicate."

Testing and Tuning Applications Test applications before installing them enterprise-wide to make sure they aren't going to swamp your network. Then tune existing applications for the same reason. Atlanta-based United Parcel Service (www.ups.com) does "extensive studies of the behavior of applications," says Mark Morelli, telecommunications director for the global shipping company. UPS not only tests but also assiduously monitors applications' bandwidth use, he says. "We have to, a lot of our sites only have 56K connections," Morelli says.

"Many of the Web-based HTML applications have become real bandwidth hogs," he adds. Those that demand too much bandwidth are simply banned from the network. "We're waiting for the day when true class-of-service network management can be done to automatically prioritize all applications use of network resources in real time," Morelli says. "Meanwhile, the business determines the importance of applications. Based on those priorities, we use network management tools to carve out specified amounts of bandwidth that each application can use."

Case Study Questions

1. How do the network bandwidth problems experienced by the companies in this case affect their business performance?

2. What network management tactics are used to help solve these problems? How effective are they? Explain your answer.

3. What other network management tactics would you recommend to help solve the business problems identified in this case?

Source: Adapted from Sami Lais, "Coping with Bandwidth Hogs," *Computerworld*, September 16, 2002, pp. 36–37. Reprinted with permission from *Computerworld*.

FIGURE 4.11

Key telecommunications network components and alternatives.

Network Alternative	Examples of Alternatives
Networks	Internet, intranet, extranet, wide area, local area, client/server, network computing, peer-to-peer
Media	Twisted-pair wire, coaxial cable, fiber optics, microwave radio, communications satellites, cellular and PCS systems, wireless mobile and LAN systems
Processors	Modems, multiplexers, switches, routers, hubs, gateways, front-end processors, private branch exchanges
Software	Network operating systems, telecommunications monitors, Web browsers, middleware
Channels	Analog/digital, switched/nonswitched, circuit/message/packet/cell switching, bandwidth alternatives
Topology/architecture	Star, ring, and bus topologies, OSI and TCP/IP architectures and protocols

Figure 4.11 outlines key telecommunications components and alternatives. Remember, a basic understanding and appreciation, not a detailed knowledge, are sufficient for most business professionals.

A Telecommunications Network Model

Before we begin our discussion of telecommunications network alternatives, we should understand the basic components of a **telecommunications network.** Generally, a *communications network* is any arrangement where a *sender* transmits a message to a *receiver* over a *channel* consisting of some type of *medium.* Figure 4.12 illustrates a simple conceptual model of a telecommunications network, which shows that it consists of five basic categories of components:

- **Terminals,** such as networked personal computers, network computers, or information appliances. Any input/output device that uses telecommunications networks to transmit or receive data is a terminal, including telephones and the various computer terminals that are discussed in Chapter 13.

- **Telecommunications processors,** which support data transmission and reception between terminals and computers. These devices, such as modems, switches, and routers, perform a variety of control and support functions in a telecommunications network. For example, they convert data from digital to analog and back, code and decode data, and control the speed, accuracy, and efficiency of the communications flow between computers and terminals in a network.

FIGURE 4.12

The five basic components in a telecommunications network: (1) terminals, (2) telecommunications processors, (3) telecommunications channels, (4) computers, and (5) telecommunications software.

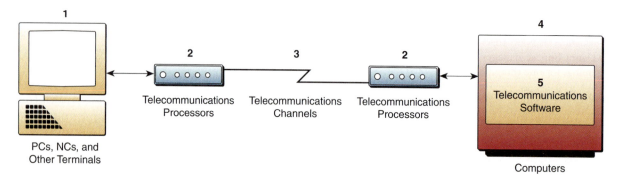

PCs, NCs, and Other Terminals

Telecommunications Processors

Telecommunications Channels

Telecommunications Processors

Telecommunications Software

Computers

- **Telecommunications channels** over which data are transmitted and received. Telecommunications channels may use combinations of **media,** such as copper wires, coaxial cables, or fiber-optic cables, or use wireless systems like microwave, communications satellite, radio, and cellular systems to interconnect the other components of a telecommunications network.

- **Computers** of all sizes and types are interconnected by telecommunications networks so that they can carry out their information processing assignments. For example, a mainframe computer may serve as a *host computer* for a large network, assisted by a midrange computer serving as a *front-end processor,* while a microcomputer may act as a *network server* in a small network.

- **Telecommunications control software** consists of programs that control telecommunications activities and manage the functions of telecommunications networks. Examples include network management programs of all kinds, such as *telecommunications monitors* for mainframe host computers, *network operating systems* for network servers, and *Web browsers* for microcomputers.

No matter how large and complex real world telecommunications networks may appear to be, these five basic categories of network components must be at work to support an organization's telecommunications activities. This is the conceptual framework you can use to help you understand the various types of telecommunications networks in use today.

Types of Telecommunications Networks

Many different types of networks serve as the telecommunications infrastructure for the Internet and the intranets and extranets of internetworked enterprises. However, from an end user's point of view, there are only a few basic types, such as wide area and local area networks and client/server, network computing, and peer-to-peer networks.

Wide Area Networks

Telecommunications networks covering a large geographic area are called **wide area networks** (WANs). Networks that cover a large city or metropolitan area *(metropolitan area networks)* can also be included in this category. Such large networks have become a necessity for carrying out the day-to-day activities of many business and government organizations and their end users. For example, WANs are used by many multinational companies to transmit and receive information among their employees, customers, suppliers, and other organizations across cities, regions, countries, and the world. Figure 4.13 illustrates an example of a global wide area network for a major multinational corporation.

Local Area Networks

Local area networks (LANs) connect computers and other information processing devices within a limited physical area, such as an office, classroom, building, manufacturing plant, or other work site. LANs have become commonplace in many organizations for providing telecommunications network capabilities that link end users in offices, departments, and other workgroups.

LANs use a variety of telecommunications media, such as ordinary telephone wiring, coaxial cable, or even wireless radio and infrared systems, to interconnect microcomputer workstations and computer peripherals. To communicate over the network, each PC usually has a circuit board called a *network interface card.* Most LANs use a more powerful microcomputer having a large hard disk capacity, called a *file server* or **network server,** that contains a **network operating system** program that controls telecommunications and the use and sharing of network resources. For example, it distributes copies of common data files and software packages to the other microcomputers in the network and controls access to shared laser printers and other network peripherals. See Figure 4.14.

FIGURE 4.13   A global wide area network (WAN): The Chevron MPI (Multi-Protocol Internetwork).

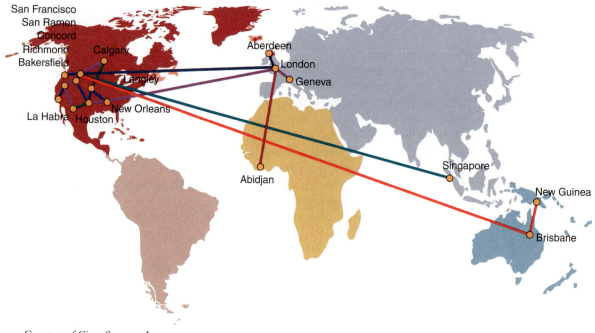

Source: Courtesy of Cisco Systems, Inc.

Virtual Private Networks

Many organizations use *virtual private networks* (VPNs) to establish secure intranets and extranets. A **virtual private network** is a secure network that uses the Internet as its main *backbone network*, but relies on the fire walls and other security features of its Internet and intranet connections and those of participating organizations. Thus, for example, VPNs would enable a company to use the Internet to establish

FIGURE 4.14

A local area network (LAN). Note how the LAN allows users to share hardware, software, and data resources.

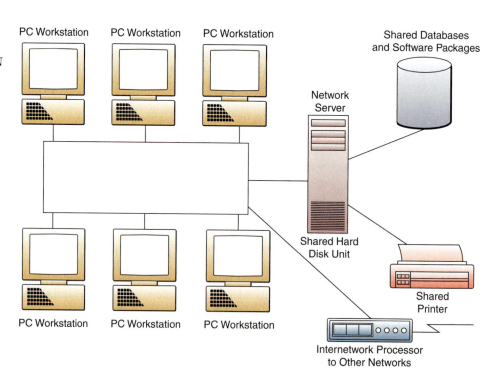

secure intranets between its distant branch offices and manufacturing plants, and secure extranets between itself and its customers and suppliers. See Figure 4.15. Let's look at a real world example.

On Command Corporation: Benefits of a VPN	On Command Corporation has replaced its low-speed private-line network with a quicker virtual private network (VPN) so it can provide faster customer service to hotels worldwide that have bought its in-room TV. The VPN service is managed by Internet service provider Concentrick Networks Corporation. The virtual network has slashed the time it takes agents to access data from customer support systems from several minutes to just seconds. The virtual net links 12 far-flung regional offices with the $225 million firm's San Jose, California, headquarters.

Because VPN links are much cheaper than dedicated connections, On Command was able to afford much higher bandwidth—24 times the bandwidth of its 56K bit/sec. private-line network—for about the same price: $1,200 per site per month. The 1.544M bit/sec. lines that On Command now use give its agents access to technical data, information on trouble tickets, and contracts to handle customer inquiries faster. Before the virtual network, agents had to take information from customers, hang up, wait several minutes for the data to arrive, and then call customers back to answer their questions. Now the data arrives in a matter of seconds [24]. |

Client/Server Networks

Client/server networks have become the predominant information architecture of enterprisewide computing. In a client/server network, end user PC or NC workstations are the **clients.** They are interconnected by local area networks and share application processing with network **servers,** which also manage the networks. (This

FIGURE 4.15

An example of a virtual private network.

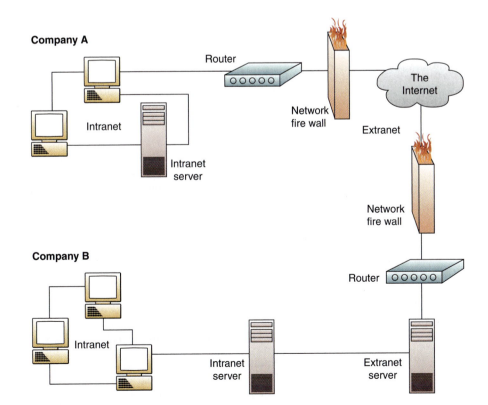

FIGURE 4.16

The functions of the computer systems in client/server networks.

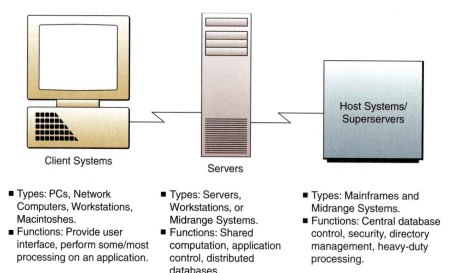

Client Systems

Servers

Host Systems/
Superservers

- Types: PCs, Network Computers, Workstations, Macintoshes.
- Functions: Provide user interface, perform some/most processing on an application.

- Types: Servers, Workstations, or Midrange Systems.
- Functions: Shared computation, application control, distributed databases.

- Types: Mainframes and Midrange Systems.
- Functions: Central database control, security, directory management, heavy-duty processing.

arrangement of clients and servers is sometimes called a *two-tier* client/server architecture.) Local area networks are also interconnected to other LANs and wide area networks of client workstations and servers. Figure 4.16 illustrates the functions of the computer systems that may be in client/server networks, including optional host systems and superservers.

A continuing trend is the **downsizing** of larger computer systems by replacing them with client/server networks. For example, a client/server network of several interconnected local area networks may replace a large mainframe-based network with many end user terminals. This typically involves a complex and costly effort to install new application software that replaces the software of older, traditional mainframe-based business information systems, now called **legacy systems.** Client/server networks are seen as more economical and flexible than legacy systems in meeting end user, workgroup, and business unit needs, and more adaptable in adjusting to a diverse range of computing workloads.

Network Computing

The growing reliance on the computer hardware, software, and data resources of the Internet, intranets, extranets, and other networks has emphasized that for many users, "the network is the computer." This **network computing** or *network-centric* concept views networks as the central computing resource of any computing environment.

Figure 4.17 illustrates that in network computing, **network computers** and other *thin clients* provide a browser-based user interface for processing small application programs called *applets.* Thin clients include network computers, Net PCs, and other low-cost network devices or information appliances. Application and database servers provide the operating system, application software, applets, databases, and database management software needed by the end users in the network. Network computing is sometimes called a *three-tier* client/server model, since it consists of thin clients, application servers, and database servers.

Peer-to-Peer Networks

Peer-to-peer networking is a civilization-altering event for the media industry. Every consumer now is a producer, distributor, and marketer . . . of intellectual property and information content . . . a "human node" with vast new powers [3].

The emergence of peer-to-peer (P2P) networking technologies and applications is being hailed as a development that will revolutionize e-business and e-commerce and the Internet itself. Whatever the merits of such claims, it is clear that peer-to-peer

FIGURE 4.17

The functions of the computer systems in network computing.

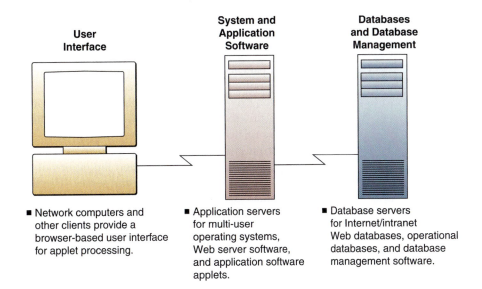

User Interface

System and Application Software

Databases and Database Management

■ Network computers and other clients provide a browser-based user interface for applet processing.

■ Application servers for multi-user operating systems, Web server software, and application software applets.

■ Database servers for Internet/intranet Web databases, operational databases, and database management software.

networks are a powerful telecommunications networking tool for many business applications.

Figure 4.18 illustrates two major models of **peer-to-peer networking** technology. In the central server architecture, P2P file-sharing software connects your PC to a central server that contains a directory of all of the other users *(peers)* in the network. When you request a file, the software searches the directory for any other users who have that file and are online at that moment. It then sends you a list of user names that are active links to all such users. Clicking on one of these user names prompts the software to connect your PC to their PC (making a *peer-to-peer* connection) and automatically transfers the file you want from their hard drive to yours.

FIGURE 4.18

The two major forms of peer-to-peer networks.

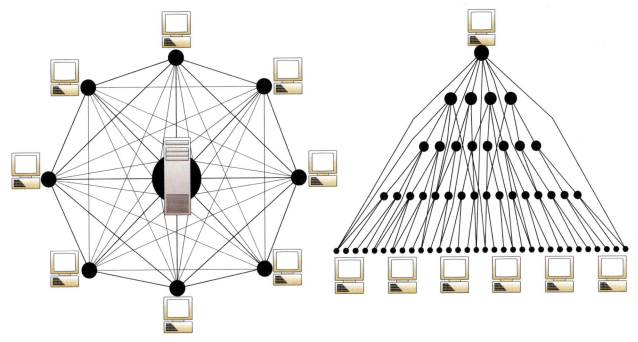

■ A peer-to-peer network architecture with a directory of all peers on a central server

■ A pure peer-to-peer network architecture with no central directory server

The *pure* peer-to-peer network architecture has no central directory or server. First, the file-sharing software in the P2P network connects your PC with one of the online users in the network. Then an active link to your user name is transmitted from peer to peer to all the online users in the network that the first user (and the other online users) encountered in previous sessions. In this way, active links to more and more peers spread throughout the network the more it is used. When you request a file, the software searches every online user and sends you a list of active file names related to your request. Clicking on one of these automatically transfers the file from their hard drive to yours.

One of the major advantages and limitations of the central server architecture is its reliance on a central directory and server. The directory server can be slowed or overwhelmed by too many users or technical problems. However, it also provides the network with a platform that can better protect the integrity and security of the content and users of the network. Some applications of pure P2P networks, on the other hand, have been plagued by slow response times and bogus and corrupted files containing viruses, junk, static, and empty code [3, 12].

Telecommunications Media

Telecommunications channels make use of a variety of **telecommunications media.** These include twisted-pair wire, coaxial cables, and fiber-optic cables, all of which physically link the devices in a network. Also included are terrestrial microwave, communications satellites, cellular phone systems, and packet and LAN radio, all of which use microwave and other radio waves. In addition, there are infrared systems, which use infrared light to transmit and receive data.

Twisted-Pair Wire

Ordinary telephone wire, consisting of copper wire twisted into pairs (**twisted-pair wire**), is the most widely used medium for telecommunications. These lines are used in established communications networks throughout the world for both voice and data transmission. Thus, twisted-pair wiring is used extensively in home and office telephone systems and many local area networks and wide area networks.

Coaxial Cable

Coaxial cable consists of a sturdy copper or aluminum wire wrapped with spacers to insulate and protect it. The cable's cover and insulation minimize interference and distortion of the signals the cable carries. Groups of coaxial cables may be bundled together in a big cable for ease of installation. These high-quality lines can be placed underground and laid on the floors of lakes and oceans. They allow high-speed data transmission and are used instead of twisted-pair wire lines in high-service metropolitan areas, for cable TV systems, and for short-distance connection of computers and peripheral devices. Coaxial cables are also used in many office buildings and other work sites for local area networks.

Fiber Optics

Fiber optics uses cables consisting of one or more hair-thin filaments of glass fiber wrapped in a protective jacket. They can conduct pulses of visible light elements (*photons*) generated by lasers at transmission rates as high as 320 billion bits per second. This is about 640 times greater than coaxial cable and 32,000 times better than twisted-pair wire lines. Fiber-optic cables provide substantial size and weight reductions as well as increased speed and greater carrying capacity. A half-inch-diameter fiber-optic cable can carry over 500,000 channels, compared to about 5,500 channels for a standard coaxial cable.

Fiber-optic cables are not affected by and do not generate electromagnetic radiation; therefore, multiple fibers can be placed in the same cable. Fiber-optic cables have less need for repeaters for signal retransmissions than copper wire media. Fiber optics also has a much lower data error rate than other media and is harder to tap than electrical wire and cable. Fiber-optic cables have already been installed in many parts of the world, and they are expected to replace other communications media in many applications.

New optical technologies such as *dense wave division multiplexing* (DWDM) can split a strand of glass fiber into 40 channels, which enables each strand to carry 5 million calls. In the future, DWDM technology is expected to split each fiber into 1,000 channels, enabling each strand to carry up to 122 million calls. In addition, newly developed *optical routers* will be able to send optical signals up to 2,500 miles without needing regeneration, thus eliminating the need for repeaters every 370 miles to regenerate signals [17, 22].

Wireless Technologies

Wireless telecommunications technologies rely on radio wave, microwave, infrared, and visible light pulses to transport digital communications without wires between communications devices. Wireless technologies include terrestrial microwave, communications satellites, cellular and PCS telephone and pager systems, mobile data radio, wireless LANs, and various wireless Internet technologies. Each technology utilizes specific ranges within the electromagnetic spectrum (in megahertz) of electromagnetic frequencies that are specified by national regulatory agencies to minimize interference and encourage efficient telecommunications. Let's briefly review some of these major wireless communications technologies. See Figure 4.19.

Terrestrial Microwave

Terrestrial microwave involves earthbound microwave systems that transmit high-speed radio signals in a line-of-sight path between relay stations spaced approximately 30 miles apart. Microwave antennas are usually placed on top of buildings, towers, hills, and mountain peaks, and they are a familiar sight in many sections of the country. They are still a popular medium for both long-distance and metropolitan area networks.

Communications Satellites

Communications satellites also use microwave radio as their telecommunications medium. Many communications satellites are placed in stationary geosynchronous orbits approximately 22,000 miles above the equator. Satellites are powered by solar panels and can transmit microwave signals at a rate of several hundred million bits per second. They serve as relay stations for communications signals transmitted from earth

FIGURE 4.19
The Ericsson Smartphone gives users wireless Internet access for e-mail and website services.

Source: Courtesy of Ericsson

stations. Earth stations use dish antennas to beam microwave signals to the satellites that amplify and retransmit the signals to other earth stations thousands of miles away.

While communications satellites were used initially for voice and video transmission, they are now also used for high-speed transmission of large volumes of data. Because of time delays caused by the great distances involved, they are not suitable for interactive, real-time processing. Communications satellite systems are operated by several firms, including Comsat, American Mobile Satellite, and Intellsat.

A variety of other satellite technologies are being implemented to improve global business communications. For example, many companies use networks of small satellite dish antennas known as VSAT (very-small-aperture terminal) to connect their stores and distant work sites via satellite. Other satellite networks use many low-earth orbit (LEO) satellites orbiting at an altitude of only 500 miles above the earth. Companies like Globalstar offer cellular phone, paging, and messaging services to users anywhere on the globe. Let's look at a real world example.

Bob Evans Farms: The Case for Satellite Networks

The network connecting the Bob Evans Farms, Inc., 459 restaurants and six food production plants to each other and the Internet runs via satellite, a technology choice that came as something of a surprise to company executives. "Truthfully, we didn't want to do satellite at first," says Bob Evans Farms CIO Larry Beckwith. The company looked at frame relay, ISDN lines, a virtual private network over the Internet, and DSL services. But a VSAT (very small aperture terminal) communications satellite network was the only technology that supported Bob Evans' goals, was available at all sites, and was cost-effective, Beckwith says.

But until last year, the computers at Bob Evans restaurants dialed in daily over ordinary phone lines to the Columbus, Ohio, headquarters to report sales, payroll, and other data. That worked well enough, Beckwith says. Credit card authorization, especially on busy weekend mornings, was another story. "With dial-up, every time you swipe a credit card, a modem dials the credit card authorization site, makes the connection, then verifies the card, which takes another 15 seconds," Beckwith says. If the connection fails, it restarts after timing out for 30 seconds, "a long time when you've got a line of people waiting to pay. We needed a persistent IP connection."

Satellite would give the restaurants the connection and sufficient bandwidth—8M bit/second outbound from remote sites, and 153K bit/second inbound. After talks with satellite network vendors, Beckwith ran tests for two months, first in the lab, then in one restaurant, on a Skystar Advantage system from Spacenet Inc. Only after a further month-long pilot project with 10 stores was Beckwith sold on satellite. During the next five weeks, Spacenet rolled out earth stations to 440 stores, and the network went live in September 2000.

"Average time to do a credit card authorization is about three seconds now, including getting your printed receipt," Beckwith says. Also running over satellite are nightly automatic polling of financial data from the point-of-sale (POS) systems, Lotus Notes e-mail to managers, and online manuals of restaurant procedures, restaurant POS systems, facilities and physical plant maintenance, "things the restaurants never had live access to before," Beckwith says.

To use its VSAT network to collect sales data from its 459 restaurants, Bob Evans headquarters initiates a request that travels via a T1 line to the master Earth station at a Spacenet hub. The hub sends it to a satellite, which is both a wireless receiver and transmitter, and then to Earth stations at each of the restaurants. A three- to five-foot diameter dish antenna mounted on the roof of each restaurant sends the message to the indoor unit, which provides the interface to an NT server. The server polls the restaurants' POS terminals and sends the data back along the same route.

The response time benefits and savings from dropping one phone line per store justify the costs of the satellite network, Beckwith says. Also important for Bob Evans Farms was the ability to easily add stores or applications. "We open about 30 new restaurants a year," Beckwith says.

New applications planned include online inventory management, with XML-based electronic ordering to follow. In-store audio for music and promotional messages, and video broadcasting for employee training and corporate communications (Skystar supports IP multicasting) are also in the works for the near future [12].

Cellular and PCS Systems

Cellular and PCS telephone and pager systems use several radio communications technologies. However, all of them divide a geographic area into small areas, or *cells*, typically from one to several square miles in area. Each cell has its own low-power transmitter or radio relay antenna device to relay calls from one cell to another. Computers and other communications processors coordinate and control the transmissions to and from mobile users as they move from one area to another.

Cellular phone systems have long used analog communications technologies operating at frequencies in the 800 to 900 MHz cellular band. Newer cellular systems use digital technologies, which provide greater capacity and security, and additional services such as voice mail, paging, messaging, and caller ID. These capabilities are also available with PCS (Personal Communications Services) phone systems. PCS operates at 1,900 MHz frequencies using digital technologies that are related to digital cellular. However, PCS phone systems cost substantially less to operate and use than cellular systems and have lower power consumption requirements [20].

Wireless LANs

Wiring an office or a building for a local area network is often a difficult and costly task. Older buildings frequently do not have conduits for coaxial cables or additional twisted-pair wire, and the conduits in newer buildings may not have enough room to pull additional wiring through. Repairing mistakes and damages to wiring is often difficult and costly, as are major relocations of LAN workstations and other components. One solution to such problems is installing a **wireless LAN,** using one of several wireless technologies. Examples include a high-frequency radio technology similar to digital cellular, and a low-frequency radio technology called *spread spectrum*. The other wireless LAN technology is called infrared because it uses beams of infrared light to establish network links between LAN components.

The use of wireless LANs is growing rapidly as new high-speed technologies are implemented. A prime example is a new open-standard wireless radio-wave technology technically known as IEEE 802.11b, or more popularly as Wi-Fi (for wireless fidelity). Wi-Fi is faster and less expensive than Standard Ethernet and other common wire-based LAN technologies. Thus, Wi-Fi wireless LANs enable laptop PCs and other devices with Wi-Fi modems to easily connect to the Internet and other networks in a rapidly increasing number of business, public, and home environments [23].

The Wireless Web

Wireless access to the Internet, intranets, and extranets is growing as more Web-enabled information appliances proliferate. Smart telephones, pagers, PDAs, and other portable communications devices have become *very thin clients* in wireless networks. Agreement on a standard *wireless application protocol* (WAP) has encouraged the development of many wireless Web applications and services. The telecommunications industry continues to work on *third generation* (3G) wireless technologies whose goal is to raise wireless transmission speeds to enable streaming video and multimedia applications on mobile devices.

For example, the Smartphone, a PCS phone shown in Figure 4.19, can send and receive e-mail and provide Web access via a "Web clipping" technology that generates

FIGURE 4.20   The wireless application protocol (WAP) architecture for wireless Internet services to mobile information appliances.

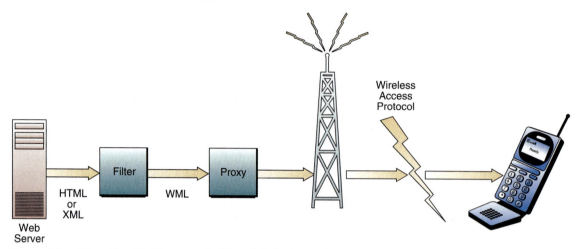

Source: Adapted from David G. Messerschmitt, *Network Applications: A Guide to the New Computing Infrastructure* (San Francisco: Morgan Kaufmann Publishers, 1999), p. 350.

custom-designed Web pages from many popular financial, securities, travel, sport, entertainment, and e-commerce websites. Another example is the Sprint PCS Wireless Web phone, which delivers similar Web content and e-mail services via a Web-enabled PCS phone [7].

Figure 4.20 illustrates the wireless application protocol that is the foundation of wireless mobile Internet and Web applications. The WAP standard specifies how Web pages in HTML or XML are translated into a *wireless markup language* (WML) by *filter* software and preprocessed by *proxy* software to prepare the Web pages for wireless transmission from a Web server to a Web-enabled wireless device [15].

UPS: Wireless LANs and M-Commerce	Atlanta-based UPS uses wireless as part of UPScan, a companywide, global initiative to streamline and standardize all scanning hardware and software used in their package distribution centers. For package tracking, UPScan will consolidate multiple scanning applications into one wireless LAN application, while maintaining interfaces with critical control and repository systems. The project is part of a $100 million upgraded and expanded effort throughout the decade.

UPS will use Bluetooth, a short-range wireless networking protocol for communications with cordless peripherals (such as ring-mounted wireless manual scanners), linked to wireless LANs, which communicate with corporate systems. The project calls for fixed-mount, wearable, and portable devices, which are expected to serve most UPS applications, from package tracking to equipment monitoring to two-way communications, Salzman says. UPS will also install advanced wireless LANs at all of its 2,000 facilities worldwide.

UPS has also developed application programming interfaces (APIs) in-house to link its legacy tracking systems to business customers, such as retailers that wanted to provide order-status information on their websites from UPS to their customers. When UPS decided to offer its customers wireless shipment tracking as part of a mobile commerce/information services package, it hired Air2Web, Inc., a wireless application service provider in Atlanta. The company used the existing APIs to link UPS business applications to multiple types of wireless networks from different providers and configure them for a range of wireless devices, from PDAs to cell phones [21].

Telecommunications Processors

Telecommunications processors such as modems, multiplexers, switches, and routers perform a variety of support functions between the computers and other devices in a telecommunications network. Let's take a look at some of these processors and their functions. See Figure 4.21.

Modems

Modems are the most common type of communications processor. They convert the digital signals from a computer or transmission terminal at one end of a communications link into analog frequencies that can be transmitted over ordinary telephone lines. A modem at the other end of the communications line converts the transmitted data back into digital form at a receiving terminal. This process is known as *modulation* and *demodulation*, and the word *modem* is a combined abbreviation of those two words. Modems come in several forms, including small stand-alone units, plug-in circuit boards, and removable modem cards for laptop PCs. Most modems also support a variety of telecommunications functions, such as transmission error control, automatic dialing and answering, and a faxing capability.

Modems are used because ordinary telephone networks were first designed to handle continuous analog signals (electromagnetic frequencies), such as those generated by the human voice over the telephone. Since data from computers are in digital form (voltage pulses), devices are necessary to convert digital signals into appropriate analog transmission frequencies and vice versa. However, digital communications networks that use only digital signals and do not need analog/digital conversion are becoming commonplace. Since most modems also perform a variety of telecommunications support functions, devices called digital modems are still used in digital networks. Figure 4.22 compares several new modem and telecommunications technologies for access to the Internet and other networks by home and business users [16].

FIGURE 4.21   The communications processors involved in a typical Internet connection.

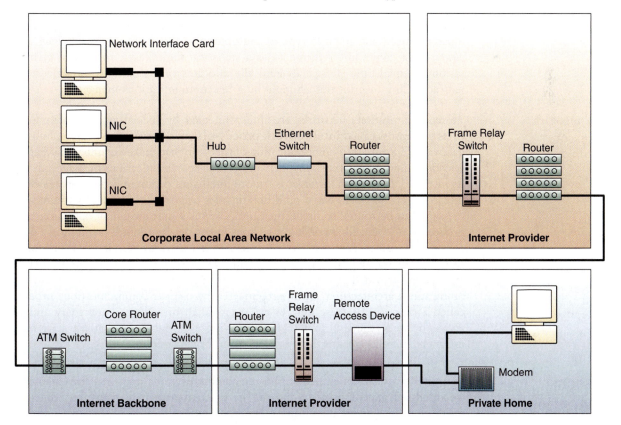

FIGURE 4.22

Comparing modem and telecommunications technologies for Internet and other network access.

Modem (56K bit/sec)	DSL (Digital Subscriber Line) Modem
• Receives at 56K bit/sec.	• Receives at up to 256K bit/sec.
• Sends at 28.8K bit/sec.	• Sends at 64K bit/sec.
• Slowest technology	• Users must be near switching centers
ISDN (Integrated Services Digital Network)	**Cable Modem**
• Sends and receives at 128K bit/sec.	• Receives at 1.5 to 3M bit/sec.
• Users need extra lines	• Sends at 128K bit/sec.
• Becoming obsolete	• Cable systems need to be upgraded
Home Satellite	**Local Microwave**
• Receives at 400K bit/sec.	• Sends and receives at 512K to 1.4M bit/sec.
• Sends via phone modem	• Higher cost alternative
• Slow sending, higher cost	• May require line of sight to base antenna

Multiplexers

A **multiplexer** is a communications processor that allows a single communications channel to carry simultaneous data transmissions from many terminals. Thus, a single communications line can be shared by several terminals. Typically, a multiplexer merges the transmissions of several terminals at one end of a communications channel, while a similar unit separates the individual transmissions at the receiving end.

This is accomplished in two basic ways. In *frequency division multiplexing* (FDM), a multiplexer effectively divides a high-speed channel into multiple slow-speed channels. In *time division multiplexing* (TDM), the multiplexer divides the time each terminal can use the high-speed line into very short time slots, or time frames. The most advanced and popular type of multiplexer is the *statistical time division multiplexer*, most commonly referred to as a statistical multiplexer. Instead of giving all terminals equal time slots, it dynamically allocates time slots only to active terminals according to priorities assigned by a telecommunications manager.

Internetwork Processors

Telecommunications networks are interconnected by special-purpose communications processors called **internetwork processors** such as switches, routers, hubs, and gateways. A *switch* is a communications processor that makes connections between telecommunications circuits in a network so a telecommunications message can reach its intended destination. A *router* is a more intelligent communications processor that interconnects networks based on different rules or *protocols*, so a telecommunications message can be routed to its destination. A *hub* is a port switching communications processor. Advanced versions of hubs provide automatic switching among connections called *ports* for shared access to a network's resources. Workstations, servers, printers, and other network resources are connected to ports, as are switches and routers provided by the hub to other networks. Networks that use different communications architectures are interconnected by using a communications processor called a *gateway*. All these devices are essential to providing connectivity and easy access between the multiple LANs and wide area networks that are part of the intranets and client/server networks in many organizations.

Telecommunications Software

Software is a vital component of all telecommunications networks. In Chapter 14, we discussed telecommunications and network management software, which may reside in PCs, servers, mainframes, and communications processors like multiplexers and routers. For example, mainframe-based wide area networks frequently use *telecommunications monitors or teleprocessing* (TP) monitors. CICS (Customer Identification Control System) for IBM mainframes is a typical example. Servers in local area networks frequently rely on Novell NetWare, Sun's Solaris, UNIX, Linux, or Microsoft Windows 2000 Servers.

Telecommunications functions built into Microsoft Windows and other operating systems provide a variety of communications support services. For example, they work with a communications processor (such as a modem) to connect and disconnect communications links and establish communications parameters such as transmission speed, mode, and direction.

Corporate intranets use network management software like the iPlanet Portal Server, which is one of several programs for network management, electronic commerce, and application development in Sun Microsystems and Netscape's iPlanet software servers for the Internet, intranets, and extranets. Many software vendors also offer telecommunications software known as *middleware*, which can help diverse networks communicate with each other.

Network Management

Network management packages such as network operating systems and telecommunications monitors determine transmission priorities, route (switch) messages, poll terminals in the network, and form waiting lines (queues) of transmission requests. They also detect and correct transmission errors, log statistics of network activity, and protect network resources from unauthorized access. See Figure 4.23.

Examples of major **network management** functions include:

- **Traffic management.** Manage network resources and traffic to avoid congestion and optimize telecommunications service levels to users.

- **Security.** Provide authentication, encryption, and auditing functions, and enforce security policies.

- **Network monitoring.** Troubleshoot and watch over the network, informing network administrators of potential problems before they occur.

FIGURE 4.23

Network management software monitors and manages network performance. This CA Unicenter display shows a group of Web servers and their relationships.

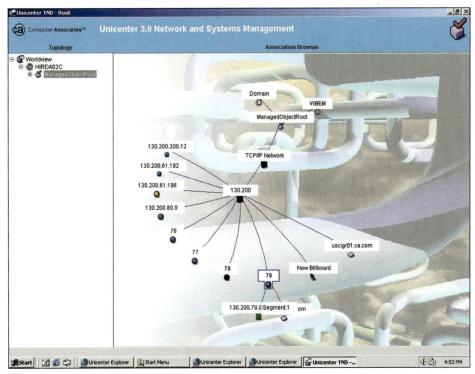

Source: Computer Associates

● **Capacity planning.** Survey network resources and traffic patterns and users' needs to determine how best to accommodate the needs of the network as it grows and changes.

Network Topologies

There are several basic types of network *topologies*, or structures, in telecommunications networks. Figure 4.24 illustrates three basic topologies used in wide area and local area telecommunications networks. A star network ties end user computers to a central computer. A *ring* network ties local computer processors together in a ring on a more equal basis. A *bus* network is a network in which local processors share the same bus, or communications channel. A variation of the ring network is the *mesh* network. It uses direct communications lines to connect some or all of the computers in the ring to each other. Another variation is the *tree* network, which joins several bus networks together.

Client/server networks may use a combination of star, ring, and bus approaches. Obviously, the star network is more centralized, while ring and bus networks have a more decentralized approach. However, this is not always the case. For example, the central computer in a star configuration may be acting only as a *switch*, or message-switching computer, that handles the data communications between autonomous local computers. Star, ring, and bus networks differ in their performances, reliabilities, and costs. A pure star network is considered less reliable than a ring network, since the other computers in the star are heavily dependent on the central host computer. If it fails, there is no backup processing and communications capability, and the local computers are cut off from each other. Therefore, it is essential that the host computer be highly reliable. Having some type of multiprocessor architecture to provide a fault tolerant capability is a common solution.

Ring and bus networks are most common in local area networks. Ring networks are considered more reliable and less costly for the type of communications in such

FIGURE 4.24   The ring, star, and bus network topologies.

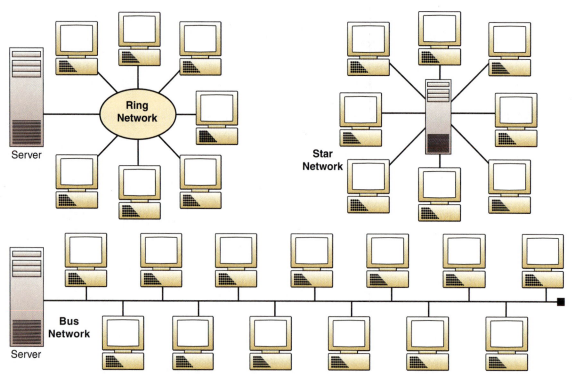

networks. If one computer in the ring goes down, the other computers can continue to process their own work as well as to communicate with each other.

Network Architectures and Protocols

Until quite recently, there was a lack of sufficient standards for the interfaces between the hardware, software, and communications channels of telecommunications networks. This situation hampered the use of telecommunications, increased its costs, and reduced its efficiency and effectiveness. In response, telecommunications manufacturers and national and international organizations have developed standards called *protocols* and master plans called *network architectures* to support the development of advanced data communications networks.

Protocols. A protocol is a standard set of rules and procedures for the control of communications in a network. However, these standards may be limited to just one manufacturer's equipment, or to just one type of data communications. Part of the goal of communications network architectures is to create more standardization and compatibility among communications protocols. One example of a protocol is a standard for the physical characteristics of the cables and connectors between terminals, computers, modems, and communications lines. Other examples are the protocols that establish the communications control information needed for *handshaking*, which is the process of exchanging predetermined signals and characters to establish a telecommunications session between terminals and computers. Other protocols deal with control of data transmission reception in a network, switching techniques, internetwork connections, and so on.

Network Architectures. The goal of network architectures is to promote an open, simple, flexible, and efficient telecommunications environment. This is accomplished by the use of standard protocols, standard communications hardware and software interfaces, and the design of a standard multilevel interface between end users and computer systems.

The OSI Model

The International Standards Organization (ISO) has developed a seven-layer Open Systems Interconnection (OSI) model to serve as a standard model for network architectures. Dividing data communications functions into seven distinct layers promotes the development of modular network architectures, which assists the development, operation, and maintenance of complex telecommunications networks. Figure 4.25 illustrates the functions of the seven layers of the OSI model architecture.

The Internet's TCP/IP

The Internet uses a system of telecommunications protocols that has become so widely used that it is equivalent to a network architecture. The Internet's protocol suite is called Transmission Control Protocol/Internet Protocol and is known as TCP/IP. As Figure 4.25 shows, TCP/IP consists of five layers of protocols that can be related to the seven layers of the OSI architecture. TCP/IP is used by the Internet and by all intranets and extranets. Many companies and other organizations are thus converting their client/server networks to TCP/IP technology, which are now commonly called IP networks.

Bandwidth Alternatives

The communications speed and capacity of telecommunications networks can be classified by **bandwidth.** This is the frequency range of a telecommunications channel; it determines the channel's maximum transmission rate. The speed and capacity of data transmission rates are typically measured in bits per second (BPS). This is sometimes referred to as the *baud* rate, though baud is more correctly a measure of signal changes in a transmission line.

Narrow-band channels typically provide low-speed transmission rates up to 64K BPS, but can now handle up to 2 million BPS. They are usually unshielded

FIGURE 4.25   The seven layers of the OSI communications network architecture, and the five layers of the Internet's TCP/IP protocol suite.

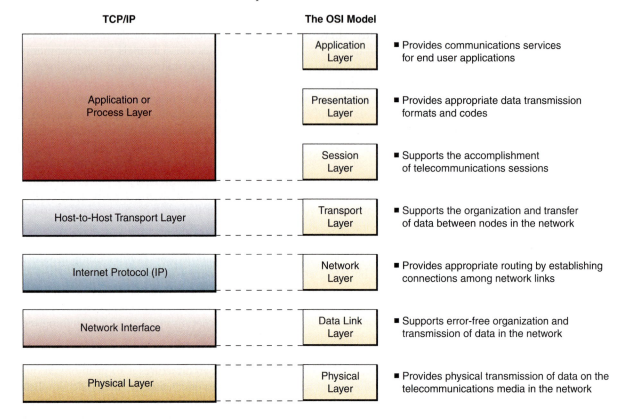

twisted-pair lines commonly used for telephone voice communications, and for data communications by the modems of PCs and other devices. Medium-speed channels (*medium-band*) use shielded twisted-pair lines for transmission speeds up to 100 MBPS.

Broadband channels provide high-speed transmission rates at intervals from 256,000 BPS to several billion BPS. Typically, they use microwave, fiber optics, or satellite transmission. Examples are 1.54 million BPS for T1 and 45M BPS for T3 communications channels, up to 100 MBPS for communications satellite channels, and between 52 MBPS and 10 GBPS for fiber-optic lines. See Figure 4.26.

Switching Alternatives

Regular telephone service relies on *circuit switching*, in which a switch opens a circuit to establish a link between a sender and receiver; it remains open until the communication session is completed. In message switching, a message is transmitted a block at a time from one switching device to another.

Packet switching involves subdividing communications messages into fixed or variable groups called packets. For example, in the X.25 protocol, packets are 128 characters long, while they are of variable length in the *frame relay* technology. Packet switching networks are frequently operated by *value-added carriers* who use computers and other communications processors to control the packet switching process and transmit the packets of various users over their networks.

Early packet switching networks were X.25 networks. The X.25 protocol is an international set of standards governing the operations of widely used, but relatively slow, packet switching networks. *Frame relay* is another popular packet switching protocol, and is used by many large companies for their wide area networks. Frame relay is considerably faster than X.25, and is better able to handle the heavy

FIGURE 4.26

Examples of telecommunications transmission speeds by type of media and network technology.

Type of Media	Maximum BPS
Twisted pair—unshielded/shielded	2M/100M
Coaxial cable—baseband/broadband	264M/550M
Satellite/terrestrial microwave	200M
Wireless LAN: radio wave	11M
Wireless LAN: infrared	4M
Fiber-optic cable	320G

Network Technologies	Typical–Maximum BPS
Standard Ethernet or token ring	10–16M
High-speed Ethernet	100M–1G
FDDI: fiber distributed data interface	100M
DDN: digital data network	2.4K–2M
PSN: packet switching network	2.4K–64K
Frame relay network	1.5M–45M
ISDN: integrated services digital network	64K/128K–2M
ATM: asynchronous transfer mode	25/155M–2.4G
OC: Optical Carrier	52M–10G

KBPS = thousand BPS or kilobits per second.   GBPS = billion BPS or gigabits per second.
MBPS = million BPS or megabits per second.

telecommunications traffic of interconnected local area networks within a company's wide area client/server network. ATM *(asynchronous transfer mode)* is an emerging high-capacity *cell switching* technology. An ATM switch breaks voice, video, and other data into fixed cells of 53 bytes (48 bytes of data and 5 bytes of control information) and routes them to their next destination in the network. ATM networks are being developed by many companies needing their fast, high-capacity multimedia capabilities for voice, video, and data communications. See Figure 4.27.

FIGURE 4.27

Why four large retail chains chose different network technologies to connect their stores.

Company	Technology	Why
Sears	Frame relay	Reliable, inexpensive, and accommodates mainframe and Internet protocols
Rack Room	VSAT	Very inexpensive way to reach small markets and shared satellite dishes at malls
Hannaford	ATM	Very high bandwidth; combines voice, video, and data
7-Eleven	ISDN	Can use multiple channels to partition traffic among different uses

Source: Adapted from David Orenstein, "Price, Speed, Location All Part of Broadband Choice," *Computerworld*, July 26, 1999, p. 62. Copyright 1999 by Computerworld, Inc., Framingham, MA 01701. Reprinted from *Computerworld*.

Summary

- **Telecommunications Trends.** Organizations are becoming internetworked enterprises that use the Internet, intranets, and other telecommunications networks to support e-business operations and collaboration within the enterprise, and with their customers, suppliers, and other business partners. Telecommunications has entered a deregulated and fiercely competitive environment with many vendors, carriers, and services. Telecommunications technology is moving toward open, internetworked digital networks for voice, data, video, and multimedia. A major trend is the pervasive use of the Internet and its technologies to build interconnected enterprise and global networks, like intranets and extranets, to support enterprise collaboration, electronic commerce, and other e-business applications.

- **The Internet Revolution.** The explosive growth of the Internet and the use of its enabling technologies have revolutionized computing and telecommunications. The Internet has become the key platform for a rapidly expanding list of information and entertainment services and business applications, including enterprise collaboration and electronic commerce systems. Open systems with unrestricted connectivity using Internet technologies are the primary telecommunications technology drivers in e-business systems. Their primary goal is to promote easy and secure access by business professionals and consumers to the resources of the Internet, enterprise intranets, and interorganizational extranets.

- **The Business Value of the Internet.** Companies are deriving strategic business value from the Internet, which enables them to disseminate information globally, communicate and trade interactively with customized information and services for individual customers, and foster collaboration of people and integration of business processes within the enterprise and with business partners. These capabilities allow them to generate cost savings from using Internet technologies, revenue increases from electronic commerce, and better customer service and relationships through interactive marketing and customer relationship management.

- **The Role of Intranets.** Businesses are installing and extending intranets throughout their organizations (1) to improve communications and collaboration among individuals and teams within the enterprise; (2) to

publish and share valuable business information easily, inexpensively, and effectively via enterprise information portals and intranet websites and other intranet services; and (3) to develop and deploy critical applications to support business operations and decision making.

- **The Role of Extranets.** The primary role of extranets is to link the intranet resources of a company to the intranets of its customers, suppliers, and other business partners. Extranets can also provide access to operational company databases and legacy systems to business partners. Thus, extranets provide significant business value by facilitating and strengthening the business relationships of a company with customers and suppliers, improving collaboration with its business partners, and enabling the development of new kinds of Web-based service for its customers, suppliers, and others.

- **Telecommunications Networks.** The major generic components of any telecommunications network are (1) terminals, (2) telecommunications processors, (3) communications channels, (4) computers, and (5) telecommunications software. There are several basic types of telecommunications networks, including wide area networks (WANs) and local area networks (LANs). Most WANs and LANs are interconnected using client/server, network computing, peer-to-peer, and Internet networking technologies.

- **Network Alternatives.** Key telecommunications network alternatives and components are summarized in Figure 4.11 for telecommunications media, processors, software, channels, and network architectures. A basic understanding of these major alternatives will help business end users participate effectively in decisions involving telecommunications issues. Telecommunications processors include modems, multiplexers, internetwork processors, and various devices to help interconnect and enhance the capacity and efficiency of telecommunications channels. Telecommunications networks use such media as twisted-pair wire, coaxial cables, fiber-optic cables, terrestrial microwave, communications satellites, cellular and PCS systems, wireless LANs, and other wireless technologies. Telecommunications software, such as network operating systems and telecommunications monitors, controls and manages the communications activity in a telecommunications network.

Key Terms and Concepts

These are the key terms and concepts of this chapter. The page number of their first explanation is in parentheses.

1. Bandwidth alternatives (131)
2. Business applications of the Internet (106)
3. Business value of the Internet (109)
4. Business value of telecommunications networks (106)
5. Cellular phone systems (125)
6. Client/server networks (119)
7. Coaxial cable (122)
8. Communications satellites (123)
9. Downsizing (120)
10. Extranets (112)

11. Fiber optics (122)
12. Internet revolution (107)
13. Internet technologies (104)
14. Internetwork processors (128)
15. Intranets (110)
16. Legacy systems (120)
17. Local area network (117)
18. Modem (127)
19. Multiplexer (128)
20. Network architectures (131)
    a. OSI (131)
    b. TCP/IP (131)

21. Network computing (120)
22. Network management (129)
23. Network operating system (117)
24. Network server (117)
25. Network topologies (130)
26. Open systems (105)
27. Peer-to-peer networks (121)
28. Protocol (131)
29. Switching alternatives (132)
30. Telecommunications channels (117)
31. Telecommunications media (122)

32. Telecommunications network components (116)
33. Telecommunications processors (116)
34. Telecommunications software (128)
35. Trends in telecommunications (104)
36. Virtual private network (118)
37. Wide area network (117)
38. Wireless LAN (125)
39. Wireless technologies (123)

Review Quiz

Match one of the key terms and concepts listed previously with one of the brief examples or definitions that follow. Try to find the best fit for answers that seem to fit more than one term or concept. Defend your choices.

_____ 1. Fundamental changes have occurred in the competitive environment, the technology, and the application of telecommunications.

_____ 2. Telecommunications networks help companies overcome geographic, time, cost, and structural barriers to business success.

_____ 3. Companies are using the Internet for electronic commerce and enterprise collaboration.

_____ 4. Companies are cutting costs, generating revenue, improving customer service, and forming strategic business alliances via the Internet.

_____ 5. The rapid growth in the business and consumer use of the Internet, and the use of its technologies in internetworking organizations.

_____ 6. Internet-like networks that improve communications and collaboration, publish and share information, and develop applications to support business operations and decision making within an organization.

_____ 7. Provide Internet-like access to a company's operational databases and legacy systems by its customers and suppliers.

_____ 8. Includes terminals, telecommunications processors, channels, computers, and control software.

_____ 9. A communications network covering a large geographic area.

_____ 10. A communications network in an office, a building, or other work site.

_____ 11. Communications data move in these paths using various media in a network.

_____ 12. Coaxial cable, microwave, and fiber optics are examples.

_____ 13. A communications medium that uses pulses of laser light in glass fibers.

_____ 14. A wireless mobile telephone technology.

_____ 15. Includes modems, multiplexers, and internetwork processors.

_____ 16. Includes programs such as network operating systems and Web browsers.

_____ 17. A common communications processor for microcomputers.

_____ 18. Helps a communications channel carry simultaneous data transmissions from many terminals.

_____ 19. Star, ring, and bus networks are examples.

_____ 20. Cellular and PCS systems can connect mobile information appliances to the Internet.

_____ 21. A computer that handles resource sharing and network management in a local area network.

_____ 22. Intranets and extranets can use their network fire walls and other security features to establish secure Internet links within an enterprise or with its trading partners.

_____ 23. The software that manages a local area network.

_____ 24. Standard rules or procedures for control of communications in a network.

_____ 25. An international standard, multilevel set of protocols to promote compatibility among telecommunications networks.

_____ 26. The standard suite of protocols used by the Internet, intranets, extranets, and some other networks.

_____ 27. Information systems with common hardware, software, and network standards that provide easy access for end users and their networked computer systems.

_____ 28. Interconnected networks need communications processors such as switches, routers, hubs, and gateways.

_____ 29. Websites, Web browsers, HTML documents, hypermedia databases, and TCP/IP networks are examples.

_____ 30. Networks where end user PCs are tied to network servers to share resources and application processing.

_____ 31. Network computers provide a browser-based interface for software and databases provided by servers.

_____ 32. End user computers connect directly with each other to exchange files.

_____ 33. Replacing mainframe-based systems with client/server networks.

_____ 34. Older, traditional mainframe-based business information systems.

_____ 35. Telecommunications networks come in a wide range of speed and capacity capabilities.

_____ 36. Examples are packet switching using frame relay and cell switching using ATM technologies.

_____ 37. Provides wireless network access for laptop PCs in business settings.

_____ 38. Monitoring and optimizing network traffic and service.

Discussion Questions

1. The Internet is the driving force behind developments in telecommunications, networks, and other information technologies. Do you agree or disagree? Why?

2. How is the trend toward open systems, connectivity, and interoperability related to business use of the Internet, intranets, and extranets?

3. Refer to the Real World Case on FedEx versus UPS in the chapter. What other IT or Web-based services could FedEx and UPS offer their business or consumer customers? Defend the business value of your proposal.

4. How will wireless information appliances and services affect the business use of the Internet and the Web? Explain.

5. What are some of the business benefits and management challenges of client/server networks? Network computing? Peer-to-peer networks?

6. What is the business value driving so many companies to rapidly install and extend intranets throughout their organizations?

7. What strategic competitive benefits do you see in a company's use of extranets?

8. Refer to the Real World Case on Nielsen Media Research and others in the chapter. What are some network usage problems not mentioned in the case that could be solved by better network management? Give an example and propose a solution.

9. Do you think that business use of the Internet, intranets, and extranets has changed what businesspeople expect from information technology in their jobs? Explain.

10. The insatiable demand for everything wireless, video, and Web-enabled everywhere will be the driving force behind developments in telecommunications, networking, and computing technologies for the forseeable future. Do you agree or disagree? Why?

Application Exercises

Complete the following exercises as individual or group projects that apply chapter concepts to real world business situations.

1. Evaluating Capital One Financial

Web Capital One Financial Corporation is the most profitable credit card company in the United States. The secret to the success of the Falls Church, Virginia–based credit card issuer is a test-and-learn philosophy that the company has dubbed its Information Based Strategy (IBS).

"We identify people who will be positively attracted to the product, so the response rates are high, the cost of acquisition isn't outrageous, and at the same time people

are an appropriate price to charge off [write off] losses from accounts that default," says Wylie Schwieder, vice president of customer relations at Capital One. Capital One then analyzes the results of the test to determine what the appropriate prices or interest rates should be, says Schwieder. Company leaders look for relevant characteristics among the test group "and see whether we can go elsewhere in the United States to find more people who share those characteristics. Then we do a direct-mail campaign based on that," he adds.

FIGURE 4.28

Capital One opens thousands of new credit card accounts online each day at this website.

Source: Courtesy of www.capitalone.com

For example, Capital One has used IBS to track visitors' activities and offer customized promotions on its website. It has studied which online visitors it has successfully converted into customers and has used that information to buy banner ads on other websites whose visitor demographics match those of its ideal customers. Using these tactics, the company has doubled its goal of opening 1 million new accounts online. Capital One's customer base has burgeoned from 6 million in 1995 to 33 million in 2001. Capital One currently nets about 25,000 new customers each day. See Figure 4.28.

a. Visit the Capital One website (www.capitalone.com.) and evaluate the business and customer value of its content. How do you rate its effectiveness as a website? Explain your rating.

b. Visit the website for MBNA America at www.mbna.com, a leading competitor to Capital One. Which is the better website for support of their credit card business? Why?

Source: Adapted from Jackie Cohen, "Growth Formula," *Computerworld*, July 2, 2001, pp. 36, 38. Reprinted by permission.

2. Evaluating Online Banking Websites

On the Web, some of the biggest banks want your business, and options for managing your accounts and paying bills have improved.

American Express (www.americanexpress.com/banking).
Why leave home? Amex offers very attractive interest rates on deposits, lots of personal finance information, and links to online trading.

Bank of America (www.bankofamerica.com).
Sleek, no-nonsense design is pitched to retail and business customers alike.

CompuBank (www.compubank.com).
All Net, all the time. CompuBank's website gets kudos for detailed account information and security. Ranks among the low-price leaders in fees, while paying among the highest rates on deposits.

My Citi (www.myciti.com).
Citigroup wants to help you round up all your financial activity and park it here. The site updates your finances to include your latest credit card bill, for instance. Security is top-notch.

Wells Fargo (www.wellsfargo.com).
This West Coast innovator has taken its act national. Good design aimed at both consumers and commercial accounts. Color scheme looks odd unless you're a San Francisco 49ers fan.

Wingspan (www.wingspanbank.com).
After a recent overhaul, Wingspan's site makes online banking relatively painless. A good comeback for the online unit of troubled BankOne's First USA subsidiary.

a. Check out several of these online banking sites. Evaluate and rank them based on ease of use, speed, banking fees and other costs, and the amount and quality of their online banking services.

b. Write up the results of your evaluations in a one- or two-page report. Which is your favorite banking site? Why? Your least favorite? Explain.

c. How would you improve the sites you visited? Include your recommendations in your report.

Source: Adapted from "Stake Your Claim to Wealth," Technology Buyers Guide, *Fortune*, Winter 2001, p. 252.

3. MNO Incorporated Communications Network

DB MNO Incorporated is considering acquiring its own leased lines to handle its voice and data communications between its 14 distribution sites in three regions around the country. The peak load of communications for each site is expected to be a function of the number of phone lines and the number of computers at that site. You have been asked to gather this information, as shown in the first table below, and place it in a database file.

a. Create a database table with an appropriate structure to store the data above. Site Location can serve as the primary key for this table. Enter the records shown above and get a printed listing of your table.

b. Survey results suggest that the peak traffic to and from a site will be approximately 2 kilobits per second for each phone line plus 10 kilobits per second for each computer. Create a report showing the estimated peak demand for the telecommunications system at each site in kilobits. Create a second report grouped by region and showing regional subtotals and a total for the system as a whole.

4. Prioritizing Calls to Service Centers

DB ABC Products International has over 100 offices worldwide and has 12 service centers worldwide which handle computer-related problems of the company's employees. Each center is open only about 10 hours a day and calls can be placed to other centers around the globe to provide 24-hour service. You are assigned to the New Orleans office and have been asked to develop a database that will list all available service centers at a particular time of day and sort them so that the center with the lowest communications cost appears first.

The second table below summarizes this information with the hours shown reflecting local New Orleans time.

a. Create a database table structure to store the data shown in the table, and enter the set of records. (Use the short time format and a 24-hour clock for the Opening Hour and Closing Hour figures.) Print out a listing of this table.

b. Create a query that will allow the user to enter the current time and will display a list of the locations and phone numbers of service centers that are open, sorted so that the location with the lowest communication cost per minute is listed first. Test your query to be sure that it works across all hours of the day. Print out results for 3:00, 10:00, 18:00, and 23:00. (Note that centers open through midnight have a closing hour that is earlier than their opening hour and require different treatment. Hint: Centers that open after 14:00 close at times earlier than their opening time. Literal time values can be entered in Access by placing # around the values, e.g. #14:00#.)

Site Location	Region	Phone Lines	Computers
Boston	East	228	95
New York	East	468	205
Richmond	East	189	84
Atlanta	East	192	88
Detroit	East	243	97
Cincinnati	East	156	62
New Orleans	Central	217	58
Chicago	Central	383	160
Saint Louis	Central	212	91
Houston	Central	238	88
Denver	West	202	77
Los Angeles	West	364	132
San Francisco	West	222	101
Seattle	West	144	54

Site Location	Phone No.	Opening Hour	Closing Hour	Comm. Cost Per Minute
Berlin	49 348281723	15:00	1:00	$0.24
Boston	617 6792814	9:00	19:00	$0.12
Cairo	20 33721894	16:00	2:00	$0.30
Honolulu	808 373-1925	4:00	14:00	$0.18
London	44 4622649172	14:00	0:00	$0.20
Mexico City	52 273127901	8:00	18:00	$0.25
New Delhi	91 7432631952	19:00	5:00	$0.32
Rio De Janeiro	55 8202131485	11:00	21:00	$0.32
San Francisco	650 212-9047	6:00	16:00	$0.13
Seoul	82 164195023	22:00	8:00	$0.28
St. Petersburg	7 4837619103	16:00	2:00	$0.30
Sydney	61 934816120	0:00	10:00	$0.27

Link Staffing, FMC, AutoWeb, and APL Logistics: Evaluating Virtual Private Network Services

The growth of e-business, and the ever-increasing Internet-based integration between corporations and their suppliers and trading partners, has put a premium on security, user authentication, and data integrity. In addition, recent economic pressures have forced many businesses to reassess their telecommunications strategies with an eye not just toward security, but toward cost and performance as well. Thus many companies are turning to virtual private networks (VPNs) as an answer to these challenges. In addition to providing increased security over the Internet, VPNs may reduce network management costs and improve network performance. However, deploying a VPN still involves meeting many technical challenges, say business users. Let's look at several examples.

Link Staffing George Gaulda, CIO at Link Staffing Inc. (www.linkstaffing.com) wanted to securely connect 49 branch offices in 23 states to his company's Houston headquarters. Gaulda decided he needed to build a virtual private network (VPN) to tie the far-flung parts of Link Staffing together. Trouble was, he lacked the staff to design and manage the system. So Gaulda chose OpenReach Inc. to provide Link Staffing with a secure VPN over the Internet.

Link Staffing is one of many companies that are turning to outsourced VPN services. Some are pinched for security-savvy network personnel. And even some that have the staffs simply want to off-load the hassle of policing increased network infrastructure to a firm that provides VPNs for a living. The offerings of those providers, however, vary significantly and require users to evaluate their needs thoroughly and select their providers carefully. Prior to cutting a deal with OpenReach, Gaulda says, he had a "very bad experience with a major service provider." Gaulda won't name the company, but he says it was unwilling to provide the support his firm needed. His technicians ended up doing most of the VPN support work, which contradicted the idea of using a service provider in the first place, he says.

Although OpenReach manages the network, Gaulda says he never feels out of the control loop because he can view VPN performance from his own desktop PC through a special browser-based interface provided by the VPN's network management software. "I can drill down to the workstation level on a remote location to see how the VPN is performing," he says.

FMC Corporation "We were worried about the technological risk associated with changing telecom technology," says Ed Flynn, CIO at FMC Corp. (www.fmc.com), a Philadelphia-based manufacturing company with 90 locations worldwide. FMC started the move toward a VPN in early 2000 to provide what Flynn calls "secure anybody, anywhere access" for more than 1,000 employees. However, the growth of business-to-business e-commerce also increased concerns about having to enter customer systems, says Flynn, "and we didn't want to do that at all."

After researching its options, FMC chose Seattle-based Aventail Corp. for its VPN technology and remote access requirements. It came down to the technology and flexibility, says Flynn. The Aventail VPN service allows FMC to control employee access rights and also uses a noninvasive network management process that meets FMC's requirements to not enter customer systems.

AutoWeb Communications Kelly Henderson, chief operating officer at AutoWeb Communications Inc. (www.autoweb.com) in Oak Park, Michigan, agrees with the idea of having someone else do a company's VPN work. AutoWeb, which does business through a VPN managed by ANXebusiness Corp., was faced with figuring out a VPN management process for each of its 600 trading partners, including nine of the world's largest automotive manufacturers. "Most companies aren't in the business of managing telecommunications," says Henderson. "It's not their core business." And VPN network management on AutoWeb's scale "can get involved" and "can be a significant investment," she says. "It requires expertise that we didn't have," says Henderson. "The cost is well worth it to us because of the type of business we're in. But you need to identify where the real network management pain points are and whether a VPN is going to fix them."

APL Logistics ASL Logistics Ltd. (www.apllogistics.com), a contract logistics company and unit of Singapore-based shipping giant Neptune Orient Lines Ltd., wanted to hire one service provider that could provide VPN service over a network spanning 180 sites in 32 countries. Network availability is critical to APL because scheduling and shipping are time-sensitive, says Cindy Stoddard, the Oakland, California–based firm's CIO. APL recently selected Amsterdam, Netherlands–based vendor Equant NV, signing a three-year, $23 million agreement for VPN and network services. APL chose Equant, says Stoddard, because Equant has global reach and the ability to manage the whole network. Equant also uses a network routing technology that speeds up time-sensitive traffic running over their VPN.

Case Study Questions

1. Why do companies implement virtual private networks?

2. What is the business case for outsourcing VPN services?

3. What role does network management software play in implementing and managing VPNs?

Source: Adapted from James Cope, "Privacy for Hire," *Computerworld*, February 11, 2002, pp. 36–37; and Dan Verton, "Out from the Shadows," *Computerworld*, July 15, 2002, pp. 44–45. Reprinted with permission from *Computerworld*.

Dow Chemical: The Business Case for Internet Telephony

There's a good chance that The Dow Chemical Co.'s new Internet Protocol (IP) network will be remembered as the industry milestone that finally got the Internet telephony ball rolling. The $30 billion global company is building a 50,000-user integrated IP voice/data network. In partnership with outsourcer Electronic Data Systems and network equipment giant Cisco Systems, Midland, Michigan–based Dow Chemical (www.dow.com) has completed a pilot of its converged network, DowNet, at selected sites across four continents. Nearly all 450 Dow sites in 35 countries should be operational during 2002, says Ray Warmbier, DowNet program manager.

Voice over IP (VOIP) is a hot topic of discussion, but large installations are scarce, particularly in the United States. Yet Dow is making a wholesale, pioneering commitment to the technology. In fact, the size of DowNet is matched only by Cisco's own worldwide VOIP network. "People will watch this rollout carefully," predicts Larry Hettick, an independent telecommunications consultant who specializes in network convergence. "Dow's adoption of IP telephony provides serious evidence to other enterprises that VOIP might finally be ready for prime time."

Why take the plunge? It would seem tough to justify a global network overhaul during a recession. But most of Dow's existing private branch exchange (PBX) telephone systems were very old and were running different software versions, explains Warmbier. "Some were upgradable and some weren't. Getting our old PBXs upgraded, replaced, and standardized on a global scale would have cost us a great deal of money," he says.

Rather than continuing to invest heavily in a legacy technology, Dow turned to IP telephony. It's replacing traditional telephone PBXs with Cisco Call Manager IP server software, which runs on standard PC operating systems and hardware. Special routers at Dow sites will shuttle both IP telephone calls and data packets across a common IP virtual private network (VPN). The network is hosted by Equant, which is a global telecommunications network services provider and leading IP networking company based in Amsterdam, Netherlands, and a member of France Telecom Group. The IP/VPN technology that Equant uses promises to bring quality of service and privacy to IP networks. The Equant VPN replaces a mix of frame relay, Asynchronous Transfer Mode, and other wide area network services at Dow Chemical. EDS is installing and managing the entire project and is responsible for delivering on contracted telecommunications service levels.

This network is important to Dow's acquisitions strategy. "We want to be able to bring new users from acquired companies into Dow work processes as quickly as possible."

Warmbier says. Dow's ambitions also include deploying new IP-based multimedia applications. The installation of regional Web-based call centers, for example, is expected to improve customer service through real-time, multimedia collaboration between call agents and Dow customers.

Dow is also running unified messaging, whereby users can access voice, e-mail, and fax messages from a Microsoft Exchange in-box. Dow estimates that unified messaging can provide productivity gains of about 25 minutes per user per day. Dow also plans to make use of IP/TB, a Cisco capability for delivering corporate Webcasts. "Many of our senior managers want to communicate globally with their people on a regular basis, and this is a very efficient way to do it," says Warmbier.

Warmbier says savings will come partially from bypassing the public telephone network in many non-U.S. sites where phone calls are expensive. In addition, he says, upgrading and changing standard IP systems is easier than relying on a PBX vendor to change its proprietary telephony software.

One reason companies have been leery of migrating to VOIP is that they aren't convinced of an IP network's ability to guarantee application performance when voice and data—which have inherently different network performance requirements—coexist. "At this point, the service we're getting with our IP phones is on a par with what we get with our traditional phones," says Warmbier. "But we did have to work hard on tuning the routers to eliminate echo on the line." EDS is responsible for configuring the routers to classify, mark, and prioritize Dow's voice, data, and video traffic and then coordinating with Equant to make sure the network provides the high levels of service quality required by the contract.

Case Study Questions

1. Why have companies been reluctant to rely on Internet telephony instead of traditional telephone systems for business use?

2. Do the potential business benefits support Dow Chemical's decision to implement a new global VOIP network? Why or why not?

3. Visit the website of Equant at www.equant.com and view their VPN and IP telephony news and services. Would you recommend that more companies implement IP telephony services? Explain your answer.

Source: Adapted from Joanie Wexler, "Dow Blazes VOIP Trail," *Computerworld*, January 21, 2002, p. 38. Reprinted with permission from *Computerworld*.

REAL WORLD CASE 5

General Motors Corporation: The Business Value of Wireless LANs

Auto manufacturers have long used wireless networks in various settings, including on the factory floor. "The major automakers started installing wireless links in the mid-1990s, using proprietary methods until the Wi-Fi (802.11b) international wireless LAN standard appeared in 2001. General Motors Corp. (www.gm.com) has deployed wireless links around the world. "Using wire-based networks would have left important assembly lines vulnerable to hours of downtime," says Arvind Sabharwal, director of telecommunications and networks. In addition, the wireless networks give workers greater mobility.

Viewing wireless LANs as a mission-critical infrastructure for its manufacturing operations, General Motors Corp. by 2002's end will have installed them in all 25 of its North American assembly plants. GM will initially use the massive in-plant wireless LAN infrastructure to track materials and replenish parts at stations on its assembly lines. But once the wireless LANs are in place, according to Clif Triplett, global information officer for manufacturing and quality at GM, they can be used to support a wide range of other applications. Those include access to computer-aided design drawings and plant configuration information, which Triplett called a "virtual factory" database.

Larry Graham, global manager of manufacturing technologies for GM, said the factory wireless LAN infrastructure will bring about a "quantum change" in the ability of GM to send and receive information to and from workers and systems in the manufacturing environment. "It provides you with agility and flexibility that did not exist before," Graham said. GM plans to standardize on the high-speed (11MBPS) Wi-Fi wireless LAN technology in all of its plants, he added. GM is investing in rugged enclosures for all LAN access points and tuned, directional antennas required to propagate a signal inside a plant without having it spill outside that cost $1,000 each.

But Graham said GM expects a quick payback on its investment—less than one year. He declined to elaborate further on the financial details. Jack Maynard, an analyst at Boston-based Aberdeen Group Inc., said the fact that GM expects to recoup its investment so quickly indicates that the company had "a real problem" with locating parts expeditiously and efficiently. Maynard added that GM could use the wireless LAN-based materials management system to drastically change its manufacturing operation to a build-to-order model.

GM has already equipped 75 to 100 forklift trucks with wireless terminals in each plant. In its United Motor Manufacturing Inc. plant in Fremont, California, which it operates jointly with Japan-based Toyota Motor Corp., GM has installed a wireless location system that works with the wireless LAN. When workers need to replenish parts for their station, they press a button on a wireless pendant at their workstation. The request is displayed on a screen on the forklift, showing the location of the worker and the materials required. Triplett said he views vehicle-tracking information as another high-priority application for the wireless system.

GM is concerned about the security vulnerabilities of its wireless LANs, despite the contained nature of plants, whose perimeter fences and locked entry areas might seem to make them immune to sniffing of wireless transmissions by nearby hackers. GM "doesn't consider its production lines a low-security area," partly because the wireless LANs run in proximity to some office networks, Sabharwal says. To address what he calls the Achilles' heel of wireless LANs, GM has resorted to a range of approaches. GM segments its networks with firewalls and virtual private networks, and relies heavily on detailed site surveys that look at all radio interference sources, including cordless phones. "With good security software, you can survey the bleed of radio signals outside the facility to make sure it's minimized," Sabharwal says.

GM's biggest strategic weapon may be its involvement with standards bodies and vendors to see that standardized security methods are quickly incorporated into wireless gear—an important consideration for a global manufacturer that uses Wi-Fi equipment from several makers. "Because of our size and clout, we are making sure some of our partners and vendors are adopting standards quicker in the security area," Sabharwal says.

Case Study Questions

1. What is the business value of wireless LANs to GM?

2. What are the security vulnerabilities of wireless LANs? Is GM taking appropriate security measures? Why or why not?

3. What are some other possible business applications of wireless LANs? Evaluate the benefits and challenges of one of them to a large or small business.

Source: Adapted from Matt Hamblen, "IT Rolls Out Wireless LANs Despite Insecurity," *Computerworld*, March 25, 2002, pp. 46–48; and Bob Brewin, "Wireless LANs Critical for GM," *Computerworld*, May 20, 2002, pp. 1, 61. Reprinted with permission from *Computerworld*.

MODULE III

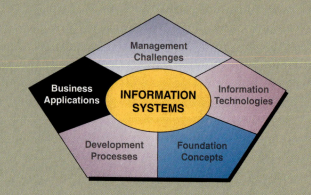

BUSINESS APPLICATIONS

How do Internet technologies and other forms of IT support business processes, electronic commerce, and business decision making? The four chapters of this module show you how such business applications of information systems are accomplished in today's networked enterprises.

- **Chapter 5: Introduction to e-Business Systems** describes how information systems integrate and support enterprisewide business processes and the business functions of marketing, manufacturing, human resource management, accounting, and finance.

- **Chapter 6: Enterprise e-Business Systems** outlines the goals and components of customer relationship management, enterprise resource planning, and supply chain management, and discusses the benefits and challenges of these major enterprise e-business applications.

- **Chapter 7: Electronic Commerce Systems** introduces the basic process components of e-commerce systems, and discusses important trends, applications, and issues in e-commerce.

- **Chapter 8: Decision Support Systems** shows how management information systems, decision support systems, executive information systems, expert systems, and artificial intelligence technologies can be applied to decision-making situations faced by business managers and professionals in today's dynamic business environment.

CHAPTER 5

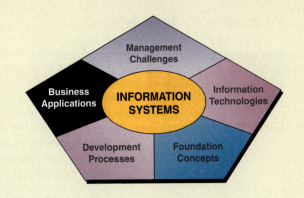

INTRODUCTION TO
e-BUSINESS SYSTEMS

Chapter Highlights

Learning Objectives

After reading and studying this chapter, you should be able to:

1. Give examples of how Internet and other information technologies support business processes within the business functions of accounting, finance, human resource management, marketing, and production and operations management.

2. Identify the following cross-functional system concepts, and give examples of how they can provide significant business value to a company.

    a. Cross-functional enterprise systems

    b. Enterprise application integration

    c. Transaction processing systems

    d. Enterprise collaboration systems

SECTION I   Functional Business Systems

Introduction

Contrary to popular opinion, e-business is not synonymous with e-commerce. E-business is much broader in scope, going beyond transactions to signify use of the Net, in combination with other technologies and forms of electronic communication, to enable any type of business activity [28].

This chapter introduces the fast-changing world of business applications of information technology, which increasingly consists of what is popularly called *e-business* applications. Remember that **e-business** is the use of the Internet and other networks and information technologies to support electronic commerce, enterprise communications and collaboration, and Web-enabled business processes both within a networked enterprise, and with its customers and business partners.

In this chapter, we will explore some of the major concepts and applications of e-business. We will begin by focusing in Section I on information systems that support activities in the functional areas of business. Section II introduces concepts and examples of cross-functional enterprise systems, which serve as a foundation for more in-depth coverage of customer relationship management, enterprise resource planning, and supply chain management in Chapter 6.

Analyzing Cypress Semiconductor and FleetBoston

Read the Real World Case on Cypress Semiconductor and FleetBoston on the next page. We can learn a lot from this case about how information technologies are transforming and improving the marketing and customer-focused processes of many companies today. See Figure 5.1.

FIGURE 5.1
Bill Verdi is VP of headquarters sales for Cyprus Semiconductor and an e-mail contact for handling customer service complaints entered at the company's website.

Source: John Harding.

REAL WORLD CASE 1	Cypress Semiconductor and FleetBoston: Benefits and Challenges of Targeted Marketing

The customer wasn't happy. He had tried several times to get in touch with someone at the local office of Cypress Semiconductor Corp. (www.cypress. com), but no one had returned his phone calls. So he filled out a customer satisfaction questionnaire at Cypress' website, and his poor rating of the company automatically triggered an e-mail to Bill Verdi, Cypress' vice president of headquarters sales. Within 24 hours, Verdi was on the phone with the customer and the local sales office. "The customer was totally amazed, and pleased," Verdi says. "We booked business with him within three days."

San Jose–based Cypress has made Web-based satisfaction surveys the cornerstone of its customer segmentation and targeted marketing efforts and its entire customer relationship management (CRM) program. In the chip-maker's eyes, nothing so distinguishes one customer from another as each customer's feelings toward the company. Cypress' real-time customer satisfaction monitoring system from Satmetrix Systems triggers the e-mails to Verdi and will soon produce the data that determine the bonuses awarded to employees, based on responsiveness to customers.

Data warehouses, data marts, data mining tools, statistical and analytical software, and CRM systems are enabling ever more sophisticated customer research, segmentation, and targeted marketing. But pitfalls abound, including alienating customers by making inappropriate pitches and ignoring customers with low current returns but high potential.

Cypress has the right idea about surveys, says Fred Reichheld, director emeritus at management consultancy Bain & Co. in Boston. He says companies often spend millions of dollars on surveys, but then don't have a system that helps their front-line employees use the results at an individual customer level. "So I could have said in a survey that I am unbelievably dissatisfied, and the next time I talk to a service rep, they have no idea I ever said that," he says.

FleetBoston Financial Corp. (www.fleetboston.com) has increased the number of analysts in its database marketing area from three to more than 30 in five years. The company says the targeted marketing that its customer segmentation allows has boosted the returns from its sales campaigns tenfold. Using time-and-motion studies and activity-based costing, Fleet has computed the cost of every kind of transaction and customer interaction. Fleet can use the information to compute and track the profitability of every customer, and it can target its marketing efforts to individual customers and households based on their current and past contributions to the bottom line.

To help predict future contributions, Fleet buys data from external sources such as credit bureaus. "We figure out what's the customer's total wallet, then we can see what's our share of the wallet," says Brian Wolf, senior vice president for corporate marketing. The possibility of getting even a small share of a big wallet makes such customers a juicy marketing target. Fleet also uses a neural network AI (artificial intelligence) system to analyze transactions in real time. It can spot patterns, such as decreasing transaction rates or balances for a high-value customer, that indicate that a customer may soon leave. "We call them," Wolf says. "We found we could cut our attrition rate in half. In most cases, we had products they didn't know we offered."

At many financial institutions, including Fleet, caller identification and routing systems linked to a database of customer histories and characteristics are used to ensure that the most valuable customers get preferential treatment. Investors with million-dollar portfolios get to bypass those endless automated voice prompts and are routed to the most experienced service representatives.

The rigor of Fleet's customer analysis isn't for everyone, says David Harding, a principal at consultancy McKinsey & Co. in Minneapolis. "Some companies spend years and years and millions of dollars building these databases, but when it comes to making a calculation around customer value, they can't pull it off," he says. Some companies fail to send the information mined by analysts to the marketing, sales, and front-line customer service people who could actually use it. He recommends having integrated teams of IT, statistical analysis, and marketing people.

Deepak Sirdeshmukh, a marketing professor at Case Western Reserve University in Cleveland, says IT-based initiatives often backfire because it's so easy to spit out promotional e-mails or make dinnertime telemarketing calls to some favored customer segment. "One of the biggest pitfalls of customer databases is that the best customers are bothered endlessly—surveys, new offers, cross-selling—sometimes by multiple people within the company," he says. "People are getting CRMed." The solution, Sirdeshmukh says: "You need smart thinking on top of the database."

Case Study Questions

1. How does the use of Internet technologies to support the marketing function at Cypress Semiconductor improve business and customer value?

2. What are the benefits and potential challenges of FleetBoston's use of IT to support their targeted marketing programs?

3. Why do IT-based targeted marketing programs sometimes produce negative business results? How can such results be avoided?

Source: Adapted from Gary Anthes, "Picking Winners & Losers," *Computerworld*, February 18, 2002, pp. 34–35. Reprinted with permission from *Computerworld*.

Cypress Semiconductor has made Web-based customer satisfaction surveys and feedback a cornerstone of their customer segmentation, direct marketing, and customer relationship management programs. Their real-time customer satisfaction system is a key driver of the company's customer focus, marketing efforts, and customer service improvement initiatives. FleetBoston makes heavy use of a variety of IT applications to drive customer segmentation, direct marketing, and customer service initiatives based on their exhaustive analysis of individual customer profitability. But such customer-focused programs can backfire if all customer-serving professionals do not share in relevant customer information and feedback, or if a company's best customers are overwhelmed with targeted marketing campaigns.

IT in Business

Business managers are moving from a tradition where they could avoid, delegate, or ignore decisions about IT to one where they cannot create a marketing, product, international, organization, or financial plan that does not involve such decisions [20].

There are as many ways to use information technology in business as there are business activities to be performed, business problems to be solved, and business opportunities to be pursued. As a business professional, you should have a basic understanding and appreciation of the major ways information systems are used to support each of the functions of business. Thus, in this section, we will discuss **functional business systems,** that is, a variety of types of information systems (transaction processing, management information, decision support, etc.) that support the business functions of accounting, finance, marketing, operations management, and human resource management. This functional or departmental view of how information technology has traditionally been used in business sets the stage for the discussion of cross-functional enterprise information systems that we will introduce in Section II.

As a business professional, it is also important that you have a specific understanding of how information systems affect a particular business function—marketing, for example—or a particular industry (e.g., banking) that is directly related to your career objectives. For example, someone whose career objective is a marketing position in banking should have a basic understanding of how information systems are used in banking and how they support the marketing activities of banks and other firms.

Figure 5.2 illustrates how information systems can be grouped into business function categories. Thus, information systems in this section will be analyzed according to the business function they support to give you an appreciation of the variety of functional business systems that both small and large business firms may use.

Marketing Systems

The business function of marketing is concerned with the planning, promotion, and sale of existing products in existing markets, and the development of new products and new markets to better attract and serve present and potential customers. Thus, marketing performs a vital function in the operation of a business enterprise. Business firms have increasingly turned to information technology to help them perform vital marketing functions in the face of the rapid changes of today's environment.

Figure 5.3 illustrates how **marketing information systems** provide information technologies that support major components of the marketing function. For example, Internet/intranet websites and services make an *interactive marketing* process possible where customers can become partners in creating, marketing, purchasing, and improving products and services. *Sales force automation* systems use mobile computing and Internet technologies to automate many information processing activities for sales support and management. Other marketing information systems assist marketing managers in customer relationship management, product planning, pricing, and other product management decisions, advertising, sales promotion, and targeted marketing strategies, and market research and forecasting. Let's take a closer look at some of the newer marketing applications.

FIGURE 5.2

Examples of functional business information systems. Note how they support the major functional areas of business.

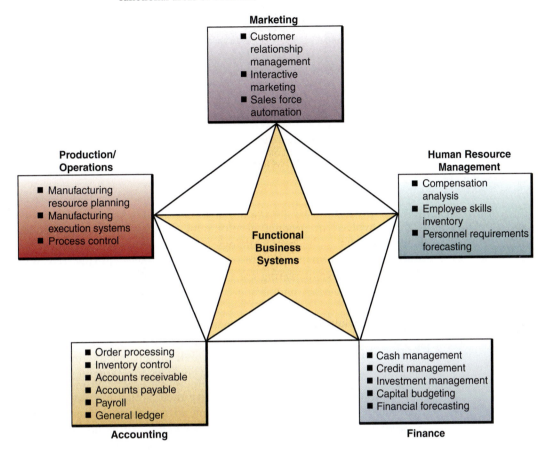

Marketing
- Customer relationship management
- Interactive marketing
- Sales force automation

Production/ Operations
- Manufacturing resource planning
- Manufacturing execution systems
- Process control

Human Resource Management
- Compensation analysis
- Employee skills inventory
- Personnel requirements forecasting

Functional Business Systems

- Order processing
- Inventory control
- Accounts receivable
- Accounts payable
- Payroll
- General ledger

Accounting

- Cash management
- Credit management
- Investment management
- Capital budgeting
- Financial forecasting

Finance

Interactive Marketing

The term **interactive marketing** has been coined to describe a customer focused marketing process that is based on using the Internet, intranets, and extranets to establish two-way transactions between a business and its customers or potential customers. The goal of interactive marketing is to enable a company to profitably use those networks to attract and keep customers who will become partners with the business in creating, purchasing, and improving products and services.

In interactive marketing, customers are not just passive participants who receive media advertising prior to purchase, but are actively engaged in a network-enabled

FIGURE 5.3

Marketing information systems provide information technologies to support major components of the marketing function.

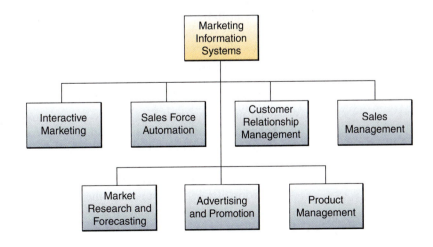

Marketing Information Systems

- Interactive Marketing
- Sales Force Automation
- Customer Relationship Management
- Sales Management
- Market Research and Forecasting
- Advertising and Promotion
- Product Management

FIGURE 5.4

The five major components of targeted marketing for electronic commerce.

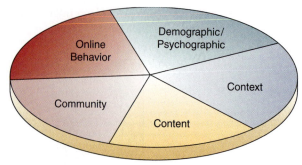

Source: Adapted from Chuck Martin, *The Digital Estate: Strategies for Competing, Surviving, and Thriving in an Internetworked World* (New York: McGraw-Hill, 1997), pp. 124–25, 206.

proactive and interactive processes. Interactive marketing encourages customers to become involved in product development, delivery, and service issues. This is enabled by various Internet technologies, including chat and discussion groups, Web forms and questionnaires, and e-mail correspondence. Finally, the expected outcomes of interactive marketing are a rich mixture of vital marketing data, new product ideas, volume sales, and strong customer relationships.

Targeted Marketing

Targeted marketing has become an important tool in developing advertising and promotion strategies for a company's e-commerce websites, as well as its traditional business venues. As illustrated in Figure 5.4, targeted marketing is an advertising and promotion management concept that includes five targeting components.

- **Community.** Companies can customize their Web advertising messages and promotion methods to appeal to people in specific communities. These can be *communities of interest*, such as *virtual communities* of online sporting enthusiasts or arts and crafts hobbyists, or geographic communities formed by the websites of a city or local newspaper.

- **Content.** Advertising such as electronic billboards or banners can be placed on various website pages, in addition to a company's home page. These messages reach the targeted audience. An ad for a movie on the opening page of an Internet search engine is a typical example.

- **Context.** Advertising appears only in Web pages that are relevant to the content of a product or service. So advertising is targeted only at people who are already looking for information about a subject matter (vacation travel, for example) that is related to a company's products (car rental services, for example).

- **Demographic/Psychographic.** Marketing efforts can be aimed only at specific types or classes of people: unmarried, twenty-something, middle income, male college graduates, for example.

- **Online Behavior.** Advertising and promotion efforts can be tailored to each visit to a site by an individual. This strategy is based on a variety of tracking techniques, such as Web "cookie" files recorded on the visitor's disk drive from previous visits. This enables a company to track a person's online behavior at a website so marketing efforts can be instantly developed and targeted to that individual at each visit to their website.

Sales Force Automation

Increasingly, computers and the Internet are providing the basis for **sales force automation.** In many companies, the sales force is being outfitted with notebook computers, Web browsers, and sales contact management software that connect them to marketing websites on the Internet, extranets, and their company intranets. This

FIGURE 5.5

This Web-based sales force automation package supports sales lead management of qualified prospects, and management of current customer accounts.

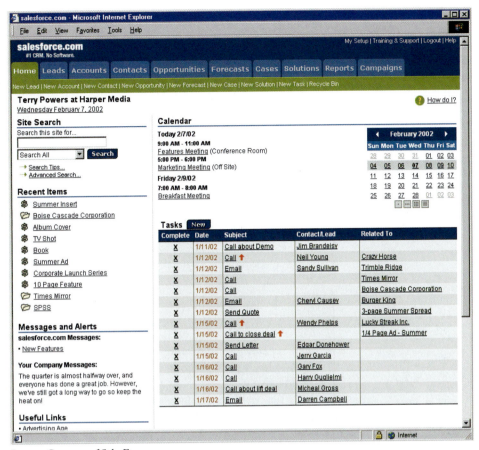

Source: Courtesy of SalesForce.com.

not only increases the personal productivity of salespeople, but dramatically speeds up the capture and analysis of sales data from the field to marketing managers at company headquarters. In return, it allows marketing and sales management to improve the delivery of information and the support they provide to their salespeople. Therefore, many companies are viewing sales force automation as a way to gain a strategic advantage in sales productivity and marketing responsiveness. See Figure 5.5.

For example, salespeople use their PCs to record sales data as they make their calls on customers and prospects during the day. Then each night, sales reps in the field can connect their computers by modem and telephone links to the Internet and extranets, which can access intranet or other network servers at their company. Then, they can upload information on sales orders, sales calls, and other sales statistics, as well as send electronic mail messages and access website sales support information. In return, the network servers may download product availability data, prospect lists of information on good sales prospects, and e-mail messages. See Figure 5.6.

Baker Tanks: Web-Based Sales Force Automation	Baker Tanks, a nationwide leader in rentals of industrial containment and transfer equipment, serves customers throughout the country in industries ranging from construction to aerospace. Because of this varied client base, it's especially important—and challenging—for salespeople to be aware of the specifics of each account every time they speak to customers. The company's 50 sales professionals are on the road four days a week visiting customers on location. That creates additional challenges when it comes to keeping track of customer information and accessing it when it's needed.

FIGURE 5.6

Sales force automation integrates IT support of sales function activities during the order life cycle.

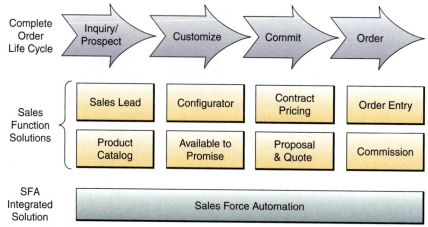

Source: Adapted from Ravi Kalakota and Marcia Robinson, *e-Business 2.0: Roadmap for Success* (Reading, MA: Addison-Wesley, 2001), p. 209.

In the past, salespeople filled out paper forms to track customer information, which was later entered into an electronic database. This left the reps with less time to do what they do best—selling. Even worse, the traveling representatives had no way of connecting to the electronic database from the customer's location. They were collecting plenty of information, but they couldn't access and use it effectively.

"They were recording everything on paper, and that's a very unproductive way of getting things done," says Scott Whitford, systems administrator and lead on the wireless salesforce.com solution. "We were looking for a solution that would improve our communications, not only between corporate and field people, but between field people and our customers." "We were looking for a tool we could implement quickly, but that would still give us the flexibility we needed to become more efficient," adds Darrell Yoshinaga, marketing manager at Baker Tanks.

Baker Tanks was immediately drawn to the salesforce.com's Web-based functionality, quick implementation time, and low capital investment. The ability to connect to sales information anywhere at anytime was also an attractive feature. Salesforce.com moved Baker Tanks from a paper-based system to a Web-based system, eliminating the extra step of transferring information from paper documents to the database. Next, sales reps were outfitted with personal digital assistants (PDAs) enabled with the salesforce.com service. "Our salespeople are real road warriors, and we needed to extend the system to them rather than make them come to the system," Whitford reflects.

Each PDA is equipped with a wireless modem that allows the salesperson to connect to salesforce.com for customer contact information, as well as sales history and anecdotal notes on the customer—all with read and write access. Salespeople can also use the PDAs to e-mail responses to customers more promptly and improve time management by integrating appointment scheduling and calendar viewing. Says Yoshinaga: "We have achieved our main objective of communicating better with our customers. And our salespeople have become more productive because they have instant access to information and electronic reporting capabilities" [27].

Manufacturing Systems

Manufacturing information systems support the *production/operations* function that includes all activities concerned with the planning and control of the processes producing goods or services. Thus, the production/operations function is concerned with the management of the operational processes and systems of all business firms. Information systems used for operations management and transaction processing support all firms that must plan, monitor, and control inventories, purchases, and the flow of goods and services. Therefore, firms such as transportation companies, wholesalers, retailers, financial institutions, and service companies must use production/operations information systems to plan and control their operations. In this section, we will concentrate on computer-based manufacturing applications to illustrate information systems that support the production/operations function.

Computer-Integrated Manufacturing

Once upon a time, manufacturers operated on a simple build-to-stock model. They built 100 or 100,000 of an item and sold them via distribution networks. They kept track of the stock of inventory and made more of the item once inventory levels dipped below a threshold. Rush jobs were both rare and expensive, and configuration options limited. Things have changed. Concepts like just-in-time inventory, build-to-order (BTO) manufacturing, end-to-end supply chain visibility, the explosion in contract manufacturing, and the development of Web-based e-business tools for collaborative manufacturing have revolutionized plant management [26].

A variety of manufacturing information systems, many of them Web-enabled, are used to support **computer-integrated manufacturing** (CIM). See Figure 5.7. CIM is an overall concept that stresses that the objectives of computer-based systems in manufacturing must be to:

- **Simplify** (reengineer) production processes, product designs, and factory organization as a vital foundation to automation and integration.

- **Automate** production processes and the business functions that support them with computers, machines, and robots.

- **Integrate** all production and support processes using computers, telecommunications networks, and other information technologies.

The overall goal of CIM and such manufacturing information systems is to create flexible, agile, manufacturing processes that efficiently produce products of the highest quality. Thus, CIM supports the concepts of *flexible manufacturing systems,*

FIGURE 5.7

Manufacturing information systems support computer-integrated manufacturing. Note that manufacturing resources planning systems are one of the application clusters in an ERP system.

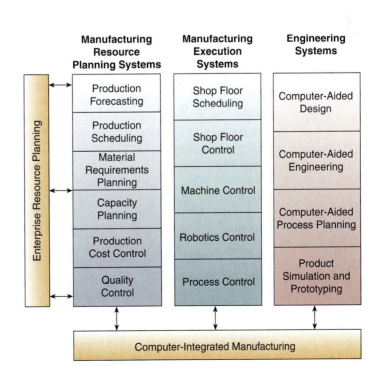

agile manufacturing, and *total quality management*. Implementing such manufacturing concepts enables a company to quickly respond to and fulfill customer requirements with high-quality products and services.

Manufacturing information systems help companies simplify, automate, and integrate many of the activities needed to produce products of all kinds. For example, computers are used to help engineers design better products using both *computer-aided engineering* (CAE) and *computer-aided design* (CAD) systems, and better production processes with *computer-aided process planning*. They are also used to help plan the types of material needed in the production process, which is called *material requirements planning* (MRP), and to integrate MRP with production scheduling and shop floor operations, which is known as *manufacturing resource planning*. Many of the processes within manufacturing resource planning systems are included in the manufacturing module of enterprise resource planning (ERP) software discussed earlier.

Computer-aided manufacturing (CAM) systems are those that automate the production process. For example, this could be accomplished by monitoring and controlling the production process in a factory (manufacturing execution systems) or by directly controlling a physical process (process control), a machine tool (machine control), or machines with some humanlike work capabilities (robots).

Manufacturing execution systems (MES) are performance monitoring information systems for factory floor operations. They monitor, track, and control the five essential components involved in a production process: materials, equipment, personnel, instructions and specifications, and production facilities. MES includes shop floor scheduling and control, machine control, robotics control, and process control systems. These manufacturing systems monitor, report, and adjust the status and performance of production components to help a company achieve a flexible, high-quality manufacturing process.

Process Control

Process control is the use of computers to control an ongoing physical process. Process control computers control physical processes in petroleum refineries, cement plants, steel mills, chemical plants, food product manufacturing plants, pulp and paper mills, electric power plants, and so on. Many process control computers are special-purpose minicomputer systems. A process control computer system requires the use of special sensing devices that measure physical phenomena such as temperature or pressure changes. These continuous physical measurements are converted to digital form by analog-to-digital converters and relayed to computers for processing.

Process control software uses mathematical models to analyze the data generated by the ongoing process and compare them to standards or forecasts of required results. Then the computer directs the control of the process by adjusting control devices such as thermostats, valves, switches, and so on. The process control system also provides messages and displays about the status of the process so a human operator can take appropriate measures to control the process. See Figure 5.8.

Machine Control

Machine control is the use of a computer to control the actions of a machine. This is also popularly called *numerical control*. The control of machine tools in factories to manufacture products of all kinds is a typical numerical control application.

Numerical control computer programs for machine tools convert geometric data from engineering drawings and machining instructions from process planning into a numerical code of commands that control the actions of a machine tool. Machine control may involve the use of special-purpose microcomputers called programmable logic controllers (PLCs). These devices operate one or more machines according to the directions of a numerical control program. Manufacturing engineers use computers to develop numerical control programs, analyze production data furnished by PLCs, and fine-tune machine tool performance.

FIGURE 5.8
This production control specialist monitors aluminum refining processes from an automated control room that overlooks the production areas of an aluminum mill.

Source: Charles Thatcher/Getty Images.

The Timken Company: Web-Based Manufacturing Systems

To outsiders, says president James W. Griffith, Timken may seem old-economy, but to people inside, it is a high-tech operation. Just walk through its huge R&D center and see the sophisticated instruments that some 450 scientists and engineers are applying to product design. The Timken Company, based in Canton, Ohio, is a global manufacturer of precision bearings and specialty alloys with operations in 24 countries. Timken has embarked on major e-business initiatives in electronic commerce, engineering design collaboration, and global e-manufacturing.

So Timken hired a GE executive, Curt J. Andersson, and named him to a new post, senior vice president for e-business. Andersson and his team have concentrated on establishing "electronic visibility" through Timken's global supply chain. Within eight weeks the team created a system that lets a Timken dealer see exactly where a part is available in any of a dozen warehouses spread around the world. Such searches previously took lots of faxing, telephoning, and paperwork. The improvement will save Timken millions of dollars annually.

Connecting design to the factory floor came next in the Andersson team's plans. Engineers in the company's main R&D center initiate, modify, and complete product designs jointly with customers in real time via the Internet. Now, newly developed e-manufacturing software allows the designs to flow immediately to Timken's sophisticated production plants all over the world.

Such instant access to information anywhere, anytime, and its meaningful manipulation, are what all e-manufacturers strive for. "We're combining the Internet benefits of speed and worldwide access with the real world capabilities of automated manufacturing plants, warehouses, freight, and global logistics management," says Timken's Andersson. "This bricks-and-clicks e-business combination is what the real Internet is all about" [2].

Human Resource Systems

The human resource management (HRM) function involves the recruitment, placement, evaluation, compensation, and development of the employees of an organization. The goal of human resource management is the effective and efficient use of the human resources of a company. Thus, **human resource information systems**

FIGURE 5.9 Human resource information systems support the strategic, tactical, and operational use of the human resources of an organization.

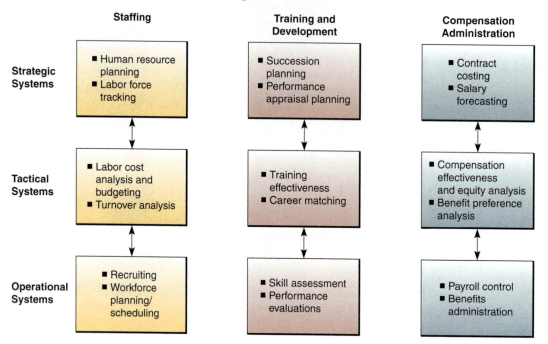

	Staffing	**Training and Development**	**Compensation Administration**
Strategic Systems	■ Human resource planning ■ Labor force tracking	■ Succession planning ■ Performance appraisal planning	■ Contract costing ■ Salary forecasting
Tactical Systems	■ Labor cost analysis and budgeting ■ Turnover analysis	■ Training effectiveness ■ Career matching	■ Compensation effectiveness and equity analysis ■ Benefit preference analysis
Operational Systems	■ Recruiting ■ Workforce planning/ scheduling	■ Skill assessment ■ Performance evaluations	■ Payroll control ■ Benefits administration

are designed to support (1) planning to meet the personnel needs of the business, (2) development of employees to their full potential, and (3) control of all personnel policies and programs. Originally, businesses used computer-based information systems to (1) produce paychecks and payroll reports, (2) maintain personnel records, and (3) analyze the use of personnel in business operations. Many firms have gone beyond these traditional *personnel management* functions and have developed human resource information systems (HRIS) that also support (1) recruitment, selection, and hiring; (2) job placement; (3) performance appraisals; (4) employee benefits analysis; (5) training and development; and (6) health, safety, and security. See Figure 5.9.

HRM and the Internet

The Internet has become a major force for change in human resource management. For example, online HRM systems may involve recruiting for employees through recruitment sections of corporate websites. Companies are also using commercial recruiting services and databases on the World Wide Web, posting messages in selected Internet newsgroups, and communicating with job applicants via e-mail.

The Internet has a wealth of information and contacts for both employers and job hunters. Top websites for job hunters and employers on the World Wide Web include Monster.com, FreeAgent.com, and Jobweb.org. These websites are full of reports, statistics, and other useful HRM information, such as job reports by industry, or listings of the top recruiting markets by industry and profession. Of course, you may also want to access the job listings and resource databases of commercial recruiting companies on the Web.

HRM and Corporate Intranets

Intranet technologies allow companies to process most common HRM applications over their corporate intranets. Intranets allow the HRM department to provide around-the-clock services to their customers: the employees. They can also disseminate valuable information faster than through previous company channels. Intranets can collect information online from employees for input to their HRM files, and they can enable employees to perform HRM tasks with little intervention by the HRM department.

For example, *employee self-service (ESS)* intranet applications allow employees to view benefits, enter travel and expense reports, verify employment and salary information, access and update their personal information, and enter data that has a time constraint to it. Through this completely electronic process, employees can use their Web browsers to look up individual payroll and benefits information online, right from their desktop PCs, mobile computers, or intranet kiosks located around a work site.

Another benefit of the intranet is that it can serve as a superior training tool. Employees can easily download instructions and processes to get the information or education they need. In addition, employees using new technology can view training videos over the intranet on demand. Thus, the intranet eliminates the need to loan out and track training videos. Employees can also use their corporate intranets to produce automated paysheets, the online alternative to time cards. These electronic forms have made viewing, entering, and adjusting payroll information easy for both employees and HRM professionals [17].

Staffing the Organization

The staffing function must be supported by information systems that record and track human resources within a company to maximize their use. For example, a personnel record-keeping system keeps track of additions, deletions, and other changes to the records in a personnel database. Changes in job assignments and compensation, or hirings and terminations, are examples of information that would be used to update the personnel database. Another example is an employee skills inventory system that uses the employee skills data from a personnel database to locate employees within a company who have the skills required for specific assignments and projects.

Training and Development

HRM systems can help human resource managers plan and monitor employee recruitment, training, and development programs by analyzing the success history of present programs. They also analyze the career development status of each employee to determine whether development methods such as training programs and periodic performance appraisals should be recommended. Computer-based multimedia training programs and appraisals of employee job performance are available to help support this area of human resource management. See Figure 5.10.

FIGURE 5.10

An example of an employee hiring review system.

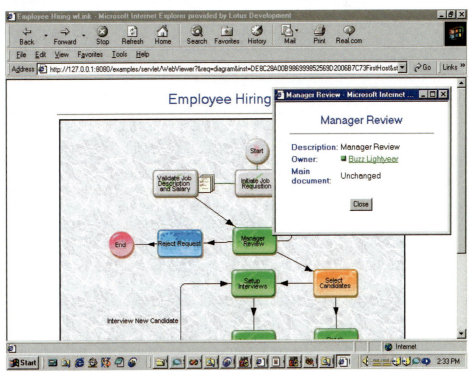

Source: Courtesy of Lotus Development Corp.

Charles Schwab & Co.: Web-Based Human Resource Systems	It receives 1.3 million page views per day, but it's not Yahoo or America Online or even CNN.com. It's an intranet created by Charles Schwab & Co. that enables Schwab's 23,000 employees to access detailed HR information about benefits, training, computer support, and scads of company information. "As a company, we're very committed to using technology to benefit our customers and to provide good services to our employees," says Anne Barr, vice president of the intranet initiative known throughout the company as the "Schweb." The Schweb provides managers with online access to accurate information about employees. Because the directory is online, it's a lot easier to update and maintain than a set of desktop applications, notes Barr. The intranet provides employees with more personalized information about themselves, their roles, and the organization than they'd otherwise be able to obtain from the company's human resources department. "The other benefit is that it helps employees find the information they need faster and serve customers faster, more effectively," says Barr. There are now 30 HR applications that link into the Schweb, including the Learning Intranet, an application that helps manage training for Schwab's customer-facing employees, and eTimesheets, which employees use to manage their own vacation time. The productivity benefits alone from the use of the Schweb are huge. Schwab is saving hundreds of thousands of dollars annually by having employees fill out benefit forms online using an application called eForms, says Barr [17].

Accounting Systems

Accounting information systems are the oldest and most widely used information systems in business. They record and report business transactions and other economic events. Accounting information systems are based on the double-entry bookkeeping concept, which is hundreds of years old, and other, more recent accounting concepts such as responsibility accounting and activity-based costing. Computer-based accounting systems record and report the flow of funds through an organization on a historical basis and produce important financial statements such as balance sheets and income statements. Such systems also produce forecasts of future conditions such as projected financial statements and financial budgets. A firm's financial performance is measured against such forecasts by other analytical accounting reports.

Operational accounting systems emphasize legal and historical record-keeping and the production of accurate financial statements. Typically, these systems include transaction processing systems such as order processing, inventory control, accounts receivable, accounts payable, payroll, and general ledger systems. Management accounting systems focus on the planning and control of business operations. They emphasize cost accounting reports, the development of financial budgets and projected financial statements, and analytical reports comparing actual to forecasted performance.

Figure 5.11 illustrates the interrelationships of several important accounting information systems commonly computerized by both large and small businesses. Many accounting software packages are available for these applications. Let's briefly review how several of these systems support the operations and management of a business firm. Figure 5.12 summarizes the purpose of six common, but important, accounting information systems.

Online Accounting Systems

It should come as no surprise that the accounting information systems illustrated in Figures 5.11 and 5.12 are being affected by Internet technologies. Using the Internet, intranets, extranets, and other networks changes how accounting information systems monitor and track business activity. The online, interactive nature of such networks calls for new forms of transaction documents, procedures, and controls.

FIGURE 5.11   Important accounting information systems for transaction processing and financial reporting. Note how they are related to each other in terms of input and output flows.

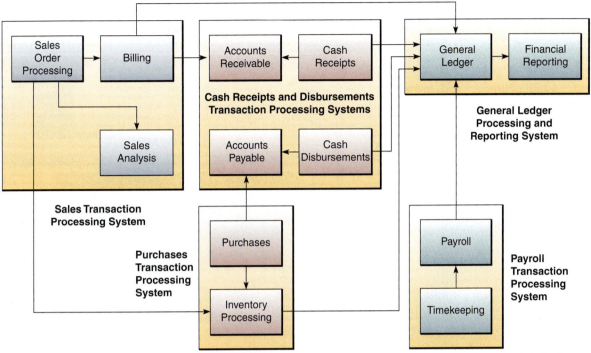

Source: Adapted from Joseph W. Wilkinson and Michael J. Cerullo, *Accounting Information Systems: Essential Concepts and Applications*, 3rd ed., p. 10. Copyright © 1997 by John Wiley & Sons, Inc. Reprinted by permission.

This particularly applies to systems like order processing, inventory control, accounts receivable, and accounts payable. These systems are directly involved in the processing of transactions between a business and its customers and suppliers. So naturally, many companies are using Internet and other network links to these trading partners for such online transaction processing systems, as discussed in Section II. Figure 5.13 is an example of an online accounting report.

FIGURE 5.12   A summary of six widely used accounting information systems.

Common Business Accounting Systems
● **Order Processing**   Captures and processes customer orders and produces data for inventory control and accounts receivable.
● **Inventory Control**   Processes data reflecting changes in inventory and provides shipping and reorder information.
● **Accounts Receivable**   Records amounts owed by customers and produces customer invoices, monthly customer statements, and credit management reports.
● **Accounts Payable**   Records purchases from, amounts owed to, and payments to suppliers, and produces cash management reports.
● **Payroll**   Records employee work and compensation data and produces paychecks and other payroll documents and reports.
● **General Ledger**   Consolidates data from other accounting systems and produces the periodic financial statements and reports of the business.

FIGURE 5.13

An example of an online accounting report.

Source: Courtesy of Hyperion Solutions Corp.

Order Processing

Order processing, or sales order processing, is an important transaction processing system that captures and processes customer orders and produces data needed for sales analysis and inventory control. In many firms, it also keeps track of the status of customer orders until goods are delivered. Computer-based sales order processing systems provide a fast, accurate, and efficient method of recording and screening customer orders and sales transactions. They also provide inventory control systems with information on accepted orders so they can be filled as quickly as possible.

Inventory Control

Inventory control systems process data reflecting changes to items in inventory. Once data about customer orders are received from an order processing system, a computer-based inventory control system records changes to inventory levels and prepares appropriate shipping documents. Then it may notify managers about items that need reordering and provide them with a variety of inventory status reports. Computer-based inventory control systems thus help a business provide high-quality service to customers while minimizing investment in inventory and inventory carrying costs.

Accounts Receivable

Accounts receivable systems keep records of amounts owed by customers from data generated by customer purchases and payments. They produce invoices to customers, monthly customer statements, and credit management reports. Computer-based accounts receivable systems stimulate prompt customer payments by preparing accurate and timely invoices and monthly statements to credit customers. They provide managers with reports to help them control the amount of credit extended and the collection of money owed. This activity helps to maximize profitable credit sales while minimizing losses from bad debts.

Accounts Payable

Accounts payable systems keep track of data concerning purchases from and payments to suppliers. They prepare checks in payment of outstanding invoices and produce cash management reports. Computer-based accounts payable systems help ensure prompt and accurate payment of suppliers to maintain good relationships, ensure a good credit standing, and secure any discounts offered for prompt payment. They provide tight financial control over all cash disbursements of the business. They also provide management with information needed for the analysis of payments, expenses, purchases, employee expense accounts, and cash requirements.

Payroll

Payroll systems receive and maintain data from employee time cards and other work records. They produce paychecks and other documents such as earning statements, payroll reports, and labor analysis reports. Other reports are also prepared for management and government agencies. Computer-based payroll systems help businesses make prompt and accurate payments to their employees, as well as reports to management, employees, and government agencies concerning earnings, taxes, and other deductions. They may also provide management with reports analyzing labor costs and productivity.

General Ledger

General ledger systems consolidate data received from accounts receivable, accounts payable, payroll, and other accounting information systems. At the end of each accounting period, they close the books of a business and produce the general ledger trial balance, the income statement and balance sheet of the firm, and various income and expense reports for management. Computer-based general ledger systems help businesses accomplish these accounting tasks in an accurate and timely manner. They typically provide better financial controls and management reports and involve fewer personnel and lower costs than manual accounting methods.

Financial Management Systems

Computer-based **financial management systems** support financial managers in decisions concerning (1) the financing of a business and (2) the allocation and control of financial resources within a business. Major financial management system categories include cash and investment management, capital budgeting, financial forecasting, and financial planning. See Figure 5.14.

Cash Management

Cash management systems collect information on all cash receipts and disbursements within a company on a real-time or periodic basis. Such information allows businesses to deposit or invest excess funds more quickly, and thus increase the income generated by deposited or invested funds. These systems also produce daily, weekly, or monthly forecasts of cash receipts or disbursements (cash flow forecasts) that are used to spot future cash deficits or surpluses. Mathematical models frequently can determine optimal cash collection programs and determine alternative financing or investment strategies for dealing with forecasted cash deficits or surpluses.

FIGURE 5.14

Examples of important financial management systems.

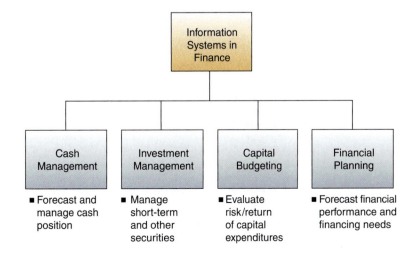

Online Investment Management

Many businesses invest their excess cash in short-term low-risk marketable securities (such as U.S. Treasury bills, commercial paper, or certificates of deposit) or in higher-return/higher-risk alternatives, so that investment income may be earned until the funds are required. The portfolio of such securities can be managed with the help of portfolio management software packages. Investment information and securities trading are available from hundreds of online sources on the Internet and other networks. Online investment management services help a financial manager make buying, selling, or holding decisions for each type of security so that an optimum mix of securities is developed that minimizes risk and maximizes investment income for the business.

Capital Budgeting

The **capital budgeting** process involves evaluating the profitability and financial impact of proposed capital expenditures. Long-term expenditure proposals for plants and equipment can be analyzed using a variety of techniques. This application makes heavy use of spreadsheet models that incorporate present value analysis of expected cash flows and probability analysis of risk to determine the optimum mix of capital projects for a business.

Financial Forecasting and Planning

Financial analysts typically use electronic spreadsheets and other **financial planning** software to evaluate the present and projected financial performance of a business. They also help determine the financing needs of a business and analyze alternative methods of financing. Financial analysts use financial forecasts concerning the economic situation, business operations, types of financing available, interest rates, and stock and bond prices to develop an optimal financing plan for the business. Electronic spreadsheet packages, DSS software, and Web-based groupware can be used to build and manipulate financial models. Answers to what-if and goal-seeking questions can be explored as financial analysts and managers evaluate their financing and investment alternatives. We will discuss such applications further in Chapter 8. See Figure 5.15.

FIGURE 5.15
An example of strategic financial planning using a multiple scenario approach.

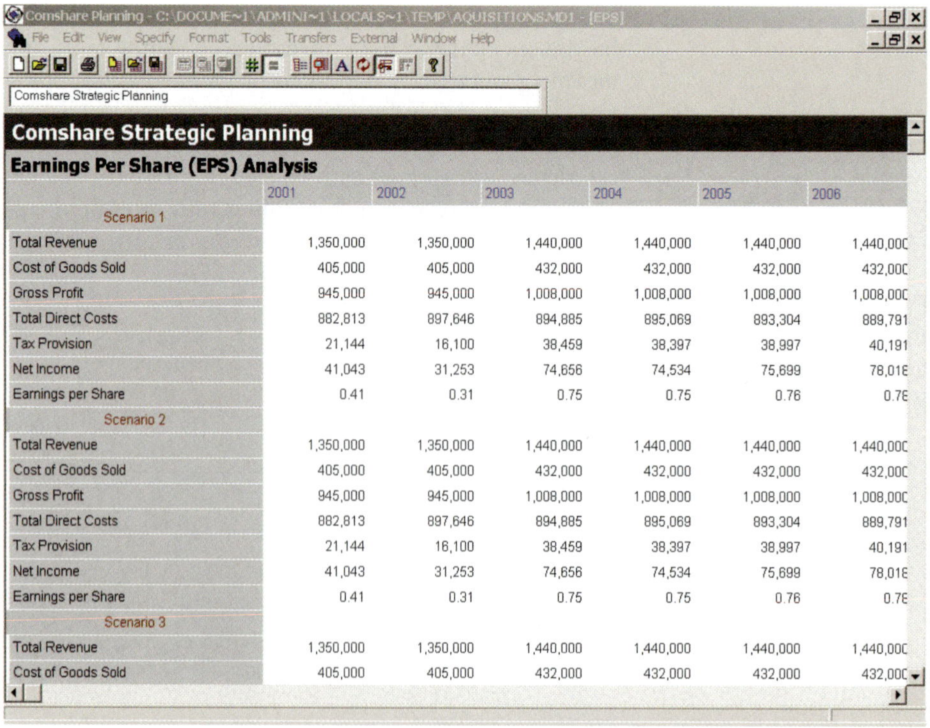

	2001	2002	2003	2004	2005	2006
Scenario 1						
Total Revenue	1,350,000	1,350,000	1,440,000	1,440,000	1,440,000	1,440,00C
Cost of Goods Sold	405,000	405,000	432,000	432,000	432,000	432,00C
Gross Profit	945,000	945,000	1,008,000	1,008,000	1,008,000	1,008,00C
Total Direct Costs	882,813	897,646	894,885	895,069	893,304	889,791
Tax Provision	21,144	16,100	38,459	38,397	38,997	40,191
Net Income	41,043	31,253	74,656	74,534	75,699	78,01E
Earnings per Share	0.41	0.31	0.75	0.75	0.76	0.7E
Scenario 2						
Total Revenue	1,350,000	1,350,000	1,440,000	1,440,000	1,440,000	1,440,00C
Cost of Goods Sold	405,000	405,000	432,000	432,000	432,000	432,00C
Gross Profit	945,000	945,000	1,008,000	1,008,000	1,008,000	1,008,00C
Total Direct Costs	882,813	897,646	894,885	895,069	893,304	889,791
Tax Provision	21,144	16,100	38,459	38,397	38,997	40,191
Net Income	41,043	31,253	74,656	74,534	75,699	78,01E
Earnings per Share	0.41	0.31	0.75	0.75	0.76	0.7E
Scenario 3						
Total Revenue	1,350,000	1,350,000	1,440,000	1,440,000	1,440,000	1,440,00C
Cost of Goods Sold	405,000	405,000	432,000	432,000	432,000	432,00C

Source: Courtesy of Comshare.

<table>
<tr><td>**SECTION II**</td><td># Cross-Functional Enterprise Systems</td></tr>
</table>

Introduction

E-business, in addition to encompassing e-commerce, includes both front- and back-office applications that form the engine for modern business. E-business is not just about e-commerce transactions; it's about redefining old business models, with the aid of technology, to maximize customer value [19].

This section introduces you to concepts and examples of cross-functional e-business applications that redefine the traditional models of the business functions we discussed in Section I. These cross-functional *enterprise* applications are integrated combinations of information subsystems that share information resources and support business processes across the functional units of the business enterprise and extend beyond to customers, suppliers, and other business partners. Thus, this section provides you with an overview and examples of several cross-functional enterprise systems. You will then be ready to explore other key enterprise e-business systems in more depth in Chapter 6.

Analyzing Johnson Controls

Read the Real World Case on Johnson Controls on the next page. We can learn a lot from this case about the vital role that enterprise collaboration systems can play in many companies today. See Figure 5.16.

Johnson Controls Inc. (JCI) manufactures almost half of the car and truck cockpits used in the 50 million vehicles produced in the world each year. Most of the products JCI produces have to be engineered and designed to order by teams of engineers, suppliers, and contractors. Thus, collaboration by team members during every stage of product design and other manufacturing processes is an absolute requirement. Therefore JCI has been a leader in the use of Web-based collaboration

FIGURE 5.16

John Waraniak is executive director of e-speed at Johnson Controls and directs their Web-based product design collaboration programs.

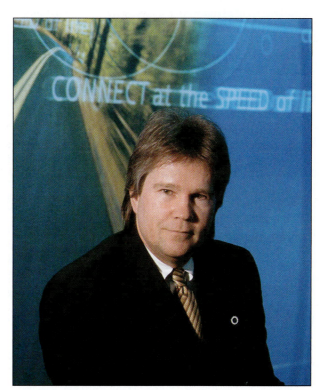

Source: Jay Asquini.

Johnson Controls: Enterprise Collaboration Systems in Manufacturing

Collaborator die. That's the unspoken motto at Johnson Controls Inc. (JCI). It permeates nearly everything from product design to delivery within the company's automotive supply division. So it comes as no surprise that Johnson Controls (www.jci.com) is well along in a Web-based application integration project that has turned collaboration into something far more than a motto.

"Collaboration connects blue sky with solid ground," says John Waraniak, executive director of e-speed at the Milwaukee manufacturer. The automotive division where he works delivered $13.6 billion of JCI's $18.4 billion in revenue last year and is a Tier 1 supplier of car and truck cockpits, which include the dashboard, seats, and other interior parts. JCI builds almost half of the cockpits used in the approximately 50 million vehicles manufactured by the world's major automakers each year.

Waraniak says product ideas must be analyzed in the early design stages by those most affected to avoid costly mistakes. Fixing a problem during engineering design, for example, costs one-tenth of what it would cost once a product reaches the prototype stage. If the product reaches the field, the cost can easily top 1,000 times what it would have taken to correct the problem on the assembly line. Waraniak says that Web-based collaboration work at JCI has saved the company a whopping 80 percent on research and development investments. "Sixty percent of our work is engineer-to-order. We conceive and then we build," he says. "That means we depend on tribal knowledge for insight into the product and the process for making it."

Throw in a multitiered supply chain with countless suppliers, and that tribal knowledge wouldn't be possible without e-business systems, including the Web-based integration of key applications as part of the collaboration process, Waraniak says. That's why the company was an early proponent of the automotive industry's Covisint business-to-business (B2B) online exchange. It's also why JCI established its own B2B exchange in 2001 using technology from MatrixOne Inc. The Johnson Controls B2B portal acts as a private B2B exchange that reduces integration hassles by supplying and supporting a variety of applications used for collaboration by JCI suppliers and contractors that enable collaborative design and manufacturing processes to work effectively.

Thus, all registered suppliers that access JCI's B2B portal use a version of MatrixOne's software on their sites. That software has extensions to popular design tools that suppliers typically employ. For example, a supplier can use computer-aided design and manufacturing data provided by JCI's B2B portal using the application it knows best, such as AutoDesk Inc.'s AutoCAD software with Catera 5, while still benefiting from collaboration with engineers who use different software. MatrixOne's integration software, which runs on each collaborator's location, takes care of the differences between users' applications.

Beyond engineering design, JCI is using MatrixOne for its manufacturing supply chain, where users inside and outside of JCI don't have to concern themselves with the source of, say, enterprise resource planning (ERP) information sent from a PeopleSoft ERP application to an Oracle ERP program. For example, JCI builds the cockpit for the Jeep Liberty using 35 suppliers, all of which can work with data from one another's various inventory applications to gauge when they will need to supply parts to JCI's manufacturing floor. "We want to provide visibility all through our supply chain," Waraniak says.

Few companies achieve the kind of supply chain visibility JCI does, says Kevin Prouty, an analyst at AMR Research Inc. in Boston. And it's paying dividends. "It's one of the few larger automotive suppliers that has grown profit margins during these down times," he says. However, Prouty says he doesn't believe MatrixOne will solve all of JCI's future integration problems. "Just when you think that you've built the last adapter you'll ever need, you acquire a new company with a different legacy ERP system," he says.

For Waraniak, the progress is tangible. Collaboration on 2003 and 2004 model-year automobiles has yielded gains in efficiency. He says engineers have used collaborative online design to reduce costs by $20 million in JCI's "core products portfolio," primarily by reducing the number of discrete parts in each cockpit component. Collaboration cuts time out of component design, Waraniak says. What once took days as overnight express packages went back and forth takes "a few hours on the Web," he says, which is critical when there are as many as 5,000 distinct parts in a vehicle.

Engineers also save time using the B2B portal by sharing drawings, revising calculations, and exchanging critical feedback on ongoing work. "Typically, engineers spend half their time engineering and the rest of the time they are looking for information," Waraniak says. "With the exchange, it's all brought together for them."

Case Study Questions

1. Why is the exchange of "tribal knowledge" important in product design? How do Web-based systems support such collaboration?

2. Why is it important to provide visibility throughout a supply chain? How is JCI attempting to accomplish this?

3. What is the business value of JCI's B2B portal?

Source: Adapted from Mark Hall, "Portal Masks Integration Complexity," *Computerworld*, July, 22, 2002, p. 32. Reprinted with permission from *Computerworld*.

systems in the auto industry, including establishing their own business-to-business exchange. The JCI B2B portal supplies a variety of applications that JCI's suppliers and contractors need to enable them to use their own systems to effectively collaborate with each other and with JCI's engineers in product design and manufacturing processes. JCI's Web-based approaches have thus produced major reductions in costs and design time and dramatically improved collaboration among all business partners.

Cross-Functional Enterprise Applications

Integration of the enterprise has emerged as a critical issue for organizations in all business sectors striving to maintain competitive advantage. Integration is the key to success. It is the key to unlocking information and making it available to any user, anywhere, anytime [19].

As we emphasized in Chapter 1, information systems in the real world typically are integrated combinations of cross-functional business systems. Such systems support **business processes,** such as product development, production, distribution, order management, customer support, and so on. Many organizations are using information technology to develop integrated **cross-functional enterprise systems** that cross the boundaries of traditional business functions in order to reengineer and improve vital business processes all across the enterprise. These organizations view cross-functional enterprise systems as a strategic way to use IT to share information resources and improve the efficiency and effectiveness of business processes, and develop strategic relationships with customers, suppliers, and business partners. See Figure 5.17.

Many companies first moved from functional mainframe-based *legacy systems* to integrated cross-functional *client/server* applications. This typically involved installing *enterprise resource planning, supply chain management,* or *customer relationship management* software from SAP America, PeopleSoft, Oracle, and others. Instead of focusing on the information processing requirements of business functions, such enterprise software focuses on supporting integrated clusters of business processes involved in the operations of a business.

Now, as we see continually in the Real World Cases in this text, business firms are using Internet technologies to help them reengineer and integrate the flow of information among their internal business processes and their customers and suppliers. Companies all across the globe are using the World Wide Web and their intranets and extranets as a technology platform for their cross-functional and inter-enterprise e-business systems.

Enterprise Application Architecture

Figure 5.18 presents an **enterprise application architecture,** which illustrates the interrelationships of the major cross-functional enterprise applications that many companies have or are installing today. This architecture does not provide a detailed

FIGURE 5.17 The new product development process in a manufacturing company. This business process must be supported by cross-functional information systems that cross the boundaries of several business functions.

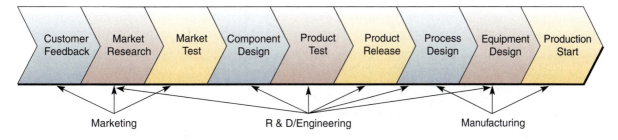

FIGURE 5.18

This enterprise application architecture presents an overview of the major cross-functional enterprise applications and their interrelationships.

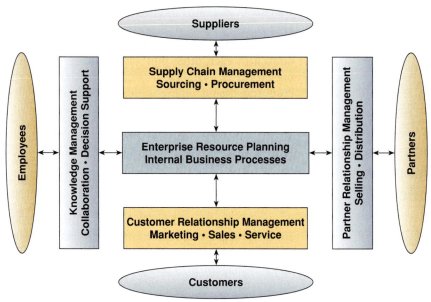

Source: Adapted from Mohan Sawhney and Jeff Zabin, *Seven Steps to Nirvana: Strategic Insights into e-Business Transformation* (New York, McGraw-Hill, 2001), p. 175.

or exhaustive application blueprint, but provides a conceptual framework to help you visualize the basic components, processes, and interfaces of these major e-business applications, and their interrelationships to each other. This application architecture also spotlights the roles these e-business systems play in supporting the customers, suppliers, partners, and employees of a business.

Notice that instead of concentrating on traditional business functions, or only supporting the internal business processes of a company, enterprise applications are focused on accomplishing fundamental business processes in concert with a company's customer, supplier, partner, and employee stakeholders. Thus, enterprise resource planning (ERP) concentrates on the efficiency of a firm's internal production, distribution, and financial processes. Customer relationship management (CRM) focuses on acquiring and retaining profitable customers via marketing, sales, and service processes. Partner relationship management (PRM) aims at acquiring and retaining partners who can enhance the selling and distribution of a firm's products and services. Supply chain management (SCM) focuses on developing the most efficient and effective sourcing and procurement processes with suppliers for the products and services needed by a business. Knowledge management (KM) applications focus on providing a firm's employees with tools that support group collaboration and decision support [28].

We will discuss CRM, ERP, PRM, and SCM applications in detail in Chapter 6, and cover knowledge management applications in Chapter 8. Now let's look at a real world example of a cross-functional enterprise system in action.

IBM Corporation: Global Cross-Functional Enterprise Systems

An enterprise e-business system requires end-to-end connectivity across all of the different processes, from the innards of a company's legacy systems to the outer reaches of its suppliers, customers, and partners. Consider the real-time, configure-to-order system that IBM has created for its personal systems division. A customer in Europe can configure a personal computer on IBM's website and get real-time availability and order confirmation. Seems simple, doesn't it? But behind the scenes, it takes a team of rocket scientists and a hundred man-years of effort to stitch together the myriad business processes and systems that need to work together to make this simple action possible.

> Here's what happens when the customer places the order: The order travels to IBM's fulfillment engine located in the United Kingdom; its e-commerce engine located in Boulder, Colorado; its ERP and production management systems located in Raleigh, North Carolina; its sales reporting system located in Southbury, Connecticut; its product database located in Poughkeepsie, New York; and back to the customer's browser in Europe. Every system updates its status and communicates with every other system in real time. And every order placed in Europe zips across the Atlantic an average of four times. In its journey, it touches dozens of geographical units, legacy systems, and databases strewn across the globe [28].

Enterprise Application Integration

How does a business interconnect some of the cross-functional enterprise systems shown in Figure 5.18? **Enterprise application integration** (EAI) software is being used by many companies to connect major e-business applications like CRM and ERP. See Figure 5.19. EAI software enables users to model the business processes involved in the interactions that should occur between business applications. EAI also provides *middleware* that performs data conversion and coordination, application communication and messaging services, and access to the application interfaces involved. Thus, EAI software can integrate a variety of enterprise application clusters by letting them exchange data according to rules derived from the business process models developed by users. For example, a typical rule might be:

> *When an order is complete, have the order application tell the accounting system to send a bill and alert shipping to send out the product.*

Thus, as Figure 5.19 illustrates, EAI software can integrate the front-office and back-office applications of a business so they work together in a seamless, integrated way. This is a vital capability that provides real business value to a business enterprise that must respond quickly and effectively to business events and customer demands. For example, the integration of enterprise application clusters has been shown to dramatically improve customer call center responsiveness and effectiveness. That's because EAI integrates access to all of the customer and product data customer reps need to quickly serve customers. EAI also streamlines sales order processing so products and services can be delivered faster. Thus, EAI improves customer and supplier experience with the business because of its responsiveness [10, 19, 24]. See Figure 5.20.

FIGURE 5.19

Enterprise application integration software interconnects front-office and back-office applications like customer relationship management and enterprise resource planning.

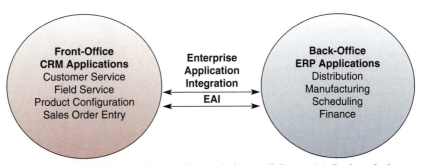

Source: Adapted from Ravi Kalakota and Marcia Robinson, *E-Business 2.0: Roadmap for Success* (Reading, MA: Addison-Wesley, 2001), p. 160. © 2001 Addison-Wesley Publishing Company, Inc. Reprinted by permission of Addison-Wesley Longman, Inc.

Dell Computer: Enterprise Application Integration

In a survey of just 75 companies it deals with, Dell Computer found they used 18 different software packages, says Terry Klein, vice president of e-business for Dell's "relationship group." This lack of integration means that companies aren't getting the seamless processing that reduces costs and speeds up customer responsiveness.

Dell knew that figuring out how to get its system to talk to each of those 18 different systems in its partners' back offices, one at a time, would be impractical, to say the least. So Dell installed software from WebMethods, a maker of industrial-strength business-to-business integration software, based in Fairfax, Virginia. WebMethods' enterprise application integration (EAI) technology acts as a software translator and creates a kind of hub that, using the Web, allows instantaneous communication among networked companies' internal business systems.

For Dell, the first fruit of installing the WebMethods software is what Dell calls e-procurement, and it goes like this. A business customer pulls product information directly from Dell's server into the customer's purchasing system, which creates an electronic requisition. After the requisition is approved online by the customer, a computer-generated purchase order shoots over the Internet back to Dell.

The entire process can take 60 seconds. Dell says the system, which went live in the spring of 2000, has automatically cut errors in its procurement processes from about 200 per million transactions to 10 per million. And Dell has been able to shave $40 to $50 off the cost of processing each order. That adds up to $5 million a year in cost savings, since thousands of orders flow to Dell through its WebMethods system daily.

The EAI software also enabled Dell to build links to 40 or so of its biggest customers, allowing a customer to buy, say, a truckload of new laptops online while Dell simultaneously enters the order for those laptops into the customer's procurement system. Think of it as one-click shopping for corporate buyers. Just as Amazon.com automates the process of entering credit card information to speed purchases by consumers, Dell is able to update its customers' procurement tracking systems every time they make a purchase [3].

FIGURE 5.20   An example of a new customer order process showing how EAI middleware connects several business information systems within a company.

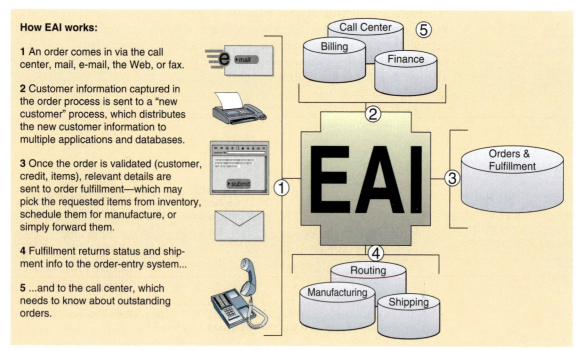

How EAI works:

1 An order comes in via the call center, mail, e-mail, the Web, or fax.

2 Customer information captured in the order process is sent to a "new customer" process, which distributes the new customer information to multiple applications and databases.

3 Once the order is validated (customer, credit, items), relevant details are sent to order fulfillment—which may pick the requested items from inventory, schedule them for manufacture, or simply forward them.

4 Fulfillment returns status and shipment info to the order-entry system...

5 ...and to the call center, which needs to know about outstanding orders.

Source: Adapted from David Orenstein, "Enterprise Application Integration," *Computerworld*, October 4, 1999, p. 72.

Transaction Processing Systems

Transaction processing systems (TPS) are cross-functional information systems that process data resulting from the occurrence of business transactions. We introduced transaction processing systems in Chapter 1 as one of the major application categories of information systems in business.

Transactions are events that occur as part of doing business, such as sales, purchases, deposits, withdrawals, refunds, and payments. Think, for example, of the data generated whenever a business sells something to a customer on credit, whether in a retail store or at an e-commerce site on the Web. Data about the customer, product, salesperson, store, and so on, must be captured and processed. This in turn causes additional transactions, such as credit checks, customer billing, inventory changes, and increases in accounts receivable balances, that generate even more data. Thus, transaction processing activities are needed to capture and process such data, or the operations of a business would grind to a halt. Therefore, transaction processing systems play a vital role in supporting the operations of an e-business enterprise.

Online transaction processing systems play a strategic role in electronic commerce. Many firms are using the Internet, extranets, and other networks that tie them electronically to their customers or suppliers for online transaction processing (OLTP). Such *real-time* systems, which capture and process transactions immediately, can help firms provide superior service to customers and other trading partners. This capability adds value to their products and services, and thus gives them an important way to differentiate themselves from their competitors.

Syntellect's Online Transaction Processing

For example, Figure 5.21 illustrates an online transaction processing system for cable pay-per-view systems developed by Syntellect Interactive Services. Cable TV viewers can select pay-per-view events offered by their cable companies using the phone or the World Wide Web. The pay-per-view order is captured by Syntellect's interactive voice response system or Web server, then transported to Syntellect database application servers. There the order is processed, customer and sales databases are updated, and the approved order is relayed back to the cable company's video server, which transmits the video of the pay-per-view event to the customer. Thus, Syntellect teams with over 700 cable companies to offer a very popular and very profitable service [30].

The Transaction Processing Cycle

Transaction processing systems, such as Syntellect's, capture and process data describing business transactions, update organizational databases, and produce a variety of information products. You should understand this as a **transaction processing cycle** of several basic activities, as illustrated in Figure 5.22.

- **Data Entry.** The first step of the transaction processing cycle is the capture of business data. For example, transaction data may be collected by point-of-sale terminals using optical scanning of bar codes and credit card readers at a retail store or other business. Or transaction data can be captured at an electronic commerce website on the Internet. The proper recording and editing of data so they are quickly and correctly captured for processing is one of the major design challenges of information systems discussed in Chapter 10.

- **Transaction Processing.** Transaction processing systems process data in two basic ways: (1) **batch processing,** where transaction data are accumulated over a period of time and processed periodically, and (2) **real-time processing** (also called online processing), where data are processed immediately after a transaction occurs. All online transaction processing systems incorporate

FIGURE 5.21   The Syntellect pay-per-view online transaction processing system.

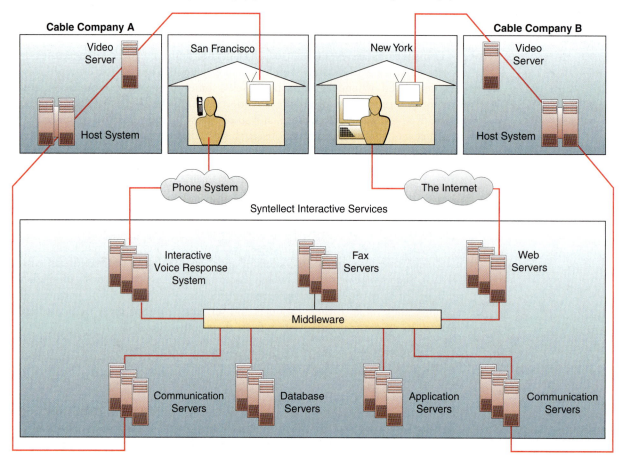

real-time processing capabilities. Many online systems also depend on the capabilities of *fault tolerant* computer systems that can continue to operate even if parts of the system fail. We will discuss this fault tolerant concept in Chapter 11.

- **Database Maintenance.** An organization's database must be maintained by its transaction processing systems so that they are always correct and up-to-date. Therefore, transaction processing systems update the corporate databases of an organization to reflect changes resulting from day-to-day business transactions. For example, credit sales made to customers will cause customer account balances to be increased and the amount of inventory on hand to be decreased. Database maintenance ensures that these and other changes are reflected in the data records stored in the company's databases.

- **Document and Report Generation.** Transaction processing systems produce a variety of documents and reports. Examples of transaction documents include purchase orders, paychecks, sales receipts, invoices, and customer statements. Transaction reports might take the form of a transaction listing such as a payroll register, or edit reports that describe errors detected during processing.

- **Inquiry Processing.** Many transaction processing systems allow you to use the Internet, intranets, extranets, and Web browsers or database management

FIGURE 5.22

The transaction processing cycle. Note that transaction processing systems use a five-stage cycle of data entry, transaction processing, database maintenance, document and report generation, and inquiry processing activities.

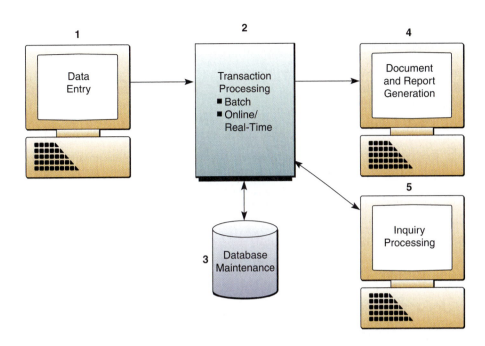

query languages to make inquiries and receive responses concerning the results of transaction processing activity. Typically, responses are displayed in a variety of prespecified formats or screens. For example, you might check on the status of a sales order, the balance in an account, or the amount of stock in inventory and receive immediate responses at your PC.

Enterprise Collaboration Systems

Enterprise collaboration systems (ECS) are cross-functional e-business systems that enhance communication, coordination, and collaboration among the members of business teams and workgroups. Information technology, especially Internet technologies, provides tools to help us collaborate—to communicate ideas, share resources, and coordinate our cooperative work efforts as members of the many formal and informal process and project teams and workgroups that make up many of today's organizations. Thus, the goal of **enterprise collaboration systems** is to enable us to work together more easily and effectively by helping us to:

- **Communicate:** Sharing information with each other.
- **Coordinate:** Coordinating our individual work efforts and use of resources with each other.
- **Collaborate:** Working together cooperatively on joint projects and assignments.

For example, engineers, business specialists, and external consultants may form a virtual team for a project. The team may rely on intranets and extranets to collaborate via e-mail, videoconferencing, discussion forums, and a multimedia database of work-in-progress information at a project website. The enterprise collaboration system may use PC workstations networked to a variety of servers on which project, corporate, and other databases are stored. In addition, network servers may provide a variety of software resources, such as Web browsers, groupware, and application packages, to assist the team's collaboration until the project is completed.

FIGURE 5.23

Electronic communications, conferencing, and collaborative work software tools enhance enterprise collaboration.

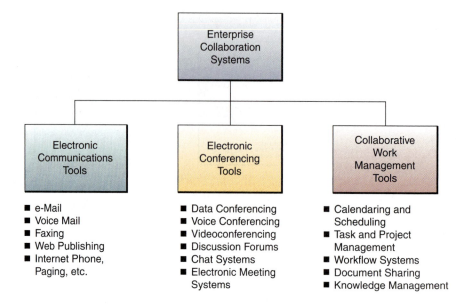

Tools for Enterprise Collaboration

The capabilities and potential of the Internet, as well as intranets and extranets, are driving the demand for better enterprise collaboration tools in business. On the other hand, it is Internet technologies like Web browsers and servers, hypermedia documents and databases, and intranets and extranets that provide the hardware, software, data, and network platforms for many of the groupware tools for enterprise collaboration that business users want. Figure 5.23 provides an overview of some of the software tools for electronic communication, electronic conferencing, and collaborative work management.

Electronic communication tools include electronic mail, voice mail, faxing, Web publishing, bulletin board systems, paging, and Internet phone systems. These tools enable you to electronically send messages, documents, and files in data, text, voice, or multimedia over computer networks. This helps you share everything from voice and text messages to copies of project documents and data files with your team members, wherever they may be. The ease and efficiency of such communications are major contributors to the collaboration process.

Electronic conferencing tools help people communicate and collaborate while working together. A variety of conferencing methods enables the members of teams and workgroups at different locations to exchange ideas interactively at the same time, or at different times at their convenience. These include data and voice conferencing, videoconferencing, chat systems, discussion forums, and electronic meeting systems. Electronic conferencing options also include *electronic meeting systems*, where team members can meet at the same time and place in a *decision room* setting. See Figure 5.24.

Collaborative work management tools help people accomplish or manage group work activities. This category of software includes calendaring and scheduling tools, task and project management, workflow systems, and knowledge management tools. Other tools for joint work, such as joint document creation, editing, and revision, are found in the software suites discussed in Chapter 14. Figure 5.25 summarizes the software tools for electronic communications, conferencing, and collaborative work management that are vital components of today's enterprise collaboration systems.

FIGURE 5.24

QuickPlace by Lotus Development helps virtual workgroups set up Web-based work spaces for collaborative work assignments.

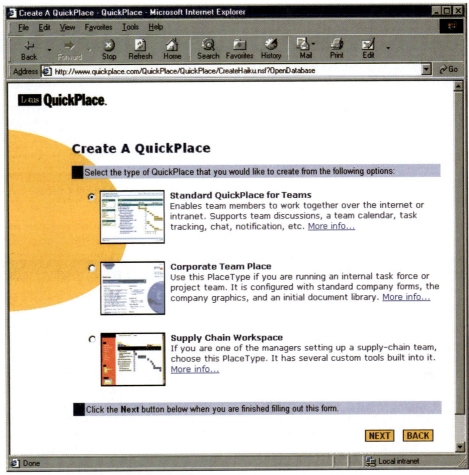

Source: Courtesy of Lotus Development Corp.

General Electric Co.: Committed to Enterprise Collaboration

GE has made a huge commitment to the Lotus Development tools QuickPlace (which lets employees set up Web-based work spaces) and Sametime (for real-time online meetings), which permit ad hoc collaboration without help from the IT department. These tools streamline the company's communication in myriad ways. Thus, GE's recruiting teams can set up QuickPlaces to trade information about prospective hires. And GE engineers share drawings, design requirements, and production schedules with supervisors on manufacturing floors. In all, GE has created almost 18,000 QuickPlaces for 250,000 users, says CTO Larry Biagini. "And if we have an engineering project with someone outside the company, we'll set up a QuickPlace or Sametime session and invite outside people."

There's also Support Central, a companywide knowledge management system developed using software from GE's Fanuc division. Employees sign on and complete a survey about their areas of expertise. The responses are added to a knowledge base so people with questions anywhere in GE can find people with answers. "Someone may have a question about, say, titanium metallurgy, and they'll be able to find documents about it, or send e-mail or initiate an online chat with someone who can help," says Stuart Scott, CIO of GE Industrial Systems. The result of all this collaboration? Faster workflow and quicker, smarter decisions, GE executives say [7].

FIGURE 5.25   A summary of the major categories of software tools used in enterprise collaboration systems.

Electronic Communication Tools

Electronic communication tools help you to communicate and collaborate with others by electronically sending messages, documents, and files in data, text, voice, or multimedia over the Internet, intranets, extranets, and other computer networks.

- **Electronic Mail and Instant Messaging.** Widely used to send and receive text messages between team members using PCs and mobile devices via the Internet. E-mail can also include data files, software, and multimedia messages and documents as attachments.
- **Voice Mail.** Unanswered telephone messages are digitized, stored, and played back to you by a voice messaging computer.
- **Faxing.** Transmitting and receiving images of documents over telephone or computer networks using PCs or fax machines.
- **Web Publishing.** Creating, converting, and storing hyperlinked documents and other material on Internet or intranet Web servers so they can easily be shared via Web browsers or netcasting with teams, workgroups, or the enterprise.

Electronic Conferencing Tools

Electronic conferencing tools help networked computer users share information and collaborate while working together on joint assignments, no matter where they are located.

- **Data Conferencing.** Users at networked PCs can view, mark up, revise, and save changes to a shared whiteboard of drawings, documents, and other material.
- **Voice Conferencing.** Telephone conversations shared among several participants via speaker phones or networked PCs with *Internet telephone* software.
- **Videoconferencing.** Realtime video- and audioconferencing (1) among users at networked PCs (desktop videoconferencing) or (2) among participants in conference rooms or auditoriums in different locations (teleconferencing). Videoconferencing can also include whiteboarding and document sharing.
- **Discussion Forums.** Provide a computer network discussion platform to encourage and manage online text discussions over a period of time among members of special interest groups or project teams.
- **Chat Systems.** Enable two or more users at networked PCs to carry on online, realtime text conversations.
- **Electronic Meeting Systems.** Using a meeting room with networked PCs, a large-screen projector, and EMS software to facilitate communication, collaboration, and group decision making in business meetings.

Collaborative Work Management Tools

Collaborative work management tools help people accomplish or manage joint work activities.

- **Calendaring and Scheduling**. Using electronic calendars and other groupware features to automatically schedule, notify, and remind the computer networked members of teams and workgroups of meetings, appointments, and other events.
- **Task and Project Management.** Managing team and workgroup projects by scheduling, tracking, and charting the completion status of tasks within a project.
- **Workflow Systems.** Helping networked knowledge workers collaborate to accomplish and manage the flow of structured work tasks and electronic document processing within a business process.
- **Knowledge Management.** Organizing and sharing the diverse forms of business information created within an organization. Includes managing and providing personalized access to project and enterprise document libraries, discussion databases, hypermedia website databases, and other types of knowledge bases.

Summary

- **Functional Business Systems.** Functional business information systems support the business functions of marketing, production/operations, accounting, finance, and human resource management through a variety of e-business operational and management information systems summarized in Figure 5.2.

- **Marketing.** Marketing information systems support traditional and e-commerce processes and management of the marketing function. Major types of marketing information systems include interactive marketing at e-commerce websites, sales force automation, customer relationship management, sales management, product management, targeted marketing, advertising and promotion, and market research. Thus, marketing information systems assist marketing managers in electronic commerce product development and customer relationship decisions, as well as in planning advertising and sales promotion strategies and developing the e-commerce potential of new and present products, and new channels of distribution.

- **Manufacturing.** Computer-based manufacturing information systems help a company achieve computer-integrated manufacturing (CIM), and thus simplify, automate, and integrate many of the activities needed to quickly produce high-quality products to meet changing customer demands. For example, computer-aided design using collaborative manufacturing networks helps engineers collaborate on the design of new products and processes. Then manufacturing resource planning systems help plan the types of resources needed in the production process. Finally, manufacturing execution systems monitor and control the manufacture of products on the factory floor through shop floor scheduling and control systems, controlling a physical process (process control), a machine tool (numerical control), or machines with some humanlike work capabilities (robotics).

- **Human Resource Management.** Human resource information systems support human resource management in organizations. They include information systems for staffing the organization, training and development, and compensation administration. HRM websites on the Internet or corporate intranets have become important tools for providing HR services to present and prospective employees.

- **Accounting and Finance.** Accounting information systems record, report, and analyze business transactions and events for the management of the business enterprise. Examples of common accounting information systems include order processing, inventory control, accounts receivable, accounts payable, payroll, and general ledger systems. Information systems in finance support financial managers in decisions regarding the financing of a business and the allocation of financial resources within a business. Financial information systems include cash management, online investment management, capital budgeting, and financial forecasting and planning.

- **Cross-Functional Enterprise Systems.** Major e-business applications and their interrelationships are summarized in the enterprise application architecture of Figure 5.18. Many e-business applications are integrated cross-functional enterprise applications such as enterprise resource planning (ERP), customer relationship management (CRM), and supply chain management (SCM), which will be covered in detail in Chapter 6.

  These systems themselves are being interconnected by enterprise application integration (EAI) systems so that the business users of these applications can more easily access the information resources they need to support the needs of customers, suppliers, and business partners. Enterprise collaboration systems (ECS) are cross-functional systems that support and enhance communication and collaboration among the teams and workgroups in an organization. Refer to Figures 5.19, 5.23, and 5.25 for summary views of the e-business applications in EAI systems and enterprise collaboration systems.

- **Transaction Processing Systems.** Online transaction processing systems play a vital role in e-commerce. Transaction processing involves the basic activities of (1) data entry, (2) transaction processing, (3) database maintenance, (4) document and report generation, and (5) inquiry processing. Many firms are using the Internet, intranets, extranets, and other networks for online transaction processing to provide superior service to their customers and suppliers. Figure 5.22 illustrates the basic activities of transaction processing systems.

Key Terms and Concepts

These are the key terms and concepts of this chapter. The page number of their first explanation is in parentheses.

1. Accounting systems (156)
2. Accounts payable (158)
3. Accounts receivable (158)
4. Batch processing (167)
5. Cash management systems (159)
6. Computer-aided manufacturing (152)
7. Computer-integrated manufacturing (151)
8. Cross-functional enterprise systems (163)
9. E-business (144)
10. Enterprise application architecture (163)
11. Enterprise application integration (165)
12. Enterprise collaboration systems (169)
13. Financial management systems (159)
14. Functional business systems (146)
15. General ledger (159)
16. Human resource systems (153)
17. Interactive marketing (147)
18. Inventory control (158)
19. Machine control (152)
20. Manufacturing execution systems (152)
21. Manufacturing systems (150)
22. Marketing systems (146)
23. Online accounting systems (156)
24. Online HRM systems (154)
25. Online investment systems (160)
26. Online transaction processing systems (167)
27. Order processing (158)
28. Payroll (159)
29. Process control (152)
30. Real-time processing (167)
31. Sales force automation (147)
32. Targeted marketing (147)
33. Transaction processing cycle (167)

Review Quiz

Match one of the key terms and concepts listed previously with one of the brief examples or definitions that follow. Try to find the best fit for the answers that seem to fit more than one term or concept. Defend your choices.

_____ 1. Using the Internet and other networks for e-commerce, collaboration, and business processes.

_____ 2. Information systems that cross the boundaries of the functional areas of a business in order to integrate and automate business processes.

_____ 3. Information systems that support marketing, production, accounting, finance, and human resource management.

_____ 4. E-business applications can be grouped into interrelated cross-functional enterprise applications.

_____ 5. Software that interconnects enterprise application systems.

_____ 6. Information systems for customer relationship management, sales management, and promotion management.

_____ 7. Collaborating interactively with customers in creating, purchasing, servicing, and improving products and services.

_____ 8. Using mobile computing networks to support salespeople in the field.

_____ 9. Information systems that support manufacturing operations and management.

_____ 10. A conceptual framework for simplifying and integrating all aspects of manufacturing automation.

_____ 11. Using computers in a variety of ways to help manufacture products.

_____ 12. Use electronic communications, conferencing, and collaborative work tools to support and enhance collaboration among teams and workgroups.

_____ 13. Using computers to operate a petroleum refinery.

_____ 14. Using computers to help operate machine tools.

_____ 15. Information systems to support staffing, training and development, and compensation administration.

_____ 16. Using the Internet for recruitment and job hunting is an example.

_____ 17. Accomplishes legal and historical record-keeping and gathers information for the planning and control of business operations.

_____ 18. An example is using the Internet and extranets to do accounts receivable and accounts payable activities.

_____ 19. Handles sales orders from customers.

_____ 20. Keeps track of items in stock.

_____ 21. Keeps track of amounts owed by customers.

_____ 22. Keeps track of purchases from suppliers.

_____ 23. Produces employee paychecks.

_____ 24. Produces the financial statements of a firm.

_____ 25. Information systems for cash management, investment management, capital budgeting, and financial forecasting.

_____ 26. Using the Internet and other networks for investment research and trading.

_____ 27. Performance monitoring and control systems for factory floor operations.

_____ 28. Customizing advertising and promotion methods to fit their intended audience.

_____ 29. Data entry, transaction processing, database maintenance, document and report generation, and inquiry processing.

_____ 30. Collecting and periodically processing transaction data.

_____ 31. Processing transaction data immediately after they are captured.

_____ 32. Systems that immediately capture and process transaction data and update corporate databases.

Discussion Questions

1. Refer to the Real World Case on Cypress Semiconductor and FleetBoston in the chapter. How can customer segmentation and targeted marketing programs that focus on customer profitability avoid "ignoring customers with low current returns but high potential"?

2. Why is there a trend toward cross-functional integrated enterprise systems in business?

3. Refer to the example on Dell Computer in the chapter. What other solutions could there be for the problem of information system incompatibility in business besides EAI systems?

4. Refer to the example on Charles Schwab & Co. in the chapter. What are the most important HR applications a company should offer to its employees via a Web-based system? Why?

5. How do you think sales force automation affects salesperson productivity, marketing management, and competitive advantage?

6. How can Internet technologies be involved in improving a process in one of the functions of business? Choose one example and evaluate its business value.

7. Refer to the Real World Case on Johnson Controls in the chapter. Can collaboration systems improve the quality of the products that are designed, as well as reducing the cost and time of the design process? Why or why not?

8. What are several e-business applications that you might recommend to a small company to help it survive and succeed in challenging economic times? Why?

9. Which of the 14 tools for enterprise collaboration summarized in Figure 5.24 do you feel are essential for any business to have today? Which of them do you feel are optional, depending on the type of business or other factor? Explain.

10. Refer to the example on General Electric in the chapter. How do enterprise collaboration systems contribute to bottom-line profits for a business?

Application Exercises

Complete the following exercises as individual or group projects that apply chapter concepts to real world business situations.

1. **QuickBooks Solutions Marketplace: Online Applications for Small Business**

   Web Why build a power plant when you can pay someone else for electricity? This is the logic behind the business models of Web-based software companies known as application service providers, or ASPs. Instead of providing electric power, ASPs deliver software applications over the Internet for monthly or per-user fees.

   ASPs provide browser-based, Web-native applications—meaning the software and data existing on the Web—and generally require high-speed Internet access. Service providers create enterprise-level software and charge customers a monthly per-user service fee, which includes all installations, upgrades, and maintenance, so small businesses can automate such critical functions as accounting, human resources, and customer management. See Figure 5.26.

FIGURE 5.26

The QuickBooks Solutions Marketplace provides online application software services from Intuit and their many business partners.

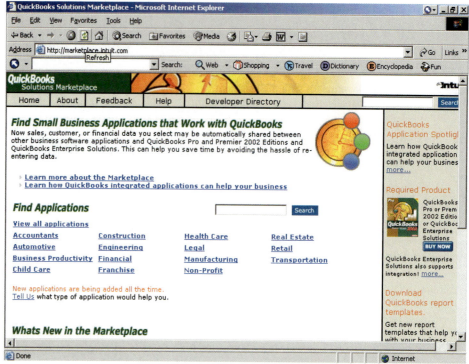

Source: Courtesy of Intuit.

a. Check out the QuickBooks Solutions Marketplace at www.marketplace.intuit.com. What is the business value of the software and services they offer?

b. Link to the websites of several of the other online application service providers in the QuickBooks Marketplace. Evaluate the business value of two of these more specialized ASPs.

c. Would you use or recommend any of the online application services to a small business? Why or why not?

2. eWork Exchange and eLance.com: Online Job Matching and Auctions

Web Many opportunities await those who troll the big job boards, the free-agent sites, the auction services where applicants bid for projects, and the niche sites for specialized jobs and skills. Examples of top job matching and auction sites are eWork Exchange and eLance.com.

eWork Exchange (www.eworkexchange.com). No more sifting through irrelevant search results: Fill out a list of your skills and let eWork Exchange's proprietary technology find the most suitable projects for you—no bidding required.

eLance.com (www.elance.com). This global auction marketplace covers more than just IT jobs; it runs the gamut from astrology and medicine to corporate work and cooking projects. Register a description of your services or go straight to browsing

the listings of open projects—and then start bidding. A feedback section lets both employers and freelancers rate one another.

a. Check out eWork Exchange and eLance, and other online job sites on the Web.

b. Evaluate several sites based on their ease of use and their value to job seekers and employers.

c. Which website was your favorite? Why?

3. Job Search Database

DB Visit websites like Monster.com and others mentioned in the chapter to gather information about available jobs. Look up and record the relevant data for at least 10 current job openings that are of interest to you or that meet criteria provided by your instructor.

a. Create a database table to store key characteristics of jobs. Include all of the job characteristics shown in the list that follows as fields in your table, but feel free to add additional fields of interest to you. If data are not available for some fields (such as, salary range) for a particular job, leave that field blank.

b. Write queries that will enable you to retrieve **(a)** just those jobs in a specified location, and **(b)** just those jobs in a specified job category.

c. Create a report that groups jobs by Location and sorts jobs within each group by Job category.

List of Fields for the Job Search Database

Job Title:	Systems Analyst
Employer:	Techron Inc.
Location:	Springfield, MA
Job Category:	Data and Information Services
Job Description:	Work with team to analyze, design, and develop e-commerce systems. Skills in systems analysis, relation database design, and Programming in Java are required.
Qualifications:	Bachelors degree in Information Systems or Computer Science
Salary Range:	$48,000–$60,000 depending on experience.

4. Performing an Industry Financial Analysis

SS Select an industry of interest to you and at least three prominent firms in that industry that you would like to investigate. Go to the websites of the firms you are investigating and obtain information about financial operations including at least net sales (or net revenue) and net after-tax income for the three most recent years available. Also, search the Web for current information affecting your firms and the industry.

a. Create a simple spreadsheet of the net sales and after-tax income data you collected. Your spreadsheet should include percentage changes between years to facilitate comparisons between companies that are of unequal size. Also, you should show the rate of after-tax income as a percentage of net sales. Add charts comparing trends in net revenue and net income for the firms you are investigating. Include a projection for net revenue and net income for the next year.

b. Write a brief report describing the income statistics of your spreadsheet, discussing current trends affecting your firms, and justifying your projections for the upcoming year.

REAL WORLD CASE 3

Union Pacific, Corporate Express, and Best Buy: Enterprise Application Integration Challenges

For some large companies, the need to tie together incompatible systems has grown to the point that the main mission of their IT departments is shifting from application development and support to application integration. Users such as Corporate Express Inc., Best Buy Co., and Union Pacific Corp. say they no longer have any choice about braving the rigors of building an enterprise application integrations (EAI) infrastructure. EAI tools still have a reputation of being difficult to use, but IT managers at those companies say trying to cope with scores of diverse, unconnected business applications—"application spaghetti"—is worse.

"We really need to make integration a central part of every IT initiative," said Marty Malley, director of information systems at Omaha-based Union Pacific (www.up.com). For example, he said, the railroad has to find a way to deliver real-time pricing information from its systems to freight customers in the oil and gas industries. "That price data touches many internal systems, and now we've got to find a way to tie it all together," Malley said. Which means that UP has to find a way to integrate those applications and connect them to their customers' systems.

In November 2001, Union Pacific began working with EAI tools developed by Tibco Software, including the Tibco BusinessWorks EAI development tool. Once the EAI framework of integrated applications and databases is developed, it will allow UP to move some of the applications of its core railroad transportation control system from its mainframes to server-based systems. But Malley said the railroad hasn't developed a full road map for the EAI applications that they want to accomplish. He also wouldn't speculate on the project's expected cost.

Monry Sooter, CIO at Corporate Express (www.corporateexpress.com), based in Broomfield, Colorado, said EAI technology will play a role in all four of the major IT projects that the office supplies distributor plans to take on this year. "We made a business decision that our integration infrastructure has to be corrected," Sooter said. "If it's not, we're not going to be able to move forward." For example, in a project that began 18 months ago, Corporate Express used EAI software tools developed by WebMethods Inc. to integrate its systems with the business-to-business applications of 120 of its largest customers.

Now, Sooter said, the company plans to use the EAI tools to support integration of i2 Technologies' online procurement and warehouse management applications. They will also be used as part of projects aimed at improving information systems to Corporate Express' suppliers and for developing an online system for paying its sales force. The EAI application will funnel data among various product, customer, and other business databases and business system interfaces, Sooter said.

Tyler McDaniel, an analyst at Hurwitz Group, says early versions of EAI tools were difficult to use. But improved business object methodologies and graphical user interface capabilities have lessened their arcane nature, he said. However, EAI projects can still be long and hard.

For example, Best Buy (www.bestbuy.com) plans to use EAI software tools from WebMethods to connect its electronic data interchange (EDI) system for transactions with its trading partners with a new application server that's being installed to run its inventory and financial systems. Best Buy, a major electronics retailer, has such a heavy volume of EDI activity for the electronic exchange of transaction documents that it's running short of the nightly downtime needed to complete batch processing of all EDI transactions, said Patricia Vessey, e-business communications manager at Best Buy. The WebMethods tools will translate data among various systems and enable real-time transaction processing of purchase orders and invoices, Vessey said. But she estimated that it will take two years to do the required data-conversion work.

The IT team at Best Buy started learning the ins and outs of WebMethods' EAI software in August. "We're finding it's complex, but we need to learn it if we want quicker account reconciliation and better accuracy in our e-commerce systems," said David Nelson, products capabilities manager at Best Buy. Best Buy wants to convert its EDI trading documents to a new Web-based XML (eXtensible Markup Language) document format. But that will require detailed data-mapping work, Nelson said. He added that the company also needs to set well-defined workflow routines for the data that it plans to funnel through the EAI infrastructure. The data come from more than 600 suppliers. Nelson noted that WebMethods has pledged to help Best Buy with any problems that may arise as they go through their data-mapping process.

Case Study Questions

1. How could an enterprise application integration system help a firm to better serve its customers? Use Union Pacific and Corporate Express as examples.

2. How could enterprise application systems improve a company's business interactions with its suppliers? Use Corporate Express and Best Buy as examples.

3. What major challenges are faced by businesses that implement EAI initiatives? How can companies meet such challenges? Use the companies in this case to illustrate your answer.

Source: Adapted from Michael Meehan, "IT Managers Make EAI Projects a Top Priority," *Computerworld*, February 4, 2002, p. 14. Reprinted with permission from *Computerworld*.

| REAL WORLD CASE 4 | Baxter International: Web-Enabled Human Resource Management |

aye Katt, VP of employee programs at medical products and services company Baxter International, has a realistic view of how HR management thinking translates into practice. "I don't buy into the theory that our core activity is only strategy," she says. "You can think as strategically as you like, but if some basics aren't happening—if employees aren't being paid properly—that's what you have to focus on first."

Katt's pragmatic view is particularly significant given that Baxter is one of the more advanced adopters of both HR-related technologies and business practices. In the early 1990s, for example, it delved into the world of employee self-service. More recently, it embarked on a major global implementation of PeopleSoft 8 HRMS pure Internet software, which is being rolled out in some 39 countries.

The company's Web-based rollout now encompasses a range of traditional HR functions, from online recruitment (including internal job posting) to compensation modeling for its North American operations. Some of the administrative functions that are typically done manually in other organizations have now been fully automated. They range from enrollment into employee stock purchase plans, to direct deposit of salary payments backed by online distribution of payment advice. "Self-service and the Web are about getting people to do things differently—you don't take the same processes and put them on the Web," says Katt.

At a structural level, meanwhile, Baxter's HR department is largely centralized, with a "relationship manager" assigned to each of its five business units. In the future, this will allow the organization to segment its services providing additional HR support where required—for example, high-growth divisions will need additional skills assessment and recruitment services. Using the Web as a prime communications vehicle has allowed the HR function to extend its reach across the global organization, giving it a better insight into the cultural differences that characterize its operations in different countries. "Much of our success has been from using the Web," she says. "You have to get close to the global community to understand how they define business value."

The next stage for Baxter is to increase adoption of analytical applications and tools. "I think you have to evolve to a certain point before you can do that—you've got to have the whole workforce up and running and you've got to have the culture to handle metrics. Baxter is on a pretty good trajectory there. There will be big demographic challenges—just in terms of finding talent over the next decade. We'll need more tools to get a better handle on the workforce and to do workforce planning." This combination of Web-based applications and business analytical infrastructure will provide the platform for the future development of HR services which, Katt believes, will become more and more challenging over time.

Although the company has been able to drive much of its transactional activity and information distribution onto the Web, it also believes that there is a strong case for retaining a live HR function alongside the self-service application to handle situations where employees require direct assistance. This requires software tools that are closer in nature to customer relationship management than traditional HR—in effect, HR becomes a service provider and its employees become the client. Baxter already has an operational service center and is discussing whether the services and functions of PeopleSoft's customer relationship management (CRM) application can be integrated into the Baxter HRMS system.

Baxter also takes a practical approach to the business philosophy that transactional activities should be outsourced wherever possible. Armed with the right service backup, Katt believes that many transactional activities can be carried out as cheaply internally as externally, and the company is looking to bring some outsourced functions back in-house. "To me, it's all about economics," says Katt. "If you're willing to have a permission culture through HR self-service, with an auditing procedure, I know you can do some HR activities cheaper in-house. You've got to be selective."

Case Study Questions

1. What key HR applications are provided by Baxter's Web-based HR system? What are some other Web-based HR applications they might implement?

2. What business value does Baxter derive from their Web-based HR approach? What value do their employees receive from such HR systems?

3. How could viewing employees as customers or clients change how HR services are provided to employees by Web-based HR systems?

Source: Adapted from PeopleSoft, "Human Capital Management: A Pragmatic Approach to Delivering Strategic Value," HRMS White Papers, PeopleSoft.com, January 2002.

IBM Corporation: The Business Value of Instant Messaging Collaboration

Anne Altman is managing director of IBM's federal government business, but she has a 16-year-old's zeal for instant messaging—because she has found a very grown-up way to leverage the technology at the bluest of blue-chip companies. "Instant messaging has made the biggest difference for me," she says. "When I'm on a sales call and the customer needs a status update or a piece of information that I don't have on hand, I just send a message to someone on my team, and I get an answer on the spot. Instant messaging eliminates the headaches of playing phone tag and constantly checking e-mail."

Altman oversees all of IBM's business with the U.S. government, which happens to be IBM's single largest customer. She works mainly with a team of 12 direct reports who each manage an account with a different department. (In total, she leads more than 2,000 IBMers.) Her team recently won a contract that could be worth up to $100 million to upgrade the finance- and accounting-service systems for the U.S. Department of Defense.

Satisfying customers as demanding as the FBI, for example, is a high-pressure job, and when a customer relationship is at stake, the phone isn't the best tool. "I can't afford to track down a piece of information," she says. "Once you lose phone contact with someone, it might take forever to reconnect with that person. Those follow-up loops are an incredible waste of time."

Often, e-mail isn't much better. Many systems require users to periodically download messages from the server, leading to lags that last from a few minutes to several hours between the times that they receive mail. Even on e-mail systems that continuously download, urgent requests can get burned in an overflowing inbox.

So Altman relies on instant messaging to get the job done. She uses Lotus Sametime, which is produced by IBM subsidiary Lotus Development Corp. and controls about 66 percent of the enterprise IM market. She keeps a buddy list of 20 to 30 people, including her 12 direct reports and various experts in such areas as contracts, legal issues, and security. With the click of a button, she can add or delete people from IBM's global employee-database list. When Altman logs on to the program, she can see who is online and available to chat.

"I received a call yesterday from a senior executive in the federal government who needed some of our white papers," recalls Altman. "While we were chatting, I shot a message to Brien Lorenz, our e-government and enterprise transformation consultant. He sent me a bunch of files which I forwarded to the customer—while he was still on the phone, explaining what he needed!"

Using IM technology in business certainly isn't new: many Silicon Valley companies have been using AOL and Yahoo Instant Messenger for years. But only recently have billion-dollar corporations jumped on the IM bandwagon. One reason for their former reluctance is that most competing IM products can't talk to each other. And the jury is still out over whether IM increases or distracts from worker productivity. A recent Gartner Group study found that 42 percent of U.S. Internet business users use IM in the workplace, even though 70 percent of IT departments refuse to support it.

But even its critics agree that there are major problems with IM's alternatives, since both e-mail and voice mail messages are frequently ignored. For example, a recent study found that more than 60 percent of business phone calls never reach their intended recipients. And there is another big reason for the recent conversion of big companies to IM: IM software and services suppliers now bundle additional enterprise collaboration tools with the traditional instant messaging technology.

"[Lotus] Sametime allows me to have an instant meeting by bringing several different people into a chat spontaneously," says Altman. The only requirement is that they all be online. "And I can say, 'Let me draw a picture to show you what I mean,'" she adds, referring to Sametime's tools for incorporating whiteboarding for sharing diagrams and other notations, as well as audio and video, in IM chats. Another feature creates transcripts of the message threads, which can be saved to keep a record of the meeting.

IM does have a downside. Chats can easily get out of control, resulting in so many pop-ups on your computer screen that real work is all but impossible. "If I really need to get work done, I go invisible," Altman says, referring to the option that allows users to appear as if they are off-line so that other people won't contact them. But if everyone is invisible on the system, the information network breaks down.

Simple IM etiquette helps avoid such snafus. "Start off a conversation with a quick, 'Do you have a moment?'" suggests Altman. "By asking permission, you help set a standard of cooperation and productivity." In any case, for Altman's team, the new IM system works so well that there's no going back to e-mail.

Case Study Questions

1. Why have many companies been reluctant to support instant messaging in the workplace?

2. What are the advantages of instant messaging over e-mail and voice mail for enterprise collaboration?

3. Do you recommend that companies encourage and support the use of IM tools for enterprise collaboration? Why or why not?

Source: Adapted from Mathew Schwartz, "The Instant Messaging Debate," *Computerworld*, January 7, 2002, pp. 40–41. Reprinted with permission from *Computerworld*; and Allison Overholt, "The Art of Multitasking," *Fast Company*, October 2002, pp. 118–124.

CHAPTER 6

APPLICATIONS IN BUSINESS AND MANAGEMENT

ENTERPRISE e-BUSINESS SYSTEMS

Chapter Highlights

Learning Objectives

After reading and studying this chapter, you should be able to:

Identify and give examples to illustrate the following aspects of customer relationship management, enterprise resource management, and supply chain management systems:

a. Business processes supported

b. Customer and business value provided

c. Potential challenges and trends

Customer Relationship Management: The Business Focus

Introduction

Today, customers are in charge. It is easier than ever for customers to comparison shop and, with a click of the mouse, to switch companies. As a result, customer relationships have become a company's most valued asset. These relationships are worth more than the company's products, stores, factories, web addresses, and even employees. Every company's strategy should address how to find and retain the most profitable customers possible [8].

The primary business value of customer relationships today is indisputable. That's why we emphasized in Chapter 2 that becoming a *customer-focused business* was one of the top business strategies that can be supported by information technology. Thus, many companies are implementing **customer relationship management** **(CRM)** business initiatives and information systems as part of a customer-focused or *customer centric* strategy to improve their chances for success in today's competitive business environment. In this section, we will explore basic CRM concepts and technologies, as well as examples of the benefits and challenges faced by companies that have implemented CRM systems as part of their customer-focused business strategy. Let's start with a real world example.

Analyzing Mitsubishi Motor Sales

Read the Real World Case on Mitsubishi Motor Sales on the next page. We can learn a lot about the many ways companies are implementing customer relationship management systems. See Figure 6.1.

Mitsubishi Motor Sales realized their business lacked a customer focus and decided to change that through a customer relationship management initiative. The CRM project involved acquiring and installing the hardware, software, network, and

FIGURE 6.1
Greg O'Neill is executive vice president and general manager of Mitsubishi Motor Sales of America and led the implementation of their customer relationship management initiative.

Source: Mark Robert Halper.

Mitsubishi Motor Sales: Implementing Customer Relationship Management Systems

Until the late 1990s, Mitsubishi Motor Sales of America Inc. (www.mitsucars.com) was only about cars, and its approach to retail customer service reflected that. There were more than 18 toll-free customer service numbers that callers had to navigate to find information on topics ranging from financing to sales to repairs. "We were fragmented in our approach, and we clearly lacked a customer focus," says Greg O'Neill, executive vice president and general manager.

Mitsubishi decided to change that. In the spring of 1999, as part of a companywide shift to an increased focus on customers, executives challenged the call center to provide "one voice and one set of ears for the customer," says CIO Tony Romero. That was the beginning of a continuing drive toward improved customer service through a customer relationship management (CRM) initiative that would eventually engage multiple departments and 18 vendors.

Today, Mitsubishi has one call center and an outsourced service provider that handles the most basic calls. The cost per call has decreased by about two-thirds, and that savings alone paid for the system in 18 months, according to Rich Donnelson, director of customer relations. The system saves agents time and uncertainty and enabled the call center to handle 38 percent more volume in 2001 than in 2000, with an even staffing level. Meanwhile, the company's customer satisfaction rate rose by 8 percent, according to a survey by J. D. Power and Associates.

Mitsubishi's call center project team included members from its sales, marketing, finance, and IT departments, all of which contributed resources as needed. Early on, the team members established some rules of the road. First, they would selectively choose best-of-breed CRM software components, not the integrated CRM suites that seemed intent on force-fitting Mitsubishi's needs into fixed product offerings. But that required a constant struggle to keep 18 vendors heading in the same direction.

The team members also decided to implement changes slowly, adding a technology only when all employees were using the last one implemented. This approach allowed call center agents to get comfortable with the new technology over time. To accommodate the deliberate, modular approach, all products had to pass the "three S" test: Is it simple? Does it satisfy? Is it scalable? "If we couldn't answer yes to all three, we didn't do it," says Greg Stahl, Mitsubishi's director of advertising.

The journey began in earnest in June 1999, when Mitsubishi chose to outsource its most basic level of customer calls to Baltimore-based Sitel Corp. Within two months, Mitsubishi's 18 toll-free customer numbers and the multiple call centers behind them were consolidated, and call center software from Siebel Systems was implemented. Also, as part of the companywide customer focus, a new customer-centric database was consolidated in-house the next year. The database

became the engine powering the call center, but unfortunately, dirty data were a major stumbling block. The project stalled for months as the data were cleansed and updated.

In early 2001, a digital phone switch from Avaya Inc. was installed that allowed flexible skills-based call routing. Callers to the single toll-free number were routed based on menu choices. About half the callers got the information they needed from an interactive voice response unit, which can answer fairly sophisticated queries without live contact. Simple calls went to Sitel, and the rest were routed to call center agents with the appropriate skills. In March 2001, graphical user interface upgrades put 11 screens' worth of customer information on one screen of call center agents. And Smart Scripts workflow software from Siebel provided agents with decision-tree scripts and automated customer correspondence.

In May 2001, Mitsubishi managers began listening to outsourced service calls, and they could see agents' screens with Avaya IP Agent software. The next month, the company started using workforce management software from Blue Pumpkin Software to hourly forecast call center coverage. Then NiceLog software from Nice Systems was installed to record agents' voice and screen activity for quality assurance and training.

Aside from happier customers, the benefits to call center employees include career growth and higher pay. Previously, agents in separate call centers handled specific areas: accounts, vehicles, titles, or retailer queries. Now the silos are gone and agents can learn new skills in multiple areas, greatly increasing call center flexibility. The workforce management software schedules training time during lags, and agents who learn multiple skills earn more money. Call center turnover, which has traditionally been more than 20 percent, was about 7 percent last year.

O'Neill says the executive team members regularly listen in on service calls to get a feel for customer concerns, and they act on what they hear. "That bubble up of information has driven more early marketing decisions and made us more effective earlier on than I could have ever thought," O'Neill says. "That's been a huge dividend."

Case Study Questions

1. What are the key application components of Mitsubishi's CRM system? What is the business purpose of each of them?

2. What are the benefits to a business and its customers of a CRM system like Mitsubishi's?

3. Do you approve of Mitsubishi's approach to acquiring and installing its CRM system? Why or why not?

Source: Adapted from "Driven to Better Service," *Computerworld,* July 8, 2002, pp. 40–41. Reprinted with permission from *Computerworld.*

data resources from 18 vendors needed to create and support one central call center system that would provide superior service to all customers, prospects, and other callers. The team of sales, marketing, finance, and IT professionals who directed the project decided to install individual CRM software components (instead of an integrated CRM suite) using a slow, phased development approach so employees could be properly trained in each new application. The new system has produced many benefits, including increased customer satisfaction, major cost savings, increased call handling capabilities and capacity, improved employee morale, decreased employee turnover, and valuable customer and marketing information for Mitsubishi management.

What Is CRM?

Managing the full range of the customer relationship involves two related objectives: one, to provide the organization and all of its customer-facing employees with a single, complete view of every customer at every touch point and across all channels; and, two, to provide the customer with a single, complete view of the company and its extended channels [23].

That's why companies are turning to **customer relationship management** to help them become customer-focused businesses. CRM uses information technology to create a cross-functional enterprise system that integrates and automates many of the *customer serving* processes in sales, marketing, and customer services that interact with a company's customers. CRM systems also create an IT framework of Web-enabled software and databases that integrates these processes with the rest of a company's business operations. CRM systems include a family of software modules that provides the tools that enable a business and its employees to provide fast, convenient, dependable, and consistent service to its customers. Siebel Systems, Oracle, PeopleSoft, SAP AG, and Epiphany are some of the leading vendors of CRM software. Figure 6.2 illustrates some of the major application components of a CRM system. Let's take a look at each of them.

Contact and Account Management

CRM software helps sales, marketing, and service professionals capture and track relevant data about every past and planned contact with prospects and customers, as

FIGURE 6.2

The major application clusters in customer relationship management.

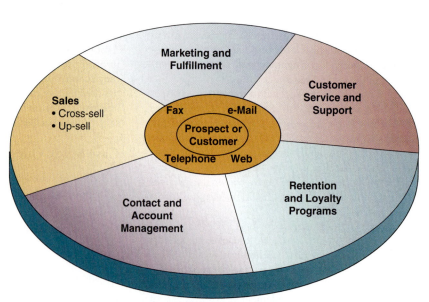

Source: Adapted from Ravi Kalakota and Marcia Robinson, *E-Business 2.0: Roadmap for Success* (Reading, MA: Addison-Wesley, 2001), p. 180. © 2001 Addison-Wesley Publishing Company, Inc. Reprinted by permission of Addison-Wesley Longman, Inc.

well as other business and life cycle events of customers. Information is captured from all customer touchpoints, such as telephone, fax, e-mail, the company's website, retail stores, kiosks, and personal contact. CRM systems store the data in a common customer database that integrates all customer account information and makes it available throughout the company via Internet, intranet, or other network links for sales, marketing, service, and other CRM applications.

Sales

A CRM system provides sales reps with the software tools and company data sources they need to support and manage their sales activities, and optimize cross-selling and up-selling. Examples include sales prospect and product information, product configuration, and sales quote generation capabilities. CRM also gives them real-time access to a single common view of the customer, enabling them to check on all aspects of a customer's account status and history before scheduling their sales calls. For example, a CRM system would alert a bank sales rep to call customers who make large deposits to sell them premier credit or investment services. Or it would alert a salesperson of unresolved service, delivery, or payment problems that could be resolved through a personal contact with a customer.

Marketing and Fulfillment

CRM systems help marketing professionals accomplish direct marketing campaigns by automating such tasks as qualifying leads for targeted marketing, and scheduling and tracking direct marketing mailings. Then the CRM software helps marketing professionals capture and manage prospect and customer response data in the CRM database, and analyze the customer and business value of a company's direct marketing campaigns. CRM also assists in the fulfillment of prospect and customer responses and requests by quickly scheduling sales contacts and providing appropriate information on products and services to them, while capturing relevant information for the CRM database.

Customer Service and Support

A CRM system provides service reps with software tools and real-time access to the common customer database shared by sales and marketing professionals. CRM helps customer service managers create, assign, and manage requests for service by customers. *Call center* software routes calls to customer support agents based on their skills and authority to handle specific kinds of service requests. *Help desk* software assists customer service reps in helping customers who are having problems with a product or service, by providing relevant service data and suggestions for resolving problems. Web-based self-service enables customers to easily access personalized support information at the company website, while giving them an option to receive further assistance online or by phone from customer service personnel.

Retention and Loyalty Programs

- It costs six times more to sell to a new customer than to sell to an existing one.
- A typical dissatisfied customer will tell eight to ten people about his or her experience.
- A company can boost its profits 85 percent by increasing its annual customer retention by only 5 percent.
- The odds of selling a product to a new customer are 15 percent, whereas the odds of selling a product to an existing customer are 50 percent.
- Seventy percent of complaining customers will do business with the company again if it quickly takes care of a service snafu [8].

That's why enhancing and optimizing customer retention and loyalty is a major business strategy and primary objective of customer relationship management. CRM systems try to help a company identify, reward, and market to their most loyal and profitable customers. CRM analytical software includes data mining tools and other analytical marketing software, while CRM databases may consist of a customer data warehouse and CRM data marts. These tools are used to identify profitable and loyal

FIGURE 6.3   A proposed report format for evaluating the customer retention performance of Charles Schwab & Co.

	Navigation	Performance	Operations	Environment
Customer Retention	Customer retention rate Household retention rate Average customer tenure	Retention rate by customer cohort Retention rate by customer segment Customer loyalty rating	Percentage of customers who are active Web users Percentage of customers who interact via e-mail Decline in customer activity Propensity to defect	Competitors' offers Share of portfolio Comparative retention Comparative customer tenure
Customer Experience	Satisfaction by customer segment Satisfaction by cohort Satisfaction by customer scenario	Customer satisfaction by: • Task • Touchpoint • Channel partner End-to-end performance by scenario Customer satisfaction with quality of information provided	Elapsed time for commonly performed tasks Accuracy of Web search results Percentage of trades executed with price improvement Percentage of e-mails answered accurately in one hour	Comparative satisfaction: Competitors: • Other online brokers • Other financial service firms • All products and services
Customer Spending	Average revenue per customer Average profitability per customer Growth in customer assets Customer lifetime value	Revenues per customer segment Profits per customer segment Growth in customer assets per segment	Daily logins at market opening Revenue trades per day Percentage increase in customer assets Cost to serve by touchpoint	Total brokerage assets Growth in brokerage assets

Source: Adapted from Patricia Seybold, *The Customer Revolution* (New York, Crown Business, 2001), p. 225.

customers and direct and evaluate a company's targeted marketing and relationship marketing programs toward them. Figure 6.3 is an example of part of a proposed Web-based report format for evaluating Charles Schwab & Co.'s customer retention performance.

Telstra Corporation: The Business Value of CRM	Australia's Telstra Corporation provides fixed, wireless, and e-commerce services to a customer base in nineteen countries. In addition, Telstra offers voice, data, Internet, multimedia, managed communications services, and customer-contact center solutions globally through its strategic alliances and partnerships. The Melbourne company is Australia's largest communications carrier and the clear market leader. To succeed in transforming its relationship with its customers, Telstra determined that it needed a CRM solution that would provide both its customer-facing employees and channel partners a single view of each customer relationship. The solution would also require the integration of more than twenty core legacy billing and operations databases across all of its product lines. After exploring several options, Telstra chose a variety of Siebel Systems products to provide its e-business solution. For its initial deployment, Telstra rolled out a Siebel Call Center to more than 250 telesales representatives and 150 telephone account managers in its outbound call centers, which are geographically dispersed throughout Australia. "This was

where we could most quickly impact our business," explains Ross Riddoch, general manager of Retail Technology Products. "We rolled out account, contact, and opportunity management modules." This Siebel CRM product was deployed in approximately three months, on time and on budget.

User acceptance and business benefits quickly followed. "Users found Siebel Call Center's Web-based interface to be extremely intuitive and easy to use," says Riddoch. "This enabled us to reduce our training time and get our users up to speed in record time. Within four months of employing Siebel Call Center, our account management team doubled its weekly revenue, and we achieved a three-fold gain in employee productivity" [22].

The Three Phases of CRM

Figure 6.4 illustrates another way to think about the customer and business value and components of customer relationship management. We can view CRM as an integrated system of Web-enabled software tools and databases accomplishing a variety of customer-focused business processes that support the three phases of the relationship between a business and its customers [8].

- **Acquire.** A business relies on CRM software tools and databases to help it acquire new customers by doing a superior job of contact management, sales prospecting, selling, direct marketing, and fulfillment. The goal of these CRM functions is to help customers perceive the value of a superior product offered by an outstanding company.

- **Enhance.** Web-enabled CRM account management and customer service and support tools help keep customers happy by supporting superior service from a responsive networked team of sales and service specialists and business partners. And CRM sales force automation and direct marketing and fulfillment tools help companies cross-sell and up-sell to their customers, thus increasing their profitability to the business. The value perceived by customers is the convenience of one-stop shopping at attractive prices.

FIGURE 6.4

How CRM supports the three phases of the relationship between a business and its customers.

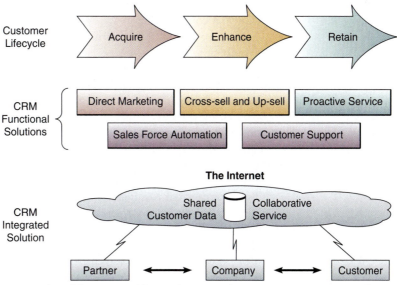

Source: Adapted from Ravi Kalakota and Marcia Robinson, *E-Business 2.0 Roadmap for Success* (Reading, MA: Addison-Wesley, 2001), p. 179 © 2001 Addison-Wesley Publishing Company, Inc. Reprinted by permission of Addison-Wesley Longman Inc.; and Craig Fellentstein and Ron Wood, *Exploring E-commerce, Global E-business, and E-societies* (Upper Saddle River, NJ: Prentice-Hall, 2000), p. 192.

- **Retain.** CRM analytical software and databases help a company proactively identify and reward its most loyal and profitable customers to retain and expand their business via targeted marketing and relationship marketing programs. The value perceived by customers is of a rewarding personalized business relationship with "their company."

Benefits and Challenges of CRM

The potential business benefits of customer relationship management are many. For example, CRM allows a business to identify and target their best customers—those who are the most profitable to the business—so they can be retained as lifelong customers for greater and more profitable services. It makes possible real-time customization and personalization of products and services based on customer wants, needs, buying habits, and life cycles. CRM can also keep track of when a customer contacts the company, regardless of the contact point. And CRM systems can enable a company to provide a consistent customer experience and superior service and support across all the contact points a customer chooses. All of these benefits would provide strategic business value to a company and major customer value to its customers [5, 6, 7].

Boise Cascade: Success in Customer Service

Boise Cascade Office Products (BCOP) is a $4 billion subsidiary of paper giant Boise Cascade, and a purveyor to large and midsize businesses of everything from paper to paper clips to office furniture. About two years ago, the company had its "eureka" moment. "Here we had tons of data on our customers and were doing nothing with it," says senior VP for Marketing Dave Goudge, the leader of BCOP's customer data initiative. "We could distinguish ourselves in an increasingly competitive industry by collecting that data in one place, organizing it, and then using it to create great customer service."

Easier said than done. For starters, BCOP's customer information was buried in dozens of separate databases that couldn't speak to one another. Liberating that data and installing a new customer relationship management (CRM) system without disrupting BCOP's ongoing business would be challenge enough. But the organizational hurdles were higher still. For BCOP to make full use of its data, service representatives would have to learn to sell, territorial sales reps would have to share data on their clients, and once-autonomous brands within BCOP would have to be consolidated.

Still, phase one of the initiative dubbed One Boise went into effect on April 1, 2001, on time and within 1 percent of the $20 million the firm had budgeted—and life began to get dramatically easier for BCOP clients. Now when you call to place an order (or log on—about 18 percent of sales come via the Web), you key up an identifying number and are soon greeted by name by a rep whose screen shows all of your most recent BCOP interactions. Based on your past dealings with the company, your call might get special routing—to a specialist in a particular kind of merchandise, say, or to a Spanish-speaking rep—all before the rep even picks up the phone.

Lost on the website? Click "Need Assistance?" and a pop-up screen asks whether you would like help by instant message or by phone. Choose the former and a rep will be on your screen immediately. Choose the latter and the phone will ring within 30 seconds. "BCOP has taken much of the aggravation out of ordering supplies," says Bob Powell, purchasing manager at Citizens Banking Corp., an $8 billion Midwestern bank [20].

CRM Failures

The business benefits of customer relationship management are not guaranteed and, instead, have proven elusive at many companies. Surveys by industry research groups include a report that over 50 percent of CRM projects did not produce the results that were promised. In another research report, 20 percent of businesses surveyed reported that CRM implementations had actually damaged long-standing customer relationships. And in a survey of senior management satisfaction with 25 management tools, CRM ranked near the bottom in user satisfaction, even though 72 percent expected to have CRM systems implemented shortly [18].

What is the reason for such a high rate of failure or dissatisfaction with CRM initiatives? Research shows that the major reason is a familiar one: lack of understanding and preparation. That is, too often, business managers rely on a major new application of information technology (like CRM) to solve a business problem without first developing the business process changes and change management programs that are required. For example, in many cases, failed CRM projects were implemented without the participation of the business stakeholders involved. Therefore, employees and customers were not prepared for the new processes or challenges that were part of the new CRM implementation. We will discuss the topic of failures in information technology management, system implementation, and change management further in Chapters 9 and 12.

Gevity HR and Monster.com: Failures in CRM Implementation	No amount of high-level cooperation will protect a CRM project from rank-and-file employees who hate it. Lisa Harris, CIO at HR-services firm Gevity HR based in Bradenton, Florida, faced rebellion from the staff when she installed Oracle CRM software that helped solve some customers' problems online—without the help of a live operator. Call-center employees felt that the software threatened their jobs, so they quietly discouraged customers from using it. "Our operators would say, 'Wouldn't you rather call up? I'll take care of everything you need,'" Harris says. She stuck with the online CRM, but also belatedly began talking to employees about software. She changed their work routines to include more customer hand-holding and less data entry, which was increasingly done online.

CRM software is complex to install because it often touches many different legacy systems. Harris says she spent millions of dollars integrating a CRM application in 1997 for a previous employer. But when the project was finished, it took operators too long to get data on screen. The company had bogged down the performance of the new CRM implementation by trying to integrate too many complex business systems. The project ended up a total failure, she says [2].

And when Monster.com rolled out a CRM program in 1998, it was sure it had a new money-making strategy on its hands. The Massachusetts-based job-listings company had invested over $1 million in customized software and integrated all its computer systems in an attempt to boost the efficiency of its sales force. These CRM applications had been specially developed to allow Monster.com's sales representatives instant access to data for prospective customers.

However, the new system proved to be frighteningly slow—so slow, in fact, that salespeople in the field found themselves unable to download customer information from the company's databases onto their laptops. Every time they tried, their machines froze. Eventually, Monster.com was forced to rebuild the entire system. It lost millions of dollars along the way, not to mention the goodwill of both customers and employees [18].

Trends in CRM

Increasingly, enterprises must create tighter collaborative linkages with partners, suppliers, and customers, squeezing out time and costs while enhancing the customer experience and the total value proposition [19].

Figure 6.5 outlines four types or categories of CRM that are being implemented by many companies today and summarizes their benefits to a business. These

FIGURE 6.5   Many companies are implementing CRM systems with some or all of these capabilities.

Types of CRM	Business Value
Operational CRM	• Supports customer interaction with greater convenience through a variety of channels, including phone, fax, e-mail, chat, and mobile devices • Synchronizes customer interactions consistently across all channels • Makes your company easier to do business with
Analytical CRM	• Extracts in-depth customer history, preferences, and profitability information from your data warehouse and other databases • Allows you to analyze, predict, and derive customer value and behavior and forecast demand • Lets you approach your customers with relevant information and offers that are tailored to their needs
Collaborative CRM	• Enables easy collaboration with customers, suppliers, and partners • Improves efficiency and integration throughout the supply chain • Allows greater responsiveness to customer needs through sourcing of products and services outside of your enterprise
Portal-based CRM	• Provides all users with the tools and information that fit their individual roles and preferences • Empowers all employees to respond to customer demands more quickly and become truly customer focused • Provides the capability to instantly access, link, and use all internal and external customer information

Source: Adapted from mySAP Customer Relationship Management, mySAP.com, 2001, p. 7; and Brian Caulfield, "Toward a More Perfect (and Realistic) E-Business," *Business 2.0*, January 2002, p. 80.

categories may also be viewed as stages or trends in how many companies implement CRM applications, and also outlines some of the capabilities of CRM software products. Most businesses start out with *operational* CRM systems such as sales force automation and customer service centers. Then *analytical* CRM applications are implemented using several analytical marketing tools, such as data mining, to extract vital data about customers and prospects for targeted marketing campaigns.

Increasingly, businesses are moving to *collaborative* CRM systems, to involve business partners as well as customers in collaborative customer services. This includes systems for customer self-service and feedback, as well as **partner relationship management** (PRM) systems. PRM applications apply many of the same tools used in CRM systems to enhance collaboration between a company and its business partners, such as distributors and dealers, to better coordinate and optimize sales and service to customers across all marketing channels. Finally, many businesses are building Internet, intranet, and extranet Web-based CRM portals as a common gateway for various levels of access to all customer information, as well as operational, analytical, and collaborative CRM tools for customers, employees, and business partners [3, 8]. Let's look at a real world example.

Telstra Corporation: Expanding the Scope of CRM	The success of Telstra's initial implementation of a CRM system led the company to expands its CRM deployment to target four work streams: sales and account management, commissions, order fulfillment, and marketing. Based on this strategy, Telstra is now managing seven concurrent projects and rolling out e-business applications to the majority of its field sales, call center, telesales, and business partners. Within its marketing organization, for example, Telstra has deployed Siebel Marketing and Siebel eAnalytics applications to more than 80 marketing

professionals. These CRM applications enable Telstra's marketing managers to perform customer segmentation analysis using customer information from across all touchpoints and create targeted campaigns that effectively reach their customers through call centers, direct mail, and e-mail. They also help Telstra manage, analyze, and track channel and marketing effectiveness through real-time reporting, enabling the company to continually refine its marketing efforts across all channels.

To better integrate partners into its channel system, Telstra also is deploying Siebel eChannel—a Web-based partner relationship management portal for communication of customer and sales data between Telstra and its many business partners. By integrating its channel partners into its CRM system, Telstra wants to ensure that it maintains a seamless view of the customer across all points of interaction between customers, partners, and Telstra customer-facing professionals [22].

SECTION II Enterprise Resource Planning: The Business Backbone

Introduction

What do Microsoft, Coca-Cola, Cisco, Eli Lilly, Alcoa, and Nokia have in common? Unlike most businesses, which operate on 25-year-old back-office systems, these market leaders reengineered their businesses to run at breakneck speed by implementing a transactional backbone called enterprise resource planning (ERP). These companies credit their ERP systems with having helped them reduce inventories, shorten cycle times, lower costs, and improve overall operations [8].

Businesses of all kinds have now implemented **enterprise resource planning** (ERP) systems. ERP serves as a cross-functional enterprise backbone that integrates and automates many internal business processes and information systems within the manufacturing, logistics, distribution, accounting, finance, and human resource functions of a company. Large companies throughout the world began installing ERP systems in the 1990s as a conceptual framework and catalyst for reengineering their business processes. ERP also served as the vital software engine needed to integrate and accomplish the cross-functional processes that resulted. Now, ERP is recognized as a necessary ingredient that many companies need in order to gain the efficiency, agility, and responsiveness required to succeed in today's dynamic business environment.

Analyzing Agilent Technologies and Russ Berrie

Read the Real World Case on Agilent Technologies and Russ Berrie on the next page. We can learn a lot about the major challenges businesses face when implementing ERP systems. See Figure 6.6.

Agilent Technologies is a large multinational company and high-tech maker of telecommunications and scientific equipment. Yet it appears to have been poorly prepared for a major change in key internal business systems when it began its implementation of a new Oracle ERP system. The ERP system failure resulted in a loss of $105 million in revenue and $70 million in profits. Agilent business and IT

FIGURE 6.6
Agilent Technologies President and CEO Ned Barnholt said the company did not expect the extensive business disruptions caused by their ERP implementation.

Source: Paul Sakuma/AP/Wide World.

Agilent Technologies and Russ Berrie: Challenges of Implementing ERP Systems

The good news is that Agilent Technologies Inc. (www.agilent.com) says its enterprise resource planning applications are stable. The bad news is they got that way only after a rocky ERP migration project that cost the company $105 million in revenue and $70 million in profits.

In mid-August 2002, the multinational communications and life sciences company, formerly a part of Hewlett-Packard Co., said problems with the ERP components in Oracle's e-Business Suite 11e software froze production for the equivalent of a week, leading to the massive losses. The Oracle system, part of which went live in June, handles about half of the company's worldwide production of test, measurement, and monitoring products and almost all of its financial operations, as well as functions such as order handling and shipping.

Agilent is in the process of migrating as many as 2,200 legacy applications that it inherited from HP to Oracle. As part of the switchover, approximately 6,000 orders in the internally developed legacy systems had to be converted to an Oracle-friendly format, an Agilent spokeswoman said from company headquarters in Palo Alto, California. She said the configuration process had problems requiring correction.

In a statement last week, Agilent President and CEO Ned Barnholt said the disruptions to the business after implementing the ERP system were "more extensive than we expected." An Agilent spokeswoman said the issue wasn't the quality of the Oracle application, but rather the "very complex nature of the enterprise resource planning implementation."

For its part, Oracle Corp. said it's working closely with Agilent. "At Oracle, we are fully committed to all of our customers for the long haul and support them in any way necessary," the company said in a statement. "We have a strong relationship with Agilent, and both companies believe the implementation is stable."

Agilent also had a take-away lesson: "Enterprise resource planning implementations are a lot more than software packages," the company said in a statement. "They are a fundamental transformation of a company's business processes. People, processes, policies, the company's culture are all factors that should be taken into consideration when implementing a major enterprise system."

According to one analyst, ERP disasters are often caused by the user company itself. Joshua Greenbaum, an analyst at Enterprise Applications Consulting, said 99 percent of such rollout fiascoes are caused by "management's inability to spec out their own requirements and the implementer's inability to implement those specs."

Russ Berrie and Co. After a three-year saga that included a $10.3 million financial hit from the failed installation of packaged applications, teddy bear maker Russ Berrie and Co. (www.russberrie.com) is taking another crack at replacing its legacy business systems. The Oakland, New Jersey–based distributor of toys and gifts last week finalized plans to roll out J. D. Edwards & Co.'s OneWorld Xe suite of enterprise resource planning (ERP), customer relationship management, and financial applications. The multimillion-dollar project is scheduled to be done in phases over the next 18 months.

Russ Berrie CIO Michael Saunders said that the company, which had sales of $225 million during the first nine months of 2001, hopes the OneWorld System will help it reach $1 billion in annual revenue in the coming years. Within the next 12 months, he said, Russ Berrie plans to begin installing the applications one department at a time, starting with a stand-alone implementation in purchasing. "We're not going big bang," Saunders said. "We're mitigating implementation risks by taking a phased-in approach."

The company has reason to be cautious. Three years ago, a Y2K-related migration from its homegrown distribution, financial, and customer service systems to packaged ERP applications experienced major system failures. Saunders said the problems were severe enough for Russ Berrie to take many of the new applications off-line and return to their old systems. Saunders wouldn't identify the software vendors that were involved in the failed implementation, but sources said that SAP AG's applications were part of the 1999 project. A spokesman at SAP confirmed that Russ Berrie was one of its customers, but he declined to offer further details because of pending litigation between the two companies.

Joshua Greenbaum of Enterprise Applications Consulting said it appears that Russ Berrie "bit off more than they could chew" on the 1999 project. Companywide rollouts are especially risky for midsize businesses like Russ Berrie, Greenbaum said.

Case Study Questions

1. What are the main reasons companies experience failures in implementing ERP systems?

2. What are several key things companies should do to avoid ERP systems failures? Explain the reasons for your proposals.

3. Why do you think ERP systems in particular are often cited as examples of failures in IT systems development, implementation, or management?

Source: Adapted from Marc Songini, "ERP Effort Sinks Agilent Revenue," *Computerworld*, August 26, 2002, pp. 1, 12; and Marc Songini, "Teddy Bear Maker Prepares for Second Attempt at ERP Rollout," *Computerworld*, February 4, 2002, p. 16. Reprinted with permission from *Computerworld*.

management obviously failed to properly plan and implement for "a fundamental transformation of a company's business processes."

Russ Berrie is attempting another installation of ERP software after a major failure in an ERP implementation project three years ago. However, this time, they are doing a phased implementation, one department at a time, of J. D. Edwards ERP software. Three years earlier they had attempted a companywide implementation of an ERP system from SAP AG, which experienced major system failures. Russ Berrie is still suing SAP for failure to properly fulfill the contract for that ERP installation, though an ERP consultant contends that Russ Berrie was not adequately prepared for a companywide ERP implementation at that time.

What Is ERP?

ERP is the technological backbone of e-business, an enterprise-wide transaction framework with links into sales order processing, inventory management and control, production and distribution planning, and finance [8].

Enterprise resource planning is a cross-functional enterprise system driven by an integrated suite of software modules that supports the basic internal business processes of a company. For example, ERP software for a manufacturing company will typically process the data from and track the status of sales, inventory, shipping, and invoicing, as well as forecast raw material and human resource requirements. Figure 6.7 presents the major application components of an ERP system. Figure 6.8 illustrates some of the key cross-functional business processes and supplier and customer information flows supported by ERP systems.

ERP gives a company an integrated real-time view of its core business processes, such as production, order processing, and inventory management, tied together by the ERP application software and a common database maintained by a database management system. ERP systems track business resources (such as cash, raw materials, and production capacity), and the status of commitments made by the business (such as customer orders, purchase orders, and employee payroll), no matter which department (manufacturing, purchasing sales, accounting, etc.) has entered the data into the system [19].

ERP software suites typically consist of integrated modules of manufacturing, distribution, sales, accounting, and human resource applications. Examples of manufacturing processes supported are material requirements planning, production planning, and capacity planning. Some of the sales and marketing processes supported by ERP are sales analysis, sales planning, and pricing analysis, while typical distribution

FIGURE 6.7

The major application components of enterprise resource planning demonstrate the cross-functional approach of ERP systems.

Source: Adapted from Ravi Kalakota and Marcia Robinson, *E-Business 2.0: Roadmap for Success* (Reading, MA: Addison-Wesley, 2001), p. 243. © 2001 Addison-Wesley Publishing Company, Inc. Reprinted by permission of Addison-Wesley Longman, Inc.

FIGURE 6.8   Some of the business process flows and customer and supplier information flows supported by ERP systems.

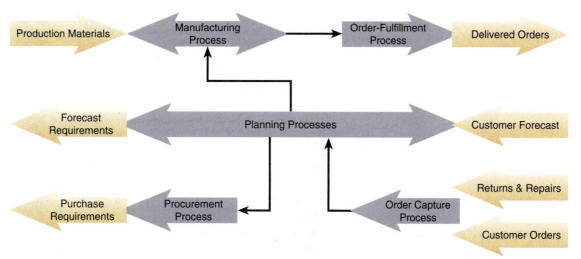

Source: Adapted from Grant Norris, James Hurley, Kenneth Hartley, John Dunleavy, and John Balls, *E-Business and ERP: Transforming the Enterprise*, p. 83. Copyright. © 2000 by John Wiley & Sons, Inc. Reprinted by permission.

applications include order management, purchasing, and logistics planning. ERP systems support many vital human resource processes, from personnel requirements planning to salary and benefits administration, and accomplish most required financial record-keeping and managerial accounting applications. Figure 6.9 illustrates the processes supported by the ERP system installed by the Colgate-Palmolive Company. Let's take a closer look at their experience with ERP.

Colgate-Palmolive: The Business Value of ERP	Colgate-Palmolive is a global consumer products company that implemented the SAP R/3 enterprise resource planning system. Colgate embarked on an implementation of SAP R/3 to allow the company to access more timely and accurate data, get the most out of working capital, and reduce manufacturing costs. An important factor for Colgate was whether it could use the software across the entire spectrum of the business. Colgate needed the ability to coordinate globally and act locally. The implementation of SAP across the Colgate supply chain contributed to increased profitability. Now installed in operations that produce most of Colgate's worldwide sales, SAP was expanded to all Colgate divisions worldwide during 2001. Global efficiencies in purchasing—combined with product and packaging standardization—also produced large savings.

- Before ERP, it took Colgate U.S. anywhere from one to five days to acquire an order, and another one to two days to process the order. Now, order acquisition and processing combined takes four hours, not up to seven days. Distribution planning and picking used to take up to four days; today, it takes 14 hours. In total, the order-to-delivery time has been cut in half.

- Before ERP, on-time deliveries used to occur only 91.5 percent of the time, and cases ordered were delivered correctly 97.5 percent of the time. After R/3 the figures are 97.5 percent and 99.0 percent, respectively.

- After ERP domestic inventories have dropped by one-third and receivables outstanding have dropped to 22.4 days from 31.4. Working capital as a percentage of sales has plummeted to 6.3 percent from 11.3 percent. Total delivered cost per case has been reduced by nearly 10 percent [8].

FIGURE 6.9   The business processes and functions supported by the ERP system implemented by the
Colgate-Palmolive Company.

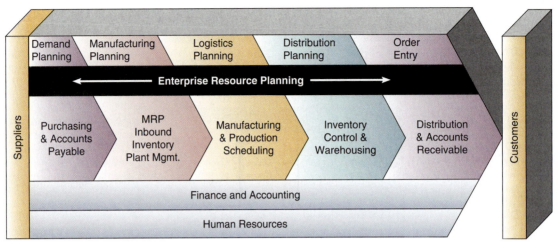

Source: Adapted from Ravi Kalakota and Marcia Robinson *E-Business 2.0: Roadmap for Success* (Reading, MA: Addison-Wesley,
2001), p. 259 © 2001 Addison-Wesley Publishing Company, Inc. Reprinted by permission of Addison-Wesley Longman, Inc.

Benefits and Challenges of ERP

As the example of Colgate-Palmolive has just shown, ERP systems can generate significant business benefits for a company. Many other companies have found major business value in their use of ERP in several basic ways [14].

- **Quality and Efficiency.** ERP creates a framework for integrating and improving a company's internal business processes that results in significant improvements in the quality and efficiency of customer service, production, and distribution.

- **Decreased Costs.** Many companies report significant reductions in transaction processing costs and hardware, software, and IT support staff compared to the nonintegrated legacy systems that were replaced by their new ERP systems.

- **Decision Support.** ERP provides vital cross-functional information on business performance quickly to managers to significantly improve their ability to make better decisions in a timely manner across the entire business enterprise.

- **Enterprise Agility.** Implementing ERP systems breaks down many former departmental and functional walls or "silos" of business processes, information systems, and information resources. This results in more flexible organizational structures, managerial responsibilities, and work roles, and therefore a more agile and adaptive organization and workforce that can more easily capitalize on new business opportunities.

The Costs of ERP

An ERP implementation is like the corporate equivalent of a brain transplant. We pulled the plug on every company application and moved to PeopleSoft software. The risk was certainly disruption of business, because if you do not do ERP properly, you can kill your company, guaranteed [8].

So says Jim Prevo, CIO of Green Mountain Coffee of Vermont, commenting on their successful implementation of an ERP system. Though the benefits of ERP are many, the costs and risks are also considerable, as we will continue to see in some of the real world cases and examples in the text. Figure 6.10 illustrates the relative size and types of costs of implementing an ERP system in a company. Notice that hardware and software costs are a small part of total costs, and that the costs of developing new business processes (reengineering) and preparing employees for the

FIGURE 6.10

Typical costs of implementing a new ERP system.

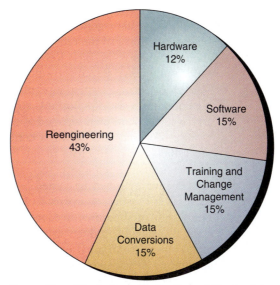

Source: Grant Norris, James Hurley, Kenneth Hartley, John Dunleavy, and John Balls, *E-Business and ERP: Transforming the Enterprise* (New York, John Wiley & Sons, 2000), p. 54.

new system (training and change management) make up the bulk of implementing a new ERP system. Converting data from previous legacy systems to the new cross-functional ERP system is another major category of ERP implementation costs [14].

The costs and risks of failure in implementing a new ERP system are substantial. Most companies have had successful ERP implementations, but a sizable minority of firms experienced spectacular and costly failures that heavily damaged their overall business. Big losses in revenue, profits, and market share resulted when core business processes and information systems failed, or did not work properly. In many cases, orders and shipments were lost, inventory changes were not recorded correctly, and unreliable inventory levels caused major stock-outs to occur for weeks or months. Companies like Hershey Foods, Nike, A-DEC, and Connecticut General sustained losses running into hundreds of millions of dollars in some instances. In the case of FoxMeyer Drugs, a $5 billion pharmaceutical wholesaler, the company had to file for bankruptcy protection, and then was bought out by its arch competitor McKesson Drugs [8]. Let's take a look at an example of a more recent failed ERP project.

Sobeys Inc.: Failure in ERP Implementation

SAP AG's software applications for retailers continue to be stung by a series of high-profile installation problems that many say illustrate the complexity of trying to fit an integrated suite of enterprise resource planning (ERP) software into a retail operation. A major example came late in January 2001, when Canadian supermarket chain Sobeys Inc. abandoned an $89.1 million SAP Retail implementation. "SAP Retail has insufficient core functionality . . . to effectively deal with the extremely high number of transactions in our retail operating environment," said Bill McEwan, president and CEO of the Stellarton, Nova Scotia–based retail chain.

Sobeys isn't alone. Jo-Ann Stores Inc. in Hudson, Ohio, and pet supply retailer Petsmart Inc. in Phoenix both attributed low financial results to problems with their SAP Retail rollouts. Both, however, said they're pleased with the system overall. SAP officials continued to defend the capabilities of SAP Retail. Geraldine McBride, general manager of the consumer sector business unit at SAP America Inc., said the German vendor has signed up 264 retailers as customers,

128 of which have gone live. But Greg Girard, an analyst at AMR Research in Boston, said most of the retailers are running SAP's financial and human resources applications, not the SAP Retail core ERP application itself. "I can't point to a single happy SAP Retail account in North America," said Girard.

Canada's second largest supermarket chain abandoned the $80 million implementation of SAP AG's business applications for retailers after a five-day database and systems shutdown affected the company's business operations for nearly a month. McEwan said during a conference that all "growing pains" expected by the 1,400-store retail chain in the two-year-old project became "in fact systemic problems of a much more serious nature." McEwan, who inherited the SAP implementation when he joined Sobeys in November 2000, added that it would have taken another two years to finish the software rollout.

The system shutdown in December 2000 resulted in "unprecedented" out-of-stock issues with products at many of Sobeys' corporate-owned stores, McEwan said. The disruption also forced Sobeys to implement work-arounds for its accounting department. Sobeys plans to replace the SAP applications with software that can be installed more quickly and that "will fully meet all the business requirements" at the company, McEwan said [13].

Causes of ERP Failures

What have been the major causes of failure in ERP projects? In almost every case, the business managers and IT professionals of these companies underestimated the complexity of the planning, development, and training that were needed to prepare for a new ERP system that would radically change their business processes and information systems. Failure to involve affected employees in the planning and development phases and change management programs, or trying to do too much too fast in the conversion process, were typical causes of failed ERP projects. Insufficient training in the new work tasks required by the ERP system, and failure to do enough data conversion and testing, were other causes of failure. In many cases, ERP failures were also due to overreliance by company or IT management on the claims of ERP software vendors or the assistance of prestigious consulting firms hired to lead the implementation [10]. The following experiences of companies that did it right give us a helpful look at what is needed for a successful ERP implementation.

Reebok and Home Depot: Success with ERP

SAP Retail is a good ERP product, argues Kevin Restivo, a Canada-based analyst who works for IDC in Framingham, Massachusetts. But technology is never a "silver bullet, just part of a larger puzzle" that includes making sure internal business processes are in tune with the software's capabilities, Restivo said. That's especially true given the processing complexities faced by retailers, he added.

In late 1998, Reebok International Ltd. was the first U.S. company to go live with SAP Retail, which now supports 115 outlet stores run by the Stoughton, Massachusetts–based footwear maker. Peter Burrows, Reebok's chief technology officer, said the SAP ERP system is producing "a very high level of stock accuracy" in the stores. But the yearlong development and installation process wasn't easy and required some adjustments as the project went along, Burrows said.

The Home Depot Inc. recently completed a SAP ERP installation in the company's Argentina operations. Gary Cochran, vice president of information services at the Atlanta-based home improvement retailer, said he made "limited use" of SAP's consulting services. Instead Cochran put together a team of fifty top employees—IT personnel and end users. Because of the team's familiarity with their traditional legacy systems, he said, it didn't have to "face some of the configuration issues that have been problematic for other people." "It went so smoothly there was literally no ripple in corporate organization," Cochran said [12].

Trends in ERP

Today, ERP is still evolving—adapting to developments in technology and the demands of the market. Four important trends are shaping ERP's continuing evolution: improvements in integration and flexibility, extensions to e-business applications, a broader reach to new users, and the adoption of Internet technologies [8].

Figure 6.11 illustrates four major developments and trends that are evolving in ERP applications [8, 11]. First, the ERP software packages that were the mainstay of ERP implementations in the 1990s, and were often criticized for their inflexibility, have gradually been modified into more flexible products. Companies who installed ERP systems pressured software vendors to adopt more open, flexible, standards-based software architectures. This makes the software easier to integrate with other application programs of business users, as well as making it easier to make minor modifications to suit a company's business processes. An example is SAP R/3 Enterprise, released in 2002 by SAP AG as a successor to earlier versions of SAP R3. Other leading ERP vendors, including Oracle, PeopleSoft, and J. D. Edwards, have also developed more flexible ERP products.

Web-enabling ERP software is a second development in the evolution of ERP. The growth of the Internet and corporate intranets and extranets prompted software companies to use Internet technologies to build Web interfaces and networking capabilities into ERP systems. These features make ERP systems easier to use and connect to other internal applications, as well as the systems of a company's business partners. This Internet connectivity led to the development of interenterprise ERP systems that provide Web-enabled links between key business systems (such as inventory and production) of a company and its customers, suppliers, distributors, and others. These external links signaled a move toward the integration of internal-facing ERP applications with the external-focused applications of supply chain management (SCM) and a company's supply chain partners. We will discuss supply chain management in Section III.

All of these developments have provided the business and technological momentum for the integration of ERP functions into **e-business suites.** The major ERP software companies have developed modular, Web-enabled software suites that integrate ERP, customer relationship management, supply chain management, procurement, decision support, enterprise portals, and other business applications and functions. Examples include Oracle's e-Business Suite and SAP's mySAP. Some e-business suites disassemble ERP components and integrate them into other modules, while

FIGURE 6.11

Trends in the evolution of ERP applications.

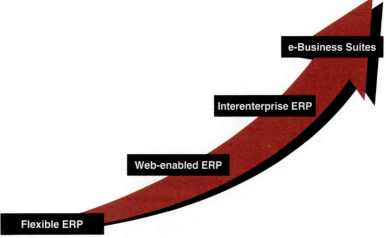

Source: Adapted from Ravi Kalakota and Marcia Robinson *E-Business 2.0: Roadmap for Success* (Reading, MA: Addison-Wesley, 2001), p. 244 © 2001 Addison-Wesley Publishing Company, Inc. Reprinted by permission of Addison-Wesley Longman, Inc.

FIGURE 6.12   The application components in Oracle's e-Business Suite software product.

ORACLE E-BUSINESS SUITE

Advanced Planning	Business Intelligence	Contracts
E-Commerce	Enterprise Asset Management	Exchanges
Financials	Human Resources	Interaction Center
Manufacturing	Marketing	Order Fulfillment
Procurement	Product Development	Professional Services Automation
Projects	Sales	Service
Training	Treasury	

Source: Adapted from Oracle Corporation, "E-Business Suite: Manage by Fact with Complete Automation and Complete Information," Oracle.com, 2002.

other products keep ERP as a distinct module in the software suite. Of course, the goal of these software suites is to enable companies to run most of their business processes using one Web-enabled system of integrated software and databases, instead of a variety of separate e-business applications. See Figure 6.12. Let's look at a real world example.

Visa International: Implementing an e-Business Suite

Despite the innovations brought to global commerce by Visa's sophisticated consumer payments processing system, Visa International had surprisingly outdated systems managing some of its most critical internal business processes. "KPMG did an analysis of our business and found that our internal systems were becoming a risk to our organization," said Gretchen McCoy, senior vice president of Visa International. "We were in the red zone."

McCoy found that Visa's internal systems were unnecessarily complex and utilized few of the advantages that technology can bring to an enterprise. The financial management infrastructure was fragmented, complex, and costly to maintain. Data were not standardized, resulting in many different databases making disparate interpretations of business data. Corporate purchasing, accounts payable, and asset management were managed manually, resulting in time-consuming delays and discrepancies. Fragmented internal systems are not unusual in a company that experiences rapid growth. Visa experienced double digit growth for eleven consecutive years. Visa chose Oracle e-Business Suite to remedy the problems that come with a complex and inefficient back office.

The resulting implementation turned Visa's cumbersome, outdated desktop procedures into Web-based e-business solutions that met Visa's demands for all roles and processes. For example, Oracle Financials automated Visa's old organization and created a more agile system capable of accounting for the impact of financial activities on a global scale. Accounts payable was transformed from a cumbersome manual process into a streamlined system that automatically checks invoices against outgoing payments and requests review of any discrepancies via e-mail. And Oracle iProcurement helped automate Visa's requisitioning and purchasing system by streamlining the entire purchasing process and implementing a self-service model to increase processing efficiency, said McCoy [16].

SECTION III Supply Chain Management: The Business Network

Introduction

Starting an e-business takes ideas, capital, and technical savvy. Operating one, however, takes supply chain management (SCM) skills. A successful SCM strategy is based on accurate order processing, just-in-time inventory management, and timely order fulfillment. SCM's increasing importance illustrates how a tool that was a theoretical process 10 years ago is now a hot competitive weapon [8].

That's why many companies today are making supply chain management (SCM) a top strategic objective and major e-business application development initiative. Fundamentally, supply chain management helps a company get the right products to the right place at the right time, in the proper quantity and at an acceptable cost. The goal of SCM is to efficiently manage this process by forecasting demand; controlling inventory; enhancing the network of business relationships a company has with customers, suppliers, distributors, and others, and receiving feedback on the status of every link in the supply chain. To achieve this goal, many companies today are turning to Internet technologies to Web-enable their supply chain processes, decision making, and information flows. Let's take a look at a real world example.

Analyzing TaylorMade Golf and HON Industries

Read the Real World Case on TaylorMade Golf and HON Industries on the next page. We can learn a lot about the different ways companies are implementing supply chain management systems. See Figure 6.13.

TaylorMade Golf spent $10 million to develop a secure extranet website to integrate its dealings with its supplier and distributor systems and to share production forecasts and inventory information with them. The new system shortened Taylor-Made's production schedule dramatically, and the company estimates that it will save $50 million in production costs in 2002. HON Industries successfully completed a challenging implementation of a new production scheduling and logistics application to correct major inefficiencies in their previous warehousing and inventory

FIGURE 6.13
Malcolm Fields is vice president and CIO of HON Industries, and led the implementation of a new supply chain logistics management system for the company.

Source: Michael Kreiser.

TaylorMade Golf and HON Industries: The Business Value of Supply Chain Management

Although golf-equipment makers generally stage their competition in the public eye, with star-studded ads or with logos that are plastered on players as thickly as on racing cars, TaylorMade Golf Co. (www.taylormadegolf.com) took a less glamorous approach. It spent the past two years moving its key business information systems with its network of suppliers and distributors to the Web. The concept turned out to be as simple as a two-foot putt—and far more lucrative than a championship-winning stroke.

Of course, to implement its Web strategy, TaylorMade did spend $10 million to develop a secure extranet website to efficiently handle the administrative details of dealing with the systems of its suppliers and distributors, and to more easily share forecasts and inventory information with them. Mark Leposky, the vice president of global operations, says that TaylorMade may save $50 million in production costs in 2002—Tiger Woods–type money—based on just that $10 million investment in moving online.

The new Web-based system has compressed Taylor-Made's production schedule for a set of off-the-shelf golf clubs by more than half. And the company can now make a set of custom clubs in less than seven days, instead of taking six weeks. As a result, TaylorMade's custom-club business has doubled in the past year. "In a supply chain, how you execute creates competitive advantage," Leposky says. "We definitely see ours as a competitive weapon."

HON Industries HON Industries Inc. (www.honindustries.com), headquartered in Muscatine, Iowa, is a major manufacturer of office furniture and gas- and wood-burning fireplaces, with annual revenue of $2 billion and an IT department of approximately 100. The old legacy systems at HON Industries Inc. were unable to accurately measure the capacity of the manufacturer's warehouses. That lack of understanding led to errors like sending more products to a particular facility than it could store. To address the problem, a new system was designed to be more flexible and to take into account more variables, such as the size of the trucks and warehouse dock schedules.

CIO and Vice President Malcolm C. Fields says the optimization system has cut distribution costs, improved the timeliness of shipments, and reduced the amount of finished inventory that the manufacturer has to carry to "unbelievable lows."

The implementation team achieved its results despite considerable obstacles, including a shake-up in company structure and management and resistance from employees who were wedded to traditional processes. HON Industries began its advance-planning and scheduling system project in October 1999 and wrapped it up in March 2001 at a cost of about $2 million. Though the project ran past its original deadline by six months, it also far exceeded the expectations of the project team, says Fields.

The project, which involved replacing legacy distribution mainframe programs, used supply chain management (SCM) software from SynQuest, Inc. The SynQuest-based application allows HON to take a product order, factor in shipping and scheduling variables, then decide which factory could build and ship the product for the least amount of money. What's unique about this sort of supply chain management initiative is the focus on logistics and transportation factors, says Steve Banker, an analyst at ARC Advisory Group. SCM deployments typically focus on different parts of the supply chain, such as sourcing or procurement, he says.

Without offering exact numbers, Fields says the new system has contributed to a drop in freight costs from 6.5 to 5.8 percent as part of the firm's overall sales revenue. Scheduling accuracy has improved by 20 percent, and there are now 19 inventory turns a year, up from 16, he says.

One major challenge to the project was the constant shifting of business processes at HON, which meant projects had "to be implemented in short, intensive phases," says Fields. For instance, during the middle of the rollout, the company was split into two separate divisions, and the president of the original operating company was replaced. The business executives who signed off on the project were gone, says Fields. "We had to go out and rewin some hearts and minds," he says. Although work never slowed, for about 30 days the project's fate was uncertain. In the end, project advocates successfully educated the new executive team, and the rollout was a success.

Fields says he learned from this project just how tough it is to persuade people to change their way of thinking. "Never underestimate the difficulty of shifting a paradigm," he says.

Case Study Questions

1. How could moving business information systems with suppliers and distributors to the Web result in such dramatic business benefits as experienced by Taylor-Made Golf?

2. How does HON Industries' new SCM system improve the efficiency of their supply chain?

3. What other SCM initiatives would you recommend that TaylorMade Golf or HON Industries implement to improve their supply chain performance and business value? Explain the business value of your proposals.

Source: Adapted from Bob Diddlebock, "Share and Share Alike," *Context*, December 2001–January 2002, pp. 35–37; and Marc L. Songlini, "Supply System Grows Smarter," *Computerworld Premiere 100 Best in Class*, Supplement to *Computerworld*, March 11, 2002, pp. 10–11. Reprinted with permission from *Computerworld*.

systems. The new SCM system has resulted in significant decreases in freight costs, improved scheduling accuracy, and led to major reductions in finished goods inventory requirements.

What Is SCM?

Legacy supply chains are clogged with unnecessary steps and redundant stockpiles. For instance, a typical box of breakfast cereal spends an incredible 104 days getting from factory to supermarket, struggling its way through an unbelievable maze of wholesalers, distributors, brokers, and consolidators, each of which has a warehouse. The e-commerce opportunity lies in the fusing of each company's internal systems to those of its suppliers, partners, and customers. This fusion forces companies to better integrate interenterprise supply chain processes to improve manufacturing efficiency and distribution effectiveness [8].

So supply chain management is a cross-functional interenterprise system that uses information technology to help support and manage the links between some of a company's key business processes and those of its suppliers, customers, and business partners. The goal of SCM is to create a fast, efficient, and low-cost network of business relationships, or *supply chain*, to get a company's products from concept to market.

What exactly is a company's supply chain? Let's suppose a company wants to build and sell a product to other businesses. Then it must buy raw materials and a variety of contracted services from other companies. The interrelationships with suppliers, customers, distributors, and other businesses that are needed to design, build, and sell a product make up the network of business entities, relationships, and processes that is called a supply chain. And since each supply chain process should add value to the products or services a company produces, a supply chain is frequently called a *value chain*, a different but related concept we discussed in Chapter 2. In any event, many companies today are using Internet technologies to create interenterprise e-business systems for supply chain management that help a company streamline its traditional supply chain processes.

Figure 6.14 illustrates the basic business processes in the supply chain life cycle and the functional SCM processes that support them. It also emphasizes how many companies today are reengineering their supply chain processes, aided by Internet technologies and supply chain management software. For example, the demands of today's competitive business environment are pushing manufacturers to use their intranets, extranets, and e-commerce Web portals to help them reengineer their relationships with their suppliers, distributors, and retailers. The objective is to significantly reduce costs, increase efficiency, and improve their supply chain cycle times. SCM software can also help to improve interenterprise coordination among supply chain process players. The result is much more effective distribution and channel networks among business partners. The Web initiatives of Moen Inc. illustrate these developments.

Moen Inc.: Web-Enabling the Supply Chain

In late 1998, faucet maker Moen Inc. started sending electronic files of new product designs by e-mail. A few months later, it launched ProjectNet, an online extranet site where Moen can share digital designs simultaneously with suppliers worldwide. Every supplier can make changes immediately. Moen consolidates all the design changes on a master Web file. That way, design problems are discovered instantly and adjustments can be made just as fast, cutting the time it takes to lock in a final design to three days.

Next, the company attacked the cumbersome process of ordering parts from suppliers and updating them by fax or phone. In October 2000, the company launched its SupplyNet extranet site that allows parts suppliers to check the status of Moen's orders online. Every time Moen changes an order, the supplier receives

FIGURE 6.14

Supply chain management software and Internet technologies can help companies reengineer and integrate the functional SCM processes that support the supply chain life cycle.

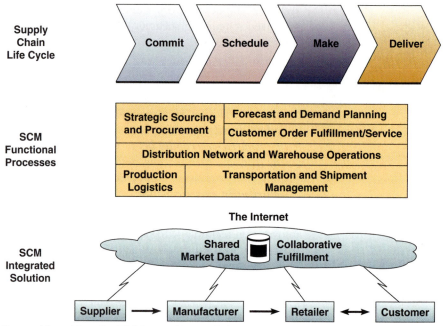

Supply Chain Life Cycle

Commit → Schedule → Make → Deliver

SCM Functional Processes

Strategic Sourcing and Procurement	Forecast and Demand Planning
	Customer Order Fulfillment/Service
Distribution Network and Warehouse Operations	
Production Logistics	Transportation and Shipment Management

SCM Integrated Solution

The Internet

Shared Market Data Collaborative Fulfillment

Supplier → Manufacturer → Retailer ↔ Customer

Source: Adapted from Ravi Kalakota and Marcia Robinson, *E-Business 2.0: Roadmap for Success* (Reading, MA: Addison-Wesley, 2001), pp. 280–289. © 2001 Addison-Wesley Publishing Company, Inc. Reprinted by permission of Addison-Wesley Longman, Inc.; and Craig Fellenstein and Ron Wood, *Exploring E-commerce, Global E-business, and E-societies* (Upper Saddle River, NJ: Prentice-Hall, 2000), p. 192.

an e-mail. If a supplier can't fill an order in time, it can alert Moen right away so the faucet maker can search elsewhere for the part. Today, the 40 key suppliers who make 80 percent of the parts that Moen buys use SupplyNet. The result: The company has shaved $3 million, or almost 6 percent, off its raw materials and work-in-progress inventories since October.

Moen's approach is like high-speed compared with competitors. Many still rely on fax machines to do most of their business. The percentage of companies using the Net to speed the supply chain in the construction/home improvement field, which includes plumbing, is expected to rise to just 7.7 percent in 2004, up from 3.2 percent in 2000, according to Forrester Research. "Moen is a step ahead of its peers in embracing Internet technologies," says analyst Navi Radjou of Forrester Research.

Moen may be ahead of its peers, but there's plenty of work to do. Technology chief Baker's most sensitive task is CustomerNet, the company's attempt to wire wholesalers, which account for 50 percent of the company's business. Unlike suppliers, who depend on Moen for most of their business, the company has little sway with wholesalers that buy plumbing, heating, and other products—not just faucets—from many manufacturers. Most still order by fax, even though that process causes errors up to 40 percent of the time. Moen execs are undaunted. They're courting wholesalers with the same methodical determination that has made Moen a Web-smart company [9].

Electronic Data Interchange

Electronic data interchange (EDI) was one of the earliest uses of information technology for supply chain management. EDI involves the electronic exchange of business transaction documents over the Internet and other networks between supply chain trading partners (organizations and their customers and suppliers). Data representing a variety of business transaction documents (such as purchase orders,

FIGURE 6.15 A typical example of electronic data interchange activities, an important form of business-to-business electronic commerce. EDI over the Internet is a major B2B e-commerce application.

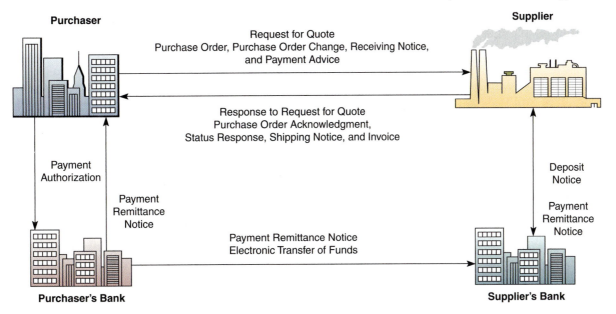

invoices, requests for quotations, and shipping notices) are automatically exchanged between computers using standard document message formats. Typically, EDI software is used to covert a company's own document formats into standardized EDI formats as specified by various industry and international protocols. Thus, EDI is an example of the almost complete automation of an e-commerce supply chain process. And EDI over the Internet, using secure *virtual private networks*, is a growing B2B e-commerce application.

Formatted transaction data are transmitted over network links directly between computers without paper documents or human intervention. Besides direct network links between the computers of trading partners, third-party services are widely used. Value-added network companies like GE Global Exchange Services and Computer Associates offer a variety of EDI services for relatively high fees. But many EDI service providers now offer secure, lower cost EDI services over the Internet. Figure 6.15 illustrates a typical EDI system [22].

EDI is still a popular data-transmission format among major trading partners, primarily to automate repetitive transactions, though it is slowly being replaced by XML-based Web services. EDI automatically tracks inventory changes; triggers orders, invoices, and other documents related to transactions; and schedules and confirms delivery and payment. By digitally integrating the supply chain, EDI streamlines processes, saves time, and increases accuracy. And by using Internet technologies, lower cost Internet-based EDI services are now available to smaller businesses [25, 28].

Telefonica TSAI: Internet EDI

Telefonica is Spain's largest supplier of telecommunications services, serving the Spanish-speaking and Portuguese-speaking world with affiliates in Latin America and the United States. Telefonica Servicios Avanzados de Informacion (TSAI) is a subsidiary of Telefonica that handles 60 percent of Spain's electronic data interchanged (EDI) traffic. TSAI's customers are supply chain trading partners—merchants, suppliers, and others involved in business supply chains from design to delivery.

To tap into the sizable market of smaller businesses that can't afford standard EDI services, TSAI offers an Internet EDI service, InfoEDI, based on ECXpert electronic commerce software. InfoEDI allows transactions to be entered and processed on the Internet, so smaller trading partners no longer have to buy and install special connections, dedicated workstations, and proprietary software. Instead, they can access the EDI network through the Internet via TSAI's Web portal.

InfoEDI's forms-based interface lets businesses connect with the InfoEDI simply by using modems and Web browsers. They can then interact with the largest suppliers and retailers to send orders, issue invoices based on orders, send invoice summaries, track status of documents, and receive messages. InfoEDI also provides a product database that lists all details of trading partners' products. Once a trading relationship has been established, each partner has encrypted access to details of its own products. Because those details remain accessible on TSAI's Web server, users need enter only minimal information to create links to that data, which are then plugged in as needed [28].

The Role of SCM

Figure 6.16 helps us understand the role and activities of supply chain management in business more clearly. The top three levels of Figure 6.16 show the strategic, tactical, and operational objectives and outcomes of SCM planning, which are then accomplished by the business partners in a supply chain at the execution level of SCM. The role of information technology in SCM is to support these objectives with interenterprise information systems that produce many of the outcomes a business needs to effectively manage its supply chain. That's why many companies today are installing SCM software and developing Web-based SCM information systems [15].

Until recently, SCM software products have typically been developed for either supply chain planning or execution applications. SCM planning software from vendors such as I2 and Manugistics support a variety of applications for supply and demand forecasting. SCM execution software from vendors such as EXE Technologies and

FIGURE 6.16   The objectives and outcomes of supply chain management are accomplished for a business with the help of interenterprise SCM information systems.

SCM Objectives		SCM Outcomes
What? Establish objectives, policies, and operating footprint	**Strategic**	• Objectives • Supply policies (service levels) • Network design
How much? Deploy resources to match supply to demand	**Tactical**	• Demand forecast • Production, procurement, logistics plan • Inventory targets
When? Where? Schedule, monitor, control, and adjust production	**Operational**	• Work center scheduling • Order/inventory tracking
Do Build and transport	**Execution**	• Order cycle • Material movement

Source: Adapted from Keith Oliver, Anne Chung, and Nick Samanach, "Beyond Utopia: The Realist's Guide to Internet-Enabled Supply Chain Management," *Strategy and Business*, Second Quarter, 2001, p. 99.

FIGURE 6.17   The supply chain management functions and potential benefits offered by the SCM module in the mySAP e-business software suite.

SCM Functions	SCM Outcomes
Planning	
Supply chain design	● Optimize network of suppliers, plants, and distribution centers
Collaborative demand and supply planning	● Develop an accurate forecast of customer demand by sharing demand and supply forecasts instantaneously across multiple tiers
	● Internet-enable collaborative scenarios, such as collaborative planning, forecasting, and replenishment (CPFR), and vendor-managed inventory
Execution	
Materials management	● Share accurate inventory and procurement order information
	● Ensure materials required for production are available in the right place at the right time
	● Reduce raw material spending, procurement costs, safety stocks, and raw material and finished goods inventory
Collaborative manufacturing	● Optimize plans and schedules while considering resource, material, and dependency constraints
Collaborative fulfillment	● Commit to delivery dates in real time
	● Fulfill orders from all channels on time with order management, transportation planning, and vehicle scheduling
	● Support the entire logistics process, including picking, packing, shipping, and delivery in foreign countries
Supply chain event management	● Monitor every stage of the supply chain process, from price quotation to the moment the customer receives the product, and receive alerts when problems arise
Supply chain performance management	● Report key measurements in the supply chain, such as filling rates, order cycle times, and capacity utilization

Source: Adapted from SAP AG, mySAP Supply Chain Management, mySAP.com, 2002, p. 8.

Manhattan Associates support applications like order management, logistics management, and warehouse management. However, big ERP vendors like Oracle and SAP are now offering Web-enabled software suites of e-business applications that include SCM modules. Examples include Oracle's e-Business Suite and SAP AG's mySAP [3].

Figure 6.17 gives you a good idea of the major planning and execution functions and outcomes that can be provided by SCM software as promised by mySAP's supply chain management module. Now let's look at a real world example of an SCM execution system.

| **Cardinal Glass: Supply Chain Event Management** | Two-and-a-half years ago, Cardinal Glass's legacy systems were making it a weak link in one of its key customer's supply chain. The system, a hodgepodge of custom and purchased applications, caused so many errors that it was "shameful and embarrassing," says Dan Peterson, director of corporate information systems at the Minneapolis-based maker of glass products. So when the customer decided that its products required delivery on a just-in-time basis, with lead times of just hours, there was no way the existing supply chain management applications could keep up the pace.

Luckily, Cardinal found that by installing supply chain event management (SCEM) applications from Minneapolis-based HighJump Software, it could deliver products at nearly 100 percent accuracy. "We probably cut the error rate by 90 percent," Peterson says. |

SCEM applications let companies see—in real-time, or as close as possible—if their existing supply chain management (SCM) systems are working. The applications are attached to an SCM server and get updates on supply chain activity through middleware connectors. Depending on preset rules and benchmarks, SCEM software can monitor SCM applications, run simulations of supply chain scenarios, automatically take control of supply chain processes, or send out alerts to customers, suppliers, and company management. Anomalies, such as a discrepancy in an order, will trigger appropriate alert and order fulfillment responses, making the system more sensitive to real-time needs.

Cardinal did contemplate replacing its legacy enterprise resources planning (ERP) system, but Cardinal officials decided that they needed SCM execution software. Cardinal wanted to address errors in the system on the fly, he explains—something traditional supply chain management and ERP systems wouldn't be able to do.

At Cardinal, when an order is received, inventory is checked immediately for availability. If a shortage is detected, the HighJump SCEM system will send alerts via e-mail to the customer and appropriate Cardinal managers. This speeds up the supply chain, reducing lead times and meeting their customer responsiveness goals, says Peterson. There were bottom-line benefits, too. The SCM execution system cut by about two-thirds the amount of personnel needed to compensate for errors such as inventory erroneously being marked "in" when it wasn't there, or shipments being sent incorrectly [26].

Benefits and Challenges of SCM

Creating a real-time SCM infrastructure is a daunting and ongoing issue and quite often, a point of failure, for several reasons. The chief reason is that the planning, selection, and implementation of SCM solutions is becoming more complex as the pace of technological change accelerates and the number of a company's partners increases [8].

The real world experiences of companies like Cardinal Glass and the promised outcomes that are outlined in Figure 6.17 emphasize the major business benefits that are possible with effective supply chain management systems. Companies know that SCM systems can provide them with key business benefits such as faster, more accurate order processing, reductions in inventory levels, quicker time to market, lower transaction and materials costs, and strategic relationships with their suppliers. All of these benefits of SCM are aimed at helping a company achieve agility and responsiveness in meeting the demands of their customers and the needs of their business partners.

But developing effective SCM systems has proven to be a complex and difficult application of information technology to business operations. So achieving the business value and customer value goals and objectives of supply chain management, as illustrated in Figure 6.18, has been a major challenge for most companies.

What are the causes of problems in supply chain management? Several reasons stand out. A lack of proper demand planning knowledge, tools, and guidelines is a major source of SCM failure. Inaccurate or overoptimistic demand forecasts will cause major production, inventory, and other business problems, no matter how efficient the rest of the supply chain management process is constructed. Inaccurate production, inventory, and other business data provided by a company's other information systems are a frequent cause of SCM problems. And lack of adequate collaboration among marketing, production, and inventory management departments within a company, and with suppliers, distributors, and others, will sabotage any SCM system. Even the SCM software tools themselves are considered to be immature, incomplete, and hard to implement by many companies who are installing SCM systems [1]. These problems are spotlighted in the real world example of Solectron Corporation.

FIGURE 6.18

Achieving the goals and objectives of supply chain management is a major challenge for many companies today.

Objectives of Supply Chain Management

Source: Adapted from Ravi Kalakota and Marcia Robinson, *E-Business 2.0: Roadmap for Success* (Reading, MA: Addison-Wesley, 2001), pp. 273–79. © 2001 Addison-Wesley Publishing Company, Inc. Reprinted by permission of Addison-Wesley Longman, Inc.

Solectron Corp.: Failures in SCM

SCM theory contends that technologically driven improvements in inventory management—like "just-in-time" production, direct online sales, and supply-chain management software—will prompt increased efficiency and allow managers to tailor output to match demand exactly. That, in turn, would increase working capital, boost margins, and help companies smooth out the ups and downs in the business cycle.

SCM lesson one is that killer software applications can't compensate for old-fashioned business judgment. There's a flaw in the premise that technology can synchronize every party in the product chain by providing a transparent view of supply and demand: The forecasts driving the entire flow of work are still concocted by people, not by real-time blips of data from retail shelves. No matter how mechanized the system becomes, sales managers and CEOs still shoot for the moon in a boom and don't share internal market intelligence with outsiders.

The experience of Solectron Corp., the world's biggest electronics contract manufacturer, is a case in point. In the fall of 2000, company officials say they could tell a supply glut of telecom equipment was brewing. Each of their big customers, which include Cisco, Ericsson, and Lucent, was expecting explosive growth for wireless phones and networking gear. But since Solectron supplies every major player, it knew the numbers didn't add up, even under the rosiest scenario.

Nevertheless, the telecom giants told Solectron and other contractors to produce flat out, assuring them that they would pay for excess materials. But when the bottom finally fell out and its clients ordered production cutbacks, it was too late for Solectron to halt orders from all of its 4,000 suppliers. By the spring of 2001, Solectron was left holding the bag for $4.7 billion in inventory [4].

Trends in SCM

The supplier-facing applications arena will see the continued growth of public as well as private networks that transform linear and inflexible supply chains into nonlinear and dynamic fulfillment networks. Supplier-facing applications will also evolve along another dimension: from automation and integration of supply chains to collaborative sourcing, planning, and design across their supplier networks [19].

Figure 6.19 illustrates the trends in the use of supply chain management today as three possible stages in a company's implementation of SCM systems. In the first stage, a company concentrates on making improvements to its internal supply chain processes and its external processes and relationships with suppliers and customers. Its e-commerce website and those of some of its trading partners provide access to

FIGURE 6.19 Stages in the use of supply chain management.

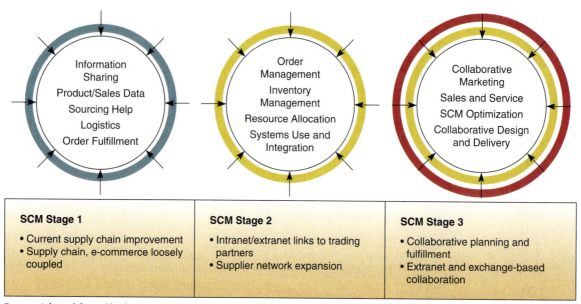

SCM Stage 1	SCM Stage 2	SCM Stage 3
• Current supply chain improvement • Supply chain, e-commerce loosely coupled	• Intranet/extranet links to trading partners • Supplier network expansion	• Collaborative planning and fulfillment • Extranet and exchange-based collaboration

Source: Adapted from Charles Poirier and Michael Bauer, *E-Supply Chain: Using the Internet to Revolutionize Your Business* (San Francisco, Berrett-Koehler Publishers, 2000), p. 79.

online catalogs and useful supply chain information, while supporting limited online transactions.

In stage two, a company accomplishes substantial supply chain management applications by using selected SCM software programs internally, as well as externally via intranet and extranet links among suppliers, distributors, customers, and other trading partners. Companies in this stage also concentrate on expanding the business network of Web-enabled SCM-capable trading partners in their supply chain to increase its operational efficiency and effectiveness in meeting their strategic business objectives.

In the third stage, a company begins to develop and implement cutting-edge collaborative supply chain management applications using advance SCM software, full-service extranet links, and private and public e-commerce exchanges. Examples include collaborative supply chain planning and fulfillment applications like collaborative product design and delivery, and collaborative planning, forecasting, and replenishment (CPFR). In addition, collaborative marketing sales, and service applications with trading partners, including customer and partner relationship management systems, may be developed. Companies in this third stage strive to optimize the development and management of their supply chains in order to meet their strategic customer value and business value goals [17]. Let's look at two real world examples.

CVS, McKesson, and MPT: Web-Based SCM Integration

CVS is a leading drug retail chain, while McKesson is the largest U.S. distributor of pharmaceuticals, health care products, and medical/surgical supplies, with annual sales in excess of $20 billion. Better integration with McKesson is a key strategic move for CVS, as management sees significant potential for improving sales and margins through its enhanced pricing and promotional forecasting systems. Supply chain integration helps the retailer move from pull to push promotions by allowing marketing managers to plan promotions more effectively, using item history taken from historical point-of-sale data on a store-by-store basis. The integration with McKesson substantially reduces the amount of time needed to plan and to stock inventory for individual promotions.

A major objective in the CVS–McKesson chain is to improve business performance through better supply chain integration. This requires much closer cooperation between McKesson and CVS, with McKesson even taking responsibility for CVS stock levels. McKesson monitors CVS's store-level consumption via Web extranet links and replenishes the inventory to meet the agreed on service levels—true supply chain integration. This cooperative process between supplier and customer is achieved through seamless interenterprise process integration and advanced SCM applications that link CVS directly to McKesson's production department [8].

But not every supply chain application requires a hefty up-front investment. Modern Plastics Technology (MPT), an injection mold manufacturer in Port Huron, Michigan, spends just several hundred dollars per month to access the i-Supply Service Web-based supply chain application from SupplySolution Inc. The company had been using electronic data interchange transmissions to fill its orders and was having a tough time keeping up with unscheduled changes in orders, says Doug Archer, vice president of Modern Plastics.

Then a large sealant manufacturer that was one of their customers persuaded Modern Plastics to connect with its i-Supply Service application. This Web-based SCM system enables them to see what their customers need on a real-time basis. Modern Plastics runs 30 to 40 different products through its presses, and i-Supply now allows management to better plan long production runs or prioritize specific product runs. Additionally, i-Supply helps MPT accomplish more accurate demand forecasting and production scheduling [27].

Summary

- **Customer Relationship Management: The Business Focus.** Customer relationship management is a cross-functional enterprise system that integrates and automates many of the customer serving processes in sales, marketing, and customer services that interact with a company's customers. CRM systems use information technology to support the many companies who are reorienting themselves into customer-focused businesses as a top business strategy. The major application components of CRM include contact and account management, sales, marketing and fulfillment, customer service and support, and retention and loyalty programs, all aimed at helping a company acquire, enhance, and retain profitable relationships with its customers as a primary business goal. However, many companies have found CRM systems difficult to properly implement due to lack of adequate understanding and preparation by management and affected employees. Finally, many companies are moving toward collaborative CRM systems that support the collaboration of employees, business partners, and the customers themselves in enhancing profitable customer relationships.

- **Enterprise Resource Planning: The Business Backbone.** Enterprise resource planning is a cross-functional enterprise system that integrates and automates many of the internal business processes of a company, particularly those within the manufacturing, logistics, distribution, accounting, finance, and human resource functions of the business. Thus, ERP serves as the vital backbone information system of the enterprise, helping a company achieve the efficiency, agility, and responsiveness required to succeed in a dynamic business environment. ERP software typically consists of integrated modules that give a company a real-time cross-functional view of its core business processes, such as production, order processing, and sales, and its

resources, such as cash, raw materials, production capacity, and people. However, properly implementing ERP systems is a difficult and costly process that has caused serious business losses for some companies, who underestimated the planning, development, and training that were necessary to reengineer their business processes to accommodate their new ERP systems. However, continuing developments in ERP software, including Web-enabled modules and e-business software suites, have made ERP more flexible and user-friendly, as well as extending it outward to a company's business partners.

- **Supply Chain Management: The Business Network.** Supply chain management is a cross-functional inter-enterprise system that integrates and automates the network of business processes and relationships between a company and its suppliers, customers, distributors, and other business partners. The goal of SCM is to help a company achieve agility and responsiveness in meeting the demands of their customers and needs of their suppliers, by enabling it to design, build, and sell its products using a fast, efficient, and low cost network of business partners, processes, and relationships, or supply chain. SCM is frequently subdivided into supply chain planning applications, such as demand and supply forecasting, and supply chain execution applications, such as inventory management, logistics management, and warehouse management. Developing effective supply chain systems and achieving the business goals of SCM has proven to be a complex and difficult challenge for many firms. But SCM continues to be a major concern and top e-business initiative as companies increase their use of Internet technologies to enhance integration and collaboration with their business partners, and improve the operational efficiency and business effectiveness of their supply chains.

Key Terms and Concepts

These are the key terms and concepts of this chapter. The page number of their first explanation is in parentheses.

1. Customer relationship management (182)
   - *a.* Application components (184)
   - *b.* Business benefits (188)
   - *c.* Challenges (188)
   - *d.* Trends (189)
2. E-business suites (199)

3. Electronic data interchange (204)
4. Enterprise resource planning (192)
   - *a.* Application components (194)
   - *b.* Business benefits (196)
   - *c.* Challenges (196)
   - *d.* Trends (199)

5. Supply chain (203)
6. Supply chain management (201)
   - *a.* Application components (203)
   - *b.* Business benefits (208)
   - *c.* Challenges (208)
   - *d.* Trends (209)

Review Quiz

Match one of the key terms and concepts listed previously with one of the brief examples or definitions that follow. Try to find the best fit for answers that seem to fit more than one term or concept. Defend your choices.

_____ 1. A cross-functional enterprise system that helps a business develop and manage its customer-facing business processes.

_____ 2. A cross-functional enterprise system that helps a business integrate and automate many of its internal business processes and information systems.

_____ 3. A cross-functional interenterprise system that helps a business manage its network of relationships and processes with its business partners.

_____ 4. Includes contact and account management, sales, marketing and fulfillment, and customer service and support systems.

_____ 5. Includes order management, production planning, accounting, finance, and human resource systems.

_____ 6. Includes demand forecasting, inventory management, logistics management, and warehouse management systems.

_____ 7. Acquiring, enhancing, and retaining profitable relationships with customers.

_____ 8. Improvements in the quality, efficiency, cost, and management of internal business processes.

_____ 9. Development of a fast, efficient, and low cost network of business partners to get products from concept to market.

_____ 10. Resistance from sales and customer service professionals who are not adequately involved in the development of the system.

_____ 11. Failure of order processing and inventory accounting systems that are reengineered to accommodate a new cross-functional system.

_____ 12. A lack of adequate demand planning knowledge, tools, and guidelines may cause major overproduction and excess inventory problems.

_____ 13. Toward Web portals and collaborative systems involving business partners as well as customers to coordinate sales and service across all marketing channels.

_____ 14. Toward more flexible, user-friendly, Web-enabled software, integrated into e-business software suites.

_____ 15. Toward the use of Internet technologies to integrate and enhance collaboration with a company's network of business partners.

_____ 16. An integrated system of software modules for customer relationship management, enterprise resource planning, supply chain management, and other business applications.

_____ 17. The automatic exchange of electronic business documents between the networked computers of business partners.

_____ 18. A network of business partners, processes, and relationships that supports the design, manufacture, distribution, and sale of a company's products.

Discussion Questions

1. Should every company become a customer-focused business? Why or why not?

2. Why would systems that enhance a company's relationships with customers have such a high rate of failure?

3. Refer to the Real World Case on Mitsubishi Motor Sales in the chapter. Why have many CRM systems failed to provide promised benefits like those generated by Mitsubishi's system?

4. How could some of the spectacular failures of ERP systems have been avoided?

5. Should companies continue to use EDI systems? Why or why not?

6. Refer to the Real World Case on Agilent Technologies and Russ Berrie in the chapter. What do you think caused the major failure of Agilent's ERP

implementation? Explain your reasons for their failure, and why they did not act to avoid the reasons you specify.

7. How can the problem of overenthusiastic demand forecasts in supply chain planning be avoided?

8. What challenges do you see for a company that wants to implement collaborative SCM systems? How would you meet such challenges?

9. Refer to the Real World Case on TaylorMade Golf and HON Industries in the chapter. What are several ways a small business could use supply chain management to improve the efficiency and business value of their supply chain? Give several examples to illustrate your answer.

10. Should companies install e-business software suites or "best of breed" e-business software components? Why?

Application Exercises

Complete the following exercises as individual or group projects that apply the chapter concepts to real world business situations.

1. Oracle Corporation: Small Business Suite

Web The Oracle Small Business Suite is developed and marketed for Oracle Corporation by NetLedger Inc. The websites at www.netledger.com and www.oraclesmallbusiness.com present extensive information on this e-business software suite for small business. Check out the multimedia Quick Tour, the information on specific business applications in the Learn More section, and the detailed information in the FAQ (frequently asked questions). See Figure 6.20.

a. What are the business benefits of this suite of online business software and services?

b. What are the limitations and disadvantages of this and similar online software applications?

c. Would you recommend this suite to a small business owner? Why or why not?

2. SAP versus Oracle: mySAP versus E-Business Suite

Web Check out the websites of SAP's mySAP (www.mysap.com) and Oracle's E-Business Suite (www.oracle.com/applications), the e-business software suites of these two major ERP, CRM, and SCM competitors. Review the extensive information on the features and capabilities of both suites.

a. What are the business benefits offered by such suites?

b. What are the limitations and disadvantages of such suites compared to individual "best of breed" business application software?

c. Which one of the two suites do you prefer? Give at least three reasons to substantiate your selection.

FIGURE 6.20

The home page of NetLedger Inc., developer of the Oracle Small Business Suite.

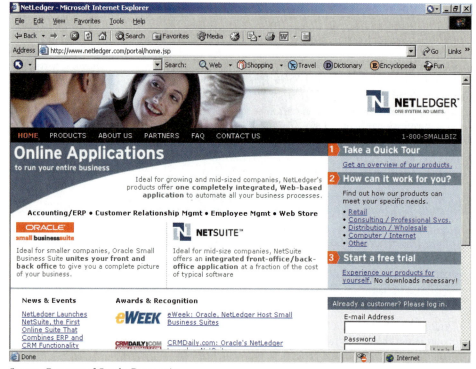

Source: Courtesy of Oracle Corporation.

REAL WORLD CASE 4

H-P, Eastman Chemical, and Others: The Benefits and Challenges of SCM Systems

Computer maker Hewlett-Packard Co. (www.hp.com) began moving its supply chain online in 1999 and has already seen significant benefits. To pick one small example, H-P linked together all the companies whose products go into making its computer monitors, reaching all the way back to the suppliers of the resins that are used to make the casings. In the process, H-P says, the price of the resins has dropped as much as 5 percent because H-P handles all the purchasing and gets a bulk rate; in the past, the numerous companies that H-P used to make casings placed their own, far smaller orders.

H-P says the number of people required to manage the supply chain for its monitors has been cut in half. The time it takes to fill an order for a monitor has also been cut in half because every company in the supply chain can communicate more easily and thus cooperate better. H-P says that moving the supply chain online has even increased monitor sales by 2 percent. The reason is that the company is no longer losing orders because it couldn't deliver the right product at the right time.

You don't have to be a goliath like H-P to see the benefits, says Bernard Cheng, chief executive of Advanced International Multitech Co. (www.adgroup.com.tw), a Taiwan-based manufacturer of golf club heads and shafts with $70 million in annual revenue. He estimates that his company spent $3 million in the past five years digitizing its internal operations, as well as its links with buyers such as Taylor-Made Golf. "That's a lot of money for a company our size," Cheng says. "But we believe in the technology. It's what an offshore company like ours needs to get involved with businesses in the West."

Eastman Chemical Co. (www.eastman.com), which generates revenue of $5.3 billion a year and orders huge quantities of propane, ethane, and hundreds of other raw materials on a daily basis, believes so strongly in online procurement that it has bought stakes in a handful of software developers that specialize in that area. Eastman—which spent upward of $10 million on its own e-procurement system, launched two years ago—asks its software partners to make presentations to its suppliers pointing up the advantages of going digital.

Eastman will sometimes retrofit a supplier's website so Eastman can send purchase orders to the supplier and handle other exchanges of data electronically. Eastman also has established a central extranet website to allow for at least minimal online contact with suppliers that may use nothing more sophisticated than spreadsheets, personal computers, and browsers. "We bend over backward to bring someone into the loop," says Peter Roueche, a senior procurement engineer at Eastman. "We can't live in a vacuum." In 2000, Eastman forged direct Web connections into the procurement operations of 15 suppliers. Their 2001 goal: 40.

W. W. Grainger Inc. (www.grainger.com) says a fast-growing piece of its business likely couldn't exist without online connections. The unit, FindMRO.com, lets customers of the industrial-parts distributor locate even oddball items that they rarely use, such as bear repellent for workers on the Alaska pipeline. The company deals with 14,000 suppliers hawking more than five million products. "We take the messy, random, and overwhelming tasks that you don't want to do, and do them," says Ron Paulson, the general manager of FindMRO.com.

If the benefits are so clear, does that mean that every company is rushing to link up with suppliers and distributors online? Hardly. Mark Leposky, of TaylorMade Golf, says suppliers have been "under-interested" in doing anything technologically. "I'd say 50% of [prospective] vendors will walk away" from business with TaylorMade rather than go online, he adds. Paulson of FindMRO.com agrees that persuading suppliers to take the e-train is often easier said than done. "There is still some fighting and screaming," Paulson says.

Suppliers—particularly the smaller ones, employing fewer than 500 people—say that the software and procedures prescribed by manufacturers can be confusing, often contradictory, and not necessarily sculpted to their needs. These smaller companies, which make up 95 percent of the 6.6 million businesses in the United States, also say they are concerned about the cost of the new systems, a worry that has been magnified in a slack economy.

Then there's the often impenetrable technical jargon used to describe the online processes. For example, a small business in the sheet-metal industry thinks about classic supply-chain issues in simple terms. Do you have the part? How many can I get? When can you deliver? How much will it cost?

But the software companies and consultants that often help implement moves to the Web often use buzzwords like "transparency," "visibility," "tagging and flagging," "exception management," "CPFR," and "XRM." "The smaller suppliers feel threatened by the whole thing," says Bill Burke, the president of First Index USA, which sets up online marketplaces for suppliers.

Case Study Questions

1. Why can both large and small businesses cut costs and increase revenues by moving their supply chains online? Use the companies in this case as examples.

2. What is the business value to Eastman Chemical and W. W. Grainger of their initiatives to help their suppliers and customers do business online?

3. Why are many small suppliers reluctant to do business online with their large customers? What can be done to encourage small suppliers online?

Source: Adapted from Bob Diddlebock, "Share and Share Alike," *Context*, December 2001–January 2002, pp. 35–37.

Wal-Mart and Mattel: Supply Chain Management Best Practices

"**B**eing a supplier to Wal-Mart is a two-edged sword," says Joseph R. Eckroth Jr., CIO at Mattel Inc. (www.mattel.com). "They're a phenomenal channel but a tough customer. They demand excellence."

It's a lesson that the El Segundo, California–based toy manufacturer and thousands of other suppliers learned as the world's largest retailer, Wal-Mart Stores (www.walmart. com), built an inventory and supply chain management system that changed the face of business. By investing early and heavily in cutting-edge technology to identify and track sales on the individual item level, the Bentonville Arkansas–based retail giant made its IT infrastructure a key competitive advantage that has been studied and copied by companies around the world.

"We view Wal-Mart as the best supply chain operator of all time," says Pete Abell, retail research director at high-tech consultancy AMR Research in Boston. Abell says he expects the company to remain in the vanguard. "Wal-Mart is evolving; they're not standing still," he says. The company is still pushing the limits of supply chain management, he says, searching for and supporting better technology that promises to make its IT infrastructure more efficient. Radio frequency identification (RFID) microchips, for example, may replace bar codes and security tags with a combination technology that costs less money.

Early on, Wal-Mart saw the value of sharing that data with suppliers, and it eventually moved that information online on its Retail Link website. Opening its sales and inventory databases to suppliers is what made Wal-Mart the powerhouse it is today, says Rena Granofsky, a senior partner at J. C. Williams Group, a Toronto-based retail consulting firm. While its competition guarded sales information, Wal-Mart approached its suppliers as if they were partners, not adversaries, says Granofsky. By implementing a collaborative planning, forecasting, and replenishment (CPFR) program, Wal-Mart began a just-in-time inventory program that reduced carrying costs for both the retailer and its suppliers. "There's a lot less excess inventory in the supply chain because of it," says Granofsky.

That efficiency is the key factor in maintaining Wal-Mart's low-price leadership among retailers, says Abell. "Their margins can be far lower than other retailers' because they have such an efficient supply chain," he says. The company's cost of goods is 5 to 10 percent less than that of most of its competitors, Abell estimates.

Wal-Mart's success with supply chain management has inspired other retail companies, which are now playing catch-up, says Abell. "Others are now just starting. They've all had inventory systems, but sharing the data with their partners hasn't been easy," he says. Wal-Mart's influence has extended beyond the retail sector. Mattel's Eckroth says that he studied Wal-Mart's supply chain best practices when he worked at a manufacturing division of General Electric Co. "They're a benchmark company," he says.

One reason Wal-Mart is studied so closely is that it gets buy-in from its suppliers to an incredible degree. That's because its programs and practices benefit not just the retailer but its partners as well, says Eckroth. CPFR, he says has "blurred the lines between supplier and customer. You're both working to the same end: To sell as much product as possible without either of us having too much inventory. We've learned that if we listen to Wal-Mart, take their initiatives seriously, and align our strategies with making them successful, we both can succeed," he says.

Mattel has learned a lot from working with Wal-Mart and is bringing those lessons to bear in its relationship with other channels, says Eckroth. "Getting the supply chain optimized inside of Mattel is only 50% of the equation," he says. "The other 50% is getting tightly linked with every one of our customers so that we're reacting as quickly as they're giving us data." Tight links, Eckroth says, will enable Mattel to tackle the next big business problem: increasing manufacturing efficiency.

"My ability to get information about the sales pace of a toy and either ramping up or shutting down manufacturing depends on my having data," he says. Having sales data on a daily or hourly basis is necessary to figure out on a micro level what is selling best where and tailor manufacturing accordingly. The greatest efficiencies will appear when the kind of trusting mutually beneficial relationship Mattel has with Wal-Mart is duplicated with the rest of the manufacturer's retail outlets.

"Having that data on a global basis from every one of my customers allows me to optimize the sales of my products and the fill rates of my customers," Eckroth says. "The theme for the future is that at the end of the day, there can be a symbiotic relationship between companies."

Case Study Questions

1. Do you agree that Wal-Mart is "the best supply chain operator of all time"? Why or why not?

2. What has Mattel learned from Wal-Mart? How well are they applying it to their own business? Explain your evaluation.

3. What can other businesses learn from the experiences of Wal-Mart and Mattel that could improve their supply chain performance? Use an example to illustrate your answer.

Source: Adapted from Amy Johnson, "A New Supply Chain Forged," *Computerworld*, September 30, 2002, pp. 38–39. Reprinted with permission from *Computerworld*.

CHAPTER 7

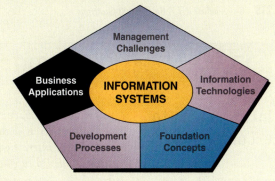

APPLICATIONS IN BUSINESS AND MANAGEMENT

ELECTRONIC COMMERCE SYSTEMS

Chapter Highlights

Learning Objectives

After reading and studying this chapter, you should be able to:

1. Identify the major categories and trends of e-commerce applications.

2. Identify the essential processes of an e-commerce system, and give examples of how they are implemented in e-commerce applications.

3. Identify and give examples of several key factors and Web store requirements needed to succeed in e-commerce.

4. Identify and explain the business value of several types of e-commerce marketplaces.

5. Discuss the benefits and trade-offs of several e-commerce clicks and bricks alternatives.

Electronic Commerce Fundamentals

Introduction to e-Commerce

Few concepts have revolutionized business more profoundly than e-commerce. E-commerce is changing the shape of competition, the speed of action, and the streamlining of interactions, products, and payments from customers to companies and from companies to suppliers [17].

For most companies in the age of the Internet, electronic commerce is more than just buying and selling products online. Instead, it encompasses the entire online process of developing, marketing, selling, delivering, servicing, and paying for products and services transacted on internetworked, global marketplaces of customers, with the support of a worldwide network of business partners. As we will see in this chapter, electronic commerce systems rely on the resources of the Internet, intranets, extranets, and other technologies to support every step of this process.

Analyzing Yahoo! Inc.

Read the Real World Case on Yahoo! Inc. on the next page. We can learn a lot about the challenges and opportunities of retail electronic commerce from this example. See Figure 7.1.

Yahoo! Inc. is fighting its way back to profitability after a year and a half of losses. CEO Terry Semel has crafted an e-commerce business plan whose main strategy is to make Yahoo! less dependent on Internet advertising revenues by offering new online services to Yahoo's 200 million users, most of whom are not paying customers. This includes offering high-speed Internet service through a partnership with SBC Communications as a way to lure customers to more lucrative entertainment, job placement, and other higher-margin online services. Only time will tell whether Semel's strategy will transform Yahoo! into an online portal services company that rivals AOL and MSN.

The Scope of e-Commerce

Figure 7.2 illustrates the range of business processes involved in the marketing, buying, selling, and servicing of products and services in companies that engage in e-commerce. Companies involved in e-commerce as either buyers or sellers rely on

FIGURE 7.1
Yahoo CEO Terry Semel is the architect of their new business plan for e-commerce profitability.

Source: Richard Morgenstein

REAL WORLD CASE 1	Yahoo! Inc.: Striving for Success in e-Commerce

It's a blistering August morning in Silicon Valley, and Terry S. Semel, chief executive of Yahoo! Inc. (www.yahoo.com), sits back sipping a Diet Coke. Under Semel's leadership, the legendary Internet portal has slogged its way through a Death Valley of Web advertising, posting in July a second-quarter 2002 profit of $21.4 million. Those are Yahoo's first profit numbers since the last gasp escaped from the Net bubble in late 2000. But Semel, a former top studio executive at Warner Bros. Inc., doesn't waste much breath on his rescue work at Yahoo. Instead, he focuses on the transformation ahead. Leaning forward on his elbows, Semel says: "We're going to change the way people access the Internet."

That's the linchpin of Yahoo's strategy—and could well determine whether the pioneer e-commerce portal's turnaround is fleeting or just getting its legs. In the fall of 2002, Yahoo began selling high-speed Internet access through an exclusive partnership with regional telco giant SBC Communications Inc. SBC subscribers who sign up for the service will automatically reach the Web through a Yahoo portal. Yahoo will take a cut of the subscription fees, an average of $3 to $5 a month, predict analysts.

Once broadband customers are on board, Semel plans to sell them a host of offerings from entertainment downloads to its online personals. Add it all up, and this could generate $125 million next year for Yahoo—46 percent of the company's projected 2003 growth. If the broadband offering is a winner, Yahoo could prove that a stand-alone Net-content company can compete in a world of media conglomerates.

Such an idea long seemed far-fetched, especially after AOL acquired Time Warner in 2000 and promised to cross-sell online advertising with print and television ads—something Yahoo can't match. But AOL Time Warner Inc.'s struggle to integrate its offerings lends Yahoo's simpler model renewed credence. "Yahoo's not at a disadvantage," says Kelly Corroon, e-business director of Miller Brewing Co., a big Yahoo advertiser. "We would love to see better integrated media offerings, but nobody has shown us one."

Still, Yahoo's broadband offering is no slam dunk. SBC spans 18 states and 37 percent of the territory covered by the regional telcos. Microsoft Corp.'s MSN, by contrast, beat out Yahoo and AOL to create a partnership with Verizon Communications. Add that to Microsoft's earlier deal with Qwest Communications International, and the software giant has 45 percent of the U.S. regional telephone business tied up.

To gain greater access to customers, Semel has to create a rich high-speed channel to the Internet. Only then are other cable and phone carriers likely to ink deals with Yahoo. To entice them, Semel's planning to offer enhanced e-mail with mammoth storage capacity and a host of entertainment services. Still, rivals say Yahoo is facing a rough slog. "Yahoo's too far out from their field of expertise," says Bob Visse, director of MSN. "We've been at the Net-access game for seven or eight years, and a long learning curve goes into being successful."

Semel can't afford to get this wrong. So far, he has managed to prop up Yahoo's financials by cutting costs and pushing into new businesses. But these successes mask his most serious problem. Yahoo, an e-commerce company built on Web advertising, is seeing its core business continue to shrivel. Ad sales, which account for 60 percent of its business, are lagging behind the rest of the market. Industry spending on such ads climbed 1 percent in the first half of 2002, according to researcher CME, yet Yahoo's ad sales tumbled 14 percent in the same period. "It's still too early to get excited about Yahoo's performance," says WR Hambrecht analyst Derek Brown.

Semel is undaunted. Despite Yahoo's challenges, he's on pace to meet one major goal: making half of Yahoo's money from beyond Net advertising by 2004. Non-ad revenues are expected to jump from 23 to 41 percent by year-end. Semel has done this by pounding a money-making philosophy into the 3,500-person business. It has prompted everything from the $436 million acquisition of online job search company HotJobs.com to Yahoo taking a bigger slice of transactions from its online mall. "Terry has turned Yahoo into a company that acts like adults. It's going to become a great selling mechanism," says Barry Diller, CEO of USA Interactive Inc.

This means Semel must turn more of Yahoo's passersby into paying customers. Currently, the number reaches 1 million—or 0.5 percent of Yahoo's 200 million quarterly users. Bolstered by broadband customers, Semel hopes to double the number of paying customers by the end of this year. SBC is a formidable partner with the largest DSL customer base among the regional telcos. And the phone company's 3 percent stake in Yahoo should bolster its commitment to the deal. Already, a preliminary Internet dial-up partnership launched by the two companies in June has boosted SBC's Internet subscription rates 20 percent above its anticipated levels.

So far, it's Semel's execution that has nudged Yahoo into profitability. But to turn Yahoo's short-term gains into a full-blown comeback, the ex-movie mogul needs a powerful dose of execution—and a healthy shot of good fortune.

Case Study Questions

1. Review the services offered by Yahoo at their website. Also, click on their Company Information and Investor Relations links. How is Yahoo doing financially right now?

2. Is Yahoo making the right moves toward continuing e-commerce profitability? Why or why not?

3. What are several other things Terry Semel could do to make Yahoo more successful? Explain the business value of your proposals.

Source: Adapted from Ben Elgin "Can Yahoo Make Them Pay?" *Business Week*, September 9, 2002, pp. 92–94.

FIGURE 7.2 E-commerce involves accomplishing a range of business processes to support the electronic buying and selling of goods and services.

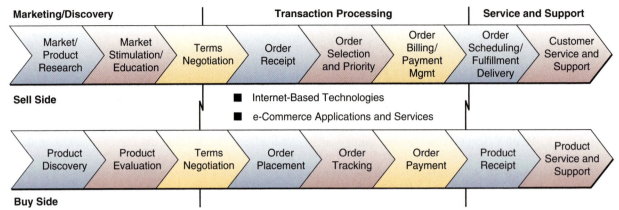

Marketing/Discovery **Transaction Processing** **Service and Support**

Market/Product Research → Market Stimulation/Education → Terms Negotiation → Order Receipt → Order Selection and Priority → Order Billing/Payment Mgmt → Order Scheduling/Fulfillment Delivery → Customer Service and Support

Sell Side

■ Internet-Based Technologies
■ e-Commerce Applications and Services

Product Discovery → Product Evaluation → Terms Negotiation → Order Placement → Order Tracking → Order Payment → Product Receipt → Product Service and Support

Buy Side

Source: Adapted from Craig Fellenstein and Ron Wood, *Exploring E-Commerce, Global E-Business, and E-Societies* (Upper Saddle River, N J Prentice-Hall, 2000) p. 28.

Internet-based technologies, and e-commerce applications and services to accomplish marketing, discovery, transaction processing, and product and customer service processes. For example, electronic commerce can include interactive marketing, ordering, payment, and customer support processes at e-commerce catalog and auction sites on the World Wide Web. But e-commerce also includes e-business processes such as extranet access of inventory databases by customers and suppliers (transaction processing), intranet access of customer relationship management systems by sales and customer service reps (service and support), and customer collaboration in product development via e-mail exchanges and Internet newsgroups (marketing/discovery).

Many companies today are participating in or sponsoring three basic categories of electronic commerce applications: business-to-consumer, business-to-business, and consumer-to-consumer e-commerce. Note: We will not explicitly cover business-to-government (B2G) and *e-government* applications in this text. However, many e-commerce concepts apply to such applications.

Business-to-Consumer (B2C) e-Commerce. In this form of electronic commerce, businesses must develop attractive electronic marketplaces to entice and sell products and services to consumers. For example, many companies offer e-commerce websites that provide virtual storefronts and multimedia catalogs, interactive order processing, secure electronic payment systems, and online customer support.

Business-to-Business (B2B) e-Commerce. This category of electronic commerce involves both electronic business marketplaces and direct market links between businesses. For example, many companies offer secure Internet or extranet e-commerce catalog websites for their business customers and suppliers. Also very important are B2B e-commerce portals that provide auction and exchange marketplaces for businesses. Others may rely on electronic data interchange (EDI) via the Internet or extranets for computer-to-computer exchange of e-commerce documents with their larger business customers and suppliers.

Consumer-to-Consumer (C2C) e-Commerce. The huge success of online auctions like eBay, where consumers (as well as businesses) can buy and sell with each other in an auction process at an auction website, makes this e-commerce model an important e-commerce business strategy. Thus, participating in or sponsoring consumer or business auctions is an important e-commerce alternative for B2C, C2B (consumer-to-business), or B2B e-commerce. Electronic personal advertising of products or services to buy or sell by consumers at electronic newspaper sites, consumer e-commerce portals, or personal websites is also an important form of C2C e-commerce.

Electronic Commerce Technologies

What technologies are necessary for electronic commerce? The short answer is that most information technologies and Internet technologies that we discuss in this text are involved in electronic commerce systems. A more specific answer is illustrated in Figure 7.3.

Figure 7.3 illustrates an electronic commerce architecture developed by Sun Microsystems and its business partners. If you examine this architecture, you will notice that:

- The Internet, intranets, and extranets are the network infrastructure or foundation of electronic commerce.

- Customers must be provided with a range of secure information, marketing, transaction processing, and payment services.

- Trading and business partners rely on the Internet and extranets to exchange information and accomplish secure transactions, including electronic data interchange (EDI) and other supply chain and financial systems and databases.

FIGURE 7.3

The software components and functions of an integrated e-commerce system. This architecture would enable a business to use the Internet, intranets, and extranets to accomplish e-commerce transactions with consumers, business customers, and business partners.

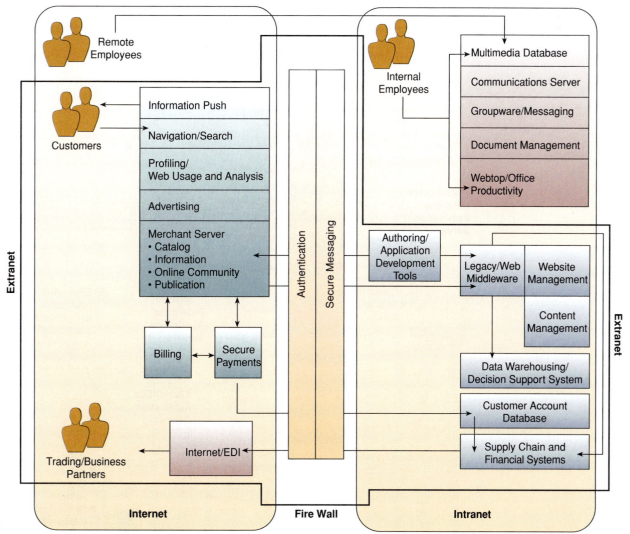

Source: Adapted courtesy of Sun Microsystems.

● Company employees depend on a variety of Internet and intranet resources to communicate and collaborate in support of their EC work activities.

● IS professionals and end users can use a variety of software tools to develop and manage the content and operations of the websites and other EC resources of a company.

Figure 7.4 is an example of the technology resources required by e-commerce systems. The figure illustrates some of the hardware, software, data, and network components used by Free Markets Inc. to provide B2B online auction e-commerce services.

FIGURE 7.4

The e-commerce technology components and architecture of B2B online auctions provider FreeMarkets Inc. are illustrated in this example of their Internet-based QuickSource auction service.

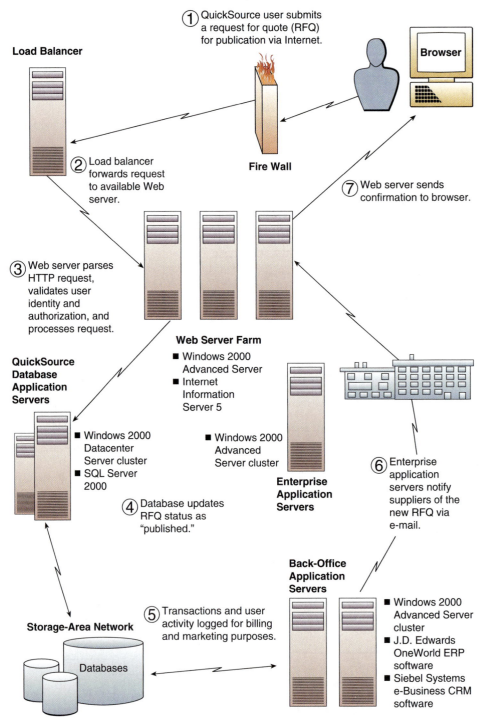

Source: Adapted from David Essex, "Betting on Win 2K," *Computerworld*, February 26, 2001, p. 57.

FIGURE 7.5   This e-commerce process architecture highlights nine essential categories of e-commerce processes.

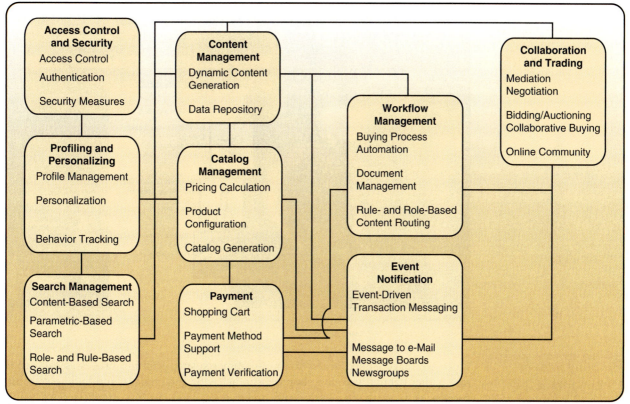

Source: Adapted from Faisal Hoque, *E-Enterprise: Business Models, Architecture, and Components* (Cambridge, UK: Cambridge University Press, 2000), p. 207.

Essential e-Commerce Processes

The essential **e-commerce processes** required for the successful operation and management of e-commerce activities are illustrated in Figure 7.5. This figure outlines the nine key components of an *e-commerce process architecture* that is the foundation of the e-commerce initiatives of many companies today [15]. We will concentrate on the role these processes play in e-commerce systems, but you should recognize that many of these components may also be used in internal, noncommerce e-business applications. An example would be an intranet-based human resource system used by a company's employees, which might use all but the catalog management and product payment processes shown in Figure 7.5. Let's take a brief look at each essential process category.

Access Control and Security

E-commerce processes must establish mutual trust and secure access between the parties in an e-commerce transaction by authenticating users, authorizing access, and enforcing security features. For example, these processes establish that a customer and e-commerce site are who they say they are through user names and passwords, encryption keys, or digital certificates and signatures. The e-commerce site must then authorize access to only those parts of the site that an individual user needs to accomplish his or her particular transactions. Thus, you usually will be given access to all resources of an e-commerce site except for other people's accounts, restricted company data, and webmaster administration areas. Companies engaged in B2B e-commerce may rely on secure industry exchanges for procuring goods and services, or Web trading portals that allow only registered customers access to trading information and applications. Other security processes protect the resources of e-commerce sites from threats such as hacker attacks, theft of passwords or credit card numbers, and system failures. We discuss many of these security threats and features in Chapter 11.

FIGURE 7.6

Bselect software gathers and analyzes the behavior of visitors to the Supergo Bike Shops website to help them personalize a customer's Web shopping experience.

Source: Courtesy of www.supergo.com.

Profiling and Personalizing

Once you have gained access to an e-commerce site, profiling processes can occur that gather data on you and your website behavior and choices, and build electronic profiles of your characteristics and preferences. User profiles are developed using profiling tools such as user registration, cookie files, website behavior tracking software, and user feedback. These profiles are then used to recognize you as an individual user and provide you with a personalized view of the contents of the site, as well as product recommendations and personalized Web advertising as part of a *one-to-one marketing* strategy. Profiling processes are also used to help authenticate your identity for account management and payment purposes, and to gather data for customer relationship management, marketing planning, and website management. Some of the ethical issues in user profiling are discussed in Chapter 11. See Figure 7.6.

Be Free and Supergo Bike Shops: Personalizing e-Commerce

If you're looking to give your customers a unique experience at your e-store, Bselect by Be Free offers a personalization service at affordable prices. Setup costs around $5,000; after that you pay $5,000 per month, plus 15 cents every time someone buys a suggested sale item. Bselect works by tagging and tracking each page of your site. Frequent guests to your online store see products based on where they've been in the past and what they've bought. Bselect saves profile information by key, not a name or address. The system tracks customers anonymously, and they can delete profile details or opt out of future profiles through an online control panel (although Bselect saves customer purchase information indefinitely).

Steven Laff, Web developer for Santa Monica, California–based Supergo Bike Shops, started using Bselect about a year ago for the company's e-commerce site, Supergo.com. Before that Laff had developed his own recommendation tool, which didn't allow him to keep track of sale items. "If you have 600 items, manually recommending something becomes a nightmare," he says. "Bselect is ingenious. It doesn't recommend the same thing twice, and if it's a consumable product, you can set it up to be recommended again. Best of all, Bselect pays for itself 5, 10, 15 times over per month." Before Bselect, e-commerce orders made up only 33 percent of Supergo's overall mail-order sales; now they make up 60 percent.

Search Management

Efficient and effective search processes provide a top e-commerce website capability that helps customers find the specific product or service they want to evaluate or buy. E-commerce software packages can include a website search engine component, or a company may acquire a customized e-commerce search engine from search technology companies like Excite and Requisite Technology. Search engines may use a combination of search techniques, including searches based on content (a product description, for example), or by parameters (above, below, or between a range of values for multiple properties of a product, for example).

Content and Catalog Management

Content management software helps e-commerce companies develop, generate, deliver, update, and archive text data and multimedia information at e-commerce websites. For example, German media giant Bertelsmann, part owner of BarnesandNoble.com, uses StoryServer content manager software to generate Web page templates that enable online editors from six international offices to easily publish and update book reviews and other product information, which are sold (syndicated) to other e-commerce sites.

E-commerce content frequently takes the form of multimedia catalogs of product information. So generating and managing catalog content is a major subset of content management. For example, W.W. Grainger & Co., a multibillion-dollar industrial parts distributor, uses the CenterStage catalog management software suite to retrieve data from more than 2,000 supplier databases, standardize the data and translate it into HTML or XML for Web use, and organize and enhance the data for speedy delivery as multimedia Web pages at their www.grainger.com website.

Content and catalog management software work with the profiling tools we mentioned earlier to personalize the content of Web pages seen by individual users. For example, Travelocity.com uses OnDisplay content manager software to push personalized promotional information about other travel opportunities to users while they are involved in an online travel-related transaction.

Finally, content and catalog management may be expanded to include *product configuration* processes that support Web-based customer self-service and the *mass customization* of a company's products. Configuration software helps online customers select the optimum feasible set of product features that can be included in a finished product. For example, both Dell Computer and Cisco Systems use configuration software to sell build-to-order computers and network processors to their online customers [6].

Cabletron Systems: e-Commerce Configuration

When $3 billion network equipment maker Cabletron Systems began selling its wares online, its sales reps knew full well that peddling made-to-order routers was not as simple as the mouse-click marvel of online book selling. Cabletron's big business customers—whether ISP EarthLink or motorcycle maker Harley-Davidson—did not have the technical expertise to build their own router (which can be as small as a breadbox or as large as a television, depending upon the customer, and can include hundreds of components). Worse, Cabletron's website listed thousands of parts that presented users with nearly infinite combinations, most of which would work only when assembled in a certain way.

That's why part of Cabletron's new online sales team consists of a set of complex Web-based product configuration tools made by Calico Commerce of San Jose, California. Called eSales Configuration Workbench, it prompts customers the same way a salesperson might: It walks them through product features; analyzes their needs, budgets, and time constraints; and considers only components and options compatible with existing systems. The configurator also suggests various options—different kinds of backup power, the number of parts, types of connecting wires—and generates price quotes for up to 500 concurrent online users. When a customer clicks the Buy button, the configurator generates an order that is passed on to Cabletron's back-end order fulfillment systems, which update inventory, accounting, and shipping databases.

Within a year of completing a six-month implementation of Calico's software, Cabletron saw staggering results. Some 60 percent of the businesses using its website now use the configurator. Kirk Estes, Cabletron's director of e-commerce, estimates Calico's software saved $12 million in one year by whittling down the percentage of misconfigured orders—and subsequent returns—to nearly nothing. "We think it's 99.8 percent accurate," Estes says. Order processing costs also dropped 96 percent, and customers can now place online orders in 10 to 20 minutes—a fraction of the two to three days it takes through a sales rep [5].

Workflow Management

Many of the business processes in e-commerce applications can be managed and partially automated with the help of workflow management software. E-business workflow systems for enterprise collaboration help employees electronically collaborate to accomplish structured work tasks within knowledge-based business processes. Workflow management in both e-business and e-commerce depends on a *workflow software engine* containing software models of the business processes to be accomplished. The workflow models express the predefined sets of business rules, roles of stakeholders, authorization requirements, routing alternatives, databases used, and sequence of tasks required for each e-commerce process. Thus, workflow systems ensure that the proper transactions, decisions, and work activities are performed, and the correct data and documents are routed to the right employees, customers, suppliers, and other business stakeholders.

For example, Figure 7.7 illustrates the e-commerce procurement processes of the MS Market system of Microsoft Corporation. Microsoft employees use their global intranet and the catalog/content management and workflow management software engines built into MS Market to electronically purchase more than $3 billion annually of business supplies and materials from approved suppliers connected to the MS Market system by their corporate extranets [17].

Microsoft Corporation: e-Commerce Purchasing Processes

MS Market is an internal e-commerce purchasing system that works on Microsoft's intranet. MS Market drastically reduced the personnel required to manage low-cost requisitions and gives employees a quick, easy way to order materials without being burdened with paperwork and bureaucratic processes. These high-volume, low-dollar transactions represent about 70 percent of total volume, but only 3 percent of Microsoft's accounts payable. Employees were wasting time turning requisitions into purchase orders (POs) and trying to follow business rules and processes. Managers wanted to streamline this process, so the decision was made to create a requisitioning tool that would take all the controls and validations used by requisition personnel and push them onto the Web. Employees wanted an easy-to-use online form for ordering supplies that included extranet interfaces to procurement partners, such as Boise Cascade and Marriott.

FIGURE 7.7

The role of catalog/content management and workflow management in a Web-based procurement process: the MS Market system used by Microsoft Corporation.

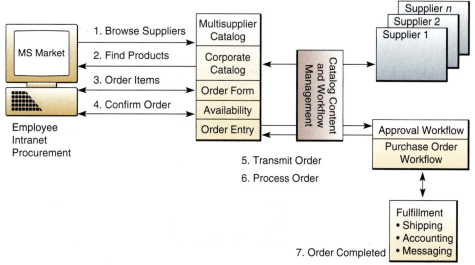

Source: Adapted from Ravi Kalakota and Marcia Robinson, *E-Business: Roadmap for Success* (Reading, MA: Addison-Wesley, 1999), p. 243, © 1999 Addison-Wesley Publishing Company, Inc. Reprinted by permission of Addison-Wesley Longman Inc.

How does this system work? Let's say a Microsoft employee wants a technical book. He goes to the MS Market site on Microsoft's intranet, and MS Market immediately identifies his preferences and approval code through his log-on ID. The employee selects the Barnes & Noble link, which brings up a catalog, order form, and a list of hundreds of books with titles and prices that have been negotiated between Microsoft buyers and Barnes & Noble. He selects a book, puts it in the order form, and completes the order by verifying his group's cost center number and manager's name.

The order is transmitted immediately to the supplier, cutting down on delivery time as well as accounting for the payment of the supplies. Upon submission of the order, MS Market generates an order tracking number for reference, sends notification via e-mail to the employee's manager, and transmits the order over the Internet to Barnes & Noble for fulfillment. In this case, since the purchase total is only $40, the manager's specific approval is not required. Two days later, the book arrives at the employee's office. Thus, MS Market lets employees easily order low-cost items in a controlled fashion at a low cost, without going through a complicated PO approval process [17].

Event Notification

Most e-commerce applications are *event-driven* systems that respond to a multitude of events—from a new customer's first website access, to payment and delivery processes, and to innumerable customer relationship and supply chain management activities. That is why **event notification** processes play an important role in e-commerce systems, since customers, suppliers, employees, and other stakeholders must be notified of all events that might affect their status in a transaction. Event notification software works with the workflow management software to monitor all e-commerce processes and record all relevant events, including unexpected changes or problem situations. Then it works with user-profiling software to automatically notify all involved stakeholders of important transaction events using appropriate user-preferred methods of electronic messaging, such as e-mail, newsgroup, pager, and fax communications. This includes notifying a company's management so they can monitor their employees' responsiveness to e-commerce events and customer and supplier feedback.

For example, when you purchase a product at a retail e-commerce website like Amazon.com, you automatically receive an e-mail record of your order. Then you may receive e-mail notifications of any change in product availability or shipment status, and finally, an e-mail message notifying you that your order has been shipped and is complete.

Collaboration and Trading

This major category of e-commerce processes are those that support the vital collaboration arrangements and trading services needed by customers, suppliers, and other stakeholders to accomplish e-commerce transactions. Thus, in Chapter 2, we discussed how a customer-focused e-business uses tools such as e-mail, chat systems, and discussion groups to nurture online *communities of interest* among employees and customers to enhance customer service and build customer loyalty in e-commerce. The essential collaboration among business trading partners in e-commerce may also be provided by Internet-based trading services. For example, B2B e-commerce Web portals provided by companies like Ariba and Commerce One support matchmaking, negotiation, and mediation processes among business buyers and sellers. In addition, B2B e-commerce is heavily dependent on Internet-based trading platforms and portals that provide online exchange and auctions for e-business enterprises. Therefore, the online auctions and exchange developed by companies like FreeMarkets are revolutionizing the procurement processes of many major corporations. We will discuss these and other e-commerce applications in Section II.

Electronic Payment Processes

Payment for the products and services purchased is an obvious and vital set of processes in electronic commerce transactions. But payment processes are not simple, because of the near-anonymous electronic nature of transactions taking place between the networked computer systems of buyers and sellers, and the many security issues involved. Electronic commerce payment processes are also complex because of the wide variety of debit and credit alternatives and financial institutions and intermediaries that may be part of the process. Therefore, a variety of **electronic payment systems** have evolved over time. In addition, new payment systems are being developed and tested to meet the security and technical challenges of electronic commerce over the Internet.

Web Payment Processes

Most e-commerce systems on the Web involving businesses and consumers (B2C) depend on credit card payment processes. But many B2B e-commerce systems rely on more complex payment processes based on the use of purchase orders, as was illustrated in Figure 7.7. However, both types of e-commerce typically use an electronic *shopping cart* process, which enables customers to select products from website catalog displays and put them temporarily in a virtual shopping basket for later checkout and processing. Figure 7.8 illustrates and summarizes a B2C electronic payment system with several payment alternatives.

Electronic Funds Transfer

Electronic funds transfer (EFT) systems are a major form of electronic payment systems in banking and retailing industries. EFT systems use a variety of information technologies to capture and process money and credit transfers between banks and businesses and their customers. For example, banking networks support teller terminals at all bank offices and automated teller machines (ATMs) at locations throughout the world. Banks, credit card companies, and other businesses may support pay-by-phone services. Very popular also are Web-based payment services, such as PayPal and BillPoint for cash transfers, and CheckFree and PayTrust for automatic bill payment which enable the customers of banks and other bill payment services to use the Internet to electronically pay bills. In addition, most point-of-sale terminals in retail stores are networked to bank EFT systems. This makes it possible for you to use a credit card or debit card to instantly pay for gas, groceries, or other purchases at participating retail outlets.

FIGURE 7.8

An example of a secure
electronic payment system
with many payment
alternatives.

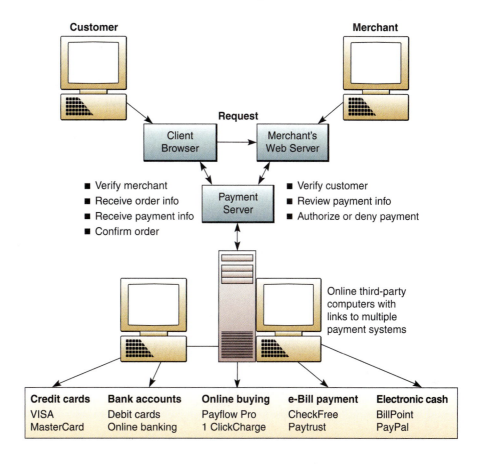

Secure Electronic Payments

When you make an online purchase on the Internet, your credit card information is vulnerable to interception by *network sniffers*, software that easily recognizes credit card number formats. Several basic security measures are being used to solve this security problem: (1) encrypt (code and scramble) the data passing between the customer and merchant, (2) encrypt the data passing between the customer and the company authorizing the credit card transaction, or (3) take sensitive information offline. (Note: Because encryption and other security issues are discussed in Chapter 11, we will not explain how they work in this section.)

For example, many companies use the Secure Socket Layer (SSL) security method developed by Netscape Communications that automatically encrypts data passing between your Web browser and a merchant's server. However, sensitive information is still vulnerable to misuse once it's decrypted (decoded and unscrambled) and stored on a merchant's server. So a digital wallet payment system was developed. In this method, you add security software add-on modules to your Web browser: That enables your browser to encrypt your credit card data in such a way that only the bank that authorizes credit card transactions for the merchant gets to see it. All the merchant is told is whether your credit card transaction is approved or not.

The Secure Electronic Transaction, or SET, standard for electronic payment security extends this digital wallet approach. In this method, EC software encrypts a digital envelope of digital certificates specifying the payment details for each transaction. SET has been agreed to by VISA, MasterCard, IBM, Microsoft, Netscape, and most other industry players. Therefore, SET is expected to eventually become the standard for secure electronic payments on the Internet. However, SET has been stalled by the reluctance of companies to incur its increased hardware, software, and cost requirements [28]. See Figure 7.9.

FIGURE 7.9

VeriSign provides electronic payment, security, and many other e-commerce services.

Source: Courtesy of VeriSign.

SECTION II	# e-Commerce Applications and Issues

e-Commerce Application Trends

E-commerce is here to stay. The Web and e-commerce are key industry drivers. It's changed how many companies do business. It's created new channels for our customers. Companies are at the e-commerce crossroads and there are many ways to go [17].

Thus, e-commerce is changing how companies do business both internally and externally with their customers, suppliers, and other business partners. How companies apply e-commerce to their business is also subject to change as their managers confront a variety of e-commerce alternatives. The applications of e-commerce by many companies have gone through several major stages as e-commerce matures in the world of business. For example, e-commerce between businesses and consumers (B2C) moved from merely offering multimedia company information at corporate websites *(brochureware)*, to offering products and services at Web storefront sites via electronic catalogs and online sales transactions. B2B e-commerce, on the other hand, started with website support to help business customers serve themselves, and then moved toward automating intranet and extranet procurement systems. But before we go any further, let's look at a real world example.

Analyzing ChemConnect and Heritage Services

Read the Real World Case on ChemConnect and Heritage Services on the next page. We can learn a lot about the challenges that companies face as they develop major e-commerce marketplaces. See Figure 7.10.

ChemConnect is an example of a successful public B2B e-commerce exchange specializing in the chemical industry. ChemConnect offers its business customers an efficient way to conduct online auctions with prequalified business suppliers or other companies. This saves time and effort and lowers their customers' cost of acquiring needed chemicals or other materials. However, Heritage Environmental Services is an example of a company that did not like participating as a supplier in a public B2B exchange. It did not like the downward pressure on the prices it was willing to offer for its services, and the public disclosure of its business information that was

FIGURE 7.10
CEO John Robinson's solid business experience has helped lure more business customers to the ChemConnect B2B exchange.

Source: Courtesy of ChemConnect.

REAL WORLD CASE 2

ChemConnect and Heritage Services: Public versus Private B2B Exchanges

The pricing was becoming cutthroat in the closing minutes of the online auction. A North American chemical producer offered to sell a plastics stabilizer to a Fortune 20 firm for $4.35 per kilogram. But with two minutes left, a lower price from a Chinese company flashed across the computer screens at ChemConnect (www.chemconnect.com), the San Francisco operator of a public online marketplace for the chemical industry. The North American producer lowered its price. Back and forth the two firms went as ChemConnect officials saw the price drop penny by penny. The Chinese offered $4.23. Finally, the North American company won the $500,000 contract with an offer of $4.20. The auction was just one of 20 taking place on ChemConnect's website one August morning, as companies from North America, Europe, and Asia bid on the lucrative six-month contracts.

ChemConnect hosted the event during several hours on a recent Monday morning. The same bidding process without the online auction would have taken at least three months, according to the company that held the event—even using e-mail. In the past, this company sent e-mail to all the suppliers it wanted to bid on its business. Then in a few days those companies would respond with their opening bids. The buyer would counter. Up to a week elapsed between every round.

The company doing the buying in this case requested anonymity for fear of tipping off competitors about its buying habits and suppliers. The open nature of the bidding process with public exchanges is a serious challenge. It's also a reason larger companies often set up their own private exchanges.

Not only does ChemConnect help save companies time when they're buying, but it offers a central hub in a fragmented industry. More than 89,000 companies around the world produce chemicals, according to the American Chemical Council. ChemConnect, housed on one floor of a San Francisco high-rise, allows many of them to find suppliers or buyers they did not know existed.

Unlike some of the other B2B dot-coms that flourished and failed, ChemConnect named an industry veteran as its chief executive. CEO John Robinson was an executive with global oil giant BP for 18 years, holding various jobs in the company's research, sales, procurement, and e-commerce divisions. Robinson's past experience has helped lure customers who might have been skeptical of the Net as a venue for million-dollar deals. Still, Robinson says, "We need to . . . broaden our customer base."

Private B2B Exchanges Day after day, e-commerce salespeople called Heritage Environmental Services (www.heritage-enviro.com), a hazardous-waste management firm in Indianapolis, to promote the potential of Internet-based business exchanges. These online bazaars, they said, would introduce the company's services to hundreds of new customers and help Heritage boost sales almost effortlessly. Finally last year, Heritage President Ken Price agreed to enter two B2B Web auctions, hosted by FreeMarkets, to bid on contracts. But Heritage didn't end up winning. Not only that, the online-auction process emphasized price, meaning Heritage had to lower its fee to compete.

Heritage managers quickly concluded that this flavor of Net commerce wasn't for them. Instead, they decided on a different strategy: building their own online portal to link Heritage with existing customers. Heritage's B2B Web-based exchange lets customers order services and keep tabs on their accounts. It also speeds up the billing process because it accepts payment for services online. "What we've got is a nice central focal point where everyone in the process can see what's going on," says Price, who expects his company to book up to 15 percent of its business this year through the private portal.

Heritage is at the forefront of a new development in business-to-business commerce on the Net: so-called private exchanges. This form of online link appeals to a growing number of large and small companies disappointed by public Internet markets intended to facilitate auctions and group purchasing. Like Heritage, many suppliers have been unhappy with the downward price pressures they encounter in public Internet markets.

Businesses concerned that participating in public B2B exchanges would put sales information and other critical data in the hands of customers and competitors are also turning to private exchanges. Smaller companies such as Heritage as well as giants like Dell Computer, Intel, and Wal-Mart have set up private online exchanges to link to suppliers and customers, help streamline the business, and boost sales. Private exchanges offer more control, say executives at these companies, and permit easier customization—allowing automation of processes such as sending purchase orders or checking delivery schedules. And the exchange owner can set its hub to swap data instantly with key suppliers and customers.

Case Study Questions

1. What are the business benefits and limitations of using public B2B exchanges like ChemConnect?

2. What is the business value of private B2B exchanges for a company?

3. Should a small business use public or private B2B exchanges, or should they use exchanges like eBay, that attract both consumers and small businesses? Explain.

FIGURE 7.11   Trends in B2C and B2B e-commerce, and the business strategies and value driving these trends.

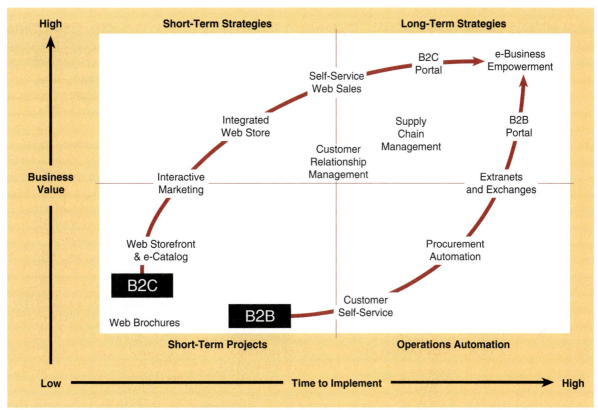

Source: Adapted from Jonathan Rosenoer, Douglas Armstrong, and J. Russell Gates, *The Clickable Corporation: Successful Strategies for Capturing the Internet Advantage* (New York: The Free Press, 1999), p. 24.

required. So Heritage has chosen to establish its own private B2B online exchange as a convenient Web focal point for conducting business electronically with its business customers.

e-Commerce Trends

Figure 7.11 illustrates some of the trends taking place in the e-commerce applications that we introduced at the beginning of this section. Notice how B2C e-commerce moves from simple Web storefronts to interactive marketing capabilities that provide a personalized shopping experience for customers, and then toward a totally integrated Web store that supports a variety of customer shopping experiences. B2C e-commerce is also moving toward a self-service model where customers configure and customize the products and services they wish to buy, aided by configuration software and online customer support as needed.

B2B e-commerce participants moved quickly from self-service on the Web to configuration and customization capabilities and extranets connecting trading partners. As B2C e-commerce moves toward full-service and wide-selection retail Web portals, B2B is also trending toward the use of e-commerce portals that provide catalog, exchange, and auction markets for business customers within or across industries. Of course, both of these trends are enabled by e-business capabilities like customer relationship management and supply chain management, which are the hallmarks of the customer-focused and internetworked supply chains of a fully e-business-enabled company [30].

e-Commerce Sectors

Another way to look at how companies have moved into e-commerce is to organize present and potential online services and products into a variety of **e-commerce sectors** that go beyond simple classifications like B2B and B2C. Figure 7.12 defines

FIGURE 7.12 The six major sectors of e-commerce activities differ in the online services and products they offer and the customer values that drive them.

e-Commerce Sectors			
Sector	**Online Products and Services**	**Key Value Drivers**	**Companies That Target the Sector**
Infrastructure	Access, communication, interpretation, digitization, interconnectedness, display, storage, retrieval, and processing	Availability, security, coverage, speed, scalability, mobility, and price	Akamai, AOL, BEA Systems, IBM, Sun Microsystems, Telefonica, Tibco Software, and VeriSign
Applications	Organization, simplification, presentation, manipulation, analysis, tracking, matching, and reception and transmission of information	Functionality, reliability, efficiency, compatibility, upgradability, privacy, and price	Adobe, Ariba, Commerce One, DoubleClick, IBM, Inktomi, Intuit, Microsoft, Oracle, and SAP
Portals	Internet gateway, search and navigation, links to services and content, and broadcast medium (for advertising)	Exhaustiveness, speed, convenience, privacy, community experience, customizability, size and attractiveness of user base, and price	AOL, CEOExpress, Excite, iVillage, StarMedia Networks, TerraLycos, and Yahoo!
Content	Information (general and specific, current and archived), news, entertainment (including games), and databases	Accuracy, timeliness, completeness, appeal, interactivity, and price	AOL Time Warner, CNN, Bloomberg, EMI, Multex, Newscorp, Pearson, and Reuters
Services	An act that satisfies a need or want	Quality of experience, efficiency, reliability, convenience, customization, privacy, and price	Amazon, bfinance, btrade, E*Trade, W.W. Grainger, Media Metrix, Merck-Medco, and Travelocity
Exchanges	A virtual trading place, and matching and creation of supply and demand	Transaction density, trust, transaction security, privacy, support services (such as insurance and delivery), and price	ChemConnect, Covisint, eBay, Elemica, QXL, FreeMarkets, and Ventro

Source: Adapted from Subramanian Rangan and Ron Adner, "Profits and the Internet: Seven Misconceptions," *MIT Sloan Management Review*, Summer 2001, p. 48.

and describes six major e-commerce sectors that companies have chosen or can choose to operate in as they formulate their e-commerce strategies. Notice how each sector differs in the online services and products they offer and the key customer values that drive their e-commerce activities. For example, in the e-commerce infrastructure sector, compatibility, availability, and scalability of online networks and support services are major value drivers for customers. In the e-commerce content sector, on the other hand, the accuracy, timeliness, and appeal of online content are key customer value drivers. Examples of companies that have a major presence in each sector are also shown in Figure 7.12. This should give you a good idea of some of the major opportunities and challenges facing companies and entrepreneurs who wish to develop or expand e-commerce services and products.

Business-to-Consumer e-Commerce

E-commerce applications that focus on the consumer share an important goal: to attract potential buyers, transact goods and services, and build customer loyalty through individual courteous treatment and engaging community features [15].

What does it take to create a successful B2C e-commerce business venture? That's the question that many are asking in the wake of the failures of many pure B2C *dot-com* companies. One obvious answer would be to create a Web business initiative that offers attractive products or services of great customer value, and whose business plan

FIGURE 7.13

Examples of a few top-rated retail websites.

Top Retail Websites
● **Amazon.com   www.amazon.com** Amazon.com is the exception to the rule that consumers prefer to shop "real world" retailers online. The mother of all shopping sites, Amazon features a vast selection of books, videos, DVDs, CDs, toys, kitchen items, electronics, and even home and garden goods sold to millions of loyal customers.
● **eBay   www.ebay.com** The fabled auction site operates the world's biggest electronic flea market, with everything from antiques, computers, and coins to Pez dispensers and baseball cards. This site boasts billions of page views per month, and millions of items for sale in thousands of categories supported by thousands of special-interest groups.
● **Eddie Bauer   www.eddiebauer.com** Sportswear titan Eddie Bauer has integrated its retail channels-store, website, and catalog. Shoppers can return an item to any Eddie Bauer store, no matter where it was purchased—a policy other merchants should follow.
● **Lands' End   www.landsend.com** With several seasons as an online retailer, Lands' End is a pro at meeting shoppers' expectations. One of the best features: Specialty Shoppers. A customer service rep will help you make your selections and answer questions by phone or via a live chat.

Source: Adapted from "Tech Lifestyles: Shopping," Technology Buyers Guide, *Fortune*, Winter 2001, pp. 288–90. © 2001 Time Inc. All rights reserved.

is based on realistic forecasts of profitability within the first year or two of operation—a condition that was lacking in many failed dot-coms. But such failures have not stemmed the tide of millions of businesses, both large and small, that are moving at least part of their business to the Web. So let's take a look at some essential success factors and website capabilities for companies engaged in either B2C or B2B e-commerce. Figure 7.13 provides examples of a few top-rated retail Web companies.

e-Commerce Success Factors

On the Internet, the barriers of time, distance, and form are broken down, and businesses are able to transact the sale of goods and services 24 hours a day, 7 days a week, 365 days a year with consumers all over the world. In certain cases, it is even possible to convert a physical good (CDs, packaged software, a newspaper) to a virtual good (MP3 audio, downloadable software, information in HTML format) [15].

A basic fact of Internet retailing (*e-tailing*) is that all retail websites are created equal as far as the "location, location, location" imperative of success in retailing is concerned. No site is any closer to its Web customers, and competitors offering similar goods and services may be only a mouse click away. This makes it vital that businesses find ways to build customer satisfaction, loyalty, and relationships, so customers keep coming back to their Web stores. Thus the key to e-tail success is to optimize several key factors such as selection and value, performance and service efficiency, the look and feel of the site, advertising and incentives to purchase, personal attention, community relationships, and security and reliability. Let's briefly examine each of these factors that are essential to the success of a B2C Web business. See Figure 7.14.

Selection and Value. Obviously, a business must offer Web shoppers a good selection of attractive products and services at competitive prices or they will quickly click away from a Web store. But a company's prices don't have to be the lowest on the Web if they build a reputation for high quality, guaranteed satisfaction, and top customer support while shopping and after the sale. For example, top-rated e-tailer REI.com helps you select quality outdoor gear for hiking and other activities with a "How to Choose" section, and gives a money-back guarantee on your purchases.

FIGURE 7.14
Some of the key factors for
success in e-commerce.

e-Commerce Success Factors
● **Selection and Value.** Attractive product selections, competitive prices, satisfaction guarantees, and customer support after the sale.
● **Performance and Service.** Fast, easy navigation, shopping, and purchasing, and prompt shipping and delivery.
● **Look and Feel.** Attractive Web storefront, website shopping areas, multimedia product catalog pages, and shopping features.
● **Advertising and Incentives.** Targeted Web page advertising and e-mail promotions, discounts and special offers, including advertising at affiliate sites.
● **Personal Attention.** Personal Web pages, personalized product recommendations, Web advertising and e-mail notices, and interactive support for all customers.
● **Community Relationships.** Virtual communities of customers, suppliers, company representatives, and others via newsgroups, chat rooms, and links to related sites.
● **Security and Reliability.** Security of customer information and website transactions, trustworthy product information, and reliable order fulfillment.

Performance and Service. People don't want to be kept waiting when browsing, selecting, or paying in a Web store. A site must be efficiently designed for ease of access, shopping, and buying, with sufficient server power and network capacity to support website traffic. Web shopping and customer service must also be friendly and helpful, as well as quick and easy. In addition, products offered should be available in inventory for prompt shipment to the customer.

Look and Feel. B2C sites can offer customers an attractive Web storefront, shopping areas, and multimedia product catalogs. These could range from an exciting shopping experience with audio, video, and moving graphics, to a more simple and comfortable look and feel. Thus, most retail e-commerce sites let customers browse product sections, select products, drop them into a virtual shopping cart, and go to a virtual checkout station when they are ready to pay for their order.

Advertising and Incentives. Some Web stores may advertise in traditional media, but most advertise on the Web with targeted and personalized banner ads and other Web page and e-mail promotions. Most B2C sites also offer shoppers incentives to buy and return. Typically, this means coupons, discounts, special offers, and vouchers for other Web services, sometimes with other e-tailers at cross-linked websites. Many Web stores also increase their market reach by being part of Web banner advertising exchange programs with thousand of other Web retailers. Figure 7.15 compares major marketing communications choices in traditional and e-commerce marketing to support each step of the buying process.

Personal Attention. Personalizing your shopping experience encourages you to buy and make return visits. Thus, e-commerce software can automatically record details of your visits and build user profiles of you and other Web shoppers. Many sites also encourage you to register with them and fill out a personal interest profile. Then, whenever you return, you are welcomed by name or with a personal Web page, greeted with special offers, and guided to those parts of the site that you are most interested in. This *one-to-one marketing* and relationship building power is one of the major advantages of personalized Web retailing.

Community Relationships. Giving online customers with special interests a feeling of belonging to a unique group of like-minded individuals helps build customer loyalty and value. Thus, website relationship and affinity marketing programs build

FIGURE 7.15   How traditional and Web marketing communications differ in supporting each step of the buying process.

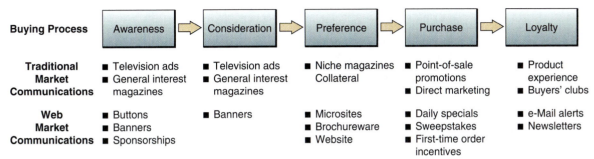

Buying Process	Awareness	Consideration	Preference	Purchase	Loyalty
Traditional Market Communications	■ Television ads ■ General interest magazines	■ Television ads ■ General interest magazines	■ Niche magazines Collateral	■ Point-of-sale promotions ■ Direct marketing	■ Product experience ■ Buyers' clubs
Web Market Communications	■ Buttons ■ Banners ■ Sponsorships	■ Banners	■ Microsites ■ Brochureware ■ Website	■ Daily specials ■ Sweepstakes ■ First-time order incentives	■ e-Mail alerts ■ Newsletters

Source: Adapted from Jeffrey Rayport and Bernard Jaworski, *Introduction to e-Commerce*, McGraw-Hill/Irwin, 2001, p. 242.

and promote virtual communities of customers, suppliers, company representatives, and others via a variety of Web-based collaboration tools. Examples include discussion forums or newsgroups, chat rooms, message board systems, and cross-links to related website communities.

Security and Reliability. As a customer of a successful Web store, you must feel confident that your credit card, personal information, and details of your transactions are secure from unauthorized use. You must also feel that you are dealing with a trustworthy business, whose products and other website information you can trust to be as advertised. Having your orders filled and shipped as you requested, in the time frame promised, and with good customer support are other measures of an e-tailer's reliability.

Amazon.com: Tops in B2C Retailing

Amazon (www.amazon.com) is rated as one of the biggest and best virtual retailers on the Web, and has regained some of its luster with investors because it is finally making operating profits after many years of losses. The site is designed to speed you through the process of browsing and ordering merchandise while giving you reassuring, personal service at discount prices. For example, the search engine for finding the products you want is quick and accurate, and the ordering process easy and fast. Confirmation is quick, notifications are accurate and friendly, and delivery is prompt. Buyers are e-mailed both when their order is confirmed, as well as the day their order is shipped. The company also offers customers a complete money-back guarantee.

In creating this potential powerhouse of shopping services and offerings, Amazon.com wants to be not simply a Wal-Mart of the Web but rather a next-generation retail commerce portal. Imagine a customized site where—through a personalized shopping service and communities of other shoppers—you will not only shop easily with a trusted brand for books, videos, gifts, and more, but you will also research the features, price, and availability of millions of products from a single storefront that has Amazon's—and your—name on it.

That's what has gotten Amazon this far in its first years of business: exhaustive focus on convenience, selection, and personalization. It lived up to its billing as "Earth's Biggest Selection" by building an inventory of millions of products. It was also among the first Net stores to facilitate credit card purchases; greet customers by name and offer customized home pages; send purchase recommendations via e-mail; and number and explain each step in the purchasing process. This combination of vast selection, efficiency, discount prices, and personal service is why Amazon is frequently mentioned as the top retailer on the Web [6, 36].

FIGURE 7.16   These Web store requirements must be implemented by a company or its website hosting service, in order to develop a successful e-commerce business.

Developing a Web Store		
Build	**Market**	
Website design tools	Web page advertising	
Site design templates	E-mail promotions	
Custom design services	Web advertising exchanges with affiliate sites	
Website hosting	Search engine registrations	
Serving Your Customers		
Serve	**Transact**	**Support**
Personalized Web pages	Flexible order process	Website online help
Dynamic multimedia catalog	Credit card processing	Customer service e-mail
Catalog search engine	Shipping and tax calculations	Discussion groups and chat rooms
Integrated shopping cart	E-mail order notifications	Links to related sites
Managing a Web Store		
Manage	**Operate**	**Protect**
Website usage statistics	24x7 website hosting	User password protection
Sales and inventory reports	Online tech support	Encrypted order processing
Customer account management	Scalable network capacity	Encrypted website administration
Links to accounting system	Redundant servers and power	Network fire walls and security monitors

Web Store Requirements

Most business-to-consumer e-commerce ventures take the form of retail business sites on the World Wide Web. Whether a huge retail Web portal like Amazon.com, or a small specialty Web retailer, the primary focus of such e-tailers is to develop, operate, and manage their websites so they become high-priority destinations for consumers who will repeatedly choose to go there to buy products and services. Thus, these websites must be able to demonstrate the key factors for e-commerce success that we have just covered. In this section, let's discuss the essential Web store requirements that you would have to implement to support a successful retail business on the Web, as summarized and illustrated in Figure 7.16.

Developing a Web Store

Before you can launch your own retail store on the Internet, you must build an e-commerce website. Many companies use simple website design software tools and predesigned templates provided by their website hosting service to construct their Web retail store. That includes building your Web storefront and product catalog Web pages, as well as tools to provide shopping cart features, process orders, handle credit card payments, and so forth. Of course, larger companies can use their own software developers or hire an outside website development contractor to build a custom-designed e-commerce site. Also, like most companies, you can contract with your ISP (Internet service provider) or a specialized Web hosting company to operate and maintain your B2C website.

Once you build your website, it must be developed as a retail Web business by marketing it in a variety of ways that attract visitors to your site and transform them into loyal Web customers. So your website should include Web page and e-mail advertising and promotions for Web visitors and customers, and Web advertising exchange programs with other Web stores. Also, you can register your Web business with its own domain name (for example, yourstore.com), as well as registering your website with the major Web search engines and directories to help Web surfers find your site more easily. In addition, you might consider affiliating as a small business partner with large Web portals like Yahoo! and Netscape, large e-tailers and auction sites like Amazon and eBay, and small business Web centers like Microsoft bCentral and Prodigy Biz.

Freemerchant and Prodigy Biz: Getting Started	Freemerchant and Prodigy Biz are examples of the many companies that help small businesses get on the Web. Freemerchant.com enables you to set up a Web store for free by choosing from nearly 60 design templates. That includes Web hosting on secure networks, shopping cart and order processing, and providing common database software for importing your product catalog data. Fee-based services include banner ad exchanges, domain and search engine registrations, and enabling product data to be listed on eBay and sales data to be exported to the QuickBooks accounting system.

Prodigybiz.com is designed to serve small e-tail businesses with a full range of Web store development services. Prodigy Biz features both free and fee-based site design and Web publishing tools, website hosting and site maintenance, full e-commerce order and credit card processing, Internet access and e-mail services, and a variety of management reports and affiliate marketing programs [34]. See Figure 7.17.

Serving Your Customers

Once your retail store is on the Web and receiving visitors, the website must help you welcome and serve them personally and efficiently so that they become loyal customers. So most e-tailers use several website tools to create user profiles, customer files, and personal Web pages and promotions that help them develop a one-to-one relationship with their customers. This includes creating incentives to encourage visitors to register, developing *Web cookie files* to automatically identify returning visitors, or contracting with website tracking companies like DoubleClick and others for software to automatically record and analyze the details of the website behavior and preferences of Web shoppers.

FIGURE 7.17

Prodigy Biz is one of many companies offering retail website development and hosting services.

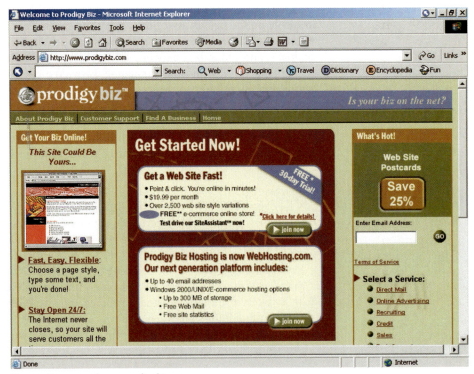

Source: Courtesy of www.prodigybiz.com.

Of course, your website should have the look and feel of an attractive, friendly, and efficient Web store. That means having e-commerce features like a dynamically changing and updated multimedia catalog, a fast catalog search engine, and a convenient shopping cart system that is integrated with Web shopping, promotions, payment, shipping, and customer account information. Your e-commerce order processing software should be fast and able to adjust to personalized promotions and customer options like gift handling, special discounts, credit card or other payments, and shipping and tax alternatives. Also, automatically sending your customers e-mail notices to document when orders are processed and shipped is a top customer service feature of e-tail transaction processing.

Providing customer support for your Web store is an essential website capability. So many e-tail sites offer help menus, tutorials, and lists of FAQs (frequently asked questions) to provide self-help features for Web shoppers. Of course, e-mail correspondence with customer service representatives of your Web store offers more personal assistance to customers. Establishing website discussion groups and chat rooms for your customers and store personnel to interact helps create a more personal community that can provide invaluable support to customers, as well as building customer loyalty. Providing links to related websites from your Web store can help customers find additional information and resources, as well as earning commission income from the affiliate marketing programs of other Web retailers. For example, the Amazon.com Affiliate program pays commissions of up to 15 percent for purchases made by Web shoppers clicking to their Web store from your site.

Managing a Web Store

A Web retail store must be managed as both a business and a website, and most e-commerce hosting companies offer software and services to help you do just that. For example, companies like Freemerchant, Prodigy Biz, and Verio provide their hosting clients with a variety of management reports that record and analyze Web store traffic, inventory, and sales results. Other services build customer lists for e-mail and Web page promotions, or provide customer relationship management features to help retain Web customers. Also, some e-commerce software includes links to download inventory and sales data into accounting packages like QuickBooks for bookkeeping and preparation of financial statements and reports.

Of course, Web hosting companies must enable their Web store clients to be available online twenty-four hours a day and seven days a week all year. This requires them to build or contract for sufficient network capacity to handle peak Web traffic loads, and redundant network servers and power sources to respond to system or power failures. Most hosting companies provide e-commerce software that uses passwords and encryption to protect Web store transactions and customer records, and employ network fire walls and security monitors to repel hacker attacks and other security threats. Many hosting services also offer their clients twenty-four hour tech support to help them with any technical problems that arise. We will discuss these and other e-commerce security management issues in Chapter 11.

NTT/Verio Inc.: Website Management

NTT/Verio Inc. (www.verio.com) is an example of one of the world's leading Web hosting companies. Verio provides complete software, computing, and network resources to Web hosting companies, as well as offering e-commerce development and hosting services to Web retailers. Verio also offers a Web startup and development service for small businesses called SiteMerlin (www.sitemerlin.com). Verio guarantees 99.9 percent website uptime to its e-commerce customers, with 24 × 7 server monitoring and customer support. Verio hosts more than 10,000 small and medium-sized Web businesses; has a network hosting alliance with Sun Microsystems, an Oracle Web database application service; and provides hosting services to Terra Lycos and other Web hosting companies [34].

Business-to-Business e-Commerce

Business-to-business electronic commerce is the wholesale and supply side of the commercial process, where businesses buy, sell, or trade with other businesses. B2B electronic commerce relies on many different information technologies, most of which are implemented at e-commerce websites on the World Wide Web and corporate intranets and extranets. B2B applications include electronic catalog systems, electronic trading systems such as exchange and auction portals, electronic data interchange, electronic funds transfers, and so on. All of the factors for building a successful retail website we discussed earlier also apply to wholesale websites for business-to-business electronic commerce.

In addition, many businesses are integrating their Web-based e-commerce systems with their e-business systems for supply chain management, customer relationship management, and online transaction processing, as well as to their traditional, or legacy, computer-based accounting and business information systems. This ensures that all electronic commerce activities are integrated with e-business processes and supported by up-to-date corporate inventory and other databases, which in turn are automatically updated by Web sales activities. Let's look at a successful example.

Cisco Systems: B2B Marketplace Success

The e-commerce website Cisco Connection Online enables corporate users to purchase routers, switches, and other hardware that enables customers to build high-speed information networks. Over 70 percent of Cisco's sales take place at this site.

So what has made Cisco so successful? Some would argue that its market—networking hardware—is a prime product to sell online because the customer base is composed almost entirely of IT department staffers and consultants. To some degree, this is certainly true. On the other hand, competitors initially scoffed at Cisco's efforts due to the inherent complexity of its product. However, it's difficult to dispute that Cisco has built an online store with functionality and usefulness that is a model of success in the B2B commerce world.

Cisco was able to achieve success largely due to the variety of service offerings made available throughout its purchasing process. In addition to simply providing a catalog and transaction processing facilities, Cisco includes a personalized interface for buyers, an extensive customer support section with contact information, technical documents, software updates, product configuration tools, and even online training and certification courses for Cisco hardware. Also, Cisco provides direct integration with its internal back-end systems for frequent customers, and makes software available that customers can use to design custom links to their own line-of-business software from such players as SAP America, PeopleSoft, and Oracle.

Cisco has also made a concerted effort to ensure that post-sale customer support is available to buyers of every kind. For most large corporations, this means diligent account management and dedicated support representatives to troubleshoot problems and aid in complex network design. For smaller businesses that may be installing their first routers or switches, Cisco includes recommended configurations and simple FAQs to get users up and running.

Like any mature virtual marketplace, Cisco Connection Online integrates directly with Cisco's internal applications and databases to automatically manage inventory and production. Cisco even allows vendors such as HP, PeopleSoft, and IBM to exchange design data to enable easy network configuration troubleshooting online [15].

e-Commerce Marketplaces

The latest e-commerce transaction systems are scaled and customized to allow buyers and sellers to meet in a variety of high-speed trading platforms: auctions, catalogs, and exchanges [23].

FIGURE 7.18

Types of e-commerce marketplaces.

e-Commerce Marketplaces
● **One to many:** Sell-side marketplaces. Host one major supplier, who dictates product catalog offerings and prices. Examples: Cisco.com and Dell.com.
● **Many to one:** Buy-side marketplaces. Attract many suppliers that flock to these exchanges to bid on the business of a major buyer like GE or AT&T.
● **Some to many:** Distribution marketplaces. Unite major suppliers who combine their product catalogs to attract a larger audience of buyers. Examples: VerticalNet and Works.com
● **Many to some:** Procurement marketplaces. Unite major buyers who combine their purchasing catalogs to attract more suppliers and thus more competition and lower prices. Examples: the auto industry's Covisint and energy industry's Pantellos.
● **Many to many:** Auction marketplaces used by many buyers and sellers that can create a variety of buyers' or sellers' auctions to dynamically optimize prices. Examples are eBay and FreeMarkets.

Source: Adapted from Edward Robinson, "Battle to the Bitter End (-to-End)," *Business 2.0*, July 25, 2000, pp. 140–141.

Businesses of any size can now buy everything from chemicals to electronic components, excess electrical energy, construction materials, or paper products at business-to-business **e-commerce marketplaces.** Figure 7.18 outlines five major types of e-commerce marketplaces used by businesses today. However, many B2B **e-commerce portals** provide several types of marketplaces. Thus they may offer an electronic **catalog** shopping and ordering site for products from many suppliers in an industry. Or they may serve as an **exchange** for buying and selling via a bid-ask process, or at negotiated prices. Very popular are electronic **auction** websites for business-to-business auctions of products and services. Figure 7.19 illustrates a B2B trading system that offers exchange, auction, and reverse auction (where sellers bid for the business of a buyer) electronic markets.

Many of these B2B **e-commerce portals** are developed and hosted by third-party *market-maker* companies who serve as **infomediaries** that bring buyers and

FIGURE 7.19

This is an example of a B2B e-commerce Web portal that offers exchange, auction, and reverse auction electronic markets.

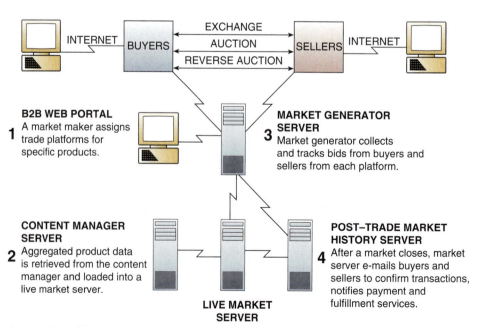

Source: Adapted from Mark Leon, "Trading Spaces," *Business 2.0*, February 2000, p. 129.

FIGURE 7.20 Examples of the B2B procurement marketplaces formed by major corporations in various industries.

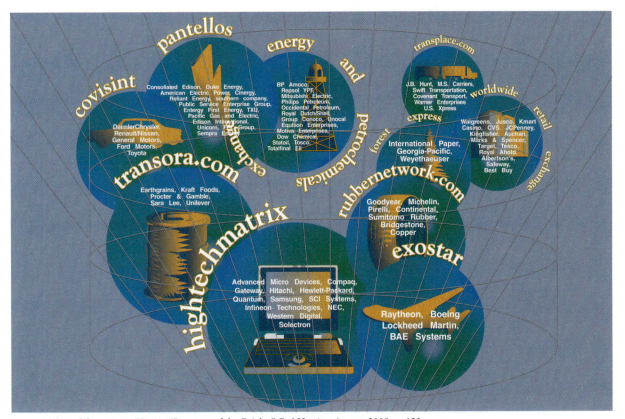

Source: Adapted from Peter Henig, "Revenge of the Bricks," *Red Herring*, August 2000, p. 123.

sellers together in catalog, exchange, and auction markets. Infomediaries are companies that serve as intermediaries in e-business and e-commerce transactions. Examples are Ariba, Commerce One, VerticalNet, and FreeMarkets, to name a few. All provide e-commerce marketplace software products and services to power their Web portals for e-commerce transactions.

These B2B e-commerce sites make business purchasing decisions faster, simpler, and more cost effective, since companies can use Web systems to research and transact with many vendors. Business buyers get one-stop shopping and accurate purchasing information. They also get impartial advice from infomediaries that they can't get from the sites hosted by suppliers and distributors. Thus, companies can negotiate or bid for better prices from a larger pool of vendors. And of course, suppliers benefit from easy access to customers from all over the globe [23, 25]. Figure 7.20 illustrates the huge B2B procurement marketplaces formed by consortiums of major corporations in various industries to trade with their thousands of suppliers. Now, let's look at a real world example.

| **Covisint, Johnson Controls, and FreeMarkets.com: B2B Marketplaces** | In just about every industry—from automobile manufacturing to chemical production—electronic marketplaces have been created to handle the buying and selling of goods and services between manufacturers and suppliers. One common bond that unites these B2B e-commerce markets is the hope that the automation of exchange processes will dramatically cut time, cost, and waste. But while information technology is a key enabler behind the scenes, one of the biggest challenges |

online e-market creators face is translating paper-based processes to more efficient, electronic approaches that support strategic relationships with their suppliers, customers, and even competitors.

A prime example of that is Covisint LLC, a business-to-business e-marketplace created by Ford Motor, General Motors, and DaimlerChrysler in February 2000. The automotive exchange could potentially handle more than $240 billion in annual procurements of raw materials and vehicle parts by these manufacturers alone.

Detroit-based GM plans to reduce the average cost of processing a purchase order from $100 to $10 by using Covisint. The world's largest automaker spends more than $80 billion in procurements each year, so even a minor improvement in how these activities are handled could save the company billions.

Most of the big automotive suppliers acknowledge that they'll work with Covisint, but that hasn't stopped them from creating e-marketplaces of their own. For example, Johnson Controls, Inc., a manufacturer of car parts and environmental systems in Milwaukee, launched a design and collaboration exchange for its 600 suppliers in March 2001.

Mike Suman, group vice president for e-business and marketing at Johnson Controls, says the company needed to replace its homegrown product development software with a B2B exchange that will address the bidding process with suppliers and the management of design collaboration. E-commerce software from MatrixOne forms the bulk of the technology infrastructure for the e-marketplace.

Auction sites like MetalSite and PlasticsNet.com create lively global spot markets for standard processed materials like steel, chemicals, and plastics. On MetalSite, for example, Weirton or LTV can put sheet or rolled steel on the block anytime the market looks hungry. Buyers then enter their bids over two or three days, and the highest price wins. This is called a sellers' auction: Think of it as the business version of the familiar estate sale for rugs or antiques.

The FreeMarkets online auction model takes the Internet into a much bigger, far more complex kind of corporate purchase: the individually crafted parts—the motors, gears, circuit boards, and plastic casings that producers forge into their finished automobiles, washing machines, and locomotives—that are purchased on contracts typically running three or four years.

General Motors, United Technologies, Raytheon, and Quaker Oats have saved more than 15 percent on average buying parts, materials, and even services at FreeMarkets auctions. Says Kent Brittan, vice president of supply management for United Technologies: "This FreeMarkets auction idea is revolutionizing procurement as we know it" [41].

Clicks and Bricks in e-Commerce

Companies are recognizing that success in the new economy will go to those who can execute clicks-and-mortar strategies that bridge the physical and virtual worlds. Different companies will need to follow very different paths in deciding how closely—or loosely—to integrate their Internet initiatives with their traditional operations [13].

Figure 7.21 illustrates the spectrum of alternatives and benefit trade-offs that e-business enterprises face when choosing an e-commerce "clicks and bricks" strategy. E-business managers must answer this question: Should we integrate our e-commerce virtual business operations with our traditional physical business operations, or keep them separate? As Figure 7.21 shows, companies have been implementing a range

FIGURE 7.21   Companies have a spectrum of alternatives and benefits trade-offs when deciding upon an integrated or separate e-commerce business.

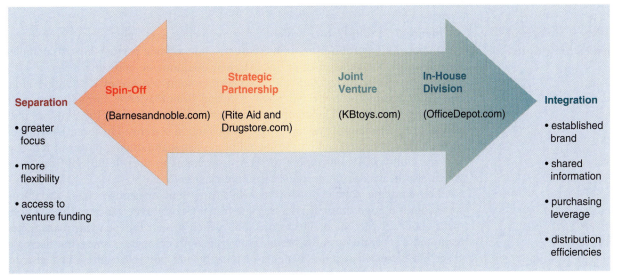

Source: Adapted from Ranjay Gulati and Jason Garino, "Get the Right Mix of Bricks and Clicks," *Harvard Business Review*, May–June 2000, p. 110.

of integration/separation strategies and made key benefits trade-offs in answering that question. Let's take a look at several alternatives [13].

e-Commerce Integration

The Internet is just another channel that gets plugged into the business architecture [13].

So says CIO Bill Seltzer of office supply retailer Office Depot, which fully integrates their OfficeDepot.com e-commerce sales channel into their traditional business operations. Thus, Office Depot is a prime example of why many companies have chosen integrated clicks and bricks strategies, where their e-commerce business is integrated in some major ways into the traditional business operations of a company. The business case for such strategies rests on:

- Capitalizing on any unique strategic capabilities that may exist in a company's traditional business operations that could be used to support an e-commerce business.

- Gaining several strategic benefits of integrating e-commerce into a company's traditional business; such as the sharing of established brands and key business information, and joint buying power and distribution efficiencies.

For example, Office Depot already had a successful catalog sales business with a professional call center and a fleet of over 2,000 delivery trucks. Its 1,825 stores and 30 warehouses were networked by a sophisticated information system that provided complete customer, vendor, order, and product inventory data in real time. These business resources made an invaluable foundation for coordinating Office Depot's e-commerce activities and customer services with its catalog business and physical stores. Thus, customers can shop at OfficeDepot.com at their home or business, or at in-store kiosks. Then they can choose to pick up their purchases at the stores or have them delivered. In addition, the integration of Web-enabled e-commerce applications within Office Depot's traditional store and catalog operations has helped to increase the traffic at their physical stores and improved the catalog operation's productivity and average order size.

Other Clicks and Bricks Strategies

As Figure 7.21 illustrates, other clicks and bricks strategies range from partial e-commerce integration using joint ventures and strategic partnerships, to complete separation via the spin-off of an independent e-commerce company.

For example, KBtoys.com is an e-commerce joint venture of KB Online Holdings LLC, created by toy retailer KB Toys and BrainPlay.com, formerly an e-tailer of children's products. The company is 80 percent owned by KB Toys, but has independent management teams and separate distribution systems. However, KBtoys.com has successfully capitalized on the shared brand name and buying power of KB Toys, and the ability of its customers to return purchases to over 1,300 KB Toys stores which also heavily promote their e-commerce site.

The strategic partnership of the Rite-Aid retail drugstore chain and Drugstore.com is a good example of a less integrated e-commerce venture. Rite-Aid only owns about 25 percent of Drugstore.com, which has an independent management team and a separate business brand. However, both companies share the decreased costs and increased revenue benefits of joint buying power, an integrated distribution center, co-branded pharmacy products, and joint prescription fulfillment at Rite-Aid stores.

Finally, let's look at an example of the benefits and challenges of a completely separate clicks and bricks strategy. Barnesandnoble.com was created as an independent e-commerce company that was spun off by the Barnes & Noble book retail chain. This enabled it to gain several hundred million dollars in venture capital funding, create an entrepreneurial culture, attract quality management, maintain a high degree of business flexibility, and accelerate decision making. But the book e-retailer has done poorly since its founding, and has failed to gain market share from Amazon.com, its leading competitor. Many business analysts say that the failure of Barnes & Noble to integrate some of the marketing and operations of Barnesandnoble.com within their thousands of bookstores forfeited a key strategic business opportunity.

e-Commerce Channel Choices

Some of the key questions that the management of companies must answer in making a clicks and bricks decision and developing the resulting e-commerce channel are outlined in Figure 7.22. The different ways companies can generate e-commerce revenue, summarized in Figure 7.23, help to spotlight the alternatives

FIGURE 7.22
Key questions for developing an e-commerce channel strategy.

A Checklist for Channel Development
1. What audiences are we attempting to reach?
2. What action do we want those audiences to take?—to learn about us, to give us information about themselves, to make an inquiry, to buy something from our site, to buy something through another channel?
3. Who owns the e-commerce channel within the organization?
4. Is the e-commerce channel planned alongside other channels?
5. Do we have a process for generating, approving, releasing, and withdrawing content?
6. Will our brands translate to the new channel or will they require modification?
7. How will we market the channel itself?

Source: Paul May, *The Business of e-Commerce: From Corporate Strategy to Technology* (Cambridge, UK, Cambridge University Press, 2001), p. 66.

FIGURE 7.23

Key revenue-generating alternatives for a company's e-commerce channel.

e-Commerce Revenue Alternatives	
Additive channel	Sell more of our traditional lines to new markets
New offer channel	Invent a new product or service for the e-commerce channel
Subscription	Charge for access to content
Advertising	Sell ad space on the site
Sponsorship	Apply a brand to a content offering
Licensing	Restrict your channel to paying carriers
Portaling	Charge destinations for sending users there (also seen in "click-through" advertising)
Commission	Take a percentage on transactions effected through the channel
Tolling	Take a percentage on transactions effected through your mechanism

Source: Paul May, *The Business of e-Commerce: From Corporate Strategy to Technology* (Cambridge, UK, Cambridge University Press, 2001), p. 67.

companies have in developing a profitable business model for their e-commerce channel.

An **e-commerce channel** is the marketing or sales channel created by a company to conduct and manage its chosen e-commerce activities. How this e-commerce channel is integrated with a company's traditional sales channels (retail/wholesale outlets, catalog sales, direct sales, etc.) is a major consideration in developing its e-commerce strategy. We will discuss e-business and e-commerce strategy further in Chapter 9.

Thus, the examples in this section emphasize that there is no universal clicks and bricks e-commerce strategy or e-commerce channel choice for every company, industry, or type of business. Both e-commerce integration and separation have major business benefits and shortcomings. Thus, deciding on a clicks and bricks strategy and e-commerce channel depends heavily on whether or not a company's unique business operations provide strategic capabilities and resources to successfully support a profitable business model for their e-commerce channel. As these examples show, most companies are implementing some measure of clicks and bricks integration, because "the benefits of integration are almost always too great to abandon entirely" [13].

Citigroup: From Failure to Success in e-Commerce Integration Strategies

Few companies blew more money trying to build independent e-commerce divisions than Citigroup, parent company of Citibank, Salomon Smith Barney, and Travelers Insurance. In 1997, it launched e-Citi with high hopes and a big task. e-Citi's job was to keep all of Citigroup on its toes—partly by competing with the very bank, credit card company, and other businesses that made Citigroup a $230 billion giant. There was to be an e-Citibank called Citi.f/i and a financial portal called Finance.com. The e-Citi unit soon had 1,600 employees and more than 100 U.S. websites. The idea: to cannibalize your business before someone else did.

The only thing e-Citi gobbled was money. Citigroup's e-commerce effort lost over $1 billion between 1998 and 2000. In online banking, for example, Citigroup was so determined to make Citi.f/i an independent operation that customers of the online bank couldn't use Citibank branches. That turned off depositors. The online bank drew 30,000 accounts versus 146 million for the rest of Citigroup's banking operation. By March 2000, word came down from Citigroup Chairman Sandy Weill: E-commerce initiatives must be part of the existing business, not self-appointed upstarts trying to overturn them. "At the beginning of 2000, people were dreaming that you could take e-Citi public," says Deryck C. Maughan, Citigroup's vice-chairman. "I looked very carefully and asked, could it make a profit? Not in our lifetime."

Still, Citigroup wanted to keep e-commerce innovation humming. So in 2000, the company formed an Internet Operating Group of top execs to help Citigroup units share e-business technology and to ensure that they all have a common look and feel.

By 2001, the results were easy to see. The number of online customers are up 80 percent because Citibank and Citi's credit card operations are pushing Web services themselves, instead of leaving that mostly to e-Citi. Citigroup now serves 10 million customers online. e-Citi has scaled back to only 100 people, who implement projects the operating groups propose. The 100 websites have been trimmed to 38. The reported loss for online efforts in the first half of this year was down 41 percent, to $67 million, from $114 million a year ago. And counting savings from moving procurement, human resources, and other back-office functions online, Citigroup says e-business systems will cut $1 billion off annual costs by the end of 2002. "I promise you, we are going to be saving a lot more than we are spending," Maughan pledges [21].

Summary

- **Electronic Commerce.** Electronic commerce encompasses the entire online process of developing, marketing, selling, delivering, servicing, and paying for products and services. The Internet and related technologies and e-commerce websites on the World Wide Web and corporate intranets and extranets serve as the business and technology platform for e-commerce marketplaces for consumers and businesses in the basic categories of business-to-consumer (B2C), business-to-business (B2B), and consumer-to-consumer (C2C) e-commerce. The essential processes that should be implemented in all e-commerce applications—access control and security, personalizing and profiling, search management, content management, catalog management, payment systems, workflow management, event notification, and collaboration and trading—are summarized in Figure 7.5.

- **e-Commerce Issues.** Many e-business enterprises are moving toward offering full-service B2C and B2B e-commerce portals supported by integrated customer-focused processes and internetworked supply chains as illustrated in Figure 7.11. In addition, companies must evaluate a variety of e-commerce sector choices as outlined in Figure 7.12, and integration or separation alternatives and benefit trade-offs when choosing a clicks and bricks strategy and e-commerce channel, as summarized in Figures 7.21, 7.22, and 7.23.

- **B2C e-Commerce.** Businesses typically sell products and services to consumers at e-commerce websites that provide attractive Web pages, multimedia catalogs, interactive order processing, secure electronic payment systems, and online customer support. However, successful e-tailers build customer satisfaction and loyalty by optimizing factors outlined in Figure 7.14, such as selection and value, performance and service efficiency, the look and feel of the site, advertising and incentives to purchase, personal attention, community relationships, and security and reliability. In addition, a Web store has several key business requirements, including building and marketing a Web business, serving and supporting customers, and managing a Web store, as summarized in Figure 7.16.

- **B2B e-Commerce.** Business-to-business applications of e-commerce involve electronic catalog, exchange, and auction marketplaces that use Internet, intranet, and extranet websites and portals to unite buyers and sellers, as summarized in Figure 7.18 and illustrated in Figure 7.19. Many B2B e-commerce portals are developed and operated for a variety of industries by third-party market-maker companies called infomediaries, which may represent consortiums of major corporations.

Key Terms and Concepts

These are the key terms and concepts of this chapter. The page number of their first explanation is in parentheses.

1. Clicks and bricks alternatives (244)
2. E-commerce channel (247)
3. E-commerce marketplaces (241)
   a. Auction (231)
   b. Catalog (242)
   c. Exchange (242)
   d. Portal (242)
4. E-commerce success factors (235)
5. E-commerce technologies (221)

6. Electronic commerce (218)
   a. Business-to-business (220)
   b. Business-to-consumer (220)
   c. Consumer-to-consumer (220)
   d. Sectors (233)
7. Electronic funds transfer (228)
8. Essential e-commerce processes (223)
   a. Access control and security (223)
   b. Catalog management (225)

   c. Collaboration and trading (228)
   d. Content management (225)
   e. Electronic payment systems (228)
   f. Event notification (227)
   g. Profiling and personalizing (224)
   h. Search management (225)
   i. Workflow management (226)
9. Infomediaries (242)
10. Trends in e-commerce (233)
11. Web store requirements (238)

Review Quiz

Match one of the key terms and concepts listed previously with one of the brief examples or definitions that follow. Try to find the best fit for the answers that seem to fit more than one term or concept. Defend your choices.

_____ 1. The online process of developing, marketing, selling, delivering, servicing, and paying for products and services.

_____ 2. Business selling to consumers at retail Web stores is an example.

_____ 3. Using an e-commerce portal for auctions by business customers and their suppliers is an example.

_____ 4. Using an e-commerce website for auctions among consumers is an example.

_____ 5. E-commerce depends on the Internet and the World Wide Web, and on other networks of browser-equipped client/server systems and hypermedia databases.

_____ 6. E-commerce applications must implement several major categories of interrelated processes such as search management and catalog management.

_____ 7. Helps to establish mutual trust between you and an e-tailer at an e-commerce site.

_____ 8. Tracks your website behavior to provide you with an individualized Web store experience.

_____ 9. Develops, generates, delivers, and updates information to you at a website.

_____ 10. Ensures that proper e-commerce transactions, decisions, and activities are performed to better serve you.

_____ 11. Sends you an e-mail when what you ordered at an e-commerce site has been shipped.

_____ 12. Includes matchmaking, negotiation, and mediation processes among buyers and sellers.

_____ 13. Companies that serve as intermediaries in e-commerce transactions.

_____ 14. A website for e-commerce transactions.

_____ 15. An e-commerce marketplace that may provide catalog, exchange, or auction service for businesses or consumers.

_____ 16. Buyers bidding for the business of a seller.

_____ 17. Marketplace for bid (buy) and ask (sell) transactions.

_____ 18. The most widely used type of marketplace in B2C e-commerce.

_____ 19. The marketing or sales channel created by a company to conduct and manage its e-commerce activities.

_____ 20. The processing of money and credit transfers between businesses and financial institutions.

_____ 21. Ways to provide efficient, convenient, and secure payments in e-commerce.

_____ 22. E-businesses are increasingly developing full-service B2C and B2B e-commerce portals.

_____ 23. E-businesses can evaluate and choose from several e-commerce integration alternatives.

_____ 24. Successful e-tailers build customer satisfaction and loyalty in several key ways.

_____ 25. Successful e-commerce ventures must build, market, and manage their Web businesses while serving their customers.

Discussion Questions

1. Most businesses should engage in electronic commerce on the Internet. Do you agree or disagree with this statement? Explain your position.

2. Are you interested in investing in, owning, managing, or working for a business that is primarily engaged in electronic commerce on the Internet? Explain your position.

3. Refer to the Real World Case on Yahoo! in the chapter. Will Yahoo! be able to compete successfully with AOL and MSN as an online service and e-commerce portal? Why or why not?

4. Why do you think there have been so many business failures among "dot-com" companies that were devoted only to retail e-commerce?

5. Do the e-commerce success factors listed in Figure 7.14 guarantee success for an e-commerce business venture? Give a few examples of what else could go wrong and how you would confront such challenges.

6. If personalizing a customer's website experience is a key success factor, then electronic profiling processes to track visitor website behavior are necessary. Do you agree or disagree with this statement? Explain your position.

7. All corporate procurement should be accomplished in e-commerce auction marketplaces, instead of using B2B websites that feature fixed-price catalogs or negotiated prices. Explain your position on this proposal.

8. Refer to the Real World Case on ChemConnect and Heritage Services in the chapter. How can ChemConnect broaden its customer base? Visit their website for information to help you defend your answer.

9. If you were starting an e-commerce Web store, which of the business requirements summarized in Figure 7.16 would you primarily do yourself, and which would you outsource to a Web development or hosting company? Why?

10. Which of the e-commerce clicks and bricks alternatives illustrated in Figure 7.21 would you recommend to Barnes & Noble? Amazon.com? Wal-Mart? Any business? Explain your position.

Application Exercises

Complete the following exercises as individual or group projects that apply chapter concepts to real world business situations.

1. bCentral.com: Small Business e-Commerce Portals

Web On the net, small businesses have become big news. And a really big business, Microsoft, wants a piece of the action. The company's bCentral Web portal (www.bcentral.com) is one of many sites offering advice and services for small businesses moving online. Most features, whether free or paid, are what you'd expect: lots of links and information along the lines established by Prodigy Biz (www.prodigybiz.com), and other competitors like Entrabase.com or GoBizGo.com. BCentral, however, stands out for its affordable advertising and marketing services. See Figure 7.24.

One bCentral program allows you to put banner ads on other sites in exchange for commissions from click-throughs and sales. As on other sites, a banner ad exchange program lets you place one ad on a member site in exchange for displaying two ads on your own. For as little as $20 a month, you can buy a marketing package that includes ads on sites such as Yahoo! and Excite, and get help with direct e-mail campaigns, as well as track all activities on your personal "my business" page.

a. Check out bCentral and the other e-commerce portals mentioned. Identify several benefits and limitations for a business using their websites.

b. Which is your favorite. Why?

c. Which site would you recommend or use to help a small business wanting to get into e-commerce? Why?

Source: Adapted from Anush Yegazarian, "BCentral.com Puts Your Business on the Web," *PC World*, December 1999, p. 64.

2. Microsoft, Ford, GM, and Others: e-Commerce Websites for Car Buying

Web Nowadays, you can configure the car of your dreams on Microsoft's MSN Autos website, and those of Ford, GM, and other auto giants. Many independent online car purchase and research companies offer similar services. See Figure 7.25.

For now, the majority of car buyers are still using the Internet as a place to research rather than buy. Most auto sites simply put consumers in touch with a local dealer, where they test drive a vehicle and negotiate a price. Autobytel.com of Irvine, Calif., for example, has been referring buyers to new and used car dealers since 1995, as well as offering online financing and insurance. General Motors' BuyPower site provides access to a vast inventory of cars, though shoppers still have to go to a dealer to close the sale.

Online car buying sites on the Web make consumers less dependent on what cars a dealer has on the lot. At online sites, buyers can customize a car—or van, truck, or sport utility vehicle—by selecting trim,

FIGURE 7.24

Microsoft's bCentral is a small business e-commerce portal.

Source: Courtesy of Microsoft Corporation.

paint color, and other options before purchase. Buyers will still pick up and pay for the cars at local dealerships.

a. Check out several of the websites shown in Figure 7.25. Evaluate them based on ease of use, response times, relevance of information provided, and other criteria you feel are important. Don't forget the classic: "Did they make you want to buy?"

b. Which sites would you use or recommend if you or a friend actually wanted to buy a car? Why?

Source: Adapted from "E-commerce Cars," in Technology Review, *Fortune*, Winter 2000, p. 42. © 2000 Time Inc. All rights reserved.

3. Comparing e-Commerce Sites

SS In this exercise you will experiment with electronic shopping and compare alternative electronic commerce sites. First you will need to select a category of product widely available on the Web, such as books, CDs, toys, etcetera. Next select five specific products to price on the Internet, e.g., five specific CDs

you might be interested in buying. Search three prominent electronic commerce sites selling this type of product and record the price charged for each product by each site.

a. Using a spreadsheet record a set of information similar to that shown below for each product. (Categories describing the product will vary depending upon the type of product you select— CDs might require the title of the CD and the performer[s], while toys or similar products would require the name of the product and its description.)

b. For each product rank each company based on the price charged. Give a rating of 1 for the lowest price and 3 for the highest and split the ratings for ties—two sites tying for 1st and 2nd lowest price would each receive a 1.5. If a site does not have one of the products available for sale, give that site a rating of 4 for that product. Add the ratings across your products to produce an overall price/availability rating for each site.

Title of Book	Author	Price at: Site A	Site B	Site C	Rating A	B	C
The Return of Little Big Man	Berger, T.	$15.00	$16.95	$14.50	2	3	1
Learning Perl/Tk	Walsh, N. & Mui, L.	$26.36	$25.95	$25.95	3	1.5	1.5
Business at the Speed of Thought	Gates, W.	$21.00	$22.95	$21.00	1.5	3	1.5
Murders for the Holidays	Smith, G.		$ 8.25	$ 7.95	4	2	1
Design for Dullards	Jones	$17.95	$18.50	$18.50	1	2.5	3
Sum of ratings (low score represents most favorable rating)					11.5	12	8

FIGURE 7.25
FIGURE 7.25
Some of the top
e-commerce websites for
car buying and researching.

Top Car Buying Websites
● **Autobytel.com   www.autobytel.com** Enter make and model, and a local dealer will contact you with a price offer. Home delivery is an option.
● **AutoNation   www.autonation.com** Every make and model available, as well as financing and insurance information, home delivery, and test drives.
● **Microsoft MSN Autos   www.autos.msn.com** Auto reviews, detailed vehicle specifications, safety ratings, and buying services for new and used cars, including customizing your very own Ford.
● **cars.com   www.cars.com** Research tools include automotive reviews, model reports, dealer locators, and financing information.
● **CarsDirect.com   www.carsdirect.com** Research price and design, then order your car. CarsDirect will deliver it to your home. A top-rated site.
● **Edmunds.com   www.edmunds.com** For an objective opinion, Edmunds.com provides reviews, safety updates, and rebate news for car buyers.
● **FordVehicles.com   www.fordvehicles.com** Research, configure, price, and order your new Ford car, minivan, truck, or SUV at this website.
● **GM BuyPower   www.gmbuypower.com** With access to nearly 6,000 GM dealerships, car shoppers can get a price quote, schedule a test drive, and buy.

c. Based on your experience with these sites rate them on their ease of use, completeness of information, and order-filling and shipping options. As in part B, give a rating of 1 to the site you feel is best in each category, a 2 to the second best and a 3 to the poorest site.

d. Prepare a set of PowerPoint slides or similar presentation materials summarizing the key results and including an overall assessment of the sites you compared.

4. Evaluating the Market for B2C Electronic Commerce

In assessing the potential for business-to-consumer (B2C), electronic commerce, it is important to know how many people are using the Internet for business transactions and what segments of the population are using the Internet in this manner. In August of 2000 the U.S. Census Bureau asked a number of questions about Internet use as a part of its monthly Current Population Survey. This survey is administered to over 100,000 individuals and its results are used to create projected rates of use for the full population. Among the questions was one that asked each respondent whether they used the Internet to shop, to pay bills, or for other commercial purposes. A number of general demographic characteristics, such as age, education level, and household income level are also gathered for each respondent.

The sample table below shows summary results for different education levels. Data showing the

	Have Used Internet to Shop / Pay Bills		% Using Internet to
Education Level	**Yes**	**No**	**Shop / Pay Bills**
Less than High School	598824	32354711	1.8%
High School Grad	5104952	60930000	7.7%
Some College No Degree	6613400	32290000	17.0%
Associate Degree	7840540	38855612	16.8%
Bachelors Degree	9581979	22830000	29.6%
Masters Degree or Higher	5196040	10280934	33.6%

distribution of Internet use for shopping across age categories and levels of family income have also been collected from this survey data and are available as a download file for this application exercise in the website for this textbook. The textbook website is at www.mhhe.com/business/mis/obrien. Click on downloads under the student resources section of the website.

a. Download the initial spreadsheet file for this exercise and modify it to include percentage use calculations for each age, education level, and income category.

b. Create appropriate graphs to illustrate how the distribution of use of the Internet for shopping varies across age, income, and education level categories.

c. Write a short memorandum to your instructor summarizing your results and describing their implications for a Web-based retailer that is designing a marketing strategy.

Staples, Steelcase, Countrywide, and HSN: Evaluating e-Commerce Website ROI

Despite the dot-com disasters of 2001, the Web continues to be a part of virtually every company's marketing strategy. The questions isn't whether or not to have an online presence; it's how to tell whether—and by how much—the Internet increases market share and fattens the bottom line. The problem is that most companies have no idea how to accurately measure return on investment when it comes to their websites. Counting hits and monitoring visitor behavior have become de rigueur, but neither one answers the thorny question of how much a company earns—or saves—by marketing on the Web.

Meanwhile, even in the midst of a down economy, companies continue to invest money in their websites. But now top managers are pushing harder than they once did for proof that the sites are more than glitzy money pits, according to Lisa Melsted, an analyst at The Yankee Group in Boston. The average company budget allocation for a website is about $500,000 annually, according to a survey of 200 companies that The Yankee Group conducted in August 2001. While overall expenditures have likely come down somewhat recently due to cutbacks and layoffs, website maintenance is still a large expenditure, Melsted says.

Staples. Comparing Web sales with sales generated by other channels is an important ROI metric that can help a company determine how online activities stack up against overall business goals. At $10.7 billion Staples Inc. (www.staples.com) in Framingham, Massachusetts, the value of a customer is based in part on how many channels he uses to buy products. That means analyzing sales generated over the Web, at retail stores, and from the catalog.

"We focus on integrating sales data across all our channels to create metrics that refer to the lifetime value of the customer," says Mike Ragunas, chief technology officer at the office supplies retailer. "We've found that in terms of sales, a three-channel shopper is worth 4.5 times that of a retail-only shopper."

Home Shopping Network. Similarly, St. Petersburg, Florida–based HSN LP, (www.hsn.com) a $1.8 billion multichannel retailer best known for its Home Shopping Network, has found that customers who shop both online and from television spend 26 percent more than those who shop through a single channel.

Steelcase.com. If a company experiences an increase in website visitors that doesn't result in increased sales, something is wrong, says Eileen Raphael, manager of Steelcase.com, (www.steelcase.com) the online arm of $3.9 billion office-furniture maker Steelcase Inc. in Grand Rapids, Michigan. After launching the company's first website in 1995, Raphael watched site traffic double every year, but the number of sales leads didn't double. Steelcase learned from customer feedback that visitors to the site were frustrated by its design and felt that it didn't provide enough information to place orders. "When we decided to relaunch our website, we were getting 110,000 to 120,000 visitors per month, so there was a tremendous opportunity to build our customer base," Raphael says.

Now, Steelcase looks at both revenue and cost savings to measure the ROI of its relaunched website. For example, a salesperson at one of the company's 800 outlets might earn $75,000 per year. If Steelcase.com can provide product information without getting a salesperson involved, it saves an hour of the salesperson's time, or about $36. "If we can save one hour of time for a dealer salesperson every week, that adds up to millions of dollars per year in people's time," says Raphael.

Countrywide. Countrywide Credit Industries Inc. (www.countrywide.com), a $2 billion financial services company based in Calabasas, California, is also seeing increased sales online as a result of a website overhaul. The company redesigned its site two years ago based on customer feedback and website performance. Countrywide's IT group built software that lets the company track "events," such as how many people fill out loan applications online and how many applications result in loans. To do that, Countrywide had to integrate the website with back-end databases and enterprise applications.

The new system now lets the company more easily measure website activity in terms of its overall business objectives, says Larry Gentry, vice president of e-commerce. For example, Countrywide now knows that its websites account for 48 percent of overall loan funding, up from only 5 percent two years ago. Also, providing services such as electronic statements and online rate calculations via the website has yielded cost savings. Previously, Countrywide provided those services at a higher cost via mail and fax. "The immediate ROI is cost reduction. Now that we put those services online customers get the information sooner and we get the cost savings," says Gentry.

Case Study Questions

1. Does the fact that customers who shop online and in other channels generate more sales, as Staples and HSN have found, mean that most companies should have an e-commerce website? Explain your position.

2. Do you agree with Steelcase that it is better for people to get product information online than from a salesperson? Why or why not?

3. Evaluate the redesigned websites of Steelcase and Countrywide. Do they do a good job of encouraging customers and visitors to buy their products and use their services? Explain your evaluation.

Source: Adapted from John Webster, "Calculating Web Site Payoff," *Computerworld*, February 4, 2002, p. 34. Reprinted with permission from *Computerworld*.

REAL WORLD CASE 4

eBags, Economy.com, and Classmates Online: Evaluating e-Commerce Business Models

No Inventory. Like eBay, eBags Inc. (www.ebags. com) doesn't have to worry about inventory. The privately held company sells handbags, computer cases, backpacks, luggage, and other gear but has manufacturers—including Samsonite Corp., JanSport, and Adirenne Vittadini—ship directly to eBags' customers. "We let the brand manufacturers maintain the inventory. That's what they do best. They know what's going to sell," says Peter Cobb, eBags' vice president of marketing.

The company does have to spend on marketing, however. It mostly uses promotional contests that people can enter, such as a free ski trip to the Grand Tetons, to build its list of prospective customers. As of April, it had more than two million names in its database, up from 292,000 in January 2001. eBags had its first monthly profit in December 2001. The company says it expects to achieve "sustained profitability" during the second half of 2002.

Unlike many online companies, eBags has won high marks for its customer service as well as for tools on its website that make it easier to comparison shop or to design your own bag by picking favorite colors, fabrics, and accessories such as laptop sleeves or cellphone holsters. eBags "wasn't started by technology types. It was started by people from Samsonite who understood the luggage business," says Don McCubbrey, director of the Center for the Study of Electronic Commerce at the University of Denver's Daniels College of Business.

Customized, Yet Cheap. Economic research firm Economy.com Inc. (www.economy.com) is using the Internet's reach to expand beyond its traditional base of clients in Fortune 500 companies. The 770-person firm is reeling in foreign central banks, smaller businesses such as money managers, consumers, and charities. How? The Internet has let Economy.com offer customized reports that cost a fraction of what reports used to cost.

The private company, which sells economic reports detailing the health of the 50 states, 320 U.S. metropolitan areas, and 65 industries, used to mail bound reports to clients. A few years ago, a 50- to 60-page report on 100 metro areas would cost $15,000, regardless of whether a customer was interested in only a handful of the localities. In 1997, though, the firm—previously called Regional Financial Associates Inc.—began putting its data on the Internet. Today, customers can log on to the Economy.com site and pick and choose, selecting, say, the Sacramento or Denver report at $200 each.

"They don't have to pay for what they don't want," says Paul Getman, chief executive of Economy.com. The change has opened a new market for smaller customers. Individuals moving to a new city are able to buy reports to find out about the local job and home markets in their future locales. Economy.com also has attracted a growing international client base.

In addition to increasing revenue, using the Internet lets the company better target its research, helping it operate more efficiently because it can see what clients pull off its site. The company is now pumping out more foreign stats; for example. Economy.com says it earned an operating profit last year and expects to be profitable this year "in every sense of the word."

Connections. Classmates Online Inc. (www.classmates. com) was born in 1995 after its founder, Randy Conrads, tried unsuccessfully to locate a high school friend using online listing services and the white pages. The site is a sort of lost and found for old school chums and sweethearts, as well as military buddies. "If eBay is like a co-op for garage sales, we're a co-op for finding old friends," says Michael Schutzler, the company's chief executive.

The comparison is apt. Classmates' minimal expenses mostly consist of advertising and payroll. As with eBay, each new Classmates member improves the list and makes it more attractive to anyone thinking of joining. The site has more than 27 million members and is adding 50,000 daily. More than two million are paying $36 a year, which gives them free e-mail contact with anyone else in the site's directory, as well as access to special message boards and chat rooms and the ability to share photos. (Nonpaying members just have their names listed, usually by school and year of graduation. They can be contacted but can't contact others. No e-mail addresses are listed on-site, so Classmates is the only medium for initiating contact with someone.)

Classmates does spend quite a bit on marketing itself, mostly through arrangements with other websites. The company, which employs 135, turned profitable in November (on a net-income basis) and expects to remain so. Schutzler says part of this company's success stems from the strong feelings that get ignited when someone checks out names of old classmates. Customers recount stories of how they found their long-lost sweethearts or were reunited with their birth mothers and spread the word to others about Classmates Online—a classic example of "viral marketing."

Case Study Questions

1. Do you feel that eBags will be able to sustain its recent profitability? Visit their website to help you explain your answer.

2. Visit the website of Economy.com. How else could they increase their products, markets, and profitability? Defend your proposals.

3. How could other kinds of businesses use the Classmates Online business model to help strengthen their e-commerce success? Give an example to illustrate your answer.

Source: Adapted from Roger Fillion, "Rising from the Ashes," *Context*, June–July 2002, pp. 32–35.

Office Depot, Lands' End, and Others: Trends in e-Commerce Website Capabilities

They are mostly gone now, those early online retailers. They believed profits didn't matter. They saw advanced technology as the silver bullet. And their business plans ran to just six words: "Build it, and they will come." Now the dot-com survivors say there's a new focus on basics, such as how to attract customers to a site once it's been built and how to make them happy there. There's a big push to integrate websites with back-end systems and brick-and-mortar retail operations. And, yes, there's still a drive toward the latest technologies, such as wireless, 3-D, and website personalization.

"The first use of a new technology is always imitation of the old," says Michael Shamos, co-director of the Institute for eCommerce at Carnegie Mellon University in Pittsburgh. "So what we see in e-tailing is the first thing you do with your Web site is replicate your catalog." Although understandable, that's a huge mistake because an online catalog is harder to use than a paper one, Shamos says. "A catalog can't ask you questions. So Web sites are generally terrible at eliciting consumer needs," he says.

Office Depot. But the best sites are moving far beyond catalog-like presentations. A year ago, Shamos asked his e-commerce graduate students to see how many Web pages they had to traverse on Delray Beach, Florida–based Office Depot Inc.'s website (www.officedepot.com) to find the heaviest-duty stapler offered. Results ranged from 23 to 56 pages. But now you can get the answer (a $70 behemoth that will staple 210 sheets at once) in just five clicks. "They now have a beautiful new interface I haven't seen anywhere else," Shamos says. The advanced "search by attributes" option lets you select and search product characteristics. There are 23 listed for staplers, such as color, staple size, grip materials, sheet capacity, and warranty.

Lands' End. Another e-retailer that Shamos says heralds the future is Lands' End Inc. (www.landsend.com) in Dodgeville, Wisconsin. The online clothing store allows shoppers to build virtual models of themselves and then use the models to try on and display clothing. Lands' End buys the modeling service from Montreal-based My Virtual Model Inc., which stores a shopper's model and lets him use it at a number of clothing websites. The next step, which Shamos says is the subject of research at Carnegie Mellon and elsewhere, will be true 3-D images of models and products.

MarthaStewart. Martha Stewart Living Omnimedia Inc. (www.marthastewart.com) in New York uses Consumer Commerce Suite from Art Technology Group to tie together its four major businesses. "We built a data mart for all the information about our customers from magazine subscriptions, television viewers, buyers of our books and people ordering through catalogs," says Raffaele Pisacane, vice president of Internet development at Martha Stewart. "We integrated this into a single view, and we leverage it through our Internet channel." For example, Pisacane says, Martha Stewart's online system can generate e-mails to people whose magazine subscriptions are about to expire, or it can flash an expiration warning to a subscriber who happens to be shopping or looking for information online.

Matsushita. Matsushita Electric Corp. of America has an even tougher integration challenge: how to tie its Panasonic website (www.panasonic.com) to the inventory systems of the retail chains that sell Panasonic gear. "If your Web site sends someone to a dealer down the street that doesn't have the model they are looking for, they'll buy something from someone else," says Tom Popp, eBusiness applications manager.

The Panasonic website now lists those stores that have received a shipment of the requested item within the past two weeks. "That's about as close as we can get right now," Popp says. Developing a real-time online inventory capability for a dozen major retail chains is one of two major projects under way at Panasonic now, he says.

NextWine.com. When wine seller NextWine (www.nextwine.com) LLC in Napa, California, built its e-commerce site two years ago using IBM's WebSphere e-commerce software, it insisted on providing real-time inventory views to its shoppers, even though few online retailers did that. But at the time, NextWine couldn't afford an automated inventory system, so it manually posted stock balances on some 5,000 items to the website so that the site always showed current stock on hand.

But the company recently migrated from the Windows NT version of WebSphere to the Linux version. NextWine President Dain Dunston says Linux and other open standards made it easy to interface the website to a new automated inventory system that posts inventory updates every 10 minutes to the website using a very simple interface, Dunston says. "Because it's an open system, we were able to do this for an extraordinarily low cost," he says.

Case Study Questions

1. Visit the Office Depot and Lands' End websites. Which one does a better job of helping users find the products they want? Explain the reasons for your evaluation.

2. Compare the business value of the integration of customer information at Martha Stewart, retailer information at Panasonic, and inventory information at NextWine. Which capability is of greatest importance to the success of an e-commerce business? Why?

3. Which website capability or feature would you most like to see added to e-commerce websites? Explain the customer value and business value of your proposal.

Source: Adapted from Gary Anthes, "e-Retailing 2.0," *Computerworld*, June 17, 2002, pp. 26–27. Reprinted with permission from *Computerworld*.

CHAPTER 8

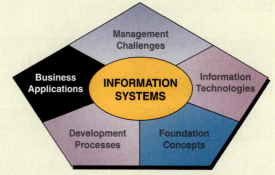

APPLICATIONS IN BUSINESS AND MANAGEMENT

DECISION SUPPORT SYSTEMS

Chapter Highlights

Learning Objectives

After reading and studying this chapter, you should be able to:

1. Identify the changes taking place in the form and use of decision support in business.

2. Identify the role and reporting alternatives of management information systems.

3. Describe how online analytical processing can meet key information needs of managers.

4. Explain the decision support system concept and how it differs from traditional management information systems.

5. Explain how the following information systems can support the information needs of executives, managers, and business professionals:

   a. Executive information systems

   b. Enterprise information portals

   c. Knowledge management systems

6. Identify how neural networks, fuzzy logic, genetic algorithms, virtual reality, and intelligent agents can be used in business.

7. Give examples of several ways expert systems can be used in business decision-making situations.

<table>
<tr><td>

SECTION I

Business and Decision Support

</td></tr>
</table>

Decision Support in Business

As companies migrate toward responsive e-business models, they are investing in new data-driven decision support application frameworks that help them respond rapidly to changing market conditions and customer needs [32].

So to succeed in business today, including any e-business initiatives, companies need information systems that can support the diverse information and decision-making needs of their managers and business professionals. In this section, we will explore in more detail how this is accomplished by several types of management information, decision support, and executive information systems. We will concentrate our attention on how the Internet, intranets, and other Web-enabled information technologies have significantly strengthened the role information systems play in supporting the decision-making activities of every manager and knowledge worker in business.

Analyzing AmeriKing and Others

Read the Real World Case on AmeriKing and Others on the next page. We can learn a lot from this case about how a variety of information technologies have become key components of successful decision support systems. See Figure 8.1.

AmeriKing relied on an antiquated corporate information system that involved copying and then mailing or faxing paper reports to managers and business professionals. This was replaced with an intranet-based enterprise information portal that enables employees to use Web browsers to instantly access financial, marketing, human resource, and other reports and over 71,000 corporate documents. Employees

FIGURE 8.1

Hernando Manrique is CIO of AmeriKing and led the development of their AKInet enterprise information portal.

Source: Courtesy of Hernando Manrique.

| REAL WORLD CASE 1 | AmeriKing and Others: The Business Value of Enterprise Portals |

When Chief Information Officer Hernando Manrique arrived at AmeriKing three years ago, technology wasn't exactly on the front burner for the Westchester, Illinois–based Burger King franchisee. Though AmeriKing (www.ameriking.com) claims to be the largest Burger King franchisee in the country with some 376 stores and 13,000 employees scattered across the United States, its technology and applications infrastructures definitely weren't whoppers. Information ranging from financial reports to human resource policies was manually photocopied and distributed via monthly or bimonthly mailings and fax. "The technology side of the business was definitely underdeveloped," says Manrique.

So Manrique teamed with Carol Swanson, manager of Business Data & Intelligence, and Patti Cahanin, manager of Business Applications and Solutions, to help AmeriKing put its technology efforts into overdrive. At the beginning of 2001, the company began testing of its intranet portal, which is powered by Plumtree's Portal Server. And in June 2001, Manrique and his team officially launched AKInet, as the portal is called, to some 180 district managers, marketing directors, and marketing managers. And a rollout of the portal to the managers of all 376 stores began during 2002. Field personnel can now use Web browsers to access daily and monthly financial reports and over 71,000 corporate documents, use e-mail accounts, and order supplies from Boise Cascade online via the portal. Just the ability to access these reports and human resource information online is saving AmeriKing about $500,000 per year in reduced printing and distribution costs. "Those savings alone enabled us to justify the entire project, and we see it as just the beginning," he says.

While the portal is now providing tangible benefits to this far-flung company, it wasn't an easy sell. Because AmeriKing is in a business sector known for its low profit margins, each penny spent had to be justified and payback had to be almost immediate. Manrique also faced the additional hurdle of a general aversion to technology within the company. "There was little understanding that information systems and technology can be at the very center of a sound strategy, not simply an afterthought," he says.

The AKInet portal provides several "communities" of applications accessible by all or selected employees, including an HR community of employee profiles and employee contact information; a Myinet community of personalized employee information; a Finance and Accounting community with access to sales and inventory data, P&L, payroll, and a decision support system; and a Marketing community with regional calendars and timely promotional information. Other portal components include an AKNews community with corporate content such as Burger King press releases, partner company news, and executive news; and a Training community with access to course scheduling and materials and the AmeriKing University for online training.

According to a 2002 study by the Meta Group, 90 percent of companies are going to emulate AmeriKing by deploying an enterprisewide portal in the next few years. Here's why eight leading companies have already done so.

Merrill Lynch built an enterprisewide portal because the company could no longer afford to finance all the websites and portal sites being built across the company. **Guess** installed a portal because it had become too expensive to train its retail associates and partners on how to use all of the applications it wanted to roll out from headquarters. **ChevronTexaco** implemented a portal because it wanted an integrated Web environment but could not afford to convert every system from the newly merged units of Chevron and Texaco into common Web applications. And **Boeing** installed an enterprise portal because the security and content changes that poured into its intranet every day overwhelmed the Web producers and developers that built the site.

Starbucks implemented a portal because it was the most comprehensive way to eliminate all sorts of paperwork required to keep its retail outlets humming. **Beringer** Wine Estates estimates that its salespeople spend hours more in the field each week meeting wine retailers because they can easily find everything they need from headquarters in their portal. **FirstEnergy** plans to eliminate millions from its training budget for HR self-service by delivering the key HR functions in a portal that is already widely used by employees. And **Washington Mutual** implemented a portal so that every business unit could draw on a common set of foundation services for building Web applications within the portal at lower cost. This centralized knowledge management and content management, and created consistent business processes that can span different departments.

Case Study Questions

1. What is the business value to a company of an enterprise portal like AmeriKing's?

2. What are several ways AmeriKing could improve the business value of its portal? Review the reasons why other companies in the case have implemented portals to help you answer.

3. How might an enterprise portal help you as a business professional or manager in your work activities? Give several examples to illustrate your answer.

Source: Adapted from Sarah Roberts-Witt, "Plumtree Helps Fast Food Firm Build a Whopper of a Portal," ZDNet Update, February 19, 2002; Plumtree Software, "Why Deploy a Portal Now?" White Paper, Plumtree.com, August 30, 2002; and "AmeriKing," Customer Profile, Plumtree.com, October 25, 2002.

can also use the portal for e-mail, online training, ordering supplies, and corporate news. This has resulted in major cost savings and greatly improved information access within the company. These are some of the many reasons why a great number of companies are now installing enterprise portals. For example, some of the other companies in the case are implementing enterprise portals to reduce the number of development projects and their cost, and reduce the number of applications and their training costs. Other companies are focused on the ease and time saved in accessing required business information via an enterprise portal.

Information, Decisions, and Management

Figure 8.2 emphasizes that the type of information required by decision makers in a company is directly related to the **level of management decision making** and the amount of structure in the decision situations they face. You should realize that the framework of the classic *managerial pyramid* shown in Figure 8.2 applies even in today's *downsized* organizations and *flattened* or nonhierarchical organizational structures. Levels of management decision making still exist, but their size, shape, and participants continue to change as today's fluid organizational structures evolve. Thus, the levels of managerial decision making that must be supported by information technology in a successful organization are:

● **Strategic Management.** Typically, a board of directors and an executive committee of the CEO and top executives develop overall organizational goals, strategies, policies, and objectives as part of a strategic planning process. They also monitor the strategic performance of the organization and its overall direction in the political, economic, and competitive business environment.

● **Tactical Management.** Increasingly, business professionals in self-directed teams as well as business unit managers develop short- and medium-range plans, schedules, and budgets and specify the policies, procedures, and business objectives for their subunits of the company. They also allocate resources and monitor the performance of their organizational subunits, including departments, divisions, process teams, project teams, and other workgroups.

● **Operational Management.** The members of self-directed teams or operating managers develop short-range plans such as weekly production schedules.

FIGURE 8.2

Information requirements of decision makers. The type of information required by directors, executives, managers, and members of self-directed teams is directly related to the level of management decision making involved and the structure of decision situations they face.

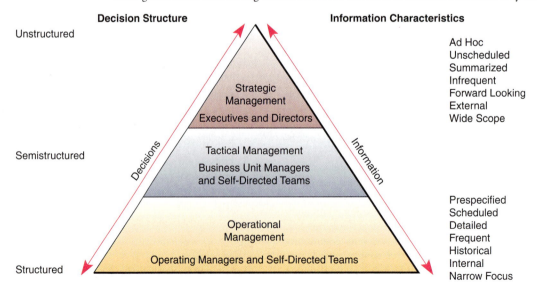

They direct the use of resources and the performance of tasks according to procedures and within budgets and schedules they establish for the teams and other workgroups of the organization.

Information Quality

What characteristics would make information products valuable and useful to you? One way to answer this important question is to examine the characteristics or attributes of **information quality.** Information that is outdated, inaccurate, or hard to understand would not be very meaningful, useful, or valuable to you or other business professionals. People want information of high quality, that is, information products whose characteristics, attributes, or qualities make the information more valuable to them. It is useful to think of information as having the three dimensions of time, content, and form. Figure 8.3 summarizes the important attributes of information quality and groups them into these three dimensions.

Decision Structure

Decisions made at the operational management level tend to be more *structured*, those at the tactical level more *semistructured*, and those at the strategic management level more *unstructured*. Structured decisions involve situations where the procedures to follow when a decision is needed can be specified in advance. The inventory reorder

FIGURE 8.3

A summary of the attributes of information quality. This outlines the attributes that should be present in high-quality information products.

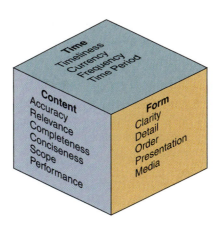

Time Dimension

Timeliness	Information should be provided when it is needed.
Currency	Information should be up-to-date when it is provided.
Frequency	Information should be provided as often as needed.
Time Period	Information can be provided about past, present, and future time periods.

Content Dimension

Accuracy	Information should be free from errors.
Relevance	Information should be related to the information needs of a specific recipient for a specific situation.
Completeness	All the information that is needed should be provided.
Conciseness	Only the information that is needed should be provided.
Scope	Information can have a broad or narrow scope, or an internal or external focus.
Performance	Information can reveal performance by measuring activities accomplished, progress made, or resources accumulated.

Form Dimension

Clarity	Information should be provided in a form that is easy to understand.
Detail	Information can be provided in detail or summary form.
Order	Information can be arranged in a predetermined sequence.
Presentation	Information can be presented in narrative, numeric, graphic, or other forms.
Media	Information can be provided in the form of printed paper documents, video displays, or other media.

FIGURE 8.4   Examples of decisions by the type of decision structure and by level of management.

Decision Structure	Operational Management	Tactical Management	Strategic Management
Unstructured	Cash management	Business process reengineering Workgroup performance analysis	New e-business initiatives Company reorganization
Semistructured	Credit management Production scheduling Daily work assignment	Employee performance appraisal Capital budgeting Program budgeting	Product planning Mergers and acquisitions Site location
Structured	Inventory control	Program control	

decisions faced by most businesses are a typical example. Unstructured decisions involve decision situations where it is not possible to specify in advance most of the decision procedures to follow. At most, many decision situations are semistructured. That is, some decision procedures can be prespecified, but not enough to lead to a definite recommended decision. For example, decisions involved in starting a new line of e-commerce services or making major changes to employee benefits would probably range from unstructured to semistructured. Figure 8.4 provides a variety of examples of business decisions by type of decision structure and level of management [27].

Therefore, information systems must be designed to produce a variety of information products to meet the changing needs of decision makers throughout an organization. For example, decision makers at the strategic management level require more summarized, ad hoc, unscheduled reports, forecasts, and external intelligence to support their more unstructured planning and policy-making responsibilities. Decision makers at the operational management level, on the other hand, may require more prespecified internal reports emphasizing detailed current and historical data comparisons that support their more structured responsibilities in day-to-day operations.

Decision Support Trends

The emerging class of applications focuses on personalized decision support, modeling, information retrieval, data warehousing, what-if scenarios, and reporting [32].

As we discussed in Chapter 1, using information systems to support business decision making has been one of the primary thrusts of the business use of information technology. However, during the 1990s, both academic researchers and business practitioners began reporting that the traditional managerial focus originating in classic management information systems (1960s), decision support systems (1970s), and executive information systems (1980s) was expanding. The fast pace of new information technologies like PC hardware and software suites, client/server networks, and networked PC versions of DSS/EIS software made decision support available to lower levels of management, as well as to nonmanagerial individuals and self-directed teams of business professionals [25, 46, 50].

This trend has accelerated with the dramatic growth of the Internet and intranets and extranets that internetwork companies and their stakeholders. The e-business and e-commerce initiatives that are being implemented by many companies are also expanding the information and decision support uses and expectations of a company's employees, managers, customers, suppliers, and other business partners. Figure 8.5 illustrates that all business stakeholders expect easy and instant access to information and Web-enabled self-service data analysis. Today's businesses are responding with a variety of personalized and proactive Web-based analytical techniques to support the decision-making requirements of all of their constituents.

Thus, the growth of corporate intranets, extranets, as well as the Web, has accelerated the development and use of "executive class" information delivery and decision

FIGURE 8.5

A business must meet the information and data analysis requirements of their stakeholders with more personalized and proactive Web-based decision support.

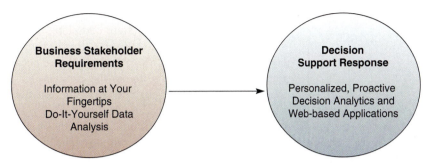

Source: Adapted from Ravi Kalakota and Marcia Robinson, *E-Business: Roadmap for Success* (Reading, MA: Addison-Wesley, 1999), p. 270. © 1999 Addison-Wesley Publishing Company, Inc. Reprinted by permission of Addison-Wesley Longman, Inc.

support software tools by lower levels of management and by individuals and teams of business professionals. In addition, this dramatic expansion has opened the door to the use of such *business intelligence* (BI) tools by the suppliers, customers, and other business stakeholders of a company for customer relationship management, supply chain management, and other e-business applications.

Figure 8.6 highlights several of the major e-business applications for which decision support is being customized, personalized, and Web-enabled for use in business [24, 25, 32, 46]. We will highlight the trend toward such decision support applications in the various types of information and decision support systems that are discussed in this chapter.

Target Corporation: DSS in Business	Target Corporation's decision support system is composed of several applications known collectively as the Decision Maker's Workbench, which use Decision Suite tools and WebOLAP software from Information Advantage. The DSS tools and Target's corporate intranet support more than 1,700 active users creating more than 60,000 adhoc online analytical processing (OLAP) reports each month. During the Christmas season, more than 20,000 analytic OLAP reports are produced each day. By integrating the Web with its corporate data warehouse, Target Stores enable its vendors to access its data warehouse to monitor the sales and performance of their own products via secure extranet links across the Internet.

FIGURE 8.6

Personalized Web-based decision support is now being provided in e-business applications that are available to employees, managers, customers, suppliers, and other business partners.

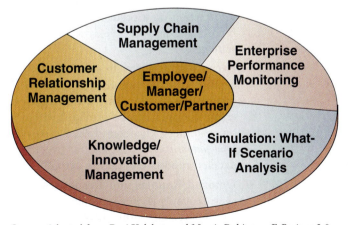

Source: Adapted from Ravi Kalakota and Marcia Robinson, *E-Business 2.0: Roadmap for Success* (Reading, MA: Addison-Wesley, 2001), p. 361. © 2001 Addison-Wesley Publishing Company, Inc. Reprinted by permission of Addison-Wesley Longman, Inc.

With the Target Stores system complete, the corporation has standardized it as a model for the entire company. Already the standardized data warehouse has enabled Target Corporation to obtain more accurate data on how items are performing across divisions, across the company. This has improved vendor negotiations considerably by enabling the different divisions to consolidate orders and receive a better price. The suite of DSS applications also allow for cross-referencing of fashion trends across divisions, and they have helped validate merchandising hunches through the data mining of cross-company data in the data warehouse [14, 43].

Management Information Systems

Management information systems were the original type of information system developed to support managerial decision making. An MIS produces information products that support many of the day-to-day decision-making needs of managers and business professionals. Reports, displays, and responses produced by management information systems provide information that these decision makers have specified in advance as adequately meeting their information needs. Such predefined information products satisfy the information needs of decision makers at the operational and tactical levels of the organization who are faced with more structured types of decision situations. For example, sales managers rely heavily on sales analysis reports to evaluate differences in performance among salespeople who sell the same types of products to the same types of customers. They have a pretty good idea of the kinds of information about sales results they need to manage sales performance effectively.

Managers and other decision makers use an MIS to request information at their networked workstations that supports their decision-making activities. This information takes the form of periodic, exception, and demand reports and immediate responses to inquiries. Web browsers, application programs, and database management software provide access to information in the intranet and other operational databases of the organization. Remember, operational databases are maintained by transaction processing systems. Data about the business environment are obtained from Internet or extranet databases when necessary.

Management Reporting Alternatives

Management information systems provide a variety of information products to managers. Four major reporting alternatives are provided by such systems.

- **Periodic Scheduled Reports.** This traditional form of providing information to managers uses a prespecified format designed to provide managers with information on a regular basis. Typical examples of such periodic scheduled reports are daily or weekly sales analysis reports and monthly financial statements.

- **Exception Reports.** In some cases, reports are produced only when exceptional conditions occur. In other cases, reports are produced periodically but contain information only about these exceptional conditions. For example, a credit manager can be provided with a report that contains only information on customers who exceed their credit limits. Exception reporting reduces *information overload*, instead of overwhelming decision makers with periodic detailed reports of business activity.

- **Demand Reports and Responses.** Information is available whenever a manager demands it. For example, Web browsers and DBMS query languages and report generators enable managers at PC workstations to get immediate responses or find and obtain customized reports as a result of their requests for the information they need. Thus, managers do not have to wait for periodic reports to arrive as scheduled.

FIGURE 8.7

An example of the push components in a marketing intelligence system that uses the Internet and a corporate intranet system to provide information to employees.

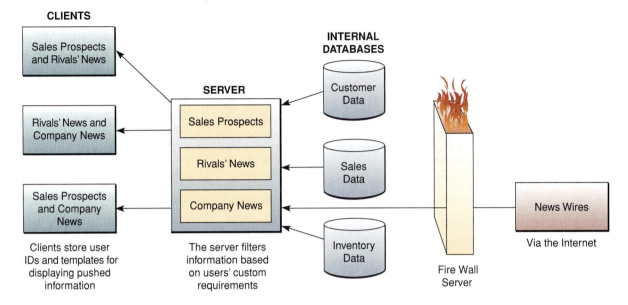

CLIENTS

Sales Prospects and Rivals' News

Rivals' News and Company News

Sales Prospects and Company News

Clients store user IDs and templates for displaying pushed information

SERVER

Sales Prospects

Rivals' News

Company News

The server filters information based on users' custom requirements

INTERNAL DATABASES

Customer Data

Sales Data

Inventory Data

Fire Wall Server

News Wires

Via the Internet

- **Push Reporting.** Information is *pushed* to a manager's networked workstation. Thus, many companies are using webcasting software to selectively broadcast reports and other information to the networked PCs of managers and specialists over their corporate intranets. See Figure 8.7.

Online Analytical Processing

At a recent stockholder meeting, the CEO of PepsiCo, D. Wayne Calloway, said: "Ten years ago I could have told you how Doritos were selling west of the Mississippi. Today, not only can I tell you how well Doritos sell west of the Mississippi, I can also tell you how well they are selling in California, in Orange County, in the town of Irvine, in the local Vons supermarket, in the special promotion, at the end of Aisle 4, on Thursdays" [55].

The competitive and dynamic nature of today's global business environment is driving demands by business managers and analysts for information systems that can provide fast answers to complex business queries. The IS industry has responded to these demands with developments like analytical databases, data marts, data warehouses, data mining techniques, and multidimensional database structures (discussed in Chapter 3), and with specialized servers and Web-enabled software products that support **online analytical processing** (OLAP).

Online analytical processing enables managers and analysts to interactively examine and manipulate large amounts of detailed and consolidated data from many perspectives. OLAP involves analyzing complex relationships among thousands or even millions of data items stored in multidimensional databases to discover patterns, trends, and exception conditions. An OLAP session takes place online in real time, with rapid responses to a manager's or analyst's queries, so that their analytical or decision-making process is undisturbed [21]. See Figure 8.8.

Online analytical processing involves several basic analytical operations, including consolidation, "drill-down," and "slicing and dicing" [20]. See Figure 8.9.

- **Consolidation.** Consolidation involves the aggregation of data. This can involve simple roll-ups or complex groupings involving interrelated data. For example, sales offices can be rolled up to districts and districts rolled up to regions.

FIGURE 8.8

Online analytical processing may involve the use of specialized servers and multidimensional databases. OLAP provides fast answers to complex queries posed by managers and analysts using traditional and Web-enabled OLAP software.

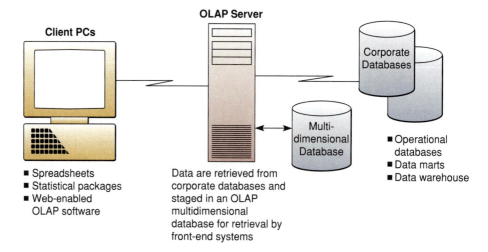

- **Drill-Down.** OLAP can go in the reverse direction and automatically display detail data that comprise consolidated data. This is called drill-down. For example, the sales by individual products or sales reps that make up a region's sales totals could be easily accessed.
- **Slicing and Dicing.** Slicing and dicing refers to the ability to look at the database from different viewpoints. One slice of the sales database might show all sales of product type within regions. Another slice might show all sales by sales channel within each product type. Slicing and dicing is often performed along a time axis in order to analyze trends and find time-based patterns in the data.

FIGURE 8.9

Comshare's Management Planning and Control software enables business professionals to use Microsoft Excel as their user interface for Web-enabled online analytical processing.

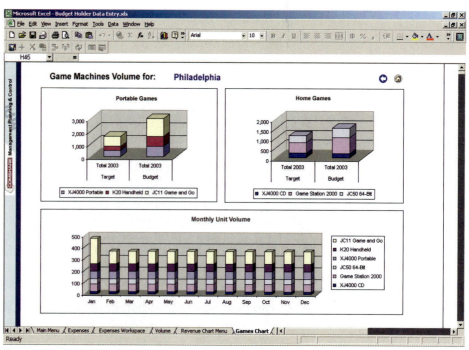

Source: Courtesy of Comshare.

International Rectifier: OLAP for Decision Support

At International Rectifier Corp., an El Segundo, California–based producer of power management semiconductors, manager of financial analytics Doug Burke says Hyperion Solutions' Essbase software has enabled the company to "get a lot more out of our IBM AS/400" midrange system by allowing the company to extract and analyze sales data very inexpensively. Rather than being forced to manipulate and e-mail each other huge spreadsheets, which ties up network bandwidth, users at networked PC workstations can now dynamically retrieve calculated views of just the data they need from the AS/400's databases using the online analytical processing (OLAP) features of Essbase.

Burke says he expects more cost savings in a few weeks when he deploys Essbase Version 6.1, which includes attributes that will allow users to dynamically analyze data across additional dimensions (such as sales areas) without having to store those calculations and thus increase the size of the database. "That's a big payoff," he says, "especially when you want to scale this thing up to hundreds of thousands or even millions of products" to analyze.

International Rectifier is using Essbase not only to cut the costs and time it takes to collect data but also to standardize how the data is created to improve decision making, says Burke. Using Essbase, the company has built a multidimensional data cube for inventory analysis and will soon roll out another to analyze sales by market sector. Using these common databases, "you don't have costs defined three different ways or revenue defined four different ways by different divisions," Burke says. "Whether people like the numbers or not, everyone agrees on the numbers," and can focus more on analyzing the data than gathering it, he explains [49].

Decision Support Systems

Decision support systems are computer-based information systems that provide interactive information support to managers and business professionals during the decision-making process. Decision support systems use (1) analytical models, (2) specialized databases, (3) a decision maker's own insights and judgments, and (4) an interactive, computer-based modeling process to support the making of semistructured and unstructured business decisions. See Figure 8.10.

Example. An example might help at this point. Sales managers typically rely on management information systems to produce sales analysis reports. These reports contain sales performance figures by product line, salesperson, sales region, and so on. A decision support system, on the other hand, would also interactively show a sales manager the effects on sales performance of changes in a variety of factors (such

FIGURE 8.10

Comparing decision support systems and management information systems. Note the major differences in the information and decision support they provide.

	Management Information Systems	Decision Support Systems
● Decision support provided	Provide information about the performance of the organization	Provide information and decision support techniques to analyze specific problems or opportunities
● Information form and frequency	Periodic, exception, demand, and push reports and responses	Interactive inquiries and responses
● Information format	Prespecified, fixed format	Ad hoc, flexible, and adaptable format
● Information processing methodology	Information produced by extraction and manipulation of business data	Information produced by analytical modeling of business data

as promotion expense and salesperson compensation). The DSS could then use several criteria (such as expected gross margin and market share) to evaluate and rank several alternative combinations of sales performance factors.

Therefore, DSS are designed to be ad hoc, quick-response systems that are initiated and controlled by business decision makers. Decision support systems are thus able to directly support the specific types of decisions and the personal decision-making styles and needs of individual executives, managers, and business professionals.

DSS Components

Unlike management information systems, decision support systems rely on **model bases** as well as databases as vital system resources. A DSS model base is a software component that consists of models used in computational and analytical routines that mathematically express relationships among variables. For example, a spreadsheet program might contain models that express simple accounting relationships among variables, such as Revenue − Expenses = Profit. Or a DSS model base could include models and analytical techniques used to express much more complex relationships. For example, it might contain linear programming models, multiple regression forecasting models, and capital budgeting present value models. Such models may be stored in the form of spreadsheet models or templates, or statistical and mathematical programs and program modules. See Figure 8.11.

DSS software packages can combine model components to create integrated models that support specific types of decisions. DSS software typically contains built-in analytical modeling routines and also enables you to build your own models. Many DSS packages are now available in microcomputer and Web-enabled versions. Of course, electronic spreadsheet packages also provide some of the model building (spreadsheet models) and analytical modeling (what-if and goal-seeking analysis) offered by more powerful DSS software. See Figure 8.12.

FIGURE 8.11

Components of a Web-enabled marketing decision support system. Note the hardware, software, model, data, and network resources involved.

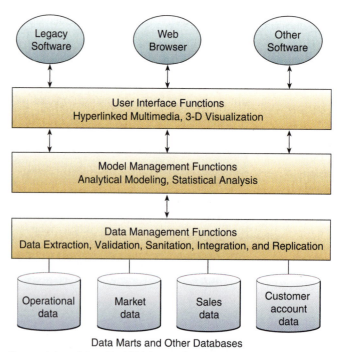

Source: Adapted from Ravi Kalakota and Andrew Whinston, *Electronic Commerce: A Manager's Guide* (Reading, MA: Addison-Wesley, 1997), p. 343. © 1997 by Addison-Wesley Publishing Company, Inc. Reprinted by permission of Addison-Wesley Longman, Inc.

FIGURE 8.12

Examples of special-purpose DSS packages.

DSS Packages
● **Retail:** Information Advantage and Unisys offer the Category Management Solution Suite, an OLAP decision support system and industry-specific data model.
● **Insurance:** Computer Associates offers RiskAdvisor, an insurance risk decision support system whose data model stores information in insurance industry specific tables designed for optimal query performance.
● **Telecom:** NCR and SABRE Decision Technologies have joined forces to create the NCR Customer Retention program for the communications industry including data marts for telephone companies to use for decision support in managing customer loyalty, quality of service, network management, fraud, and marketing.

Source: Adapted from Charles B. Darling, "Ease Implementation Woes with Packaged Data Marts," *Datamation*, March 1997, p. 103. © 1997 by Cahners Publishing Co.

Web-Enabled DSS at PepsiCo

PepsiCo and Sedgwick James Inc., the world's second largest insurance broker, developed a risk management DSS to help minimize PepsiCo's losses from accidents, theft, and other causes. Every week, Sedgwick loads the latest casualty claims data from the nation's leading insurance carriers into a DSS database resident on IBM RS/6000 servers in the PepsiCo intranet. The database is then accessed by managers and analysts using desktop PCs and remote laptops equipped with the INFORM risk management system. Both the RS/6000 servers and local PCs use Information Builders' middleware to provide PepsiCo managers and business analysts with transparent data access from a variety of hardware/software configurations.

The INFORM risk management system combines the analytical power of FOCUS decision support modeling with the graphical analysis capabilities of FOCUS/EIS for Windows. As a result, PepsiCo managers and business analysts at all levels can pinpoint critical trends, drill down for detailed backup information, identify potential problems, and plan ways to minimize risks and maximize profits [41].

Geographic Information and Data Visualization Systems

Geographic information systems (GIS) and *data visualization systems* (DVS) are special categories of DSS that integrate computer graphics with other DSS features. A geographic information system is a DSS that uses *geographic databases* to construct and display maps and other graphics displays that support decisions affecting the geographic distribution of people and other resources. Many companies are using GIS technology along with *global positioning system* (GPS) devices to help them choose new retail store locations, optimize distribution routes, or analyze the demographics of their target audiences. For example, companies like Levi Strauss, Arby's, Consolidated Rail, and Federal Express use GIS packages to integrate maps, graphics, and other geographic data with business data from spreadsheets and statistical packages. GIS software such as MapInfo and Atlas GIS is used for most business GIS applications [36].

Data visualization systems represent complex data using interactive three-dimensional graphical forms such as charts, graphs, and maps. DVS tools help users to interactively sort, subdivide, combine, and organize data while it is in its graphical form. This helps users discover patterns, links, and anomalies in business or scientific data in an interactive knowledge discovery and decision support process. Business applications like data mining typically use interactive graphs that let users drill down in real time and manipulate the underlying data of a business model to help clarify its meaning for business decision making [15, 28]. Figure 8.13 is an example of website activity data displayed by a data visualization system.

FIGURE 8.13

Using a data visualization system to analyze user activity on an e-commerce website.

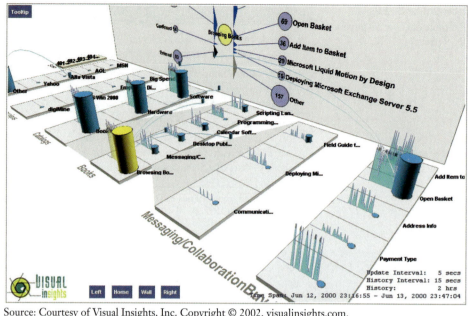

Source: Courtesy of Visual Insights, Inc. Copyright © 2002, visualinsights.com.

Ely Lilly: Data Visualization for Decision Support

A new idea in software is beginning to help companies reduce the time and money they spend searching for patterns and meaning in their data oceans. It's an approach that started as a doctoral thesis by Christopher Ahlberg, the 32-year-old Swedish-born founder of software company Spotfire, in Somerville, Massachusetts.

Spotfire's software is the first to combine both "data visualization" and a powerful database querying flexibility. Known as DecisionSite, the data visualization system (DVS) software isn't cheap—installations start at $100,000. That hasn't stopped customers in a wide range of industries from buying more than 16,000 licenses.

The magic in Spotfire's software is that it lets users easily do what-if queries and comparisons of data from different sources by moving sliders on a computer screen with a mouse. The results appear as brightly colored bar graphs, pie charts, scatter plots, and even maps.

When Spotfire rolled out its software in 1997, it aimed first at the drug industry, where the data explosion has been immense. An early adopter was Sheldon Ort, Eli Lilly's information officer for manufacturing and supply services. Ort now has some 1,500 company scientists around the world hooked up to Spotfire's software. "We primarily use it to facilitate decision making," Ort says. "With its ability to represent multiple sources of information and interactively change your view, it's helpful for homing in on specific molecules and deciding whether we should be doing further testing on them."

Using Spotfire, researchers avoid having to construct multiple queries in perfect syntax. Dragging the sliders to and fro, the user is actually launching a sequence of queries in rapid succession and seeing the outcomes expressed graphically onscreen. Lilly uses the software to conduct meetings among researchers at multiple sites who are linked on a computer network. As the person making a presentation moves the sliders on his or her screen, everyone can see the families, clusters, outliers, gaps, anomalies, and other statistical nuggets that database users fish for. Ideas can be tried out collaboratively in real time [9].

Using Decision Support Systems

Using a decision support system involves an interactive **analytical modeling** process. For example, using a DSS software package for decision support may result in a series of displays in response to alternative what-if changes entered by a manager. This differs from the demand responses of management information systems, since

FIGURE 8.14

Activities and examples of the major types of analytical modeling.

Type of Analytical Modeling	Activities and Examples
What-if analysis	Observing how changes to selected variables affect other variables. *Example:* What if we cut advertising by 10 percent? What would happen to sales?
Sensitivity analysis	Observing how repeated changes to a single variable affect other variables. *Example:* Let's cut advertising by $100 repeatedly so we can see its relationship to sales.
Goal-seeking analysis	Making repeated changes to selected variables until a chosen variable reaches a target value. *Example:* Let's try increases in advertising until sales reach $1million.
Optimization analysis	Finding an optimum value for selected variables, given certain constraints. *Example:* What's the best amount of advertising to have, given our budget and choice of media?

decision makers are not demanding prespecified information. Rather, they are exploring possible alternatives. Thus, they do not have to specify their information needs in advance. Instead, they use the DSS to find the information they need to help them make a decision. That is the essence of the decision support system concept.

Using a decision support system involves four basic types of analytical modeling activities: (1) what-if analysis, (2) sensitivity analysis, (3) goal-seeking analysis, and (4) optimization analysis. Let's briefly look at each type of analytical modeling that can be used for decision support. See Figure 8.14.

What-If Analysis

In **what-if analysis,** an end user makes changes to variables, or relationships among variables, and observes the resulting changes in the values of other variables. For example, if you were using a spreadsheet, you might change a revenue amount (a variable) or a tax rate formula (a relationship among variables) in a simple financial spreadsheet model. Then you could command the spreadsheet program to instantly recalculate all affected variables in the spreadsheet. A managerial user would be very interested in observing and evaluating any changes that occurred to the values in the spreadsheet, especially to a variable such as net profit after taxes. To many managers, net profit after taxes is an example of *the bottom line*, that is, a key factor in making many types of decisions. This type of analysis would be repeated until the manager was satisfied with what the results revealed about the effects of various possible decisions. Figure 8.15 is an example of what-if analysis.

Sensitivity Analysis

Sensitivity analysis is a special case of what-if analysis. Typically, the value of only one variable is changed repeatedly, and the resulting changes on other variables are observed. So sensitivity analysis is really a case of what-if analysis involving repeated changes to only one variable at a time. Some DSS packages automatically make repeated small changes to a variable when asked to perform sensitivity analysis. Typically, sensitivity analysis is used when decision makers are uncertain about the assumptions made in estimating the value of certain key variables. In our previous spreadsheet example, the value of revenue could be changed repeatedly in small increments, and the effects on other spreadsheet variables observed and evaluated. This would help a manager understand the impact of various revenue levels on other factors involved in decisions being considered.

Goal-Seeking Analysis

Goal-seeking analysis reverses the direction of the analysis done in what-if and sensitivity analysis. Instead of observing how changes in a variable affect other variables, goal-seeking analysis (also called *how can* analysis) sets a target value (a goal) for a

FIGURE 8.15

This what-if analysis involves the evaluation of probability distributions of net income and net present value (NPV) generated by changes to values for sales, competitors, product development, and capital expenses.

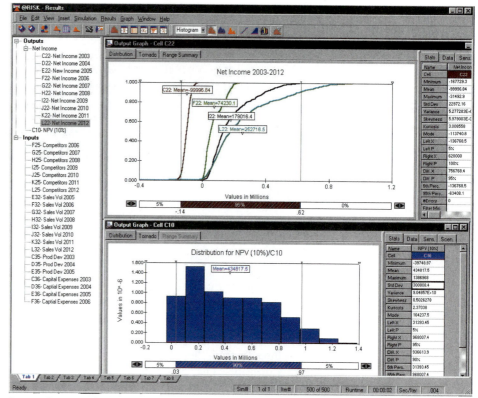

Source: Courtesy of Palisade Software.

variable and then repeatedly changes other variables until the target value is achieved. For example, you could specify a target value (goal) of $2 million for net profit after taxes for a business venture. Then you could repeatedly change the value of revenue or expenses in a spreadsheet model until a result of $2 million is achieved. Thus, you would discover what amount of revenue or level of expenses the business venture needs to achieve in order to reach the goal of $2 million in after-tax profits. Therefore, this form of analytical modeling would help answer the question, "How can we achieve $2 million in net profit after taxes?" instead of the question, "What happens if we change revenue or expenses?" Thus, goal-seeking analysis is another important method of decision support.

Optimization Analysis

Optimization analysis is a more complex extension of goal-seeking analysis. Instead of setting a specific target value for a variable, the goal is to find the optimum value for one or more target variables, given certain constraints. Then one or more other variables are changed repeatedly, subject to the specified constraints, until the best values for the target variables are discovered. For example, you could try to determine the highest possible level of profits that could be achieved by varying the values for selected revenue sources and expense categories. Changes to such variables could be subject to constraints such as the limited capacity of a production process or limits to available financing. Optimization typically is accomplished by special-purpose software packages for optimization techniques such as linear programming, or by advanced DSS generators.

Lexis-Nexis: Web Tools for Decision Support

"Our new subscribers will grow geometrically with Web-based access to our information services," explains Keith Hawk, vice president of sales for the Nexis division of Lexis-Nexis. "And therefore our business model is changing from selling primarily to organizations to selling to individual users." To track their 1.7

million subscribers of legal and news documents, Lexis-Nexis replaced its old decision support system with new DSS tools and an NCR Teradata data warehouse system. The new customer data warehouse lets 475 salespeople and in-house analysts use the corporate intranet and Web browsers to look up daily detailed customer usage data.

The type of data that the company's salespeople sort through and analyze includes subscriber usage patterns—what they look up, what sources they use most often, when they're connecting—along with customer contract details. To get to that data, Lexis-Nexis uses decision support software from MicroStrategy Inc. Field sales representatives who need ad hoc reporting capabilities use MicroStrategy DSS WebPE, a Web-based reporting tool. Power users, such as market research analysis, use DSS Agent, an analytical modeling tool with Web access, to closely analyze and model business processes [16, 24].

Data Mining for Decision Support

We discussed data mining and data warehouses in Chapter 3 on data resource management. However, data mining's main purpose is knowledge discovery leading to decision support. Data mining software analyzes the vast stores of historical business data that have been prepared for analysis in corporate data warehouses. Data mining attempts to discover patterns, trends, and correlations hidden in the data that can give a company a strategic business advantage.

Data mining software may perform regression, decision tree, neural network, cluster detection, or market basket analysis for a business. See Figure 8.16. The data mining process can highlight buying patterns, reveal customer tendencies, cut

FIGURE 8.16

Data mining software can provide data visualization capabilities to help discover patterns in business data like this analysis of customer demographic information.

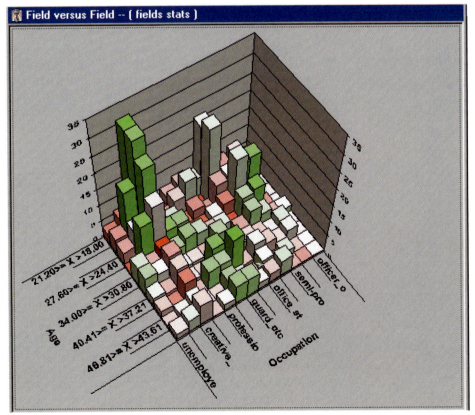

Source: Courtesy of Attar Software.

redundant costs, or uncover unseen profitable relationships and opportunities. For example, many companies use data mining to find more profitable ways to perform successful direct mailings, including e-mailings, or to discover better ways to display products in a store, design a better e-commerce website, reach untapped profitable customers, or recognize customers or products that are unprofitable or marginal [18].

KeyCorp and Peoples Bank: Data Mining DSS	Quick payback and support for some surprising, counterintuitive decisions have been among the benefits users have found with IBM's DecisionEdge for Relationship Marketing decision support software. "We had a full return on our investment 14 months after installing the data mining component," said Jo Ann Boylan, an executive vice president in the Key Technology Service division at KeyCorp, one of the largest retail banks in the United States. She added that the data mining and analysis system helped raise the bank's direct-mail response rate from 1 to as high as 10 percent. It also helped identify unprofitable product lines. The DecisionEdge decision support package includes application suites, analytical tools, a mining data tool, industry-specific data models, and consulting services. Pricing begins at around $150,000. Peoples Bank & Trust Co. in Indianapolis used the DecisionEdge for Relationship Marketing to delve into some highly profitable bank offerings that turned out to be prohibitively expensive, said Bob Connors, a senior vice president of information services. The DSS pointed out how much it actually costs to bring in each highly profitable home equity loan customer. "Because those loans can be so profitable, it seems like a no-brainer that you'd want to market them," Connors explained. "But we found that the costs to bring them in were far too high, so we've cut way back on that spending. We still offer the loans, but we don't spend so much on advertising or direct mail any more" [17].

Executive Information Systems

Executive information systems (EIS) are information systems that combine many of the features of management information systems and decision support systems. When they were first developed, their focus was on meeting the strategic information needs of top management. Thus, the first goal of executive information systems was to provide top executives with immediate and easy access to information about a firm's *critical success factors* (CSFs), that is, key factors that are critical to accomplishing an organization's strategic objectives. For example, the executives of a retail store chain would probably consider factors such as its e-commerce versus traditional sales results, or its product line mix to be critical to its survival and success.

However, executive information systems are becoming so widely used by managers, analysts, and other knowledge workers that they are sometimes humorously called "everyone's information systems." More popular alternative names are enterprise information systems (EIS) and executive support systems (ESS). These names also reflect the fact that more features, such as Web browsing, electronic mail, groupware tools, and DSS and expert system capabilities, are being added to many systems to make them more useful to managers and business professionals [23, 25, 50].

Features of an EIS

In an EIS, information is presented in forms tailored to the preferences of the executives using the system. For example, most executive information systems stress the use of a graphical user interface and graphics displays that can be customized to the

FIGURE 8.17

Web-based executive information systems can provide managers and business professionals with personalized information and analytical tools for decision support.

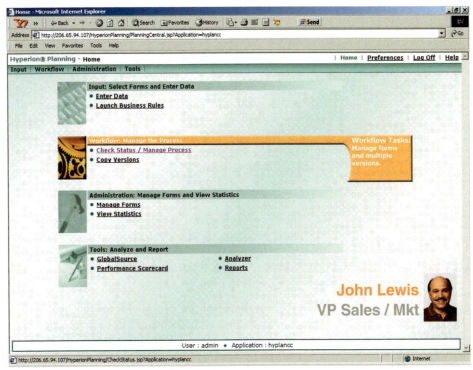

Source: Courtesy of Hyperion Solutions Corp.

information preferences of executives using the EIS. Other information presentation methods used by an EIS include exception reporting and trend analysis. The ability to *drill down*, which allows executives to quickly retrieve displays of related information at lower levels of detail, is another important capability. And of course, the growth of Internet and intranet technologies has added Web browsing to the list of EIS capabilities.

Figure 8.17 shows one of the displays provided by the Web-enabled Hyperion executive information system. Notice how simple and brief this display is. Also note how it provides users of the system with the ability to drill down quickly to lower levels of detail in areas of particular interest to them. Beside the drill-down capability, the Hyperion EIS also stresses trend analysis and exception reporting. Thus, a business user can quickly discover the direction key factors are heading and the extent to which critical factors are deviating from expected results [53].

EIS have spread into the ranks of middle management and business professionals as they recognized their feasibility and benefits, and as less-expensive systems for client/server networks and corporate intranets became available. For example, one popular EIS software package reports that only 3 percent of its users are top executives. Another example is the EIS of Conoco, one of the world's largest oil companies. Conoco's EIS is used by most senior managers, and by over 4,000 employees located at corporate headquarters in Houston and throughout the world [4, 51, 54].

EIS at Conoco and KeyCorp

As we just mentioned, Conoco, Inc., has a widely used EIS. Conoco's EIS is a large system with 75 different applications and hundreds of screen displays. Senior executives and over 4,000 managers and analysts worldwide use EIS applications ranging from analyzing internal operations and financial results to viewing external events that affect the petroleum industry. Conoco's EIS is popular with its users and has resulted in improved employee productivity and decision making, and significant cost savings compared to alternative methods of generating information for managers and analysts [4].

KeyCorp is a large banking and financial services holding company. It developed Keynet, a corporate intranet that transformed their mainframe-based EIS into a new EIS—a Web-enabled system they call "everyone's information system." Now more than 1,000 managers and analysts have Web access to 40 major business information areas within Keynet, ranging from sales and financial statistics to human resource management [45].

Enterprise Portals and Decision Support

Don't confuse portals with the executive information systems that have been used in some industries for many years. Portals are for everyone in the company, and not just for executives. You want people on the front lines making decisions using browsers and portals rather than just executives using specialized executive information system software [45].

We mentioned earlier in this chapter that major changes and expansion are taking place in traditional MIS, DSS, and EIS tools for providing the information and modeling managers need to support their decision making. Decision support in business is changing, driven by rapid developments in end user computing and networking; Internet and Web technologies, and Web-enabled business applications.

Enterprise Information Portals

A user checks his e-mail, looks up the current company stock price, checks his available vacation days, and receives an order from a customer—all from the browser on his desktop. That is the next-generation intranet, also known as a corporate or enterprise information portal. With it, the browser becomes the dashboard to daily business tasks [44].

An **enterprise information portal** (EIP) is a Web-based interface and integration of intranet and other technologies that gives all intranet users and selected extranet users access to a variety of internal and external business applications and services. For example, internal applications might include access to e-mail, project websites, and discussion groups; human resources Web self-services; customer, inventory, and other corporate databases; decision support systems, and knowledge management systems. External applications might include industry, financial, and other Internet news services; links to industry discussion groups; and links to customer and supplier Internet and extranet websites. Enterprise information portals are typically tailored or personalized to the needs of individual business users or groups of users, giving them a personalized *digital dashboard* of information sources and applications. See Figure 8.18.

The business benefits of enterprise information portals include providing more specific and selective information to business users, providing easy access to key corporate intranet website resources, delivering industry and business news, and providing better access to company data for selected customers, suppliers, or business partners. Enterprise information portals can also help avoid excessive surfing by employees across company and Internet websites by making it easier for them to receive or find the information and services they need, thus improving the productivity of a company's workforce [45].

Figure 8.19 illustrates how companies are developing enterprise information portals as a way to provide Web-enabled information, knowledge, and decision support to their executives, managers, employees, suppliers, customers, and other business partners. The enterprise information portal is a customized and personalized Web-based interface for corporate intranets, which gives users easy access to a variety of internal and external business applications, databases, and services. For example, the

FIGURE 8.18

An enterprise information portal can provide a business professional with a personalized workplace of information sources, administrative and analytical tools, and relevant business applications.

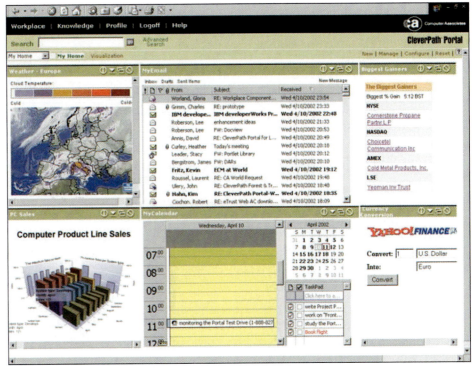

Source: Courtesy of Computer Associates.

EIP in Figure 8.19 might give a qualified user secure access to DSS, data mining, and OLAP tools, the Internet and the Web, the corporate intranet, supplier or customer extranets, operational and analytical databases, a data warehouse, and a variety of business applications [43, 44, 45].

Procter & Gamble: How an EIP Provides Decision Support	Back in 1996, when a portal was just a fancy name for a door, Procter & Gamble Co.'s IT division began developing a rudimentary system for sharing documents and information over the company's intranet. As the demands of users and the number of Web pages supported by the system grew, the IT team expanded the scope of this Global Knowledge Catalog. The larger system is a storehouse of information that lets all 97,000 Procter & Gamble employees worldwide find information specific to their needs.

But although the system helped make sense of volumes of data, it still led to information overload. What Procter & Gamble really needed was a way to personalize the information of each employee, based on his or her job, says Dan Gerbus, project manager for the portal project in the Cincinnati company's IT division. "Users wanted one tool on their browser that would consolidate and deliver all the information they needed to do their work without having to navigate through 14 websites," he says.

So in January 2000, Procter & Gamble awarded a contract to Plumtree Software for 100,000 seats of the Plumtree Corporate Portal. Procter & Gamble, which became an investor in Plumtree, uses the portal to deliver marketing, product, and strategic information, as well as industry-news documents in thousands of Lotus Notes databases to its employees. The portal's document directory pulls data from more than 1 million Web pages.

By early 2001, Procter & Gamble's enterprise-wide portal included Web links to the company's SAP R/3 enterprise resource planning system and a wide range of Oracle data warehousing and decision support products. Customer data analyzed

FIGURE 8.19

The components of this enterprise information portal identify it as an e-business decision support system that can be personalized for executives, managers, employees, suppliers, customers, and other business partners.

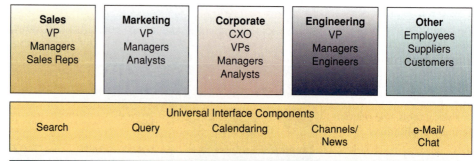

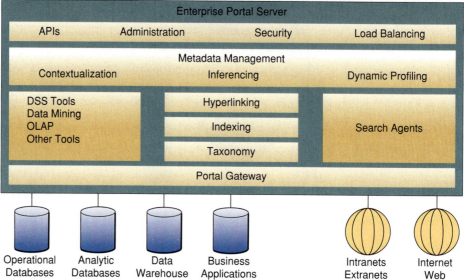

Source: Adapted from Gerry Murray, "Making Connections with Enterprise Knowledge Portals," White Paper, *Computerworld*, September 6, 1999, p. 6. Copyright 1999 by Computerworld, Inc., Framingham, MA 01701. Reprinted from *Computerworld*.

by E.piphany's customer relationship management application is also incorporated. The idea, Gerbus says, is to give employees one place to get the information and applications they need. "They used to have to scan multiple intranet sites to find ways to get that. The portal is one-stop shopping," he says.

Gerbus says that Procter & Gamble employees will be able to glance at their "dashboard," which will deliver a preset view into various information sources and find all the up-to-date information they need to make decisions about new products, advertising compaigns, or other initiatives. "If a business manager always needs to track some key pieces of information, we'll be able to build a dashboard for that," Gerbus says. "But we'll also provide the tools for them to get to the application or data source for a more-in-depth analysis" [47].

Knowledge Management Systems

We introduced **knowledge management systems** in Chapter 2 as the use of information technology to help gather, organize, and share business knowledge within an organization. In many organizations, hypermedia databases at corporate intranet websites have become the *knowledge bases* for storage and dissemination of business knowledge. This frequently takes the form of best practices, policies, and business solutions at the project, team, business unit, and enterprise levels of the company.

For many companies, enterprise information portals are the entry to corporate intranets that serve as their knowledge management systems. That's why such portals are called **enterprise knowledge portals** by their vendors. Thus, enterprise knowledge portals play an essential role in helping companies use their intranets as knowledge management systems to share and disseminate knowledge in support of business decision making by managers and business professionals [29, 43]. See Figure 8.20.

Qwest Communications: Web Knowledge Management System

At Qwest Communications, knowledge management (KM) was the only way to be sure that call center representatives had the information they needed, when they needed it. Relying on print documentation or a supervisor's directive did not ensure cross-company accuracy or even that the information was delivered to all who needed it. Knowledge management was the only way to ensure that support would be available for every conceivable situation, and that the information was accurate and complete. Qwest has had an online procedures database for quite some time, but it was just online documentation. Each document looked different. Design was in the hands of the individual author, and there were lots of authors. Compounding the problem, authors had their own view about the content and the appropriate level of detail. Generally speaking, they wrote what *they* thought the representative needed to know, not necessarily what the representative *actually* needed to know.

In 1999 the old system was replaced by *InfoBuddy*, Qwest's Web-based knowledge management system. It supports a wide variety of job functions in addition to customer service representatives, including technical repair, installation and

FIGURE 8.20   This example of the capabilities and components of an enterprise knowledge portal emphasizes its use as a Web-based knowledge management system.

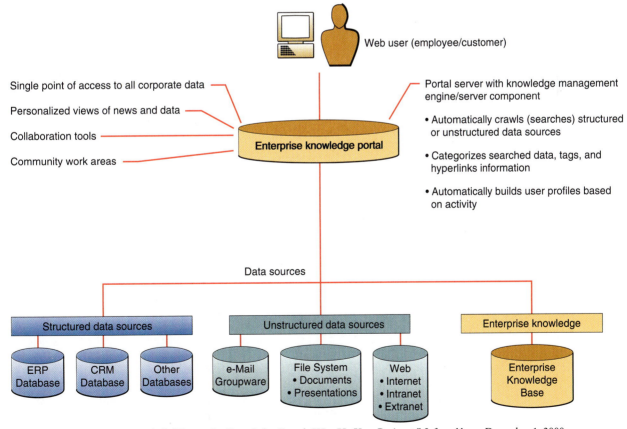

Source: Adapted from Lori Mitchell, "Enterprise Knowledge Portals Wise Up Your Business," *Infoworld.com*, December 1, 2000.

maintenance, etc. InfoBuddy uses a methods and procedures database with intelligent KM capabilities, such as searching, tagging, and customizable interface. It can reorder the information presentation based on who the user is.

When users identify themselves and their job function or role, the InfoBuddy intranet portal knows how to configure its user interface to provide information of most value to each person. In addition, users have the ability to personalize their portal through the "MyBuddy" feature, enabling representatives to place bookmarks on their home pages to the information they feel is most important. Over time, as users "learn" from the system, they can replace learned material with new, usually more advanced information.

In addition, the InfoBuddy system "pushes" information to specific users based on their needs. For example, if a new promotion were initiated, specific information—products, pricing, etc.—would appear on the "desktop" of those representatives who are involved in the marketing initiative [48].

| SECTION II | # Artificial Intelligence Technologies in Business |

Business and AI

Artificial intelligence is making its way back to the mainstream of corporate technology. Designed to leverage the capabilities of humans rather than replace them, today's AI technology enables an extraordinary array of applications that forge new connections among people, computers, knowledge, and the physical world. AI-enabled applications are at work in information distribution and retrieval, database mining, product design, manufacturing, inspection, training, user support, surgical planning, resource scheduling, and complex resource management.

Indeed, for anyone who schedules, plans, allocates resources, designs new products, uses the Internet, develops software, is responsible for product quality, is an investment professional, heads up IT, uses IT, or operates in any of a score of other capacities and arenas, new AI technologies already may be in place and providing competitive advantage [56].

Analyzing BAE Systems

Read the Real World Case on BAE Systems on the next page. We can learn a lot about the business value of using the Internet and artificial intelligence technologies from this example. See Figure 8.21.

BAE Systems found that its top decision makers did not have the right information at key stages and most of their employees were wasting time trying to find

FIGURE 8.21

Richard West is organizational and e-learning manager for BAE Systems and led the development of its knowledge management system.

Source: Phil Rudge/BAE Systems.

REAL WORLD CASE 2

BAE Systems: The Benefits of AI in Knowledge Management Systems

It's one of those blue-sky goals to which many big companies only aspire: capturing the seemingly infinite amount of intellectual capital that's carried by tens of thousands of employees around the world and using it to achieve competitive advantage. But it's a flight that's well under way at London-based BAE Systems PLC (www.baesystems.com), formerly British Aerospace, which is getting solid returns on a knowledge management intranet-based system. Thousands of BAE engineers scattered across five continents in 100 offices are using the system to search for information that may be vital to big initiatives and to identify and eliminate redundant project work.

Like other far-flung multinationals, the $20 billion-plus aerospace and engineering giant suspected that its engineers and other workers might be wasting a lot of time searching for information scattered across the enterprise. So in early 1999, BAE Systems invested roughly $150,000 to study its global operations to see whether "we had the right information to support decision-making processes and if people had the right learning systems to help them support their day-to-day jobs," says Richard West, BAE's organizational and e-learning manager in Farnborough, England.

The results, says West, "were certainly eye-opening." BAE Systems discovered that nearly two-thirds of its top 120 decision makers didn't have the right information at key stages. The company also found that 80 percent of employees were "wasting" an average of 30 minutes each day trying to find the information they needed to do their jobs. Another 60 percent were spending an hour or more duplicating the work of others.

"In an organization as massive as BAE Systems, we seemed to be working in silos where we didn't seem to know what was going on elsewhere," says West. One of the problems BAE Systems officials discovered through the study was information overload on its intranets. The information itself was often unstructured, and the search engines were inadequate for conducting keyword searches to find information, says West. The company decided to test two or three of the top intranet search engines over three months and compare their ability to find information, says West.

One of the search engines BAE Systems tested was from San Francisco–based Autonomy Corp. The Autonomy search engine uses advanced pattern matching, intelligent agents, and other artificial intelligence (AI) technologies whose "ability to retrieve information was second to none," says West. What sold BAE Systems on Autonomy's AI-based technology was its ability to flag whether other people in the organization are searching against similar information and, perhaps, working on common problems.

That kind of matching identification helped the Autonomy system pay for itself just seven months after it was installed in late 1999. One of the system's first big payoffs came soon after, when two disparate groups of engineers in the

U.K. were working on wing construction issues for the company's Harrier 2 military aircraft. After using the Autonomy system to search for wing specification information across the company's intranet, one of the engineering groups discovered that the other group was working on the same problem. Catching the redundancy early in the cycle helped save the company millions, which ultimately paid for the licensing and maintenance of the Autonomy search engine, says West. He declined to say how much BAE Systems paid for the search engine.

A year into using the Autonomy search engine, BAE Systems evaluated its performance and determined that it was able to reduce the time needed to retrieve information from its intranet by 90 percent. Christopher Tree, a systems engineer in Farnborough and one of 20,000 regular users of the search engine, says it is "helping me do my day-to-day job." For instance, the central IT organization at BAE Systems is conducting a software capability maturity model audit throughout its global offices over the next several weeks. Tree plans to use the software to "determine where the audit has taken place before and assist me in preparing for it," he says.

One of the features Tree likes best about the search engine is its ability to "scan the network and draw upon that information" so he doesn't have to log in and send engineering or project information into the portal himself. Using previous search engines on the company's intranet, Tree says, it would often take seven days out of a monthlong project to search for and find best-practices information. Using the Autonomy system's matching identification capabilities, "I can now literally find a name and contact information within minutes," he says.

In fact, because it took so long to find that kind of information before, Tree says he rarely invested the time to do the research. The upshot was that a lot of BAE's intellectual capital was never tapped. For a knowledge management portal to succeed, "it's got to form part of an information sharing process with measurable benefits," says West. "You can have a whiz-bang solution, but if you say, 'Here's a great search engine; use it if you want to,' will they come? Not likely."

Case Study Questions

1. What problems was BAE having in knowledge sharing? Are such problems common to many companies? Why or why not?

2. How does BAE's knowledge management system help solve such problems?

3. What are some of the business benefits and potential limitations of BAE's knowledge management system?

Source: Adapted from Thomas Hoffman, "In the Know," *Computerworld*, October 14, 2002, p. 42.

information to do their jobs, or duplicating the work of others. The fault lay with information overload and inadequate search engines on its company intranets. So BAE developed an intranet-based knowledge management system using the Autonomy search engine that uses artificial intelligence techniques to search for information and information sources, as well as identifying other employees working on similar or related problems. The new knowledge management system has already resulted in a 90 percent reduction in the time needed to find information on the intranet, and saved millions of dollars in discovering and eliminating redundant design work on major aircraft construction projects.

An Overview of Artificial Intelligence

What is artificial intelligence? **Artificial intelligence** (AI) is a field of science and technology based on disciplines such as computer science, biology, psychology, linguistics, mathematics, and engineering. The goal of AI is to develop computers that can think, as well as see, hear, walk, talk, and feel. A major thrust of artificial intelligence is the development of computer functions normally associated with human intelligence, such as reasoning, learning, and problem solving, as summarized in Figure 8.22.

Debate has raged around artificial intelligence since serious work in the field began in the 1950s. Not only technological, but moral and philosophical questions abound about the possibility of intelligent, thinking machines. For example, British AI pioneer Alan Turing in 1950 proposed a test for determining if machines could think. According to the Turing test, a computer could demonstrate intelligence if a human interviewer, conversing with an unseen human and an unseen computer, could not tell which was which [37, 50].

Though much work has been done in many of the subgroups that fall under the AI umbrella, critics believe that no computer can truly pass the Turing test. They claim that developing intelligence to impart true humanlike capabilities to computers is simply not possible. But progress continues, and only time will tell if the ambitious goals of artificial intelligence will be achieved and equal the popular images found in science fiction.

The Domains of Artificial Intelligence

Figure 8.23 illustrates the major domains of AI research and development. Note that AI applications can be grouped under three major areas: cognitive science, robotics, and natural interfaces, though these classifications do overlap each other, and other classifications can be used. Also note that expert systems are just one of many important AI applications. Let's briefly review each of these major areas of AI and some of their current technologies. Figure 8.24 outlines some of the latest developments in commercial applications of artificial intelligence.

FIGURE 8.22

Some of the attributes of intelligent behavior. AI is attempting to duplicate these capabilities in computer-based systems.

Attributes of Intelligent Behavior
● Think and reason.
● Use reason to solve problems.
● Learn or understand from experience.
● Acquire and apply knowledge.
● Exhibit creativity and imagination.
● Deal with complex or perplexing situations.
● Respond quickly and successfully to new situations.
● Recognize the relative importance of elements in a situation.
● Handle ambiguous, incomplete, or erroneous information.

FIGURE 8.23

The major application areas of artificial intelligence. Note that the many applications of AI can be grouped into the three major areas of cognitive science, robotics, and natural interfaces.

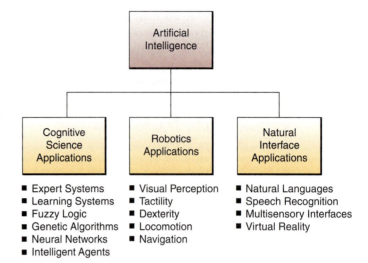

Cognitive Science. This area of artificial intelligence is based on research in biology, neurology, psychology, mathematics, and many allied disciplines. It focuses on researching how the human brain works and how humans think and learn. The results of such research in *human information processing* are the basis for the development of a variety of computer-based applications in artificial intelligence.

Applications in the cognitive science area of AI include the development of *expert systems* and other *knowledge-based systems* that add a knowledge base and some reasoning capability to information systems. Also included are *adaptive learning systems* that can modify their behaviors based on information they acquire as they operate. Chess-playing systems are primitive examples of such applications, though many more applications are being implemented. *Fuzzy logic* systems can process data that are incomplete or ambiguous, that is, *fuzzy data*. Thus, they can solve unstructured problems with incomplete knowledge by developing approximate inferences and answers, as humans do. *Neural network* software can learn by processing sample problems and their solutions. As neural nets start to recognize patterns, they can begin to program themselves to solve such problems on their own. *Genetic algorithm* software uses Darwinian (survival of the fittest), randomizing, and other mathematics functions to simulate evolutionary processes that can generate increasingly better solutions to problems. And *intelligent agents* use expert system and other AI technologies to serve as software surrogates for a variety of end user applications.

Robotics. AI, engineering, and physiology are the basic disciplines of robotics. This technology produces robot machines with computer intelligence and computer-controlled, humanlike physical capabilities. This area thus includes applications designed to give robots the powers of sight, or visual perception; touch, or tactile capabilities; dexterity, or skill in handling and manipulation; locomotion, or the physical ability to move over any terrain; and navigation, or the intelligence to properly find one's way to a destination [37]. The use of robotics in computer-aided manufacturing was discussed in Chapter 5.

Natural Interfaces. The development of natural interfaces is considered a major area of AI applications and is essential to the natural use of computers by humans. For example, the development of *natural languages* and speech recognition are major thrusts of this area of AI. Being able to talk to computers and robots in conversational human languages and have them "understand" us as easily as we understand each other is a goal of AI research. This involves research and development in linguistics, psychology, computer science, and other disciplines. Other natural interface

FIGURE 8.24

Examples of some of the latest commercial applications of AI.

Commercial Applications of AI
Decision Support
● Intelligent work environment that will help you capture the *why* as well as the *what* of engineered design and decision making
● Intelligent human-computer interface (HCI) systems that can understand spoken language and gestures, and facilitate problem solving by supporting organizationwide collaborations to solve particular problems
● Situation assessment and resource allocation software for uses that range from airlines and airports to logistics centers
Information Retrieval
● AI-based intra- and Internet systems that distill tidal waves of information into simple presentations
● Natural language technology to retrieve any sort of online information, from text to pictures, videos, maps, and audio clips, in response to English questions
● Database mining for marketing trend analysis, financial forecasting, maintenance cost reduction, and more
Virtual Reality
● X-raylike vision enabled by enhanced-reality visualization that allows brain surgeons to "see through" intervening tissue to operate, monitor, and evaluate disease progression
● Automated animation and haptic interfaces that allow users to interact with virtual objects via touch (i.e., medical students can "feel" what it's like to suture severed aortas)
Robotics
● Machine vision inspections systems for gauging, guiding, identifying, and inspecting products and providing competitive advantage in manufacturing
● Cutting-edge robotics systems from micro robots and hands and legs to cognitive robotic and trainable modular vision systems

Source: Adapted from Patrick Winston, "Rethinking Artificial Intelligence," Program Announcement: Massachusetts Institute of Technology, September 1997, p. 3.

research applications include the development of multisensory devices that use a variety of body movements to operate computers. This is related to the emerging application area of *virtual reality*. Virtual reality involves using multisensory human-computer interfaces that enable human users to experience computer-simulated objects, spaces, activities, and "worlds" as if they actually exist.

Neural Networks

Neural networks are computing systems modeled after the brain's meshlike network of interconnected processing elements, called *neurons*. Of course, neural networks are a lot simpler in architecture (the human brain is estimated to have over 100 billion neuron brain cells!). However, like the brain, the interconnected processors in a neural network operate in parallel and interact dynamically with each other. This enables the network to "learn" from data it processes. That is, it learns to recognize patterns and relationships in the data it processes. The more data examples it receives as input, the better it can learn to duplicate the results of the examples it processes. Thus, the neural network will change the strengths of the interconnections between the processing elements in response to changing patterns in the data it receives and the results that occur [8, 50]. See Figure 8.25.

For example, a neural network can be trained to learn which credit characteristics result in good or bad loans. Developers of a credit evaluation neural network could provide it with data from many examples of credit applications and loan results

FIGURE 8.25

Evaluating the training status of a neural network application.

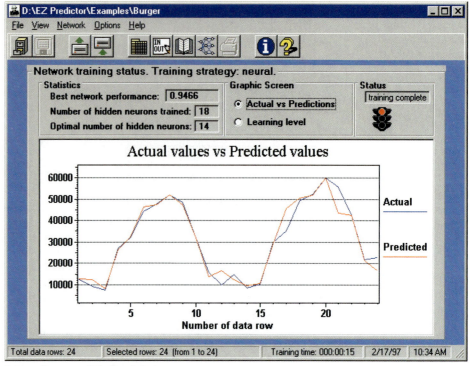

Source: Courtesy of Trading Solutions.

to process, and opportunities to adjust the signal strengths between its neurons. The neural network would continue to be trained until it demonstrated a high degree of accuracy in correctly duplicating the results of recent cases. At that point it would be trained enough to begin making credit evaluations of its own.

Neural networks can be implemented on microcomputers and other traditional computer systems by using software packages that simulate the activity of a neural network. Specialized neural network coprocessor circuit boards for PCs are also available that provide significantly greater processing power. In addition, special-purpose neural net microprocessor chips are being used in specific application areas such as military weapons systems, image processing, and voice recognition. However, most business applications depend primarily on neural net software packages to accomplish applications ranging from credit risk assessment to check signature verification, investment forecasting, data mining, and manufacturing quality control [8, 55].

Neural Nets at Go.com

Go.com has a targeted marketing service that more closely targets advertising on its Internet search engine to users' interests by keeping track of every search that a user makes. The service uses neural network technology from Aptex Software to observe all the searches users run every time they use the Go.com search engine. The neural net software then calculates a numeric value, or "vector," that describes users' interests. Go.com uses that information to match users to the online ads it sells to advertisers on its Web search pages.

Other commercial World Wide Web sites use this technology to build up the usefulness of their websites or encourage repeat business. Many electronic commerce websites use customizing software to track user behavior and predict what a user will be interested in seeing in the future. For example, Aptex has a version of its neural net software designed for sites that sell products and services

FIGURE 8.26 An example of fuzzy logic rules and a fuzzy logic SQL query in a credit risk analysis application.

Fuzzy Logic Rules

Risk should be acceptable
If debt-equity is very high
   then risk is positively increased
If income is increasing
   then risk is somewhat decreased
If cash reserves are low to very low
   then risk is very increased
If PE ratio is good
   then risk is generally decreased

Fuzzy Logic SQL Query

Select companies
   from financials
      where revenues are very large
         and pe_ratio is acceptable
         and profits are high to very high
         and (income/employee_tot) is reasonable

online. Select-Cast for Commerce Servers analyzes customer buying patterns, and predicts products and services the customer will be likely to buy, based on past behavior [52].

Fuzzy Logic Systems

In spite of the funny name, **fuzzy logic** systems represent a small, but serious and growing, application of AI in business. Fuzzy logic is a method of reasoning that resembles human reasoning since it allows for approximate values and inferences (fuzzy logic) and incomplete or ambiguous data (fuzzy data) instead of relying only on *crisp data*, such as binary (yes/no) choices. For example, Figure 8.26 illustrates a partial set of rules (fuzzy rules) and a fuzzy SQL query for analyzing and extracting credit risk information on businesses that are being evaluated for selection as investments.

Notice how fuzzy logic uses terminology that is deliberately imprecise, such as *very high, increasing, somewhat decreased, reasonable,* and *very low.* This enables fuzzy systems to process incomplete data and quickly provide approximate, but acceptable, solutions to problems that are difficult for other methods to solve. Fuzzy logic queries of a database, such as the SQL query shown in Figure 8.26, promise to improve the extraction of data from business databases. Queries can be stated more naturally in words that are closer to the way business specialists think about the topic for which they want information [11, 31].

Fuzzy Logic in Business

Examples of applications of fuzzy logic are numerous in Japan, but rare in the United States. The United States has tended to prefer using AI solutions like expert systems or neural networks. But Japan has implemented many fuzzy logic applications, especially the use of special-purpose fuzzy logic microprocessor chips, called fuzzy process controllers. Thus, the Japanese ride on subway trains, use elevators, and drive cars that are guided or supported by fuzzy process controllers made by Hitachi and Toshiba. They can even trade shares on the Tokyo Stock Exchange using a stock-trading program based on fuzzy logic rules. Many new models of Japanese-made products also feature fuzzy logic microprocessors. The list is growing, but includes autofocus cameras, autostabilizing camcorders, energy-efficient air conditioners, self-adjusting washing machines, and automatic transmissions [42].

Genetic Algorithms

The use of **genetic algorithms** is a growing application of artificial intelligence. Genetic algorithm software uses Darwinian (survival of the fittest), randomizing, and other mathematical functions to simulate an evolutionary process that can yield

FIGURE 8.27

Risk Optimizer software combines genetic algorithms with a risk simulation function in this airline yield optimization application.

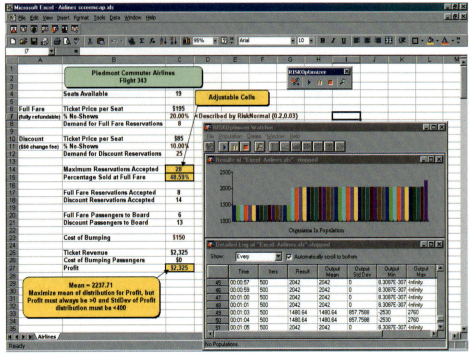

Source: Courtesy of Palisade Software.

increasingly better solutions to a problem. Genetic algorithms were first used to simulate millions of years in biological, geological, and ecosystem evolution in just a few minutes on a computer. Now genetic algorithm software is being used to model a variety of scientific, technical, and business processes [3, 26].

Genetic algorithms are especially useful for situations in which thousands of solutions are possible and must be evaluated to produce an optimal solution. Genetic algorithm software uses sets of mathematical process rules (*algorithms*) that specify how combinations of process components or steps are to be formed. This may involve trying random process combinations (*mutation*), combining parts of several good processes (*crossover*), and selecting good sets of processes and discarding poor ones (*selection*) in order to generate increasingly better solutions. Figure 8.27 illustrates a business use of genetic algorithm software.

GE's Engeneous	General Electric's design of a more efficient jet engine for the Boeing 777 is a classic example of a genetic algorithm application in business. A major engineering challenge was to develop more efficient fan blades for the engine. GE's engineers estimated that it would take billions of years, even with a supercomputer, to mathematically evaluate the astronomical number of performance and cost factors and combinations involved. Instead, GE used a hybrid genetic algorithm/expert system, called Engeneous, that produced an optimal solution in less than a week [3].

Virtual Reality

Virtual reality (VR) is a computer-simulated reality. Virtual reality is a fast-growing area of artificial intelligence that had its origins in efforts to build more natural, realistic, multisensory human-computer interfaces. So virtual reality relies on multisensory input/output devices such as a tracking headset with video goggles and stereo earphones, a *data glove* or jumpsuit with fiber-optic sensors that track your

FIGURE 8.28

Using a virtual reality system to design the interiors of an office building.

Source: Corbis Sygma.

body movements, and a *walker* that monitors the movement of your feet. Then you can experience computer-simulated "virtual worlds" three-dimensionally through sight, sound, and touch. Thus, virtual reality is also called *telepresence*. For example, you can enter a computer-generated virtual world, look around and observe its contents, pick up and move objects, and move around in it at will. Thus, virtual reality allows you to interact with computer-simulated objects, entities, and environments as if they actually exist [2, 46]. See Figure 8.28.

VR Applications

Current applications of virtual reality are wide ranging and include computer-aided design (CAD), medical diagnostics and treatment, scientific experimentation in many physical and biological sciences, flight simulation for training pilots and astronauts, product demonstrations, employee training, and entertainment, especially 3-D video arcade games. CAD is the most widely used industrial VR application. It enables architects and other designers to design and test electronic 3-D models of products and structures by entering the models themselves and examining, touching, and manipulating sections and parts from all angles. This scientific-visualization capability is also used by pharmaceutical and biotechnology firms to develop and observe the behavior of computerized models of new drugs and materials, and by medical researchers to develop ways for physicians to enter and examine a virtual reality of a patient's body.

VR designers are creating everything from virtual weather patterns and virtual wind tunnels to virtual cities and virtual securities markets. For example, by converting stock market and other financial data into three-dimensional graphic form, securities analysts can use VR systems to more rapidly observe and identify trends and exceptions in financial performance. Also promising are applications in information technology itself. This includes the development of 3-D models of telecommunications networks and databases. These virtual graphical representations of networks and databases make it easier for IS specialists to visualize the structure and relationships of an organization's telecommunications networks and corporate databases, thus improving their design and maintenance.

VR becomes *telepresence* when users who can be anywhere in the world use VR systems to work alone or together at a remote site. Typically, this involves using a VR system to enhance the sight and touch of a human who is remotely manipulating equipment to accomplish a task. Examples range from virtual surgery, where surgeon and patient may be on either side of the globe, to the remote use of equipment in hazardous environments such as chemical plants or nuclear reactors.

VR Limitations. The use of virtual reality seems limited only by the performance and cost of its technology. For example, some VR users develop *cybersickness*, such as eyestrain and motion sickness, from performance problems in the realism of VR systems. The cost of a virtual reality system is another limitation. A VR system consisting of a headset with goggles and headphones, a fiber-optic data glove, motion-sensing devices, and a powerful engineering workstation with top-quality 3-D modeling software can exceed $50,000. If you want less cumbersome devices, more realistic displays, and a more natural sense of motion in your VR world, costs can escalate into several hundred thousand dollars. CAVEs *(cave automatic virtual environments)*, virtual reality rooms that immerse you in a virtual reality experience, cost several million dollars to set up [10, 46].

However, the cost of highly realistic multisensory VR systems is dropping each year. In the meantime some VR developers are using the VRML *(virtual reality modeling language)* to develop 3-D hypermedia graphics and animation products that provide a primitive VR experience for PC users on the World Wide Web and corporate intranets. Further advances in these and other VR technologies are expected to make virtual reality useful for a wide array of business and end user applications [2, 5, 46].

| **VR at Morgan Stanley** | The Market Risks Department of Morgan Stanley & Co. uses Discovery virtual reality software by Visible Decisions to model risks of financial investments in varying market conditions. Discovery displays three-dimensional results using powerful Silicon Graphics workstations.

Morgan Stanley also uses VRML (virtual reality modeling language) as a way to display the results of risk analyses in three dimensions on PCs in their corporate intranet. (VRML allows developers to create hyperlinks between 3-D objects in files and databases on the World Wide Web and corporate intranets.) 3-D results are displayed on ordinary PCs in a virtual reality experience over an intranet connection to a Sun Microsystems SPARCstation server running a Sun VRML browser. Seeing data in three dimensions and experiencing relationships among data in a virtual reality process make it easier for analysts to make intuitive connections than it would be with a 2-D chart or table of numbers [53]. |

Intelligent Agents

Intelligent agents are growing in popularity as a way to use artificial intelligence routines in software to help users accomplish many kinds of tasks in e-business and e-commerce. An intelligent agent is a *software surrogate* for an end user or a process that fulfills a stated need or activity. An intelligent agent uses its built-in and learned knowledge base about a person or process to make decisions and accomplish tasks in a way that fulfills the intentions of a user. Sometimes an intelligent agent is given a graphic representation or persona, such as Einstein for a science advisor, Sherlock Holmes for an information search agent, and so on. Thus, intelligent agents (also called *software robots* or "bots") are special-purpose knowledge-based information systems that accomplish specific tasks for users. Figure 8.29 summarizes major types of intelligent agents [30, 40].

One of the most well-known uses of intelligent agents is the wizards found in Microsoft Office and other software suites. These wizards are built-in capabilities

FIGURE 8.29

Examples of different types of intelligent agents.

Types of Intelligent Agents
User Interface Agents
● **Interface Tutors.** Observe user computer operations, correct user mistakes, and provide hints and advice on efficient software use.
● **Presentation Agents.** Show information in a variety of reporting and presentation forms and media based on user preferences.
● **Network Navigation Agents.** Discover paths to information and provide ways to view information that are preferred by a user.
● **Role-Playing Agents.** Play what-if games and other roles to help users understand information and make better decisions.
Information Management Agents
● **Search Agents.** Help users find files and databases, search for desired information, and suggest and find new types of information products, media, and resources.
● **Information Brokers.** Provide commercial services to discover and develop information resources that fit the business or personal needs of a user.
● **Information Filters.** Receive, find, filter, discard, save, forward, and notify users about products received or desired, including e-mail, voice mail, and all other information media.

that can analyze how an end user is using a software package and offer suggestions on how to complete various tasks. Thus, wizards might help you change document margins, format spreadsheet cells, query a database, or construct a graph. Wizards and other software agents are also designed to adjust to your way of using a software package so that they can anticipate when you will need their assistance. See Figure 8.30.

FIGURE 8.30

Intelligent agents like those in Ask Jeeves help you find information in a variety of categories from many online sources.

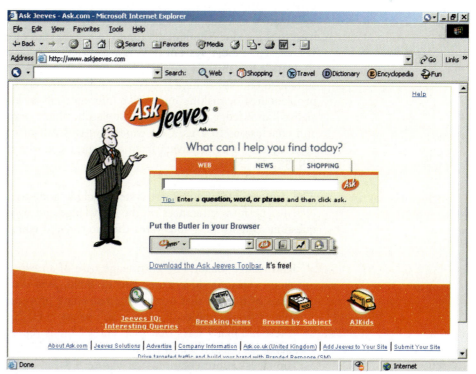

Source: Courtesy of Ask Jeeves, Inc., © 2000.

The use of intelligent agents is growing rapidly as a way to simplify software use, search websites on the Internet and corporate intranets, and help customers do comparison shopping among the many e-commerce sites on the Web. Intelligent agents are becoming necessary as software packages become more sophisticated and powerful, as the Internet and the World Wide Web become more vast and complex, and as information sources and e-commerce alternatives proliferate exponentially. In fact, some commentators forecast that much of the future of computing will consist of intelligent agents performing their work for users. So instead of using agents to help us accomplish computing tasks, we will be managing the performance of intelligent agents as they perform computing tasks for us [34].

Dow Jones & Co.: Intelligent Web Agents	Websites such as Amazon.com's Shop the Web, Excite's Jango.com, and MySimon's MySimon.com use intelligent agent technology to help users compare prices for fragrances, book titles, or other items on multiple sites. Other types of agents can answer e-mail, conduct intelligent searches, or help users find news reports and useful sites based on stated preferences. For example, dozens of sites can show you the news, but Dow Jones & Co.'s Dow Jones Interactive (www.djinteractive.com) is different. Nearly 600,000 customers pay to search through stories from its 6,000 licensed and internal publications. That's a huge amount of data to filter and the company has applied intelligent agent and other artificial intelligence (AI) technologies to manage the task. One of the site's most important features is Custom Clips, which allows users to create folders based on predefined topics—such as agribusiness or IBM—or to build their own using custom key words. When the site IS agent retrieves relevant articles, it can post them to a database-generated Web page or send the stories to the user's e-mail address [39, 40].

Expert Systems

One of the most practical and widely implemented applications of artificial intelligence in business is the development of expert systems and other knowledge-based information systems. A *knowledge-based information system* (KBIS) adds a knowledge base to the major components found in other types of computer-based information systems. An **expert system** (ES) is a knowledge-based information system that uses its knowledge about a specific, complex application area to act as an expert consultant to end users. Expert systems provide answers to questions in a very specific problem area by making humanlike inferences about knowledge contained in a specialized knowledge base. They must also be able to explain their reasoning process and conclusions to a user. So expert systems can provide decision support to end users in the form of advice from an expert consultant in a specific problem area [19, 37].

Components of an Expert System

The components of an expert system include a knowledge base and software modules that perform inferences on the knowledge and communicate answers to a user's questions. Figure 8.31 illustrates the interrelated components of an expert system. Note the following components:

- **Knowledge Base.** The knowledge base of an expert system contains (1) facts about a specific subject area (for example, *John is an analyst*) and (2) heuristics (rules of thumb) that express the reasoning procedures of an expert on the subject (for example: IF John is an analyst, THEN he needs a workstation). There are many ways that such knowledge is represented in expert systems. Examples are *rule-based*, *frame-based*, *object-based*, and *case-based* methods of knowledge representation. See Figure 8.32.

FIGURE 8.31

Components of an expert system. The software modules perform inferences on a knowledge base built by an expert and/or knowledge engineer. This provides expert answers to an end user's questions in an interactive process.

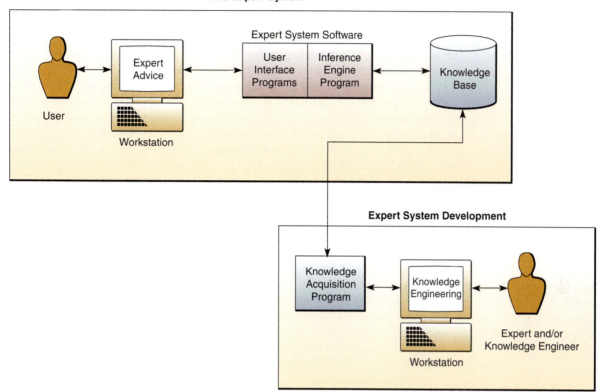

Software Resources. An expert system software package contains an inference engine and other programs for refining knowledge and communicating with users. The **inference engine** program processes the knowledge (such as rules and facts) related to a specific problem. It then makes associations and inferences resulting in recommended courses of action for a user. User interface programs for communicating with end users are also needed, including an explanation program to explain the reasoning process to a user if requested. Knowledge acquisition programs are not part of an expert system

FIGURE 8.32

A summary of four ways that knowledge can be represented in an expert system's knowledge base.

Methods of Knowledge Representation
● **Case-Based Reasoning.** Representing knowledge in an expert system's knowledge base in the form of cases, that is, examples of past performance, occurrences, and experiences.
● **Frame-Based Knowledge.** Knowledge represented in the form of a hierarchy or network of *frames*. A frame is a collection of knowledge about an entity consisting of a complex package of data values describing its attributes.
● **Object-Based Knowledge.** Knowledge represented as a network of objects. An object is a data element that includes both data and the methods or processes that act on those data.
● **Rule-Based Knowledge.** Knowledge represented in the form of rules and statements of fact. Rules are statements that typically take the form of a premise and a conclusion such as: If (condition), Then (conclusion).

but are software tools for knowledge base development, as are *expert system shells*, which are used for developing expert systems.

Expert System Applications

Using an expert system involves an interactive computer-based session in which the solution to a problem is explored, with the expert system acting as a consultant to an end user. The expert system asks questions of the user, searches its knowledge base for facts and rules or other knowledge, explains its reasoning process when asked, and gives expert advice to the user in the subject area being explored. For example, Figure 8.33 illustrates an expert system application.

Expert systems are being used for many different types of applications, and the variety of applications is expected to continue to increase. However, you should realize that expert systems typically accomplish one or more generic uses. Figure 8.34 outlines six generic categories of expert system activities, with specific examples of actual expert system applications. As you can see, expert systems are being used in many different fields, including medicine, engineering, the physical sciences, and business. Expert systems now help diagnose illnesses, search for minerals, analyze compounds, recommend repairs, and do financial planning. So from a strategic business standpoint, expert systems can and are being used to improve every step of the product cycle of a business, from finding customers to shipping products to providing customer service.

Cutler-Hammer: Strategic Expert System

Cutler-Hammer's IT people were pioneers when they began work in 1995 on an expert system software program called Bid Manager. Its original purpose was to let customers' engineers deal more directly with the factory. Today Bid Manager has grown into a giant software package with six million lines of code, a far-reaching all-embracing e-manufacturing weapon with a sharp competitive edge. Not surprisingly, Cutler-Hammer has kept it largely under wraps.

To start with, the program allows a customer, a distributor, or one of the company's sales engineers in the field to easily configure the sometimes devilishly complex innards of Cutler-Hammer equipment with its convoluted wiring patterns and precise placement of dozens of electronic and electrical components. The software automatically checks that the engineer does everything right. If he places a switch or a wire in the wrong spot, he gets a gentle electronic slap on the wrist—an onscreen message pointing out the mistake. Bid Manager contains literally thousands of rules to ensure that designs are done correctly; at the same time, it allows for idiosyncrasies—a user may want the equipment to turn on electric motors in a certain way, for instance.

"No outsider could possibly know an industry such as ours well enough to cover it the way Bid Manager does," says Barbara J. Riesmeyer, manager of IT at Cutler-Hammer's power and control systems division and a developer of Bid Manager. To create the software, the company enlisted not only 15 software writers but also experts at the plants, sales engineers, and many others. Director of e-business Ray L. Huber led the team and, with Riesmeyer, created what they call the design-to-delivery (D2D) vision.

With more than 61,000 orders processed electronically last year at Cutler-Hammer, the expert system unquestionably has proved itself. Plant managers Frank C. Campbell at Sumter and Steven R. Kavanaugh at Fayetteville overflow with praise for the software. It's easy to see why. Where in the past paperwork stifled production flow, now Bid Manager takes care of even small but significant details. What's more, says Huber, "Bid Manager has helped us think differently about products." For example, Cutler-Hammer has standardized its products and models, slimming down the number of steel enclosure sizes from more than 400 to only 100.

FIGURE 8.33

Tivoli Systems Manager by IBM automatically monitors and manages the computers in a network with proactive software components that use expert system technology.

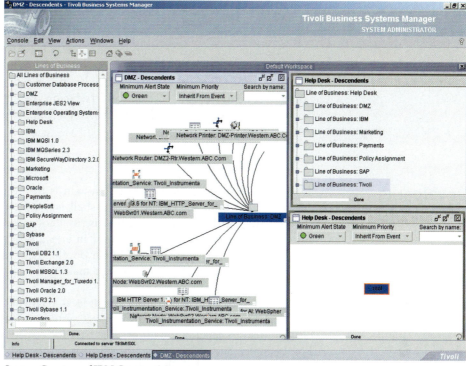

Source: Courtesy of IBM Corporation.

FIGURE 8.34

Major application categories and examples of typical expert systems. Note the variety of applications that can be supported by such systems.

Application Categories of Expert Systems

● **Decision management**—Systems that appraise situations or consider alternatives and make recommendations based on criteria supplied during the discovery process:
    Loan portfolio analysis
    Employee performance evaluation
    Insurance underwriting
    Demographic forecasts

● **Diagnostic/troubleshooting**—Systems that infer underlying causes from reported symptoms and history:
    Equipment calibration
    Help desk operations
    Software debugging
    Medical diagnosis

● **Design/configuration**—Systems that help configure equipment components, given existing constraints:
    Computer option installation
    Manufacturability studies
    Communications networks
    Optimum assembly plan

● **Selection/classification**—Systems that help users choose products or processes, often from among large or complex sets of alternatives:
    Material selection
    Delinquent account identification
    Information classification
    Suspect identification

● **Process monitoring/control**—Systems that monitor and control procedures or processes:
    Machine control (including robotics)
    Inventory control
    Production monitoring
    Chemical testing

There's no question that the expert system has decisively helped Cutler-Hammer's business. CEO Randy Carson reports that Bid Manager has increased Cutler-Hammer's market share for configured products—motor control centers, control panels, and the like—by 15 percent. He adds that Bid Manager has boosted sales of the larger assemblies by 20 percent, doubling profits, increasing productivity by 35 percent, and reducing quality costs by 26 percent. He concludes, "Bid Manager has transformed Cutler-Hammer into a customer-driven company [10]."

Developing Expert Systems

The easiest way to develop an expert system is to use an **expert system** shell as a developmental tool. An expert system shell is a software package consisting of an expert system without its kernel, that is, its knowledge base. This leaves a *shell* of software (the inference engine and user interface programs) with generic inferencing and user interface capabilities. Other development tools (such as rule editors and user interface generators) are added in making the shell a powerful expert system development tool.

Expert system shells are now available as relatively low-cost software packages that help users develop their own expert systems on microcomputers. They allow trained users to develop the knowledge base for a specific expert system application. For example, one shell uses a spreadsheet format to help end users develop IF-THEN rules, automatically generating rules based on examples furnished by a user. Once a knowledge base is constructed, it is used with the shell's inference engine and user interface modules as a complete expert system on a specific subject area. Other software tools may require an IT specialist to develop expert systems. See Figure 8.35.

FIGURE 8.35

Using the Visual Rule Studio and Visual Basic to develop rules for a credit management expert system.

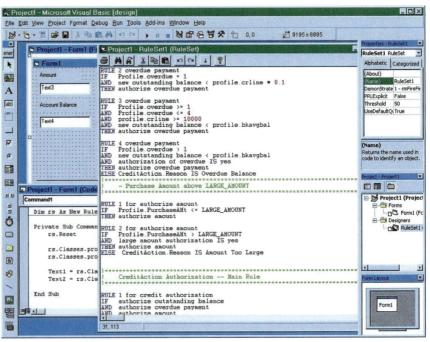

Source: Courtesy of MultiLogic, Inc.

Knowledge Engineering

A **knowledge engineer** is a professional who works with experts to capture the knowledge (facts and rules of thumb) they possess. The knowledge engineer then builds the knowledge base (and the rest of the expert system if necessary), using an iterative, prototyping process until the expert system is acceptable. Thus, knowledge engineers perform a role similar to that of systems analysts in conventional information systems development.

Once the decision is made to develop an expert system, a team of one or more domain experts and a knowledge engineer may be formed. Or experts skilled in the use of expert system shells could develop their own expert systems. If a shell is used, facts and rules of thumb about a specific domain can be defined and entered into a knowledge base with the help of a rule editor or other knowledge acquisition tool. A limited working prototype of the knowledge base is then constructed, tested, and evaluated using the inference engine and user interface programs of the shell. The knowledge engineer and domain experts can modify the knowledge base, then retest the system and evaluate the results. This process is repeated until the knowledge base and the shell result in an acceptable expert system.

ES Development at MacMillan Bloedel

MacMillan Bloedel Corp. is a forest products conglomerate in British Columbia, Canada, that produces particleboard used in building items such as bookshelves, furniture, and kitchen cupboards. Due to high staff turnover and a reorganization of divisional personnel at the particleboard plant, only two senior employees had the comprehensive, operational know-how and training needed to operate the facility. After they retired, MacMillan had to call back a former manager, named Herb, as a very expensive consultant to keep the mill running. So MacMillan decided to develop an expert system to capture his knowledge of plant operations. The expert system that resulted documents the procedures needed to efficiently run the facility, and is also used for training and upgrading employees.

Knowledge engineers used the ACQUIRE expert system shell from Acquired Intellup the particleboard coating line. The line consisted of machines whose operations parameters changed according to the coating to be applied. Herb was able to provide expert information, in the form of facts and rules, that was captured in the expert system's knowledge base. The resulting expert system consistently provides quality maintenance and operations advice to the mill operators [19].

The Value of Expert Systems

Obviously, expert systems are not the answer to every problem facing an organization. People using other types of information systems do quite well in many problem situations. So what types of problems are most suitable to expert system solutions? One way to answer this is to look at examples of the applications of current expert systems, including the generic tasks they can accomplish, as were summarized in Figure 8.34. Another way is to identify criteria that make a problem situation suitable for an expert system. Figure 8.36 outlines some important criteria.

Figure 8.36 should emphasize that many real world situations do not fit the suitability criteria for expert system solutions. Hundreds of rules may be required to capture the assumptions, facts, and reasoning that are involved in even simple problem situations. For example, a task that might take an expert a few minutes to accomplish might require an expert system with hundreds of rules and take several months to develop. A task that may take a human expert several hours to do may require an expert system with thousands of rules and take several years to build [1, 50].

FIGURE 8.36

Criteria for applications that are suitable for expert systems development.

Suitability Criteria for Expert Systems
● **Domain:** The domain, or subject area, of the problem is relatively small and limited to a well-defined problem area.
● **Expertise:** Solutions to the problem require the efforts of an expert. That is, a body of knowledge, techniques, and intuition is needed that only a few people possess.
● **Complexity:** Solution of the problem is a complex task that requires logical inference processing, which would not be handled as well by conventional information processing.
● **Structure:** The solution process must be able to cope with ill-structured, uncertain, missing, and conflicting data, and a problem situation that changes with the passage of time.
● **Availability:** An expert exists who is articulate and cooperative, and who has the support of the management and end users involved in the development of the proposed system.

Benefits of Expert Systems

An expert system captures the expertise of an expert or group of experts in a computer-based information system. Thus, it can outperform a single human expert in many problem situations. That's because an expert system is faster and more consistent, can have the knowledge of several experts, and does not get tired or distracted by overwork or stress.

Expert systems also help preserve and reproduce the knowledge of experts. They allow a company to preserve the expertise of an expert before she leaves the organization. This expertise can then be shared by reproducing the software and knowledge base of the expert system. This allows novices to be trained and supported by copies of an expert system distributed throughout an organization. Finally, expert systems can have the same competitive advantages as other types of information technology. That is, the effective use of expert systems can allow a firm to significantly improve the efficiency of its business processes, or produce new knowledge-based products and services.

Limitations of Expert Systems

The major limitations of expert systems arise from their limited focus, inability to learn, maintenance problems, and developmental cost. Expert systems excel only in solving specific types of problems in a limited domain of knowledge. They fail miserably in solving problems requiring a broad knowledge base and subjective problem solving. They do well with specific types of operational or analytical tasks, but falter at subjective managerial decision making. For example, an expert system might help a financial consultant develop alternative investment recommendations for a client. But it could not adequately evaluate the nuances of current political, economic, and societal developments, or the personal dynamics of a session with a client. These important factors would still have to be handled by the human consultant before a final investment decision could be reached.

Expert systems may also be difficult and costly to develop and maintain properly. The costs of knowledge engineers, lost expert time, and hardware and software resources may be too high to offset the benefits expected from some applications. Also, expert systems can't maintain themselves. That is, they can't learn from experience but must be taught new knowledge and modified as new expertise is needed to match developments in their subject areas. However, some of these limitations can be overcome by combining expert systems with AI technologies such as fuzzy logic and neural networks or by the use of expert system developmental tools that make the job of development and maintenance easier.

Summary

- **Information, Decisions, and Management.** Information systems can support a variety of management decision-making levels and decisions. These include the three levels of management activity (strategic, tactical, and operational decision making) and three types of decision structures (structured, semistructured, and unstructured). Information systems provide a wide range of information products to support these types of decisions at all levels of the organization.

- **Decision Support Trends.** Major changes are taking place in traditional MIS, DSS, and EIS tools for providing the information and modeling managers need to support their decision making. Decision support in business is changing, driven by rapid developments in end user computing and networking; Internet and Web technologies; and Web-enabled business applications. The growth of corporate intranets, extranets, as well as the Web, has accelerated the development of "executive class" interfaces like enterprise information portals, enterprise knowledge portals, and Web-enabled decision support software tools, and their use by lower levels of management and by individuals and teams of business professionals. In addition, the growth of e-commerce and e-business applications has expanded the use of enterprise portals and DSS tools by the suppliers, customers, and other business stakeholders of a company for applications like customer relationship and supply chain management.

- **Management Information Systems.** Management information systems provide prespecified reports and responses to managers on a periodic, exception, demand, or push reporting basis, to meet their need for information to support decision making.

- **OLAP and Data Mining.** Online analytical processing interactively analyzes complex relationships among large amounts of data stored in multidimensional databases. Data mining analyzes the vast amounts of historical data that have been prepared for analysis in data warehouses. Both technologies discover patterns, trends, and exception conditions in a company's data that support their business analysis and decision making.

- **Decision Support Systems.** Decision support systems are interactive, computer-based information systems that use DSS software and a model base and database to provide information tailored to support semistructured and unstructured decisions faced by individual managers. They are designed to use a decision maker's own insights and judgments in an ad hoc, interactive, analytical modeling process leading to a specific decision.

- **Executive Information Systems.** Executive information systems are information systems originally designed to support the strategic information needs of top management. However, their use is spreading to lower levels of management and business professionals.

EIS are easy to use and enable executives to retrieve information tailored to their needs and preferences. Thus, EIS can provide information about a company's critical success factors to executives to support their planning and control responsibilities.

- **Enterprise Information and Knowledge Portals.** Enterprise information portals provide a customized and personalized Web-based interface for corporate intranets to give their users easy access to a variety of internal and external business applications, databases, and information services that are tailored to their individual preferences and information needs. Thus, an EIP can supply personalized Web-enabled information, knowledge, and decision support to executives, managers, and business professionals, as well as customers, suppliers, and other business partners. An enterprise knowledge portal is a corporate intranet portal that extends the use of an EIP to include knowledge management functions and knowledge base resources so that it becomes a major form of knowledge management system for a company.

- **Artificial Intelligence.** The major application domains of artificial intelligence (AI) include a variety of applications in cognitive science, robotics, and natural interfaces. The goal of AI is the development of computer functions normally associated with human physical and mental capabilities, such as robots that see, hear, talk, feel, and move, and software capable of reasoning, learning, and problem solving. Thus, AI is being applied to many applications in business operations and managerial decision making, as well as in many other fields.

- **AI Technologies.** The many application areas of AI are summarized in Figure 8.23, including neural networks, fuzzy logic, genetic algorithms, virtual reality, and intelligent agents. Neural nets are hardware or software systems based on simple models of the brain's neuron structure that can learn to recognize patterns in data. Fuzzy logic systems use rules of approximate reasoning to solve problems where data are incomplete or ambiguous. Genetic algorithms use selection, randomizing, and other mathematics functions to simulate an evolutionary process that can yield increasingly better solutions to problems. Virtual reality systems are multisensory systems that enable human users to experience computer-simulated environments as if they actually existed. Intelligent agents are knowledge-based software surrogates for a user or process in the accomplishment of selected tasks.

- **Expert Systems.** Expert systems are knowledge-based information systems that use software and a knowledge base about a specific, complex application area to act as expert consultants to users in many business and technical applications. Software includes an inference engine program that makes inferences based on the facts and rules stored in the knowledge base. A knowledge base consists of facts about a specific subject area and heuristics (rules of thumb) that express the reasoning procedures of an expert. The benefits of expert systems (such as preservation and replication of expertise) must be balanced with their limited applicability in many problem situations.

Key Terms and Concepts

These are the key terms and concepts of this chapter. The page number of their first explanation is in parentheses.

1. Analytical modeling (270)
   a. Goal-seeking analysis (271)
   b. Optimization analysis (272)
   c. Sensitivity analysis (271)
   d. What-if analysis (271)
2. Artificial intelligence (283)
   a. Application areas (284)
   b. Domains (283)
3. Data mining (273)
4. Data visualization system (269)
5. Decision structure (261)
6. Decision support versus management reporting (264)
7. Decision support system (267)
8. Decision support trends (262)
9. DSS components (268)

10. Enterprise information portal (276)
11. Enterprise knowledge portal (278)
12. Executive information system (274)
13. Expert system (292)
    a. Applications (294)
    b. Benefits and limitations (298)
    c. Components (292)
    d. System development (296)
14. Expert system shell (294)
15. Fuzzy logic (287)
16. Genetic algorithms (287)
17. Geographic information system (269)
18. Inference engine (293)

19. Intelligent agent (290)
20. Knowledge base (292)
21. Knowledge engineer (297)
22. Knowledge management system (278)
23. Level of management decision making (260)
24. Management information system (264)
25. Model base (268)
26. Neural network (285)
27. Online analytical processing (265)
28. Reporting alternatives (264)
29. Robotics (284)
30. Virtual reality (288)

Review Quiz

Match one of the key terms and concepts listed previously with one of the brief examples or definitions that follow. Try to find the best fit for answers that seem to fit more than one term or concept. Defend your choices.

_____ 1. Internet technologies and e-business developments have expanded the form and use of decision support in business.

_____ 2. Decision support systems rely on DSS software, model bases, and databases as system resources.

_____ 3. A CEO and a production team may have different needs for decision making.

_____ 4. Decision-making procedures cannot be specified in advance for some complex decision situations.

_____ 5. Information systems for the strategic information needs of top and middle managers.

_____ 6. Systems that produce predefined reports for management.

_____ 7. Managers can receive reports periodically, on an exception basis, or on demand.

_____ 8. Provide an interactive modeling capability tailored to the specific information needs of managers.

_____ 9. Interactive responses to ad hoc inquiries versus prespecified information.

_____ 10. A collection of mathematical models and analytical techniques.

_____ 11. Analyzing the effect of changing variables and relationships and manipulating a mathematical model.

_____ 12. Changing revenues and tax rates to see the effect on net profit after taxes.

_____ 13. Changing revenues in many small increments to see revenue's effect on net profit after taxes.

_____ 14. Changing revenues and expenses to find how you could achieve a specific amount of net profit after taxes.

_____ 15. Changing revenues and expenses subject to certain constraints in order to achieve the highest profit after taxes.

_____ 16. Realtime analysis of complex business data.

_____ 17. Attempts to find patterns hidden in business data in a data warehouse.

_____ 18. Represents complex data using three-dimensional graphical forms.

_____ 19. A customized and personalized Web interface to internal and external information resources available through a corporate intranet.

_____ 20. Using intranets to gather, store, and share a company's best practices among employees.

_____ 21. An enterprise information portal that can access knowledge management functions and company knowledge bases.

_____ 22. Information technology that focuses on the development of computer functions normally associated with human physical and mental capabilities.

_____ 23. Applications in cognitive science, robotics, and natural interfaces.

_____ 24. Development of computer-based machines that possess capabilities such as sight, hearing, dexterity, and movement.

_____ 25. Computers can provide you with computer-simulated experiences.

_____ 26. An information system that integrates computer graphics, geographic databases, and DSS capabilities.

_____ 27. A knowledge-based information system that acts as an expert consultant to users in a specific application area.

_____ 28. Applications such as diagnosis, design, prediction, interpretation, and repair.

_____ 29. These systems can preserve and reproduce the knowledge of experts but have a limited application focus.

_____ 30. A collection of facts and reasoning procedures in a specific subject area.

_____ 31. A software package that manipulates a knowledge base and makes associations and inferences leading to a recommended course of action.

_____ 32. A software package consisting of an inference engine and user interface programs used as an expert system development tool.

_____ 33. One can either buy a completely developed expert system package, develop one with an expert system shell, or develop one from scratch by custom programming.

_____ 34. An analyst who interviews experts to develop a knowledge base about a specific application area.

_____ 35. AI systems that use neuron structures to recognize patterns in data.

_____ 36. AI systems that use approximate reasoning to process ambiguous data.

_____ 37. Knowledge-based software surrogates that do things for you.

_____ 38. Software that uses mathematical functions to simulate an evolutionary process.

Discussion Questions

1. Is the form and use of information and decision support in e-business changing and expanding? Why or why not?

2. Has the growth of self-directed teams to manage work in organizations changed the need for strategic, tactical, and operational decision making in business?

3. What is the difference between the ability of a manager to retrieve information instantly on demand using an MIS and the capabilities provided by a DSS?

4. Refer to the Real World Case on AmeriKing and others in the chapter. Is it becoming necessary for all companies to provide an enterprise information portal to their employees? Why or why not?

5. In what ways does using an electronic spreadsheet package provide you with the capabilities of a decision support system?

6. Are enterprise information portals making executive information systems unneccessary? Explain your reasoning.

7. Refer to the Real World Case on BAE Systems in the chapter. What is the difference between a corporate intranet and a knowledge management system? What is the difference in their business value?

8. Can computers think? Will they ever be able to? Explain why or why not.

9. What are some of the most important applications of AI in business? Defend your choices.

10. What are some of the limitations or dangers you see in the use of AI technologies such as expert systems, virtual reality, and intelligent agents? What could be done to minimize such effects?

Application Exercises

Complete the following exercises as individual or group projects that apply chapter concepts to real world business situations.

1. BizRate: e-Commerce Website Reviews

Web Visit *www.bizrate.com* and you instantly have information about hundreds of online stores and what thousands of previous shoppers at those stores think about them. See Figure 8.37.

Looking to buy a Miles Davis music CD, I entered *CDnow.com* at BizRate.com's Rapid Reports section. What I got back was an overall customer satisfaction rating of four and a half stars out of a possible five. I scrolled down farther to find individual ratings of the online music store's product selection, pricing, customer support, and on-time delivery record. The rating was based on reports from 22,034 shoppers who had already been to the CDnow site.

BizRate.com users who don't know the name of an online music retailer can go to the site's categories section. Here, I typed in *music* and was given the choice of shopping by product, store, or personal preferences. I wanted to pay by check and receive my CD the next day. Two sites—Cdconnection.com and Playback.com—met my criteria. The first had been reviewed by more than 1,200 shoppers. The other had received 911 reviews.

a. Check out the reviews of online stores for a product you want to buy at the bizrate.com site. How thorough, valid, and valuable were they to you? Explain.

b. How could similar Web-enabled reporting systems be used in other business situations? Give an example.

Source: Adapted from Julia King, "Infomediary," *Computerworld*, November 1, 1999, p. 58. Copyright 1999 by Computerworld, Inc., Framingham, MA 01701. Reprinted from *Computerworld*.

2. Jango and mySimon: Intelligent Web Price Comparison Agents

Web **Jango/Excite Product Finder**
The Jango award-winning intelligent agent software is used in the Excite shopping area. This agent can use presupplied templates to search categories or adapt new templates from past experiences. The Excite shopping area (www.excite.com) covers a range of product categories, although the merchant list in the standard categories is a bit shorter than some others. One nice touch is that some of Jango's price comparisons also list shipping costs along with the product price, so you can compare the total price. You also can search for product reviews in addition to finding merchants that sell a given product.

mySimon
The mySimon site (www.mysimon.com) starts from a category listing that covers many different kinds of merchandise. After you find the subcategory that interests you, you can search by manufacturer and product keywords. mySimon also offers shopping

FIGURE 8.37
The BizRate website offers customer reviews of online stores.

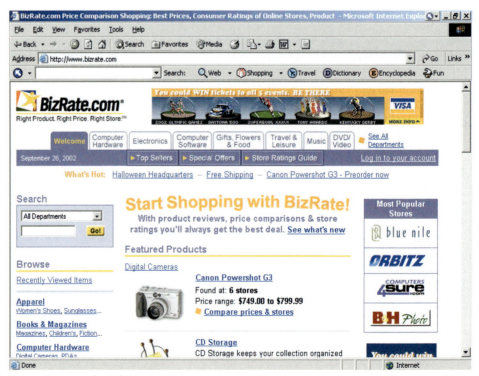

Source: Courtesy of www.bizrate.com.

guides for areas such as Winter Sports or product guides such as Coffeemaker/Espresso. You can register with the site to receive its newsletter, use the talk forums, and save your searches.

a. Visit the Jango and mySimon sites. Which price comparison agent do you prefer? Why?

b. Are these sites examples of Web-enabled decision support systems? Why or why not?

c. How could this technology be used in business situations? Give an example.

Source: Adapted from Jennifer Powell, "Streamline Your Shopping," *Smart Computing*, February 2000, pp. 88–90.

3. Retail Electronic Commerce System for Pinnacle Products

SS Pinnacle Products is considering developing a strategic system to allow it to sell products through its website. None of Pinnacle's direct competitors currently utilize electronic retailing, but the president of Pinnacle feels that business to consumer electronic commerce is appropriate for Pinnacle's industry and wants to be in a leadership position. You have been asked to assist in preparing a preliminary feasibility study for the system. Your analysis is to be restricted to the first five years of operation.

The Information Systems and Marketing departments have developed estimates for your use. The marketing department estimates that sales will be $1,000,000 in year 2 (the system is expected to take one full year for initial development) and that sales will grow 50 percent per year thereafter. The department also estimates that each dollar of electronic sales will contribute 25 cents to profit. The IS department has estimated the cost of developing and maintaining this system across it first five years of operation, as shown below.

	Year 1	Year 2	Year 3	Year 4	Year 5
System Cost:	$900,000	$400,000	$400,000	$500,000	$600,000
Projected Sales $:	$2,000,000 (50 percent growth per year)				
Sales Contribution Rate:	(25 percent contribution to profits in all years 1–5)				

a. Based upon these figures construct a spreadsheet to analyze the costs and benefits of the proposed system. Projected sales for year 3 will be 1.5 times year 2 sales, year 4's sales will be 1.5 times year 3's and so on. The benefits of the system are equal to new sales times the 25 percent contribution to profits. Your spreadsheet should include a column showing the net contribution (benefits minus system cost) for each year.

b. Assume that ABC Company requires a return of 25 percent on this type of investment. Add an internal rate of return estimate to your spreadsheet and determine whether the return exceeds the 25 percent requirement.

c. This type of investment is risky largely because sales growth is very hard to predict. To assess risk,

marketing has been asked to provide worst-case and best-case estimates for the rate of growth in sales. Their worst-case estimate is a growth of only 10 percent per year while their best-case estimate is 100 percent growth per year. Calculate the returns under best case and worst case assumptions and add these estimates to your spreadsheet.

d. Prepare a set of PowerPoint slides or similar presentation materials summarizing your key results and including a recommendation as to whether this project should be pursued.

4. Palm City Police Department

SS The Palm City Police Department has eight defined precincts. The police station in each precinct has primary responsibility for all activities in its precinct area. The current population of each precinct, the number of violent crimes committed in each precinct, and the number of officers assigned to each precinct are shown below. The department has established a goal of equalizing access to police services. Ratios of population per police officer and violent crimes per police officer should be calculated for each precinct. These ratios for the city as a whole are shown below.

a. Build a spreadsheet to perform the analysis described above and print it out.

Currently, no funds are available to hire additional officers. Based on the citywide ratios the department has decided to develop a plan to shift resources as needed in order to ensure that no precinct has more than 1,100 residents per police officer and no precinct has more than seven violent crimes per police officer. The department will transfer officers from precincts, that easily meet these goals to precincts that violate one or both of these ratios.

b. Use goal seeking on your spreadsheet to move police officers between precincts until the goals are met. (You can use the goal seek function to see how many officers would be required to bring each precinct into compliance and then judgmentally reduce officers in precincts that are substantially within the criteria.) Print out a set of results that allow the department to comply with these ratios and a memorandum to your instructor summarizing your results and the process you used to develop them.

Precinct	Population	Violent Crimes	Police Officers
Shea Blvd.	96,552	318	85
Lakeland Heights	99,223	582	108
Sunnydale	68,432	206	77
Old Town	47,732	496	55
Mountainview	101,233	359	82
Financial District	58,102	511	70
Riverdale	78,903	537	70
Cole Memorial	75,801	306	82
Total	625,978	3,315	629
Per officer	995.196	5.270	

Cisco Systems, NetFlix, and Office Depot: The Business Value of Real-Time Web Decision Support

There are compelling reasons for using real-time Web information to make business decisions. Many of them are related to trying to keep up with the behavior of online customers at e-commerce websites. Other real-time uses are emerging in e-business application areas like collaborative product development and supply chain management. But the complex nature of the application requirements involved means that most companies are only dipping their toes into real-time Web analytic waters. A few companies, however, are wading more deeply into the technology.

Cisco Systems. At Cisco (www.cisco.com), company executives say that ideally, everyone in the business should have access to real-time information. "The whole corporation is moving to real time," says Mike Zill, director sales finance IT at Cisco. "It's difficult to have the applications stay in batch mode when the business architecture is message-based."

According to Zill, channel account managers in the sales department use a Web-based "dashboard," or graphical user interface-based view, from OneChannel Inc. that gives them real-time views of their accounts' activities. When a business condition hits a predetermined threshold, the OneChannel software triggers an alert, sending a message or warning to the user's dashboard. For example, if Cisco's sales department has a top-10 list of new products it wants sold through, say, Ingram Micro, the application will let the Cisco channel manager know the instant the distributor's sales fall outside target levels.

To achieve this, Cisco had to build deep hooks into its supply chain, which wasn't easy, acknowledges Zill. The firm has established agreements with its partners to receive point-of-sale data via the Internet or, in some cases, through electronic data interchange. However, most of the data are batched. Few partners will feed real-time point-of-sale data to the company, Zill says.

Once it receives the data, Cisco couples it with real-time Web-based inventory information and processes it using analytics software from Hyperion Solutions Corp. Channel managers can then query the Hyperion software in detail through the OneChannel dashboard to find the underlying causes of any distribution problem. "The response time is fast enough so you're not waiting," Zill says. And that's the essence of real time for any user.

NetFlix.com. Your critiques of films starring Jack Nicholson or Nicole Kidman get thrown back at you in real time if you're one of the 500,000 subscribers to NetFlix.com's (www.netflix.com) website. A critical review, a thumbs up, past rentals, your profile, and current Web activity all contribute to the pages served up by the "recommendation engine" from the Los Gatos, California–based online movie services company.

Initially, the IT department started with purchased application software. That work stopped, says Neil Hunt, the company's vice president of e-commerce, because the canned software was ill-suited for evaluating the subjective world of tens of thousands of movie critics in real time. Yet, the capability was critical in order for NetFlix to distinguish itself online. "We felt we needed to own the technology," says Hunt.

So he hired mathematicians with C++ experience to write the algorithms and code to define movie clusters, relate opinions to the clusters, evaluate thousands of ratings per second, and factor in current website behavior to deliver a specially configured Web page before a site visitor can click again. Hunt says NetFlix's "significant" investment in proprietary technology was only made after it was deemed critical to the company's added value to the market.

He says the real-time analytics can also tell marketing managers that Web page design is working best for a given promotion and allow them to make changes immediately based on dynamic feedback. "It's a good tool for effective design," he says.

Office Depot. Linda Belanger's company has been edging toward developing real-time alerts for its sales and customer data. "On our application development radar is to do alarm reports so we can give instant information to our sales force about a customer in his territory," says Belanger, senior manager of decision support at Office Depot Inc. (www.officedepot.com) in Delray Beach, Florida.

She envisions the appropriate pagers beeping with information and instructions as soon as the proposed real-time sales alert system reaches a rules-defined threshold. In this way, Belanger says, real-time tools will make her company's sales force more effective. But she adds that while real-time updates to the sales force are a plus, staffers must still evaluate the information before responding to customer issues. However, Belanger says, the quicker the sales staff gets customer data, the more effective it is at generating revenue.

Case Study Questions

1. What are the business benefits and limitations of Cisco's Web-based system for its channel managers?

2. Visit the NetFlix website. Do you agree with them that their real-time personalization system is critical to their business success? Explain the reasons for your answer.

3. Do you think salespeople will appreciate and benefit from the real-time alert system envisioned for Office Depot? Why or why not?

Source: Adapted from Mark Hall, "Get Real," *Computerworld*, April 1, 2002, pp. 42–43. Reprinted with permission from *Computerworld*.

**REAL WORLD
CASE 4**

Producers Assistance, Kinko's, and Champion Printing: Using Spatial Information Systems

Your data are operating at a disadvantage if they don't know where they are. Data that are "location-aware" can quickly draw connections between customers and stores or available workers and remote job sites, for example, creating revenue streams in the process. But as more businesses discover the value of location-aware data, they aren't turning to traditional geographic information systems (GIS). Companies are looking at new technology: spatial information management software. Use of this new technology to add location awareness to existing databases and business software is on the rise.

Finding Workers. By making its data location-aware, Producers Assistance Corp. (PAC), a Houston-based staffing service for oil and gas producers, has trimmed the time it takes to find the right employees for its customers from days to minutes. To speed searches of its Lotus database, the company turned to MapInfo Corp., says Gary Dean, PAC's vice president of operations.

Typically, when PAC (www.pachouston.com) had to supply workers for offshore oil operations, they would be at the job site for a week or two, so their location wasn't very important, Dean says. PAC staff could search the database for workers with the needed skills and simply draw from that pool. "But then we started to see more business development inland, where workers would have to report to the same site every day," Dean says. With a pool of more than 3,000 employees, finding the right worker for what is usually a remote job site could take one or two people two or three days, he says.

After unsuccessfully trying several geocoding products, "we contemplated abandoning that feature," says John Knapp, PAC's executive vice president. Then a PAC software developer found MapInfo's MapX software. PAC embedded MapX in its LotusNotes groupware, and now it takes one person 10 minutes to locate workers with the appropriate skills by ZIP code, Knapp says.

"Mapping is bringing our database alive," he says. "We were having a hard time getting anyone to use it as a database. Now we don't have to encourage anybody. The thing that made it so cheap [about $5,000] to add is that ZIP codes are something you already have in your database." The time between deciding to go ahead with the implementation to delivering it to user desktops was about 45 days, Knapp says.

PAC is just beginning to calculate the return on investment, says Dean. "But it comes down to this: We don't make money if we don't fill positions, and the faster we can do it, the more money we can make," he says.

Finding Services. For Dallas-based Kinko's Inc. (www.kinkos.com), letting customers visit its website to find the nearest store wasn't enough. The company needed to extend that capability to wireless phone users, says Richard Maranville, Kinko's vice president of e-commerce and field services. But Kinko's wanted to stay focused on its core mission, selling photocopying and other business services, Maranville says, explaining, "We didn't want to have to geocode our own data." Kinko's turned to Vicinity Corp. in Sunnyvale, California, in July 2001 to help with that.

Potential customers who go to Kinko's website can now find the nearest stores and get maps and directions to them. "It was relatively painless to implement," Maranville says. "We feed the data nightly to Vicinity, and they geocode it," says Michael Dekel, Kinko's product manager. "And as we add product lines, it'll be simple to add new attributes." For example, Kinko's is considering letting stores customize their sites to advertise new or unique services. Thus, a store in Los Angeles could offer special script-copying services and need to give online directions on how to get there.

"Cost avoidance is another bottom line," Dekel says. "This implementation means there are thousands of hits a day not going to our call center. We saw that traffic flatten out, and that means we can manage the calls we have coming in without hiring new staff."

Finding Customers. By combining insights into its customers' data and demographic information, Champion Printing and Advertising Inc. (www.championprinting.net) in Jackson, Michigan, has grown from a small local printing company to an advertising and printing operation spanning several Midwestern states. Three years ago, the company was seeing a return of sometimes less than 2 percent on direct mail marketing campaigns for its financial institution customers, says Mike Shutler, Champion's president.

By combining customer demographic data in MapInfo Corp.'s TargetPro with the mapping capabilities of MapInfo Professional, Champion was able to offer better-focused mailing lists, Shutler says. "We got returns of better than 15 percent," he notes. Now, when a bank picks a location for a new branch, for example, it can "come to us and say, 'Find us some business in this area,'" Shutler says. "MapInfo paid for itself within six months."

Case Study Questions

1. What is the business value of spatial information systems? Use the examples of the companies in this case to help you answer.

2. How else could spatial information systems be used in business? Give several examples to illustrate your answer.

3. Visit the Kinko's website. How helpful is their location finder service? What else can Kinko's do to improve this spatial information management application?

Source: Adapted from Sami Lais, "The Power of Location," *Computerworld*, April 15, 2002, pp. 48–50. Reprinted with permission from *Computerworld*.

Schneider National: The Business Value of Business Intelligence

In summer 1998, Bill Braddy joined Schneider National (www.schneider.com), a huge transportation and logistics company headquartered in Green Bay, Wisconsin. The former Army colonel's mission at Schneider: figure out how to search through and harness mountains of valuable but disorganized corporate data quickly enough to make the business more efficient. "We were drowning in data but starving for information," he says of the crisis Schneider faced.

To attack Schneider's problem, Braddy did what a lot of corporate IT folks are trying these days. He installed business intelligence software. BI, as it's often called, helps businesses view and catch and dissect and reassemble and write reports about all sorts of information lurking in the dark corners of their databases. If BI is linked to clean, carefully tended data—a really big "if"—it can work very well. At Schneider, Braddy is counting on BI to show managers where outsized costs (and benefits) exist and why. So far, it's off to a good start.

To understand why a trucking company cares about gargantuan databases, it helps to understand what Schneider does. The family-owned company's main business used to be renting out its signature pumpkin-colored trucks. Today Schneider is the biggest transportation and logistics company in North America, sending goods by truck, rail, and sea all over the world; it also brokers freight to other carriers and provides some financial services. A big chunk of its $2.4 billion in annual revenues comes from Schneider Logistics, a division that makes sure its customer's wares get to the right place at the right time—taking care of freight payments for the likes of Wal-Mart and chemical giant BASF, coordinating shipment of aftermarket parts for General Motors and Ford.

Logistics and transportation are two of the most data-intensive pieces of Schneider's business. So when Braddy signed on, he turned to their information woes first. The company's computers were high powered, but they had to run complicated analyses on almost ten terabytes of data strewn across eight different databases. Schneider collected all kinds of documents, invoices, tracking paperwork, and late-payment notices, as well as delivery information zapped in via satellite from truckers, warehouse operators, and accounting offices all over the world, every minute of every day.

With the advice of technology-consulting firm Meta Group and a team of as many as 30 people from Schneider, Braddy spent five months evaluating some 23 BI solutions, eventually zeroing in on eight finalists. In February 1999, an executive group voted unanimously to use a suite of software from an Ottawa, Canada, company called Cognos, mainly because one of the products in the suite, PowerPlay seemed to offer the most advanced data-analysis capabilities.

PowerPlay excels at two things: presenting key data to laypeople and making it easy for them to analyze those data in depth. To do this the software takes records from a company's databases (specified by people in IT) and pours them into specialized information arrays it calls cubes—which are basically stacks of manipulable spreadsheets.

A cube that the business analyst uses today, for instance, houses all kinds of data about load status—if a shipment is waiting to be assigned to a carrier, picked up, in transit, delivered, or paid for. Using the software she can look at the average time that loads spend in transit to the Ford dealership, click on a button to sort the data, see immediately that the problem lies somewhere else, and then—this is the beauty part—run a second analysis instantaneously. Once she finds where the problem is, she can drill down on elements in the cube until she gets to a single smoking-gun document. The entire process takes less than ten minutes.

Just five months after they chose the software, it was up and running—thanks in part to the fact that Schneider had already devoted two years and 60 people to a complete overhaul of its massive databases. Technicians, for example, had worked to smooth out the ten terabytes of information item by item (making sure that dates were written uniformly and so on). "That required real intestinal fortitude," says Bob Grawien, vice president of applications development, who worked with Braddy on the cleanup.

A few weeks after the PowerPlay launch, Braddy began seeing results. A business analyst in the trucking division was trying to track down reimbursements owed to Schneider for certain kinds of auto work—money that had been practically impossible to collect in the past. Using PowerPlay, the analyst was able to pinpoint, in a matter of two weeks, hundreds of cases in which payments had fallen through the cracks. From that one sweep, Schneider was able to recoup all the money it spent on Cognos software in the first place. (While Schneider won't reveal how much it spent, a similar large installation, says Cognos, might cost as much as $2 million.) Over the past two years, Braddy estimates, the software has helped Schneider grab a total of $2.5 million in "hard, quantifiable savings."

Case Study Questions

1. What problems was Schneider National having with their business data? How did business intelligence software solve such problems?

2. What are the benefits and limitations of business intelligence software as demonstrated by Schneider National?

3. Visit the Cognos website at www.cognos.com. What is the business value of business intelligence as defined by Cognos and illustrated in this case?

MODULE IV

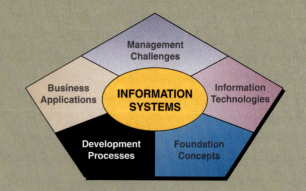

DEVELOPMENT PROCESSES

How can business professionals plan, develop, and implement strategies and solutions that use information technologies to help meet the challenges and opportunities faced in today's business environment? Answering that question is the goal of the chapters of this module, which concentrate on the processes for planning, developing, and implementing IT-based business strategies and applications.

- Chapter 9, **Developing Business/IT Strategies,** emphasizes the importance of the planning process in developing IT/business strategies, and the implementation challenges that arise when introducing new IT-based business strategies and applications into an organization.

- Chapter 10, **Developing Business/IT Solutions,** introduces the traditional, prototyping, and end user approaches to the development of information systems, and discusses the processes and managerial issues in the implementation of new business applications of information technology.

CHAPTER 9

APPLICATIONS IN BUSINESS AND MANAGEMENT

DEVELOPING BUSINESS/IT STRATEGIES

Chapter Outline

Learning Objectives

After reading and studying this chapter, you should be able to:

1. Discuss the role of planning in the business use of information technology, using the scenario approach and planning for competitive advantage as examples.

2. Discuss the role of planning and business models in the development of business/IT strategies, architectures, and applications.

3. Identify several change management solutions for end user resistance to the implementation of new IT-based business strategies and applications.

Planning Fundamentals

Introduction

Imagine taking a caravan of thousands of people on a journey with no map, no plan, no one in charge, no logistical support, no way to keep everyone informed, no scouting reports to assess and update progress, and no navigational instruments. Sheer madness, yet that's how most companies are handling the transition to e-business.

Information technology has created a seismic shift in the way companies do business. Just knowing the importance and structure of e-business is not enough. You need to create and implement an action plan that allows you to make the transition from an old business design to a new e-business design [18].

That is why you need to learn some fundamental planning concepts, which is the goal of this section. We will first discuss several strategic planning concepts, and then talk more specifically about developing IT-based business strategies and other planning issues. In Section II, we will discuss the process of implementing IT-based business plans, and the challenges that arise when introducing new IT strategies and applications into a company.

Analyzing The Rowe Cos. and Merrill Lynch

Read the Real World Case on The Rowe Cos. and Merrill Lynch on the next page. We can learn a lot about the business value of various business/IT planning methodologies from this case. See Figure 9.1

Faced with budget cutbacks from changing economic conditions, CIO Suzanne Krupa prioritizes proposed IT projects using a variety of ROI methodologies in the business/IT planning process. This has resulted in decisions to drop or postpone some IT projects, and helped to evaluate possible reengineering initiatives for cost savings or quality improvements at the Rowe Cos. Merrill Lynch has a more formalized ROI planning methodology for its proposed IT investments. Merrill uses a standard planning document that a business unit proposing an IT project must complete with the help of IT specialists, and have evaluated by standing review

FIGURE 9.1
Suzanne Krupa, CIO at the Rowe Cos., uses a variety of ROI methodologies to prioritize IT projects in business/IT planning.

Source: Katherine Lambert.

The Rowe Cos. and Merrill Lynch: The ROI Process in Business/IT Planning

At the Rowe Cos. (www.therowecompanies.com) in McLean, Virginia, sales were falling and budget planners were slashing. The $400 million furniture maker and retailer cut its $8 million IT budget to slightly less than $6 million in 2002, says CIO Suzanne Krupa. So any project at Rowe that can't promise a 17-month payback will be scrapped or postponed, says Krupa. Interoffice telephone lines are being clipped because Internet telephony is cheaper. Two point-of-sale systems will be combined, saving the company $250,000 a year in licensing and support costs. Krupa also plans to postpone upgrades for software such as Microsoft Windows and Office by two years. "We did a pay-now vs. pay-later analysis on Microsoft, and guess what? We are going to pay later," she says. That will net Rowe $300,000 a year in smaller license fees and support costs.

Krupa says she uses simple ROI calculations to help prioritize IT projects for planning purposes—but it isn't enough. She also uses Economic Value Added (EVA) analysis, which is broader in scope and is geared to maximizing shareholder value. EVA takes into consideration the cost of capital for a project, risk factor associated with the project, and a targeted value return percentage. For example, Krupa says she used EVA analysis to evaluate a proposed enterprise resource planning system for a manufacturing subsidiary. It enabled her to estimate the cost of delaying the project, and when she found that it would be less than the computed cost of the business disruption associated with the system, she decided to postpone the project indefinitely.

Krupa has recently begun using a newer measurement called return on opportunity (ROO). ROO combines more than a dozen factors to assess the rate of change in the business environment, the rate of change in business processes and IT infrastructure, the competitive environment, and the value of intangible assets. It focuses on the potential gains in new business from, say, attracting new customers or boosting revenue from existing customers.

Krupa is also spearheading reengineering planning at Rowe. "Instead of looking at new technologies, we are taking an introspective look at each of our businesses," she says. Those efforts, each assisted by IT people, are intended to find ways to reengineer processes for cost savings or quality improvements. Says Krupa, "As IT executives, we have to first and foremost look at the business units and say, 'Here are the things that can help you improve your performance and your budget.'"

Merrill Lynch. New York–based Merrill Lynch (www.ml.com) has ROI evaluations at the core of its IT project planning processes. "This process has clearly lowered our technology spending on what I'd call non-strategic investments and redirected spending to more strategic areas," says Marvin Balliet, chief financial officer for the technology group at Merrill Lynch. The financial services company now requires that the businesspeople who will use the technology are involved in budgeting and planning for IT.

For the past three years, Merrill Lynch has required a risk-and-payback analysis for every technology initiative that costs more than $2.5 million. The process is similar to how Merrill Lynch would measure a capital investment in real estate, for example. This year, there will be 50 to 100 IT projects evaluated, quite a bit fewer than the 230 the brokerage reviewed in 2000, given the restraints of the recessionary economy.

Merrill Lynch launched its ROI methodology three years ago. Before then, every technology purchasing decision was made by technologists. Now, other than technology infrastructure investments, all IT decisions are "made by businesspeople, with technology people sitting next to them," Balliet says. Standing review committees in each of Merrill Lynch's business units are made up of managers from the business, finance, and technology departments who meet monthly and assign low, medium, or high probabilities to the expected benefits of a project.

When Balliet started the process in late 1998, there were seven review standards, or templates, that management at Merrill Lynch used to evaluate projects, each one favoring its own business area. Now a single standard six-page template is used that poses yes-or-no questions to evaluate project success factors. The document is coupled with a detailed five-page financial report. Questions asked include, "Is the success of this project dependent on another business or technology unit?" and "Have the business functions and the data requirements been identified and agreed to with the business units?"

"The businessperson and the technology person sit down together, and it's an agreement between the two sides before we start to spend," says Balliet. "The only rule to this is that the process has to be assigned to the businesspeople; it cannot be assigned to the technology people." Before Merrill Lynch launched its ROI program, about half of its projects ran above cost and never delivered all the promised benefits, Balliet says. Now the number of individual projects that exceed costs is down to 10 percent.

Case Study Questions

1. What are the benefits and limitations of the Rowe Companies' ROI methods for IT project planning?

2. What is the business value of the ROI methodology required for project planning by Merrill Lynch?

3. Do you agree with the IT investment decisions being made by the Rowe Companies in response to changing economic conditions? Why or why not?

Source: Adapted from Gary Anthes, "The Budget Squeeze," *Computerworld*, December 10, 2001, pp. 40–41; and Matt Hamblen, "In Search of ROI Measurements," *Computerworld*, March 25, 2002, pp. 32–33. Reprinted with permission from *Computerworld*.

FIGURE 9.2 The components of an organizational planning process.

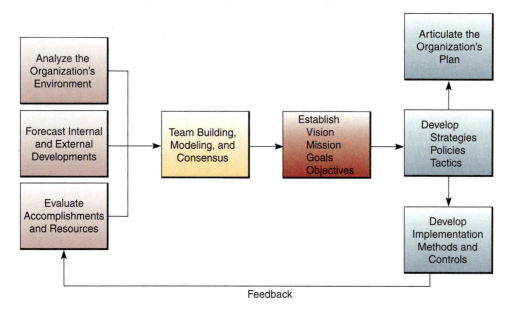

Feedback

committees of business unit and IT department heads. The result has been a big drop in the number of projects that exceed their budgeted cost.

Organizational Planning

Figure 9.2 illustrates the components of an **organizational planning** process. This fundamental planning process consists of (1) team building, modeling, and consensus, (2) evaluating what an organization has accomplished and the resources they have acquired, (3) analyzing their business, economic, political, and societal environment, (4) anticipating and evaluating the impact of future developments, (5) building a shared vision and deciding on what goals they want to achieve, and (6) deciding what actions to take to achieve their goals.

The result of this planning process is what we call a *plan*, which formally articulates the actions we feel are necessary to achieve our goals. Thus, a plan is an action statement. Plans lead to actions, actions produce results, and part of planning is learning from results. In this context, the planning process is followed by implementation, which is monitored by control measures, which provide feedback for planning.

Strategic planning deals with the development of an organization's mission, goals, strategies, and policies. Corporations may begin the process by developing a shared vision using a variety of techniques, including team building, scenario modeling, and consensus creating exercises. Team planning sessions frequently include answering *strategic visioning* questions such as those shown in Figure 9.3. *Tactical planning* involves the setting of objectives and the development of procedures, rules, schedules, and budgets. *Operational planning* is planning done on a short-term basis to implement and control day-to-day operations. Typical examples are project planning and production scheduling.

Many organizational planning methodologies are used in business today. However, in this section, let's concentrate on two of the most popular methodologies: the scenario approach, and planning for competitive advantage.

The Scenario Approach

Planning and budgeting processes are notorious for their rigidity and irrelevance to management action. Rigid adherence to a process of rapid or efficient completion may only make the process less relevant to the true management agenda [8].

FIGURE 9.3   Examples of strategic visioning questions in planning for e-business initiatives.

Strategic Business Visioning	
● **Understanding the Customer**	Who are our customers? How are our customers' priorities shifting? Who should be our target customer? How will an e-business help reach our target customer segments?
● **Customer Value**	How can we add value for the customer with e-business services? How can we become the customer's first choice?
● **Competition**	Who are our real competitors? What is our toughest competitor's business model? What are they doing in e-business and e-commerce? Are our competitors potential partners, suppliers, or customers in an e-business venture?
● **Value Chain**	How would we design a value chain if we were just starting an e-business? Who would be our supply chain partners? What roles should we play: e-commerce website, B2C portal, B2B marketplace, or partner in an e-commerce alliance?

Source: Adapted from Ravi Kalakota and Marcia Robinson, *E-Business 2.0: Roadmap for Success* (Reading, MA: Addison-Wesley, 2001), p. 396, © 2001 Addison-Wesley Publishing Company, Inc. Reprinted by permission of Addison-Wesley Longman Inc.; and Peter Fingar, Harsha Kumar, and Tarun Sharma, *Enterprise E-Commerce: The Software Component Breakthrough for Business to Business Commerce* (Tampa, FL: Meghan-Kiffer Press, 2000), p. 229.

Managers and planners continually try different approaches to make planning easier, more accurate, and more relevant to the dynamic, real world of business. The **scenario approach** to planning has gained in popularity as a less formal, but more realistic, strategic planning methodology for use by business professionals.

In the scenario approach, teams of managers and other planners participate in what management author Peter Senge calls *microworld*, or *virtual world*, exercises. A microworld is a simulation exercise that is a microcosm of the real world. In a microworld exercise, managers can safely create, experience, and evaluate a variety of scenarios of what might be happening, or what might happen in the real world.

> *When a work team goes white-water rafting or engages in some other outdoor team-building exercise, they are creating a microworld to reflect on and improve the way they work together. When personnel staff create a role-playing exercise to be used in a supervisory training, they are creating a microworld. Many team retreats serve as microworlds* [26].

Thus, in the scenario approach to strategic IS planning, teams of business and IS managers create and evaluate a variety of business scenarios. For example, they make assumptions on what a business will be like three to five years or more into the future, and the role that information technology can or will play in those future scenarios. Alternative scenarios are created by the teams or by business simulation software, based on combining a variety of developments, trends, and environmental factors, including political, social, business, and technological changes that might occur [11]. For example, Figure 9.4 outlines key business, political, and technological trends that could help guide business/IT planning.

Royal Dutch Shell and Dennys: Scenario Planning	Royal Dutch Shell, one of the world's largest oil companies, changed their planning process to a scenario approach over 20 years ago. They shifted from the idea that planning involves "producing a documented view of the future," to a scenario approach where planning involves "designing scenarios so managers would question their own model of reality and change it when necessary." Royal Dutch Shell believes this change to scenario-based planning was a major reason for their successful business decisions during the oil market upheavals of the 1970s and 1980s [8, 9].

FIGURE 9.4   Converging business, political, and technological trends that are shaping strategic business/IT planning.

Technology	Deregulation
• Electronic Commerce • Customer Information Technology • "Death of Distance" • Digital Everything, Technology Convergence • Information Content of Products and Services Increasing Steadily	• Regulated Markets Opening Up • Fewer Regulatory Impediments in Business • Single Currency Zones • Regulators Outflanked by Changing Boundaries and Unstoppable Forces (Internet and e-Business)
Competitive Imperatives	**Customer Sophistication/ Expectations**

• Imperatives:
  - Real Growth
  - Globalization
  - Customer Orientation
  - Knowledge and Capability as Key Assets
  - New Entrants
• Enablers:
  - Alliances
  - Outsourcing
	• Demand for Better and More Convenient Solutions
	• Increased Emphasis on Service
	• Demand for Added Value
	• Less Tolerance for Poor Standards
	• Just-in-Time Delivery
	• Global Influences
	• Brand "Savvy"

Converging Trends

Source: Adapted from Martin Diese, Conrad Nowikow, Patrick King, and Amy Wright, *Executive's Guide to E-Business: From Tactics to Strategy*, 2000, p. 139. Reprinted with permission of John Wiley & Sons, Inc. Copyright © 2000 by John Wiley & Sons, Inc.

Denny's, the nationwide restaurant corporation, uses scenario-based planning to develop five-year plans for the business use of information technology. Department managers gather off-site for several days to create business and IS scenarios. They assess the success of scenarios from the past, to help them anticipate what the company might be like five years into the future. The managers create several most-likely business scenarios, and develop a high-level IS plan for the information technology needed to support each one. Then the IS director analyzes these IS plans to identify the common IT resources required by each one. The managers then reconvene to discuss these findings, and decide on one IS plan for Denny's [11].

Planning for Competitive Advantage

Betting on new IT innovations can mean betting the future of the company. Leading-edge firms are sometimes said to be on the "bleeding edge." Almost any business executive is aware of disastrous projects that had to be written off, often after large cost overruns, because the promised new system simply did not work [19].

Planning for competitive advantage is especially important in today's competitive business arena and complex information technology environment. So strategic business/IT planning involves an evaluation of the potential benefits and risks a company faces when using IT-based strategies and technologies for competitive advantage. In Chapter 2, we introduced a model of *competitive forces* (competitors, customers, suppliers, new entrants, and substitutes) and *competitive strategies* (cost leadership, differentiation, growth, innovation, and alliances), as well as a value chain model of basic business activities. These models can be used in a strategic planning process to help generate ideas for the strategic use of information technologies to support new e-business initiatives.

Also popular in strategic business/IT planning is the use of a *strategic opportunities matrix* to evaluate the strategic potential of proposed business/IT opportunities, as measured by their risk/payoff probabilities. See Figure 9.5.

FIGURE 9.5

A strategic opportunities matrix helps to evaluate the strategic risk/payoff potential of proposed business/IT opportunities.

SWOT Analysis

SWOT analysis (strengths, weaknesses, opportunities, and threats) is used to evaluate the impact that each possible strategic opportunity can have on a company and its use of information technology [7,19]. A company's strengths are its core competencies and resources in which it is one of the market or industry leaders. Weaknesses are areas of substandard business performance compared to others in their industry or market segments. Opportunities are the potential for new business markets or innovative breakthroughs that might greatly expand present markets. Threats are the potential for business and market losses posed by the actions of competitors and other competitive forces, changes in government policies, disruptive new technologies, and so on. Now let's look at a real world example of how a company used SWOT analysis to evaluate a strategic opportunity.

Dell Computer: Using SWOT Analysis

Dell Computer Corp. is a good example of how a company can use SWOT analysis to carve out a strong business strategy to meet a strategic opportunity: the huge demand for PCs by Internet-connected consumers and businesses. Dell recognized that its strength was selling directly to consumers and businesses and keeping its costs lower than those of other hardware vendors. As for weaknesses, the company acknowledged that it lacked solid dealer relationships.

Identifying opportunities was an easier task. Dell looked at the marketplace and saw that customers increasingly valued convenience and one-stop shopping and that they knew what they wanted to purchase. Dell also saw the Internet as a powerful marketing tool. On the threats side, Dell realized that competitors like IBM and Compaq Computer Corp. had stronger brand names, which put Dell in a weaker position with dealers.

Dell put together a business strategy that included mass customization and just-in-time manufacturing (letting customers use the Web to design their own computers, and then custom-building their systems). Dell also stuck with its direct sales plan and developed a world-class e-commerce website to showcase and sell its products [23].

Business Models and Planning

"Business model" was one of the great buzzwords of the Internet boom, routinely invoked, as the writer Michael Lewis put it, "to invoke all manner of half-baked plans." But a good business model remains essential to every successful organization, whether it's a new venture or an established player [23].

FIGURE 9.6

Questions that illustrate the components of all business models. A good business model effectively answers these questions.

Component of Business Model	Questions for All Business Models
Customer value	Is the firm offering its customers something distinctive or at a lower cost than its competitors?
Scope	To which customers (demographic and geographic) is the firm offering this value? What is the range of products/services offered that embody this value?
Pricing	How does the firm price the value?
Revenue source	Where do the dollars come from? Who pays for what value and when? What are the margins in each market and what drives them? What drives value in each source?
Connected activities	What set of activities does the firm have to perform to offer this value and when? How connected (in cross section and time) are these activities?
Implementation	What organizational structure, systems, people, and environment does the firm need to carry out these activities? What is the fit between them?
Capabilities	What are the firm's capabilities and capabilities gaps that need to be filled? How does a firm fill these capabilities gaps? Is there something distinctive about these capabilities that allows the firm to offer the value better than other firms and that makes them difficult to imitate? What are the sources of these capabilities?
Sustainability	What is it about the firm that makes it difficult for other firms to imitate it? How does the firm keep making money? How does the firm sustain its competitive advantage?

Source: Adapted from Allan Afuah and Christopher Tucci, *Internet Business Models and Strategies* (New York, McGraw-Hill/Irwin, 2001), p. 49.

A **business model** is a conceptual framework that expresses the underlying economic logic and system that prove how a business can deliver value to customers at an appropriate cost and make money. A business model answers vital questions about the fundamental components of a business, such as: Who are our customers? What do our customers value? How much will it cost to deliver that value to our customers? How do we make money in this business [23]?

A business model specifies what value to offer customers, and which customers to provide this value to using which products and services at what prices. It also specifies how the business will organize and operate to have the capability to provide this value and sustain any advantage from providing this value to its customers. Figure 9.6 outlines more specific questions about the components of a business that all business models must answer. Figure 9.7 lists questions that illustrate the essential components of e-business models [1].

A business model is a valuable planning tool because it focuses attention on how all the essential components of a business fit into a complete system. Done properly, it forces entrepreneurs and managers to think rigorously and systemically about the value and viability of the business initiatives they are planning. Then the strategic planning process can be used to develop unique business strategies that capitalize on a firm's business model to help it gain competitive advantages in its industry and the markets it wants to dominate [23].

FIGURE 9.7
Questions that illustrate the components of e-business models that can be developed as part of the strategic business/IT planning process.

Component of Business Model	Questions Specific to e-Business Models
Customer value	What is it about Internet technologies that allows your firm to offer its customers something distinctive? Can Internet technologies allow you to solve a new set of problems for customers?
Scope	What is the scope of customers that Internet technologies enable your firm to reach? Does the Internet alter the product or sevice mix that embodies the firm's products?
Pricing	How does the Internet make pricing different?
Revenue source	Are revenue sources different with the Internet? What is new?
Connected activities	How many new activities must be performed as a result of the Internet? How much better can Internet technologies help you to perform existing activities?
Implementation	How do Internet technologies affect the strategy, structure, systems, people, and environment of your firm?
Capabilities	What new capabilities do you need? What is the impact of Internet technologies on existing capabilities?
Sustainability	Do Internet technologies make sustainability easier or more difficult? How can your firm take advantage of it?

Source: Adapted from Allan Afuah and Christopher Tucci, *Internet Business Models and Strategies* (New York, McGraw-Hill/Irwin, 2001), p. 49.

Webvan and Webhouse: When Business Models Fail

When business models don't work, it's because they fail either the narrative test (the story doesn't make sense) or the numbers test (the P&L doesn't add up). The business model of online grocers, for instance, failed the numbers test. The grocery industry has very thin margins to begin with, and online merchants like Webvan incurred new costs for marketing, service, delivery, and technology. Since customers weren't willing to pay significantly more for groceries bought online than in stores, there was no way the math could work. Internet grocers had plenty of company. Many ventures in the first wave of electronic commerce failed simply because the basic business math was flawed.

Other business models failed the narrative test. Consider the rapid rise and fall of Priceline Webhouse Club. This was an offshoot of Priceline.com, the company that introduced name-your-own pricing to the purchase of airline tickets. Wall Street's early enthusiasm encouraged CEO Jay Walker to extend his concept to groceries and gasoline.

Here's the story Walker tried to tell. Via the Web, millions of consumers would tell him how much they wanted to pay for, say, a jar of peanut butter. Consumers could specify the price but not the brand, so they might end up with Jif or they might end up with Skippy. Webhouse would then aggregate the bids and go to companies like P&G and Bestfoods and try to make a deal: Take 50 cents off the price of your peanut butter, and we'll order a million jars this week. Webhouse wanted to be a power broker for individual consumers: Representing millions of shoppers, it would negotiate discounts and then pass on the savings to its customers, taking a fee in the process.

What was wrong with the story? It assumed that companies like P&G, Kimberly-Clark, and Exxon wanted to play this game. Think about that for a minute. Big consumer companies have spent decades and billions of dollars building brand loyalty. The Webhouse model teaches consumers to buy on price alone. So why would the manufacturers want to help Webhouse undermine both their prices and the brand identities they'd worked so hard to build? They wouldn't. The story just didn't make sense. To be a power broker, Webhouse needed a huge base of loyal customers. To get those customers, it first needed to deliver discounts. Since the consumer product companies refused to play, Webhouse had to pay for those discounts out of its own pocket. A few hundred million dollars later, in October 2000, it ran out of cash—and out of investors who still believed the story [23].

Business/IT Planning

Figure 9.8 illustrates the **business/IT planning** process, which focuses on discovering innovative approaches to satisfying a company's customer value and business value goals. This planning process leads to development of strategies and business models for new e-business and e-commerce platforms, processes, products, and services. Then a company can develop IT strategies and an IT architecture that supports building and implementing their newly planned business applications.

Both the CEO and the chief information officer (CIO) of a company must manage the development of complementary business and IT strategies to meet its customer value and business value vision. This *co-adaptation* process is necessary because as we have seen so often in this text, information technologies are a fast changing, but vital component in many strategic business initiatives. The business/IT planning process has three major components:

- **Strategy development.** Developing business strategies that support a company's business vision. For example, use information technology to create innovative e-business systems that focus on customer and business value. We will discuss this process in more detail shortly.

- **Resource management.** Developing strategic plans for managing or outsourcing a company's IT resources, including IS personnel, hardware, software, data, and network resources.

- **Technology architecture.** Making strategic IT choices that reflect an information technology architecture designed to support a company's e-business and other business/IT initiatives.

FIGURE 9.8

The business/IT planning process emphasizes a customer and business value focus for devoloping business strategies and models, and an IT architecture for business applications.

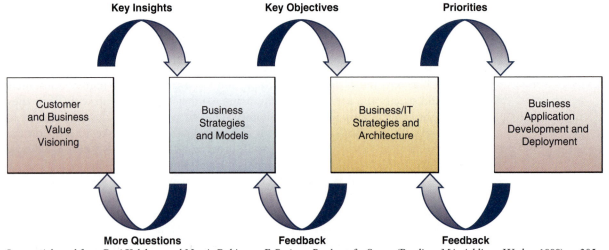

Information Technology Architecture

The **IT architecture** that is created by the strategic business/IT planning process is a conceptual design, or blueprint, that includes the following major components:

- **Technology platform.** The Internet, intranets, extranets, and other networks, computer systems, system software, and integrated enterprise application software provide a computing and communications infrastructure, or platform, that supports the strategic use of information technology for e-business, e-commerce, and other business/IT applications.

- **Data resources.** Many types of operational and specialized databases, including data warehouses and Internet/intranet databases (as reviewed in Chapter 3) store and provide data and information for business processes and decision support.

- **Applications architecture.** Business applications of information technology are designed as an integrated architecture of enterprise systems that support strategic business initiatives, as well as cross-functional business processes. For example, an applications architecture should include support for developing and maintaining interenterprise supply chain applications, and integrated enterprise resource planning and customer relationship management applications we discussed in Chapter 6.

- **IT organization.** The organizational structure of the IS function within a company and the distribution of IS specialists are designed to meet the changing strategies of a business. The form of the IT organization depends on the managerial philosophy and business/IT strategies formulated during the strategic planning process. We will discuss the IT organization in Chapter 12.

Identifying Business/IT Strategies

Companies need a strategic framework that can bridge the gap between simply connecting to the Internet and harnessing its power for competitive advantage. The most valuable Internet applications allow companies to transcend communication barriers and establish connections that will enhance productivity, stimulate innovative development, and improve customer relations [9].

Internet technologies and e-business and e-commerce applications can be used strategically for competitive advantage, as this text repeatedly demonstrates. However, in order to optimize this strategic impact, a company must continually assess the strategic value of such applications. Figure 9.9 is a strategic positioning matrix that can help a company identify where to concentrate its strategic use of Internet technologies to gain a competitive advantage. Let's take a look at the strategies that each quadrant of this matrix represents [9].

- **Cost and Efficiency Improvements.** This quadrant represents a low amount of internal company, customer, and competitor connectivity and use of IT via the Internet and other networks. So one recommended strategy would be to focus on improving efficiency and lowering costs by using the Internet and the World Wide Web as a fast, low-cost way to communicate and interact with customers, suppliers, and business partners. The use of e-mail, chat systems, discussion groups, and a company website are typical examples.

- **Performance Improvement in Business Effectiveness.** Here a company has a high degree of internal connectivity and pressures to substantially improve its business processes, but external connectivity by customers and competitors is still low. A strategy of making major improvements in business effectiveness is recommended. For example, widespread internal use of Internet-based technologies like intranets and extranets can substantially improve information sharing and collaboration within the business and with its trading partners.

FIGURE 9.9

A strategic positioning matrix helps a company optimize the strategic impact of Internet technologies for electronic business and commerce applications.

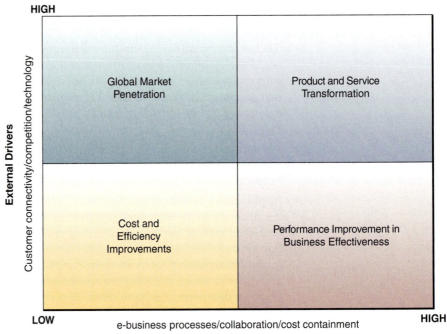

- **Global Market Penetration.** A company that enters this quadrant of the matrix must capitalize on a high degree of customer and competitor connectivity and use of IT. Developing e-business and e-commerce applications to optimize interaction with customers and build market share is recommended. For example, e-commerce websites with value-added information services and extensive online customer support would be one way to implement such a strategy.

- **Product and Service Transformation.** Here a company and its customers, suppliers, and competitors are extensively networked. Internet-based technologies, including e-commerce websites and e-business intranets and extranets, must now be implemented throughout the company's operations and business relationships. This enables a company to develop and deploy new Internet-based products and services that strategically reposition it in the marketplace. Using the Internet for electronic commerce transaction processing with customers at company websites, and e-commerce auctions and exchanges for suppliers are typical examples of such strategic e-business applications. Let's look at more specific examples.

e-Business Strategy Examples	**Market creator.** Use the Internet to define a new market by identifying a unique customer need. This model requires you to be among the first to market and to remain ahead of competition by continuously innovating. Examples: Amazon.com and E*TRADE.
	Channel reconfiguration. Use the Internet as a new channel to directly access customers, make sales, and fulfill orders. This model supplements, rather than replaces, physical distribution and marketing channels. Example: Cisco and Dell.

Transaction intermediary. Use the Internet to process purchases. This transactional model includes the end-to-end process of searching, comparing, selecting, and paying online. Examples: Microsoft Expedia and eBay.

Infomediary. Use the Internet to reduce the search cost. Offer the customer a unified process for collecting information necessary to make a large purchase. Examples: HomeAdvisor and Auto-By-Tel.

Self-service innovator. Use the Internet to provide a comprehensive suite of services that the customer's employees can use directly. Self-service affords employees a direct, personalized relationship. Examples: Employease and Healtheon.

Supply chain innovator. Use the Internet to streamline the interactions among all parties in the supply chain to improve operating efficiency. Examples: McKesson and Ingram Micro.

Channel mastery. Use the Internet as a sales and service channel. This model supplements, rather than replaces, the existing physical business offices and call centers. Example: Charles Schwab [23].

Business Application Planning

The **business application planning** process begins after the strategic phase of business/IT planning has occurred. Figure 9.10 shows that the application planning process includes the evaluation of proposals made by the IT management of a company for using information technology to accomplish the strategic business priorities developed earlier in the planning process as was illustrated in Figure 9.8. Then, the business case for investing in proposed e-business development projects is evaluated by company executives and business unit managers based on the strategic business priorities that they decide are most desirable or necessary at that point in time. Finally, business application planning involves developing and implementing business applications of IT, and managing their development projects. We will cover the application development and implementation process in Chapter 10. Now, let's examine a real world example.

FIGURE 9.10

A business application planning process includes consideration of IT proposals for addressing the strategic business priorities of a company and planning for application development and implementation.

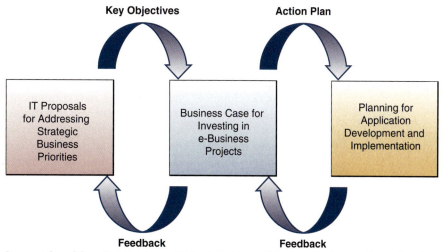

Source: Adapted from Ravi Kalakota and Marcia Robinson, *E-Business: Roadmap for Success* (Reading, MA: Addison-Wesley, 1999), p. 341. © 1999 Addison-Wesley Publishing Company, Inc. Reprinted by permission of Addison-Wesley Longman Inc.

FIGURE 9.11

Comparing conventional and e-business strategic and application planning approaches.

Conventional IT Planning	Avnet Marshall's e-Business Planning
• Strategic alignment: IT strategy tracks specified enterprise strategy	• Strategic improvisation: IT strategy and enterprise business strategy co-adaptively unfold based on the clear guidance of a focus on customer value
• CEO endorses IT vision shaped through CIO	• CEO proactively shapes IT vision jointly with CIO as part of e-business strategy
• IT application development projects functionally organized as technological solutions to business issues	• IT application development projects co-located with e-business initiatives to form centers of IT-intensive business expertise
• Phased application development based on learning from pilot projects	• Perpetual application development based on continuous learning from rapid deployment with incomplete functionality and end user involvement

Source: Adapted from Omar El Sawy, Arvind Malhotra, Sanjay Gosain, and Kerry Young, "IT-Intensive Value Innovation in the Electronic Economy: Insights from Marshal Industries," *MIS Quarterly*, September 1999, p. 324. Reprinted with permission from the *MIS Quarterly*.

Avnet Marshall: e-Business Planning

Figure 9.11 outlines Avnet Marshall's planning process for e-business initiatives, and compares it to conventional IT planning approaches. Avnet Marshall is the giant electronics distributor we first mentioned in Chapter 2. Avnet Marshall weaves both e-business and IT strategic planning together *co-adaptively* under the guidance of the CEO and the CIO, instead of developing IT strategy by just tracking and supporting business strategies. Avnet Marshall also locates IT application development projects within the business units that are involved in an e-business initiative to form centers of business/IT expertise throughout the company. Finally, Avnet Marshall uses an application development process with rapid deployment of e-business applications, instead of a traditional systems development approach. This application development strategy trades the risk of implementing incomplete applications with the benefits of gaining competitive advantages from early deployment of e-business services to employees, customers, and other stakeholders, and of involving them in the "fine-tuning" phase of application development [12].

Business/IT Architecture Planning

Another way to look at the business/IT planning process, which is growing in acceptance and use in industry, is shown in Figure 9.12. **E-business architecture planning** combines contemporary strategic planning methods like SWOT analysis and alternative planning scenarios with more recent business modeling and application development methodologies like component-based development. As illustrated in Figure 9.12, strategic e-business initiatives, including strategic goals, constraints, and requirements, are developed based on SWOT analysis and other planning methods. Then application developers use business process engineering methods to define how strategic business requirements are to be implemented, using organizational, process, and data models to create new internal and interenterprise e-business processes among a company's customers, suppliers, and other business partners.

Component-based e-business and e-commerce applications are then developed to implement the new business processes using application software and data components stored in a *repository* of reusable business models and application components. Of course, the business process engineering and component-based

FIGURE 9.12   E-business architecture planning integrates business strategy development and business process engineering to produce e-business and e-commerce applications using the resources of the IT architecture, component development technologies, and a repository of business models and application components.

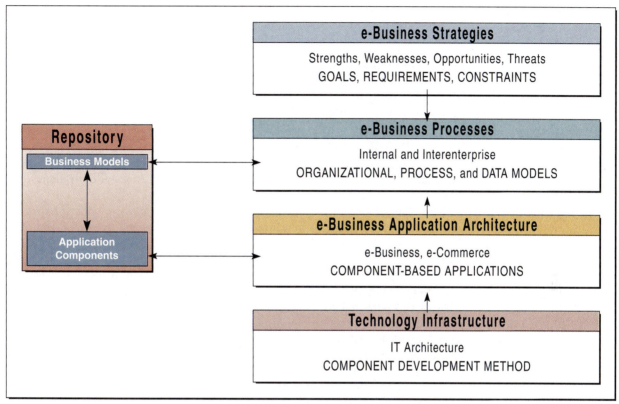

Source: Adapted from Peter Fingar, Harsha Kumar, and Tarun Sharma, *Enterprise E-Commerce: The Software Component Breakthrough for Business to Business Commerce* (Tampa, FL: Meghan-Kiffer Press, 2000), p. 68.

application development activities are supported by a company's technology infrastructure, which includes all the resources of its IT architecture, as well as the necessary component development technologies. So e-business architecture planning links strategy development to business modeling and component development methodologies in order to produce the strategic e-business applications needed by a company [14].

Implementation Challenges

Implementation

Many companies plan really well, yet few translate strategy into action, even though senior management consistently identifies e-business as an area of great opportunity and one in which the company needs stronger capabilities [18].

Implementation is an important managerial responsibility. Implementation is doing what you planned to do. You can view **implementation** as a process that carries out the plans for changes in business/IT strategies and applications that were developed in the planning process we covered in Section I.

Analyzing Verizon, F.X. Coughlin, and A-dec

Read the Real World Case on Analyzing Verizon, F.X. Coughlin, and A-dec on the next page. We can learn a lot from this case about the important implementation challenges that arise when implementing new business/IT strategies. See Figure 9.13.

CIO Roger Gurnani is responsible for managing the massive consolidation and integration of the business applications, computer systems and networks, and other IT resources and services of the nine companies that merged into Verizon Wireless. Ed Winfield, CIO at F.X. Coughlin, supervised the overhaul and integration of the company's supply chain applications. And CIO Keith Bearden of A-dec led the integration of their ERP and sales forecasting applications. All of them had to be sensitive to the potential for business disruption and user resistance caused by the changes required by these integration projects. Thus they all used a variety of project management and change management methods to help maximize the success and acceptance of their new systems by all of the business stakeholders involved.

FIGURE 9.13
Roger Gurnani is CIO at Verizon Wireless and leads their massive IT integration project.

Source: John Rae.

Verizon, F.X. Coughlin, and A-dec: Implementation Challenges of Application Integration

Death, taxes, IT integration projects. Few things are more certain on life's road. The CIOs who drive massive, ambitious, and sometimes scary integration projects need to be take-charge individuals with loads of technology and management experience who are willing to take risks but know when to stop racing ahead. They also need to have a keen understanding of the business in order to earn the trust of everyone involved.

"The first thing to consider with an integration project is the potential disruption to the business," advises Roger Gurnani, vice president and CIO at Bedminster, New Jersey–based telecommunications provider Verizon Wireless (www.verizonwireless.com), a subsidiary of telecom giant Verizon Communications.

Eliminating redundancy in IT operations was a core concept behind the final merger in April 2000 of nine companies' sprawling wireless businesses that came together to form the 28 million-customer operation of Verizon Wireless, now the largest U.S. wireless telecommunications company. "Integration was needed to deliver the synergies and to leverage the economies of scale," says Gurnani, who reports directly to the CEO, Dennis Strigl.

The nine companies used more than 150 major applications for billing, inventory, point of sale, financial management, customer care, and all other aspects of business. Gurnani's team has consolidated that number to 70 within 18 months, with an end goal of 25 to 30 core applications. Concurrent with that effort has been data center consolidation work and the development of companywide standards for desktop PCs, e-mail, and wide area network services. "We're not all done, but we've made significant progress," Gurnani says.

Many CIOs would be daunted by the project's scope, but Gurnani says his 15 years' integration experience from other mergers and acquisitions while an executive at Bell Atlantic Mobile and WilTel (now WorldCom Inc.) gives him the confidence that his staff will get the job done. He also says his experience means he knows the risks and how to create a "rigorous methodology"—a kind of project management checklist to get past the pitfalls that he has discovered over the years.

Although it's important to be comfortable discussing all levels of technology changes during an integration, Gurnani says, IT managers should be focused on business users during these projects because "it's not just the technology, but the business processes that are changed." For example, during any application change he has made sure that business experts were on hand with IT staff to handle any concerns from end users after they'd gone through extensive training.

Ed Winfield echoes the sentiment. As CIO at F.X. Coughlin Co. (www.fxcoughlin.com), a $300 million shipping company in Southfield, Michigan, Winfield recently oversaw a major overhaul and the integration of the company's supply chain applications. He says it's natural for peo-

ple to get comfortable with old ways of doing things that may be inefficient. It's the CIO's job to improve the processes while updating the technology. For example, Winfield recalls that his company once had 107 codes for freight designations. It now has three.

"A lot of people were entrenched in the way things were done. They took pride in knowing all the codes," he says. "And they worried that change would jeopardize customer service." To get them on board, Winfield led a relentless communications campaign, keeping people who would be affected by the changes informed "while we were in process, not after the fact."

Of course, business managers often demand that IT initiate an integration project. That's what happened at Newberg, Oregon–based A-dec Inc. (www.a-dec.com), a leading supplier of dental equipment that recently tied together its enterprise resource planning and sales forecast applications. "We were spending an extraordinary amount of money on overtime in manufacturing because of inaccurate forecasts," says B. Keith Bearden, A-dec's director of information services and CIO. "We had the dollar forecasts right, but we had the product mix wrong." Top management wanted to correct the problem and looked to Bearden's team to improve the timeliness of data from field sales. The result has been an impressive reduction in sales lead times by two months and a 20 to 25 percent decrease in overtime.

But even with enthusiastic buy-in from all departments and top management, Bearden notes, you can't assume that you know exactly what people want, nor can you assume that a particular improvement will be considered the right one. For example, field salespeople will want reports designed to illuminate regional or even customer-specific information, while in-house sales managers will want reports designed with more aggregate information. "You can never satisfy everyone," he observes.

Case Study Questions

1. What business benefits resulted from the integration projects of Verizon Wireless, F.X. Coughlin, and A-dec?

2. What change management challenges surfaced in each project? Were they handled properly by the companies involved? Why or why not?

3. What are several change management actions these companies could have taken to increase the acceptance of their IT integration challenges? Explain.

Source: Adapted from Mark Hall, "Integration: IT's Albatross," *Computerworld*, January 1, 2002, pp. 22–24. Reprinted with permission from *Computerworld*.

Implementing Information Technology

Moving to an e-business environment involves a major organizational change. For many large, global companies, becoming an e-business is the fourth or fifth major organizational change they have undergone since the early 1980s. Many companies have gone through one or more rounds of business process reengineering (BPR); installation and major upgrades of an ERP system; upgrading legacy systems to be Y2K compliant; creating shared service centers; implementing just-in-time (JIT) manufacturing; automating the sales force; contract manufacturing; and the major challenges related to the introduction of Euro currency [24].

So implementing new e-business strategies and applications is only the latest catalyst for major organizational changes enabled by information technology. Figure 9.14 illustrates the impact and the levels and scope of business changes that applications of information technology introduce into an organization. For example, implementing an application like online transaction processing brings efficiency to single-function or core business processes. However, implementing e-business applications such as enterprise resource management or customer relationship management requires a reengineering of core business processes internally and with supply chain partners, thus forcing a company to model and implement business practices being implemented by leading firms in their industry. Of course, any major new business initiatives can enable a company to redefine its core lines of business and precipitate dramatic changes within the entire interenterprise value chain of a business.

As we will see in this section, implementing new business/IT strategies requires managing the effects of major changes in key organizational dimensions such as business processes, organizational structures, managerial roles, employee work assignments, and stakeholder relationships that arise from the deployment of new business information systems. For example, Figure 9.15 emphasizes the variety and extent of the challenges reported by 100 companies that developed and implemented new enterprise information portals and ERP systems.

End User Resistance and Involvement

Any new way of doing things generates some resistance by the people affected. For example, the implementation of new work support technologies can generate fear and resistance to change by employees. Let's look at a real world example that demonstrates the challanges of implementing major business/IT strategies and applications,

FIGURE 9.14   The impact and the levels and scope of business change introduced by implementations of information technology.

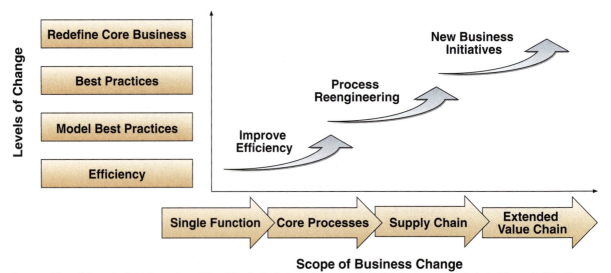

Source: Adapted from Craig Fellenstein and Ron Wood, *Exploring E-Commerce, Global E-Business and E-Societies* (Upper Saddle River, NJ: Prentice-Hall, 2000), p. 97.

FIGURE 9.15

The ten greatest challenges of developing and implementing intranet enterprise portals and enterprise resource planning systems reported by 100 companies.

Intranet Enterprise Portal Challenges	Enterprise Resource Planning Challenges
• Security, security, security	• Getting end-user buy-in
• Defining the scope and purpose of the portal	• Scheduling/planning
• Finding the time and the money	• Integrating legacy systems/data
• Ensuring consistent data quality	• Getting management buy-in
• Getting employees to use it	• Dealing with multiple/international sites and partners
• Organizing the data	• Changing culture/mind-sets
• Finding technical expertise	• IT training
• Integrating the pieces	• Getting, keeping IT staff
• Making it easy to use	• Moving to a new platform
• Providing all users with access	• Performance/system upgrades

Source: Adapted from Kathleen Melymuka, "An Expanding Universe," *Computerworld*, September 14, 1998, p. 57; and Tim Ouellette, "Opening Your Own Portal," *Computerworld*, August 9, 1999. p. 79. Copyright 1998 and 1999 by Computerworld, Inc., Framingham, MA 01701, Reprinted from *Computerworld*.

and the change management challenges that confront management. Customer relationship management (CRM) is a prime example of a key e-business application for many companies today. It is designed to implement a business strategy of using IT to support a total customer care focus for all areas of a company. Yet CRM projects have a history of a high rate of failure in meeting their objectives. For example, according to a report from Meta Group, a staggering 55% to 75% of CRM projects fail to meet their objectives, often as a result of sales force automation problems and "unaddressed cultural issues"—sales staffs are often resistant to, or even fearful of, using CRM systems.

Crane Engineering: Overcoming User Resistance to CRM

"Our biggest challenge was our sales guys—changing their habits, getting them to use it for planning. They'd make comments like, 'I don't have time to enter the information.' Some are afraid of using Windows, not to mention CRM," says Jeff Koeper, vice president of operations at Crane Engineering, a Kimberly, Wisconsin–based industrial equipment distributor.

Crane initially had formed a cross-functional team with IT sales and customer service staffers to hear sales automation software vendors' presentations and mutually decide on the desired goals. After a vendor was chosen in 1999, a cross-functional pilot project was formed to iron out any kinks before the system was rolled out company wide. Two full-day training classes have been held since the initial implementation. But now, Crane is requiring sales managers to ride herd on foot-draggers, and using peer pressure from salespeople selling different products to the same accounts. A cross-functional CRM steering committee meets monthly to discuss problem areas.

"Salespeople want to know what's in it for them; it's not enough to tell them they have to do it. But give them a panoramic view of what their customer is doing in call centers and on the company Web site, such as buying other products or complaints. That's a very powerful motivator—they respond to revenue potential and growing their customer base," says Liz Shahnam, a Meta Group analyst.

But companies face a bigger challenge: CRM is a mind-set—a business philosophy that reshapes a company's sales, marketing, customer service and analytics and presents a radical cultural shift for many organizations. "It's a change from a product-centered or internal focus to a customer-centered or external focus. It's a change from a monologue to a dialogue with the customer; with the advent of the Internet, customers want to converse with a company. Also, it's a change from targeting customers to becoming the target. Customers are now the hunters," says Ray McKenzie, Seattle-based director of management consulting at DMR Consulting.

This switch means getting IT professionals to "think customer" and breaking down the barriers between IT and the employees who interact with customers. It also means structural changes in how the company operates, like sharing information and resources across departments and job functions, which translates into giving up control over who "owns" it; retraining employees in new roles, responsibilities and skills; and measuring their job performance, and even how they're paid.

One of the keys to solving problems of **end user resistance** to new information technologies is proper education and training. Even more important is **end user involvement** in organizational changes, and in the development of new information systems. Organizations have a variety of strategies to help manage business change, and one basic requirement is the involvement and commitment of top management and all business stakeholders affected by the planning processes we described in Section I.

Direct end user participation in business planning and application development projects before a new system is implemented is especially important in reducing the potential for end user resistance. That is why end users frequently are members of systems development teams or do their own development work. Such involvement helps ensure that end users assume ownership of a system, and that its design meets their needs. Systems that tend to inconvenience or frustrate users cannot be effective systems, no matter how technically elegant they are and how efficiently they process data. For example, Figure 9.16 illustrates some of the major obstacles to knowledge management systems in business. Notice that end user resistance to sharing knowledge is the biggest obstacle to the implementation of knowledge management applications. Let's look at a real world example that spotlights end user resistance and some of its solutions.

Qwest and Others: User Resistance and Involvement

In the mid-1980s, Shirley Wong was part of a team developing software for an automated 411 system at a large West Coast telephone company that is now part of Qwest Communications. After a great deal of work, the team unveiled the system to telephone operators and were greeted with universal hisses and boos. "The operators didn't want it," recalls Wong, who is now the webmaster at Optodyne, Inc. The company had wasted at least $1 million on the effort, and as a result of the fiasco, the project director and three managers were fired.

The problem: The operators who would be using the system were never consulted about their needs.

Times change and many IT project managers realize how crucial users are to a project's success. But how do you get users to take system requirements seriously? "This is probably the biggest problem at most companies," says Bill Berghel, a project manager at FedEx Corp. in Memphis.

To get users engaged, start by educating their bosses, says Naomi Karten, president of Karten Associates, a customer service consulting firm. Demonstrate how important user input is to the success of systems. Use real examples to show the

FIGURE 9.16
Obstacles to knowledge management systems. Note that end user resistance to knowledge sharing is the biggest obstacle.

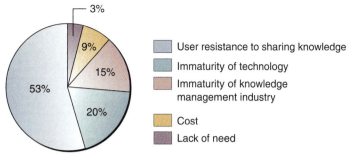

Source: Adapted from Barb Cole-Gomolski, "Users Loathe to Share Their Know-How," *Computerworld*, November 17, 1997, p. 6. Copyright 1997 by Computerworld, Inc. Framingham, MA. 01701. Reprinted from *Computerworld*.

benefits of doing things right and the consequences of doing things wrong. Once they get it, make sure they buy in on every project, she says. "Senior managers have to make sure that people below them make the time," says Peter Goundry, MIS manager at Aircast Inc., a medical device maker in Summit, New Jersey.

Don't just ask what users want; find out what they need. "Focus on what ails the user, not just what the user wants in a system," says Rob Norris, CIO at Pinocol Assurance in Denver. "Users don't always know what they want," says Sue McKay, CIO at Aircast. "Sometimes, you have to help them understand that what they think they want won't give them what they need." For example, end users may have heard about some cool system to produce management reports and may not realize the same information is already easily available through existing databases.

And don't make the mistake Wong's group made. Talk with enough people to really understand the business process you're trying to facilitate. "If you are creating a new sales system and you're only dealing with the VP of sales, you're doomed," Aircast's McKay says. Don't forget the sales representatives, sales assistants, and customers.

One of the best ways to get users interested and keep them engaged is to make them partners in application development. "We show a series of prototypes to the users and work toward what they do want," says Berghel of FedEx. And each iteration should take only a few days, to keep up the momentum, he says.

Change Management

Figure 9.17 illustrates some of the key dimensions of **change management,** and the level of difficulty and business impact involved. Notice some of the people, process, and technology factors involved in the implementation of business/IT strategies and applications, or other changes caused by introducing new information technologies into a company. Some of the technical factors listed, such as systems integrators, outsourcing, and hardware and software technology selection, will be discussed in more detail in the next few chapters. For example, systems integrators are consulting firms or other outside contractors who may be paid to assume the responsibility for developing and implementing a new e-business application, including designing and leading its change management activities. And notice that people factors have the highest level of difficulty and longest time to resolve of any dimension of change management.

Thus, people are a major focus of organizational change management. This includes activities such as developing innovative ways to measure, motivate, and reward performance. So is designing programs to recruit and train employees in the core competencies required in a changing workplace. Change management also

FIGURE 9.17

Some of the key dimensions of change management. Examples of the people, process, and technology factors involved in managing the implementation of IT-based changes to an organization.

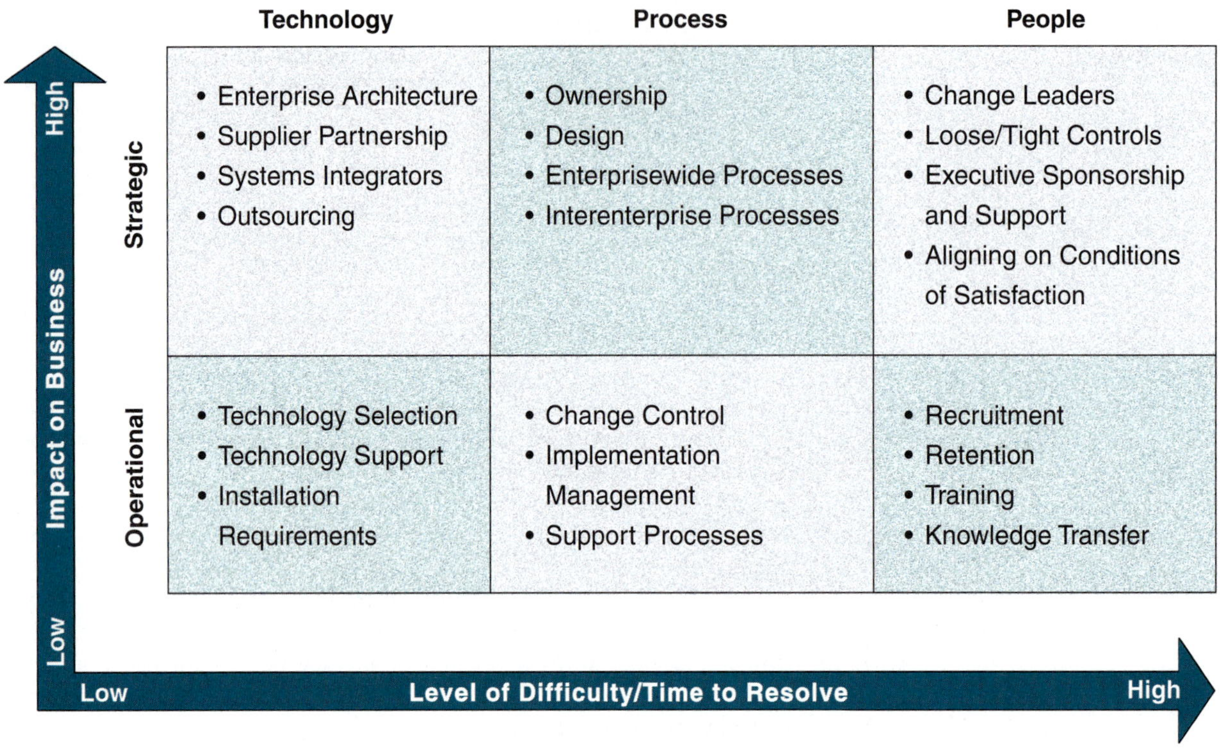

	Technology	Process	People
Strategic	• Enterprise Architecture • Supplier Partnership • Systems Integrators • Outsourcing	• Ownership • Design • Enterprisewide Processes • Interenterprise Processes	• Change Leaders • Loose/Tight Controls • Executive Sponsorship and Support • Aligning on Conditions of Satisfaction
Operational	• Technology Selection • Technology Support • Installation Requirements	• Change Control • Implementation Management • Support Processes	• Recruitment • Retention • Training • Knowledge Transfer

Impact on Business — High / Low

Level of Difficulty/Time to Resolve — Low / High

Source: Adapted from Grant Norris, James Hurley, Kenneth Hartley, John Dunleavy, and John Balls, *E-Business and ERP: Transforming the Enterprise*, p. 120. Copyright © 2000 by John Wiley & Sons, Inc. Reprinted by permission.

involves analyzing and defining all changes facing the organization, and developing programs to reduce the risks and costs and to maximize the benefits of change. For example, implementing a new e-business application such as customer relationship management might involve developing a *change action plan*, assigning selected managers as *change sponsors*, developing employee *change teams*, and encouraging open communications and feedback about organizational changes. Some key tactics change experts recommend include:

- Involve as many people as possible in e-business planning and application development.
- Make constant change an expected part of the culture.
- Tell everyone as much as possible about everything as often as possible, preferably in person.
- Make liberal use of financial incentives and recognition.
- Work within the company culture, not around it [22].

Duke Energy: A Guerrilla Approach to e-Business Change

Duke Energy initiated a guerrilla approach to e-business. A small band of advocates began to roam the utility, living in the business units, seeding pilot projects, assisting with implantations, coordinating resources, and spreading success stories. Eighteen months later in the summer of 2001, having launched more than a dozen successful Internet initiatives that saved the company $52 million last year alone, the "e-team" handed off the projects to the business units.

Duke's corporate policy committee, at the urging of CIO Cecil Smith, authorized senior vice president and chief e-business officer A. R. Mullinax to begin to harness the Internet. The goal was to weave e-business into the Duke fabric. "We didn't want to turn Duke into a dot-com," Mullinax recalls. "We wanted to find uses of the Internet that would advance our existing business."

Mullinax, then senior vice president for procurement, was given free reign to recruit a team and carry out the mission. He chose Ted Schultz from strategic planning; Steve Bush, finance and administration; Dave Davies, IT project management; Amy Baxter and Dennis Wood, procurement; Elizabeth Henry, customer focus; and Anne Narang, Web design. "Everybody brought strengths to the table," Mullinax says, "and the other ingredient was chemistry. We worked well as a team."

Team members literally moved into the businesses. If a unit had already launched an Internet initiative, a team member would advise on strategy and implementation. If a unit was new to the Web, a team member would spearhead an initiative.

The e-team had a budget, but its mantra was "Invest little, save big." It looked for business units that could use Internet tools in the most effective way, particularly those units where customers were dependent on information, and easy access to that information would add value to the relationship. "We could have taken on hundreds of initiatives, but we looked for the ones that would give us the most return compared with the level of effort it was going to take," Mullinex explains.

For example, Henry worked at Duke Solutions, which advises very large industrial, commercial, and institutional customers, such as Northfield, Illinois–based Kraft Foods, Inc., on energy management. "I was attached at the hip to Duke Solutions' e-business strategist Jeffrey Custer," she recalls. "It worked so well to be with them, hearing what their issues were every day." Custer, director of corporate development at Duke Solutions, agrees. "You have a fear when you hear that corporate is going to create a new group, but they were different," he says. "I was the lead; they were here to provide support and seed money. They kept the focus and kept me moving."

A Change Management Process

An eight-level process of change management for organizations is illustrated in Figure 9.18. This change management model is only one of many that could be applied to manage organizational changes caused by new business/IT strategies and applications and other changes in business processes. For example, this model suggests that the business vision created in the strategic planning phase should be communicated in a compelling *change story* to the people in the organization. Evaluating the readiness for changes within an organization and then developing change strategies and choosing and training change leaders and champions based on that assessment could be the next steps in the process.

These change leaders are the change agents that would then be able to lead change teams of employees and other business stakeholders in building a business case for changes in technology, business processes, job content, and organizational structures. They could also communicate the benefits of these changes and lead training programs on the details of new business applications. Of course, many change management models include methods for performance measurement and rewards to provide financial incentives for employees and stakeholders to cooperate with changes that may be required. In addition, fostering a new e-business culture within an organization by establishing communities of interest for employees and other business stakeholders via Internet, intranet, and extranet discussion groups could also be a valuable change management strategy. Such groups would encourage stakeholder involvement and buy-in for the changes brought about by implementing new e-business applications of information technology.

FIGURE 9.18

A process of change management. Examples of the activities involved in successfully managing organizational change caused by the implementation of new business processes.

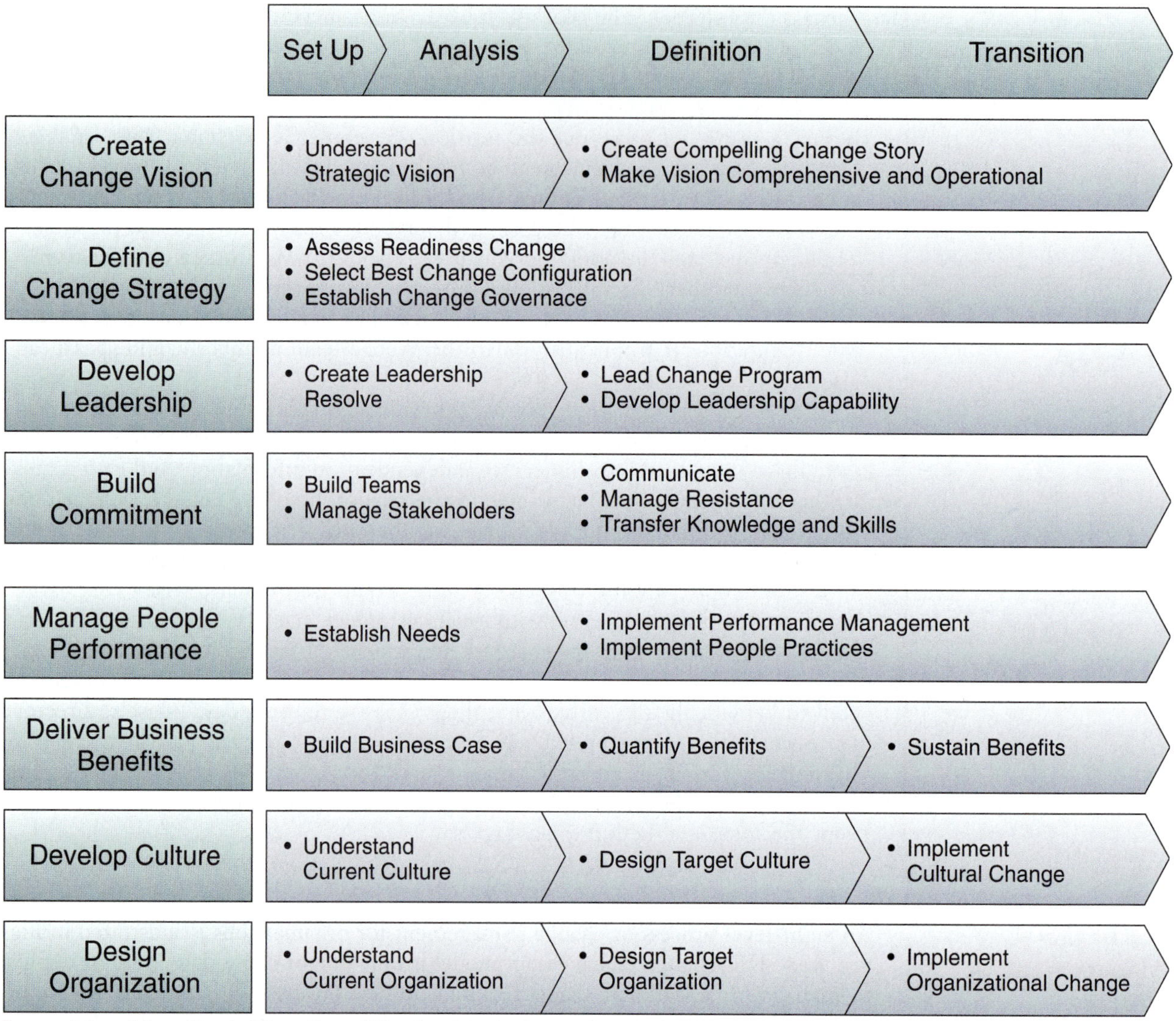

	Set Up	Analysis	Definition	Transition
Create Change Vision	• Understand Strategic Vision		• Create Compelling Change Story • Make Vision Comprehensive and Operational	
Define Change Strategy	• Assess Readiness Change • Select Best Change Configuration • Establish Change Governace			
Develop Leadership	• Create Leadership Resolve		• Lead Change Program • Develop Leadership Capability	
Build Commitment	• Build Teams • Manage Stakeholders		• Communicate • Manage Resistance • Transfer Knowledge and Skills	
Manage People Performance	• Establish Needs		• Implement Performance Management • Implement People Practices	
Deliver Business Benefits	• Build Business Case	• Quantify Benefits	• Sustain Benefits	
Develop Culture	• Understand Current Culture	• Design Target Culture	• Implement Cultural Change	
Design Organization	• Understand Current Organization	• Design Target Organization	• Implement Organizational Change	

Source: Adapted from Martin Diese, Conrad Nowikow, Patric King, and Amy Wright, *Executive's Guide to E-Business: From Tactics to Strategy,* p. 190. Copyright © 2000 by John Wiley & Sons, Inc. Reprinted by permission.

Avnet Marshall: Organizational Transformation

Figure 9.19 illustrates how a company like Avnet Marshall can transform itself via information technology. Notice how Avnet Marshall moved through several stages of organizational transformation as they implemented various e-business and e-commerce applications. Throughout this change process, they were driven by their commitment to the customer value focus of the Free.Perfect.Now business model that we introduced in Chapter 2.

First, Avnet Marshall implemented an automated shipping and receiving system (AS/RS) and a quality order booking, resell application (QOBRA) as they focused on achieving customer value through cost savings generated by the efficiencies of automating these core business processes. Then they focused on achieving interconnectivity internally and building a platform for enterprise collaboration and knowledge management by implementing their AvNet intranet and a data warehouse. The second step was building an Avnet Marshall website on the Internet to offer customers 24 × 7 online e-commerce transactions and customer support services. In addition, the company built a customized website for customers of its European partner SEI.

Next Avnet Marshall connected with their suppliers by building a Partnernet extranet and the Distribution Resource Planner (DRP) system, a supply chain management application that enables the company and its suppliers to help manage a customer's purchases and inventories. Avnet Marshall also implemented a customer relationship management and market intelligence system known as the Manufacturing Account Profile Planner (MAP), which integrates and uses all the customer information from other systems to better target its marketing activities and manage its customer contacts. As Figure 9.19 illustrates, Avnet Marshall's other innovative e-business applications help its customers (1) simulate online and design custom special-purpose microprocessor chips (Electronic Design Center), (2) design new products online with suppliers, as well as take online training classes using real-time streaming video and audio and online chat (NetSeminar), and (3) let customers themselves offer online seminars and push broadcasts to their employees and customers—the Education News and Entertainment Network (ENEN).

All of the new technologies and applications we have mentioned now enable Avnet Marshall to provide more value to its customers with fast delivery of high-quality customized products. And all of these initiatives created many new inter-enterprise business links between Avnet Marshall and its customers and business partners. These major technological and business changes required the organizational change phases noted in Figure 9.19. In a little over five years, Avnet Marshall had transformed itself into a premier example of an internetworked customer value focused business [12].

FIGURE 9.19   Avnet Marshall moved through several stages of organizational transformation as they implemented various e-business and e-commerce applications, driven by the customer value focus of their Free.Perfect.Now business model.

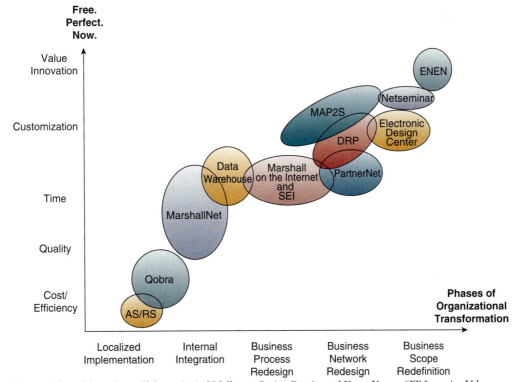

Source: Adapted from Omar El Sawy, Arvind Malhotra, Sanjay Gosain, and Kerry Young, "IT-Intensive Value Innovation in the Electronic Economy: Insights from Marshall Industries," *MIS Quarterly*, September 1999, p. 316. Reprinted by permission from the *MIS Quarterly*.

Summary

- **Organizational Planning.** Managing information technology requires planning for changes in business goals, processes, structures, and technologies. Planning is a vital organizational process that uses methods like the scenario approach and planning for competitive advantage to evaluate an organization's internal and external environments; forecast new developments; establish an organization's vision, mission, goals, and objectives; develop strategies, tactics, and policies to implement its goals; and articulate plans for the organization to act upon. A good planning process helps organizations learn about themselves and promotes organizational change and renewal.

- **Business/IT Planning.** Strategic business/IT planning involves aligning investment in information technology with a company's business vision and strategic goals such as reengineering business processes or gaining competitive advantages. It results in a strategic plan that outlines a company's business/IT strategies and technology architecture. The technology architecture is a conceptual blueprint that specifies a company's technology platform, data resources, applications architecture, and IT organization.

- **Implementing Business Change.** Implementation activities include managing the introduction and implementation of changes in business processes, organizational structures, job assignments, and work relationships resulting from business/IT strategies and applications such as e-business initiatives, reengineering projects, supply chain alliances, and the introduction of new technologies. Companies use change management tactics such as user involvement in business/IT planning and development to reduce end user resistance and maximize acceptance of business changes by all stakeholders.

Key Terms and Concepts

These are the key terms and concepts of this chapter. The page number of their first explanation is in parentheses.

1. Business model (316)
2. Business/IT planning (318)
   a. Application planning (321)
   b. Architecture planning (322)
   c. Strategic planning (312)
3. Change management (329)
4. End user involvement (326)
5. End user resistance (328)
6. Implementation (324)
7. Implementing business/IT change (326)
8. Information technology architecture (319)
9. Organizational planning (312)
10. Planning for competitive advantage (314)
11. Scenario approach to planning (313)
12. SWOT analysis (315)

Review Quiz

Match one of the key terms and concepts listed previously with one of the brief examples or definitions that follow. Try to find the best fit for answers that seem to fit more than one term or concept. Defend your choices.

_____ 1. An organization should create a shared business vision and mission, and plan how it will achieve its strategic goals and objectives.

_____ 2. Outlines a business vision, business/IT strategies, and technical architecture for a company.

_____ 3. A blueprint for information technology in a company that specifies a technology platform, applications architecture, data resources, and IT organization structure.

_____ 4. Evaluating strategic business/IT opportunities based on their risk/payoff potential for a company.

_____ 5. Planning teams simulate the role of information technology in various hypothetical business situations.

_____ 6. Evaluating IT proposals for new business application development projects.

_____ 7. Evaluating strategic business opportunities based on a company's capabilities and the competitive environment.

_____ 8. Accomplishing the strategies and applications developed during organizational planning.

_____ 9. Evaluating proposals for new business/IT applications within a company.

_____ 10. End users frequently resist the introduction of new technology.

_____ 11. End users should be part of planning for organizational change and business/IT project teams.

_____ 12. Companies should try to minimize the resistance and maximize the acceptance of major changes in business and information technology.

_____ 13. Expresses how a business can deliver value to customers and make money.

_____ 14. Identifying and developing e-business strategies for a company would be an example.

Discussion Questions

1. Planning is a useless endeavor, because developments in e-business and e-commerce, and in the political, economic, and societal environment are moving too quickly nowadays. Do you agree or disagree with this statement? Why?

2. "Planning and budgeting processes are notorious for their rigidity and irrelevance to management action." How can planning be made relevant to the challenges facing a business?

3. Refer to the Real World Case on the Rowe Cos. and Merrill Lynch in the chapter. How can a company identify, measure, and compare the business/IT innovation as well as the profitability of IT projects in their planning process?

4. What planning methods would you use to develop business/IT strategies and applications for your own business? Explain your choices.

5. What are several e-business and e-commerce strategies and applications that should be developed and implemented by many companies today? Explain your reasoning.

6. Refer to the Real World Case on Verizon Wireless, F.X. Coughlin, and A-dec in the chapter. What other change management methods could be used to improve the acceptance of business/IT changes like those implemented at each company?

7. How can a company use change management to minimize the resistance and maximize the acceptance of changes in business and technology? Give several examples.

8. "Many companies plan really well, yet few translate strategy into action." Do you think this statement is true? Why or why not?

9. Review the real world examples on end user resistance (Crane Engineering) and user involvement (Qwest and Others) in the chapter. What else would you recommend to encourage user acceptance in both cases? Explain your recommendations.

10. What major business changes beyond e-business and e-commerce do you think most companies should be planning for in the next ten years? Explain your choices.

Application Exercises

Complete the following exercises as individual or group projects that apply chapter concepts to real world business situations.

1. Business Insight: Analyzing Your Business Plan

Web
Having a machine assess your revolutionary idea may seem like a bad idea. But Business Resource Software (www.brs-inc.com) wants to assess and screen business plans with something it calls Business Insight, a program that analyzes your model online or off. "There are a number of advantages over the more conventional method of actually asking a so-called knowledgeable human," says Jerry Spencer, a co-founder of BRS. "Human consultants often have a different agenda. They want to get more business, so they tell you what you want to hear." Business Insight and its database, however, have the advantage of being brutally honest. "We think it's better to tell you your weaknesses rather than your strengths," Spencer says.

Business Insight, the analysis software, includes 500 questions, costs $800, and has been sold to half of the Fortune 500 companies, according to Spencer. The program, which uses economic principles drawn from the works of business gurus Michael Porter of Harvard and Philip Kotler of Northwestern University, also has been sold to thousands of smaller business. The free online service, called Business Insight Online, is a scaled-down version.

Here's how it works: Clients answer 30 questions about their business plan, on such topics as the potential market, the company's experience, and the perceived competition. BRS's database then goes to work, spitting out your free summary analysis. See Figure 9.20.

FIGURE 9.20

The Business Resource Software website provides a variety of business planning resources.

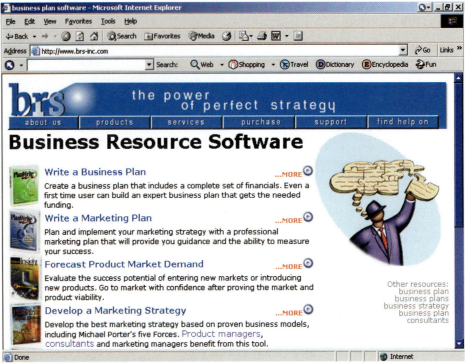

Source: Courtesy of Business Resource Software.

a. Visit the BRS website, scroll to their Web Resources, and click on the "Analyze your business strategy" link. Register and begin answering the questions asked by the Business Insight software about a business idea you have.

b. Evaluate the list of 30 questions you are asked. How well do they cover the key points of business planning? Explain your reasoning.

c. Evaluate the analysis results you are given. How effective is the Business Insight service as a planning tool? Explain your answer.

Source: Adapted from Andy Goldberg, "Does Your Model Go?" *Business 2.0*, August 8, 2000, p. 35.

2. BRS Inc.: Evaluating Business Plans

Web The BRS website at www.brs-inc.com provides links to many business planning Web resources, including how to prepare and evaluate business plans, and examples of many business plans submitted in the Moot Corp. Competition by MBA students from top U.S. and international business schools.

a. Visit the BRS website. Click on Business Planning Resources and link to sites providing information you can review on preparing and evaluating business plans. Then click on Sample Business Plans and review the world champion and runner-up winning business plans, and any others you prefer.

b. How well do these plans meet the goal of presenting an outstanding business case for a business idea? Explain your answer.

c. How could you improve any of the business ideas presented in the business plans you reviewed, or the business plans themselves? Give several examples to illustrate how you might be able to do so.

3. Developing an EDI System for Beta Business Products

SS Beta Business Products (BBP) sells business supplies directly to large corporations and wholesales its products to large business supply retailers. BBP has asked you to investigate the costs and benefits of developing an electronic data interchange system to connect with its customers.

You find that the cost of hardware and software to support this system would be approximately $540,000 the first year, with maintenance costs of $40,000 per year thereafter. Additional training and personnel costs in the IS department are estimated to be $200,000 the first year and $150,000 each year thereafter.

Benefits from the system will come from a reduction in the clerical time required to process orders and from improved market share. Since the impact on market share is difficult to quantify, you must base your quantitative analysis only on the savings in clerical time. BBP processes 275,000 orders per year. The processing time that could be saved by the EDI system is 20 minutes per order and the average cost of clerical labor is $12 including benefits. Turnover in clerical workers is currently running 40 percent per year. It is expected that the new system would process 20 percent of all orders the first year, 40 percent the second year, and 50 percent in the third and succeeding years.

a. Based on the data described above develop a spreadsheet comparing the costs and benefits of the EDI system over the first 5 years of operation. Use a column for each year and develop total cost and benefit estimates and net benefit (benefits minus costs) for each year based on the information above. Then compute an internal rate of return for this project.

b. Would you expect to see substantial resistance within the organization to this new system? Why or why not? Are there things the organization could do to reduce any resistance to the new system? Prepare a set of power point slides or similar presentation materials summarizing issues of resistance to the new system and measures that could be used to overcome this resistance.

4. Managing Salary Adjustments

DB You are director of IT services at a company that gives departments a great deal of flexibility in allocating merit raise funds. Departments are given a fixed pot of funds for merit raises and allowed to allocate them as they see fit. This year your department has received $55,000 to be distributed among your department's 25 employees. You, in consultation with your staff, have developed a process for allocating merit that contains three components.

1. Any employee completing a degree or a professional certificate during the year receives a $1,800 raise for that accomplishment.

2. 60% of the remaining merit funds are dispersed to employees receiving a good or excellent rating on their departmental annual evaluation. A fixed dollar amount is to be paid for good performance and those with an excellent performance will receive twice that amount.

3. The remaining merit funds, after step 2, are paid out by allocating a fixed dollar amount to each employee who received a peer evaluation of excellent.

An employee database table like the sample shown below, but including all 25 records is available to you from the website for this textbook. The textbook website is www.mhhe.com/business/mis/obrien/obrien5e/index.html. Click on downloads under the student resources section of that page.

a. Download the full employee table containing the records for all 25 of your employees from the website for this textbook. You may either perform a set of queries to determine the allocation of raises based on the criteria above, or you may copy the data to a spreadsheet and perform the manipulations to determine the amount of the various merit bonus components that will appropriately allocate the available pot of $55,000. Be sure to fully document the process you use—show all queries if you do your computations in the database—show appropriate intermediate result columns if you do your calculations in a spreadsheet.

b. Once you have determined the procedures needed to allocate the merit funds appropriately, write an updated query that will actually change each person's salary to reflect the merit raise they are to receive.

Employee_name	Employee_id	Salary	Performance_Eval	Team_Eval	Cert_Degree_Completed
Ann Adams	1234	$39,500.00	G	E	No
Bob Bates	2345	$43,250.00	A	G	No
Carl Combs	3456	$38,400.00	E	G	No
Dawn Davis	4567	$52,000.00	G	E	Yes
Ellen Eads	5678	$43,250.00	A	A	No

REAL WORLD CASE 3

PeopleFirst, Cessna, Allstate, and Sprint: Challenges of Implementing CRM Systems

You've been warned: Putting in a decent customer relationship management (CRM) system is as perilous as installing enterprise resource planning (ERP) systems used to be. CRM projects fail more often than not, analysts say. The software is hard to install. It forces a lot of change, quickly, on business units. And even when companies manage to install and link applications that hold client information, they often don't serve customers any better, reports Gartner Inc. Mercer Management Consulting calls CRM a "money pit."

But some companies have gotten CRM to work well—on the second or third try. Some of the disappointment can be chalked up to classic bad habits in IT, such as not listening—sometimes not even talking—to end users about what they want. Or the CRM team may try to do too much at once, which almost guarantees delays and cost overruns.

PeopleFirst Finance LLC (www.peoplefirst.com), an online car loan company in San Diego, dived into CRM in June 2000, when it tried to install a complete CRM suite. It was clear about three months into the installation that things weren't going well, says Sharon Spooler, vice president of business intelligence at PeopleFirst. For example, there was no easy, automated way to manage bouncebacks from e-mail sales pitches that didn't reach intended recipients, she says. Also the software couldn't properly track multiple versions of e-mail sales letters. The result: PeopleFirst couldn't get an accurate view of which campaigns worked.

"We tried problem-solving with the vendor. We tried a lot of different things to make it work. Every time you'd think you had a problem solved, another one would pop up," Spooler says. "It was like a game of whack-a-mole." Spooler declined to name the vendor, citing a deal struck when PeopleFirst killed the project in March 2001.

Now PeopleFirst outsources many problematic CRM tasks. Digital Impact Inc. handles the administrative part of e-mail sales efforts, such as making sure messages look good in HTML and rich text, managing bouncebacks, and tracking how many messages were undeliverable. PeopleFirst, meanwhile, handles the content side of campaigns. It keeps databases on things such as which letters produce which results and which customers respond to which pitches.

Cessna Aircraft Co. (www.cessna.com) had a couple of unsuccessful rollouts of CRM systems before successfully going live recently with StayinFront Inc.'s Visual Elk sales force automation product and Panorama decision-support tool. Cessna learned some "bitter lessons" during its first two CRM attempts, in 1995 and 1996, says Dave Turner, manager of network systems at the airplane maker. Cessna rolled out the first phase of its CRM system but had to delay the next stage until a revision of the vendor's application shipped. It never did, he says, declining to name the supplier. Cessna killed the project with that vendor.

Dennis DeGregor, vice president of CRM at Allstate Insurance Co. (www.allstate.com), has avoided the CRM full-suite option. Such packages are less expensive to maintain, he says, but suites can lack key pieces, which means buying a separate package to add on and integrate anyway.

In late 2000 Allstate requested proposals from the major suite vendors. "None of them came remotely close to having the functionality that matched our CRM vision," he says. Siebel Systems, for example, doesn't have a sales campaign management module, he says, and SAP AG doesn't offer predictive modeling. Allstate, therefore, went the best-of-breed route. It uses at least six packages from five vendors, including analytics and campaign tools from Xchange Inc. and lead-management software from MarketSoft Corp. Allstate's internal IT staff is responsible for integration.

One key to CRM, say those who have gotten it right, is having a facilitator between IT and marketing, customer service, or whatever business unit is supporting the project. This person typically doesn't come from IT but has a good grasp of technology. Ideally, he should report to the CEO or some other manager outside the groups he's trying to unite. Spooler and DeGregor play that role. So does Stephen Nehring, marketing integration manager at Sprint Corp. (www.sprint.com).

The telecommunications provider built a top-to-bottom CRM system in-house. When a request comes from marketing to capture more data about customers, Nehring explains to IT why it makes sense to free up storage or servers. Nehring also coaxes marketing to examine whether it really needs all the data it wants, citing how expensive it is to store and access those data quickly. All sides go to all CRM meetings. "By having all those individuals in the same room, we all put in our input without months of e-mail back and forth" before a decision is made, he says. "We won't meet unless everyone can be there. There's too much at risk."

Case Study Questions

1. What are several major reasons for the high failure rate in implementing CRM systems?

2. What could PeopleFirst and Cessna have done to avoid the failures in their first tries at implementing CRM systems? Defend your proposals.

3. How have Allstate and Sprint Corp. helped to ensure their successful CRM implementations? What are several other things companies could do to help implement CRM systems? Explain your suggestions.

Source: Adapted from Kim Nash and Marc Songini, "Try, Try Again," *Computerworld*, February 18, 2002, pp. 30–31. Reprinted with permission from *Computerworld*.

REAL WORLD CASE 4

Corning Inc.: Business/IT Planning Strategies in Challenging Times

To be sure that his IT department would be ready for an economic downturn, Richard J. Fishburn, vice president and CIO at Corning, New York–based glass products manufacturer Corning Inc. (www.corning.com), started planning back when the economy was on an upswing. "You plan for success, but you also take into account what happens if conditions change," he says. That's certainly been the case at Corning, that had $7 billion in sales in 2000, as the "telecommunications depression" cut into the company's fiber-optic product business, which accounts for 70 percent of its sales.

Fishburn's strategy to cope? Create "rings of defense" that include core IT employees on the inside ring, contract service providers at the middle ring, and contract employees on the outermost ring. With 25 percent of IT workers on contract and another 25 percent of work performed by shared-services contractors, Fishburn estimates that he has saved as many jobs as he has had to reduce while the economy continues to falter.

When it comes to defending IT initiatives, Fishburn, 56, says he plans ahead by aligning projects with business objectives from the start. "We want IT people to be talking with the business team about what we are doing to increase the value of the business" and focus on projects that either make positive change in the business or help take costs out or improve asset performance, he explains. And getting management buy-in is critical. "We're not talking about an IT project," Fishburn says. "We force the dialog back to where you have a set of joint objectives with the business team." "Dick has done a phenomenal job of getting the IT management structure to look at what the business requirements are," says Suzee Woods, IT director of application services.

This strategic thinking pays off in budgeting meetings, Fishburn says. "When you go through this short decision-making process during a downturn, you're not discussing the value of the project to the organization," he says. "They have already internalized why it's important." Woods has seen that strategy bear fruit. "We're implementing a major project in the financial area, and that project has stayed on the radar screen and continues to have support . . . because we've been able to put it in terms of value to the corporation," she says.

Fishburn acknowledges that getting technical people to discuss business rather than technology issues can be a challenge. "There is an adjustment period people go through," he says. But ultimately, when staffers see how presenting business benefits increases the probability of their programs being successful, "you build the trust," Fishburn says.

For example, in the late 1990s, manufacturing operations at Corning Inc.'s display technologies division were aligned with customers on a regional level—the plant in Japan served Japanese customers; the U.S. plant served U.S. customers. But when customers wanted more computer displays than ever, the business model wasn't scaling. "As we looked at the plan, we learned that our existing model just wasn't cutting it," says Fishburn.

In 1999, Corning set about improving supply chain efficiency, but technology was the last aspect discussed. In fact, when brainstorming better models, Corning first asks managers to "listen to what their operational people are saying," says Fishburn. Only then are opportunities defined, followed by business benefits and finally mechanisms to determine whether goals were met.

Corning was a pioneer in putting business processes first in evaluating a business/IT project, rather than following the classic enterprise resource planning (ERP) philosophy of making business fit the technology. Only then was technology assigned to solve the problem in this case: A supply chain module was added to Corning's PeopleSoft Inc. ERP software.

The project has stayed on schedule and under budget, and is paying for itself, even though the rollout won't be completed until next year, says Fishburn. "It used to take us five days to do the planning for tomorrow's production. Now we can do it in an hour," he says. Improved production planning efficiency meant Corning didn't have to build excess capacity. Also, fewer orders have to be rushed to reach customers on time.

Fishburn says he knew he had business sponsorship for the project from the beginning. In senior management meetings, for example, one former critic "would very clearly articulate the fact that this was the premier project that exists for this division," he says. "As the CIO, your greatest success is to sit in the background and let your operating peers talk about their projects."

Case Study Questions

1. Do you agree with how CIO Richard Fishburn has defended Corning's IT department from an economic downturn? Why or why not?

2. Why is aligning IT projects with business objectives a good business/IT strategy in challenging economic times? And in good times?

3. Does Corning's business/IT planning process for its new supply chain system prove the value of aligning IT with business goals? Why or why not?

Source: Adapted from Robert Mitchell, "The Strategists," *Computerworld*, January 1, 2002, p. 37; and Mathew Schwartz, "ERP Plan Cuts Costs at Factories," Premier 100 Best in Class, Supplement to *Computerworld*, March 11, 2002, p. 19. Reprinted with permission from *Computerworld*.

Cincinnati Bell: Change Management Challenges of Business Convergence

As president and chief operating officer of Cincinnati Bell, Jack Cassidy generates a steady stream of revenue from his 127-year-old local phone business. Even when facing rivals, the unit of Broadwing Inc. (www.broadwing.com) wins: It captured a whopping 70 percent of the Cincinnati area's consumer long-distance business just 18 months after entering the market, and the company's recent foray into the wireless arena was similarly auspicious.

So why did Cassidy announce an overhaul of Cincinnati Bell (www.cincinnatibell.com) in early 2001? He was in pursuit of nothing less than the Holy Grail of the telecom industry: He wanted to "bundle all his services onto a single bill and be the sole provider of telecom services for his customers." That required a complete reorganization of the business. Many other telecom companies had tried to bundle and failed. Still, Cincinnati Bell succeeded—and has been reaping the benefits by not only simplifying customers' lives and making them happier but also creating opportunities to sell them more services through package deals tailored to their situations.

A detailed study convinced Cassidy that reorganizing would both increase revenue and cut expenses, so he huddled with all his managers for three days to work through a plan. In a process that Cincinnati Bell calls convergence—more commonly known as "synchronization"—the company reorganized itself by starting with the needs of particular groups of customers and then working backward to see what the company should look like. Cassidy disbanded his product and service units and established divisions serving businesses and residential customers.

That caused plenty of tension. Heads of business units were stripped of their "general manager" and "resident manager" titles, and some dropped as many as three levels in terms of titles, so Cassidy had to explain that many of them were, in fact, gaining responsibility. For example, a business unit head who was reassigned to running a key function of the new customer business now has much more revenue responsibility.

Ann Crable, head of call-center operations, needed to prepare her customer service reps to handle phone calls about any or all services, rather than have to hand phone calls back and forth across corporate boundaries. If convergence was to provide all the projected revenue growth, Crable also needed to train reps to sell big-ticket items such as wireless and high-speed Internet access to customers who called with a question or problem. Before the push to converge, the reps had been peddling add-on services such as voice mail and call waiting, but they had little experience in "cross-selling" to customers.

Even together, the change had to occur in an environment where lots of Cincinnati Bell's employees feared they would lose their jobs—and where some did. Among other changes, the company reduced its number of call centers to 11 from 16. The company brought in outside experts in the field of "change acceleration" to help people through the process. "You can't have people drink from a firehose," Cassidy says.

"As much as I'd like to think that everybody could understand very quickly why we had to merge all these businesses together, nobody could."

Change didn't happen quickly. It has taken some time to move everyone's thinking from a "product point of view" to talking in terms of "one company serving the customer," says Don Daniels, vice president of consumer marketing. But change did happen. "We're finally starting to talk about things in the same way," Daniels says. Not only did the call-center reps get retrained, but even linemen and repairmen—everyone but the operators who dispense directory listings—pitch products whenever they come into contact with customers.

Chip Burke, head of IT in the new organization, drew the task of making sure the company's computer systems could adapt to and keep up with this newly unified approach to customers. He said there was no system available in the market that would handle this problem. And he estimated that if there were such a system, it would probably cost between $50 million and $100 million. "We were basically told to make it happen with the resources that we had already," Burke said.

Before convergence, each business unit had its own computer system, its own website, its own IT staff, and its own call center. Many parts of the business used different technology and incompatible software. Without the money to build a system that would make all the company's systems speak the same language, Burke used what Cassidy calls "spit and baling wire."

Burke developed an automated process to pull information from all the different databases, translate it into a common form, and build an aggregate picture of each customer—what he was currently buying and what he might be willing to buy. For the smaller base of business customers, Burke had the same process done manually. To put all changes on a single bill, Burke had each of the existing billing systems send data to a central repository that now churns out all bills. It wasn't pretty, but it worked. And in the process, Burke says, the company's IT budget actually declined.

Case Study Questions

1. Was the reorganization of Cincinnati Bell as revealed in this case a good business strategy? Why or why not?

2. Were the change management methods revealed in this case adequate for the changes being made? Why or why not?

3. What further changes should be made in IT systems to better support Cincinnati Bell's business convergence? Defend your proposals.

Source: Adapted from Joanne Kelley, "Cincinnati Bell Wether," *Context*, June/July 2002, pp. 29–31.

CHAPTER 10

APPLICATIONS IN BUSINESS AND MANAGEMENT

DEVELOPING BUSINESS/IT SOLUTIONS

Chapter Highlights

Learning Objectives

After reading and studying this chapter, you should be able to:

1. Use the systems development process outlined in this chapter, and the model of IS components from Chapter 1 as problem-solving frameworks to help you propose information systems solutions to simple business problems.

2. Describe and give examples to illustrate how you might use each of the steps of the information systems development cycle to develop and implement a business information system.

3. Explain how prototyping improves the process of systems development for end users and IS specialists.

4. Identify the activities involved in the implementation of new information systems.

5. Describe several evaluation factors that should be considered in evaluating the acquisition of hardware, software, and IS services.

<table>
<tr><td>

SECTION I

</td><td>

Developing Business Systems

</td></tr>
</table>

IS Development

Suppose the chief executive of the company where you work asks you to find a Web-enabled way to get information to and from the salespeople in your company. How would you start? What would you do? Would you just plunge ahead and hope you could come up with a reasonable solution? How would you know whether your solution was a good one for your company? Do you think there might be a systematic way to help you develop a good solution to the CEO's request? There is. It's a problem-solving process called *the systems approach*.

When the systems approach to problem solving is applied to the development of information system solutions to business problems, it is called *information systems development or application development*. This section will show you how the systems approach can be used to develop e-business systems and applications that meet the business needs of a company and its employees and stakeholders.

Analyzing Fidelity Investments and Others

Read the Real World Case on Fidelity Investments and Others on the next page. We can learn a lot about the challenges of good Web systems design for e-commerce websites. See Figure 10.1.

Fidelity Investments places a major emphasis on website usability design, since over 75 percent of their customer interactions come from the Fidlity.com website. That's why they depend on a usability lab to test user reactions before implementing new website features that can result in increased business to Fidelity. Other practices

FIGURE 10.1

Thomas Tullis is senior VP at Fidelity Investments' Center for Applied Technology and directs their website usability lab.

Source: Jason Grow.

Fidelity Investments and Others: Evaluating Usability in Website Design

Now more than ever, Fidelity Investments (www. fidelity.com) depends on its website with 75 percent of the company's customer interactions coming via Fidelity.com. The site has earned kudos for usability from J.D. Power Associates and Gomez Inc., but such recognition doesn't happen by accident. Thomas Tullis, senior vice president of Fidelity's Center for Applied Technology, explains how a usability "lab" keeps Fidelity's development team focused on the user experience. The lab is actually two identical suites. There's a room in each where the user sits with the computer, a room next to it with video equipment running behind a one-way mirror, and a bigger observation room on the other side for everyone involved with the project being tested.

Says Tullis: "We give the user a thorough briefing about what's going to happen. We stress this is not a test of them, but a test of the website. We give them a set of realistic tasks—say to find the highest price for XYZ stock over the past year—and encourage them to think aloud as they navigate. For example, before they click on a link, they might say out loud what they expect to find there. That way we have an idea of how they think the site should be organized. One useful measure is what we call 'lostness'—how many clicks the user makes beyond the minimum needed.

"I've seen developers get religion after just one of these sessions. If you've been working for months on developing some site, there's no way you can see it objectively. The lab gives you a pair of fresh eyes.

"From the beginning, we found ways to improve our website. Early on, it was organized more around how Fidelity was set up internally, while the users wanted a clear delineation between products and services. More recently, we brought people into the lab to test prototypes of our online brokerage application, to increase the percentage of prospects who finish filling it out. Among other things, we learned we needed to make clearer up front what information applicants would need to have handy. Within a month, completed applications rose by 4 percentage points. That's a lot of business for us."

Ditching stock art and choosing more appropriate images is a sure way to enliven a site. "You can put human faces on your site, but it's so much more impressive if you have real employees, real customers," says Marie Tahir, director of user experience at Intuit Inc. (www.intuit.com). A.G. Edwards & Sons Inc., (www.agedwards.com) for example, dramatically sharpened the look of its client home page by enabling its financial consultants to upload pictures of themselves, creating a more personalized experience. For transactional sites, show what's for sale. "If you have a real product to sell, show the product," says Tahir. "It makes people feel good and grounded and in the right place when they see the product they're looking for."

Want to quickly freshen up a site? Start with the writing. It's a surefire way to improve usability, which in itself is a great goal. "Rather than just putting more lipstick on the pig, I always urge people doing redesigns to invest in real good writing and editing skills," says Tahir. "People think design, and they separate from content."

Fidelity Investments has a "jargon clip" on a video that it uses for training, says Eleri Dixon, vice president for usability at Fidelity E-Business. In it, a real customer is asked whether she understands the words on the site. Dixon says the customer replies, "Well, if you use all buzzwords, I understand what you're saying but they're not my words." Customers' words are now used whenever possible, she says.

At A.G. Edwards, wording on the navigation bar was made more intuitive, and the client home page was reorganized to suit the needs of visitors, says Betsy Lueg, site manager. Another way to quickly freshen up a site, especially a corporate site, is to consolidate. "Group all the company information in one place, rather than scattering it," says Tahir. "People's minds try to group things, and if they don't see it in the place where they think it should be, then they'll think it's not there."

The natural tendency when freshening a site is to give users more—more features, more options—but by simplifying an interface and making it more visually compelling. Priceline.com (www.priceline.com) saw a 50 percent increase in the number of visitors to its ticket site. On the old Priceline.com home page, customers had to click a specific button to order a plane ticket, rent a car, or make hotel reservation. A new feature, packaged prominently in a gold box on the home page, asks customers where they are going and when. This change paid off. Now 50 percent more people start down the path to buying a ticket, and 5 to 10 percent of them actually finish the process. The old format is still available, but only 1 percent of people who use it buy a ticket. In this case, simplicity rules. "Anytime you can take a thought out of the process for the user, it's always a good thing," says Brian Harniman, vice president of marketing at Priceline.com.

Case Study Questions

1. Is a usability lab like Fidelity's necessary, or are there other alternatives for testing usability in website design? Which is the better approach? Why?

2. Evaluate the suggestions for good website design shared by the companies in this case. Which are the most important for you? Explain your choices.

3. Visit the websites of Fidelity, Intuit, A.G. Edwards, and Priceline. How would you rank them in order of the best website design? Explain your rankings.

Source: Adapted from Mathew Schwarts, "Time for a Makeover!" *Computerworld*, August 19, 2002, pp. 38–39; and Bob Tedeschi, "How Fidelity Gets That Usability Religion," *Business 2.0*, October 2002, p. 54. Reprinted with permission from *Computerworld*.

of good website design that brought success to companies like Intuit, A.G. Edwards, and Priceline are described in the case. Examples include more realistic product images, customer-style writing, and consolidating and simplifying Web page content.

The Systems Approach

The systems approach to problem solving uses a systems orientation to define problems and opportunities and develop solutions. Studying a problem and formulating a solution involves the following interrelated activities:

1. Recognize and define a problem or opportunity using *systems thinking*.
2. Develop and evaluate alternative system solutions.
3. Select the system solution that best meets your requirements.
4. Design the selected system solution.
5. Implement and evaluate the success of the designed system.

Systems Thinking

Using **systems thinking** to understand a problem or opportunity is one of the most important aspects of the systems approach. Management consultant and author Peter Senge calls systems thinking *the fifth discipline*. Senge argues that mastering systems thinking (along with the disciplines of personal mastery, mental models, shared vision, and team learning) is vital to personal fulfillment and business success in a world of constant change. The essence of the discipline of systems thinking is "seeing the forest *and* the trees" in any situation by:

- Seeing *interrelationships* among *systems* rather than linear cause-and-effect chains whenever events occur.
- Seeing *processes* of change among *systems* rather than discrete "snapshots" of change, whenever changes occur [32].

One way of practicing systems thinking is to try to find systems, subsystems, and components of systems in any situation you are studying. This is also known as using a *systems context*, or having a *systemic view* of a situation. For example, the business organization or business process in which a problem or opportunity arises could be viewed as a system of input, processing, output, feedback, and control components. Then to understand a problem and solve it, you would determine if these basic systems functions are being properly performed. See Figure 10.2.

Example The sales process of a business can be viewed as a system. You could then ask: Is poor sales performance (output) caused by inadequate selling effort (input), out-of-date sales procedures (processing), incorrect sales information (feedback), or inadequate sales management (control)? Figure 10.2 illustrates this concept.

FIGURE 10.2

An example of systems thinking. You can better understand a sales problem or opportunity by identifying and evaluating the components of a sales system.

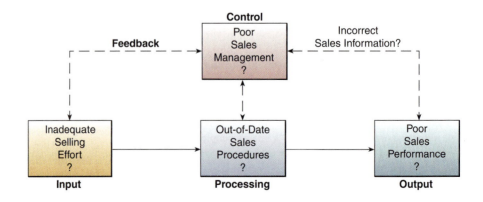

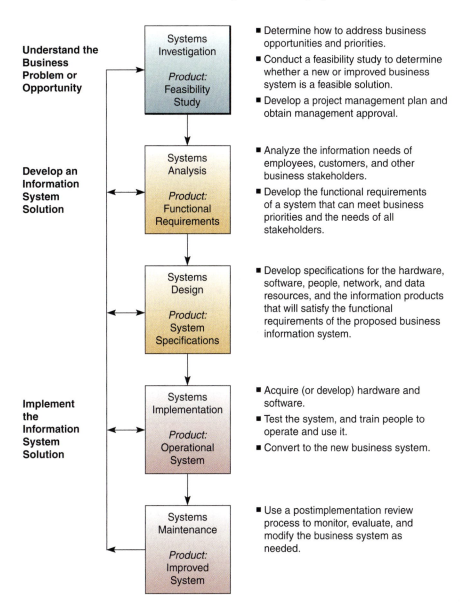

FIGURE 10.3

The traditional information systems development cycle. Note how the five steps of the cycle are based on the stages of the systems approach. Also note the products that result from each step in the cycle, and that you can recycle back to any previous step if more work is needed.

Understand the Business Problem or Opportunity

Systems Investigation

Product: Feasibility Study

- Determine how to address business opportunities and priorities.
- Conduct a feasibility study to determine whether a new or improved business system is a feasible solution.
- Develop a project management plan and obtain management approval.

Develop an Information System Solution

Systems Analysis

Product: Functional Requirements

- Analyze the information needs of employees, customers, and other business stakeholders.
- Develop the functional requirements of a system that can meet business priorities and the needs of all stakeholders.

Systems Design

Product: System Specifications

- Develop specifications for the hardware, software, people, network, and data resources, and the information products that will satisfy the functional requirements of the proposed business information system.

Implement the Information System Solution

Systems Implementation

Product: Operational System

- Acquire (or develop) hardware and software.
- Test the system, and train people to operate and use it.
- Convert to the new business system.

Systems Maintenance

Product: Improved System

- Use a postimplementation review process to monitor, evaluate, and modify the business system as needed.

The Systems Development Cycle

Using the systems approach to develop information system solutions can be viewed as a multistep process called the **information systems development cycle,** also known as the *systems development life cycle* (SDLC). Figure 10.3 illustrates what goes on in each stage of this process, which includes the steps of (1) investigation, (2) analysis, (3) design, (4) implementation, and (5) maintenance.

You should realize, however, that all of the activities involved are highly related and interdependent. Therefore, in actual practice, several developmental activities can occur at the same time, so different parts of a development project can be at different stages of the development cycle. In addition, you and IS specialists may recycle back at any time to repeat previous activities in order to modify and improve a system you are developing.

Prototyping

The systems development process frequently takes the form of, or includes, a *pro-totyping* approach. **Prototyping** is the rapid development and testing of working models, or **prototypes,** of new applications in an interactive, iterative process that

FIGURE 10.4

Application development using prototyping. Note how prototyping combines the steps of the systems development cycle and changes the traditional roles of IS specialists and end users.

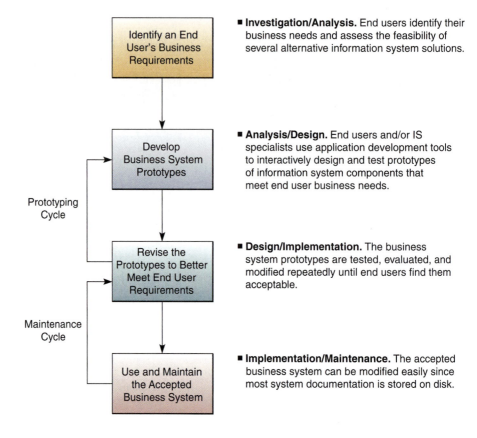

Identify an End User's Business Requirements

■ **Investigation/Analysis.** End users identify their business needs and assess the feasibility of several alternative information system solutions.

Develop Business System Prototypes

Prototyping Cycle

■ **Analysis/Design.** End users and/or IS specialists use application development tools to interactively design and test prototypes of information system components that meet end user business needs.

Revise the Prototypes to Better Meet End User Requirements

■ **Design/Implementation.** The business system prototypes are tested, evaluated, and modified repeatedly until end users find them acceptable.

Maintenance Cycle

Use and Maintain the Accepted Business System

■ **Implementation/Maintenance.** The accepted business system can be modified easily since most system documentation is stored on disk.

can be used by both IS specialists and business professionals. Prototyping makes the development process faster and easier, especially for projects where end user requirements are hard to define. Thus, prototyping is sometimes called *rapid application design* (RAD). Prototyping has also opened up the application development process to end users because it simplifies and accelerates systems design. Thus prototyping has enlarged the role of end users and changed the methods of IS specialists in systems development. See Figure 10.4.

The Prototyping Process

Prototyping can be used for both large and small applications. Typically, large business systems still require using a traditional systems development approach, but parts of such systems can frequently be prototyped. A prototype of a business application needed by an end user is developed quickly using a variety of application development software tools. The prototype system is then repeatedly refined until it is acceptable.

As Figure 10.4 illustrates, prototyping is an iterative, interactive process that combines steps of the traditional systems development cycle. End users with sufficient experience with application development tools can do prototyping themselves. Alternatively, you could work with an IS specialist to develop a prototype system in a series of interactive sessions. For example, you could develop, test, and refine prototypes of management reports, data entry screens, or output displays.

Usually, a prototype is modified several times before end users find it acceptable. Any program modules that are not generated by application development software can then be coded by programmers using conventional programming languages. The final version of the application system is then turned over to its end users for operational use. Figure 10.5 outlines a typical prototyping-based systems development process for a business application.

FIGURE 10.5

An example of a typical prototyping-based systems development process for a business application.

Example of Prototyping Development
● **Team.** A few end users and IS developers form a team to develop a business application.
● **Schematic.** The initial prototype schematic design is developed.
● **Prototype.** The schematic is converted into a simple point-and-click prototype using prototyping tools.
● **Presentation.** A few screens and routine linkages are presented to users.
● **Feedback.** After the team gets feedback from users, the prototype is reiterated.
● **Reiteration.** Further presentations and reiterations are made.
● **Consultation.** Consultations are held with IT consultants to identify potential improvements and conformance to existing standards.
● **Completion.** The prototype is converted into a finished application.
● **Acceptance.** Users review and sign off on their acceptance of the new business system.
● **Installation.** The new business software is installed on network servers.

Frito-Lay Inc.: Failure and Success in Prototyping

Frito-Lay created national sales teams to focus on top customers such as supermarket chains. But the teams, used to working regionally, found nationwide collaboration difficult. Although Frito-Lay had rich stores of market research and other pertinent customer information housed in databases at its headquarters, there was no easy way for team members to find what they needed. Frustration rose, performance suffered, and sales team turnover reached 25 percent.

So Mike Marino, Frito-Lay's vice president for category and customer development engaged Dallas-based Navigator Systems to help. Navigator consultants envisioned a Web-based enterprise knowledge portal that would combine tools for knowledge management and collaboration, enabling the team to better serve the customer while helping reduce frustration and turnover.

A portal development project team was formed to work with the national supermarket sales team because it had the most centralized and demanding customers. "We knew if we could deliver there, we could satisfy any customer," Marino says. The supermarket sales team told the project team what kind of knowledge they needed. The request ranged from simple information, such as why Frito-Lay merchandises Lays and Ruffles products in one part of a store and Doritos in another, to more complex research on what motivates shoppers as they move through a store.

A few months later, the project team presented a working prototype they had developed to a group of beta users from the supermarket sales team only to find that in the quest for speed, a classic and crippling error had been made. Because the project team had not involved the Frito-Lay team in the design of the prototype, the portal they had built wasn't specific enough for the supermarket sales team.

"Conceptually, it was a great idea," says Frito-Lay sales team leader Joe Ackerman. "But when folks are not on the front line, their view of what is valuable is different from those running 100 miles an hour in the field." The project team needed to backtrack and plug in the missing features, but it also had to win back the sales force, who now suspected that even a revised tool would be a waste of time.

The project team then spent the next four months working with salespeople to evolve the prototype into a system they would embrace. For example, a call-reporting feature was added. "So many people want to know what happened on a sales call, the account manager involved can be on the phone for days," Ackerman explains. "Now, we're able to post that to a website. It frees up the account manager to document the call once and move on."

Other changes included enabling users to analyze and manipulate data rather than just viewing it, and developing reports tailored to customers' needs. "The original reports were very general," Ackerman says, so users would have had to spend lots of time reformatting them for customer presentations. Ackerman was also enlisted for the official rollout of the portal.

Now Ackerman says that better collaboration with the portal has helped to significantly reduce turnover, while improved access to knowledge-base data has enabled account managers to present themselves to customers as consultants with important data to share.

Starting the Systems Development Process

Do we have business opportunities? What are our business priorities? How can information technologies provide information system solutions that address our business priorities? These are the questions that have to be answered in the **systems investigation stage**—the first step in the systems development process. This stage may involve consideration of proposals generated by a business/IT planning process, which we discussed in Chapter 9. The investigation stage also includes the preliminary study of proposed information system solutions to meet a company's business priorities and opportunities.

Feasibility Studies

Because the process of development can be costly, the systems investigation stage may require a preliminary study called a **feasibility study.** A feasibility study is a preliminary study where the information needs of prospective users and the resource requirements, costs, benefits, and feasibility of a proposed project are determined. Then you might formalize the findings of this study in a written report that includes preliminary specifications and a developmental plan for a proposed business application. If management approves the recommendations of the feasibility study, the development process can continue.

The goal of feasibility studies is to evaluate alternative system solutions and to propose the most feasible and desirable business application for development. The feasibility of a proposed business system can be evaluated in terms of four major categories, as illustrated in Figure 10.6.

The focus of **organizational feasibility** is on how well a proposed system supports the strategic business priorities of the organization. **Economic feasibility** is concerned with whether expected cost savings, increased revenue, increased profits,

FIGURE 10.6

Organizational, economic, technical, and operational feasibility factors. Note that there is more to feasibility than cost savings or the availability of hardware and software.

Organizational Feasibility	Economic Feasibility
• How well the proposed system supports the business priorities of the organization	• Cost savings • Increased revenue • Decreased investment requirements • Increased profits
Technical Feasibility	**Operational Feasibility**
• Hardware, software, and network capability, reliability and availability	• Employee, customer, supplier acceptance • Management support • Government or other requirements

FIGURE 10.7

Examples of how a feasibility study might measure the feasibility of a proposed e-commerce system.

Organizational Feasibility	Economic Feasibility
• How well a proposed e-commerce system fits the company's plans for developing sales, marketing, and financial e-business systems	• Savings in labor costs • Increased sales revenue • Decreased investment in inventory • Increased profits
Technical Feasibility	**Operational Feasibility**
• Capability, reliability and availability of e-commerce hardware, software, and website management services	• Acceptance of employees • Management support • Customer and supplier acceptance

reductions in required investment, and other types of benefits will exceed the costs of developing and operating a proposed system. For example, if a proposed human resource system can't cover its development costs, it won't be approved, unless mandated by government regulations or strategic business considerations.

Technical feasibility can be demonstrated if reliable hardware and software capable of meeting the needs of a proposed system can be acquired or developed by the business in the required time. Finally, **operational feasibility** is the willingness and ability of the management, employees, customers, suppliers, and others to operate, use, and support a proposed system. For example, if the software for a new e-commerce system is too difficult to use, customers or employees may make too many errors and avoid using it. Thus, it would fail to show operational feasibility. See Figure 10.7.

Cost/Benefit Analysis. Feasibility studies typically involve **cost/benefit analysis.** If costs and benefits can be quantified, they are called tangible; if not, they are called intangible. Examples of tangible costs are the costs of hardware and software, employee salaries, and other quantifiable costs needed to develop and implement an IS solution. **Intangible costs** are difficult to quantify; they include the loss of customer goodwill or employee morale caused by errors and disruptions arising from the installation of a new system.

Tangible benefits are favorable results, such as the decrease in payroll costs caused by a reduction in personnel or a decrease in inventory carrying costs caused by reduction in inventory. **Intangible benefits** are harder to estimate. Such benefits as better customer service or faster and more accurate information for management fall into this category. Figure 10.8 lists typical tangible and intangible benefits with examples. Possible tangible and intangible costs would be the opposite of each benefit shown.

Systems Analysis

What is **systems analysis?** Whether you want to develop a new application quickly or are involved in a long-term project, you will need to perform several basic activities of systems analysis. Many of these activities are an extension of those used in conducting a feasibility study. However, systems analysis is not a preliminary study. It is an in-depth study of end user information needs that produces *functional requirements* that are used as the basis for the design of a new information system. Systems analysis traditionally involves a detailed study of:

- The information needs of a company and end users like yourself.
- The activities, resources, and products of one or more of the present information systems being used.

FIGURE 10.8
Possible benefits of
new information systems,
with examples. Note that an
opposite result for each of
these benefits would be a
cost or disadvantage of
e-commerce systems.

Tangible Benefits	Example
● Increase in sales or profits	● Development of IT-based products
● Decrease in information processing costs	● Elimination of unnecessary documents
● Decrease in operating costs	● Reduction in inventory carrying costs
● Decrease in required investment	● Decrease in inventory investment required
● Increased operational efficiency	● Less spoilage, waste, and idle time

Intangible Benefits	Example
● Improved information availability	● More timely and accurate information
● Improved abilities in analysis	● OLAP and data mining
● Improved customer service	● More timely service response
● Improved employee morale	● Elimination of burdensome job tasks
● Improved management decision making	● Better information and decision analysis
● Improved competitive position	● Systems that lock in customers
● Improved business image	● Progressive image as perceived by customers, suppliers, and investors

● The information system capabilities required to meet your information needs, and those of other business stakeholders that may use the system.

Organizational Analysis

An **organizational analysis** is an important first step in systems analysis. How can anyone improve an information system if they know very little about the organizational environment in which that system is located? They can't. That's why the members of a development team have to know something about the organization, its management structure, its people, its business activities, the environmental systems it must deal with, and its current information systems. Someone on the team must know this information in more detail for the specific business units or end user workgroups that will be affected by the new or improved information system being proposed. For example, a new inventory control system for a chain of department stores cannot be designed unless someone on a development team knows a lot about the company and the types of business activities that affect its inventory. That's why business end users are frequently added to systems development teams.

Analysis of the Present System

Before you design a new system, it is important to study the system that will be improved or replaced (if there is one). You need to analyze how this system uses hardware, software, network, and people resources to convert data resources, such as transactions data, into information products, such as reports and displays. Then, you should document how the information system activities of input, processing, output, storage, and control are accomplished.

For example, you might evaluate the format, timing, volume, and quality of input and output activities. Such *user interface* activities are vital to effective interaction between end users and a computer-based system. Then, in the systems design stage, you can specify what the resources, products, and activities should be to support the user interface in the system you are designing. Figure 10.9 presents a Web page from the analysis of an e-commerce website.

FIGURE 10.9

A Web page from BuyerZone's e-commerce site at www.buyerzone.com.

Source: Courtesy of BuyerZone.com.

BuyerZone and OfficeMax: Evaluating an e-Commerce Website

Customers of business-to-business sites are faced with much more difficult decisions than the customers of business-to-consumer sites. Jakob Nielsen of Nielsen Norman Group recently studied the reactions of users who were trying to decide whether to lease or buy office equipment.

BuyerZone.com and OfficeMax both failed in the study because they didn't support users going through a process. In order to support a customer's process, businesses need to understand it from the user's perspective. If users feel pushed through a process or can't figure out what to do next, you're skipping steps that matter to them. Don't just design Web pages. Design support for users' tasks. Here's how:

Support Processes before Pushing Transactions. Customers need compelling reasons to complete complex tasks on the Web. It's usually easier to pick up the phone and deal with a salesperson than to go it alone on the Web. Users often say that the Web is OK for preliminary research, but useless for closing deals. Most B2B sites overlook their users' perspectives in their eagerness to move them to the checkout line. For example, users don't want to click Buy Now until they select their payment options on BuyerZone.com. Unfortunately, clicking Buy Now is the only way to see both leasing and purchase prices.

Provide the Right Tools at the Right Time. Complex processes require different tools for different stages of the process. Early in a process, customers need ways to quickly look at their purchasing options in many ways, without commitment. Let users easily manipulate data they care about, and carry that forward to their transaction when they're ready. For example, while it's good that BuyerZone.com offers a calculator to explore leasing prices, users struggle to understand the leasing terminology and want more guidance and recommendations from the tool.

Integrate Related Tasks. From a customer's prospective, leasing is just a payment option and is a part of a larger acquisition process, not a separate task. Yet OfficeMax separates leasing from purchasing, as if a user would get leases in an independent project. A user who has selected office equipment on OfficeMax's website can't explore how to lease that equipment. Instead, she must abandon her selection, find leasing services from the site's Business Services section, and then suffer through an awkward registration process.

Don't Push the Cart. The only purpose of a shopping cart is to hold items until users are ready for checkouts. Yet many B2B sites inappropriately use shopping carts as mandatory gateways to vital sales information, such as shipping costs or availability. If your shopping cart plays a larger role than a holding tank on your site, you're probably forcing users to do things out of their preferred sequence. For example, in order to compare leasing and purchase payments on BuyerZone.com, users must add an item to their cart by clicking a Buy Now button. Imagine how quickly you would spurn a human salesperson who forced you to "buy now" every time you wanted a question answered [25, 26].

Functional Requirements Analysis

This step of systems analysis is one of the most difficult. You may need to work as a team with IS analysts and other end users to determine your specific business information needs. For example, first you need to determine what type of information each business activity requires; what its format, volume, and frequency should be; and what response times are necessary. Second, you must try to determine the information processing capabilities required for each system activity (input, processing, output, storage, control) to meet these information needs. *Your main goal is to identify what should be done, not how to do it.*

Finally, you should try to develop **functional requirements.** Functional requirements are end user information requirements that are not tied to the hardware, software, network, data, and people resources that end users presently use or might use in the new system. That is left to the design stage to determine. For example, Figure 10.10 shows examples of functional requirements for a proposed e-commerce application.

Systems Design

Systems analysis describes *what* a system should do to meet the information needs of users. **Systems design** specifies *how* the system will accomplish this objective. Systems design consists of design activities that produce system specifications satisfying the functional requirements that were developed in the systems analysis process.

A useful way to look at systems design is illustrated in Figure 10.11. This concept focuses on three major products, or *deliverables* that should result from the

FIGURE 10.10

Examples of functional requirements for a proposed e-commerce system.

Examples of Functional Requirements
● **User Interface Requirements**   Automatic entry of product data and easy-to-use data entry screens for Web customers.
● **Processing Requirements**   Fast, automatic calculation of sales totals and shipping costs.
● **Storage Requirements**   Fast retrieval and update of data from product, pricing, and customer databases.
● **Control Requirements**   Signals for data entry errors and quick e-mail confirmation for customers.

FIGURE 10.11   Systems design can be viewed as the design of user interfaces, data, and processes.

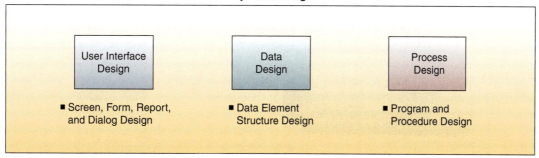

design stage. In this framework, systems design consists of three activities: user interface, data, and process design. This results in specifications for user interface methods and products, database structures, and processing and control procedures.

User Interface Design

Let's take a closer look at user interface design, since it is the system component closest to business end users, and the one they will most likely help design. The user interface design activity focuses on supporting the interactions between end users and their computer-based applications. Designers concentrate on the design of attractive and efficient forms of user input and output, such as easy-to-use Internet or intranet Web pages.

As we mentioned earlier, user interface design is frequently a *prototyping* process, where working models or prototypes of user interface methods are designed and modified several times with feedback from end users. The user interface design process produces detailed design specifications for information products such as display screens, interactive user/computer dialogues (including the sequence or flow of dialogue), audio responses, forms, documents, and reports. Figure 10.12 gives examples of user interface design elements and other guidelines suggested for the multimedia Web pages of e-commerce websites. Figure 10.13 presents actual before and after screen displays of the user interface design process for a work scheduling application of State Farm Insurance Company [27].

FIGURE 10.12   Useful guidelines for the design of business websites.

Checklist for Corporate Websites

- **Remember the Customer:** Successful websites are built solely for the customer, not to make company vice presidents happy.
- **Aesthetics:** Successful designs combine fast-loading graphics and simple color palettes for pages that are easy to read.
- **Broadband Content:** The Web's coolest stuff can't be accessed by most Web surfers. Including a little streaming video isn't bad, but don't make it the focus of your site.
- **Easy to Navigate:** Make sure it's easy to get from one part of your site to another. Providing a site map, accessible from every page, helps.

- **Searchability:** Many sites have their own search engines; very few are actually useful. Make sure yours is.
- **Incompatibilities:** A site that looks great on a PC using Internet Explorer can often look miserable on an iBook running Netscape.
- **Registration Forms:** Registration forms are a useful way to gather customer data. But make your customers fill out a three-page form, and watch them flee.
- **Dead Links:** Dead links are the bane of all Web surfers—be sure to keep your links updated. Many Web-design software tools can now do this for you.

FIGURE 10.13a & b An example of the user interface design process. State Farm developers changed this work scheduling and assignment application's interface after usability testing showed that end users working with the old interface (at left) didn't realize that they had to follow a six-step process. If users jumped to a new page out of order, they would lose their work. The new interface (at right) made it clearer that a process had to be followed.

(a) 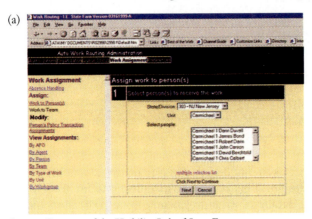 (b)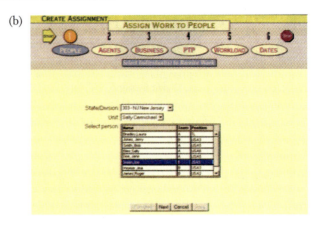

Source: Courtesy of the Usability Lab of State Farm.

Quicken Loans: Web Page Design

One yellow box. A measly 150 by 72 pixels on the QuickenLoans.com home page. Fifteen minutes of coding on a Tuesday afternoon. Yet it boosted Quicken Loans Inc.'s user return rates from 2 percent to 11 percent. Talk about an inexpensive way to recapture customer loyalty. That's the power of proper Web design. The problem isn't so much the coding but knowing what to code. And that's where Web redesign plans like those of QuickenLoans.com come in.

Creating a good design is a challenge all e-commerce sites face because a poor design can frustrate customers and have a bad financial impact. As studies from Zona Research have shown, more than one-third of online shoppers who have trouble finding a product just give up altogether. And really dissatisfied customers don't just stay away; they discourage their friends from visiting, too.

QuickenLoans.com, a leader in the booming online mortgage business, has been through the website redesign trenches and has deduced three key lessons: keep testing to see what works and what's wrong, keep tweaking (modifying features) to fix what's wrong and, when necessary, tell customers what they should buy instead of giving them too many choices [31].

System Specifications

System specifications formalize the design of an application's user interface methods and products, database structures, and processing and control procedures. Therefore, systems designers will frequently develop hardware, software, network, data, and personnel specifications for a proposed system. Figure 10.14 shows examples of system specifications that could be developed for an e-commerce system.

End User Development

In a traditional systems development cycle, your role as a business end user is similar to that of a customer or a client. Typically, you make a request for a new or improved system, answer questions about your specific information needs and information processing problems, and provide background information on your existing e-business systems. IS professionals work with you to analyze your problem and suggest alternative solutions. When you approve the best alternative, it is designed and implemented. Here again, you may be involved in a prototyping design process or be on an implementation team with IS specialists.

However, in **end user development**, IS professionals play a consulting role, while you do your own application development. Sometimes a staff of user consultants

FIGURE 10.14

Examples of system specifications for a new e-commerce system.

Examples of System Specifications
● **User Interface Specifications** Use personalized screens that welcome repeat Web customers and make product recommendations.
● **Database Specifications** Develop databases that use object/relational database management software to organize access to all customer and inventory data, and multimedia product information.
● **Software Specifications** Acquire an e-commerce software engine to process all e-commerce transactions with fast responses, i.e., retrieve necessary product data, and compute all sales amounts in less than one second.
● **Hardware and Network Specifications** Install redundant networked Web servers and sufficient high-bandwidth telecommunications lines to host the company e-commerce website.
● **Personnel Specifications** Hire an e-commerce manager and specialists and a webmaster and Web designer to plan, develop, and manage e-commerce strategies.

may be available to help you and other end users with your application development efforts. This may include training in the use of application packages; selection of hardware and software; assistance in gaining access to organization databases; and, of course, assistance in analysis, design, and implementing your e-business application.

Focus on IS Activities

It is important to remember that end user development should focus on the fundamental activities of any information system: input, processing, output, storage, and control, as we described in Chapter 1. Figure 10.15 illustrates these system components and the questions they address.

FIGURE 10.15

End user development should focus on the basic information processing activity components of an information system.

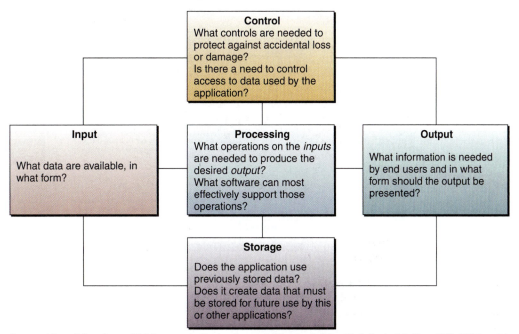

Source: Adapted from James N. Morgan, *Application Cases in MIS*, 4th ed. (New York: Irwin/McGraw-Hill, 2002), p. 31.

In analyzing a potential application, you should focus first on the **output** to be produced by the application. What information is needed and in what form should it be presented? Next, look at the **input** data to be supplied to the application. What data are available? From what sources? In what form? Then you should examine the **processing** requirements. What operations or transformation processes will be required to convert the available inputs into the desired output? Among software packages the developer is able to use, which package can best perform the operations required?

You may find that the desired output cannot be produced from the inputs that are available. If this is the case, you must either make adjustments to the output expected, or find additional sources of input data, including data stored in files and databases from external sources. The **storage** component will vary in importance in end user applications. For example, some applications require extensive use of stored data or the creation of data that must be stored for future use. These are better suited for database management development projects than for spreadsheet applications.

Necessary **control** measures for end user applications vary greatly depending upon the scope and duration of the application, the number and nature of the users of the application, and the nature of the data involved. For example, control measures are needed to protect against accidental loss or damage to end user files. The most basic protection against this type of loss is simply to make backup copies of application files on a frequent and systematic basis. Another example is the cell protection feature of spreadsheets that protects key cells from accidental erasure by users.

Doing End User Development

In end user development, you and other business professionals can develop new or improved ways to perform your jobs without the direct involvement of IS specialists. The application development capabilities built into a variety of end user software packages have made it easier for many users to develop their own computer-based solutions. For example, Figure 10.16 illustrates a website development tool

FIGURE 10.16

Microsoft FrontPage is an example of an easy-to-use end user website development tool.

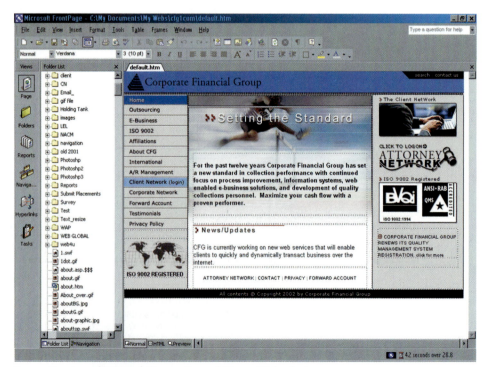

Source: Courtesy of Microsoft Corporation and Murnet Technologies.

you could use to help you develop, update, and manage an intranet website for your business unit. Or you might use an electronic spreadsheet package as a tool to develop a way to easily analyze weekly sales results for the sales managers in a company. Or you could use a website development package to design Web pages for a small business e-commerce Web store or a departmental intranet website. Let's take a look at a real world example of how many companies are encouraging business end users to do their own website development. See Figure 10.17.

Providence Health Systems: End User Web Development

Business groups at Providence Health systems in Portland, Oregon, complained to information technology staff about the sometimes outdated and incorrect content of the company's intranet websites. That was especially frustrating to IT workers, because the content originated from and belonged to the business groups, says Erik Sargent, lead Internet developer at the health care provider. So Providence Health's IT and Web development group did what many companies are considering. They gave up some of their central power to let business personnel in different departments contribute directly to corporate Internet and intranet sites with the help of Web content development tools.

More IT groups can do this because the tools have made it easier for users to create, manage, and update websites without knowing the intricacies of the Internet programming language HTML. Sargent and his team at Providence Health used Microsoft FrontPage on their development efforts. And because the company standardized on Microsoft Office productivity tools, it made sense to stay with FrontPage when allowing employees to do the intranet publishing duties.

One reason was that FrontPage maintained the same look and feel as Office, so there was a gentler learning curve. The other reason: FrontPage was cheaper to roll out to the 108 non-IT people now contributing to the intranet, rather than buying high-end tools with big price tags [28].

FIGURE 10.17
How companies are encouraging and managing intranet website development by business end users.

Encouraging End User Web Development
• **Look for Tools That Make Sense.** Some Web development tools may be too powerful and more costly than what your business end users really need.
• **Spur Creativity.** Consider a competition among business departments for the best website, to help spur users to more creative uses of their intranet sites.
• **Set Some Limits.** Yes, you have to keep some control. Consider putting limits on exactly what parts of a Web page users can change and who can change what pages. You still want some consistency across the organization.
• **Give Managers Responsibility.** Make business unit managers sign off on who will be Web publishing from their groups, and make the managers personally responsible for the content that goes on their websites. That will help prevent the publishing of inappropriate content by some users.
• **Make Users Comfortable.** Training users well on the tools will help users become confident in their ability to properly manage and update their sites—and save IT the trouble of fixing problems later on or providing continuous support for minor problems.

Source: Adapted from Tim Ouellette, "Giving Users the Key to Their Web Content," *Computerworld*, July 26, 1999, p. 67. Copyright 1999 by Computerworld, Inc., Framingham, MA 01701. Reprinted from *Computerworld*.

Implementing Business Systems

Implementation

Once a new e-business system has been designed, it must be implemented and maintained. The implementation process we will cover in this section follows the investigation, analysis, and design stages of the systems development cycle we discussed in Section I. Implementation is a vital step in the deployment of information technology to support the business information systems developed by a company for employees, customers, and other business stakeholders.

Analyzing PacifiCorp, Reynolds, and Zurich NA

Read the Real World Case on PacifiCorp, Reynolds, and Zurich NA on the next page. We can learn a lot from this case about the challenges of implementing business systems. See Figure 10.18.

This case describes a change in focus in IT project management from time to market and market share goals to profitable projects completed on time and on budget. One example is the $10 million, 18-month customer service and call center project of PacifiCorp managed by Jann Davis. The project achieved its business goals through frequent meetings of businesspeople and IT developers to hammer out agreements on business and system requirements. Pat Freeman rescued an IT project to develop a software system for car dealerships by Reynolds&Reynolds that was off schedule and over budget through weekly meetings that focused on issues that might put the project at risk. And Dave Patterson keeps his projects at Zurich NA in line by insisting on a formal project agreement and project transparency to all stakeholders via project status reporting over the corporate intranet.

Implementing New Systems

Figure 10.19 illustrates that the **systems implementation** stage involves hardware and software acquisition, software development, testing of programs and procedures, development of documentation, and a variety of conversion alternatives. It also involves the education and training of end users and specialists who will operate a new system.

FIGURE 10.18
Jann Davis is an IT project manager for PacifiCorp, and led the development of a successful customer service and call center initiative.

Source: Robbie McClaran.

REAL WORLD CASE 2

PacifiCorp, Reynolds, and Zurich NA: IT Project Management Requirements

Believe it or not, some sanity appears to be returning to IT project management. Gone are the days of bottomless-pit project funding and caffeine-pumped software developers sequestered off-site and working around the clock to be first to market with a glitzy website. Instead, experts say, economic pressures have prompted IT departments to return to traditional, hands-on "block-and-tackle" project management, with a heavy emphasis on things like strict budgeting, daily progress reports, continual user feedback, and codified processes and methodologies.

"There's been a fundamental shift," says Bob Wourms, director of the IT practice at PM Solutions, a project management consulting firm in Havertown, Pennsylvania. "A couple of years ago, time to market and market share were very critical. The focus now is on what is profitable." Experienced project leaders who have recently produced profitable projects on time and on budget attribute a good part of their success in dusting off and putting in place certain project management requirements, such as securing visible and active executive support for an endeavor early on. But along the way, they've also developed a few best-practice rules to keep their projects not only on track but in the black as well. Here's how they've done it.

PacifiCorp. Profitability requires you to keep projects not only on time and on budget, but also on target to deliver no less or more than what they were designed to accomplish. This was a key challenge for Jann Davis, manager of Project Discovery, a $10 million customer service and call center initiative at PacifiCorp (www.pcificorp.com), a Portland, Oregon–based electric utility with 1.5 million customers. One of the goals of the 18-month project, which involved implementing a new Web-based billing system and automating many call center activities, was for 325 call center agents to handle 80 percent of incoming calls in less than 20 seconds. This entailed scripting different responses that would pop up on an operator's computer screen, depending on the type of call request that came into the company's two call centers.

"The problem was keeping the team to the 80/20 rule," Davis says, noting that certain team members wanted to script responses for the rarest types of customer issues. "I had to keep pointing out the goals of the project. We don't need a Ferrari." Knowing when you're done is critical to keeping a project on time, on budget, and on track, Davis says. But how do you do it? "I had to throw people together in a room constantly and have businesspeople and developers sit together to come up with, agree on and then stick to the requirements," she explains.

Reynolds & Reynolds. "I wouldn't characterize it as brute force, but rather as paying relentless attention to detail," says project leader Pat Freeman, describing his style of managing a $55 million, 15-month project to develop a next-generation software system for car dealerships at automotive software developer Reynolds & Reynolds (www.reyrey.com)

in Dayton, Ohio. Initially, Freeman's role was that of project rescuer, because the development effort was off schedule and over budget. There were also no clearly defined project management processes and procedures.

Freeman tackled the problem by instituting what he describes as "very intense" weekly reviews, during which each and every detail of any slipping task, deliverable, schedule, or cost was scrutinized. "The meetings lasted two to four hours, and we had a structured agenda every week, looking at the same series of things," he says. "We always approached issues in terms of risk and what effect they'd have on the schedule and business case" before developing solutions. This enabled the team to focus first on higher-risk tasks that could set the project back, Freeman says.

Zurich NA. Dave Patterson is a big believer in what he describes as full transparency. "Every project we're working on and its status is reported through the intranet," says Patterson, vice president of IT at Zurich North America, the Baltimore–based insurance arm of Zurich Financial Services (www.zurich.com). "The status of projects is all very fact-based. You're either making your dates or you're not; you're on budget or you're not; you either have an issue or you don't."

Patterson says Zurich applies the same black-and-white, fact-based thinking when it comes to paying salaries and bonuses to members of an IT project team. The bulk of each project team member's salary is based on market pay rates and the worker's competency. "But about 10 to 20 percent of compensation is based on whether the company makes money and whether we deliver a project as promised," Patterson says.

His other financial rule of thumb is to always get the budget and funding arrangements of a project in writing. "At the start of every project, there is a project agreement," Patterson says. "It needs to contain the full scope of the project plans, risk analysis, costs and benefits, and it has to be signed by the business partners willing to pay for the project. I will not allow a project to initiate if I don't have a customer who is willing to pay for it."

Case Study Questions

1. Why has there been a change of focus in IT project management? Is this change necessary? Why or why not?

2. What are the reasons for the difference in the project management focus of the meetings held by PacifiCorp and Reynolds? Which is more important? Explain.

3. What are the benefits to IT project management of project status transparency and the project agreement as practiced by Zurich NA?

Source: Adapted from Julia King, "Back to Basics," *Computerworld*, April 22, 2002, pp. 36–37. Reprinted with permission from *Computerworld*.

FIGURE 10.19

An overview of the implementation process. Implementation activities are needed to transform a newly developed information system into an operational system for end users.

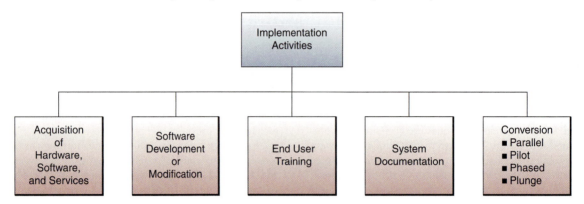

Implementation can be a difficult and time-consuming process. However, it is vital in ensuring the success of any newly developed system, for even a well-designed system will fail if it is not properly implemented. Figure 10.20 illustrates the activities and time lines that might be required to implement an intranet for a new employee benefits system in the human resources department of a company.

Evaluating Hardware, Software, and Services

How do companies evaluate and select hardware, software, and IT services, such as those shown in Figure 10.21? Large companies may require suppliers to present bids and proposals based on system specifications developed during the design stage of systems development. Minimum acceptable physical and performance characteristics for all hardware and software requirements are established. Most large business firms and all government agencies formalize these requirements by listing them in a document called an RFP (request for proposal) or RFQ (request for quotation). Then they send the RFP or RFQ to appropriate vendors, who use it as the basis for preparing a proposed purchase agreement.

Companies may use a *scoring* system of evaluation when there are several competing proposals for a hardware or software acquisition. They give each **evaluation factor** a certain number of maximum possible points. Then they assign each competing proposal points for each factor, depending on how well it meets the user's

FIGURE 10.20

An example of the implementation process activities and time lines for a company installing an intranet-based employee benefits system in its human resource management department.

Intranet Implementation Activities	Month 1	Month 2	Month 3	Month 4
Acquire and install server hardware and software				
Train administrators				
Acquire and install browser software				
Acquire and install publishing software				
Train benefits employees on publishing software				
Convert benefits manuals and add revisions				
Create Web-based tutorials for the intranet				
Hold rollout meetings				

Source: Adapted from Mclanie Hills, *Intranet Business Strategy* (New York: John Wiley & Sons, 1997), p. 193. Reprinted by permission of John Wiley & Sons, Inc. Copyright © 1997 by John Wiley & Sons, Inc.

FIGURE 10.21

Example of e-commerce hardware, software, and services offered by the IBM Corporation. These are the kinds of hardware, software, and IS services that many companies are evaluating and acquiring to support their moves into e-commerce.

Hardware
Full range of offerings, including Netfinity servers, AS/400 midrange for small and midsize businesses, RS6000 servers for UNIX customers and z900 mainframes for large enterprises. Also has full range of storage options.

Software
Web server: Lotus DominoGo Web server. **Storefront:** WebSphere Commerce Suite (formerly known as Net.Commerce) for storefront and catalog creation, relationship marketing, and order management. Can add Commerce Integrator to integrate with back-end systems and Catalog Architect for content management. **Middleware/transaction services:** WebSphere application server manages transactions. MQ Series queues messages and manages connections. CICS processes transactions. **Database:** DB2 Universal Database. **Tools:** WebSphere Studio includes set of predefined templates and common business logic. **Other applications include:** IBM Payment Suite for handling credit cards and managing digital certificates.

Services
IBM Global Services, which includes groups organized by each major industry, including retail and financial. Can design, build, and host e-commerce applications.

specifications. Scoring evaluation factors for several proposals helps organize and document the evaluation process. It also spotlights the strengths and weaknesses of each proposal.

Whatever the claims of hardware manufacturers and software suppliers, the performance of hardware and software must be demonstrated and evaluated. Independent hardware and software information services (such as Datapro and Auerbach) may be used to gain detailed specification information and evaluations. Other users are frequently the best source of information needed to evaluate the claims of manufacturers and suppliers. That's why Internet newsgroups established to exchange information about specific software or hardware vendors and their products have become one of the best sources for obtaining up-to-date information about the experiences of users of the products.

Large companies frequently evaluate proposed hardware and software by requiring the processing of special *benchmark* test programs and test data. Benchmarking simulates the processing of typical jobs on several computers and evaluates their performances. Users can then evaluate test results to determine which hardware device or software package displayed the best performance characteristics.

Hardware Evaluation Factors

When you evaluate the hardware needed by a new business application, you should investigate specific physical and performance characteristics for each computer system or peripheral component to be acquired. Specific questions must be answered concerning many important factors. Ten of these **hardware evaluation factors** and questions are summarized in Figure 10.22.

Notice that there is much more to evaluating hardware than determining the fastest and cheapest computing device. For example, the question of obsolescence must be addressed by making a technology evaluation. The factor of ergonomics is also very important. Ergonomic factors ensure that computer hardware and software are user-friendly, that is, safe, comfortable, and easy to use. Connectivity is another

FIGURE 10.22

A summary of ten major hardware evaluation factors. Notice how you can use this to evaluate a computer system or a peripheral device.

Hardware Evaluation Factors	Rating
Performance What is its speed, capacity, and throughput?	
Cost What is its lease or purchase price? What will be its cost of operations and maintenance?	
Reliability What are the risk of malfunction and its maintenance requirements? What are its error control and diagnostic features?	
Compatibility Is it compatible with existing hardware and software? Is it compatible with hardware and software provided by competing suppliers?	
Technology In what year of its product life cycle is it? Does it use a new untested technology or does it run the risk of obsolescence?	
Ergonomics Has it been "human factors engineered" with the user in mind? Is it user-friendly, designed to be safe, comfortable, and easy to use?	
Connectivity Can it be easily connected to wide area and local area networks that use different types of network technologies and bandwidth alternatives?	
Scalability Can it handle the processing demands of a wide range of end users, transactions, queries, and other information processing requirements?	
Software Is system and application software available that can best use this hardware?	
Support Are the services required to support and maintain it available?	
Overall Rating	

important evaluation factor, since so many network technologies and bandwidth alternatives are available to connect computer systems to the Internet, intranet, and extranet networks.

Software Evaluation Factors

You should evaluate software according to many factors that are similar to those used for hardware evaluation. Thus, the factors of performance, cost, reliability, availability, compatibility, modularity, technology, ergonomics, and support should be used to evaluate proposed software acquisitions. In addition, however, **the software evaluation factors** summarized in Figure 10.23 must also be considered. You should answer the questions they generate in order to properly evaluate software purchases. For example, some software packages are notoriously slow, hard to use, bug-filled, or poorly documented. They are not a good choice, even if offered at attractive prices.

Evaluating IS Services

Most suppliers of hardware and software products and many other firms offer a variety of **IS services** to end users and organizations. Examples include assistance during e-commerce website development, installation or conversion of new hardware and software, employee training, and hardware maintenance. Some of these services are provided without cost by hardware manufacturers and software suppliers.

Other types of IS services needed by a business can be outsourced to an outside company for a negotiated price. For example, *systems integrators* take over complete responsibility for an organization's computer facilities when an organization

FIGURE 10.23

A summary of selected software evaluation factors. Note that most of the hardware evaluation factors in Figure 10.22 can also be used to evaluate software packages.

Software Evaluation Factors	Rating
Quality Is it bug free, or does it have many errors in its program code?	
Efficiency Is the software a well-developed system of program code that does not use much CPU time, memory capacity, or disk space?	
Flexibility Can it handle our e-business processes easily, without major modification?	
Security Does it provide control procedures for errors, malfunctions, and improper use?	
Connectivity Is it *Web-enabled* so it can easily access the Internet, intranets, and extranets, on its own, or by working with Web browsers or other network software?	
Language Is it written in a programming language that is familiar to our own software developers?	
Documentation Is the software well documented? Does it include help screens and helpful software agents?	
Hardware Does existing hardware have the features required to best use this software?	
Other Factors What are its performance, cost, reliability, availability, compatibility, modularity, technology, ergonomics, scalability, and support characteristics? (Use the hardware evaluation factor questions in Figure 10.22)	
Overall Rating	

outsources its computer operations. They may also assume responsibility for developing and implementing large systems development projects that involve many vendors and subcontractors. Value-added resellers (VARs) specialize in providing industry-specific hardware, software, and services from selected manufacturers. Many other services are available to end users, including systems design, contract programming, and consulting services. Evaluation factors and questions for IS services are summarized in Figure 10.24.

Microsoft and IBM: Customer Service Satisfaction	**Microsoft** The effectiveness of Microsoft's support depends on who you are, or whom you know, according to a recent *Computerworld* survey. The company is highly selective in determining who receives its Premier Support plan, the very attentive service it's using to get deeper into the corridors of Fortune 500 corporations. Very large—2,500 users or more—companies fortunate enough to be included in Premier Support receive Microsoft's undivided and very effective attention. But the mediocre grades Microsoft received from *Computerworld*'s survey come largely from the rank-and-file companies that don't qualify for Premier class. These users, the vast majority of Microsoft business customers, are bounced to one of the company's many support partners. One bright spot for Microsoft: Users really like its website support and gave it the highest grade of any in the survey. Respondents said that between its website and its TechNet informational CD-ROM service, Microsoft is the best at letting its users help themselves.

FIGURE 10.24

Evaluation factors for IS services. These factors focus on the quality of support services business users may need.

Evaluation Factors for IS Services	Rating
Performance What has been their past performance in view of their past promises?	
Systems Development Are website and other e-business developers available? What are their quality and cost?	
Maintenance Is equipment maintenance provided? What are its quality and cost?	
Conversion What systems development and installation services will they provide during the conversion period?	
Training Is the necessary training of personnel provided? What are its quality and cost?	
Backup Are similar computer facilities available nearby for emergency backup purposes?	
Accessibility Does the vendor provide local or regional sites that offer sales, systems development, and hardware maintenance services? Is a customer support center at the vendor's website available? Is a customer hot line provided?	
Business Position Is the vendor financially strong, with good industry market prospects?	
Hardware Do they provide a wide selection of compatible hardware devices and accessories?	
Software Do they offer a variety of useful e-business software and application packages?	
Overall Rating	

IBM

IBM's whatever-the-customer-wants approach to service has made it the benchmark by which other vendors are measured, according to several *Computerworld* survey respondents. Big Blue scored highest in six of eight rating categories and achieved the highest customer-satisfaction grade in the entire survey for its emergency and mission-critical service. IT managers gave the highest grades to the responsiveness and knowledge demonstrated by IBM's phone staff. IBM, they said, best follows the priorities users set when calling in problems. Priority 1 means a system is down. When that happens, IBM's goal is to connect the user to the person best qualified to fix the system within the hour.

IBM lost ground in *Computerworld*'s survey over website support, however. Surveyed managers said IBM's site is OK for logging minor problems into a queue but not among the best when users need to quickly locate specific solutions. IBM wasn't alone in the area of weak Web-based support, but it's certainly one place that IBM needs to work on [2].

Other Implementation Activities

Testing

Testing, documentation, and training are keys to successful implementation of a new business system.

System testing may involve testing website performance, testing and debugging software, and testing new hardware. An important part of testing is the review of prototypes of displays, reports, and other output. Prototypes should be reviewed by end users of the proposed systems for possible errors. Of course, testing should not occur only during the system's implementation stage, but throughout the system's development process. For example, you might examine and critique prototypes of input documents, screen displays, and processing procedures during the systems design stage. Immediate end user testing is one of the benefits of a prototyping process.

Documentation

Developing good user **documentation** is an important part of the implementation process. Sample data entry display screens, forms, and reports are good examples of documentation. When *computer-aided systems engineering* methods are used, documentation can be created and changed easily since it is stored and accessible on disk in a *system repository*. Documentation serves as a method of communication among the people responsible for developing, implementing, and maintaining a computer-based system. Installing and operating a newly designed system or modifying an established application requires a detailed record of that system's design. Documentation is extremely important in diagnosing errors and making changes, especially if the end users or systems analysts who developed a system are no longer with the organization.

Training

Training is a vital implementation activity. IS personnel, such as user consultants, must be sure that end users are trained to operate a new e-business system or its implementation will fail. Training may involve only activities like data entry, or it may also involve all aspects of the proper use of a new system. In addition, managers and end users must be educated in how the new technology impacts the company's business operations and management. This knowledge should be supplemented by training programs for any new hardware devices, software packages, and their use for specific work activities. Figure 10.25 illustrates how one business coordinated its end user training program with each stage of its implementation process for developing intranet and e-commerce access within the company.

Clarke American Checks: Web-Based ERP Training

If it's 10 A.M., workers at Clarke American Checks Inc. are firing up their Web browsers for a collaborative training lesson on how to perform purchasing with their new SAP AG enterprise resource planning (ERP) software. During the daily sessions, end users in more than 20 locations either watch their colleagues perform simulated transactions with the software, or do it themselves.

Self-paced ERP training delivered via the Web is becoming a popular concept. Users say training eats up 10 to 20 percent of an ERP project's budget and is one of the more vexing parts of an ERP development project. Many ERP systems have tricky user interfaces and are highly customized, making generic, computer-based training courses ineffective. Clarke American, a San Antonio–based check printer, is in a growing group of companies using Web-based training to get workers up to speed on enterprise resource planning applications. Doing so can trim up to 75 percent off the cost of traditional training methods, such as instructor-led sessions, users said [4].

Conversion Methods

The initial operation of a new business system can be a difficult task. This typically requires a **conversion** process from the use of a present system to the operation of a new or improved application. Conversion methods can soften the impact of introducing new information technologies into an organization. Four major forms of system conversion are illustrated in Figure 10.26. They include:

- Parallel conversion.
- Phased conversion.
- Pilot conversion.
- Plunge or direct cutover.

FIGURE 10.25   How one company developed training programs for the implementation of Internet
e-commerce and intranet access for its employees.

Source: Adapted and reprinted by permission of The Harvard Business School Press from Mary Cronin, *The Internet Strategy Handbook* (Boston: 1996), p. 198. Copyright © 1996 by the President and Fellows of Harvard College; all rights reserved.

Conversions can be done on a *parallel* basis, whereby both the old and the new systems are operating until the project development team and end user management agree to switch completely over to the new system. It is during this time that the operations and results of both systems are compared and evaluated. Errors can be identified and corrected, and the operating problems can be solved before the old system is abandoned. Installation can also be accomplished by a direct cutover or *plunge* to a newly developed system.

Conversion can also be done on a *phased basis*, where only parts of a new application or only a few departments, branch offices, or plant locations at a time are converted. A phased conversion allows a gradual implementation process to take place within an organization. Similar benefits accrue from using a *pilot conversion*, where one department or other work site serves as a test site. A new system can be tried out at this site until developers feel it can be implemented throughout the organization.

Nike Inc.: Failure in System Implementation	Early in 2001, Beaverton, Oregon–based footwear maker Nike, Inc., faced serious inventory reduction and misplacement when it implemented a highly customized retail supply chain system that included applications from Dallas-based i2 Technologies Inc. At the time, i2 said the difficulties arose during the conversion process when tying the customized applications to Nike's enterprise resource planning (ERP) and back-end systems.

FIGURE 10.26

The four major forms of conversion to a new system.

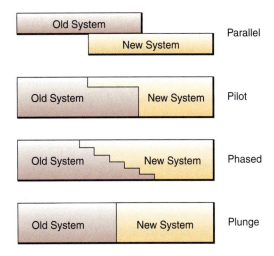

And this case isn't unique, say those who advise against tinkering with ERP applications. While customizing may give you industry-specific capabilities, it can be expensive and difficult, and the custom software may require special maintenance, say critics. It may also make the core application unstable and prone to glitches.

The trouble, of course, is that botched customization jobs can lead to disaster—as in Nike's case. The wide range of footwear products Nike sells also led to further difficulties in mapping the supply chain software to internal business processes. Nike Chairman and CEO Philip Knight, facing a drop in stock price and revenue, told shareholders, "I guess my immediate reaction is, 'This is what we get for $400 million?'"

Such crises discourage users from venturing out onto the thin ice of customization. "It's a risky strategy," says Walter Taylor, ERP program director at Atlanta-based Delta Air Lines Inc. Taylor is overseeing an SAP R/3 implementation for Delta. He says he opposes customizing because SAP already has solid applications with best practices built in. When you start tinkering with the code, you make the application unstable and start losing benefits. "It's far better for a company to reengineer its business processes than to rewrite code," Taylor says. [34]

IS Maintenance

Once a system is fully implemented and is being used in business operations, the maintenance function begins. **Systems maintenance** is the monitoring, evaluating, and modifying of operational business systems to make desirable or necessary improvements. For example, the implementation of a new system usually results in the phenomenon known as the *learning curve*. Personnel who operate and use the system will make mistakes simply because they are not familiar with it. Though such errors usually diminish as experience is gained with a new system, they do point out areas where a system may be improved.

Maintenance is also necessary for other failures and problems that arise during the operation of a system. End users and information systems personnel then perform a *troubleshooting* function to determine the causes of and solutions to such problems.

The maintenance activity includes a **postimplementation review** process to ensure that newly implemented systems meet the business objectives established for them. Errors in the development or use of a system must be corrected by the maintenance process. This includes a periodic review or audit of a system to ensure that it is operating properly and meeting its objectives. This audit is in addition to continually monitoring a new system for potential problems or necessary changes.

Maintenance also includes making modifications to an established system due to changes in the business organization or the business environment. For example, new tax legislation, company reorganizations, and new e-business and e-commerce initiatives may require major changes to current business systems.

Farmland Industries and Lockheed Martin: Implementing ERP Systems	Farmland Industries, a $10.7 billion farmer-owned cooperative in Kansas City, Missouri, installed a version of the SAP R/3 enterprise resource planning (ERP) software tailored for oil and gas users two years ago. Farmland has had only minor problems with the software, said Dick Weaver, technology manager at its petroleum and crop production units. But changing the way the company does business to take full advantage of R/3 has been a sticky proposition. Because Farmland didn't do much of that work up front, its finance and order-entry operations didn't see the kind of savings they were looking for. Now the cooperative is going back and making the business-process changes that were put off earlier in the project. "If you just put in SAP, you haven't gained a whole lot," Weaver said. "Two years into it, we're getting a lot of value. The first year, we didn't."

At Lockheed Martin Aeronautics, 900 business users from its three aircraft manufacturing companies have been working to design common ways to enter orders and process other transactions in using R/3. When that's done, several hundred users will test the system for another six months. Lockheed Martin first rolled out R/3 at an aircraft maintenance operation, and installed SAP's human resources module a few months later, to get its feet wet before bigger installations at the manufacturing units. Its project team also sought advice from Pratt & Whitney Canada, an aircraft engine supplier that had previously done an R/3 rollout [34]. |

Summary

- **The Systems Development Cycle.** Business end users and IS specialists may use a systems approach to help them develop information system solutions to meet business opportunities. This frequently involves a systems development cycle where IS specialists and end users conceive, design, and implement business systems. The stages, activities, and products of the information systems development cycle are summarized in Figure 10.3.

- **Prototyping.** Prototyping is a major alternative methodology to the traditional information systems development cycle. It includes the use of prototyping tools and methodologies, which promote an iterative, interactive process that develops prototypes of user interfaces and other information system components. See Figure 10.4.

- **End User Development.** The application development capabilities built into many end user software packages have made it easier for end users to develop their own business applications. End users should

focus their development efforts on the system components of business processes that can benefit from the use of information technology, as summarized in Figure 10.15.

- **Implementing IS.** The implementation process for information system projects is summarized in Figure 10.27. Implementation involves acquisition, testing, documentation, training, installation, and conversion activities that transform a newly designed business system into an operational system for end users.

- **Evaluating Hardware, Software, and Services.** Business professionals should know how to evaluate the acquisition of information system resources. IT vendors' proposals should be based on specifications developed during the design stage of systems development. A formal evaluation process reduces the possibility of incorrect or unnecessary purchases of hardware or software. Several major evaluation factors, summarized in Figures 10.22, 10.23, and 10.24, can be used to evaluate hardware, software, and IS services.

FIGURE 10.27

An overview of the implementation process. Implementation activities are needed to transform a newly developed information system into an operational system for end users.

Implementing New Systems
● **Acquisition** Evaluate and acquire necessary hardware and software resources and information system services. Screen vendor proposals.
● **Software Development** Develop any software that will not be acquired externally as software packages. Make any necessary modifications to software packages that are acquired.
● **Training** Educate and train management, end users, customers and other business stakeholders. Use consultants or training programs to develop user competencies.
● **Testing** Test and make necessary corrections to the programs, procedures, and hardware used by a new system.
● **Documentation** Record and communicate detailed system specifications, including procedures for end users and IS personnel and examples of input screens and output displays and reports.
● **Conversion** Convert from the use of a present system to the operation of a new or improved system. This may involve operating both new and old systems in *parallel* for a trial period, operation of a *pilot* system on a trial basis at one location, *phasing* in the new system one location at a time, or an immediate *plunge* or *cut over* to the new system.

Key Terms and Concepts

These are the key terms and concepts of this chapter. The page number of their first explanation is in parentheses.

1. Conversion methods (365)
2. Cost/benefit analysis (349)
3. Documentation (365)
4. Economic feasibility (348)
5. End user development (354)
6. Evaluation factors (360)
   a. Hardware (361)
   b. IS services (362)
   c. Software (362)
7. Feasibility study (348)
8. Functional requirements (352)
9. Implementation process (358)

10. Intangible (349)
    a. Benefits (349)
    b. Costs (349)
11. Operational feasibility (349)
12. Organizational analysis (350)
13. Organizational feasibility (348)
14. Postimplementation review (367)
15. Prototype (345)
16. Prototyping (345)
17. Systems analysis (349)
18. Systems approach (344)
19. Systems design (352)

20. Systems development life cycle (345)
21. Systems implementation (358)
22. Systems investigation (348)
23. Systems maintenance (367)
24. Systems specifications (354)
25. System testing (364)
26. Systems thinking (344)
27. Tangible (349)
    a. Benefits (349)
    b. Costs (349)
28. Technical feasibility (349)
29. User interface design (353)

Review Quiz

Match one of the key terms and concepts listed previously with one of the brief examples or definitions that follow. Try to find the best fit for answers that seem to fit more than one term or concept. Defend your choices.

_____ 1. Using an organized sequence of activities to study a problem or opportunity using systems thinking.

_____ 2. Trying to recognize systems and the new interrelationships and components of systems in any situation.

_____ 3. Evaluating the success of a solution after it has been implemented.

_____ 4. Your evaluation shows that benefits outweigh costs for a proposed system.

_____ 5. The costs of acquiring computer hardware, software, and specialists.

_____ 6. Loss of customer goodwill caused by errors in a new system.

_____ 7. Increases in profits caused by a new system.

_____ 8. Improved employee morale caused by efficiency and effectiveness of a new system.

_____ 9. A multistep process to conceive, design, and implement an information system.

_____ 10. The first stage of the systems development cycle.

_____ 11. Determines the organizational, economic, technical, and operational feasibility of a proposed information system.

_____ 12. Cost savings and additional profits will exceed the investment required.

_____ 13. Reliable hardware and software are available to implement a proposed system.

_____ 14. Customers will not have trouble using a proposed system.

_____ 15. The proposed system supports the strategic plan of the business.

_____ 16. Studying in detail the information needs of users and any information systems presently used.

_____ 17. A detailed description of user information needs and the input, processing, output, storage, and control capabilities required to meet those needs.

_____ 18. The process that results in specifications for the hardware, software, people, network, and data

resources and information products needed by a proposed system.

_____ 19. Systems design should focus on developing user-friendly input and output methods for a system.

_____ 20. A detailed description of the hardware, software, people, network, and data resources and information products required by a proposed system.

_____ 21. Acquiring hardware and software, testing and documenting a proposed system, and training people to use it.

_____ 22. Making improvements to an operational system.

_____ 23. A working model of an information system.

_____ 24. An interactive and iterative process of developing and refining information system prototypes.

_____ 25. Managers and business specialists can develop their own e-business applications.

_____ 26. Includes acquisition, testing, training, and conversion to a new system.

_____ 27. Performance, cost, reliability, technology, and ergonomics are examples.

_____ 28. Performance, cost, efficiency, language, and documentation are examples.

_____ 29. Maintenance, conversion, training, and business position are examples.

_____ 30. Operate in parallel with the old system, use a test site, switch in stages, or cut over immediately to a new system.

_____ 31. Checking whether hardware and software work properly for end users.

_____ 32. A user manual communicates the design and operating procedures of a system.

_____ 33. Modifying an operational system by adding e-commerce website access would be an example.

Discussion Questions

1. Why has prototyping become a popular way to develop business applications? What are prototyping's advantages and disadvantages?

2. Refer to the Real World Case on Fidelity Investments and others in the chapter. What are your choices for the top five design failures at business websites? Defend your selections.

3. Review the BuyerZone and OfficeMax and Quicken Loans real world examples in the chapter. What design changes should BuyerZone and OfficeMax make to correct the design flaws at their site and bring their website design up to Quicken's standard? Explain your reasoning.

4. What are the three most important factors you would use in evaluating computer hardware? Computer software? Explain why.

5. Assume that in your first week on a new job you are asked to use a type of business software that you have never used before. What kind of user training should your company provide to you before you start?

6. Refer to the Real World Case on PacifiCorp, Reynolds, and Zurich NA in the chapter. Will the change in focus in IT project management stifle creativity and innovation in business system design? Why or why not?

7. What is the difference between the parallel, plunge, phased, and pilot forms of IS conversion? Which conversion strategy is best? Explain why.

8. What are several key factors in designing a successful e-commerce or intranet website? Refer to Figure 10.12 as a starting point. Explain why the design factors you chose are important to Web success.

9. Review the Frito-Lay and Nike real world examples in the chapter. How could these failures have been avoided?

10. Pick a business task you would like to computerize. How could you use the steps of the information systems development cycle as illustrated in Figure 10.3 to help you? Use examples to illustrate your answer.

Application Exercises

Complete the following exercises as individual or group projects that apply chapter concepts to real world business situations.

1. The Sports Authority and Others: Website Design Requirements

Web Depending on which survey you choose, customers abandon online shopping carts at a rate of between 25 percent and 77 percent. Shoppers abandon their online carts for many reasons. Turn-offs include poor site navigation, hard-to-find shopping carts, and time-consuming checkouts. Let's look at how several companies are confronting this e-commerce problem.

Web Site Navigation

Consistent design throughout your site makes it easier for your customers to find their way: Users can always click on product images for most information. Buttons use a consistent color. Links are always underlined. If your site is simple for users to understand, they will happily keep moving toward the checkout. Walmart.com's recent redesign came under fire by industry critics for being too boring. However, the changes made the site cleaner, simpler, and easier for shoppers to master.

Shopping Cart Design

Whatever you do, make sure your site's shopping cart is a clearly identified link placed on the top right corner of the page, traditionally a high-click area. Moreover, make it available on every page in the same place.

Also try bringing your site's shopping cart area to life. Sports retailer The Sports Authority (*www.thesportsauthority.com*) does that with its dynamic shopping cart. The cart displays the latest item added, allowing the customer to keep a running tab more easily. The company also made sure customers could click on the cart icon to start shopping.

Don't expect people to instantly notice items added to a dynamic cart. When shoppers add items, route them to a cart summary page each time—even if it seems redundant. This page indicates confirmation and invites the shopper to check out.

Checkout Process

Shopping online is all about convenience, and nothing is a bigger pain than lengthy forms that extend the checkout process. No wonder people click away in disgust. While there may be no way around forms for the time being, keep information that you request to a minimum. Demographics are nice to know, but they can also kill sales.

A winning checkout system needs to be fast and easy. Any good checkout process makes a distinction between a repeat shopper and a first-time buyer. Greet returning customers by getting them as close as possible to single-click shopping process. Amazon.com leads in this area with the fastest possible checkout. The Gap (www.gap.com) also offers shoppers two clear shopping tracks, as well as an easy way to retrieve an account password.

Trust and Security

Shoppers demand more than security online. Getting customers to trust you must happen throughout the site, not just when they use their credit card. Establishing trust with your customers means making service a priority by giving them multiple ways to contact you and providing them with a timely reply.

The human touch, especially in a faceless online world, is important to customers. Lands' End (www.landsend.com) has 250 sales reps ready to answer questions live online—and it pays: Their Internet orders end up averaging $10 more than catalog orders.

Ensure the privacy of your customer data in a clearly worded and easy-to-find policy. Also, make sure you spell out your encryption standard by using recognizable signs such as the VeriSign logo, and explain how credit card information is transmitted to your site's servers.

Website Speed

As long as shoppers use dial-up modems to access the Web, overall site speed will be a fundamental measurement to live and die by. Browse the top ten Media Metrix sites with stopwatch in hand and you can almost feel the wind in your hair. You won't get a gratuitous 20-second splash screen on Yahoo or wait for graphic after graphic to download. The fastest sites help you get in and get out by making each subsequent click and page view as fast-loading as possible. How fast is fast enough? There is no set rule, but taking no more than a few seconds to display a Web page to a dial-up modem user is the goal of many Web designers.

a. Visit the Walmart.com and SportsAuthority.com websites. Which one has the better website navigation and shopping cart design? Why?

b. Compare the Amazon.com website with one of the websites mentioned in this case. Which one has the fastest website and checkout processes? Defend your choices.

c. Evaluate the LandsEnd.com privacy and security policies at their website. Does this information help build trust in the security of their e-commerce transactions? Explain.

Source: Adapted from Alice Hill, "Top 5 Reasons Your Customers Abandon Their Shopping Carts," *Smart Business*, March 2001, pp. 80–84.

2. Amazon and eBay: Evaluating e-Commerce Website Behavior

Web Stanford University communications professors and NetSage officers Byron Reeves and Clifford Nass evaluate e-commerce websites for their human interfaces and social behavior. Their position is that people dislike some websites not because they are badly designed, but because the sites behave badly during people's visits. Here's their evaluation of Amazon and eBay.

Amazon.com Inc.: Overall Grade = **A−**
Bottom Line: *Successfully applies social rules to create a bookstore rather than a warehouse or a library.*

Befitting its reputation as the premier e-commerce player, Amazon's book-buying site follows many social rules to great effect. The consistent style and tone throughout the site communicates a reliable personality that builds comfort and trust in the business relationship. Appropriate for its products, the tone of the site is casual.

For example, Amazon tells users, "For now, you just need to . . ." Visitors have a sense that the same person is communicating with them consistently throughout their visit at the site. This promotes a feeling that customers have a single personal assistant rather than a confusing group of merchants—all with different methods and personalities—to help with purchases. Amazon maximizes personalization with minimal information by offering suggestions based on previous purchases, discussing what people in geographic areas are buying and offering one-click shopping that uses information previously stored on the site.

It continually tells users where they are in the ordering and registration process, particularly when they're about to purchase something. A confirmation to customers that they're "doing the right things" to accomplish a transaction—commonplace in real-life transactions—is used effectively at Amazon.

Amazon also effectively uses physical places on its site to let people know what to expect of the information presented in those places. For example, the largest column of information (the middle two-thirds of each page from the top to the bottom) is devoted to product information. And regardless of whether a shopper is looking for books, music, or electronic gear, the function of the space is unchanged. Even the details of price, shipping, and discounts are identical among products.

Amazon-generated book reviews and postings from customers are mixed with book reviews (from, for example, *The New York Times*) to produce commentary relevant to many items. Through careful use of language for related groups of customers (for example, *Purchase Circles* rather than, say, folksier *Neighbors*) and

the avoidance of visual clutter around the buttons that execute the purchase, they remind the customer that this isn't a library.

eBay Inc.: Overall Grade = **D**
Bottom Line: *An expert auctioneer that doesn't behave like one.*

People labeled as experts, whether by others or themselves, are perceived as more competent, more trusting, and more likely to provide unique knowledge and expertise. But eBay's reputation as an expert suffers because it doesn't correct sellers' mistakes and is considered to be complicit in these errors. For example, typographical errors in product descriptions reduce credibility, yet eBay doesn't edit that text. There are trade-offs among image size, picture quality, and details of the background in product presentations, but eBay doesn't make suggestions or offer ways to improve them.

A lesson here is that people hopelessly confuse the errors of the "message" with the competence of the "messenger"; poor presentation undermines eBay as well as the sale items. eBay is also impolite. For example, signing up for an account can take as long as 24 hours for confirmation. eBay users also aren't alerted when they omit a field during registration. Instead of dismissing people during that period, eBay should invite customers to browse. A good social partner tries to own the problems and makes an attempt at resolution.

eBay also fails to carry through on the notion of a "personal" shopper. It's unclear how to submit the initial form that activates the personal shopper, and the shopper doesn't save a list of items on which the customer might want to bid. Having someone remember things for you is essential in personalization. Finally, eBay users must traverse many pages to find the personal shopper—the exact opposite of what a "personal" shopper should be. The idea of an automatic bidder, someone working on your behalf, is a social plus. However, eBay should place more attention and emphasis on making the bidding process personal rather than simply automatic.

a. Visit the Amazon.com and eBay.com websites. Do you agree with the evaluations of Professors Reeves and Nass? Why or why not?

b. How could Amazon improve the experience it offers its e-commerce shoppers? Give several examples.

c. What should eBay do to improve the experience it provides to customers at its auction site? Give several examples.

Source: Adapted from Kevin Fogarty, "Net Manners Matter: How Top Sites Rank in Social Behavior," *Computerworld*, October 18, 1999, pp. 40–41. Copyright 1999 by Computerworld, Inc., Framingham, MA 01701. Reprinted from *Computerworld*.

3. e-Business System Report

Study an e-business application described in a case study in this text or one used by an organization to which you

FIGURE 10.28　　　　　Outline of an e-business system report.

- **Introduction to the organization and e-business application.** Briefly describe the organization you selected and the type of e-business application you have studied.

- **Analysis of an e-business system.** Identify the following system components of a current business use of the Internet, intranets, or extranets for an e-business or e-commerce application.
  - Input, processing, output, storage, and control methods currently used.
  - Hardware, software, networks, and people involved.
  - Data captured and information products produced.
  - Files and databases accessed and maintained

- **Evaluation of the system.**
  - **Efficiency:** Does it do the job right? Is the system well organized? Inexpensive? Fast? Does it require minimum resources? Process large volumes of data, produce a variety of information products?
  - **Effectiveness:** Does it do the right job? The way the employees, customers, suppliers, or other end users want it done? Does it give them the information they need, the way they want it? Does it support the business objectives of the organization? Provide significant customer and business value?

- **Design and implementation of a system proposal.**
  - Do end users need a new system or just improvements? Why?
  - What exactly are you recommending they do?
  - Is it feasible? What are its benefits and costs?
  - What will it take to implement your recommendations?

have access. Write up the results in an e-business system report. Make a presentation to the class based on the results of your study of an e-business application. Use the outline in Figure 10.28 as a table of contents for your report and the outline of your presentation. Use presentation software and/or overhead transparencies to display key points of your analysis.

4. Alternative Web Page Targets and Styles

Web　The appropriate look and feel of a Web page are very much affected by its purpose and target audience. Web pages can be developed for a variety of purposes, including marketing or direct sales of a company's products; provision of online technical support for customers; providing effective online access to information sources such as a library or documents of a government agency; providing a variety of personnel or other job-related information to employees through an intranet; or providing a meeting place for computer users sharing common interests, such as a hobby or sport. The computer

skills of users and the degree of formality of the environment in which the Web pages will be used will also substantially affect the structure and style of a Web page.

Identify three successful websites that differ substantially in their purpose and style. Identify and describe the principal purpose of each site. Find examples illustrating differences in the style and approach of each site, and assess how well these differences fit the varying purposes and target audiences of the three websites.

a. Prepare a set of presentation materials summarizing your results and highlighting key findings. Include sample screen captures from the sites or links that can be used to call up the appropriate pages in an oral presentation. Be prepared to present your results.

b. Prepare a short report summarizing your results, including website addresses to key Web pages illustrating your main points.

Source: Adapted from James N. Morgan, *Application Cases in MIS*, 4th ed. (New York, McGraw-Hill/Irwin, 2002), p. 20.

IMG Worldwide and Others:
IT Resource Acquisition Strategies

An end-to-end, state-of-the-art, leading-edge solution that blah, blah, blah. Face it, every IT vendor says they offer an end-to-end, state-of-the-art, leading-edge blah, blah, blah. So Gergely Tapolyai, global network and telecommunications director at Cleveland-based sports, entertainment, and literary marketing firm IMG Worldwide Inc. (www.imgworld.com), cuts to the chase. "We're not looking for the positive feedback," he explains. "We're looking for the negative feedback."

Take the time Tapolyai was shopping for an Internet service provider that could offer IMG high-speed connections in 37 countries. He had narrowed his search to two finalists. Then he got the real dirt from his peers. Which vendors fudge on the numbers when it comes to uptime? Who's inflexible with their contracts?

Tapolyai turned to Chiefofficer.com, a closed online community of senior executives that he helped create. "They did sway me a lot," he says of the advice he got there. So much so that he chose a company that wasn't even in the running: UUNet. The Ashburn, Virginia–based ISP was the firm with which his peers seemed to have the fewest and least significant problems, says Tapolyai.

Call it survival of the fittest, but with so many IT vendors making so many pitches about so many products, IT managers need a strategy to filter out all the noise and identify the products that will give them the IT resources to do the best job for their users. The best way to get started? "Research, research, research," says Jamie Gruener, a senior analyst at the Yankee Group in Boston. First, make sure the project offers a quantifiable return on investment. "And don't just accept figures that vendors toss out," Gruener warns. Make sure you understand how they come up with those numbers, and determine your budget ahead of time so you know exactly what your return on investment will be. "Everybody's jumping on the bandwagon about ROI," says Gruener. "But other numbers are required, like total cost of ownership (TCO). People need to be wary."

Tapolyai says that before he even looks at products, he weeds out the vendors. He finds out the direction the industry appears to be heading and determines whether all of the vendors are moving in that direction. Then he weighs the vendor's stability versus its ability to provide personalized service. Start-ups can offer good value and innovation, says Gruener. But it's important to question the risk. "What kind of funding do they have? How is support handled?" he says, adding, "Sometimes it isn't worth the risk."

Wilma Kumar-Rubock, vice president and CIO at Washington Gas Light Co. in Washington (www.washgas.com), suggests visiting vendors' development sites to make sure they're not fly-by-night operations. Sometimes, there are no behind-the-scenes people, and what you see is what you get, she says. She also suggests hiring research firms to look under the hood to find the details that vendors may be trying to hide.

Another way to reduce the risk of working with a start-up is to plan an exit strategy so you can get out of a contract if things don't go as planned, advises Dorothy Hawkins, vice president of IT for the energy distribution group at NiSource Inc. in Merrillville, Indiana. Also, be sure you and the vendor agree up front on a clear set of deliverables, she says.

Tapolyai says he makes it a point to get past the salespeople and speak directly to the engineers during the buying process to learn exactly what he can expect from them. "Once the signature is on the contract, they're gone," he says of the salespeople. "I want to see a structured layout—what happens if this person gets hit by a bus? Who's going to take over?—I am pretty much a pain in the ass."

Jon Dell'Antonia, vice president of MIS at OshKosh B'Gosh Inc. (www.oshkoshbgosh.com) in Oshkosh, Wisconsin, starts the buying process by working with end users to determine exactly what they want the system to do. Then Dell'Antonia and the end users come up with a list of potential vendors, rank their top two or three priorities, and meet with the vendors. "If you've got your requirements defined, then it's 'Here's what we need, tell us what your product can do to help us,'" he says. If vendors "waltz around" the topic, Dell'Antonia says he just asks flat out if they're able to meet a specific requirement. If they can't, he'll end the meeting right there.

He also recommends that you ask vendors for customer references and then check with those customers to find out how their products were installed, how the support was, whether the product still works and so on. "If they can't give you good, solid, positive references, then you've got to wonder," Dell'Antonia says. Finally, before making a decision, Dell'Antonia sits down with his entire team—IT staffers and end users—to review the offerings and take a vote. "It is not just an IT-driven process," he says. "It's not, 'We pick it, you get it.' If you don't involve your end user in the selection of your system, it ain't going to work. You're just setting yourself up for failure."

Case Study Questions

1. Do you agree with the methods and criteria that Gergely Tapolyai of IMG uses to evaluate IT products? Why or why not?

2. What characteristics of the OshKosh B'Gosh buying process should be implemented by other companies? Explain your reasoning.

3. What other evaluation methods and criteria (whether mentioned in this case or not) are crucial to the IT acquisition process? Why?

Source: Adapted from Melissa Solomon, "Filtering Out the Noise," *Computerworld*, February 25, 2002, p. 36. Reprinted with permission from *Computerworld*.

Macy's and Lands' End: Systems Design Criteria for Website Shopability

Most e-commerce sites rebuff at least 70 percent of the customers who visit them, passing up millions of dollars in potential sales. Even the best retail websites are doing only half the business they could be doing, researchers say. The culprit: poor website shopability. "E-commerce sites offer a simple way to prove when you're doing it right: Measure sales," says Jakob Nielsen, of Nielsen Norman Group, a website usability design consultancy. Although software tools measure some website activities, nothing beats "watching people shop to gauge the failure or success of a site," Nielsen says. "When executives of an e-commerce site see half their customers leaving because they can't shop, that's pretty compelling," he says.

Nielsen's report, "E-Commerce User Experience," lists 207 design guidelines based on usability tests of 20 e-commerce sites. But even the experts don't agree on what makes a website great for customers, says Jared Spool, author of the report "Web Site Usability: A Designer's Guide." "We've never seen a site that does everything right. The best Web sites never get more than a 42% success rate," Spool says.

Trust. Customers must believe that a company will follow through on their orders, protect their private information, and provide end-to-end transaction integrity. So the latest research focuses on how to foster trust through website design. Designers should also include merchandise costs and shipping dates as soon as possible in the buying process, which Amazon.com does well, Nielsen says. Amazon may lose a few customers when shipping dates have to be extended, he says, "but because they're honest about it, you have the feeling that when you click to buy, you'll get the package." Trust is "the ability to predict current behavior from previous experience," Spool says. "People don't care about privacy policies. In our tests, we found people didn't even read it, and those who did found it too arcane and confusing to understand."

Integrating back-office systems with the website promotes trust too, because then customers know what's in stock, Nielsen says. "If your existing system won't do it, put it on the wish list for updates," he says. At both Macys.com (www.macys.com) in San Francisco and Lands' End Inc. (www.landsend.com) in Dodgeville, Wisconsin, inventory systems are tied to company websites—in real time. "It's extremely tough to do," says Kent Anderson, president of Macys.com. "But when you're running 70,000 items through a Web site, it's important." The integration was part of a July redesign. "Online sales through the fall season doubled," Anderson says.

Categories. To move customers quickly from the home page to the product page they want to see, the pages in between must be explicitly named and well differentiated. To find sweaters at Macys.com, you have to know they're under the "tops" category, Spool points out. On LandsEnd.com they're a separate listing. "Lands' End sells five times as many sweaters as Macy's," he says. "And it's because of the design of

the site." Examine your logs to see the words users type into your search engine. Users enter their "trigger words"—what they want to know or find—and those are the words to use as category names, Spool says.

Search. Put the search box at the top of every page, Nielsen says. Make it tolerant of misspellings and accepting of common synonyms. And set it to automatically search the entire site. Usability studies show that if the first search fails, odds sharply decrease that users will find what they want, says Nielsen. With a good search engine, people will buy twice as much because they can find what they want faster.

Product Pages. The pages that sell the most products are the ones that show the most products and have the biggest pictures, experts say. At Macys.com, shoppers can zoom in on product pictures to see a close-up of the fabric weave. "The trick is to capture the image at the appropriate density so it doesn't pixelize at the smaller size," says Anderson. "We spent a lot of time and effort on that."

One of today's prevalent myths is that if a page doesn't download within seven seconds, the customer goes elsewhere. Not true, says Spool. "People complain about the download time because they're having trouble completing a task," he says. Although faster is clearly better, when the content is something the user has asked for, studies show, that user is willing to wait. As proof, he points to companies that "made their sites faster but the complaints didn't go away."

Navigation. Designers must develop navigation and content together. Many designers instead create a shell to give each page the same look and feel and navigational structure, no matter what content they pour into it. But shells require lots of generic links, Spool says. With generic links, users rarely get what they expect. For example, people don't shop for sweaters the same way they shop for bathing suits, Spool says. "For sweaters, they want to see the fabric. Their concern with a bathing suit is how it fits on the body," he notes. Daily customer input like that helps shape their website, a Lands' End spokeswoman says. Profitable for the past four years, in fiscal 2002 the site surpassed the company's catalog in sales, she says.

Case Study Questions

1. Visit the Macy's website. How does it measure up to the five shopability criteria discussed in this case?

2. Now compare Macy's to Lands' End in each criteria category. Which is better? Explain your choices.

3. What are several other website design suggestions that either website could make to improve their shopability? Explain your suggested improvements.

Source: Adapted from Sami Lais, "How to Stop Web Shopper Flight," *Computerworld*, June 17, 2002, pp. 44–45. Reprinted with permission from *Computerworld*.

GM Locomotive Group: Failure in ERP System Implementation

The more things change, the more they remain the same. Or so it seems. Big companies or their big business units are still quite capable of failing badly when it comes to implementing new enterprise resource planning (ERP) systems. With all the bad publicity about spectacular ERP implementation failures by big U.S. companies over the past ten years, one would think that today's IT departments and business units could develop and manage ERP implementation projects so failure would not be an option. Many probably do. But others continue to take major hits. Take General Motors for instance. Or more specifically, the Locomotive Group of GM's Electromotive Division (www.gmemd.com), the world's largest builder of diesel-electric locomotives.

General Motors Corp.'s locomotive unit encountered such severe problems during a rollout of SAP AG's R/3 enterprise resource planning applications in 2001 that its spare parts business virtually ground to a halt, forcing GM to launch an emergency turnaround effort six months after the software went live. Officials at GM's Locomotive Group said order backlogs and fulfillment cycle times still aren't at levels that fully meet customer demands, although business operations started to improve shortly after the rescue effort began in July 2001.

The SAP software had to be reconfigured, flushed, and repopulated with clean data, said Mike Duncan, director of worldwide aftermarket sales and development at the La-Grange, Illinois–based Electromotive Division. The $2 billion GM subsidiary hired a second consulting firm to help fix the enterprise resource planning and supply chain management systems after its first systems integrator completed the initial rollout. The GM unit, which makes locomotive, diesel engines and armored vehicles such as tanks, also had to retrain end users and remap all the business processes that were being built into the new system.

The locomotive unit launched a SAP-based ERP and supply chain system during 2001 in order to improve its financial reporting and its ability to forecast spare parts needs. The problems started when the Locomotive Group went live with R/3 in January 2001. The plan was to make aftermarket operations more efficient by replacing legacy mainframe systems with ERP system modules powered by R/3 that could handle parts distribution, order entry procurement, and financial reporting, said David Scott, the locomotive unit's executive director. He said the software wasn't configured well enough to match internal business processes, and legacy mainframe data weren't properly formatted for the new system.

Scott said there were no problems with the R/3 software itself, but the applications weren't properly configured to meet GM's needs. As a result, the aftermarket department couldn't accurately forecast demand or ensure that it

had the right mix of parts inventories on hand. "Our business processes were largely arrested by what happened," Scott said. "We spent a lot of money and expected to get something for it, and got something else instead. It was very disappointing." Scott and Duncan declined to identify the first consulting firm that worked on the project, nor would they discuss the process they used to originally configure and operate the system. They also declined to disclose the cost of the project or the financial impact of the system problems.

A spokesman at SAP America Inc. in Newtown Square, Pennsylvania, declined to comment specifically on the situation at GM. "They continue to be a productive customer at this point, and we continue to work with them," he said.

Duncan said the materials supply and forecasting modules in the ERP system were especially troublesome. The way they were configured didn't reflect the complexity of the distribution processes that the Locomotive Group uses to supply parts to customers in the United States and other countries, he said. In addition, some legacy data weren't adequately reformatted to work within the SAP applications.

The Locomotive Group brought in Chicago-based Technology Solutions Co. to help reconfigure the ERP systems. Scott said that although most aftermarket operations have returned to normal, GM is still looking for continued improvements from both IT and business process standpoints. The Locomotive Group is also outsourcing SAP-related application support, end-user training, and follow-on software implementation for the new ERP system to Technology Solutions. And despite the major start-up problems with their current ERP system, GM still plans to install SAP's enterprise resource planning software in the locomotive unit's manufacturing operations and other departments in the next few years.

Case Study Questions

1. GM Locomotive says the problem wasn't with the ERP software. Then what did cause the major failure of their ERP system? Explain.

2. What major shortcomings in systems implementation, conversion, or project management practices do you recognize in this case?

3. What would you advise GM Locomotive to do differently to avoid similar problems in their upcoming ERP implementations? Explain the reasons for your proposals.

Source: Adapted from Marc Songini, "GM Locomotive Unit Puts ERP Rollout Back on Track," *Computerworld*, February 11, 2002, p. 12. Reprinted with permission from *Computerworld*.

MODULE V

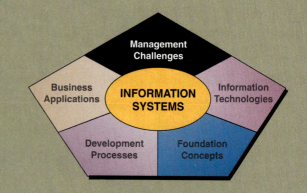

MANAGEMENT CHALLENGES

What managerial challenges do information systems pose for today's business enterprises? The two chapters of this module emphasize how managers and business professionals can manage the successful use of information technologies in a global economy.

- Chapter 11, **Security and Ethical Challenges,** discusses the threats against, and defenses needed for, the performance and security of business information systems, as well as the ethical implications and societal impacts of information technology.

- Chapter 12, **Enterprise and Global Management of Information Technology,** emphasizes the impact of business applications of information technology on management and organizations, the components of information systems management, and the managerial implications of the use of information technology in global business.

CHAPTER 11

APPLICATIONS IN BUSINESS AND MANAGEMENT
SECURITY AND ETHICAL CHALLENGES

Chapter Highlights

Section I
Security, Ethical, and Societal Challenges of IT
Introduction
Real World Case: MTV Networks and First Citizens Bank: Defending against Hacker and Virus Attacks
Ethical Responsibility of Business Professionals
Computer Crime
Privacy Issues
Other Challenges
Health Issues
Societal Solutions

Section II
Security Management of Information Technology
Introduction
Real World Case: Oppenheimer Funds, Cardinal Health, and Exodus: IT Security Management Qualifications
Tools of Security Management
Internetworked Security Defenses
Other Security Measures
System Controls and Audits

Learning Objectives

After reading and studying this chapter, you should be able to:

1. Identify several ethical issues in how the use of information technologies in business affects employment, individuality, working conditions, privacy, crime, health, and solutions to societal problems.

2. Identify several types of security management strategies and defenses, and explain how they can be used to ensure the security of business applications of information technology.

3. Propose several ways that business managers and professionals can help to lessen the harmful effects and increase the beneficial effects of the use of information technology.

SECTION I   Security, Ethical, and Societal Challenges of IT

Introduction

There is no question that the use of information technology in business presents major security challenges, poses serious ethical questions, and affects society in significant ways. Therefore, in this section we will explore the threats to businesses and individuals posed by many types of computer crime and unethical behavior. In Section II, we will examine a variety of methods that companies use to manage the security and integrity of their business systems. Now let's look at a real world example.

Analyzing MTV Networks and First Citizens Bank

Read the Real World Case on MTV Networks and First Citizens Bank on the next page. We can learn a lot from this case about the ethical and security issues and challenges that surround the business use of Internet technologies. See Figure 11.1.

MTV Networks has to protect its 15 entertainment websites from frequent attacks by hackers, especially during special events like the MTV Awards. So they use a new network security software tool to screen incoming traffic and filter out the hacker distributed denial of service (DDOS) traffic, while letting legitimate traffic into their websites. First Citizens Bank uses a new intrusion detection and prevention software tool which has successfully protected its website from several recent destructive computer viruses and hacker probes and attacks. Though these tools have their limitations, their cost is more than justified by the business that is not lost through website downtime.

Business/IT Security, Ethics, and Society

The use of information technologies in business has had major impacts on society, and thus raises ethical issues in the areas of crime, privacy, individuality, employment, health, and working conditions. See Figure 11.2.

However, you should also realize that information technology has had beneficial results as well as detrimental effects on society and people in each of these areas. For example, computerizing a manufacturing process may have the adverse effect of eliminating people's jobs, but also have the beneficial result of improving working conditions and producing products of higher quality at less cost. So your job as a

FIGURE 11.1

Brian Amirian is director of Web hosting and development for MTV Networks Online Technology, including responsibility for IT security at 15 entertainment websites.

Source: Giorgio Palmisano.

MTV Networks and First Citizens Bank: Defending against Hacker and Virus Attacks

MTV.com, the website for the cable TV music channel, is the target of distributed denial of service (DDOS) attacks each fall when the MTV Video Music Awards are televised. But the attacks, in which MTV.com's network servers are deliberately overloaded by massive automated requests for service by hackers, are now blunted because New York–based Viacom International's (www.viacom.com) MTV Networks division is protecting its 15 entertainment websites (including the MTV, VH-1, and Nickelodeon sites) with Enforcer, a network security software tool from Mazu Networks Inc. in Cambridge, Massachusetts.

"During the MTV Awards and other highly publicized TV events, some folks try to knock us out of the water," says Brian Amirian, director of Web hosting and development at MTV Networks Online Technology. So last year, MTV attached Mazu's Enforcer to telecom uplinks between the MTV websites and the company's Internet service provider.

Amirian says one reason he selected Mazu's product is the efficient way it uses proprietary hardware to filter out DDOS attacks. Some other products that he evaluated, but rejected, used software that relied on the more limited filtering capabilities of existing network routers. Mazu's Enforcer builds a statistical model of website traffic when no attack is occurring, says Carty Castaldi, vice president of engineering at Mazu Networks. During a DDOS attack, Enforcer identifies data packets associated with the attack based on their statistical differences from the norm and recommends a filter that typically blocks 80 percent of the attack packets and about 5 percent of nonattack packets, he says.

Enforcer is good but not foolproof say some security analysts. It works best when there is no variation in the attacking packets. But some attackers switch the packet types midattack, reducing Enforcer's effectiveness until it can reanalyze the situation and recommend a different filter. The more varied the attack, the less effective Enforcer is, say these analysts. But Eric Hemmendinger, research director for security and privacy at Aberdeen Group in Boston, says a key test for combating DDOS attacks "is to let the traffic that's appropriate come through to your website, and not let it be choked out by the attack. My impression is that the Mazu product meets this test." In fact, Hemmendinger says that other security vendors are likely to copy Mazu's dual detection approach: performing deep analysis of incoming data packets, while also analyzing trends to discover changes in a website's traffic.

In any event, MTV Networks' Amirian is happy. According to his calculations, he recouped the $32,000 investment in Enforcer within about two months because the Mazu device kept MTV's website from being disrupted during the heavy advertising period surrounding the Video Music Awards.

First Citizens Bank (www.firstcitizensbank.com) in Raleigh, North Carolina, also implemented a network security system to protect its website. And First Citizens installed an intrusion-detection system from Entercept Security Technologies just in time back in March 2000. The Code Red worm hit three days after the bank installed Entercept on customer-related Internet-facing servers, and the Nimda virus hit shortly after that, says Jay Ward, senior network security analyst at First Citizens. "But we kept humming along without skipping a beat, so I'd say yes, that was a definite return on investment," he says. "When the CIO asked me why we weren't hit when some of our peers' internal bank networks were down for up to three days, I told him it was Entercept."

Entercept provides intrusion-detection and prevention software for host and application servers and will soon expand the capability to database servers. The software decides whether to permit a system request into a server from an external network source based on the signature of the request or behavior rules. For example, if a hacker were seeking a password file on a Web server, that behavior would be contrary to the normal behavior of someone accessing a Web page and wouldn't be allowed.

One big advantage Entercept offered First Citizens is that it gave their network administrators time to thoroughly test patches and then apply them themselves. Some vendors had told the bank they couldn't support the servers if the patches were installed by bank personnel. First Citizens decided that waiting for the vendors to install the systems would take too long, Ward says. Because host-based intrusion prevention software must be installed on every server, it can be very expensive, notes Gartner Inc. But a $1,595 Entercept Web server product provides such good protection that it's worth the price, Ward says.

Case Study Questions

1. What are the business value and security benefits and limitations of defenses against DDOS attacks like those used by MTV Networks?

2. What are the business benefits and limitations of an intrusion-detection system like that installed at First Citizens?

3. What security defenses should small businesses have to protect their websites and internal systems? Explain your choices.

Source: Adapted from Steve Alexander and Matt Hamblen, "Top-Flight Technology," *Computerworld*, September 23, 2002, pp. 30–32. Reprinted with permission from *Computerworld*.

FIGURE 11.2

Important aspects of the security, ethical, and societal dimensions of the use of information technology in business. Remember that information technologies can support both beneficial or detrimental effects on society in each of the areas shown.

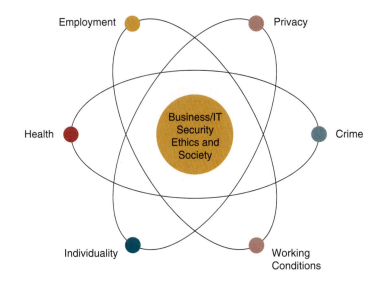

manager or business professional should involve managing your work activities and those of others to minimize the detrimental effects of business applications of information technology and optimize their beneficial effects. That would represent an ethically responsible use of information technology.

Ethical Responsibility of Business Professionals

As a business professional, you have a responsibility to promote ethical uses of information technology in the workplace. Whether you have managerial responsibilities or not, you should accept the ethical responsibilities that come with your work activities. That includes properly performing your role as a vital human resource in the business systems you help develop and use in your organization. As a manager or business professional, it will be your responsibility to make decisions about business activities and the use of information technologies, which may have an ethical dimension that must be considered.

For example, should you electronically monitor your employees' work activities and electronic mail? Should you let employees use their work computers for private business or take home copies of software for their personal use? Should you electronically access your employees' personnel records or workstation files? Should you sell customer information extracted from transaction processing systems to other companies? These are a few examples of the types of decisions you will have to make that have a controversial ethical dimension. So let's take a closer look at several ethical foundations in business and information technology.

Business Ethics

Business ethics is concerned with the numerous ethical questions that managers must confront as part of their daily business decision making. For example, Figure 11.3 outlines some of the basic categories of ethical issues and specific business practices that have serious ethical consequences. Notice that the issues of employee privacy, security of company records, and workplace safety are highlighted because they have been major areas of ethical controversy in information technology.

How can managers make ethical decisions when confronted with business issues such as those listed in Figure 11.3? Several important alternatives based on theories of corporate social responsibility can be used [38, 39]. For example, in business ethics, the **stockholder theory** holds that managers are agents of the stockholders, and their only ethical responsibility is to increase the profits of the business without violating the law or engaging in fraudulent practices.

However, the **social contract theory** states that companies have ethical responsibilities to all members of society, which allow corporations to exist based on a social contract. The first condition of the contract requires companies to enhance the

FIGURE 11.3

Basic categories of ethical business issues. Information technology has caused ethical controversy in the areas of intellectual property rights, customer and employee privacy, security of company information, and workplace safety.

Equity	Rights	Honesty	Exercise of Corporate Power
Executive Salaries	Corporate Due Process	Employee Conflicts	Product Safety
Comparable Worth	Employee Health	of Interest	Environmental Issues
Product Pricing	Screening	**Security of Company**	Disinvestment
Intellectual	**Customer Privacy**	**Information**	Corporate Contributions
Property Rights	**Employee Privacy**	Inappropriate Gifts	Social Issues Raised by
Noncompetitive	Sexual Harassment	Advertising Content	Religious Organizations
Agreements	Affirmative Action	Government Contract	Plant/Facility Closures and
	Equal Employment	Issues	Downsizing
	Opportunity	Financial and Cash	Political Action Committees
	Shareholder Interests	Management Procedures	**Workplace Safety**
	Employment at Will	Questionable Business	
	Whistle-Blowing	Practices in Foreign	
		Countries	

Source: Adapted from The Conference Board, "Defending Corporate Ethics," in Peter Madsen and Jay Shafritz, *Essentials of Business Ethics* (New York: Meridian, 1990), p. 18.

economic satisfaction of consumers and employees. They must do that without polluting the environment or depleting natural resources, misusing political power, or subjecting their employees to dehumanizing working conditions. The second condition requires companies to avoid fraudulent practices, show respect for their employees as human beings, and avoid practices that systematically worsen the position of any group in society.

The **stakeholder theory** of business ethics maintains that managers have an ethical responsibility to manage a firm for the benefit of all its stakeholders, which are all individuals and groups that have a stake in or claim on a company. This usually includes the corporation's stockholders, employees, customers, suppliers, and the local community. Sometimes the term is broadened to include all groups who can affect or be affected by the corporation, such as competitors, government agencies and special interest groups. Balancing the claims of conflicting stakeholders is obviously not an easy task for managers.

Technology Ethics

Another important ethical dimension deals specifically with the ethics of the use of any form of technology. For example, Figure 11.4 outlines four principles of technology ethics. These principles can serve as basic ethical requirements that companies

FIGURE 11.4

Ethical principles to help evaluate the potential harms or risks of the use of new technologies.

Principles of Technology Ethics
● **Proportionality.** The good achieved by the technology must outweigh the harm or risk. Moreover, there must be no alternative that achieves the same or comparable benefits with less harm or risk.
● **Informed Consent.** Those affected by the technology should understand and accept the risks.
● **Justice.** The benefits and burdens of the technology should be distributed fairly. Those who benefit should bear their fair share of the risks, and those who do not benefit should not suffer a significant increase in risk.
● **Minimized Risk.** Even if judged acceptable by the other three guidelines, the technology must be implemented so as to avoid all unnecessary risk.

FIGURE 11.5

Part of the AITP standards of professional conduct. This code can serve as a model for ethical conduct by business end users as well as IS professionals.

AITP Standards of Professional Conduct
In recognition of my obligation to my employer I shall:
● Avoid conflicts of interest and ensure that my employer is aware of any potential conflicts.
● Protect the privacy and confidentiality of all information entrusted to me.
● Not misrepresent or withhold information that is germane to the situation.
● Not attempt to use the resources of my employer for personal gain or for any purpose without proper approval.
● Not exploit the weakness of a computer system for personal gain or personal satisfaction.
In recognition of my obligation to society I shall:
● Use my skill and knowledge to inform the public in all areas of my expertise.
● To the best of my ability, ensure that the products of my work are used in a socially responsible way.
● Support, respect, and abide by the appropriate local, state, provincial, and federal laws.
● Never misrepresent or withhold information that is germane to a problem or a situation of public concern, nor will I allow any such known information to remain unchallenged.
● Not use knowledge of a confidential or personal nature in any unauthorized manner to achieve personal gain.

should meet to help ensure the ethical implementation of new information technologies and information systems in business.

Ethical Guidelines

We have outlined a few ethical principles that can serve as the basis for ethical conduct by managers, end users, and IS professionals. But what more specific guidelines might help your ethical use of information technology?

One way to answer this question is to examine statements of responsibilities contained in codes of professional conduct for IS professionals. A good example is the code of professional conduct of the Association of Information Technology Professionals (AITP), an organization of professionals in the computing field. Its code of conduct outlines the ethical considerations inherent in the major responsibilities of an IS professional. Figure 11.5 is a portion of the AITP code of conduct.

Business and IS professionals would live up to their ethical responsibilities by voluntarily following such guidelines. For example, you can be a **responsible professional** by (1) acting with integrity, (2) increasing your professional competence, (3) setting high standards of personal performance, (4) accepting responsibility for your work, and (5) advancing the health, privacy, and general welfare of the public. Then you would be demonstrating ethical conduct, avoiding computer crime, and increasing the security of any information system you develop or use.

Enron Corporation: Failure in Business Ethics	Much has been said about the driven, cultlike ethos of the organization that styled itself "the world's leading company." Truth to tell, for all its razzle-dazzle use of Internet technology, a lot of the things Enron did weren't so very exceptional: paying insanely large bonuses to executives, for example, often in the form of stock options (that practice not only hid true compensation costs but also encouraged managers to keep the stock price up by any means necessary); promising outlandish growth, year after year, and making absurdly confident predictions about every new market it entered, however untested; scarcely ever admitting a

weakness to the outside world, and showing scant interest in the questions or doubts of some in its own ranks.

Camouflaging drab facts in trendy consulto-speak was a prime Enron tactic. Woe to anyone who dared to suggest, in front of former CEO Jeffrey Skilling, that Enron was a mere *trading* company rather than a company engaged in "substituting hard-wiring with markets for the benefit of vertically integrated industries."

But credibility comes hard in business. You earn it slowly, by conducting yourself with integrity year in and year out, or by showing exceptional leadership in exceptional circumstances, such as September 11. The surest way to lose it, short of being caught in an outright lie, is to promise much and deliver little. Those, at least, are two conclusions suggested by an exclusive survey of executives conducted by Clark Martire & Bartolomeo for *Business 2.0*.

Executives rated Enron Chairman and CEO Ken Lay least credible of the business figures in the survey. Perhaps it had something to do with statements like:

- "Our performance has never been stronger; our business model has never been more robust; our growth has never been more certain ... I have never felt better about the prospects for the company." —E-mail to employees, Aug. 14, 2001

- "The company is probably in the strongest and best shape that it has ever been in." —Interview in *Business Week*, Aug. 24, 2001

- "Our 26 percent increase in [profits] shows the very strong results of our core wholesale and retail energy businesses and our natural gas pipelines." —Press release, Oct. 16, 2001

But three weeks later, Enron admitted that it had overstated earnings by $586 million since 1997. Within a few more weeks, Enron also disclosed a stunning $638 million third-quarter loss, then filed for Chapter 11 bankruptcy [23].

Computer Crime

Cyber crime is becoming one of the Net's growth businesses. Today, criminals are doing everything from stealing intellectual property and committing fraud to unleashing viruses and committing acts of cyber terrorism [36].

Computer crime is a growing threat to society caused by the criminal or irresponsible actions of individuals who are taking advantage of the widespread use and vulnerability of computers and the Internet and other networks. It thus presents a major challenge to the ethical use of information technologies. Computer crime poses serious threats to the integrity, safety, and survival of most business systems, and thus makes the development of effective security methods a top priority. See Figure 11.6.

Computer crime is defined by the Association of Information Technology Professionals (AITP) as including (1) the unauthorized use, access, modification, and destruction of hardware, software, data, or network resources; (2) the unauthorized release of information; (3) the unauthorized copying of software; (4) denying an end user access to his or her own hardware, software, data, or network resources; and (5) using or conspiring to use computer or network resources to illegally obtain information or tangible property. This definition was promoted by the AITP in a Model Computer Crime Act, and is reflected in many computer crime laws.

Exodus Communications: Cybercrime on the Internet

For Charles Neal, a 20-year veteran of the FBI, Mafiaboy was the watershed case for cybercrime. On Monday, February 7, 2000, a 15-year-old from suburban Montreal with the online moniker Mafiaboy launched a week-long Internet attack on Yahoo, CNN.com, Amazon.com, eBay, Dell, Buy.com, and several others causing

FIGURE 11.6
The threat from computer crimes and other online security breaches continues to increase, but companies still lag in implementing IT security.

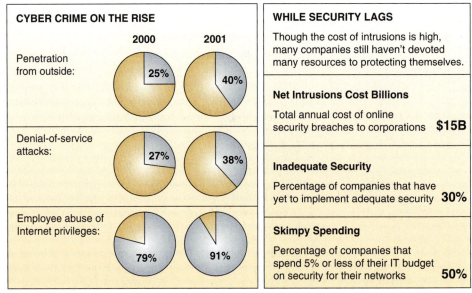

CYBER CRIME ON THE RISE

	2000	2001
Penetration from outside:	25%	40%
Denial-of-service attacks:	27%	38%
Employee abuse of Internet privileges:	79%	91%

WHILE SECURITY LAGS

Though the cost of intrusions is high, many companies still haven't devoted many resources to protecting themselves.

Net Intrusions Cost Billions

Total annual cost of online security breaches to corporations **$15B**

Inadequate Security

Percentage of companies that have yet to implement adequate security **30%**

Skimpy Spending

Percentage of companies that spend 5% or less of their IT budget on security for their networks **50%**

Data: FBI/Computer Security Institute.
Survey Based on 538 Responses from IT Security Professionals.
Source: Adapted from "In Depth: Security," *Computerworld*, July 9, 2001, p. 58.

losses estimated in the millions. The hacker hit the companies with what is now commonly known as a distributed denial-of-service attack, which flooded the victims' Internet servers with messages until they collapsed.

Mafiaboy was a newbie hacker, a "script kiddie." He begged the software—now widely available on several Internet hacker sites—from other hackers and then used it to break into and gain root access to more than 50 servers, most of them located at American universities. He then used those servers to launch his assault.

That morning, calls began coming into Neal's office at the FBI's Los Angeles computer intrusion squad. Neal sent an agent to the Irvine, California, data center of Exodus Communications, one of the world's largest providers of Internet services and network facilities, whose corporate customers included many of Mafiaboy's victims. Neal's team soon began poring over Exodus's network logs, ultimately tracing the attacks to Mafiaboy's home computer. Jill Knesek, the case agent, then flew to Montreal where the Royal Canadian Mounted Police were placing a phone tap on Mafiaboy's house.

What made Mafiaboy so important? It proved to Neal that anybody, even someone with very limited talent, could launch a massive cyberattack. And while Mafiaboy primarily targeted dot-coms, almost every company, and maybe your home, is now online and networked to some extent. The case exposed two major trends in cybercrime weapons and vulnerability. The weapons are becoming increasingly automated and easy to use, and the pool of vulnerable potential victims is expanding. Automation, Neal argues, opens up cybercrime to all sorts of groups, from hacktivists to career criminals and terrorists [4].

Hacking

Cyber thieves have at their fingertips a dozen dangerous tools, from "scans" that ferret out weaknesses in website software programs to "sniffers" that snatch passwords [36].

Hacking, in computerese, is the obsessive use of computers, or the unauthorized access and use of networked computer systems. Illegal hackers (also called *crackers*) frequently assault the Internet and other networks to steal or damage data and programs. One of the issues in hacking is what to do about a hacker who commits only *electronic breaking and entering*; that is, gets access to a computer system, reads

FIGURE 11.7
Examples of common hacking tactics to assault companies through the Internet and other networks.

Common Hacking Tactics

Denial of Service This is becoming a common networking prank. By hammering a website's equipment with too many requests for information, an attacker can effectively clog the system, slowing performance or even crashing the site. This method of overloading computers is sometimes used to cover up an attack.

Scans Widespread probes of the Internet to determine types of computers, services, and connections. That way the bad guys can take advantage of weaknesses in a particular make of computer or software program.

Sniffer Programs that covertly search individual packets of data as they pass through the Internet, capturing passwords or the entire contents.

Spoofing Faking an e-mail address or Web page to trick users into passing along critical information like passwords or credit card numbers.

Trojan Horse A program that, unknown to the user, contains instructions that exploit a known vulnerability in some software.

Back Doors In case the original entry point has been detected, having a few hidden ways back makes reentry easy—and difficult to detect.

Malicious Applets Tiny programs, sometimes written in the popular Java computer language, that misuse your computer's resources, modify files on the hard disk, send fake e-mail, or steal passwords.

War Dialing Programs that automatically dial thousands of telephone numbers in search of a way in through a modem connection.

Logic Bombs An instruction in a computer program that triggers a malicious act.

Buffer Overflow A technique for crashing or gaining control of a computer by sending too much data to the buffer in a computer's memory.

Password Crackers Software that can guess passwords.

Social Engineering A tactic used to gain access to computer systems by talking unsuspecting company employees out of valuable information such as passwords.

Dumpster Diving Sifting through a company's garbage to find information to help break into their computers. Sometimes the information is used to make a stab at social engineering more credible.

Source: Adapted from Ira Sager, Steve Hamm, Neil Gross, John Carey, and Robert Hoff, "Cyber Crime," *BusinessWeek*, February 21, 2000, p. 40. Reprinted with special permission, copyright © 2000 by The McGraw-Hill Companies, Inc.

some files, but neither steals nor damages anything. This situation is common in computer crime cases that are prosecuted. In several states, courts have found that the typical computer crime statute language prohibiting malicious access to a computer system did apply to anyone gaining unauthorized access to another's computer networks. See Figure 11.7.

Hackers can monitor e-mail, Web server access, or file transfers to extract passwords or steal network files, or to plant data that will cause a system to welcome intruders. A hacker may also use remote services that allow one computer on a network to execute programs on another computer to gain privileged access within a network. Telnet, an Internet tool for interactive use of remote computers, can help hackers discover information to plan other attacks. Hackers have used Telnet to access a computer's e-mail port, for example, to monitor e-mail messages for passwords and other information about privileged user accounts and network resources. These are just some of the typical types of computer crimes that hackers commit on the Internet on a regular basis. That's why Internet security measures like encryption and fire walls, as discussed in the next section, are so vital to the success of electronic commerce and other e-business applications.

Cyber Theft

Many computer crimes involve the theft of money. In the majority of cases, they are "inside jobs" that involve unauthorized network entry and fraudulent alteration of computer databases to cover the tracks of the employees involved. Of course, more recent examples involve the use of the Internet, such as the widely publicized theft of $11 million from Citibank in late 1994. Russian hacker Vladimir Levin and his accomplices in St. Petersburg used the Internet to electronically break into Citibank's mainframe systems in New York. They then succeeded in transferring the funds from several Citibank accounts to their own accounts at banks in Finland, Israel, and California [34].

In most cases, the scope of such financial losses is much larger than the incidents reported. Most companies don't reveal that they have been targets or victims of computer crime. They fear scaring off customers and provoking complaints by shareholders. In fact, several British banks, including the Bank of London, paid hackers more than a half million dollars not to reveal information about electronic break-ins [34].

Recourse Technologies: Insider Computer Crime	"Often, there are feelings of betrayal and grudges," particularly during times of financial hardship at companies, said Eugene Schultz, an engineer at Lawrence Berkeley National Laboratory and an adjunct professor at the University of California, Berkeley. "There's no question that there is a link between insider [computer crime] activity and bad times at organizations."

Schultz, who has written a study on the corporate use of "honey pots"—phony servers populated with false data designed to attract hackers—for Recourse Technologies Inc., a security software firm in Palo Alto, California, also said there's a clear link between job roles and insider activity. Surprisingly, systems administrators, network security personnel, and senior executives are often the culprits.

Recourse Technologies CEO Frank Huera recently conducted a live demonstration of his company's Mantrap honey pot software during a sales call at a major computer manufacturer. Within 30 seconds, the software detected that a member of the company's network security team was attempting to hack into the honey pot server.

In another case, a very large financial firm discovered it was losing money from its payroll systems. So it set up two dozen honey pots and gave each server an interesting name, such as "payroll server." The next day, the company's chief operating officer was caught trying to jury-rig another executive's payroll account [41]. |

Unauthorized Use at Work

The unauthorized use of computer systems and networks can be called *time and resource theft*. A common example is unauthorized use of company-owned computer networks by employees. This may range from doing private consulting or personal finances, or playing video games, to unauthorized use of the Internet on company networks. Network monitoring software, called *sniffers*, is frequently used to monitor network traffic to evaluate network capacity, as well as reveal evidence of improper use. See Figures 11.8 and 11.9.

According to one survey, 90 percent of U.S. workers admit to surfing recreational sites during office hours, and 84 percent say they send personal e-mail from work. So this kind of activity alone may not get you fired from your job. However, other Internet activities at work can bring instant dismissal. For example, *The New York Times* fired 23 workers in November of 1999 because they were distributing racist and sexually offensive jokes on the company's e-mail system [44].

Xerox Corporation fired more than 40 workers in 1999 for spending up to eight hours a day on pornography sites on the Web. Several employees even downloaded pornographic videos which took so much network bandwidth that it choked the company network and prevented co-workers from sending or receiving e-mail. Xerox instituted an eight-member SWAT team on computer abuse that uses software to review every website its 40,000 computer users view each day. Other companies clamp down even harder, by installing software like SurfWatch, which enables them to block, as well as monitor access to off-limit websites [29].

FIGURE 11.8

Internet abuses in the workplace.

Internet Abuses	Activity
General e-Mail Abuses	Include spamming, harassments, chain letters, solicitations, spoofing, propagations of viruses/worms, and defamatory statements.
Unauthorized Usage and Access	Sharing of passwords and access into networks without permission.
Copyright Infringement/ Plagiarism	Using illegal or pirated software that cost organizations millions of dollars because of copyright infringements. Copying of websites and copyrighted logos.
Newsgroup Postings	Posting of messages on various non-work-related topics from sex to lawn care advice.
Transmission of Confidential Data	Using the Internet to display or transmit trade secrets.
Pornography	Accessing sexually explicit sites from workplace as well as the display, distribution, and surfing of these offensive sites.
Hacking	Hacking of websites, ranging from denial-of-service attacks to accessing organizational databases.
Non-Work-Related Download/Upload	Propagation of software that ties up office bandwidth. Use of programs that allow the transmission of movies, music, and graphical materials.
Leisure Use of the Internet	Loafing around the Internet, which includes shopping, sending e-cards and personal e-mail, gambling online, chatting, game playing, auctioning, stock trading, and doing other personal activities.
Usage of External ISPs	Using an external ISP to connect to the Internet to avoid detection.
Moonlighting	Using office resources such as networks and computers to organize and conduct personal business (side jobs).

Source: Adapted from Keng Siau, Fiona Fui-Hoon Nah, and Limei Teng, "Acceptable Internet Use Policy," *Communications of the ACM*, January 2002, p. 76.

AGM Container Controls: Stealing Time and Resources

It's not hard to see why the Net provides all kinds of productivity-frittering distractions—from instant messaging socializing, to eBay, pornography, and sports scores. Worse, company secrets may be floating across your firewall. And what you dismiss as simple time wasting could be setting you up for harassment, discrimination, copyright infringement, and other lawsuits. Lawsuits are not the only risk employers face. Intellectual property can make its way out of the office more easily than ever with the help of electronic communications.

There are two ways to remedy cyber-slacking: monitoring Internet use (and making sure employees know you're doing it) and simply blocking sites deemed unrelated to work. Neither is an easy—or bulletproof—fix. If nothing else, a monitoring system with the right amount of follow-up can help employees realize how much company time they waste on the Internet—and help get them back on track.

Howard Stewart, president of AGM Container Controls in Tucson, Arizona, had a feeling that one of his employees was using her PC for personal use a little too much. "When I talked to the employee, she denied she was using e-mail or the Internet for personal use," he says, explaining that the company has a written policy against using the Internet for anything other than work. "However, I knew that this policy was ineffective because a few of my employees had come to the realization that I couldn't monitor their usage."

FIGURE 11.9

Network monitoring software (sniffers) like SurfWatch is used to monitor the use of the Internet by employees at work. SurfWatch can also block access to unauthorized websites.

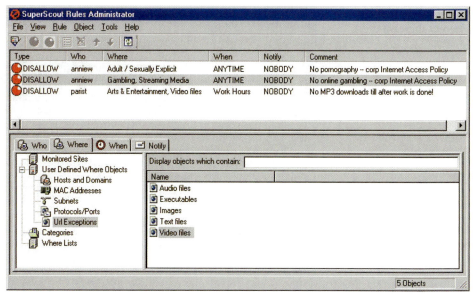

Source: Courtesy of SurfControl.

Stewart chose a simple program from Strategic Business Solutions called Resource Monitor. "Was that employee ever surprised when I was able to negate point-by-point each of her denials that she was using the computer for personal business," Stewart says. "She was shocked to discover that I could give her the exact dates and times she was on and how long she had been at inappropriate sites. Up to that point, she had claimed that she didn't have enough time to take on additional projects at work" [42].

Software Piracy

Computer programs are valuable property and thus are the subject of theft from computer systems. However, unauthorized copying of software, or **software piracy,** is also a major form of software theft. Several major cases involving the unauthorized copying of software have been widely reported. These include lawsuits by the Software Publishers Association, an industry association of software developers, against major corporations that allowed unauthorized copying of their programs.

Unauthorized copying is illegal because software is intellectual property that is protected by copyright law and user licensing agreements. For example, in the United States, commercial software packages are protected by the Computer Software Piracy and Counterfeiting Amendment to the Federal Copyright Act. In most cases, the purchase of a commercial software package is really a payment to license its fair use by an individual end user. Therefore, many companies sign *site licenses* that allow them to legally make a certain number of copies for use by their employees at a particular location. Other alternatives are *shareware*, which allows you to make copies of software for others, and *public domain software*, which is not copyrighted.

Piracy of Intellectual Property

Software is not the only intellectual property subject to computer-based piracy. Other forms of copyrighted material, such as music, videos, images, articles, books and other written works are especially vulnerable to copyright infringement, which most courts have deemed illegal. Digitized versions can easily be captured by computer systems and made available for people to access or download at Internet websites, or can be readily disseminated by e-mail as file attachments. The development of peer-to-peer (P2P) networking technologies (discussed in Chapter 4) have made digital versions of copyrighted material even more vulnerable to unauthorized use. For example, P2P file-sharing software enables direct MP3 audio file transfers of specified tracks of music between your PC and those of other users on the Internet. Thus, such software creates a *peer-to-peer network* of millions of Internet users who electronically trade digital versions of copyrighted or public domain music stored on their PC's hard drives. Let's look at the ongoing debate in this controversial area of intellectual property rights more closely with a controversial real world example.

RIAA Beats Napster: Intellectual Property Controversy	The Recording Industry Association of America (RIAA) won its suit in U.S. courts in 2001 against Napster, which went out of business in 2002. The RIAA charged that Napster's primary function is to enable and encourage copyright violations.

Napster had invented Web software which was free to anyone who wanted to download it, that allowed anyone to zap a song from their computer via the Internet to another user's hard drive in under a minute. But RIAA execs had sued, charging that Napster "has created and is operating a haven for music piracy on an unprecedented scale."

Though that seems to be exactly what Napster was doing, two intellectual-property lawyers had argued that the law favored Napster. For one thing, Napster didn't actually control any of the music—it never even passed through the website. "Napster said, 'We just put software out there,'" said John Lynch of Howrey Simon Arnold & White. "So the plaintiff had to prove Napster was inducing illegal activity. And inducing is not what they were really doing."

What's more, the RIAA had to prove that Napster was used almost exclusively for illegal activity, argued Mark Lemley, a law professor at University of California at Berkeley. That would be difficult because Napster provided access to new, uncopyrighted artists as well.

Napster argued that it was essentially powerless to prevent users from trading copyrighted music and that it shouldn't be held responsible for their misconduct. RIAA general counsel Cary Sherman had emphatically dismissed that argument. "If you have knowledge that what you are doing is causing infringement," he says, "you're liable." And the courts agreed [22]. |

Computer Viruses and Worms

One of the most destructive examples of computer crime involves the creation of **computer viruses** or *worms*. *Virus* is the more popular term but, technically, a virus is a program code that cannot work without being inserted into another program. A worm is a distinct program that can run unaided. In either case, these programs copy annoying or destructive routines into the networked computer systems of anyone who accesses computers infected with the virus or who uses copies of magnetic disks taken from infected computers. Thus, a computer virus or worm can spread destruction among many users. Though they sometimes display only humorous messages, they more often destroy the contents of memory, hard disks, and other storage devices. Copy routines in the virus or worm spread the virus and destroy the data and software of many computer users. See Figure 11.10.

Computer viruses typically enter a computer system through e-mail and file attachments via the Internet and online services, or through illegal or borrowed copies of software. Copies of *shareware* software downloaded from the Internet can be another source of viruses. A virus usually copies itself into the files of a computer's operating system. Then the virus spreads to the main memory and copies itself onto the computer's hard disk and any inserted floppy disks. The virus spreads to other computers through e-mail, file transfers, other telecommunications activities, or floppy disks from infected computers. Thus, as a good practice, you should avoid

FIGURE 11.10

Facts about recent computer viruses and worms.

Worm and Virus Facts
Nimda Worm
● It spreads via both network-based e-mail and Web browsers.
● It modifies critical system files and registry keys.
● It creates a guest account with administrator privileges for hackers to use.
Code Red Worm
● It propagated through TCP/IP Web port 80.
● It identified itself by defacing English language websites with "Welcome to www.worm.com!—Hacked by Chinese!"
● Self-propagation was controlled by means of a "random" IP address generator—that had a bug in it.
● After the initial infection and incubation periods, Code Red was programmed to unleash a denial-of-service attack on the Whitehouse.gov website.
Economic Impact
The research firm Computer Economics estimates the Code Red worm cost society about $2.6 billion in July and August 2001 alone. Add to that $8.7 billion for the Love Bug, $1.2 billion for Melissa, $1 billion for Explorer, and another $1 billion for Sir Cam. These estimates include approximately equal losses resulting from returning the computer systems to preinfection operating status and lost productivity.

Source: Adapted from Jaikumar Vijayan, "Nimda Needs Harsh Disinfectant," *Computerworld*, September 24, 2001, p. 1; and Hal Berghel," The Code Red Worm," *Communications of the ACM*, December 2001, pp. 16, 19.

using software from questionable sources without checking for viruses. You should also regularly *use antivirus programs* that can help diagnose and remove computer viruses from infected files on your hard disk. We will discuss virus defenses further in Section II.

University of Chicago: The Nimda Worm

The Nimda worm—reports of which first began flooding into mailing lists and security firms on Sept. 18, 2001, is a mass-mailed piece of malicious code that infects systems running Microsoft Corp.'s Windows 95, 98, ME, NT, and 2002. Unlike other worms and viruses, Nimda is capable of spreading via both network-based e-mail and Web browsers. It was also written to scan for and exploit back doors left behind by previous viruses such as Code Red and Sadmind.

"The newness of this is that it leverages a number of different vulnerabilities in order to propagate itself," said Allen Householder, an analyst at the CERT Coordination Center at Carnegie Mellon University in Pittsburgh. Nimda propagates via various means, including modifying Web content on vulnerable systems running Microsoft's Internet Information Server software, Householder said. In the process, Nimda last week clogged part of the Internet, slowing down or even stopping Web traffic for some users. Many sites also experienced high volumes of e-mail and network traffic as a result of the worm.

In a four-hour period, the University of Chicago's Web servers were scanned by almost 7,000 unique IP addresses looking for vulnerabilities to exploit, said Larry Lidz, a senior network security officer at the school. As a result of the attacks, about 20 university servers were infected with the Nimda worm and had to be disconnected from the network, Lidz said. He recommended to school officials that those systems be reformatted and all software reinstalled. "If somebody has used a back door left by worms such as Code Red to infect your systems, you never really know what they have done to the system," Lidz said [43].

Privacy Issues

Information technology makes it technically and economically feasible to collect, store, integrate, interchange, and retrieve data and information quickly and easily. This characteristic has an important beneficial effect on the efficiency and effectiveness of computer-based information systems. However, the power of information technology to store and retrieve information can have a negative effect on the **right to privacy** of every individual. For example, confidential e-mail messages by employees are monitored by many companies. Personal information is being collected about individuals every time they visit a site on the World Wide Web. Confidential information on individuals contained in centralized computer databases by credit bureaus, government agencies, and private business firms has been stolen or misused, resulting in the invasion of privacy, fraud, and other injustices. The unauthorized use of such information has seriously damaged the privacy of individuals. Errors in such databases could seriously hurt the credit standing or reputation of an individual.

Important privacy issues are being debated in business and government, as Internet technologies accelerate the ubiquity of global telecommunications connections in business and society. For example:

- Accessing individuals' private e-mail conversations and computer records, and collecting and sharing information about individuals gained from their visits to Internet websites and newsgroups (violation of privacy).

- Always knowing where a person is, especially as mobile and paging services become more closely associated with people rather than places (computer monitoring).

- Using customer information gained from many sources to market additional business services (computer matching).

- Collecting telephone numbers, e-mail addresses, credit card numbers, and other personal information to build individual customer profiles (unauthorized personal files).

Privacy on the Internet

If you don't take the proper precautions, any time you send an e-mail, access a website, post a message to a newsgroup, or use the Internet for banking and shopping . . . whether you're online for business or pleasure, you're vulnerable to anyone bent on collecting data about you without your knowledge. Fortunately, by using tools like encryption and anonymous remailers—and by being selective about the sites you visit and the information you provide—you can minimize, if not completely eliminate, the risk of your privacy being violated [35].

The Internet is notorious for giving its users a feeling of anonymity, when in actuality, they are highly visible and open to violations of their privacy. Most of the Internet and its World Wide Web, e-mail, chat, and newsgroups are still a wide open, unsecured electronic frontier, with no tough rules on what information is personal and private. Information about Internet users is captured legitimately and automatically each time you visit a website or newsgroup and recorded as a "cookie file" on your hard disk. Then the website owners, or online auditing services like WebTrack and DoubleClick, may sell the information from cookie files and other records of your Internet use to third parties. To make matters worse, much of the net and Web are easy targets for the interception or theft by hackers of private information furnished to websites by Internet users [29].

Of course, you can protect your privacy in several ways. For example, sensitive e-mail can be protected by encryption, if both e-mail parties use compatible encryption software built into their e-mail programs. Newsgroup postings can be made privately by sending them through *anonymous remailers* that protect your identity when you add your comments to a discussion. You can ask your Internet service provider not to sell your name and personal information to mailing list providers and other marketers. Finally, you can decline to reveal personal data and interests on online service and website user profiles to limit your exposure to electronic snooping [29].

**Acxiom Inc.:
Challenges to
Consumer Privacy**

What detail of your private life would you least like to see splashed across the Internet? Or added to a database, linked to your name and sold in a mailing list?

The privacy problem is simple. Companies need to glean information that will help target sales. Consumers want the convenience of secure e-commerce without worrying about having their identities stolen, being spammed, or having the aggregators of personal data knowing—and profiting from—every detail of their lives. As retailers and consumers force this issue, e-commerce could get squeezed in the process—particularly among companies that minimize the privacy concerns of their customers. Take Acxiom.

You may not know Acxiom. But the Conway, Arkansas, company probably knows you, having spent 30 years amassing a monster database of consumer information. It has dossiers on 160 million Americans—90 percent of U.S. households.

Acxiom has 20 million unlisted telephone numbers—gleaned mostly from those warranty cards you filled out when you bought that new coffeemaker—that it sells to law enforcement agencies, lawyers, private investigators, debt collectors, and just about anybody else willing to pay its fee. Acxiom is often better at tracking down deadbeat dads than the police. That's because Acxiom combines the most extensive public records database ever gathered by a nongovernmental entity with consumer information it purchases from the private sector.

The company's biggest clients are data-hungry telemarketers, retailers, e-commerce companies, and direct mail marketers. For example, Acxiom advises Wal-Mart on how to stock its shelves, while helping Citicorp decide the creditworthiness of potential customers [13].

Computer Matching

Computer profiling and mistakes in the **computer matching** of personal data are other controversial threats to privacy. Individuals have been mistakenly arrested and jailed, and people have been denied credit because their physical profiles or personal data have been used by profiling software to match them incorrectly or improperly with the wrong individuals. Another threat is the unauthorized matching of computerized information about you extracted from the databases of sales transaction processing systems, and sold to information brokers or other companies. A more recent threat is the unauthorized matching and sale of information about you collected from Internet websites and newsgroups you visit, as we discussed earlier. You are then subjected to a barrage of unsolicited promotional material and sales contacts as well as having your privacy violated [7, 35].

Privacy Laws

Many countries strictly regulate the collection and use of personal data by business corporations and government agencies. Many government **privacy laws** attempt to enforce the privacy of computer-based files and communications. For example, in the United States, the Electronic Communications Privacy Act and the Computer Fraud and Abuse Act prohibit intercepting data communications messages, stealing or destroying data, or trespassing in federal-related computer systems. Since the Internet includes federal-related computer systems, privacy attorneys argue that the laws also require notifying employees if a company intends to monitor Internet usage. Another example is the U.S. Computer Matching and Privacy Act, which regulates the matching of data held in federal agency files to verify eligibility for federal programs.

Computer Libel and Censorship

The opposite side of the privacy debate is the right of people to know about matters others may want to keep private (freedom of information), the right of people to express their opinions about such matters (freedom of speech), and the right of people to publish those opinions (freedom of the press). Some of the biggest battlegrounds in the debate are the bulletin boards, e-mail boxes, and online files of the Internet and public information networks such as America Online and the Microsoft Network. The weapons being used in this battle include *spamming, flame mail*, libel laws, and censorship.

Spamming is the indiscriminate sending of unsolicited e-mail messages *(spam)* to many Internet users. Spamming is the favorite tactic of mass-mailers of unsolicited advertisements, or *junk e-mail*. Spamming has also been used by cyber criminals to spread computer viruses or infiltrate many computer systems.

Flaming is the practice of sending extremely critical, derogatory, and often vulgar e-mail messages *(flame mail)*, or newsgroup postings to other users on the Internet or online services. Flaming is especially prevalent on some of the Internet's special-interest newsgroups.

There have been many incidents of racist or defamatory messages on the Web that have led to calls for censorship and lawsuits for libel. In addition, the presence of sexually explicit material at many World Wide Web locations has triggered lawsuits and censorship actions by various groups and governments.

Other Challenges

Let's now explore some other important challenges that arise from the use of information technologies in business that were illustrated in Figure 11.2. These challenges include the potential ethical and societal impacts of business applications of IT in the areas of employment, individuality, working conditions, and health.

Employment Challenges

The impact of information technologies on **employment** is a major ethical concern and is directly related to the use of computers to achieve automation of work activities. There can be no doubt that the use of information technologies has created new jobs and increased productivity, while also causing a significant reduction in some types of job opportunities. For example, when computers are used for accounting systems or for the automated control of machine tools, they are accomplishing tasks formerly performed by many clerks and machinists. Also, jobs created by information technology may require different types of skills and education than do the jobs that are eliminated. Therefore, individuals may become unemployed unless they can be retrained for new positions or new responsibilities.

However, there can be no doubt that Internet technologies have created a host of new job opportunities. Many new jobs, including Internet webmasters, e-commerce directors, systems analysts, and user consultants, have been created to support e-business and e-commerce applications. Additional jobs have been created because information technologies make possible the production of complex industrial and technical goods and services that would otherwise be impossible to produce. Thus, jobs have been created by activities that are heavily dependent on information technology, in such areas as space exploration, microelectronic technology, and telecommunications.

Computer Monitoring

One of the most explosive ethical issues concerning workplace privacy and the quality of working conditions in business is **computer monitoring.** That is, computers are being used to monitor the productivity and behavior of millions of employees while they work. Supposedly, computer monitoring is done so employers can collect productivity data about their employees to increase the efficiency and quality of service. However, computer monitoring has been criticized as unethical because it monitors individuals, not just work, and is done continually, thus violating workers' privacy and personal freedom. For example, when you call to make a reservation, an airline reservation agent may be timed on the exact number of seconds he or she took per caller, the time between calls, and the number and length of breaks taken. In addition, your conversation may also be monitored. See Figure 11.11.

FIGURE 11.11

Computer monitoring can be used to record the productivity and behavior of people while they work.

Source: Corbis.

Computer monitoring has been criticized as an invasion of the privacy of employees because, in many cases, they do not know that they are being monitored or don't know how the information is being used. Critics also say that an employee's right of due process may be harmed by the improper use of collected data to make personnel decisions. Since computer monitoring increases the stress on employees who must work under constant electronic surveillance, it has also been blamed for causing health problems among monitored workers. Finally, computer monitoring has been blamed for robbing workers of the dignity of their work. In effect, computer monitoring creates an "electronic sweatshop," where workers are forced to work at a hectic pace under poor working conditions.

Political pressure is building to outlaw or regulate computer monitoring in the workplace. For example, public advocacy groups, labor unions, and many legislators are pushing for action at the state and federal level in the United States. The proposed laws would regulate computer monitoring and protect the worker's right to know and right to privacy. In the meantime, lawsuits by monitored workers against employers are increasing. So computer monitoring of workers is one ethical issue in business that won't go away.

Challenges in Working Conditions

Information technology has eliminated monotonous or obnoxious tasks in the office and the factory that formerly had to be performed by people. For example, word processing and desktop publishing make producing office documents a lot easier to do, while robots have taken over repetitive welding and spray painting jobs in the automotive industry. In many instances, this allows people to concentrate on more challenging and interesting assignments, upgrades the skill level of the work to be performed, and creates challenging jobs requiring highly developed skills in the computer industry and within computer-using organizations. Thus, information technology can be said to upgrade the quality of work because it can upgrade the *quality of working conditions* and the content of work activities.

Of course, it must be remembered that some jobs in information technology—data entry, for example—are quite repetitive and routine. Also, to the extent that computers are utilized in some types of automation, IT must take some responsibility for the criticism of assembly-line operations that require the continual repetition of elementary tasks, thus forcing a worker to work like a machine instead of like a skilled craftsperson. Many automated operations are also criticized for relegating people to a "do-nothing" standby role, where workers spend most of their time waiting for infrequent opportunities to push some buttons. Such effects do have a detrimental effect on the quality of work, but they must be compared to the less burdensome and more creative jobs created by information technology.

Challenges to Individuality

A frequent criticism of information systems concerns their negative effect on the **individuality** of people. Computer-based systems are criticized as impersonal systems that dehumanize and depersonalize activities that have been computerized, since they eliminate the human relationships present in noncomputer systems.

Another aspect of the loss of individuality is the regimentation of the individual that seems to be required by some computer-based systems. These systems do not seem to possess any flexibility. They demand strict adherence to detailed procedures if the system is to work. The negative impact of IT on individuality is reinforced by horror stories that describe how inflexible and uncaring some organizations with computer-based processes are when it comes to rectifying their own mistakes. Many of us are familiar with stories of how computerized customer billing and accounting systems continued to demand payment and send warning notices to a customer whose account has already been paid, despite repeated attempts by the customer to have the error corrected.

However, many business applications of IT are designed to minimize depersonalization and regimentation. For example, many e-commerce systems are designed to stress personalization and community features to encourage repeated visits to e-commerce websites. Thus, the widespread use of personal computers and the Internet has dramatically improved the development of people-oriented and personalized information systems.

Health Issues

The use of information technology in the workplace raises a variety of **health issues.** Heavy use of computers is reportedly causing health problems like job stress, damaged arm and neck muscles, eye strain, radiation exposure, and even death by computer-caused accidents. For example, computer monitoring is blamed as a major cause of computer-related job stress. Workers, unions, and government officials criticize computer monitoring as putting so much stress on employees that it leads to health problems [9, 11].

People who sit at PC workstations or visual display terminals (VDTs) in fast-paced, repetitive keystroke jobs can suffer a variety of health problems known collectively as *cumulative trauma disorders* (CTDs). Their fingers, wrists, arms, necks, and backs may become so weak and painful that they cannot work. Many times strained muscles, back pain, and nerve damage may result. In particular, some computer workers may suffer from *carpal tunnel syndrome*, a painful, crippling ailment of the hand and wrist that typically requires surgery to cure.

Prolonged viewing of video displays causes eyestrain and other health problems in employees who must do this all day. Radiation caused by the cathode ray tubes (CRTs) that produce most video displays is another health concern. CRTs produce an electromagnetic field that may cause harmful radiation of employees who work too close for too long in front of video monitors. Some pregnant workers have reported miscarriages and fetal deformities due to prolonged exposure to CRTs at work. However, several studies have failed to find conclusive evidence concerning this problem. Still, several organizations recommend that female workers minimize their use of CRTs during pregnancy [9, 11].

FIGURE 11.12

Ergonomic factors in the workplace. Note that good ergonomic design considers tools, tasks, the workstation, and environment.

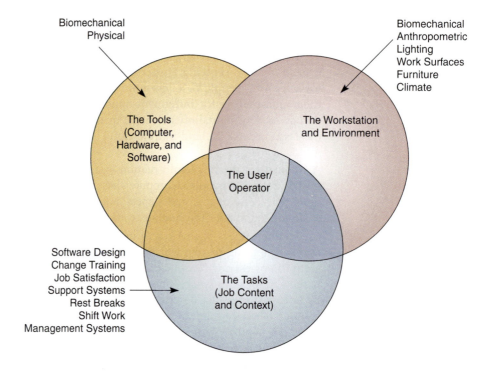

Biomechanical
Physical

Biomechanical
Anthropometric
Lighting
Work Surfaces
Furniture
Climate

The Tools
(Computer,
Hardware, and
Software)

The Workstation
and Environment

The User/
Operator

Software Design
Change Training
Job Satisfaction
Support Systems
Rest Breaks
Shift Work
Management Systems

The Tasks
(Job Content
and Context)

Ergonomics

Solutions to some of these health problems are based on the science of **ergonomics,** sometimes called *human factors engineering.* See Figure 11.12. The goal of ergonomics is to design healthy work environments that are safe, comfortable, and pleasant for people to work in, thus increasing employee morale and productivity. Ergonomics stresses the healthy design of the workplace, workstations, computers and other machines, and even software packages. Other health issues may require ergonomic solutions emphasizing job design, rather than workplace design. For example, this may require policies providing for work breaks from heavy VDT use every few hours, while limiting the CRT exposure of pregnant workers. Ergonomic job design can also provide more variety in job tasks for those workers who spend most of their workday at computer workstations.

Societal Solutions

Computers and networks like the Internet and other information technologies can have many beneficial effects on society. We can use information technologies to solve human and social problems through **societal solutions** such as medical diagnosis, computer-assisted instruction, governmental program planning, environmental quality control, and law enforcement. For example, computers can help diagnose an illness, prescribe necessary treatment, and monitor the progress of hospital patients. Computer-assisted instruction (CAI) and computer-based training (CBT) enable interactive instruction tailored to the needs of students. Distance learning is supported by telecommunications networks, video conferencing, e-mail, and other technologies.

Information technologies can be used for crime control through various law enforcement applications. For example, computerized alarm systems allow police to identify and respond quickly to evidences of criminal activity. Computers have been used to monitor the level of pollution in the air and in bodies of water, to detect the sources of pollution, and to issue early warnings when dangerous levels are reached. Computers are also used for the program planning of many government agencies in such areas as urban planning, population density and land use studies, highway planning, and urban transit studies. Computers are being used in job placement systems to help match unemployed persons with available jobs. These and other applications illustrate that information technology can be used to help solve the problems of society.

It should be obvious to you that many of the detrimental effects of information technology are caused by individuals or organizations that are not accepting the ethical responsibility for their actions. Like other powerful technologies, information technology possesses the potential for great harm or great good for all humankind. If managers, business professionals, and IS specialists accept their ethical responsibilities, then information technology can help make this world a better place for all of us.

SECTION II Security Management of Information Technology

Introduction

With Internet access proliferating rapidly, one might think that the biggest obstacle to electronic commerce would be bandwidth. But it's not; the number one problem is security. And part of the problem is that the Internet was developed for interoperability, not impenetrability [42].

As we saw in Section I, there are many significant threats to the security of e-business and e-commerce systems. That's why this section is dedicated to exploring the methods that companies can use to manage their security. Business managers and professionals alike are responsible for the security, quality, and performance of the business information systems in their business units. Like any other vital business assets, hardware, software, networks, and data resources need to be protected by a variety of security measures to ensure their quality and beneficial use. That's the business value of security management.

Analyzing Oppenheimer Funds, Cardinal Health, and Exodus

Read the Real World Case on Oppenheimer Funds, Cardinal Health, and Exodus on the next page. We can learn a lot from this case about the capabilities that security specialists need to protect corporate resources. See Figure 11.13.

This case emphasizes the wide range of technical, business, and people skills that are needed for positions as IT security specialists and executives to meet the major IT security management challenges in today's networked business world. In particular, the managers of the companies involved emphasize the business knowledge and people skills that must accompany the technical IT skills that may be required. IT security executives must also possess experience and expertise in dealing with issues in areas like government liaison, international regulations, and cyberterrorism in order to lead the IT security management function.

FIGURE 11.13
John Hartmann, VP of corporate and security services, and Ed Daniels, information protection director, lead IT security management at Cardinal Health.

Source: Andy Snow.

REAL WORLD CASE 2

Oppenheimer Funds, Cardinal Health, and Exodus: IT Security Management Qualifications

After Bruce Lobree, an information security engineer and a 20-year IT veteran, lost his job in October of 2001, he decided to work for IT contracting firms in Menlo Park, California, while waiting out the recession. Since then, Lobree has met client after client who wants a jack-of-all-trades—someone who can administer any brand and version of firewall and intrusion detection, is network-savvy, can code, and is versed in new technologies. But clients also want someone who can speak in terms of return on investment to sell projects to executives and who knows everything about the client's business, including its regulatory issues.

"Certifications and technical security expertise aren't my first criteria in placing a security specialist," says Mike Hager, vice president of network security and disaster recovery at Oppenheimer Funds Distributor Inc. (www.oppenheimer funds.com) in New York. "I'm looking for other important factors: Do you understand how the business works? Can you put this in perspective of easier, better, faster and then sell it to the company? Are you a team player? Do you understand the technology basics so I can teach you the rest?"

As at other firms, hiring at Oppenheimer Funds is flat overall. But that doesn't stop Hager from dedicating existing resources to new security problems. For example, he has sent two of his team members to the University of Denver to study database security. Hager has been assigning more training in intrusion detection and incident handling, a move that's consistent with what other firms are doing, says Bill Kasko, division director at RHI Consulting's staffing office in Dallas. Although security jobs are scarce, Kasko says he's seeing more client requests for administrators with knowledge of how to handle cyberattacks, network monitoring, and intrusion-detection programs.

Despite the specialized technical nature of IT security work, employers are more concerned with soft skills. For John Hartmann, vice president of security and corporate services at Cardinal Health Inc. (www.cardinal.com) in Dublin, Ohio, key skills include the ability to learn, build relationships, and understand business requirements. Hartmann has provided his staff with training in security policy development and implementation, compliance with government privacy regulations, and best practices that are the foundation of the company's vulnerability assessment program.

Because he possessed such core skills, Ed Daniels was propelled from telecommunications networking manager to information protection director two years ago at Cardinal, a $49 billion medical supplies and services conglomerate. His networking management work put him in daily contact with other business units, so critical relationships already existed. On top of that, Daniels has a passion for learning, says Hartmann.

Daniels builds his own staff using a similar approach. The company's intrusion-detection analyst, who transferred from Cardinal's pharmaceutical automation group, was picked for his diverse systems and customer service background. The vulnerability assessor came from another Cardinal division, where she provided Unix and database support. She was hired for her writing and relationship-building skills. Even the two analysts hired from outside the firm had little security background. "All my analysts have diverse backgrounds that would add something to the team," says Daniels.

Meanwhile, the roles of senior-level security managers are also expanding, according to Tracy Lenzner, of security executive search firm Lenzner and Associates. As is the case with other IT positions, there's very little hiring of security managers going on, she says, and those who still hold security jobs are picking up global responsibilities, particularly where government liaison and international legal issues are concerned. "Security executives must be expert in government regulations, cyberterrorism protection, private-/public-sector partnerships to support the critical IT infrastructure, and homeland security, even physical security," she says. "So a lot of these candidates come from government backgrounds."

One such person is Charles Neal, vice president of managed security services for business hosting provider Exodus (www.exodus.com), a unit of Cable & Wireless PLC. Neal was promoted to the position six months ago after having joined Santa Clara, California–based Exodus as director of its cyberattack "tiger team." Before that, Neal had been a special agent in the FBI's computer crime squad in Los Angeles.

"There's great expectations within the FBI to work with embassies around the world, a necessity in the borderless Internet world," says Neal. "There's a lot of carry-over from the FBI to the private sector that people wouldn't expect." Like his peers at Cardinal and Oppenheimer Funds, Neal also looks for business and soft skills from his technical team. And when he finds articulate security professionals who are good at relationship building and have a strong work ethic, he mentors them to take over some of his own workload.

Case Study Questions

1. What mix of skills is most sought after for IT security specialists? Why is this mix important in business?

2. Why must IT security executives in business have the mix of skills and experience outlined in the case?

3. What other skills do you think are important to have for effective IT security management? Explain your choices.

Source: Adapted from Deborah Radcliff, "Security under the Gun," *Computerworld*, June 3, 2002, pp. 36–37. Reprinted with permission from *Computerworld*.

FIGURE 11.14

Examples of important security measures that are part of the security management of information systems.

Source: Courtesy of Wang Global.

Tools of Security Management

The goal of **security management** is the accuracy, integrity, and safety of all information system processes and resources. Thus, effective security management can minimize errors, fraud, and losses in the information systems that interconnect today's companies and their customers, suppliers, and other stakeholders. As Figure 11.14 illustrates, security management is a complex task. As you can see, security managers must acquire and integrate a variety of security tools and methods to protect a company's information system resources. We will discuss many of these security measures in this section.

American Family Insurance: Security Management Issues	A few years ago, American Family Mutual Insurance Co. ran its IT operations like most other companies do: Business units would hand down an order for a new program or functionality, and IT would build it. And as in most large organizations, a security manager would attempt to advise developers on vulnerable points and security requirements. But that approach stretched the lone security manager too thin, says Mike Kleckner, who held that position at American Family three years ago.

But now, at the onset of any new project, IT security advisers meet with the business units to discuss their needs. Once the business unit fills out a project security template, a business partner document is generated. Then the IT security advisers work with the system developers to address the security areas identified by the business units.

After that, they have to find a way to bring the business mentality of budgets, policies, operational integration, and more into IT development teams, Kleckner says. It's a matter of asking the developers key questions, so they can see IT security as a strategic business enabler and overcome their misconceptions that security gets in the way of system efficiency.

The final decision still needs to be made by the business units. So once the technical specialists provide a list of solutions to meet the business units' risk requirements, the advisers return to the business units and discuss levels of risk with the business managers who make the final technical security choices [32].

Internetworked Security Defenses

Few professionals today face greater challenges than those IT managers who are developing Internet security policies for rapidly changing network infrastructures. How can they balance the need for Internet security and Internet access? Are the budgets for Internet security adequate? What impact will intranet, extranet and Web application development have on security architectures? How can they come up with best practices for developing Internet security policy? [42]

Thus, the security of today's networked business enterprises is a major management challenge. Many companies are still in the process of getting fully connected to the Web and the Internet for e-commerce, and reengineering their internal business processes with intranets, e-business software, and extranet links to customers, suppliers, and other business partners. Vital network links and business flows need to be protected from external attack by cyber criminals or subversion by the criminal or irresponsible acts of insiders. This requires a variety of security tools and defensive measures, and a coordinated security management program. Let's take a look at some of these important security defenses.

Encryption

Encryption of data has become an important way to protect data and other computer network resources especially on the Internet, intranets, and extranets. Passwords, messages, files, and other data can be transmitted in scrambled form and unscrambled by computer systems for authorized users only. Encryption involves using special mathematical algorithms, or keys, to transform digital data into a scrambled code before they are transmitted, and to decode the data when they are received. The most widely used encryption method uses a pair of public and private keys unique to each individual. For example, e-mail could be scrambled and encoded using a unique *public key* for the recipient that is known to the sender. After the e-mail is transmitted, only the recipient's secret *private key* could unscramble the message [35]. See Figure 11.15.

Encryption programs are sold as separate products or built into other software used for the encryption process. There are several competing software encryption standards, but the top two are RSA (by RSA Data Security) and PGP (pretty good privacy), a popular encryption program available on the Internet. Software products including Microsoft Windows XP, Novell Netware, and Lotus Notes offer encryption features using RSA software.

Firewalls

Another important method for control and security on the Internet and other networks is the use of **firewall** computers and software. A network firewall can be a communications processor, typically a *router*, or a dedicated server, along with firewall software. A firewall serves as a "gatekeeper" system that protects a company's intranets and other computer networks from intrusion by providing a filter and safe transfer point for access to and from the Internet and other networks. It screens all network traffic for proper passwords or other security codes, and only allows authorized transmissions in and out of the network. Firewall software has also become an essential computer system component for individuals connecting to the Internet with DSL or cable modems, because of their vulnerable, "always-on" connection status. Figure 11.16 illustrates an Internet/intranet firewall system for a company [23].

Firewalls can deter, but not completely prevent, unauthorized access (hacking) into computer networks. In some cases, a firewall may allow access only from trusted locations on the Internet to particular computers inside the firewall. Or it may allow only "safe" information to pass. For example, a firewall may permit users to read e-mail from remote locations but not to run certain programs. In other cases, it is impossible to distinguish safe use of a particular network service from unsafe use and so all requests must be blocked. The firewall may then provide substitutes for some network services (such as e-mail or file transfer) that perform most of the same functions but are not as vulnerable to penetration.

FIGURE 11.15   How public key/private key encryption works.

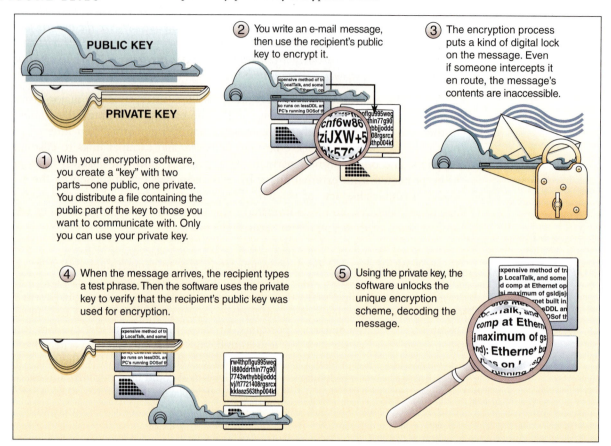

PUBLIC KEY

PRIVATE KEY

① With your encryption software, you create a "key" with two parts—one public, one private. You distribute a file containing the public part of the key to those you want to communicate with. Only you can use your private key.

② You write an e-mail message, then use the recipient's public key to encrypt it.

③ The encryption process puts a kind of digital lock on the message. Even if someone intercepts it en route, the message's contents are inaccessible.

④ When the message arrives, the recipient types a test phrase. Then the software uses the private key to verify that the recipient's public key was used for encryption.

⑤ Using the private key, the software unlocks the unique encryption scheme, decoding the message.

Barry Nance: Testing PC Firewall Security

From all over the world, and even from your hometown, the bad guys' software is constantly probing the Internet, examining consecutive IP addresses for information. Ah! The software finds an active IP address. What sort of device is it? Does it have a network management agent? Whose protocol stack is the device running? Is the IP address permanently assigned? Might the device be a good target for a virus, Trojan, or worm? Is port 23, which is used by Telnet, open? Might it be worth flooding the device with denial-of-service packets? Does the IP address correspond to a registered domain name? Is the network node running Web server, FTP server, database server, or file sharing software?

A sophisticated probe can discover a staggering amount of data and store it for future use. If an employee's home PC has a persistent Internet connection via Digital Subscriber Line (DSL) or cable, the probe's database almost certainly contains his IP address and network node data. Even dial-up users with dynamically assigned IP addresses can be at risk if connections last more than a half-day. An employee who routinely handles company business and confidential data from his home computer is also at risk.

A number of companies offer personal firewall products to help block Internet-based intruders. Software developer Barry Nance tested some of the best-known, including Norton Personal Firewall and Black Ice Defender, to find out which offers the best deterrent to Internet probes.

A software firewall to protect your home PC intercepts and examines each inbound or outbound Internet message. It distinguishes, for example, between legitimate messages that are responses to your Web browsing and illegitimate

FIGURE 11.16   An example of the Internet and intranet firewalls in a company's networks.

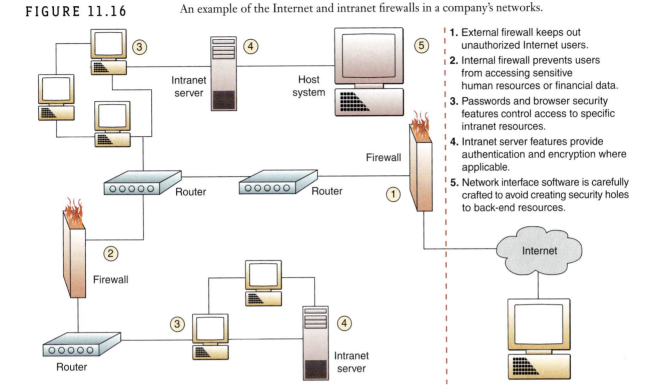

1. External firewall keeps out unauthorized Internet users.
2. Internal firewall prevents users from accessing sensitive human resources or financial data.
3. Passwords and browser security features control access to specific intranet resources.
4. Intranet server features provide authentication and encryption where applicable.
5. Network interface software is carefully crafted to avoid creating security holes to back-end resources.

messages that you never asked for. The software also uses network address translation to substitute a bogus IP address inside your computer's outgoing Internet messages. When the bad guys don't know who you are, they can't penetrate your PC.

Nance used many tools to test security, to try to penetrate each firewall and scan for ports. He also launched a 10-minute barrage of network request messages on all common ports and measured the time it took each firewall to resolve the requests.

The results were gratifying for anyone concerned about Internet security. All of the firewalls successfully blocked unsolicited Internet messages, port scans, and denial-of-service attacks. They slowed Internet access only slightly as they protected the computer from Nance's hacking efforts [28].

Denial of Service Defenses

As attacks against major e-commerce websites (described in Section I) have demonstrated, the Internet is extremely vulnerable to a variety of assaults by criminal hackers, especially **denial of service** (DOS) attacks. Figure 11.17 outlines the steps organizations can take to protect themselves from DOS attacks.

Denial of service assaults via the Internet depend on three layers of networked computer systems: (1) the victim's website, (2) the victim's Internet service provider (ISP), and (3) the sites of "zombie" or slave computers that were commandeered by the cyber criminals. For example, in the DOS attacks described in Section I, the hackers broke into hundreds of servers, mostly poorly protected servers at universities, and planted Trojan Horse .exe programs, which were then used to launch a barrage of service requests in a concerted attack at e-commerce websites like Yahoo! and eBay [31].

As Figure 11.17 shows, defensive measures and security precautions need to be taken at all three levels of the computer networks involved. These are the basic steps

FIGURE 11.17
How to defend against
denial of service attacks.

Defending against Denial of Service
● **At the zombie machines:** Set and enforce security policies. Scan regularly for Trojan Horse programs and vulnerabilities. Close unused ports. Remind users not to open .exe mail attachments.
● **At the ISP:** Monitor and block traffic spikes. Filter spoofed IP addresses. Coordinate security with network providers.
● **At the victim's website:** Create backup servers and network connections. Limit connections to each server. Install multiple intrusion-detection systems and multiple routers for incoming traffic to reduce choke points.

Source: Adapted from Deborah Radcliff, "Fighting the Flood," *Computerworld*, March 6, 2000, p. 66. Copyright 2000 by Computerworld, Inc., Framingham, MA 01701. Reprinted from *Computerworld*.

companies and other organizations can take to protect their websites from denial of service and other hacking attacks.

e-Mail Monitoring

Spot checks just aren't good enough anymore. The tide is turning toward systematic monitoring of corporate e-mail traffic using content-monitoring software that scans for troublesome words that might compromise corporate security. The reason: Users of monitoring software said they're concerned about protecting their intellectual property and guarding themselves against litigation [8].

As we mentioned in Section I, Internet and other online e-mail systems are one of the favorite avenues of attack by hackers for spreading computer viruses or breaking into networked computers. E-mail is also the battleground for attempts by companies to enforce policies against illegal, personal, or damaging messages by employees, and the demands of some employees and others, who see such policies as violations of privacy rights.

Sonalysts, Inc.: Corporate e-Mail Monitoring

John Conlin is browsing around some company's network again. This time he's searching employees' e-mail by key words. But he can also sniff out which websites workers have visited and can see how long they were there and at what time. All this snooping leaves no tracks. What Conlin does is not illegal. In fact, it's probably already happening at your company. If not, just wait. Conlin's company, eSniff, sells an electronic monitoring device that allows businesses to spy on their workers. It may sound like a scene from a movie, but as either an employee or a manager, you'd better get used to it. Some 82 percent of businesses monitor their employees in some way, according to the American Management Association.

eSniff logs all Internet traffic, recording and reporting anything that's been labeled as suspicious. For example, an administrator can view e-mail log summaries and quickly drill down to the actual content of any questionable e-mail to make sure it hasn't fallen into the wrong in-box. "It's rare for eSniff to be installed on a network and not find a lot of inappropriate activity," Conlin says, adding that close to 100 percent of workers register some kind of improper use.

But Randy Dickson, a systems analyst for the Connecticut-based multimedia production firm Sonalysts, Inc., had different results. His firm uses eSniff to monitor all Internet activity. Dickson was pleased to find there was less abuse going on than he thought. For instance, Dickson had been concerned about time wasted using instant messaging, but found that most employee IM activity was for legitimate business use and was actually saving the company money on phone bills [42].

FIGURE 11.18

An example of security suite PC software that includes antivirus and firewall protection.

Source: Courtesy of McAfee.

Virus Defenses

Is your PC protected from the latest viruses, worms, Trojan horses, and other malicious programs that can wreak havoc on your PC? Chances are it is, if it's periodically linked to the corporate network. These days, corporate antivirus protection is a centralized function of information technology. Someone installs it for you on your PC and notebook or, increasingly, distributes it over the network. The antivirus software runs in the background, popping up every so often to reassure you. The trend right now is to automate the process entirely [13].

Thus many companies are building defenses against the spread of viruses by centralizing the distribution and updating of antivirus software as a responsibility of their IS departments. Other companies are outsourcing the virus protection responsibility to their Internet service providers or to telecommunications or security management companies.

One reason for this trend is that the major antivirus software companies like Trend Micro (eDoctor and PC-cillin), McAfee (VirusScan), and Symantec (Norton Antivirus) have developed network versions of their programs which they are marketing to ISPs and others as a service they should offer to all their customers. The antivirus companies are also marketing *security suites* of software that integrate virus protection with firewalls, Web security, and content blocking features [18]. See Figure 11.18.

TrueSecure and 724 Inc.: Limitations of Antivirus Software	Much of the standard antivirus software that was available at the time the Nimda worm struck failed to keep the worm from spreading, users and analysts said. The worm does a number of insidious things, such as modifying critical system files and registry keys, making every directory available as a file share, and creating a guest account with administrator privileges, said Russ Cooper, an analyst at TruSecure Corp., a Reston, Virginia–based security firm. "These characteristics make it incredibly difficult to clean the worm from an infected system," he said.

"Running antivirus software alone will not fix the problem," said Edward York, chief technical officer at 724 Inc., an application hosting service in Lompoc, California. "The server must be secured all over again, all open shares closed, the hot fixes reapplied, the guest account disabled again and all traces of any file called root.exe or admin.dll deleted from the system," York said. Administrators also need to ensure that any registry items added by Nimda have been removed, he indicated. And, says York, until more sophisticated fixes become available, the only sure course is to disconnect infected systems from the network, reformat their hard drives, reinstall software from a clean source, and apply the appropriate security patches [43].

Other Security Measures

Let's now briefly examine a variety of security measures that are commonly used to protect business systems and networks. These include both hardware and software tools like fault tolerant computers and security monitors, and security policies and procedures like passwords and backup files. All of them are part of an integrated security management effort at many companies today.

Security Codes

Typically, a multilevel **password** system is used for security management. First, an end user logs on to the computer system by entering his or her unique identification code, or user ID. The end user is then asked to enter a password in order to gain access into the system. (Passwords should be changed frequently and consist of unusual combinations of upper- and lowercase letters and numbers.) Next, to access an individual file, a unique file name must be entered. In some systems, the password to read the contents of a file is different from that required to write to a file (change its contents). This feature adds another level of protection to stored data resources. However, for even stricter security, passwords can be scrambled, or *encrypted*, to avoid their theft or improper use, as we will discuss shortly. In addition, *smart cards*, which contain microprocessors that generate random numbers to add to an end user's password, are used in some secure systems.

Backup Files

Backup files, which are duplicate files of data or programs, are another important security measure. Files can also be protected by *file retention* measures that involve storing copies of files from previous periods. If current files are destroyed, the files from previous periods can be used to reconstruct new current files. Sometimes, several generations of files are kept for control purposes. Thus, master files from several recent periods of processing (known as *child, parent, grandparent* files, etc.) may be kept for backup purposes. Such files may be stored off-premises, that is, in a location away from a company's data center, sometimes in special storage vaults in remote locations.

Security Monitors

Security of a network may be provided by specialized system software packages known as **system security monitors.** See Figure 11.19. System security monitors are programs that monitor the use of computer systems and networks and protect them from unauthorized use, fraud, and destruction. Such programs provide the security measures needed to allow only authorized users to access the networks. For example, identification codes and passwords are frequently used for this purpose. Security monitors also control the use of the hardware, software, and data resources of a computer system. For example, even authorized users may be restricted to the use of certain devices, programs, and data files. Additionally, security programs monitor the use of computer networks and collect statistics on any attempts at improper use. They then produce reports to assist in maintaining the security of the network.

FIGURE 11.19

The eTrust security monitor manages a variety of security functions for major corporate networks, including monitoring the status of Web-based applications throughout a network.

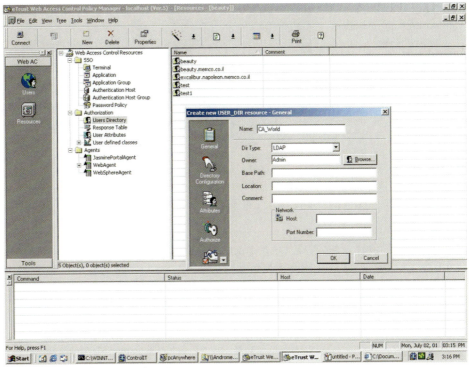

Source: Courtesy of Computer Associates.

Biometric Security

Biometric security is a fast-growing area of computer security. These are security measures provided by computer devices that measure physical traits that make each individual unique. This includes voice verification, fingerprints, hand geometry, signature dynamics, keystroke analysis, retina scanning, face recognition, and genetic pattern analysis. Biometric control devices use special-purpose sensors to measure and digitize a biometric profile of an individual's fingerprints, voice, or other physical trait. The digitized signal is processed and compared to a previously processed profile of the individual stored on magnetic disk. If the profiles match, the individual is allowed entry into a computer network and given access to secure system resources. See Figure 11.20.

FIGURE 11.20

An evaluation of common biometric security techniques based on user requirements, accuracy, and cost.

Evaluation of Biometric Techniques				
	User Criteria		System Criteria	
	Intrusiveness	Effort	Accuracy	Cost
Dynamic signature verification	Excellent	Fair	Fair	Excellent
Face geometry	Good	Good	Fair	Good
Finger scan	Fair	Good	Good	Good
Hand geometry	Fair	Good	Fair	Fair
Passive iris scan	Poor	Excellent	Excellent	Poor
Retina scan	Poor	Poor	Very good	Fair
Voice print	Very good	Poor	Fair	Very good

Source: Adapted from Gary Anthes, "Biometrics," *Computerworld*, October 12, 1998, p. 30. Copyright 1998 by Computerworld, Inc., Framingham, MA 01701. Reprinted from *Computerworld*.

FIGURE 11.21

Methods of fault tolerance in computer-based information systems.

Layer	Threats	Fault Tolerant Methods
Applications	Environment, hardware, and software faults	Application-specific redundancy and rollback to previous checkpoint
Systems	Outages	System isolation, data security, system integrity
Databases	Data errors	Separation of transactions and safe updates, complete transaction histories, backup files
Networks	Transmission errors	Reliable controllers; safe asynchrony and handshaking; alternative routing; error-detecting and error-correcting codes
Processes	Hardware and software faults	Alternative computations, rollback to checkpoints
Files	Media errors	Replication of critical data on different media and sites; archiving, backup, retrieval
Processors	Hardware faults	Instruction retry; error-correcting codes in memory and processing; replication; multiple processors and memories

Source: Adapted from Peter Neumann, *Computer-Related Risks* (New York: ACM Press, 1995), p. 231. Copyright © 1995, Association for Computing Machinery, Inc. By permission.

Computer Failure Controls

Sorry, our computer systems are down is a well-known phrase to many end users. A variety of controls can prevent such computer failure or minimize its effects. Computer systems fail for several reasons—power failure, electronic circuitry malfunctions, telecommunications network problems, hidden programming errors, computer viruses, computer operator errors, and electronic vandalism. For example, computers are available with automatic and remote maintenance capabilities. Programs of preventive maintenance of hardware and management of software updates are commonplace. A backup computer system capability can be arranged with *disaster recovery* organizations. Major hardware or software changes are usually carefully scheduled and implemented to avoid problems. Finally, highly trained data center personnel and the use of performance and security management software help keep a company's computer system and networks working properly.

Fault Tolerant Systems

Many firms also use **fault tolerant** computer systems that have redundant processors, peripherals, and software that provide a *fail-over* capability to back up components in the event of system failure. This may provide a *fail-safe* capability where the computer system continues to operate at the same level even if there is a major hardware or software failure. However, many fault tolerant computer systems offer a *fail-soft* capability where the computer system can continue to operate at a reduced but acceptable level in the event of a major system failure. Figure 11.21 outlines some of the fault tolerant capabilities used in many computer systems and networks.

Visa International: Fault Tolerant Systems

"There is no such thing as 99.9 percent reliability; it has to be 100 percent," says Richard L. Knight, senior vice president for operations at Inovant Inc., the Visa International subsidiary that runs its data centers. "Anything less than 100 percent, and I'm looking for a job." The company has had 98 minutes of downtime in 12 years. Visa fights the battle against outages and defects on two broad fronts: Its physical processing plant is protected by multiple layers of redundancy and backups, and the company's IT shop has raised software testing to a fine art.

There are more than 1 billion Visa payment cards outstanding around the world, spawning $2 trillion in transactions per year for 23 million merchants and automated teller machines and Visa's 21,000 member financial institutions. "We run the biggest payments engine in the world," says Sara Garrison, senior vice president for systems development at Visa U.S.A. Inc. in Foster City, California. "If you took all the traffic on all the stock markets in the world in 24 hours, we do that on a coffee break. And our capacity grows at 20 to 30 percent year to year, so every three years, our capacity doubles."

Visa has four global processing centers to handle that load, but the Washington, D.C., facility is the largest, with half of all global payment transactions flowing through the building. It shares U.S. traffic with a center in San Mateo, California, but it can instantly pick up the full United States if San Mateo goes down.

Indeed, everything in Visa's processing infrastructure—from entire data centers to computers, individual processors, and communications switches—has a backup. Even the backups have backups [2].

Disaster Recovery

Natural and man-made disasters do happen. Hurricanes, earthquakes, fires, floods, criminal and terrorist acts, and human error can all severely damage an organization's computing resources, and thus the health of the organization itself. Many companies, especially online e-commerce retailers and wholesalers, airlines, banks, and Internet service providers, for example, are crippled by losing even a few hours of computing power. Many firms could survive only a few days without computing facilities. That's why organizations develop **disaster recovery** procedures and formalize them in a *disaster recovery plan*. It specifies which employees will participate in disaster recovery and what their duties will be; what hardware, software, and facilities will be used; and the priority of applications that will be processed. Arrangements with other companies for use of alternative facilities as a disaster recovery site and offsite storage of an organization's databases are also part of an effective disaster recovery effort.

System Controls and Audits

Two final security management requirements that need to be mentioned are the development of information system controls and the accomplishment of business system audits. Let's take a brief look at these two security measures.

Information System Controls

Information system controls are methods and devices that attempt to ensure the accuracy, validity, and propriety of information system activities. Information system (IS) controls must be developed to ensure proper data entry, processing techniques, storage methods, and information output. Thus, IS controls are designed to monitor and maintain the quality and security of the input, processing, output, and storage activities of any information system. See Figure 11.22.

For example, IS controls are needed to ensure the proper entry of data into an e-business system and thus avoid the *garbage in, garbage out* (GIGO) syndrome. Examples include passwords and other security codes, formatted data entry screens, and audible error signals. Computer software can include instructions to identify incorrect, invalid, or improper input data as it enters the computer system. For example, a data entry program can check for invalid codes, data fields, and transactions,

FIGURE 11.22

Examples of information system controls. Note that they are designed to monitor and maintain the quality and security of the input, processing, output, and storage activities of an information system.

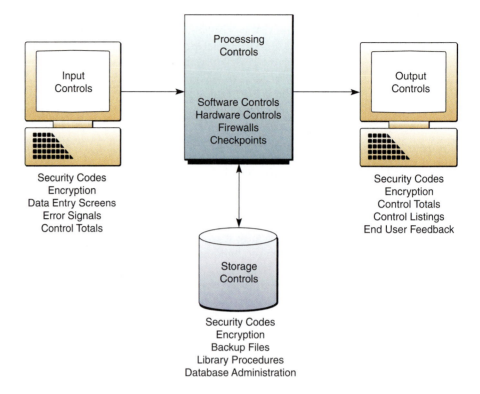

and conduct "reasonableness checks" to determine if input data exceed specified limits or are out of sequence.

Auditing Business Systems

Information systems should be periodically examined, or audited, by a company's internal auditing staff or external auditors from professional accounting firms. Such audits review and evaluate whether proper and adequate security measures and management policies have been developed and implemented. This typically involves verifying the accuracy and integrity of the software used, as well as the input of data and output produced. Some firms employ special EDP auditors for this assignment. They may use special test data to test processing accuracy and the control procedures built into the software. The auditors may develop special test programs or use audit software packages.

Another important objective of business system audits is testing the integrity of an application's *audit trail*. An **audit trail** can be defined as the presence of documentation that allows a transaction to be traced through all stages of its information processing. This journey may begin with a transaction's appearance on a source document and may end with its transformation into information on a final output document or report. The audit trail of manual information systems is quite visible and easy to trace. However, computer-based information systems have changed the form of the audit trail. Now auditors must know how to search electronically through disk and tape files of past activity to follow the audit trail of today's networked computer systems.

Many times, this *electronic audit trail* takes the form of *control logs* that automatically record all computer network activity on magnetic disk or tape devices. This audit feature can be found on many online transaction processing systems, performance and security monitors, operating systems, and network control programs. Software that records all network activity is also widely used on the Internet, especially the World Wide Web, as well as corporate intranets and

FIGURE 11.23

How to protect yourself from cybercrime and other computer security threats.

Security Management for Internet Users
1. Use antivirus and firewall software and update it often to keep destructive programs off your computer.   **6.** Send credit card numbers only to secure sites; look for a padlock or key icon at the bottom of the browser.

1. Use antivirus and firewall software and update it often to keep destructive programs off your computer.	**6.** Send credit card numbers only to secure sites; look for a padlock or key icon at the bottom of the browser.
2. Don't allow online merchants to store your credit card information for future purchases.	**7.** Confirm the site you're doing business with. Watch your typing; it's amazon.com, not amozon.com.
3. Use a hard-to-guess password that contains a mix of numbers and letters, and change it frequently.	**8.** Use a security program that gives you control over "cookies" that send information back to websites.
4. Use different passwords for different websites and applications to keep hackers guessing.	**9.** Install firewall software to screen traffic if you use DSL or a cable modem to connect to the Net.
5. Use the most up-to-date version of your Web browser, e-mail software, and other programs.	**10.** Don't open e-mail attachments unless you know the source of the incoming message.

Source: Adapted from Bill Joy, "Report from the Cyberfront," *Newsweek*, February 21, 2000, p. 44.

extranets. Such an audit trail helps auditors check for errors or fraud, but also helps IS security specialists trace and evaluate the trail of hacker attacks on computer networks.

Figure 11.23 summarizes ten security management steps you can take to protect your computer system resources from hacking and other forms of cybercrime.

Summary

- **Ethical and Societal Dimensions.** The vital role of information technologies and systems in society raises serious ethical and societal issues in terms of their impact on employment, individuality, working conditions, privacy, health, and computer crime. Managers, business professionals, and IS specialists can help solve the problems of improper use of IT by assuming their ethical responsibilities for the ergonomic design, beneficial use, and enlightened management of information technologies in our society. See Figure 11.2.

- **Ethical Responsibility in Business.** Business and IT activities involve many ethical considerations. Basic principles of technology and business ethics can serve as guidelines for business professionals when dealing with ethical business issues that may arise in the widespread use of information technology in business and society.

- **Security Management.** One of the most important responsibilities of the management of a company is to assure the security and quality of its IT-enabled business activities. Security management tools and policies can ensure the accuracy, integrity, and safety of the information systems and resources of a company, and thus minimize errors, fraud, and security losses in their e-commerce activities.

Key Terms and Concepts

These are the key terms and concepts of this chapter. The page number of their first explanation is in parentheses.

1. Antivirus software (407)
2. Audit trail (412)
3. Auditing business systems (412)
4. Backup files (408)
5. Biometric security (409)
6. Business ethics (382)
7. Computer crime (385)
8. Computer matching (394)
9. Computer monitoring (395)

10. Computer virus (391)

11. Denial of service (405)

12. Disaster recovery (411)

13. Encryption (403)

14. Ergonomics (398)

15. Ethical and societal impacts of business/IT (380)

    a. Employment (380)

    b. Health (380)

    c. Individuality (380)

    d. Societal solutions (384)

    e. Working conditions (380)

16. Ethical foundations (382)

17. Fault tolerant (410)

18. Firewall (404)

19. Flaming (395)

20. Hacking (386)

21. Information system controls (411)

22. Intellectual property piracy (390)

23. Passwords (408)

24. Privacy issues (393)

25. Responsible professional (384)

26. Security management (402)

27. Software piracy (390)

28. Spamming (395)

29. System security monitor (408)

30. Unauthorized use (388)

Review Quiz

Match one of the key terms and concepts listed previously with one of the brief examples or definitions that follow. Try to find the best fit for the answers that seem to fit more than one term or concept. Defend your choices.

_____ 1. Ensuring the accuracy, integrity, and safety of business/IT activities and resources.

_____ 2. Control totals, error signals, backup files, and security codes are examples.

_____ 3. Software that can control access and use of a computer system.

_____ 4. A computer system can continue to operate even after a major system failure if it has this capability.

_____ 5. A computer system that serves as a filter for access to and from other networks by a company's networked computers.

_____ 6. Periodically examine the accuracy and integrity of computer processing.

_____ 7. The presence of documentation that allows a transaction to be traced through all stages of information processing.

_____ 8. Using your voice or fingerprints to identify you electronically.

_____ 9. A plan to continue IS operations during an emergency.

_____ 10. Scrambling data during its transmission.

_____ 11. Ethical choices may result from decision-making processes, cultural values, or behavioral stages.

_____ 12. Managers must confront numerous ethical questions in their businesses.

_____ 13. Sending unsolicited e-mail indiscriminately.

_____ 14. Employees may have to retrain or transfer.

_____ 15. Computer-based systems may depersonalize human activities.

_____ 16. Constant long-term use of computers at work may cause health problems.

_____ 17. Computer-based monitoring of environmental quality is an example.

_____ 18. Tedious jobs are decreased and jobs are made more challenging.

_____ 19. Using computers to identify individuals that fit a certain profile.

_____ 20. Collecting information about you without your consent.

_____ 21. Using computers to monitor the activities of workers.

_____ 22. Overwhelming a website with requests for service from captive computers.

_____ 23. Using computers and networks to steal money, services, software, or data.

_____ 24. Using company computers to access the Internet during work hours for personal business.

_____ 25. Unauthorized copying of software.

_____ 26. Unauthorized copying of copyrighted material.

_____ 27. Electronic breaking and entering into a computer system.

_____ 28. A program makes copies of itself and destroys data and programs.

_____ 29. Finds and eliminates computer viruses.

_____ 30. Sending extremely critical, derogatory, and vulgar e-mail messages.

_____ 31. Designing computer hardware, software, and workstations that are safe, comfortable, and easy to use.

_____ 32. End users should act with integrity and competence in their use of information technology.

Discussion Questions

1. What can be done to improve e-commerce security on the Internet? Give several examples of security measures, and technologies you would use.

2. What potential security problems do you see in the increasing use of intranets and extranets in business? What might be done to solve such problems? Give several examples.

3. What artificial intelligence techniques can a business use to improve computer security and fight computer crime?

4. What are your major concerns about computer crime and privacy on the Internet? What can you do about it? Explain.

5. What is disaster recovery? How could it be implemented at your school or work?

6. Refer to the Real World Case on MTV Networks and First Citizens Bank in the chapter. What other network security threats besides denial of service, viruses, and

hacker attacks should businesses protect themselves against? Explain why and how.

7. Is there an ethical crisis in business today? What role does information technology play in unethical business practices?

8. What are several business decisions that you will have to make as a manager that have both an ethical and IT dimension? Give examples to illustrate your answer.

9. Refer to the Real World Case on Oppenheimer Funds, Cardinal Health, and Exodus in the chapter. How should businesses protect themselves from the spread of cyberterrorism in today's internetworked world?

10. What would be examples of one positive and one negative effect of the use of information technologies in each of the ethical and societal dimensions illustrated in Figure 11.2? Explain several of your choices.

Application Exercises

Complete the following exercises as individual or group projects that apply chapter concepts to real world business situations.

1. **Internet Privacy and Anonymity:**
   An Ethical Dilemma
   I recently came across some software that lets you cloak your identity on the Internet. It got me thinking about the whole issue of anonymity on the Net. Suppose a political activist in a country with limited civil rights sends an e-mail to an American human-rights group describing dreadful working conditions in a U.S.-owned factory. The plant's owners have to make changes—but not before local authorities, who monitor Internet traffic, throw the activist in jail. There, anonymity would have helped illuminate a problem.

   Now suppose a child pornographer delivers his wares by e-mail. Authorities intercept the transmissions, but because the pornographer has successfully hidden his identity on the Net, they are unable to identify or find him. In that case, anonymity has protected a felon.

   Whether you find these scenarios troubling will probably determine how you react to new software designed to allow people to send and receive e-mail, post messages to discussion groups, and participate in online chats in perfect anonymity. If, like me, you find both scenarios troubling, then what we have is an ethical dilemma.

   I believe fervently in the right to free speech. I'm pleased that the Internet means that freedom of the

press no longer is restricted, as A. J. Liebling once said, to the person who owns one. But I've also seen enough damage done by anonymous rumor and innuendo to recognize the danger that lurks in freedom without responsibility. I'm glad that such software for Internet anonymity will be available. But in the end, I hope that not many people will feel a need to use it.

   a. Do you share the ethical misgivings of the author on this issue? Why or why not?

   b. Should there be unrestricted use of software that provides anonymity on the Internet? Why or why not?

   c. If you were able to decide this issue now, how would you decide for yourself? Your company? For society? Explain the reasons for your decisions.

   Source: Adapted from Stephen Wildstrom, "A Big Boost for Net Privacy," *BusinessWeek*, April 5, 1999, p. 23. Reprinted with special permission, copyright © 1999 by The McGraw-Hill Companies, Inc.

2. **Your Internet Job Rights:**
   Three Ethical Scenarios
   Whether you're an employer or an employee, you should know what your rights are when it comes to Internet use in the workplace. Mark Grossman, a Florida attorney who specializes in computer and Internet law, gives answers to some basic questions.

Scenario 1

Nobody told you that your Internet use in the office was being monitored. Now you've been warned you'll be fired if you use the Internet for recreational surfing again. What are your rights?

Bottom line. When you're using your office computer, you have virtually no rights. You'd have a tough time convincing a court that the boss invaded your privacy by monitoring your use of the company PC on company time. You should probably be grateful you got a warning.

Scenario 2

Your employees are abusing their Internet privileges, but you don't have an Internet usage policy. What do you do?

Bottom line. Although the law isn't fully developed in this area, courts are taking a straightforward approach: If it's a company computer, the company can control the way it's used. You don't need an Internet usage policy to prevent inappropriate use of your company computers. To protect yourself in the future, distribute an Internet policy to your employees as soon as possible.

Scenario 3

Employee John Doe downloads adult material to his PC at work, and employee Jane Smith sees it. Smith then proceeds to sue the company for sexual harassment. As the employer, are you liable?

Bottom line. Whether it comes from the Internet or from a magazine, adult material simply has no place in the office. So Smith could certainly sue the company for making her work in a sexually hostile environment. The best defense is for the company to have an Internet usage policy that prohibits visits to adult sites. (Of course, you have to follow through. If someone is looking at adult material in the office, you must at least send the offending employee a written reprimand.) If the company lacks a strict Internet policy, though, Smith could prevail in court.

Ethical Questions

a. Do you agree with the advice of attorney Mark Grossman in each of the scenarios? Why or why not?

b. What would your advice be? Explain your positions.

c. Identify any ethical principles you may be using in explaining your position in each of the scenarios.

Source: Adapted from James Martin. "You Are Being Watched," *PC World*, November 1997, p. 258. Reprinted with the permission of *PC World* Communications Inc.

3. American Family Insurance: Evaluating Security Requirements

Web When undertaking a new development project, American Family enables the business unit project managers to set security requirements themselves. A key element is a template developed by the company's IT security advisers that outlines the following key security criteria. Business unit managers must then establish security requirements for the new business system being developed for their unit based on these ten criteria.

Authentication: Who are you?
Authorization: What can you do?
Confidentiality and reliability: Privacy and dependability
Monitoring and tracking: What did you do?
Backup and recovery: Rebuilding the system
Physical security: Locking others out
Change management: Protecting the business process
Legal requirements: What the law expects
Training and awareness: What you need to know
Contingency planning: What if?

a. Visit a popular business website such as Amazon.com or Yahoo.com, and complete their registration process if you are not already a customer. Surf the many parts of the website and evaluate several of its major features, including search, customer service, purchasing, payment, personalization, community, and privacy capabilities.

b. Evaluate the effectiveness of the security at this website based on your experience, using as many as you can of the ten security criteria developed by American Family.

c. Provide several recommendations for improving the security at this website. Explain the reasons for your recommendations.

Source: Adapted from Deborah Radcliff, "Security Ambassadors," *Computerworld*, October 1, 2001, p. 36.

4. Tracking Project Work at AAA Systems 2

DB Database systems typically involve multiple tables that are related to each other and can be combined on the basis of their logical relationship. In this exercise, we will take the database file created in **Application Exercise 3.2,** modify it, and add a second related table containing information about Employees.

The data for the Employee Table shown below is quite simple and consist only of the Employee ID, the Employee Name, and the Billing rate used when charging the employee's work against a project task. The Employee ID is used to identify the employee and to link this data to the project hours data in the existing table.

Employee_Id	Employee_Name	Billing_Rate
123	C. Davis	$70.00
234	J. Jones	$90.00
345	B. Bates	$110.00
456	B. Smith	$80.00

a. If you have not completed **Application Exercise 3.2,** complete part A of that exercise now. Open up the database file you created for **Application**

Exercise 3.2. Next create an employee table with the structure and data shown in the example on page 416. Make sure that the Employee Id column in this new table has exactly the same data type and length that you used for the Employee Id column on the previous table. Create and print a listing of a query that joins the two tables based on the common Employee ID column and displays all columns of both tables.

b. Create a report grouped by employee that lists their Id and Name and then shows the production week, hours worked that week and amount billed (hours worked times billing rate) for that week.

c. Create a report grouped project name that shows the total amount billed for each task within each

REAL WORLD CASE 3

Brandon Internet Services and PayPal: The Business Value of Cyberforensics

Businesses with intellectual property and online customers to protect are increasingly calling on cyberforensics investigators to get to the bottom of cases of employee wrongdoing and electronic crimes. Forensic techniques vary depending on the type of investigation. For example, some investigative firms simply track and trace over the Internet and sort through other publicly available electronic records. Large businesses use cyberforensic and investigative services like those offered by Predictive Systems Inc. (www.predictive.com) in New York, who can set up alarms and traps to watch and catch intruders and criminals within their networks.

"If we're tracing a scam site, we need as much information as we can gather—where the money is, where the credit card accounts are hosting companies, who's aiding and abetting, and so on," says Chris Brandon, president of Brandon Internet Services. Brandon, who doesn't post a public website for security purposes, has clients that include banks, telecom companies, and Internet service provider organizations. "We validate and document the evidence then turn it over to our clients or sometimes to the authorities, and tell them to look for themselves and check it all out." Brandon and other similar investigative firms say the work is rewarding particularly since they can get done in hours what takes weeks or months through court and law enforcement channels.

At PayPal Inc. (www.paypal.com), an online payment processing company in Palo Alto, California, security specialists noticed one day that there were too many Hudsens and Stivensons opening accounts with them. John Kothanek, PayPal's lead fraud investigator (and a former military intelligence officer), discovered 10 names opening batches of 40 or more accounts that were being used to buy high-value computer goods in auctions on eBay.com. So PayPal froze the funds used to pay for the eBay goods (all to be shipped to an address in Russia) and started an investigation. Then one of PayPal's merchants reported that it had been redirected to a mock site called PayPal.

Kothanek's team set up sniffer software, which catches packet traffic, at the mock site. The software showed that operators of the mock site were using it to capture PayPal user logins and passwords. Investigators also used the sniffer to log the perpetrators' own IP address, which they then used to search against PayPal's database. It turned out that all of the accounts under scrutiny were opened by the same Internet address.

Using two freeware network-discovery tools, TraceRoute and Sam Spade, PayPal found a connection between the fake PayPal server address and the shipping address in Russia to which the accounts were trying to send goods. Meanwhile, calls were pouring in from credit card companies disputing the charges made from the suspect PayPal accounts. The perpetrators had racked up more than $100,000

in fraudulent charges using stolen credit cards—and PayPal was fully liable to repay them.

"Carders typically buy high-value goods like computers and jewelry so they can resell them," says Ken Miller, PayPal's fraud control director. PayPal froze the funds in those accounts and began to receive e-mail and phone calls from the perpetrators, who demanded that the funds be released. "They were blatant," says Kothanek. "They thought we couldn't touch them because they were in Russia."

Then PayPal got a call from the FBI. The FBI had lured the suspects into custody by pretending to be a technology company offering them security jobs. Using a forensics tool kit called EnCase, Kothanek's team helped the FBI tie its case to PayPal's by using keyword and pattern searches familiar to the PayPal investigators to analyze the slack and ambient space—where deleted files remain until overwritten—on a mirror-image backup of the suspects' hard drives.

"We were able to establish a link between their machine's IP address, the credit cards they were using in our system, and the Perl scripts they were using to open accounts on our system," Kothanek says. The alleged perpetrators, Alexey Ivanov and Vasili Gorchkov, were charged with multiple counts of wire fraud in May. Gorchkov was convicted in September 2001 on 20 counts of wire fraud and is awaiting sentencing. Ivanov is still awaiting trial.

But PayPal's cybersleuthing also improved PayPal's bottom line by leading to the development of a pattern-matching fraud prevention system that has reduced PayPal fraud rates to 0.5 percent—well below than the average e-business fraud rate of 1.3 to 2.6 percent according to Stamford, Connecticut–based Gartner Inc. "We found tremendous value in having these skills in-house," says Ken Miller, director of the 75-person fraud control group at PayPal. "A lot of our competitors have gone out of business because of fraud. We were able to drop our fraud rate significantly."

Case Study Questions

1. What are the business benefits and limitations of the cybercrime investigative work done by firms like Brandon Internet Services?

2. When should a company use cyberforensic investigative services like those offered by Predictive Systems? Check out their website to help you answer.

3. What is the business value of their cyberforensic and investigative capabilities to PayPal? Would you trust PayPal for your online payment transactions? Why or why not?

Source: Adapted from Deborah Radcliff, "Cybersleuthing Solves the Case," *Computerworld*, January 14, 2002, pp. 36–37; and "Forensic Detectives," *Computerworld*, January 14, 2002, pp. 32–33. Reprinted with permission from *Computerworld*.

Providence Health Systems and Others: Challenges of IT Security Management

Heightened concerns about cyberterrorism and the increasing need to open internal networks to outside access are pushing corporations to bolster network and data center security, on both the IT front and physically. The goal is to add multiple layers of protection and redundancy around the data center and its hardware, software, databases, and network links, while still maintaining the levels of service demanded by the business. On the physical side, companies are boosting their business continuity and disaster recovery capabilities by buying and building redundant hardware and facilities or paying for such services, and geographically separating their IT assets. The technology effort, meanwhile, is focused on supplementing traditional network firewall protection with newer intrusion monitors, access control tools, and tougher IT usage policies.

The need for such protection is being driven by both the increasing threat of cybercrimes and the growing use of the Internet to link companies with partners and customers, says David Rymal, director of technology at Providence Health Systems (www.providence.org) in Everett, Washington. "There is an increasing pressure to enable wide and unfettered access from our business units. We are getting so many requests to open up ports in our firewall that pretty soon it is going to look like Swiss cheese," Rymal says. "The more of them you have open, the more vulnerabilities you create."

The whole notion of "Web services," under which companies will use common Web protocols to link their business systems with those of external partners and suppliers, is only going to increase the need for better security, users say. Adding to the pressures is the growing number of remote workers and the trend toward wireless applications. This has meant finding better ways of identifying and authenticating users and controlling the access they have on the network. "You have to keep in mind that the minute you open your servers or services to the Internet, you are going to have bad people trying to get in," says Edward Rabbinovitch, vice president of global networks and infrastructure operations at Cervalis Inc. (www.cervalis.com), a Stamford, Connecticut–based Internet hosting service.

Companies are also building "air gaps" between their outside-facing applications and back-end data. Providence Health, for instance, doesn't permit external Internet connections or wireless access to terminate on any internal machine. It's far safer to end such connections outside the firewall and then screen all external requests through secure network services, Rymal says.

Antivirus and e-mail filtering tools are being supplemented in many companies with new measures aimed at reducing the risk of attack via e-mail. "E-mail, to me, is always the weakest link, because you are open to just about anything and everything that comes over the Web," says George Gualda, CIO at Link Staffing Services Inc. (www.linkstaffing.com) in Houston.

Link prohibits attachments of certain types and sizes on its network. All Internet-based chatting is banned, and users aren't allowed to download and install software. Scripting functions are disabled to prevent unauthorized scripts from wreaking havoc, says Gualda. Link Staffing uses a secure virtual private network (VPN) service from OpenReach Inc. to connect its 45 remote sites. The OpenReach VPN provides firewall and encryption services, but Link placed an extra firewall in front of the VPN anyway.

While it's impossible to guarantee 100 percent security, companies should make things as difficult as possible for outsiders or insiders to steal or damage IT assets, IT managers say. Cervalis' security, for instance, begins at its ingress points—where the Internet meets its networks. The company uses strict port control and management on all of its Internet-facing routers to ensure that open ports don't provide easy access for malicious attackers. Redundant, load-balanced firewalls that are sandwiched between two layers of content switches filter all traffic coming in from the Internet. Network-based intrusion-detection systems are sprinkled throughout the Cervalis network.

Augmenting physical and electronic security measures with IT security policies that are clearly articulated and enforced is also crucial, Gualda says. Link Staffing has a tough IT usage policy that employees must abide by. Failure to comply can result in termination, says Gualda, who has fired two employees for this reason in the past. To enforce the policy, the company uses monitoring and auditing tools to inventory employee computer usage.

Securing operations also means auditing IT security by regularly going through a checklist of maintenance items, IT managers say. Periodic reviews and external audits are also needed to ensure that there is adequate security. "There is never going to be a 100% security solution; there is always a theoretical way for someone to wind their way through," Rabbinovitch of Cervalis says. "The task, therefore, is to make it as challenging as possible for the hacker."

Case Study Questions

1. Why is there a growing need for IT security defenses and management in business? What challenges does this pose to effective IT security management?

2. What are some of the IT security defenses companies are using to meet these challenges? Use each of the companies in this case as an example.

3. Do you agree with the IT usage policies of Link Staffing? The security audit policies of Cervalis? Why or why not?

Source: Adapted from Jaikumar Vijayan, "Securing the Center," *Computerworld*, May 13, 2002, pp. 56–57. Reprinted with permission from *Computerworld*.

The Doctor's Co. and Rockland Trust: Outsourcing IT Security Management

After the Nimda virus crippled his network for nearly three days in October, Richard Diamond figured there had to be a better way to protect his system. "I wanted to put in a reasonable intrusion-detection system, but I didn't have the resources in-house to integrate our security components and monitor them," says Diamond, CIO at The Doctor's Company (www.thedoctors.com), a physician-owned medical malpractice insurer in Napa, California. Diamond outsourced his security management to Symantec Corp. (www.symantec.com), a vendor of antivirus products that has joined dozens of other product vendors that are expanding their offerings to include managed security services. These vendors review and correlate audit information from different sources, weed out false security threats, and alert customers to security events and how to respond.

Managed security services providers (MSSP) are addressing a very real need as IT departments are drowning in reams of alerts and false alarms coming from virtual private networks (VPN) and firewall, intrusion-detection, antivirus, and other security monitoring systems and logs, says John Pescatore, analyst at Gartner Inc. At the same time, it's impossible for most companies to hire and keep an expert staff to sort through all of those reports on a daily basis, says Pamela O'Leary, senior vice president of information services at Rockland Trust Co. (www.rocklandtrust.com), a $2 billion bank headquartered in Rockland, Massachusetts. There's no denying the value of these services, says O'Leary, who figures she's saving 35 percent annually by outsourcing security event monitoring to Riptech Inc., which was recently acquired by Symantec. That's also true for the Regence Group (www.regence.com), an insurance administration company in Portland, Oregon, that reports saving 80 percent per year by hiring Counterpane Internet Security Inc. (www.counterpane.com) to manage its security event monitoring.

But analysts warn that relying on an MSSP is something of a double-edged sword. There's always the chance that the provider doing business today may not be around next year. This is especially true now with managed security services because providers are struggling with the traditional fallout, fragmentation, and consolidation that accompany most new technology or technology services markets. Service providers also differ widely in terms of the devices they monitor and how they correlate and analyze the information they collect. And vendors' profitability boils down to how well they automate security event correlation and analysis, which can be very time-consuming and expensive if done manually, says Peter Stapleton, director of product management at Ubizen, NV (www.ubizen.com), a monitoring services provider.

Not all providers offer equal monitoring coverage. While many customers may opt for just Web filtering, only a few providers offer the service. Other companies might want their providers to analyze audit data from nonsecurity devices. For example, the company that powered the 2002 Winter Olympics tapped Counterpane to monitor all systems and networks for security threats and other unauthorized activities. Gartner classifies Counterpane and Ubizen as leading monitoring service provider "pure plays," meaning specialized IT security providers that offer vendor-neutral coverage from a range of vendors.

A second emerging category of providers comprises vendors such as Symantec and Network Associates (www.networkassociates.com), which offer security products but are expanding to offer add-on security monitoring services. But these companies, which logically have their own competitive agendas, will service only their own antivirus and intrusion-detection products. And they monitor only third-party firewalls and VPN devices from vendors with which they have strategic partnerships. That may require some users to reinstall only supported products, which O'Leary of Rockland Trust says she was unwilling to do. But The Doctor's Co., which has little security to begin with, didn't mind installing intrusion-detection and antivirus software to conform to Symantec's monitoring capabilities, Diamond says.

It seems like everyone wants a piece of what Gartner predicts will be nearly a $6 billion managed IT security market by 2005. Telecommunications and Web hosting companies, large systems integrators, and the Big Five accounting firms all offer some managed security services. But none are as robust as the specialized IT security firms, according to Gartner. "The bottom line is that MSSPs are still getting funded with venture capital, and they're providing value," says Stapleton. "But it's tough to point anyone in the right direction, because the market is truly evolving."

Case Study Questions

1. What are the benefits and limitations for a business of outsourcing IT security management according to the companies in this case?

2. What are the benefits and limitations to a business of using "pure play" IT security management companies like Counterpane and Ubizen? Visit their websites to help you answer.

3. What are the benefits and limitations of outsourcing IT security management to vendors like Symantec and Network Associates? Visit their websites to help you answer.

Source: Adapted from Deborah Radcliff, "Choosing the Best Security Guards," *Computerworld*, August 12, 2002, p. 36. Reprinted with permission from *Computerworld*.

CHAPTER 12

ENTERPRISE AND GLOBAL MANAGEMENT OF INFORMATION TECHNOLOGY

Chapter Highlights

Learning Objectives

After reading and studying this chapter, you should be able to:

1. Identify several ways that information technology has affected the job of managers.

2. Identify the seven major dimensions of a networked organization and explain how they can affect the success of a business.

3. Identify each of the three components of information technology management and use examples to illustrate how they might be implemented in a business.

4. Explain how failures in IT management can be reduced by the involvement of business managers in IS planning and management.

5. Identify several cultural, political, and geoeconomic challenges that confront managers in the management of global information technologies.

6. Explain the effect on global business/IT strategy of the trend toward a transnational business strategy by international business organizations.

7. Identify several considerations that affect the choice of IT applications, IT platforms, data access policies, and systems development methods by a global business enterprise.

Managing Information Technology

Business and IT

The strategic and operational importance of information technology in business is no longer questioned. As the 21st century unfolds, many companies throughout the world are intent on transforming themselves into global business powerhouses via major investments in global e-business, e-commerce, and other IT initiatives. Thus, there is a real need for business managers and professionals to understand how to manage this vital organizational function. In this section, we will explore how IT affects managers and business organizations, and stress the importance of a customer and business value focus for the management of information technologies. So whether you plan to be an entrepreneur and run your own business, a manager in a corporation, or a business professional, managing information systems and technologies will be one of your major responsibilities.

Analyzing USG Corp. and Others

Read the Real World Case on USG Corp. and Others on the next page. We can learn a lot about the challenges of evaluating investments in business/IT initiatives in today's economic environment. See Figure 12.1.

This case underscores the finding that many companies fail to formally evaluate the return on investment of their IT projects and, reportedly, don't know how to approach the task. The companies mentioned in the case suggest several simple practices to encourage and enable ROI measurements of IT projects. Examples include monthly evaluations of project progress and achievement of business productivity improvements, working with the company CFO and business unit controllers, monetary incentives for project team leaders, requiring business units to justify the ROI of IT projects that will benefit their units, and requiring a review of proposed IT investments by an IT management review board of business unit managers.

FIGURE 12.1

Jean Holley is CIO of USG Corp. and responsible for monitoring the ROI status of all IT development projects.

Source: Asa Mathat.

REAL WORLD CASE 1

USG Corp. and Others: Evaluating the ROI of IT Investments

ROI might be the acronym du jour in these budget-conscious times, but how well do companies really measure returns on their IT investments? Not very well, according to an informal poll of several hundred IT executives at *Computerworld's* annual Premier 100 conference to honor outstanding IT achievements by companies. When asked during a session if their firms go back and measure the return on investment of IT projects six months after the work is completed, 68 percent of the respondents said "rarely" or "never."

"When times are tough, like they were in the third and fourth quarters of 2001, we're focused on costs and cost savings," said USG Corp. (www.usg.com) CIO Jean Holley, who was one of the panelists at the ROI session. But when business conditions are good, "you're focusing on the customer," Holley said. "The customer is king and much less ROI measurement takes place." Additional polling results supported Holley's comments. For example, 65 percent of the respondents said they don't have the knowledge or tools needed to do ROI calculations. Nearly 75 percent said their companies don't have formal processes or budgets in place for measuring the ROI of IT projects.

Still, there are effective ways to track ROI during both good and bad times, according to Holley and her fellow panelists. Among their tips: Break long-term projects into bite-sized chunks so deliverables can be measured quarterly or even monthly. For example, Holley said the IT group at her Chicago-based building materials manufacturing company conducts monthly assessments of project milestones, such as development progress and enablement of business productivity improvements. That way, she said, "If we're nine months into a project, we can be sure that we're hitting our targets." Efforts such as these can also help to ensure that funding for follow-on project phases will be approved by senior executives of the company, Holley said.

IT managers can take other fairly simple steps to justify projects, according to the panelists. "If you can't do a one-page benefit analysis on the dollars you're spending you shouldn't do the project, should you?" said Russ Lambert, director of e-commerce at Pittsburgh-based Wesco Distribution Inc. (www.wescodist.com). Cathie Kozik, CIO at Naperville, Illinois–based telecom equipment manufacturer Tellabs Inc. (www.tellabs.com), said she works with the company's chief financial officer and the controllers from its business units to examine the costs and expected returns of IT projects. The group then ties its planning work to a balanced scorecard tool that's used to track the results. The most critical part of the process: The ROI generated by projects is tied to the bonuses of the team leaders who are responsible for them, a provision that's "very important" in helping to ensure that the efforts are successful, Kozik said.

Technology professionals whose companies have put the responsibility of justifying IT projects on business managers said the transition doesn't come without some pain. "There was a lot of push-back from the business side because they didn't want ownership of that," said David Dart, CIO at HVB America Inc. in New York. Dart and his boss, HVB America's chief operating officer, pushed the bank's business units to take responsibility for calculating potential returns on IT investments two years ago. Despite initial resistance, Dart said HVB America—a division of HVB Group, a Munich, Germany–based financial services firm—has succeeded in its transition. One key step was requiring business managers to make their cases for IT investments to peers who sit on an IT management board, he added.

Chicago-based Bank One Corp. (www.bankone.com) began requiring its business units to prove the value of IT investments last year, said Nancy Toms, a technology program director at the company. As part of the change, Toms said, she and her IT counterparts have been prodding business managers "to begin including IT projects within their own budgets," including calculations of the anticipated ROI. However, Toms said, she has run into problems similar to the ones encountered by Dart. For example, Bank One's IT staffers frequently have to go back to business units after a technology project has been proposed to ask for ROI data. But now that the effort is nearly a year old, she said, "we're starting to see some acceptance and understanding that this is the way things are."

However, as business managers become increasingly IT-savvy and push for technology projects, it's only natural that they would take on the task of demonstrating the value that IT investments could yield, said Barbara Gomolski, an analyst at Gartner Inc. "He who pays becomes accountable," she noted.

Case Study Questions

1. Why do many companies fail to evaluate the return on investment of their IT projects? Is this good business practice? Why or why not?

2. What are some of the ROI measurement and incentive practices of the companies in this case that might help other companies evaluate the ROI of their IT investments? Explain how several of these might work.

3. Should business managers be responsible for justifying the ROI of IT investments that will benefit their business units? Why or why not?

Source: Adapted from Thomas Hoffman, "ROI on IT Projects Difficult to Measure," *Computerworld*, March 12, 2002; p. 6, and "'Biz Units' New Task: Prove Value of IT," *Computerworld*, October 14, 2002, pp. 1, 53. Reprinted with permission from *Computerworld*.

FIGURE 12.2   Information technology must be managed to meet the challenges of today's business and technology environment, and the customer value and business value imperatives for success in a dynamic global economy.

Business Developments

Suppliers › › › › Customers

Information Technology Developments

Customer Value Business Value

- E-business and e-commerce transformation of business strategies and processes
- Agility, flexibility, and time compression of development, manufacturing, and delivery supply chain cycles
- Reengineering and cross-functional integration of business processes using Internet technologies
- Competitive advantage, total quality, and customer value focus

- Use of the Internet, intranets, extranets, and the Web as the primary IT infrastructure
- Diffusion of technology to internetwork employees, customers, and suppliers
- Global and enterprise computing, collaboration, and decision support systems
- Integrated cross-functional enterprise software replaces legacy systems

- Give customers what they want, when and how they want it, at the lowest cost
- Interenterprise coordination of manufacturing and business processes
- Effective distribution and channel partnerships
- Responsiveness and accountability to customers

Source: Adapted in part from Ravi Kalakota and Marcia Robinson, *e-Business 2.0: Roadmap for Success* (Reading, MA: Addison-Wesley, 2001), pp. 273, 279. © 2001 Addison-Wesley Publishing Company, Inc. Reprinted by permission of Addison-Wesley Longman Inc.

The Impact of IT on Managers

Really difficult business problems always have many aspects. Often a major decision depends on an impromptu search for one or two key pieces of auxiliary information and a quick ad hoc analysis of several possible scenarios. You need software tools that easily combine and recombine data from many sources. You need Internet access for all kinds of research. Widely scattered people need to be able to collaborate and work the data in different ways [11].

So says Bill Gates, chairman of Microsoft Corporation, of his own and his management team's experience with the managerial effects of information technologies. Thus, as Figure 12.2 illustrates, the competitive pressures of today's business environment are encouraging managers to rethink their use and management of information technology. Many business executives now see information technology as an enabling platform for electronic commerce, and rely on e-business applications for managing the cross-functional and interorganizational business processes of their business units. In addition, the Internet, intranets, extranets, and the Web are interconnecting individuals, teams, business units, and business partners in close business relationships that promote the communication, collaboration, and decision making needed in today's competitive global marketplace.

Thus, information technology has become a major force for precipitating or enabling organizational and managerial change. Thanks to Internet technologies and other dynamic hardware, software, data, and network developments, computing power and information resources are now more readily available to more managers than ever before. In fact, these and other information technologies have already enabled innovative changes in managerial decision making, organizational structures, and managerial work activities [8, 16, 29].

For example, the decision support capabilities provided by Web-enabled decision support system technologies are changing the focus of managerial decision making. Managers freed from number-crunching chores must now face tougher strategic policy questions in order to develop realistic alternatives for today's dynamic e-business and e-commerce environment. In addition, many companies now use the Internet, intranets, and enterprise collaboration systems to coordinate their work activities and business processes. Middle managers no longer need to serve as conduits for the transmission of operations feedback or control directives between operational managers and teams, and top management. Thus, many companies have reduced the layers and numbers of middle management, and encouraged the growth of workgroups of task-focused teams. Let's take a look at a real world example as told by Bill Gates of Microsoft.

Microsoft: The Impact of IT on District Sales Managers	At Microsoft, our information systems have changed the role of our district sales managers. When MS Sales (our intranet-based revenue measurement and decision support system) first came online, our Minneapolis general manager ran a variety of numbers for her district at a level of detail never possible before. She discovered that excellent sales among other customer segments were obscuring a poor showing among large customers in her district. In fact, the district was dead last among U.S. districts in that category. Finding that out was a shock but also a big motivator for the large-customer teams in the district. By the end of the year Minneapolis was the top-growing district for sales to large customers. If you're a district manager at Microsoft today, you must be more than a good sales leader helping your team close the big deals, which has been the traditional district sales manager role. Now you can be a business thinker. You have numbers to help you run your business. Before, even if you were concerned about the retail store revenue in your area, you had no view whatsoever of those results. Now you can look at sales figures and evaluate where your business is strong, where your business is weak, and where your business has its greatest potential, product by product, relative to other districts. You can try out new programs and see their impact. You can talk to other managers about what they're doing to get strong results. Being a district sales manager in our organization is a much broader role than what it was five years ago because of the digital tools we've developed and their ease of use [11].

The Impact of IT on Organizations

Just as the value chain has been disintermediated, so too has the traditional organization. The Digital Age organization is no longer a single corporate entity, but rather an extended network consisting of a streamlined global core, market-focused business units and shared support services [29].

Many companies are reengineering their organizational structures and roles, as well as their business processes, as they strive to become agile, customer-focused, value-driven enterprises. One way to express this phenomenon is illustrated in Figure 12.3, which outlines several key dimensions of the new networked organization, compared to the same dimensions of a traditional organization model used by many companies. The seven dimensions of the networked model demonstrate that information technology, particularly e-business and e-commerce, appears to provide a major impetus for companies to make major changes to their organizational structures and roles. Let's look at a real world example that exemplifies and illustrates this new networked organization model [29].

Cisco Systems: The Ultimate Networked Organization	Cisco Systems Inc. may well be the best example of what we mean by a networked organization. The clear market leader in the business-to-business networking hardware industry, it is the ultimate networked enterprise. **Organization Structure:** Cisco maintains a strong web of strategic partnerships and systems integration with suppliers, contractors, and assemblers. This network of alliances provides a flexible structure that enables Cisco to shift toward new market opportunities, and away from old ones. Although it outsources functions, including a large part of its manufacturing, it also leverages its innovative

human resources and IT departments as shared services to the benefit of all its business units.

Leadership and Governance: John Chambers has proven to be a strong, visionary leader, but Cisco is led by more than just a single person. The company has made more than 40 acquisitions in its short history, and many acquired companies live on as autonomous Cisco business units. But Cisco does not install new leadership for those business units; managers of the acquired companies usually have the independence to run their business units. Even more telling, Cisco's senior management is filled with executives from acquired companies. These entrepreneurial managers are not pushed out of the company; their skills as leaders are valued at all levels of Cisco.

People and Culture: Cisco's culture is straight out of the e.org textbook, and extends all the way to the company's endless search for talent. Cisco has proven to be very effective at recruiting those whom the company calls "passive" job seekers—people who aren't actively looking for a new job. The company is a recruitment innovator in the competitive Silicon Valley marketplace. The company has a Web page, for example, to connect a potential hire with a Cisco employee who works in the same sort of position. The volunteer employee "friend," and not a trained recruiter, will then call the prospect to talk about life at Cisco. This inside view of the company is an important selling tool for recruitment; it also gives employees a voice in the continued growth of the company. And Cisco's human resources ability extends to the culture of the organization and its ability to retain talent.

Coherence: Cisco is almost religious when it comes to customer focus, and the customer focus goes right to the top. CEO John Chambers was reportedly late for his very first board meeting in 1994 because he was on the phone with an unhappy customer. The board excused him. Under Chambers, Cisco senior executives have their bonuses tied to customer satisfaction ratings, and the company has spared no expense developing its online service and support model to provide its customers with the industry's broadest range of hardware products, as well as related software and services. The customer focus permeates the entire organization—even to the engineering department, a group not traditionally thought of as customer oriented.

Knowledge: Cisco has leveraged the Internet to optimize every step in the value chain from sales to order-processing to customer service to manufacturing. The extent to which Cisco has tied its business partners together with shared knowledge is staggering. Web-based systems allow suppliers to tap directly into Cisco's manufacturing and order systems with realtime access to product logistics information, and order flow. Cisco also shares demand forecasts, intellectual capital, electronic communication tools, and volume targets. The result? Suppliers' production processes are "pulled" by Cisco's customer demand. The company's knowledge-sharing goes even further, providing online service and support to end customers; 70 percent of technical support requests are now filed electronically, generating an average customer service rating of 4+ on a 5-point scale. Cisco has saved considerable money from this online migration—an estimated $500 million a year from improved supply chain management, online technical support, software distribution via downloads and other Internet-enabled processes.

Alliances: It's not just knowledge that Cisco distributes electronically with its network of partners. Cisco's alliance partners are an integral component of the company's ability to serve customers, and Cisco treats them as part of the company. Indeed, half of customer orders that come in over its website are routed electronically to a supplier who ships directly to the customer.

FIGURE 12.3 Comparing the networked organization model to the traditional model used by many companies.

	Traditional Organization	**Networked Organization**
Organization Structure	● Hierarchical ● Command-and-control	● Centerless, networked ● Flexible structure that is easily modified
Leadership	● Selected "stars" step above ● Leaders set the agenda ● Leaders force change	● Everyone is a leader ● Leaders create environment for success ● Leaders create capacity for change
People and Culture	● Long-term rewards ● Vertical decision making ● Individuals and small teams are rewarded	● "Own your own career" mentality ● Delegated authority ● Collaboration expected and rewarded
Coherence	● Hard-wired into processes ● Internal relevance	● Embedded vision in individuals ● Impact projected externally
Knowledge	● Focused on internal processes ● Individualistic	● Focused on customers ● Institutional
Alliances	● Complement current gaps ● Ally with distant partners	● Create new value and outsource uncompetitive services ● Ally with competitors, customers, and suppliers
Governance	● Internally focused ● Top-down	● Internal and external focus ● Distributed

Source: Adapted from Gary Neilson, Bruce Pasternack, and Albert Visco, "Up the E-Organization! A Seven-Dimensional Model of the Centerless Enterprise," *Strategy & Business*, First Quarter 2000, p. 53.

Figure 12.4 provides an example of the networked organization structure of a company. Notice that there is a global executive core, four market-focused business units, and two shared support services business units. However, all six business units are customer and market focused. Even the shared support services units must provide competitive services to the global core, other business units, and external customers, since uncompetitive services may be outsourced to external vendors [29].

FIGURE 12.4

An example of the organizational structure of a networked business.

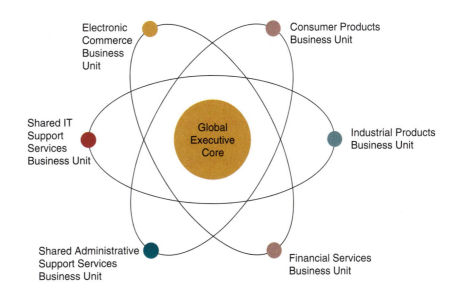

FIGURE 12.5

The major components of information technology management. Note the executives with primary responsibilities in each area.

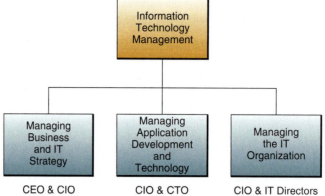

Source: Derived in part from Omar El Sawy, Arvind Malhotra, Sanjay Gosain, and Kerry Young, "IT-Intensive Value Innovation in the Electronic Economy: Insights from Marshall Industries," *MIS Quarterly*, September 1999, pp. 323–27. Reprinted with permission from the *MIS Quarterly*.

Managing Information Technology

Figure 12.5 illustrates a popular approach to managing information technology in a large company. This managerial approach has three major components:

- Managing the joint development and implementation of business and IT strategies.
- Managing the development of business/IT applications and the research and implementation of new information technologies.
- Managing the IT processes, professionals, and subunits within a company's IT organization and IS function.

Let's look at a real world example.

Avnet Marshall: Managing IT

Figure 12.6 contrasts how Avnet Marshall's information technology management differs from conventional IT management. Notice that they use the model of IT management illustrated in Figure 12.5. For example, in technology management, Avnet Marshall uses a best-of-breed approach that supports business needs, instead of enforcing a standardized and homogeneous choice of hardware, software, database, and networking technologies. In managing its IT organization, Avnet Marshall hires IS professionals who can integrate IT with business. These IS professionals are organized in workgroups around e-business initiatives that focus on building e-commerce services for customers [8].

Managing the IS Function

A radical shift is occurring in corporate computing—think of it as the recentralization of management. It's a step back toward the 1970s, when a data-processing manager could sit at a console and track all the technology assets of the corporation. Then came the 1980s and early 1990s. Departments got their own PCs and software; client/ server networks sprang up all across companies.

Three things have happened in the past few years: The Internet boom inspired businesses to connect all those networks; companies put on their intranets essential applications without which their businesses could not function; and it became apparent that maintaining PCs on a network is very, very expensive. Such changes create an urgent need for centralization [21].

Organizing IT

In the early years of computing, the development of large mainframe computers and telecommunications networks and terminals caused a **centralization** of computer hardware and software, databases, and information specialists at the corporate level of organizations. Next, the development of minicomputers and microcomputers

FIGURE 12.6

Comparing conventional and e-business-driven IT management approaches.

IT Management	Conventional Practices	Avnet Marshall's e-Business Practices
Technology Management	● Approach to IT infrastructure may sacrifice match with business needs for vendor homogeneity and technology platform choices	● Best-of-breed approach to IT infrastructure in which effective match with business needs takes precedence over commitment to technology platform choices and vender homogeneity
Managing the IT Organization	● Hire "best by position" who can bring specific IT expertise	● Hire "best athletes" IS professionals who can flexibly integrate new IT and business competencies
	● Departments organized around IT expertise with business liaisons and explicit delegation of tasks	● Evolving workgroups organized around emerging IT-intensive business initiatives with little explicit delegation of tasks
	● IT projects have separable cost/value considerations. Funding typically allocated within constraints of yearly budget for IT function	● IT funding typically based on value proposition around business opportunity related to building services for customers. IT project inseparable part of business initiative

Source: Adapted from Omar El Sawy, Arvind Malhotra, Sanjay Gosain, and Kerry Young, "IT-Intensive Value Innovation in the Electronic Economy: Insights from Marshall Industries," *MIS Quarterly*, September 1999, p. 324. Reprinted with permission from the *MIS Quarterly*.

accelerated a **downsizing** trend, which prompted a move back toward **decentralization** by many business firms. Distributed client/server networks at the corporate, department, workgroup, and team levels came into being. This promoted a shift of databases and information specialists to some departments, and the creation of *information centers* to support end user and workgroup computing.

Lately, the trend is to establish more centralized control over the management of the IS resources of a company, while still serving the strategic needs of its business units, especially their e-business and e-commerce initiatives. This has resulted in the development of hybrid structures with both centralized and decentralized components. See Figure 12.7.

FIGURE 12.7

The organizational structure of the IT function at Avnet Marshall.

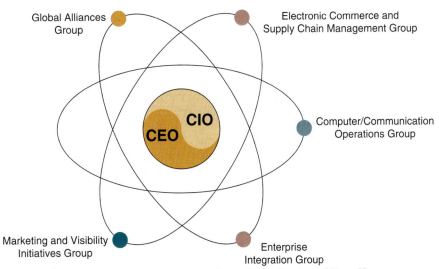

Source: Adapted from Omar El Sawy, Arvind Malhotra, Sanjay Gosain, and Kerry Young, "IT-Intensive Value Innovation in the Electronic Economy: Insights from Marshall Industries," *MIS Quarterly*, September 1999, p. 325. Reprinted with permission from the *MIS Quarterly*.

Some companies spin off their information systems function into IS *subsidiaries* that offer IS services to external organizations as well as to their parent company. Other companies created or spun off their e-commerce and Internet-related business units or IT groups into separate companies or business units. Other corporations **outsource,** that is, turn over all or parts of their IS operations to outside contractors known as *systems integrators.* In addition, some companies are outsourcing software procurement and support to *application service providers* (ASPs), who provide and support business application and other software via the Internet and intranets to all of a company's employee workstations. Let's look at some real world examples.

Premiere, Monsanto, and Fleetwood: Using ASPs

Premiere Technologies, Inc.
IT leader: Douglas B. Hadaway, vice president of finance
Goal: Rescue a failing PeopleSoft ERP project without compromising core business efforts.
ASP: TransChannel LLC, Atlanta
Solution: Premiere turned the whole project over to the ASP to manage.
Result: "We're saving about $3 million over five years by giving the work to TransChannel," Hadaway says.

Monsanto Co.
IT leader: Kathryn Kissam, director of corporate branding and identity
Goal: Centralize Monsanto's vast, very distributed library of logos, images, and branding specifications into a single library that employees can access worldwide —and do it quickly.
ASP: Imation Corp., Oakdale, Minn.
Solution: Imation created and maintains the Monsanto Image Gallery, an application that lets any company intranet user search, sort, and use Monsanto's logos and images.
Result: "We save money because we don't have to commission new images with every new project or distribute new logo updates to every office in the world," Kissam says.

Fleetwood Retail Corp.
IT leader: Don Palmour, vice president of technology.
Goal: Deploy and manage an entire suite of Lotus Domino applications in Fleetwood's more than 200 mostly rural sales centers.
ASP: Interliant Inc., Purchase, N.Y.
Solution: Fleetwood bought the Domino licenses but turned everything else over to Interliant, which centrally manages the entire suite. Everything—including tape backup—is done in the ASP's central offices.
Result: "This was the only way we could ramp up that quickly. There's no question we get better service than we could provide ourselves," Palmour says [27].

Managing Application Development

Application development management involves managing activities such as systems analysis and design, prototyping, applications programming, project management, quality assurance, and system maintenance for all major e-business/IT development projects. Managing application development requires managing the activities of teams of systems analysts, software developers, and other IS professionals working on a variety of information systems development projects. In addition, some systems development groups have established *development centers* staffed with IS professionals. Their role is to evaluate new application development tools and to help information systems specialists use them to improve their application development efforts.

FIGURE 12.8

A computer system performance monitor in action. The CA-Unicenter TNG package includes an Enterprise Management Portal module that helps IT specialists monitor and manage a variety of networked computer systems and operating systems.

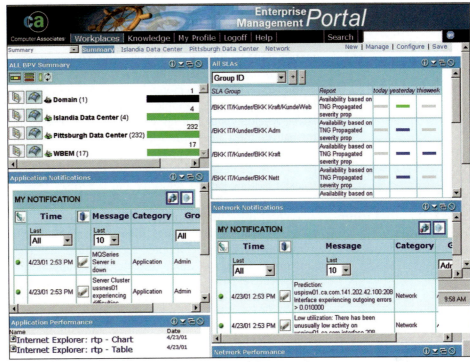

Source: Courtesy of Computer Associates International, Inc.

Managing IS Operations

IS operations management is concerned with the use of hardware, software, network, and personnel resources in the corporate or business unit **data centers** (computer centers) of an organization. Operational activities that must be managed include computer system operations, network management, production control, and production support.

Most operations management activities are being automated by the use of software packages for computer system performance management. These **system performance monitors** monitor the processing of computer jobs, help develop a planned schedule of computer operations that can optimize computer system performance, and produce detailed statistics that are invaluable for effective planning and control of computing capacity. Such information evaluates computer system utilization, costs, and performance. This evaluation provides information for capacity planning, production planning and control, and hardware/software acquisition planning. It is also used in quality assurance programs, which stress quality of services to business end users. See Figure 12.8.

System performance monitors also supply information needed by **chargeback systems** that allocate costs to users based on the information services rendered. All costs incurred are recorded, reported, allocated, and charged back to specific end user business units, depending on their use of system resources. When companies use this arrangement, the information services department becomes a service center whose costs are charged directly to business units, rather than being lumped with other administrative service costs and treated as an overhead cost.

Many performance monitors also feature **process control** capabilities. Such packages not only monitor but automatically control computer operations at large data centers. Some use built-in expert system modules based on knowledge gleaned from experts in the operations of specific computer systems and operating systems. These performance monitors provide more efficient computer operations than human-operated systems. They also enable "lights out" data centers at some companies, where computer systems are operated unattended, especially after normal business hours.

Human Resource Management of IT

The success or failure of an information services organization rests primarily on the quality of its people. Many computer-using firms consider recruiting, training, and retaining qualified IS personnel as one of their greatest challenges. Managing information services functions involves the management of managerial, technical, and clerical personnel. One of the most important jobs of information services managers is to recruit qualified personnel and to develop, organize, and direct the capabilities of existing personnel. Employees must be continually trained to keep up with the latest developments in a fast-moving and highly technical field. Employee job performances must be continually evaluated and outstanding performances rewarded with salary increases or promotions. Salary and wage levels must be set, and career paths must be designed so individuals can move to new jobs through promotion and transfer as they gain in seniority and expertise.

The CIO and Other IT Executives

The **chief information officer** (CIO) oversees all use of information technology in many companies, and brings them into alignment with strategic business goals. Thus, all traditional computer services, Internet technology, telecommunications network services, and other IS technology support services are the responsibility of this executive. Also, the CIO does not direct day-to-day information services activities. Instead, CIOs concentrate on business/IT planning and strategy. They also work with the CEO and other top executives to develop strategic uses of information technology in electronic business and commerce that help make the firm more competitive in the marketplace. Many companies have also filled the CIO position with executives from the business functions or units outside the IS field. Such CIOs emphasize that the chief role of information technology is to help a company meet its strategic business objectives.

Top IT Jobs: Requirements and Compensation

● **Chief technology officer**
Base salary range: $100,000 to $250,000-plus; varies by location
Bonus range: Up to 30% of salary

If you're second-in-command to the CIO or chief technology officer and you have years of applications development experience, your next move should be into the chief technology officer's spot. To land this job, you'll need to be a passionate problem-solver with a demonstrated record of reducing development time.

● **e-Commerce architect**
Base salary range: $120,000 to $200,000-plus; varies by location
Bonus range: Up to 20% of salary

If you know Java, Perl, C++, and Web services, have experience in systems architecture, and can design an Internet solution from concept through implementation, many companies want you to work on their e-commerce sites.

● **Technical team leader**
Base salary range: $100,000 to $200,000-plus; varies by location
Bonus range: Up to 20% of salary

Senior technical team leaders with good communication, project management, and leadership skills, as well as knowledge of Web languages and databases, are still highly sought after.

● **Practice manager**
Base salary range: $80,000 to $200,000-plus; varies by location
Bonus range: Up to 20% of salary

If you've got a background in IT assessment and a pedigree in business development (MBA preferred), you can land a job as a point person for big projects. You'll need skills in IT operations and software assessment, as well as in marketing, staffing, budgeting, and building customer relationships [10].

Technology Management

The management of rapidly changing technology is important to any organization. Changes in information technology, like the rise of the PC, client/server networks, and the Internet and intranets, have come swiftly and dramatically and are expected to continue into the future. Developments in information systems technology have had, and will continue to have, a major impact on the operations, costs, management work environment, and competitive position of many organizations.

Thus, all information technologies must be managed as a technology platform for integrated e-business and e-commerce systems. Such technologies include the Internet, intranets, and a variety of electronic commerce and collaboration technologies, as well as integrated enterprise software for customer relationship management, enterprise resource planning, and supply chain management. In many companies, technology management is the primary responsibility of a *chief technology officer* (CTO) who is in charge of all information technology planning and deployment.

Managing User Services

Teams and workgroups of business professionals commonly use PC workstations, software packages, and the Internet, intranets, and other networks to develop and apply information technology to their work activities. Thus many companies have responded by creating **user services,** or *client services,* functions to support and manage end user and workgroup computing.

End user services provide both opportunities and problems for business unit managers. For example, some firms create an *information center* group staffed with user liaison specialists, or Web-enabled intranet help desks. IS specialists with titles such as user consultant, account executive, or business analyst may also be assigned to end user work groups. These specialists perform a vital role by troubleshooting problems, gathering and communicating information, coordinating educational efforts, and helping business professionals with application development.

In addition to these measures, most organizations still establish and enforce policies for the acquisition of hardware and software by end users and business units. This ensures their compatibility with company standards for hardware, software, and network connectivity. Also important is the development of applications with proper security and quality controls to promote correct performance and safeguard the integrity of corporate and departmental networks and databases.

Failures in IT Management

Managing information technology is not an easy task. The information systems function has performance problems in many organizations. The promised benefits of information technology have not occurred in many documented cases. Studies by management consulting firms and university researchers have shown that many businesses have not been successful in managing their use of information technology. Thus, it is evident that in many organizations, information technology is not being used effectively and efficiently. For example:

- Information technology is not being used *effectively* by companies that use IT primarily to computerize traditional business processes, instead of innovative e-business processes involving customers, suppliers, and other business partners, electronic commerce, and Web-enabled decision support.

- Information technology is not being used *efficiently* by information systems that provide poor response times and frequent downtimes, or IS professionals and consultants who do not properly manage application development projects.

Let's look closer at Connecticut General as a real world example.

Connecticut General: Failure in IT Project Management

Connecticut General Life Insurance Co. sued PeopleSoft, Inc., in August 2001 over the aborted installation of a new financial system. Connecticut General claims that it was forced to develop a homegrown application after the vendor failed to deliver customized software that was promised as part of a 1999 contract. Connecticut General also charges that PeopleSoft breached an agreement for support and consulting services and falsely claimed that it could customize and install an accounts receivable billing system for the insurer. After investing more than $5 million, Connecticut General said it didn't get the promised software and had to develop its own application. The suit also claims that PeopleSoft ballooned its tab for the project from the original figure of $5.15 million to $11.7 million and indicated that the final cost could go even higher.

Connecticut General decided in 1997 that its accounts receivable billing system, which handles $5 billion in transactions annually, was outdated and needed to be replaced with a new e-business system. In mid-1999, the suit states, the company signed a $5 million-plus deal with PeopleSoft covering software licenses, technical support, and implementation and customization services. The project started in October 1999 and was supposed to be based on PeopleSoft 7.5 or a subsequent release, according to the suit. But by the following month, Connecticut General personnel "began to suspect that the PeopleSoft team was having difficulty performing the customization and implementation services." PeopleSoft replaced the workers assigned to the project and sent in a "crisis management team," the suit states.

But early in 2000, Connecticut General charged, PeopleSoft said the original project bid was flawed and raised the price to $11.76 million, with the possibility of another 20 percent increase on top of that amount. Connecticut General further claimed that PeopleSoft "failed to properly customize and implement" the promised software, leaving it "inoperable . . . and entirely useless."

PeopleSoft declined to comment on the specifics of the suit. "PeopleSoft provided CIGNA with software that it licensed and performed services that CIGNA contracted for," a PeopleSoft spokesman said. "It is unfortunate that for internal reasons, CIGNA was unable to successfully adopt our software, but this was not related to the quality of the software or services provided by PeopleSoft" [31].

Management Involvement and Governance

What is the solution to failures in the information systems function? There are no quick and easy answers. However, the experiences of successful organizations reveal that extensive and meaningful **managerial and end user involvement** is the key ingredient of high-quality information systems performance. Involving business managers in the governance of the IS function and business professionals in the development of IS applications should thus shape the response of management to the challenge of improving the business value of information technology [8, 16]. See Figure 12.9.

Involving managers in the management of IT (from the CEO to the managers of business units) requires the development of *governance structures* (such as executive councils and steering committees) that encourage their active participation in planning and controlling the business uses of IT. Thus, many organizations have policies that require managers to be involved in IT decisions that affect their business units. This helps managers avoid IS performance problems in their business units and development projects. With this high degree of involvement, managers can improve the strategic business value of information technology. Also, as we said in Chapter 10, the problems of employee resistance and poor user interface design can only be solved by direct end user participation in systems development projects. Overseeing such involvement is another vital management task.

FIGURE 12.9   Senior management needs to be involved in critical business/IT decisions to optimize the business value and performance of the IT function.

IT Decision	Senior Management's Role	Consequences of Abdicating the Decision
● **How much should we spend on IT?**	Define the strategic role that IT will play in the company and then determine the level of funding needed to achieve that objective.	The company fails to develop an IT platform that furthers its strategy, despite high IT spending.
● **Which business processes should receive our IT dollars?**	Make clear decisions about which IT initiatives will and will not be funded.	A lack of focus overwhelms the IT unit, which tries to deliver many projects that may have little companywide value or can't be implemented well simultaneously.
● **Which IT capabilities need to be companywide?**	Decide which IT capabilities should be provided centrally and which should be developed by individual businesses.	Excessive technical and process standardization limits the flexibility of business units, or frequent exceptions to the standards increase costs and limit business synergies.
● **How good do our IT services really need to be?**	Decide which features—for example, enhanced reliability or response time—are needed on the basis of their costs and benefits.	The company may pay for service options that, given its priorities, aren't worth the costs.
● **What security and privacy risks will we accept?**	Lead the decision making on the trade-offs between security and privacy on one hand and convenience on the other.	An overemphasis on security and privacy may inconvenience customers, employees, and suppliers; an underemphasis may make data vulnerable.
● **Whom do we blame if an IT initiative fails?**	Assign a business executive to be accountable for every IT project; monitor business metrics.	The business value of systems is never realized.

Source: Jeanne W. Ross and Peter Weill, "Six IT Decisions Your IT People Shouldn't Make," *Harvard Business Review*, November 2002, p. 87.

SECTION II   Managing Global IT

The International Dimension

Whether they are in Berlin or Bombay, Kuala Lumpur or Kansas, San Francisco or Seoul, companies around the globe are developing new models to operate competitively in a digital economy. These models are structured, yet agile; global, yet local; and they concentrate on maximizing the risk-adjusted return from both knowledge and technology assets [16].

Thus, international dimensions have become a vital part of managing a business enterprise in the internetworked global economies and markets of today. Whether you become a manager in a large corporation or the owner of a small business, you will be affected by international business developments, and deal in some way with people, products, or services whose origin is not from your home country.

Analyzing Agilent Technologies and Citibank

Read the Real World Case on Agilent Technologies and Citibank on the next page. We can learn a lot about the challenges and opportunities facing companies involved in global e-business. See Figure 12.10.

This case dramatizes the challenges of consolidating global IT organizations, infrastructure, and systems. It also shows how large multinational corporations like Agilent Technologies and Citibank allowed their international units in each country to develop or customize their own systems over the last thirty years. Now CIO Marty Chuck of Agilent is determined to consolidate and centralize his IT organization, infrastructure, applications, and IT projects to bring them into alignment with the business goals of the new HP-spinoff company, even in the face of major resistance from global business and IT stakeholders. But like Citibank's global banking system consolidation, the new global systems are producing hundreds of millions of dollars in reduced cost of IT operations, systems development, and maintenance.

FIGURE 12.10
Marty Chuck, CIO of Agilent Technologies, led a major consolidation of its global IT infrastructure, systems, and organizational structures.

Source: Courtesy of Agilent Technologies.

REAL WORLD CASE 2

Agilent Technologies and Citibank: The Challenges of Consolidating Global IT

When Agilent Technologies Inc. (www.agilent.com) in Palo Alto, California, spun off from Hewlett-Packard Co. in November 1999, its 2,500 IT employees were dispersed over three businesses in 40 countries. Each area had its own IT infrastructure, operations, applications, and staff. A portfolio of 1,500 applications inherited from HP was eating up 80 percent of the IT budget, and the remaining budget was scattered among too many local priorities to show much bang for the buck. Vice President and CIO Marty Chuck knew there was a better way. In November 2000, he began an initiative to consolidate IT.

The challenges were huge. Previously autonomous IT managers had to accept corporate decision making, and many pushed back. "It was very difficult," Chuck admits. But Chief Operating Officer Alain Couder put his authority behind the "One IT" initiative, and executives were clear about changes they wanted. "Once you set a clear vision, I have a high intolerance of things that don't align," Chuck explains. "We are all empowered to call things out and trim what isn't helping us win." So IT executives consolidated all IT projects and proposals into one plan, rated them on alignment with Agilent's business vision and goals, and pulled the plug on many. Many business and IT stakeholders didn't like it. "I got a lot of hate mail," Chuck says. "But that just hardened my resolve. You have to have the skill and the will to drive these things."

Moving from 1,500 applications to a few standard systems is a continuing technical challenge, and IT employees worry about the portability of their own skills, Chuck says. He meets those concerns with candor and lets his IT people decide where, how, and if they'll fit in. "We are very open and honest about what the organization will look like, what the applications portfolio will look like, what we see coming," he says.

By November 2001, a global, centralized IT was in place. It has reduced operational spending by 23 percent ($160 million over 18 months). The savings are funding the gradual replacement of old systems with standard, integrated applications. New desktop policies have saved the business units an additional $50 million, and in fiscal 2001 alone, Agilent avoided more than $300 million in expenses by saying no to unaligned IT projects.

Agilent's strong, central governance made all the difference in this effort, says Barbara Gomolski, an analyst at Gartner Inc. "Lots of companies forget about the management underpinnings, and it doesn't work," she says. And while Chuck says it might not make sense for an autonomous holding company, in an integrated enterprise like Agilent, "it drives out waste and cost and gets people focused on strategic goals." But be prepared for a long haul. "The savings we got were not due to one or two things; it was due to 150 things," he explains. "We've been on a dead run for several years. We kicked over every rock. And we're not done."

Citibank. A $100 million-plus global IT consolidation project is enabling Citibank (www.citibank.com) to replace a decades-old set of back-office corporate banking systems in all of its overseas corporate offices with a single global system with standard user interfaces and business processes. The New York–based bank has already completed changeover projects in the Asia-Pacific region, Western and Eastern Europe, and Latin America. The changeover, which began in early 2000, is expected to continue through 2004. There are still rollouts to be completed in more than 100 countries.

The bank said the project will pay for itself by letting the company avoid development costs related to a clunky legacy back-office system. Developed in-house in the 1970s, the old system has morphed into 58 disparate software applications, said Jeff Berg, executive director of program management at Citibank's parent New York–based Citigroup Inc. "In the '70s, we were growing rapidly in countries around the world. To get up and running quickly, we'd use this system call Cosmos (Consolidated Online Modulated Operating System)," Berg said. "As the bank grew, we did make a mistake in that we released the source code to each of the countries, and they changed it."

Berg said Citibank now has a single system that's customized for each country it operates in, using each nation's language, regulatory rules, and business processes. Berg said Citibank plans to reduce the number of its data centers in Europe from 18 to about 4 by standardizing on the new banking software from i-Flex Solutions Inc. in Bangalore, India. The bank anticipates an 18-month return on investment, said Berg. The software, called Flexcube, is based on an Oracle database. It automates the general ledger as well as customer accounting, deposits and withdrawals, and interest on accounts, among other services. Citibank will be able to simply change parameters in the new software to incorporate a particular country's language, regulations, and currency conversions.

Case Study Questions

1. Do you agree with Agilent's global IT consolidation goals and process? Why or why not?

2. Why did Agilent's global IT consolidation get such a strong negative response from many business and IT stakeholders? Could this reaction have been avoided? Explain.

3. What are the business benefits of Citibank's global IT consolidation project? How can a single global system still be customized for each country?

Source: Adapted from Lucas Mearian, "Citibank Overhauls Overseas Systems," *Computerworld*, February 4, 2002, p. 6; and Kathleen Melymuka, "IT Consolidation Puts Unaligned Projects on Chopping Block," *Computerworld*, June 3, 2002, p. 30. Reprinted with permission from *Computerworld*.

FIGURE 12.11
The major dimensions of global e-business technology management.

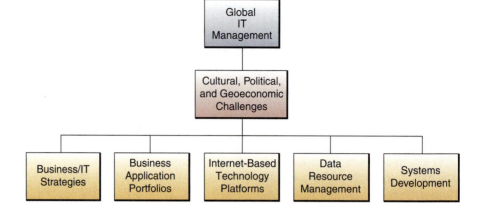

Global IT Management

Figure 12.11 illustrates the major dimensions of the job of managing global information technology that we will cover in this section. Notice that all global IT activities must be adjusted to take into account the cultural, political, and geoeconomic challenges that exist in the international business community. Developing appropriate business and IT strategies for the global marketplace should be the first step in **global information technology management.** Once that is done, end user and IS managers can move on to developing the portfolio of business applications needed to support business/IT strategies; the hardware, software, and Internet-based technology platforms to support those applications; the data resource management methods to provide necessary databases; and finally the systems development projects that will produce the global information systems required.

Cendant Corp.: Global IT Management

Lawrence Kinder faced a typical kind of global challenge. He is executive vice president and CIO with global responsibility for IT at Cendant Corp., which recently acquired Avis Group holdings. His company, a service and information provider for automotive transportation and vehicle management in Garden City, New York, grew internationally in 1999 by acquiring the U.K.'s PHH Vehicle Management Services, the world's second-largest vehicle leasing and fleet management company, and Wright Express LLC, the world's largest credit card and information services provider.

"We grew organically in North America and built a solid and stable IT foundation that we have been able to leverage in Europe," Kinder says. The key is to take the time to understand the day-to-day workings of each local IT group, he says, and to put strategic IT planning on the back burner until all groups can focus on leveraging their cultures and talents.

Kinder says he regularly brings together company leaders with similar roles from the United States, Canada, and Europe to "give each other a shot of adrenaline." He says developing and supporting global businesses is more demanding than supporting time to do strategic planning. But, he says, "Giving my global IT leaders the opportunity to think more broadly about their applications and solve international business problems has created a true learning organization" [23].

Cultural, Political, and Geoeconomic Challenges

"Business as usual" is not good enough in global business operations. The same holds true for global e-business technology management. There are too many cultural, political, and geoeconomic (geographic and economic) realities that must be confronted in order for a business to succeed in global markets. As we have just said, global information technology management must focus on developing global business IT strategies and managing global e-business application portfolios, Internet technologies, platforms, databases, and systems development projects. But managers must also accomplish that from a perspective and through methods that take into account the cultural, political, and geoeconomic differences that exist when doing business internationally.

For example, a major **political challenge** is that many countries have rules regulating or prohibiting transfer of data across their national boundaries (transborder data flows), especially personal information such as personnel records. Others severely restrict, tax, or prohibit imports of hardware and software. Still others have local content laws that specify the portion of the value of a product that must be added in that country if it is to be sold there. Other countries have reciprocal trade agreements that require a business to spend part of the revenue they earn in a country in that nation's economy [28].

Geoeconomic challenges in global business and IT refer to the effects of geography on the economic realities of international business activities. The sheer physical distances involved are still a major problem, even in this day of Internet telecommunications and jet travel. For example, it may still take too long to fly in specialists when IT problems occur in a remote site. It is still difficult to communicate in real time across the world's 24 time zones. It is still difficult to get good-quality telephone and telecommunications service in many countries. There are still problems finding the job skills required in some countries, or enticing specialists from other countries to live and work there. Finally, there are still problems (and opportunities) in the great differences in the cost of living and labor costs in various countries. All of these geoeconomic challenges must be addressed when developing a company's global business and IT strategies.

Cultural challenges facing global business and IT managers include differences in languages, cultural interests, religions, customs, social attitudes, and political philosophies. Obviously, global IT managers must be trained and sensitized to such cultural differences before they are sent abroad or brought into a corporation's home country. Other cultural challenges include differences in work styles and business relationships. For example, should one take one's time to avoid mistakes, or hurry to get something done early? Should one go it alone or work cooperatively? Should the most experienced person lead, or should leadership be shared? The answers to such questions depend on the culture you are in and highlight the cultural differences that might exist in the global workplace. Let's take a look at a real world example involving the Internet and electronic commerce.

Global Competition for IT Talent

Opportunity for professional growth is a major element of the competition between global businesses and governments for IT talent. Many IT workers understand that their résumé is their most important asset and seek out positions where they can work with modern or leading-edge technologies. While many countries offer opportunities to work in emerging technologies, the United States leads in the sheer number and variety of IT jobs working with résumé-enhancing technologies. The question that faces policy makers in other countries is where their nation has room to improve their competitiveness by attracting or retaining skilled IT talent.

Australia, for example, has a literate and affluent population, with higher Internet use than the United States, but lacks the market size and concentration of investment capital to compete with the United States in providing IT employment opportunities. As a result, there are thousands of Australians working in Silicon Valley despite a shortage of over 30,000 IT professionals at home. Some Latin American and many other countries suffer because of their limited telecommunications infrastructures. While countries like Chile have modern systems with competitive telecommunications pricing and Internet access, others have government-run telephone companies with service levels that don't support modern e-commerce development. For example, in some countries, dedicated Internet connections are not available and all telephone calls, including Internet connectivity, are priced by the duration of the connection.

With worldwide competition for IT professionals and unprecedented mobility in the IT workforce it seems that the best method for attracting or retaining IT workers involves the development of an overall program of economic, social, and technical opportunity. India and China, for example, seem to be experiencing a reverse brain drain as experienced IT professionals return home to take leadership roles in new ventures. Increased domestic demand, fueled by a combination of new domestic software needs, increased Internet connectivity, new e-commerce ventures, and local software shops developing for foreign customers, are all attracting experienced managers and entrepreneurs back home and providing rewarding employment for local entry-level technologists.

Canada, Japan, and even India have all taken recent steps to facilitate the entry of foreign professional workers, especially IT specialists. Australia and New Zealand recruit foreign professionals, including those from the United States, by promoting the natural beauty of their countries and the relaxed lifestyles. Australia has considered easing the immigration process for IT specialists and has already relaxed its rules for foreign students who wish to remain to work. Other countries are taking steps to address the outflow of companies and talented individuals.

Thus, Costa Rica has parlayed political stability, a growing educational infrastructure, and an aggressive program to recruit foreign firms such as Intel into an unemployment rate less than 5 percent and wage and job opportunities that tend to keep talented citizens at home. And Trinidad and Tobago have created a foreign investment zone aimed at high-tech industries and have eliminated import duties on computer equipment in an attempt to increase foreign investment and encourage a generation of domestic computer users [36].

Global Business/IT Strategies

Figure 12.12 illustrates that many firms are moving toward **transnational strategies** in which they integrate their global business/IT activities through close cooperation and interdependence among their international subsidiaries and their corporate headquarters. Businesses are moving away from (1) multinational strategies where foreign subsidiaries operate autonomously; (2) international strategies in which foreign subsidiaries are autonomous but are dependent on headquarters for new processes, products, and ideas; or (3) global strategies, where a company's worldwide operations are closely managed by corporate headquarters [26].

In the transnational approach, a business depends heavily on its information systems and Internet technologies to help it integrate its global business activities. Instead of having independent IS units at its subsidiaries, or even a centralized IS operation directed from its headquarters, a transnational business tries to develop an integrated and cooperative worldwide hardware, software, and Internet-based architecture for its IT platform. Figure 12.13 illustrates how transnational business and IT strategies were implemented by global companies [35].

Global Business/IT Applications

The applications of information technology developed by global companies depend on their business and IT strategies and their expertise and experience in IT. However, their IT applications also depend on a variety of **global business drivers,** that is, business requirements caused by the nature of the industry and its competitive or environmental forces. One example would be companies like airlines or hotel chains that have global customers, that is, customers who travel widely or have global operations. Such companies will need global

FIGURE 12.12   Companies operating internationally are moving toward transnational business and IT strategies. Note some of the chief differences between international, global, and transnational business and IT strategies.

Comparing Global e-Business Strategies		
International	**Global**	**Transnational**
● Autonomous operations.	● Global sourcing.	● Virtual business operations via global alliances.
● Region specific.	● Multiregional.	● World markets and mass customization.
● Vertical integration.	● Horizontal integration.	● Global e-commerce and customer service.
● Specific customers.	● Some transparency of customers and production.	● Transparent manufacturing.
● Captive manufacturing.	● Some cross regionalization.	● Global supply chain and logistics.
● Customer segmentation and dedication by region and plant.		● Dynamic resource management.
Information Technology Characteristics		
● Stand-alone systems.	● Regional decentralization.	● Logically consolidated, physically distributed, Internet connected.
● Decentralized/no standards.	● Interface dependent.	● Common global data resources.
● Heavy reliance on interfaces.	● Some consolidation of applications and use of common systems.	● Integrated global enterprise systems.
● Multiple systems, high redundancy and duplication of services and operations.	● Reduced duplication of operations.	● Internet, intranet, extranet Web-based applications.
● Lack of common systems and data.	● Some worldwide IT standards.	● Transnational IT policies and standards.

Source: Adapted and reprinted from Michael Mische, "Transnational Architecture: A Reengineering Approach," *Information Systems Management* (New York: Auerbach Publications), Winter 1995, p. 18. © 1995 Research Institute of America. Used with permission; and Nicholas Vitalari and James Wetherbe, "Emerging Best Practices in Global Systems Development," in *Global Information Technology and Systems Management*, Prashant Palvia et al., editors (Marietta, GA: Ivy League Publishing, 1996), p. 336.

FIGURE 12.13   Examples of how transnational business and IT strategies were implemented by global companies.

Tactic	Global Alliances	Global Sourcing and Logistics	Global Customer Service
Examples	British Airways / US Air KLM / Northwest Qantas / American	Benetton	American Express
IT Environment	Global network (online reservation system)	Global network, EPOS terminals in 4,000 stores, CAD/CAM in central manufacturing, robots and laser scanner in their automated warehouse	Global network linked from local branches and local merchants to the customer database and medical or legal referrals database
Results	● Coordination of schedules ● Code sharing ● Coordination of flights ● Co-ownership	● Produce 2,000 sweaters per hour using CAD/CAM ● Quick response (in stores in 10 days) ● Reduced inventories (just-in-time)	● Worldwide access to funds ● "Global Assist" hotline ● Emergency credit card replacement ● 24-hour customer service

Source: Adapted from Nicholas Vitalari and James Wetherbe, "Emerging Best Practices in Global System Development," in *Global Information Technology and Systems Management*, Prashant Palvia et al., editors (Marietta, GA: Ivy League Publishing, 1996), pp. 338–42.

FIGURE 12.14

These are some of the business reasons driving global business applications.

Business Drivers for Global IT
● **Global customers.** Customers are people who may travel anywhere or companies with global operations. Global IT can help provide fast, convenient service.
● **Global products.** Products are the same throughout the world or are assembled by subsidiaries throughout the world. Global IT can help manage worldwide marketing and quality control.
● **Global operations.** Parts of a production or assembly process are assigned to subsidiaries based on changing economic or other conditions. Only global IT can support such geographic flexibility.
● **Global resources.** The use and cost of common equipment, facilities, and people are shared by subsidiaries of a global company. Global IT can keep track of such shared resources.
● **Global collaboration.** The knowledge and expertise of colleagues in a global company can be quickly accessed, shared, and organized to support individual or group efforts. Only global IT can support such enterprise collaboration.

IT capabilities for online transaction processing so they can provide fast, convenient service to their customers or face losing them to their competitors. The economies of scale provided by global business operations are other business drivers that require the support of global IT applications. Figure 12.14 summarizes some of the business requirements that make global IT a competitive necessity [15].

Of course, many global IT applications, particularly finance, accounting, and office applications, have been in operation for many years. For example, most multinational companies have global financial budgeting and cash management systems, and office automation applications such as fax and e-mail systems. However, as global operations expand and global competition heats up, there is increasing pressure for companies to install global e-commerce and e-business applications for their customers and suppliers. Examples include global e-commerce websites and customer service systems for customers and global supply chain management systems for suppliers. In the past, such systems relied almost exclusively on privately constructed or government-owned telecommunications networks. But the explosive business use of the Internet, intranets, and extranets for electronic commerce has made such applications much more feasible for global companies.

TRW Inc: Global Business/IT Challenges

In the world of global IT operations, timing is everything. And so is knowing the ropes of the country you're in. Take, for example, Cleveland-based TRW Inc., a $17 billion technology, manufacturing, and services company with operations in 35 countries. When TRW's plant in Poland experiences a problem with its enterprise resource planning system or its global wide area network, the first wave of support comes from the local IT team. If that group is unsuccessful in righting the situation, backup is called in from a second team and even a third in the same time zone in either the U.K. or Germany.

Speed is of the essence, and local support means faster access to end users and resources, such as service providers, telephone companies, and equipment. This clustering of quick-response IT support team by time zones and proximity is just one of the lessons learned by Mostafa Mehrabani, who has served as vice president and CIO at TRW for three years and for the past two years has developed the company's global IT operations.

"For a while, we were trying to perform day-to-day support of LANs and IT development for our Asian operations from the U.S.," he says. "We came to the conclusion that while you can get someone on the phone, it isn't the same as being there and understanding the culture." So TRW developed centers of excellence, which are groups of subject-matter experts who assist employees throughout the company with their problems and requirements. "Often, we don't have the luxury of certain technical expertise in every part of the world, and we don't have the need for full-time experts in every region. Pooling resources to solve global IT issues is a major advantage." says Mehrabani [23].

Global IT Platforms

The management of technology platforms (also called the technology infrastructure) is another major dimension of global IT management—that is, managing the hardware, software, data resources, telecommunications networks, and computing facilities that support global business operations. The management of a global IT platform is not only technically complex but also has major political and cultural implications.

For example, hardware choices are difficult in some countries because of high prices, high tariffs, import restrictions, long lead times for government approvals, lack of local service or spare parts, and lack of documentation tailored to local conditions. Software choices can also present unique problems. Software packages developed in Europe may be incompatible with American or Asian versions, even when purchased from the same hardware vendor. Well-known U.S. software packages may be unavailable because there is no local distributor, or because the software publisher refuses to supply markets that disregard software licensing and copyright agreements [15].

Managing international data communications networks, including Internet, intranet, extranet, and other networks, is a key global IT challenge. Figure 12.15 outlines the top ten international data communications issues as reported by the IS executives at 300 Fortune 500 multinational companies. Notice how political issues dominate the top ten listing over technology issues, clearly emphasizing their importance in the management of global telecommunications.

FIGURE 12.15
The top ten issues in managing international data communications.

International Data Communications Issues
Network management issues
● Improving the operational efficiency of networks
● Dealing with different networks
● Controlling data communication security
Regulatory issues
● Dealing with transborder data flow restrictions
● Managing international telecommunication regulations
● Handling international politics
Technology issues
● Managing network infrastructure across countries
● Managing international integration of technologies
Country-oriented issues
● Reconciling national differences
● Dealing with international tariff structures

Source: Adapted from Vincent S. Lai and Wingyan Chung, "Managing International Data Communications," *Communications of the ACM*, March 2002, p. 91.

Establishing computing facilities internationally is another global challenge. Companies with global business operations usually establish or contract with systems integrators for additional data centers in their subsidiaries in other countries. These data centers meet local and regional computing needs, and even help balance global computing workloads through communications satellite links. However, offshore data centers can pose major problems in headquarter's support, hardware and software acquisition, maintenance, and security. That's why many global companies turn to application service providers or systems integrators like EDS or IBM to manage their overseas operations.

The Internet as a Global IT Platform

What makes the Internet and the World Wide Web so important for international business? This interconnected matrix of computers, information, and networks that reaches tens of millions of users in over one hundred countries is a business environment free of traditional boundaries and limits. Linking to an online global infrastructure offers companies unprecedented potential for expanding markets, reducing costs, and improving profit margins at a price that is typically a small percentage of the corporate communications budget. The Internet provides an interactive channel for direct communication and data exchange with customers, suppliers, distributors, manufacturers, product developers, financial backers, information providers—in fact, with all parties involved in a given business venture [6].

So the Internet and the World Wide Web have now become vital components in international business and commerce. Within a few years, the Internet, with its interconnected network of thousands of networks of computers and databases, has established itself as a technology platform free of many traditional international boundaries and limits. By connecting their businesses to this online global infrastructure, companies can expand their markets, reduce communications and distribution costs, and improve their profit margins without massive cost outlays for new telecommunications facilities. Figure 12.16 outlines key considerations for global e-commerce websites [22].

The Internet, along with its related intranet and extranet technologies, provides a low-cost interactive channel for communications and data exchange with employees, customers, suppliers, distributors, manufacturers, product developers, financial backers, information providers, and so on. In fact, all parties involved can use the Internet and other related networks to communicate and collaborate to bring a business venture to its successful completion [6]. However, as Figure 12.17 illustrates, much work needs to be done to bring secure Internet access and electronic commerce to more people in more countries. But the trend is clearly on continued expansion of the Internet as it becomes a pervasive IT platform for global business.

FIGURE 12.16

Key questions for companies establishing global Internet websites.

Key Questions for Global Websites
● Will you have to develop a new navigational logic to accommodate cultural preferences?
● What content will you translate, and what content will you create from scratch to address regional competitors or products that differ from those in the United States?
● Should your multilingual effort be an adjunct to your main site, or will you make it a separate site, perhaps with a country-specific domain name?
● What kinds of traditional and new media advertising will you have to do in each country to draw traffic to your site?
● Will your site get so many hits that you'll need to set up a server in a local country?
● What are the legal ramifications of having your website targeted at a particular country, such as laws on competitive behavior, treatment of children, or privacy?

FIGURE 12.17   Current and projected numbers of Internet users by world region.

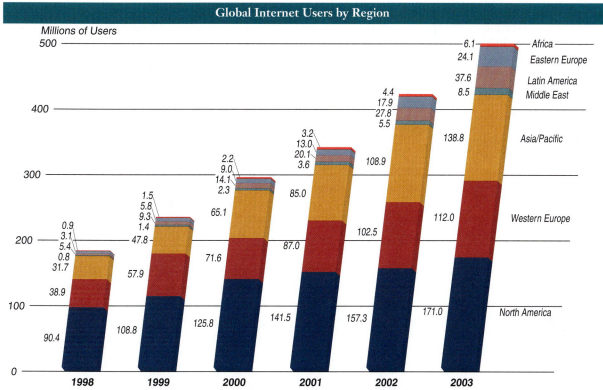

Source: Adapted from Martin VanderWeyer, "The World Debates," *Strategy & Business*, First Quarter 2000, p. 69.

Global Data Access Issues

The British and European legislative framework for e-commerce is still in its infancy, and there are large areas yet to be tackled. These include the full gamut of data protection and privacy issues. Under the European Convention on Human Rights, for example, employees are entitled to e-mail privacy; yet employers are regarded in law as the publishers of their employees' e-mails, and—as test cases against companies such as Norwich Union P.L.C. and British Gas have established—can be held legally responsible for their content [34].

Global data access issues have been a subject of political controversy and technology barriers in global business operations for many years, but have become more visible with the growth of the Internet and the pressures of e-commerce. A major example is the issue of **transborder data flows** (TDF), in which business data flow across international borders over the telecommunications networks of global information systems. Many countries view TDF as violating their national sovereignty because transborder data flows avoid customs duties and regulations for the import or export of goods and services. Others view transborder data flows as violating their laws to protect the local IT industry from competition, or their labor regulations for protecting local jobs. In many cases, the data flow business issues that seem especially politically sensitive are those that affect the movement out of a country of personal data in e-commerce and human resource applications.

Many countries, especially those in the European Union, may view transborder data flows as a violation of their privacy legislation since, in many cases, data about individuals are being moved out of the country without stringent privacy safeguards. For example, Figure 12.18 outlines the key provisions of a data privacy agreement between the United States and the European Union. The agreement exempts U.S. companies engaging in international e-commerce from EU data privacy sanctions if they join a self-regulatory program that provides EU consumers with basic information about and

U.S. – EU Data Privacy Requirements
● Notice of purpose and use of data collected
● Ability to opt out of third-party distribution of data
● Access for consumers to their information
● Adequate security, data integrity, and enforcement provisions

Source: Adapted from Patrick Thibodeau, "Europe and U.S. Agree on Data Rules," *Computerworld*,
March 20, 2000, p. 6. Copyright 2000 by Computerworld, Inc., Framingham, MA 01701. Reprinted from
Computerworld.

control over how their personal data are used. Thus, the agreement is said to provide a "safe harbor" for such companies from the requirements of the EU's Data Privacy Directive, which bans the transfer of personal information on EU citizens to countries that do not have adequate data privacy protection [32].

Council of Europe: Global Cybercrime Treaty

Some information technology managers fear that the Council of Europe's controversial cybercrime treaty, which was approved by 26 member states, plus the United States, Canada, Japan, and South Africa in November 2001, will affect their businesses from both a liability and a security perspective. But before getting all worked up over liability issues, American IT leaders need to remember that European nation-states are cooperating with the United States in terms of cyberlegislation and law enforcement, explains Martha Stansell-Gamm, chief of the Computer Crime and Intellectual Property Section at the U.S. Department of Justice (DOJ). Stansell-Gamm was the DOJ's representative in the drafting of the treaty. The United States participated because it has observer status within the Council of Europe.

"We already have many treaties—bilateral and multilateral—on law enforcement matters like extradition, mutual assistance, money laundering, and corruption," she says. "An awful lot of what's going into this treaty is not new; this just combines technology and criminal law and international law."

Just as in other international law enforcement pacts, the primary objective of the treaty is to break the bottlenecks in international cyberinvestigations, says Stansell-Gamm.

The new Convention on Cybercrime treaty contains provisions which regulate illegal access, illegal interception of electronic communications, data interference, system interference, misuse of devices, computer-related forgery and fraud, child pornography, copyright violations, and corporate liability. Treaty backers say it will serve as a foundation for legislation on such issues by the European Union and its member states, and for cooperative agreements with other countries [30].

Internet Access Issues

The Paris-based organization Reporters Without Borders (RSF) reports that there are 45 countries that "restrict their citizens' access to the Internet." At its most fundamental, the struggle between Internet censorship and openness at the national level revolves around three main means: controlling the conduits, filtering the flows, and punishing the purveyors. In countries such as Burma, Libya, North Korea, Syria, and the countries of Central Asia and the Caucasus, Internet access is either banned or subject to tight limitations through government-controlled ISPs, says the RSF [33].

Figure 12.19 outlines the restrictions to public Internet access by the governments of 20 countries deemed most restrictive by the Paris-based Reporters Without Borders (RSF). See their website at www.rsf.fr.

FIGURE 12.19

Countries that restrict or forbid Internet access by their citizens.

Global Government Restrictions on Internet Access
● **High Government Access Fees**   Kazakhstan, Kyrgyzstan
● **Government Monitored Access**   China, Iran, Saudi Arabia, Azerbaijan, Uzbekistan
● **Government Filtered Access**   Belarus, Cuba, Iraq, Tunisia, Sierra Leone, Tajikistan, Turkmenistan, Vietnam
● **No Public Access Allowed**   Burma, Libya, North Korea, Sudan, Syria

Source: Data from Reporters Without Borders in Stewart Taggart, "Censor Census," *Business 2.0*, March 2000, pp. 358–59.

So the Internet has become a global battleground over public access to data and information at business and private sites on the World Wide Web. Of course this becomes a business issue because restrictive access policies severely inhibit the growth of e-commerce with such countries. Most of the rest of the world has decided that restricting Internet access is not a viable policy, and in fact, would hurt their countries' opportunities for economic growth and prosperity. Instead, national and international efforts are being made to rate and filter Internet content deemed inappropriate or criminal, such as websites for child pornography or terrorism. In any event, countries that significantly restrict Internet access are also choosing to restrict their participation in the growth of electronic commerce [33].

> *To RSF and others, these countries' rulers face a lose-lose struggle against the Information Age. By denying or limiting Internet access, they stymie a major engine of economic growth. But by easing access, they expose their citizenry to ideas potentially destabilizing to the status quo. Either way, many people will get access to the electronic information they want. "In Syria, for example, people go to Lebanon for the weekend to retrieve their e-mail," says Virginie Locussol, RSF's desk officer for the Middle East and North Africa [33].*

Global Systems Development

Just imagine the challenges of developing efficient, effective, and responsive applications for business end users domestically. Then multiply that by the number of countries and cultures that may use a global e-business system. That's the challenge of managing global systems development. Naturally, there are conflicts over local versus global system requirements, and difficulties in agreeing on common system features such as multilingual user interfaces and flexible design standards. And all of this effort must take place in an environment that promotes involvement and "ownership" of a system by local end users. Thus, one IT manager estimates:

> *It takes 5 to 10 times more time to reach an understanding and agreement on system requirements and deliverables when the users and developers are in different countries. This is partially explained by travel requirements and language and cultural differences, but technical limitations also contribute to the problem [15].*

Other systems development issues arise from disturbances caused by systems implementation and maintenance activities. For example: "An interruption during a third shift in New York City will present midday service interruptions in Tokyo." Another major development issue relates to the trade-offs between developing one system that can run on multiple computer and operating system platforms, or letting each local site customize the software for its own platform [15]. See Figure 12.20.

FIGURE 12.20

The global use of information technology depends on international systems development efforts.

Other important global systems development issues are concerned with global standardization of data definitions. Common data definitions are necessary for sharing data among the parts of an international business. Differences in language, culture, and technology platforms can make global data standardization quite difficult. For example, a sale may be called "an 'order booked' in the United Kingdom, an 'order scheduled' in Germany, and an 'order produced' in France" [28]. However, businesses are moving ahead to standardize data definitions and structures. By moving their subsidiaries into data modeling and database design, they hope to develop a global data architecture that supports their global business objectives.

Systems Development Strategies

Several strategies can be used to solve some of the systems development problems that arise in global IT. First is transforming an application used by the home office into a global application. However, often the system used by a subsidiary that has the best version of an application will be chosen for global use. Another approach is setting up a *multinational development team* with key people from several subsidiaries to ensure that the system design meets the needs of local sites as well as corporate headquarters.

A third approach is called *parallel development*. That's because parts of the system are assigned to different subsidiaries and the home office to develop at the same time, based on the expertise and experience at each site. Another approach is the concept of *centers of excellence*. In this approach, an entire system may be assigned for development to a particular subsidiary based on their expertise in the business or technical dimensions needed for successful development. Obviously, all of these approaches require development team collaboration and managerial oversight to meet the global needs of a business. So, global systems development teams are making heavy use of the Internet, intranets, groupware, and other electronic collaboration technologies [15].

DHL Worldwide: Global Systems Development

San Francisco–based DHL Worldwide Express Inc. has opened development centers in the U.K. and in Malaysia, India, and other parts of Asia. The international delivery giant is able to take advantage of time differences between these locations and California to create an extended workday.

"For us, large-scale development is not a hothouse environment, it's an everyday reality," says Colum Joyce, a global e-business strategy manager based in DHL's offices in Brussels. That means establishing development facilities around the world, as well as working with outsourcers where necessary, he says. These realities, combined with the lower turnover rates and salaries in many foreign countries—the average salary for a skilled programmer in India, for example, is about $30,000, according to Niven—are driving global companies to open offshore facilities.

DHL's offshore developers tailor e-business applications to country-specific requirements and even take lead roles in some development efforts, such as a wireless service applications project that's under way in Europe and Asia. Joyce says the company looks at several factors when hiring in these locations, including the technical and linguistic skills of local workers, long-term business viability, and knowledge transfer. "A mastery of English is a key skill set, as it is the operating language of all cross-group communication for all development, whether it be verbal, hard copy, or electronic communication," Joyce says.

"It is not so much the knowledge but the willingness and flexibility to learn that is important in hiring global IT workers," Joyce explains. "In an incredibly dynamic environment, it is the attitude, rather than gross development capability, that counts the most in recruitment." Nonetheless, Joyce acknowledges that success in such endeavors depends heavily on adopting market standards in technology infrastructures and on ensuring that there's continual communication among development teams in disparate locations. To that end, DHL puts a great deal of effort into developing what Joyce calls "hybrid managers" who are heavily immersed in both IT and business.

"This has been a process we have engaged in for over 15 years," Joyce says. "The boundaries are really transparent now, and managers and personnel are cross-comfortable with the global business and its supporting infrastructure" [12].

Summary

- **Managers and IT.** Information technologies and new e-business applications are changing the distribution, relationships, resources, and responsibilities of managers. That is, IT is helping to eliminate layers of management, enabling more collaborative forms of management, providing managers with significant information technology resources, and confronting managers with major IT management challenges.

- **The Networked Organization.** The organizational structure and roles of today's companies are undergoing major changes as they strive to become agile, customer focused, value-driven enterprises. Figure 12.3 summarizes the major characteristics of the networked organization compared to the structure and roles of traditional organization model.

- **Failures in IT Management.** Information systems are not being used effectively or efficiently by many organizations. The experiences of successful organizations reveal that the basic ingredient of high-quality information system performance is extensive and meaningful management and user involvement in the governance and development of IT applications. Thus, managers may serve on executive IT groups and create IS management functions within their business units.

- **Managing Information Technology.** Managing IT can be viewed as having three major components: (1) managing the joint development and implementation of e-business and IT strategies, (2) managing the development of e-business applications and the research and implementation of new information technologies, and (3) managing IT processes, professionals, and subunits within a company's IT organization and IS function.

- **Managing Global IT.** The international dimensions of managing global information technologies include dealing with cultural, political, and geoeconomic challenges posed by various countries; developing appropriate business and IT strategies for the global marketplace; and developing a portfolio of global e-business and e-commerce applications and an Internet-based technology platform to support them. In addition, data access methods have to be developed and systems development projects managed to produce the global e-business applications that are required to compete successfully in the global marketplace.

● **Global Business and IT Strategies and Issues.** Many businesses are becoming global companies and moving toward transnational business strategies in which they integrate the global business activities of their subsidiaries and headquarters. This requires that they develop a global IT platform, that is, an integrated worldwide hardware, software, and Internet-based network architecture. Global companies are increasingly using the Internet and related technologies as a major component of this IT platform to develop and deliver global IT applications that meet their unique global business requirements. Global IT and end user managers must deal with limitations on the availability of hardware and software, restrictions on transborder data flows, Internet access, and movement of personal data, and difficulties with developing common data definitions and system requirements.

Key Terms and Concepts

These are the key terms and concepts of this chapter. The page number of their first explanation is in parentheses.

1. Application development management (430)
2. Centralization or decentralization of IT (428)
3. Chargeback systems (431)
4. Chief information officer (432)
5. Chief technology officer (432)
6. Cultural, political, and geoeconomic challenges (439)
7. Data center (431)
8. Downsizing (429)
9. Failures in IT management (433)
10. Global business drivers (440)
11. Global information technology management (438)
    a. e-Business applications (440)
    b. e-Business/IT strategies (440)
    c. Data access issues (445)
    d. IT platforms (443)
    e. Systems development issues (447)
12. Human resource management of IT (432)
13. Impact of IT on managers (424)
14. Internet access issues (446)
15. Internet as a global IT platform (444)
16. Management involvement in IT (434)
17. Managing information technology (428)
18. Managing the IS function (428)
19. Networked organization (427)
20. Operations management (431)
21. Outsourcing IS operations (430)
22. System performance monitor (431)
23. Technology management (433)
24. Transborder data flows (445)
25. Transnational strategy (440)
26. User services (433)

Review Quiz

Match one of the key terms and concepts listed previously with one of the brief examples or definitions that follow. Try to find the best fit for the answers that seem to fit more than one term or concept. Defend your choices.

_____ 1. Managers now have a lot of information processing power and responsibility for the use of information technologies.

_____ 2. Information systems have not been used efficiently or effectively.

_____ 3. An executive IT council is an example.

_____ 4. e-Business and e-commerce processes affect organizational roles and structures.

_____ 5. Managing business/IT planning and the IS function within a company.

_____ 6. Managing application development, data center operations, and user services are examples.

_____ 7. Many IT organizations have centralized and decentralized units.

_____ 8. Managing the creation and implementation of new business applications.

_____ 9. End users need liaison, consulting, and training services.

_____ 10. Planning and controlling data center operations.

_____ 11. Corporate locations for computer system operations.

_____ 12. Rapidly changing technological developments must be anticipated, identified, and implemented.

_____ 13. Recruiting and developing IT professionals.

_____ 14. The executive responsible for strategic business/IT planning and management.

_____ 15. The executive in charge of researching and implementing new information technologies.

____ 16. Software that helps monitor and control computer systems in a data center.

____ 17. The cost of IS services may be allocated back to end users.

____ 18. Many business firms are replacing their mainframe systems with networked PCs and servers.

____ 19. Using outside contractors to provide and manage IS operations.

____ 20. Managing IT to support a company's international business operations.

____ 21. Integrating global business activities through cooperation among international subsidiaries and corporate headquarters.

____ 22. Differences in customs, governmental regulations, and the cost of living are examples.

____ 23. Global customers, products, operations, resources, and collaboration.

____ 24. Applying IT to global e-commerce systems is an example.

____ 25. The goal of some organizations is to develop integrated Internet-based networks for global electronic commerce.

____ 26. Transborder data flows and security of personal databases are top concerns.

____ 27. Standardizing global use of computer systems, software packages, telecommunications networks, and computing facilities is an example.

____ 28. The Internet is a natural global networking choice.

____ 29. Global telecommunications networks like the Internet move data across national boundaries.

____ 30. Some countries deny or limit Internet access.

____ 31. Agreement is needed on common user interfaces and website design features in global IT.

Discussion Questions

1. What has been the impact of information technologies on the work relationships, activities, and resources of managers?

2. What can business unit managers do about performance problems in the use of information technology and the development and operation of information systems in their business units?

3. Refer to the Real World Case on USG Corp. and others in the chapter. Who should be involved in evaluating the ROI of the IT investment proposals of a company's business units? Why?

4. How are Internet technologies affecting the structure and work roles of modern organizations? For example, will middle management wither away? Will companies consist primarily of self-directed project teams of knowledge workers? Explain your answers.

5. Should the IS function in a business be centralized or decentralized? What recent developments support your answer?

6. Refer to the Real World Case on Agilent Technologies and Citibank in the chapter. What challenges might arise in managing the global IT function at Agilent Technologies from this point on? How would you meet such challenges? Give several specific examples.

7. How will the Internet, intranets, and extranets affect each of the components of global information technology management, as illustrated in Figure 12.11? Give several examples.

8. How might cultural, political, or geoeconomic challenges affect a global company's use of the Internet? Give several examples.

9. Will the increasing use of the Internet by firms with global business operations change their move toward a transnational business strategy? Explain.

10. How might the Internet, intranets, and extranets affect the business drivers or requirements responsible for a company's use of global IT, as shown in Figure 12.14? Give several examples to illustrate your answer.

Application Exercises

Complete the following exercises as individual or group projects that apply chapter concepts to real world business situations.

1. CEO Express: Top-Rated Website for Executives

Web Check out this top-rated site (www.ceoexpress.com) for busy executives. See Figure 12.21. Membership is free and open to students and professors, too. Great news from hundreds of links to top U.S. and international newspapers, business and technology magazines, and news services. Hundreds of links to business and technology research sources and references are provided, as well as to travel services, online shopping, and recreational websites.

    a. Evaluate the CEO Express website as a source of useful links to business and technology news,

FIGURE 12.21
The CEO Express website.

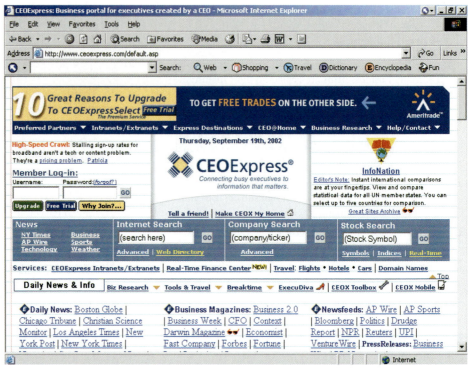

Source: Courtesy of CEO Express.

analysis, and research sources for business executives and professionals.

b. Report on one item of business or IT news, analysis, or research that might have value for your present or future career in business.

2. The World Bank: Global Information and Communications Technologies

`Web` The World Bank Group's Global Information & Communication Technologies Department (GICT) plays an important role in developing and promoting access to information and communications technologies (ICT) in developing countries. See Figure 12.22.

GICT brings together the private investment practice of the International Finance Corporation and the public sector advisory and funding arms of the World Bank to provide governments, private companies, and community organizations with the capital and expertise needed to develop and exploit information and communications technologies to accelerate the participation of all countries in the global information economy and thus reduce poverty and foster economic and social development.

a. Explore the World Bank's GICT website at www.worldbank.org/ict and investigate several of their projects to help countries participate in the global information economy.

b. Evaluate the effectiveness of two of the GICT's projects. Explain the reasons for your evaluations.

3. Tracking Shopping-Related Internet Use across the United States

`DB` The U.S. Census Bureau has surveyed households concerning their use of the Internet in December of 1998 and in August of 2000. The sample records shown below illustrate the structure of a database table based on data from these surveys that has been extracted and is available on the website for this textbook. The Use98 column indicates the estimated number of individuals in each state who regularly used the Internet to shop, pay bills, or for some other commercial purpose in December of 1998. The No_Use98 column provides an estimate of the number not using the Internet for those purposes in December of 1998. The Use00 and No_Use00 columns provide the same type of data for August of 2000. These figures are based on survey data and may be subject to significant error, especially for less populous states, but they do allow you to assess the degree of state-to-state variation in e-commerce related Internet use. Download the database file for this exercise from the website for this textbook. The textbook website is *www.mhhe.com/business/mis/obrien*. Click on downloads under the student resources section of that page.

a. Create and print a query that shows the proportion of the population in each state who used the Internet for shopping and related activities in August of 2000: Use00/(Use00/No_Use00) and sort the states in descending order by this usage proportion.

FIGURE 12.22

The website of the World Bank's Global Information and Communications Technologies Department.

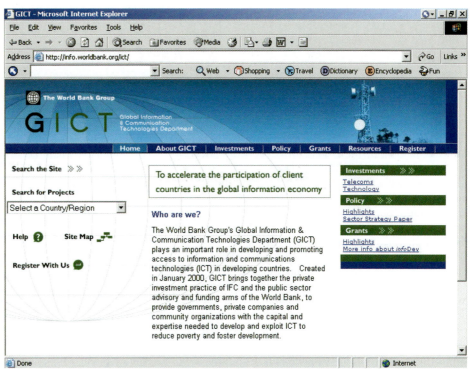

Source: Courtesy of info.worldbank.org/ict.

State	Use98	No_Use98	Use00	No_Use00
AL	183641	4107068	447023	4132225
AK	61261	533460	102968	481889
AZ	258602	4500880	528993	4417750
AR	53658	2448054	183010	2323339
CA	2036246	30804742	4475743	29460000

b. Calculate the usage proportion described in part A for the country as a whole for both December of 1998 and August of 2000 and determine the change in the commercial usage proportion between the two periods. Produce similar proportions for your home state and at least two adjacent states. (You may use database queries to find these proportions or you may copy the data to a spreadsheet and perform the calculations there.)

c. Prepare a set of PowerPoint slides or similar presentation materials summarizing the results in parts A and B and describing their implications for Web-based marketing.

4. Worldwide Internet Users

SS Figure 12.17 provides a set of estimates and projections of the numbers of Internet users in various regions of the world. Record the data from that table into a spreadsheet for further analysis or copy it from the download file for this exercise in the website for this textbook at *www.mhhe.com/business/mis/ obrien*. To download the file click on downloads under the student resources section of that page and find the file for this exercise.

a. Add a section to the spreadsheet showing the percentage growth from year to year for each region. Then create an appropriate chart of this data.

b. Add a section showing the absolute change in users each year for each region. For instance, the absolute change figures for North America would be 108.8–90.4 or 18.4 for 1999, 125.8–108.8 or 17 for 2000, and so on. Create pie charts to show the distribution of projected Internet growth for the years 2002 and 2003.

c. Create a memorandum to your instructor summarizing your results and their implications. Include an assessment of how accurate you feel these projections are likely to be.

REAL WORLD CASE 3

Cisco Systems: Failure in Supply Chain Management

As corporate humiliations go, it had to be one of the worst. In May 2001, Cisco Systems (www.cisco.com) announced the largest inventory write-down in history—$2.2 billion erased from its balance sheet for components it ordered but couldn't use. The gaffe was made all the more embarrassing by waves of prior publicity about Cisco's brilliant integration of its vast information systems. The network was so responsive, gushed CEO John Chambers, that the company could close its books in 24 hours, any day of the year. Yet the system wasn't responsive enough to stop building billions of dollars' worth of stuff nobody wanted.

Cisco blamed the fiasco on a plunge in technology spending that Chambers called as unforeseeable as "a 100-year flood." If company forecasters had only been able to see this coming, Cisco implied, the supply-chain system would have worked perfectly. But *Business 2.0* has learned that, in fact, flaws in the system contributed significantly to the breakdown.

During the late 1990s, Cisco became famous for being the hardware maker that doesn't make hardware. Instead, Cisco farms out most of its routers and switches to electronics contract manufacturers. This arrangement has several advantages. For one, it allows Cisco to concentrate on marketing and product innovation. It also liberates Cisco from much of the hassle and expense of maintaining inventory, as Cisco's information systems make it possible to ship fully assembled machines directly from the factory to buyers more or less on demand.

But the Great Inventory Wreck of 2001 highlighted some ugly bugs in the system. Cisco's supply chain is basically structured like a pyramid, with Cisco at the point. On the second tier reside a handful of contract manufacturers—including Celestica, Flextronics, and Solectron—responsible for final assembly. These manufacturers are fed by a larger sub-tier supplying components such as processor chips (Intel and Xiliox) and optical gear (JDS Uniphase and Corning). Those companies, in turn, draw on an even larger base of commodity suppliers scattered all over the globe.

Communication gaps between the tiers eventually got Cisco into trouble. To lock in supplies of scarce components during the boom, Cisco ordered large quantities well in advance, based on demand projections from the company's sales force. What the forecasters didn't notice, however, was that many of their projections were inflated artificially. With network gear hard to come by, many Cisco customers also ordered similar equipment from Cisco's competitors, knowing that they'd ultimately make just one purchase—from whoever could deliver the goods first.

The result was double and triple ordering, which bloated demand forecasts and put the squeeze on component supplies. A missing link in Cisco's supply-chain management system magnified this problem. Suppose Cisco projected sales of 10,000 units of a particular router. Each of the company's contract manufacturers would compete to fill the

entire order, and to gain an edge, they often tried to lock up supplies of scarce components.

Suppliers would be swamped with orders, but Cisco's supply-chain system couldn't show that the spike in demand represented overlapping orders. If, say, three manufacturers were competing to build those 10,000 routers, to chipmakers it looked like a sudden demand for 30,000 machines. Cisco became enmeshed in a vicious cycle of artificially inflated demand for key components, higher costs, and bad communication throughout the supply chain. Eventually, the bubble burst.

Cisco's inventory woes highlighted the shortcomings of a system that stopped only partway down the pyramid. That's where eHub, Cisco's new supply chain system which it recently unveiled, is supposed to make it all better. Under eHub, Cisco's production cycle begins when a demand forecast is sent out, showing cumulative orders. That forecast goes not only to contract manufacturers but also to chipmakers like Philips Semiconductors and Altera Corp.

"Before, if Celestica, Flextronics, and Solectron all came to Philips at the same time, and each said they wanted 10,000 of a certain chip, that was a total of 30,000 chips," says one senior engineer who worked on the eHub project. "Now Philips can say, 'Hold on, I'm on eHub. I know that total aggregated demand is only 10,000.'" By requiring all the systems in the supply network to talk to each other, eHub supposedly ferrets out inventory shortfalls, production blackouts, and other screw-ups almost as fast as they occur.

eHub is just the first stage of Cisco's plans for the future. Ultimately, Cisco hopes to automate the whole enchilada. A customer purchases a product online, and that order goes into both Cisco's financial database and supply-chain system simultaneously. For now, however, eHub will be plagued by a timeless software limitation—it's only as good as the data it receives. Garbage in, garbage out.

"If the inputs are wrong, the world's best supply chain can't save you," says Steve Kammen, an analyst who covers Cisco for CIBC World Markets.

Case Study Questions

1. What caused Cisco's $2.2 billion loss in unneeded inventory? Could this situation have been avoided? Why or why not?

2. How is eHub supposed to avoid such losses in the future? What problems might arise with this new system?

3. What can be done in the supply chain management process of any company to avoid situations like Cisco's?

REAL WORLD CASE 4   Merrill Lynch & Co.: The Business Case for Global IT Consolidation

Merrill Lynch & Co. (www.merrilllynch.com) is replacing its order processing software around the world as part of a multi-million-dollar project aimed at eliminating a hodgepodge of in-house and acquired systems. Marvin Balliet, the chief financial officer for Merrill Lynch's technology group, said he expects the project—the cost of which he ballparked at "tens of millions of dollars"—to generate a return on investment within three years through cost reductions and additional sales. Still, he said, the actual ROI will be difficult to measure because "part of why you do it is cost reduction, part of why you do it is system enhancement, and part of why you do it is revenue retention. Today, my revenue may be down in a country where I put it in, but that has nothing to do with the fact that I now have a new platform," said Balliet.

Centralizing systems has become a trend among financial services companies as the Internet and globalization—combined with the industry's push to do straight-through processing—are forcing brokerages and their clients to communicate across borders in near-real-time, according to analysts. "It was an interest of companies before. Now it's a real driver," said Shaw Lively, an analyst at IDC. "It's not necessarily always an upgrade but more about trying to get common stems, common platforms, common interfaces," he said.

Merrill's system consolidation is similar in scope to another financial services firm that's part of the global systems consolidation trend. That's its New York-based neighbor, Citibank, which is currently replacing a decades-old set of back-office corporate banking systems with a single platform in all of its overseas corporate offices.

Balliet said Merrill Lynch is initially focusing on its equity cash businesses in overseas operations because those systems offer the greatest opportunity for increased efficiency. He said the new platform will establish a global network of trading desks that can execute orders from regional exchanges instead of local connections. Merrill Lynch's current vendor-built order entry systems require middleware interfaces to allow far-flung offices to communicate with one another.

Balliet said Merrill Lynch is still evaluating what it will do with its U.S. order entry system "because we have a reasonably robust system from one of our acquisitions in the U.S., and the question is, do we have one global system or two?" Overseas, however, Merrill's international trade order entry systems have been put together piecemeal, with some added through acquisitions of other firms, according to Balliet.

In May, Merrill Lynch partnered with Royalblue Financial PLC, the London-based maker of the global financial trading software that supports Merrill Lynch's global trading requirements in the European, Japanese, Asia-Pacific, and U.S. markets. The deal included Royalblue's Fidessa

trading platform and consultancy services. Royalblue's software supports order management, trade management, and market execution across some 20 markets, according to Royalblue officials.

The Royalblue order management system rollout has been completed at Merrill Lynch offices in Japan and the rest of Asia; the system is now being introduced at the firm's European offices. If Merrill Lynch decides not to replace its U.S.-based order entry systems, the project is expected to be completed within the next year, according to Balliet.

Big global systems replacement efforts like Merrill Lynch's typically cost tens of millions of dollars to complete, but companies may find that such projects are worthwhile because "biting the bullet" now helps avoid the cost of developing interfaces in the future, said Larry Tabb, an analyst at the Tower Group. "In a period of business earnings pressure, it can force firms to look at how to reduce overall cost and centralize technology, reduce redundancy and streamline their processing," said Tabb.

The global consolidation of Merrill Lynch continued when Chief Technology Officer John McKinley was named head of Global Technology & Services at the brokerage. Merrill created the new division by merging its technology and global services units. When asked why Merrill Lynch merged its IT and global operations divisions, McKinley commented: "There are a few trends that cross the entire enterprise. One is that you need to have a competitive cost structure. The second thing is world-class customer services. While I think we've done some really great things with that, I think there's even further ground for us to hoe here. Technology can play a huge role as an enabler for a radical redesign of business processes. I think the third thing is that we're in a heavily regulated environment on a global basis. All three of these things point to a very tight connection of the global operations and technology functions."

Case Study Questions

1. Why has there been a trend toward centralizing systems among financial services firms? What are the potential benefits and limitations of this trend?

2. What are the business benefits of Merrill Lynch's new global order processing system? What implementation challenges are involved?

3. Does the merger of Merrill's global services division and its IT division make good business sense? Why or why not?

Source: Adapted from Lucas Merian, "Merrill Lynch Replacing Global Order Entry Systems," *Computerworld*, March 11, 2002, p. 9. Reprinted with permission from *Computerworld*.

REAL WORLD CASE 5

Fireman's Fund, Allmerica Financial and FMC: The Business Case for IT Outsourcing

Fireman's Fund Insurance Co. (www.firemansfund.com) in Novato, California, last fall signed a 10-year $380 million outsourcing deal with CGI Group Inc. (www.cgi.com) in Montreal, Canada. As part of the agreement, CGI will provide Fireman's Fund with IT support services to some 80 locations across the U.S. CGI has taken over the insurance company's Phoenix data center, and about 300 Fireman's Fund employees have become CGI employees.

The growing challenge of maintaining and staffing Fireman's vital-but-aging legacy systems was a primary driver of the deal, says CIO Bill McCarter. The decision to hand over legacy operations to CGI has left Fireman's with a leaner IT organization focused on developing new applications that it hopes will give it a competitive market edge. But the contract with CGI has also resulted in a substantial 21% savings in infrastructure costs—a benefit that has assumed even bigger significance in today's economy, McCarter says.

The huge fixed costs associated with owning an 800-MIPS data center have been eliminated because CGI owns it instead. Most of Fireman's infrastructure costs today are based on actual usage, an arrangement that has proved to be a far more efficient and economic model, according to McCarter. And CGI uses Fireman's data center to deliver services to other customers as well; so the costs are spread among multiple customers. For instance, a large printing operation that Fireman's Fund previously ran at half capacity out of its data center is now being used around the clock to deliver print services to other customers, resulting in lower printing costs per customer. "We are not unlike any other company that's being asked to contain IT expenditures during these critical times. If we can reduce infrastructure costs, we can shift the savings to our development organization while we retain a budget," McCarter says.

For users that have already outsourced IT operations for other reasons, the cost savings are a welcome bonus in tight times. For example, the economy had little to do with Allmerica Financial Corp.'s (www.allmerica.com) original decision to outsource legacy computer operations to Keane Inc. (www.keane.com) in Boston two years ago. But since then, the recession has sharply accelerated the company's efforts to off-load work to Keane, says Allmerica CIO Greg Tranter. Over the past six months, the Worcester, Massachusetts–based insurer has transferred 139 IT employees from its payroll to Keane's. The transfer was originally supposed to occur in about two years, but if those employees had remained at Allmerica, the insurer would have had to lay off 42 of them by now, Tranter says.

Allmerica's outsourcing strategy has allowed it to off-load legacy applications to Keane while freeing its IT organization to focus on developing cutting-edge applications, such as Internet-based point-of-sale application, he adds. Cost wasn't the most important consideration when Allmerica signed up with Keane. But the resulting 20% savings in application development and maintenance costs has been vital, Tranter says.

Technology complexity is another consideration, says Ed Flynn, CIO at Philadelphia-based FMC Corp. (www.fmc.com), a $2 billion chemicals manufacturer. Handing over complex technologies to companies with the know-how is both economical and efficient, Flynn says. It eliminates the risk and time involved in developing the knowledge in-house. FMC uses a variety of outsourcing vendors including IBM, Digex Inc., Genuity Inc. and Aventail Corp. "Cost has been an important priority in all these relationships. But our view on costs doesn't change based on the economy," says Flynn. "We are in some very competitive industries, and we look at costs all the time."

Beyond the usual domestic and offshore outsourcing options, Keane, CGI and several other outsourcing firms offer "near-shore" application outsourcing, meaning the IT services are performed in nearby countries such as Canada. Keane's near-shore services—from a facility in Nova Scotia—are targeted at customers who want the cost savings of an offshore model but want it close to home, Barry says. Because of the favorable currency exchange rate and the lower cost of labor in Canada, U.S.-based companies can deliver some services from Canada for 20% to 30% less than they could from the U.S.

"People are looking for opportunities to go near-shore and offshore much more than they have done in the past," Barry says. Some of the computer processing services that Keane is delivering to Allmerica are provided from Canada. Similarly, CGI is using its Canadian data centers to support some 500 Windows NT servers and large Unix platforms for Fireman's Fund. "Right now, we are bidding on more projects than we have ever bid before," says Michael Flak, a senior vice president at CGI. "We have $5 billion worth of orders in the pipeline," driven largely by companies hoping to save money, he says. "A recession many times is very good for outsourcing companies," he says.

Case Study Questions

1. What is the business value to Fireman's Fund and Allmerica of outsourcing their computer operations? What are some potential limitations of such outsourcing arrangements?

2. What is FMC's motivation for its IT outsourcing? What is the role of an IT organization at companies like those in this case, if much of their IT operations are outsourced?

3. What are the benefits and potential limitations of offshore and near-shore IT outsourcing arrangements?

Source: Adapted from Jaikumar Vijayan, "The Outsourcing Boom," *Computerworld*, March 18, 2002, pp. 42–43. Reprinted with permission from *Computerworld*.

MODULE VI

REVIEW OF HARDWARE AND SOFTWARE TECHNOLOGIES

Management Challenges

Business Applications

INFORMATION SYSTEMS

Information Technologies

Development Processes

Foundation Concepts

This module contains important material on computer hardware and software technologies that you may have covered in previous computer courses. At the option of your instructor, you may be assigned one of the following chapters to review before covering other chapters in the text.

- **Chapter 13: Computer Hardware** reviews trends and developments in microcomputer, midrange, and mainframe computer systems; basic computer system concepts; and the major types of technologies used in peripheral devices for computer input, output, and storage.

- **Chapter 14: Computer Software** reviews the basic features and trends in the major types of application software and system software used to support enterprise and end user computing.

CHAPTER 13

APPLICATIONS IN BUSINESS AND MANAGEMENT

COMPUTER HARDWARE

Chapter Highlights

Learning Objectives

After reading and studying this chapter, you should be able to:

1. Identify the major types and uses of microcomputer, midrange, and mainframe computer systems.

2. Outline the major technologies and uses of computer peripherals for input, output, and storage.

3. Identify and give examples of the components and functions of a computer system.

4. Identify the computer systems and peripherals you would acquire or recommend for a business of your choice, and explain the reasons for your selections.

Computer Systems: End User and Enterprise Computing

All computers are systems of input, processing, output, storage, and control components. In this section, we will discuss the trends, applications, and some basic concepts of the many types of computer systems in use today. In Section II, we will cover the changing technologies for input, output, and storage that are provided by the peripheral devices that are part of modern computer systems.

Analyzing City of Richmond and Tim Beaty Builders

Read the Real World Case on the City of Richmond and Tim Beaty Builders on the next page. We can learn a lot about innovative business uses of PDAs from this case. See Figure 13.1.

This case underscores that personal digital assistants (PDAs) are capable of much more than serving as electronic appointment books and personal organizers. Instead, the organizations in this case are using PDAs for a wide range of diverse business applications. The City of Richmond in British Columbia uses Web-enabled wireless PDAs to help their mobile workers perform equipment usage tracking, inventory control, dike and pump monitoring, and other applications that link to their PC-based systems. The PDAs enable quick responses to emergency situations and save city workers hundreds of hours each week compared to their previous systems. About 25 of Tim Beaty Builders' 40 workers use PDAs to track payroll and other construction project information, which is then input into their PC-based business systems for payroll, accounting, and project management applications. The PDA systems have produced major cost and time savings and much better information for improved construction project bidding and management.

FIGURE 13.1

Edward Hung is manager of advanced research and technology in the City of Richmond's IT department and coordinated the development of their PDA applications.

Source: Gary Benson.

REAL WORLD CASE 1

City of Richmond and Tim Beaty Builders: The Business Value of PDAs

Sure they're cool. But a growing number of companies are finding that personal digital assistants (PDAs) are also more versatile than Swiss Army Knives for solving a wide variety of business needs on the cheap. Edward Hung, a manager in the IT department for the City of Richmond, British Columbia, Canada (www.city.richmond.bc.ca), says the city uses Web-enabled wireless PDAs to track heavy-duty equipment use and manage $1.3 million in inventory. He says the hundreds of hours that the city saves using PDAs are devoted to other projects.

The city is working with its second PDA application after finding that the hand-helds were ideal for monitoring the dikes and the 30 jet-engine-like pumps that hold back the surrounding waters for the almost-sea-level city. About 18 employees, mostly in the city's water department, use PDAs to track and chart pump failures, tide levels, road temperatures, the weather, and wastewater and rain levels. Pumps routinely fail, and workers need to be alerted fast; 65 alarms in 24 hours isn't unusual, whether it's raining or not. "There's always an emergency around here," says Hung, manager of advanced research and technology in Richmond's IT department. The PDAs enable workers to identify problems such as aged pumps and potential trouble spots long before flooding starts, he adds.

Richmond's PDA application is part of an Internet-based system that connects to desktop PCs. To execute the integration, the IT team worked closely with Information Builders Inc., which provided its WebFocus software for the Internet-data connection and wireless services. "Definitely, the pump system PDAs were an opening of the door," says Hung, adding that the city is now looking at hand-helds rather than PCs for other uses. "We don't have those numbers, but I can guess we're operating two to three times as efficiently as before," Hung says. For pump monitoring, Hung finds that the PDAs, which send about 2 million transactions a week over the Internet to central databases, have saved hundreds of work hours, including in the IT department. However, city workers and the IT group now want to use tablet PCs at the water meter repair and equipment shops. "We have potential applications all over," says Hung.

Tim Beaty. At Tim Beaty Builders Inc. of Denton, Texas, about 25 of the company's 40 workers carry Palm hand-helds for recording work hours, equipment operations, and construction milestones, such as when cement is poured or when wiring inspections are completed. The biggest benefit has come from the payroll application. "We haven't done exhaustive calculations, but the savings in managers' time alone pay for the system. They used to spend 20% of their time on payroll; now it's considerably less," says David Morton, operations manager. "Everything else we get is gravy."

A 40-person regional construction company, Tim Beaty is one of a growing number of companies using PDAs as portable record-keeping or time-clock devices that can be linked to other data collection and corporate applications. The construction company now knows whether it's making money on a project. This is especially critical because Tim Beaty handles many projects simultaneously, including commercial and residential construction, trucking, equipment operations, and industrial construction and maintenance. "That all sounds like pretty much the same thing, except that each of those disciplines requires different information and reporting," explains Morton.

Workers now record on their PDAs how much time they spend on each job. "That increased accuracy is invaluable because it affects both costs and revenue," Morton says, noting that some jobs are bids and some are billed on a cost-plus basis. In the past, hours worked weren't tied to specific projects, so the company may have spent too many hours on the bid projects or neglected to collect for extra hours on the cost-plus jobs. In the wake of that success, Tim Beaty has added new PDA software modules from Austin Lane Technologies. The new applications link into Tim Beaty's PC-based business systems to help track equipment use and send alerts when it's time for repairs and when equipment is being underused.

"None of our competitors have anything like our PDA applications, and they don't appear to be looking at them. We are amazed," says Morton, discussing the PDA-based time-and-equipment tracking system. It has taken about two years for the system to pay for itself, thanks largely to the hours that managers no longer need to spend collecting and tracking payroll information. Managers also know which projects are making or losing money and how much. "It gives us a competitive advantage because our field personnel are more informed and, as a result, more responsive to our customers' needs—not to mention the cost savings we enjoy," says Merton.

Case Study Questions

1. What are the business benefits of PDAs for business applications? Use the City of Richmond and Tim Beaty Builders as examples.

2. What are the limitations of PDAs for business use? Compare PDAs to laptop PCs to help you answer.

3. The City of Richmond now wants to use tablet PCs for some applications. What are the advantages of tablet PCs over PDAs and laptop PCs for business applications? Checkout websites like www.cnet.com or www.pcworld.com for the latest product reviews to help you answer.

Source: Adapted from Connie Winkler, "Beyond Cool," *Computerworld*, November 4, 2002, pp. 43–44. Reprinted with permission from *Computerworld*.

FIGURE 13.2   Examples of computer system categories.

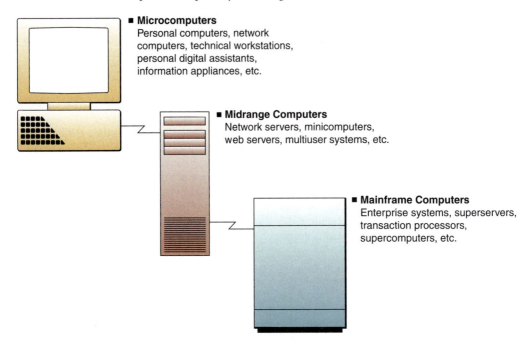

■ **Microcomputers**
Personal computers, network
computers, technical workstations,
personal digital assistants,
information appliances, etc.

■ **Midrange Computers**
Network servers, minicomputers,
web servers, multiuser systems, etc.

■ **Mainframe Computers**
Enterprise systems, superservers,
transaction processors,
supercomputers, etc.

Types of Computer Systems

Today's computer systems come in a variety of sizes, shapes, and computing capabilities. Rapid hardware and software developments and changing end user needs continue to drive the emergence of new models of computers, from the smallest hand-held personal digital assistant/cell phone combinations to the largest multiple-CPU mainframe for the enterprise.

Categories such as *mainframe, midrange computers,* and *microcomputers* are still used to help us express the relative processing power and number of end users that can be supported by different types of computers. But as Figure 13.2 illustrates, these are not precise classifications, and they do overlap each other. Thus, other names are commonly given to highlight the major uses of particular types of computers. Examples include personal computers, network servers, network computers, and technical workstations.

In addition, experts continue to predict the merging or disappearance of several computer categories. They feel, for example, that many midrange and mainframe systems have been made obsolete by the power and versatility of *client/server* networks of end user microcomputers and servers. Most recently, some industry experts have predicted that the emergence of network computers and *information appliances* for applications on the Internet and corporate intranets will replace many personal computers, especially in large organizations and in the home computer market. Only time will tell whether such predictions will equal the expectations of industry forecasters.

Microcomputer Systems

The entire center of gravity in computing has shifted. For millions of consumers and business users, the main function of desktop PCs is as a window to the Internet. Computers are now communications devices, and consumers want them to be as cheap as possible [5].

Microcomputers are the most important category of computer systems for businesspeople and consumers. Though usually called a *personal computer,* or PC, a microcomputer is much more than a small computer for use by an individual. The computing power of microcomputers now exceeds that of the mainframes of previous

FIGURE 13.3   Examples of microcomputer systems.

a. A notebook microcomputer.
Source: Courtesy of Hewlett-Packard.

b. The microcomputer as a professional workstation.
Source: Peter Kornicker/Corbis.

c. The microcomputer as a technical workstation.
Source: Richard T. Nowitz/Corbis.

computer generations at a fraction of their cost. Thus, they have become powerful networked *professional workstations* for business professionals.

Microcomputers come in a variety of sizes and shapes for a variety of purposes, as Figure 13.3 illustrates. For example, PCs are available as hand-held, notebook, laptop, portable, desktop, and floor-standing models. Or, based on their use, they include home, personal, professional, workstation, and multiuser systems. Most microcomputers are *desktops* designed to fit on an office desk, or **laptops** for those who want a small, portable PC for their work activities. Figure 13.4 offers advice on some of the key features you should consider in acquiring a high-end workstation, multimedia PC, or beginner's system. This should give you some idea of the range of features available in today's microcomputers.

Some microcomputers are powerful **workstation computers** (technical workstations) that support applications with heavy mathematical computing and graphics display demands such as computer-aided design (CAD) in engineering, or investment and portfolio analysis in the securities industry. Other microcomputers are used as **network servers.** They are usually more powerful microcomputers that coordinate telecommunications and resource sharing in small local area networks (LANs), and Internet and intranet websites.

FIGURE 13.4   Recommended features for the three types of PC users.

Business Pro	Multimedia Heavy	Newcomer
To track your products, customers, and performance, you'll need more than just a fast machine:	Media pros and dedicated amateurs will want at least a Mac G4 or a 2 GHz Intel chip, and:	Save money with a Celeron processor in the 1 GHz range. Also look for:
• 2+ Gigahertz processor	• 40 GB hard drive or more	• 128MB RAM
• 256MB RAM	• 18-inch or larger flat-screen CRT or flat-panel LCD	• 20 GB hard drive
• 40 GB hard drive	• High-end color printer	• Internal 56K modem
• 18-inch flat-panel display	• DVD-ROM or CD-RW drive	• 48X CD-ROM drive
• CD-RW drive for backup	• Deluxe speaker system	• Basic inkjet printer

Boeing, Monster.com, and Others: Corporate PC Criteria

What do you look for in a new PC system? A big, bright screen? Zippy new processor? Capacious hard drive? Acres of RAM? Sorry, none of these is a real concern for corporate PC buyers. Numerous studies have shown that the price of a new computer is only a small part of the total cost of ownership (TCO). Support, maintenance, and other intangibles contribute far more heavily to the sum. Let's take a look at three top criteria.

Solid performance at a reasonable price. Corporate buyers know that their users probably aren't mapping the human genome or plotting trajectories to Saturn. They're doing word processing, order entry, sales contact management, and other essential business tasks. They need a solid, competent machine at a reasonable price, not the latest whiz-bang. "Mainstream machines from respected vendors are going to do the job fine," says Bob Jorgenson, a spokesman for The Boeing Co. in Seattle.

Operating system ready. "A change in an operating system is the most disruptive upgrade an enterprise has to face," says Paul Neilson, vice president of technical support at Monster.com, an online job-placement service in Maynard, Massachusetts. That's why many corporate buyers want their machines to be able to handle current operating systems and anticipated new ones. While many enterprises use Windows 9x or NT, they must be able to make a possible transition to Windows 2000 or XP, or even OS versions expected three to five years out. Primarily, that means deciding what hard disk space and RAM will be sufficient.

Connectivity. Networked machines are a given in corporate life, and Internet-worked machines are becoming a given. Buyers need machines equipped with reliable network interface cards or even wireless LAN capabilities. "With fewer cables to worry about, wireless LANs, especially when combined with laptop PCs, contribute to the flexibility of the workplace and the simplicity of PC deployment," says Matt Heller, vice president of operations at GoTo.com Inc. in Pasadena, California, which provides online search services to tens of thousands of affiliate companies. Many organizations are planning for Internet-based applications and need machines ready to make fast, reliable and secure connections. "Connection performance and ports are prime factors for us," says Chris Carrara, IT manager at Sartorious AG, a global lab technology manufacturer in Goettingen, Germany [7].

Network Computers

Network computers (NCs) are a microcomputer category designed primarily for use with the Internet and corporate intranets by clerical workers, operational employees, and knowledge workers with specialized or limited computing applications. NCs are low-cost, sealed, networked microcomputers with no or minimal disk storage. Users of NCs depend primarily on Internet and intranet servers for their operating system and Web browser, Java-enabled application software, and data access and storage.

One of the main attractions of network computers is their lower cost of purchase, upgrades, maintenance, and support compared to full-featured PCs. Other benefits to business include ease of software distribution and licensing, computing platform standardization, reduced end user support requirements, and improved manageability through centralized management and enterprisewide control of computer network resources [4].

Information Appliances

PCs aren't the only option: A host of smart gadgets and information appliances—from cellular phones and pagers to hand-held PCs and Web-based game machines—promise Internet access and the ability to perform basic computational chores [5].

Hand-held microcomputer devices known as **personal digital assistants** (PDAs) are some of the most popular devices in the **information appliance category.** Web-enabled PDAs use touch screens, pen-based handwriting recognition, or keypads so mobile workers can send and receive e-mail, access the Web, and exchange information such as appointments, to-do lists, and sales contacts with their desktop PCs or Web servers. See Figure 13.5.

Information appliances may also take the form of *set-top boxes* and video-game consoles that connect to your home TV set. These devices enable you to surf the World Wide Web or send and receive e-mail and watch TV programs or play video games at the same time. Other information appliances include wireless PDAs and Internet-enabled cellular and PCS phones, and wired telephone-based home appliances that can send and receive e-mail and access the Web.

Computer Terminals

Computer terminals are undergoing a major conversion to networked computer devices. *Dumb terminals*, which are keyboard/video monitor devices with limited processing capabilities, are being replaced by *intelligent terminals*, which are modified

FIGURE 13.5

An example of a network computer: the Sun Ray I enterprise appliance.

Source: Courtesy of Sun Microsystems Inc.

networked PCs or network computers. Also included are **network terminals,** which may be *Windows terminals,* that are dependent on network servers for Windows software, processing power, and storage, or *Internet terminals,* which depend on Internet or intranet website servers for their operating systems and application software.

Intelligent terminals take many forms and can perform data entry and some information processing tasks independently. This includes the widespread use of **transaction terminals** in banks, retail stores, factories, and other work sites. Examples are automated teller machines (ATMs), factory production recorders, and retail point-of-sale (POS) terminals. These intelligent terminals use keypads, touch screens, and other input methods to capture data and interact with end users during a transaction, while relying on servers or other computers in the network for further transaction processing.

Midrange Computer Systems

Midrange computers, including high-end network servers and minicomputers, are multiuser systems that can manage networks of PCs and terminals. Though not as powerful as mainframe computers, they are less costly to buy, operate, and maintain than mainframe systems, and thus meet the computing needs of many organizations. See Figure 13.6.

> *Burgeoning data warehouses and related applications such as data mining and online analytical processing are forcing IT shops into higher and higher levels of server configurations. Similarly, Internet-based applications, such as Web servers and electronic commerce, are forcing IT managers to push the envelope of processing speed and storage capacity and other [business] applications, fueling the growth of high-end servers* [17].

FIGURE 13.6
The HP RX2600 rack-mounted server unit can hold up to twenty Itanium 2 dual-processor rack-mounted servers.

Source: Courtesy of Hewlett-Packard.

Midrange computers have become popular as powerful **network servers** to help manage large Internet websites, corporate intranets and extranets, and client/server networks. Electronic commerce and other business uses of the Internet are popular high-end server applications, as are integrated enterprisewide manufacturing, distribution, and financial applications. Other applications, like data warehouse management, data mining, and online analytical processing (which we discussed in Chapters 3 and 8), are contributing to the growth of high-end servers and other midrange systems [17].

Midrange computers first became popular as **minicomputers** for scientific research, instrumentation systems, engineering analysis, and industrial process monitoring and control. Minicomputers could easily handle such uses because these applications are narrow in scope and do not demand the processing versatility of mainframe systems. Thus, midrange computers serve as industrial process-control and manufacturing plant computers, and they still play a major role in computer-aided manufacturing (CAM). They can also take the form of powerful technical workstations for computer-aided design (CAD) and other computation and graphics-intensive applications. Midrange computers are also used as *front-end computers* to assist mainframe computers in telecommunications processing and network management.

Wyndham International: Consolidating Servers

Global hotel chain Wyndham International in Dallas is putting the application that controls guest arrivals, departures, and billing onto two IBM eServer p680 midrange computers running Unix. The same guest-management tasks used to require 165 servers scattered across 100 locations.

The Web helped push Wyndham to reevaluate the role that today's mega boxes play in a wide-ranging enterprise. A few years ago, the hotel chain picked Opera, a networked PC application from Columbia, Maryland–based Micros Systems, as its guest-management system because the program allowed IT managers to upgrade and tune the program at all of its front desks from a central administrative center in Dallas. "We then wondered, 'If that's good at the workstation level, wouldn't it be good at the server level, too,'" recalls Gary Owen, vice president of IT operations.

Although companies expect to save costs through server consolidation—Wyndham estimates it will lower its hardware bills by as much as 40 percent in the coming year—learning to live with less comes with stumbling blocks. Managing fewer servers may be easier, but when things go wrong, everyone suffers, not just the workers at a single network node. Likewise, network scalability, security, and availability become so critical to a firm's health that there's almost no room for error.

Ten years ago, the placement of servers everywhere and anywhere was considered the best way to achieve high performance and computing availability. Nowadays, corporations are taking advantage of better networking gear, lower costs for high-end components like switches, and administrative tools that manage a small number of servers in central locations.

Companies start down the consolidation trail to reduce costs. Besides lower hardware costs, Wyndham expects to save "several hundred percent" over five years in reduced travel and training costs, according to a Wyndham spokesman.

Also, rather than buying midrange or mainframe computing power packed into towers, many large companies are putting together racks of servers that fill a central data center much like the telecommunications gear that hums in communication closets. "By consolidating 50 one-processor servers into new-generation server racks, companies save not just on equipment costs but on the costs of power management and maintenance contracts," says Jonathan Eunice, principal server technology analyst at Illuminata, a technology research firm [11].

Mainframe Computer Systems

Several years after dire pronouncements that the mainframe was dead, quite the opposite is true: Mainframe usage is actually on the rise. And it's not just a short-term blip. One factor that's been driving mainframe sales is cost reductions [of 35 percent or more]. Price reductions aren't the only factor fueling mainframe acquisitions. IS organizations are teaching the old dog new tricks by putting mainframes at the center stage of emerging applications such as data mining and warehousing, decision support, and a variety of Internet-based applications, most notably electronic commerce [17].

Mainframe computers are large, fast, and powerful computer systems. For example, mainframes can process hundreds of million instructions per second (MIPS). Mainframes also have large primary storage capacities. Their main memory capacity can range from hundreds of megabytes to many gigabytes of primary storage. And mainframes have slimmed down drastically in the last few years, dramatically reducing their air-conditioning needs, electrical power consumption, and floor space requirements, and thus their acquisition and operating costs. Most of these improvements are the result of a move from water-cooled mainframes to a newer air-cooled technology for mainframe systems [15]. See Figure 13.7.

Thus, mainframe computers continue to handle the information processing needs of major corporations and government agencies with high transaction processing volumes or complex computational problems. For example, major international banks, airlines, oil companies, and other large corporations process millions of sales transactions and customer inquiries each day with the help of large mainframe systems. Mainframes are still used for computation-intensive applications such as analyzing seismic data from oil field explorations or simulating flight conditions in designing aircraft. Mainframes are also widely used as *superservers* for the large client/server networks and high-volume Internet websites of large companies. And as previously mentioned, mainframes are becoming a popular business computing platform for data mining and warehousing, and electronic commerce applications [15].

Supercomputer Systems

Supercomputers have now become "scalable servers" at the top end of the product lines that start with desktop workstations. Market-driven companies, like Silicon Graphics,

FIGURE 13.7

Mainframe computer systems are the heavy lifters of corporate computing.

Source: Corbis.

Hewlett-Packard, and IBM, have a much broader focus than just building the world's fastest computer, and the software of the desktop computer has a much greater overlap with that of the supercomputer than it used to, because both are built from the same cache-based microprocessors [12].

The term **supercomputer** describes a category of extremely powerful computer systems specifically designed for scientific, engineering, and business applications requiring extremely high speeds for massive numeric computations. The market for supercomputers includes government research agencies, large universities, and major corporations. They use supercomputers for applications such as global weather forecasting, military defense systems, computational cosmology and astronomy, microprocessor research and design, large-scale data mining, and so on.

Supercomputers use *parallel processing* architectures of interconnected microprocessors (which can execute many instructions at the same time in parallel). They can easily perform arithmetic calculations at speeds of billions of floating-point operations per second (*gigaflops*). Supercomputers that can calculate in *teraflops* (trillions of floating-point operations per second), which use massively parallel processing (MPP) designs of thousands of microprocessors, are now in use. Purchase prices for large supercomputers are in the $5 million to $50 million range.

However, the use of symmetric multiprocessing (SMP) and distributed shared memory (DSM) designs of smaller numbers of interconnected microprocessors has spawned a breed of *minisupercomputers* with prices that start in the hundreds of thousands of dollars. For example IBM's RS/6000 SP starts at $150,000 for a one-processing-node SMP computer. However, it can be expanded to hundreds of processing nodes, which drives its price into the tens of millions of dollars. For example, Blue Horizon, an IBM RS/6000 SP with 156 processing nodes and a total of 1,152 Power 3+ microprocessors, was installed at the San Diego Supercomputer Center during 2000. The system cost $50 million (less a substantial education discount), and has a peak processing capacity of 1.7 teraflops [18]. Thus, supercomputers continue to advance the state of the art for the entire computer industry. See Figure 13.8.

FIGURE 13.8

The Blue Horizon IBM RS/6000 SP at the University of California at San Diego Supercomputer Center.

Source: Spencer Grant/PhotoEdit.

FIGURE 13.9   The computer system concept. A computer is a system of hardware components and functions.

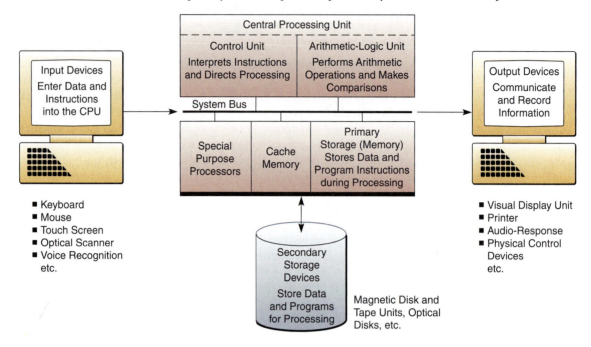

Technical Note: The Computer System Concept

As a business professional, you do not need a detailed technical knowledge of computers. However, you do need to understand some basic concepts about computer systems. This should help you be an informed and productive user of computer system resources.

A computer is more than a high-powered collection of electronic devices performing a variety of information processing chores. A computer is a *system*, an interrelated combination of components that performs the basic system functions of input, processing, output, storage, and control, thus providing end users with a powerful information processing tool. Understanding the computer as a **computer system** is vital to the effective use and management of computers. You should be able to visualize any computer this way, from the smallest microcomputer device, to a large computer network whose components are interconnected by telecommunications network links throughout a building complex or geographic area.

Figure 13.9 illustrates that a computer is a system of hardware devices organized according to the following system functions:

- **Input.** The input devices of a computer system include keyboards, touch screens, pens, electronic mouses, optical scanners, and so on. They convert data into electronic form for direct entry or through a telecommunications network into a computer system.

- **Processing.** The **central processing unit** (CPU) is the main processing component of a computer system. (In microcomputers, it is the **main microprocessor.** See Figure 13.10.) Conceptually, the circuitry of a CPU can be subdivided into two major subunits: the arithmetic-logic unit and the control unit. It is the electronic circuits (known as *registers*) of the **arithmetic-logic** unit that perform the arithmetic and logic functions required to execute software instructions.

- **Output.** The output devices of a computer system include video display units, printers, audio response units, and so on. They convert electronic information produced by the computer system into human-intelligible form for presentation to end users.

FIGURE 13.10

This Intel Mobile Pentium 4-M microprocessor operates at 2 GHz clock speeds to bring desktop power to laptop PCs.

Source: Courtesy of Intel Corporation.

- **Storage.** The storage function of a computer system takes place in the storage circuits of the computer's **primary storage unit,** or *memory,* supported by **secondary storage** devices such as magnetic disk and optical disk drives. These devices store data and software instructions needed for processing. Computer processors may also include circuitry called *cache memory* for high-speed, temporary storage of instruction and data elements.

- **Control.** The control unit of a CPU is the control component of a computer system. Its register and other circuits interpret software instructions and transmit directions to the other components of the computer system.

Computer Processing Speeds

How fast are computer systems? Early computer operating speeds were measured in **milliseconds** (thousandths of a second) and **microseconds** (millionths of a second). Now computers operate in the **nanosecond** (billionth of a second) range, with **picosecond** (trillionth of a second) speed being attained by some computers. Such speeds seem almost incomprehensible. For example, an average person taking one step each nansecond would circle the earth about 20 times in one second!

We have already mentioned the *teraflop* speeds of some supercomputers. However, most computers can now process program instructions at *million instructions per second* (MIPS) speeds. Another measure of processing speed is *megahertz* (MHz), or millions of cycles per second, and *gigahertz* (GHz), or billions of cycles per second. This rating is commonly called the *clock speed* of a microprocessor, since it is used to rate microprocessors by the speed of their timing circuits or internal clock.

However, such ratings can be misleading indicators of the effective processing speed of microprocessors. That's because processing speed depends on a variety of factors including the size of circuitry paths, or *buses* that interconnect microprocessor components; the capacity of instruction processing *registers;* the use of high-speed *memory caches;* and the use of specialized microprocessors such as a math co-processor to do arithmetic calculations faster.

SECTION II Computer Peripherals: Input, Output, and Storage Technologies

The right peripherals can make all the difference in your computing experience. A top-quality monitor will be easier on your eyes—and may change the way you work. A scanner can edge you closer to that ever-elusive goal—the paperless office. Backup-storage systems can offer bank-vault security against losing your work. CD-ROM drives can be essential for education and entertainment. Memory cards, 3-D graphics, and other devices will help you configure your computer to meet your needs. Some may be the digital equivalent of chrome bumpers and tailfins, but the right choice of peripherals can make a big difference [10].

Analyzing United Technologies and Eastman Kodak

Read the Real World Case on United Technologies and Eastman Kodak on the next page. We can learn a lot about the business value of consolidating computer operations and systems from this case. See Figure 13.11

United Technologies is a giant conglomerate of several large companies, and is involved in a major consolidation of its computer systems, data centers, help centers, and other hardware and software resources. Examples include standardizing on 45,000 new Dell PCs, reducing 20 U.S. data centers to three, going from eight mainframe systems to two, and reducing 15 help desks to one help center. Major gains in efficiency and security management and $1 billion in cost savings are expected. Eastman Kodak is consolidating from diverse PC systems to 40,000 new

FIGURE 13.11
John Doucette is CIO of United Technologies and is leading the consolidation of their computer operations and systems.

Source: Courtesy of United Technologies.

REAL WORLD CASE 2

United Technologies and Eastman Kodak: The Business Case for Consolidating Computer Operations and Systems

United Technologies Corp. (UTC) announced in mid-2002 that it is undergoing a complete IT infrastructure overhaul and consolidation that will cost $4.5 billion but will save the company $1 billion through efficiencies over the next 15 years. UTC (www.utc.com), a $28 billion Hartford, Connecticut–based conglomerate, has outsourced management of the process to Computer Sciences Corp. (CSC). The project includes changing 45,000 PCs to new Dell PC standard models, standardizing on a single backup-and-recovery platform, and consolidating the business-critical workloads in 20 major data centers into 3. The majority of the work is expected to be completed by the end of 2002.

United Technologies includes companies like Pratt & Whitney, Hamilton Sundstrand Corp., Sikorsky Aircraft Corp., Carrier Corp., Otis Elevator Co., and UTC Fuel Cells. UTC had been operating many data centers running on proprietary platforms. After decades of growth, UTC's data centers and server farms were dispersed throughout the United States. Its 8 mainframes, 11 IBM AS/400 midrange servers, and 2,950 other servers were also dispersed among those data centers. Since having consolidated them into a data center on its Pratt & Whitney campus in East Hartford and two other data centers owned by CSC in Meriden, Connecticut, and Norwich, Connecticut, the company needs only two mainframes and two AS/400 systems. It expects to drop about 350 servers by the end of the year.

"We identified 160,000 pieces of software and probably ended up putting 5,000 pieces of software back," said John Doucette, CIO of UTC. "The other thing we did with our PCs was to lock them down. People can't go out on the Internet and download software onto them. There's just tons of inefficiencies with that." UTC is also creating two storage-area networks to be located on the East Hartford campus that will include Hitachi Data Systems and EMC Symmetrix RAID storage units.

In another move, UTC consolidated 15 help desks running nine applications into one center running one system. Henning Kerger, director of transformation for CSC's UTC account, said the CSC site in Newington, Connecticut, will also be used for UTC's Web hosting facility. "The biggest challenge was to get away from a disparate situation, where every business unit was unique and had its own standards and quality of people varying from unit to unit," Kerger said.

For example, UTC found itself supporting multiple PC platforms. While it had considered changing out 20 percent of its workstations and platforms each year, Doucette said that would have made it more difficult to standardize. The company has completed about 95 percent of a changeover to Dell PCs running Windows 2000 and Office 2000. Doucette said that along with the remote control of systems, that's "the biggest part of reducing cost."

Eastman Kodak. Total cost of ownership (TCO) for PCs has dropped substantially at Eastman Kodak Co. (www.kodak.com) midway through a three-year global deployment of 40,000 IBM laptops and desktops. There are several reasons for the reduced costs, a Kodak IT manager said recently, including buying direct from IBM, and standardizing all of Kodak's hardware and installing a set of preinstalled software on all PCs.

That standardization is replacing an older, more costly process that required Kodak's IT workers to install software on a variety of PCs, said Tony Dibitetto, director of global desktop and telecommunications services at the Rochester, New York–based company. Dibitetto declined to disclose exactly how much money Kodak has saved through the IBM deal. But he said going with IBM exclusively saves Kodak 20 to 25 percent on laptop and desktop hardware, which is still being purchased and rolled out as part of a project that's due to end in 2003.

Dibitetto said help desk staffers at Kodak are now able to resolve nearly twice as many queries by phone, addressing 58 percent of the inquiries, up from about 35 percent in 2000. Because it can cost as much as $150 for a help desk technician to look at a machine on-site, the savings add up. "If you make thousands of visits a year, that's a big number," Dibitetto said. "Saving $200 on the purchase price of an individual PC is important," he added. "But it's nothing like the savings we get from resolving a significant percentage of support issues at the service desk without having to send a technician on-site."

Case Study Questions

1. What are some of the business benefits that United Technologies will gain from the consolidation of its computer systems, data centers, software, and help centers? What limitations might there be?

2. What are the business benefits of standardizing on selected models from one manufacturer of desktop and laptop PCs as UTC did with Dell and Kodak did with IBM? What limitations might there be?

3. What are the business benefits of UTC's policy of "locking down" its new Dell PCs so employees can't download other software from the Internet? Do you agree with this policy? Why or why not?

Source: Adapted from Matt Hamblen, "Kodak Touts TCO Success Amid Global PC, Laptop Rollout," *Computerworld*, February 4, 2002, p. 7; and Lucas Mearian, "United Technologies in $4.5B IT Overhaul," *Computerworld*, June 10, 2002, p. 7. Reprinted with permission from *Computerworld*.

FIGURE 13.12
Some advice about
peripherals for a
business PC.

Peripherals Checklist
● **Monitors.** Bigger is better for computer screens. Consider a 19-inch or 21-inch CRT monitor, or LCD flat panel display. That gives you much more room to display spreadsheets, Web pages, lines of text, open windows, etc. The clarity of a monitor's image is important, too. Look for models with at least an XGA resolution of 1024 × 768 pixels.
● **Printers.** Your choice is between laser printers or color inkjet printers. Lasers are better suited for high-volume business use. Moderately priced color inkjets provide high-quality images and are well-suited for reproducing photographs. Per-page costs are higher than for laser printers.
● **Scanners.** You'll have to decide between a compact, sheet-fed scanner or a flatbed model. Sheet-fed scanners will save desktop space, while bulkier flat-bed models provide higher speed and resolution. Resolution is a key measure of quality; you'll want at least 300 dpi.
● **Hard Disk Drives.** Bigger is better; as with closet space, you can always use the extra capacity. So go 20 gigabytes at the minimum, 40 to 80 gigabytes at the max.
● **CD-ROM and DVD Drives.** CD-ROM and DVD drives are becoming a necessity for software installation and multimedia applications. Consider a high-speed variable-speed model (24X to 48X) for faster, smoother presentations.
● **Backup Systems.** Essential. Don't compute without them. Removable mag disk cartridges (like the Iomega Zip and Jazz drives) are convenient and versatile, and fast too.

IBM laptop and desktop PCs including a set of preinstalled software for each unit. Benefits for Kodak include substantial equipment savings and a major reduction in PC support costs.

Peripherals

A computer is just a high-powered "processing box" without peripherals. **Peripherals** is the generic name given to all input, output, and secondary storage devices that are part of a computer system. Peripherals depend on direct connections or telecommunications links to the central processing unit of a computer system. Thus, all peripherals are **online** devices; that is, they are separate from, but can be electronically connected to and controlled by, a CPU. (This is the opposite of **offline** devices that are separate from and not under the control of the CPU.) The major types of peripherals and media that can be part of a computer system are discussed in this section. See Figure 13.12.

Input Technologies

Input technologies now provide a more **natural user interface** for computer users. You can enter data and commands directly and easily into a computer system through pointing devices like electronic mice and touch pads, and technologies like optical scanning, handwriting recognition, and voice recognition. These developments have made it unnecessary to always record data on paper *source documents* (such as sales order forms, for example) and then keyboard the data into a computer in an additional data entry step. Further improvements in voice recognition and other technologies should enable an even more natural user interface in the future.

Pointing Devices

Keyboards are still the most widely used devices for entering data and text into computer systems. However, **pointing devices** are a better alternative for issuing commands, making choices, and responding to prompts displayed on your video screen. They work with your operating system's **graphical user interface** (GUI), which presents you with icons, menus, windows, buttons, bars, and so on, for your selection. For example, pointing devices such as electronic mouses and touchpads allow

FIGURE 13.13

The touchpad is a popular pointing device in laptop PCs.

Source: Pedro Coll/Age fotostock.

you to easily choose from menu selections and icon displays using point-and-click or point-and-drag methods. See Figure 13.13.

The **electronic mouse** is the most popular pointing device used to move the cursor on the screen, as well as to issue commands and make icon and menu selections. By moving the mouse on a desktop or pad, you can move the cursor onto an icon displayed on the screen. Pressing buttons on the mouse activates various activities represented by the icon selected.

The trackball, pointing stick, and touchpad are other pointing devices most often used in place of the mouse. A **trackball** is a stationary device related to the mouse. You turn a roller ball with only its top exposed outside its case to move the cursor on the screen. A **pointing stick** (also called a *trackpoint*) is a small button-like device, sometimes likened to the eraserhead of a pencil. It is usually centered one row above the space bar of a keyboard. The cursor moves in the direction of the pressure you place on the stick. The **touchpad** is a small rectangular touch-sensitive surface usually placed below the keyboard. The cursor moves in the direction your finger moves on the pad. Trackballs, pointing sticks, and touchpads are easier to use than a mouse for portable computer users and are thus built into most notebook computer keyboards.

Touch screens are devices that allow you to use a computer by touching the surface of its video display screen. Some touch screens emit a grid of infrared beams, sound waves, or a slight electric current that is broken when the screen is touched. The computer senses the point in the grid where the break occurs and responds with an appropriate action. For example, you can indicate your selection on a menu display by just touching the screen next to that menu item.

FIGURE 13.14
Many PDAs accept pen-based input.

Source: RNT Productions/Corbis.

Pen-Based Computing

Handwriting-recognition systems convert script into text quickly and are friendly to shaky hands as well as those of block-printing draftsmen. The pen is more powerful than the keyboard in many vertical markets, as evidenced by the popularity of pen-based devices in the utilities, service, and medical trades [10].

Pen-based computing technologies are being used in many hand-held computers and personal digital assistants. *Tablet* PCs and PDAs contain fast processors and software that recognizes and digitizes handwriting, handprinting, and hand drawing. They have a pressure-sensitive layer like a graphics pad under their slate-like liquid crystal display (LCD) screen. So instead of writing on a paper form fastened to a clipboard or using a keyboard device, you can use a pen to make selections, send e-mail, and enter handwritten data directly into a computer. See Figure 13.14.

A variety of other penlike devices are available. One example is the *digitizer pen* and *graphics tablet*. You can use the digitizer pen as a pointing device, or use it to draw or write on the pressure-sensitive surface of the graphics tablet. Your handwriting or drawing is digitized by the computer, accepted as input, displayed on its video screen, and entered into your application.

Speech Recognition Systems

Speech recognition is gaining popularity in the corporate world among nontypists, people with disabilities, and business travelers, and is most frequently used for dictation, screen navigation, and Web browsing [3].

Speech recognition promises to be the easiest method for data entry, word processing, and conversational computing, since speech is the easiest, most natural means of human communication. Speech input has now become technologically and economically feasible for a variety of applications. Early speech recognition products used *discrete speech recognition*, where you had to pause between each spoken word. New *continuous speech recognition* (CSR) software recognizes continuous, conversationally paced speech. See Figure 13.15.

Speech recognition systems digitize, analyze, and classify your speech and its sound patterns. The software compares your speech patterns to a database of sound patterns in its vocabulary and passes recognized words to your application software.

FIGURE 13.15

Using speech recognition technology for word processing.

Source: Courtesy of Plantronics, Inc.

Typically, speech recognition systems require training the computer to recognize your voice and its unique sound patterns in order to achieve a high degree of accuracy. Training such systems involves repeating a variety of words and phrases in a training session, as well as using the system extensively.

Most continuous speech recognition software products like Dragon Naturally-Speaking and ViaVoice by IBM have 30,000-word vocabularies expandable to 60,000 words, and sell for less than $200. Training to 95 percent accuracy may take several hours. Longer use, faster processors, and more memory make 99 percent accuracy possible [3].

Speech recognition devices in work situations allow operators to perform data entry without using their hands to key in data or instructions and to provide faster and more accurate input. For example, manufacturers use speech recognition systems for the inspection, inventory, and quality control of a variety of products; and airlines and parcel delivery companies use them for voice-directed sorting of baggage and parcels. Speech recognition can also help you operate your computer's operating systems and software packages through voice input of data and commands. For example, such software can be voice-enabled so you can send e-mail and surf the World Wide Web.

Speaker-independent voice recognition systems, which allow a computer to understand a few words from a voice it has never heard before, are being built into products and used in a growing number of applications. Examples include *voice-messaging computers*, which use speech recognition and voice response software to verbally guide an end user through the steps of a task in many kinds of activities. Typically, they enable computers to respond to verbal and Touch-Tone input over the telephone. Examples of applications include computerized telephone call switching, telemarketing surveys, bank pay-by-phone bill-paying services, stock quotations services, university registration systems, and customer credit and account balance inquiries.

FIGURE 13.16
This multifunction unit serves as an optical scanner, copier, fax, and printer.

Source: Courtesy of Hewlett-Packard.

Optical Scanning

Few people understand how much scanners can improve a computer system and make your work easier. Their function is to get documents into your computer with a minimum of time and hassle, transforming just about anything on paper—a letter, a logo, or a photograph—into the digital format that your PC can make sense of. Scanners can be a big help in getting loads of paper off your desk and into your PC [10].

Optical scanning devices read text or graphics and convert them into digital input for your computer. Thus, optical scanning enables the direct entry of data from source documents into a computer system. For example, you can use a compact desktop scanner to scan pages of text and graphics into your computer for desktop publishing and Web publishing applications. Or you can scan documents of all kinds into your system and organize them into folders as part of a *document management* library system for easy reference or retrieval.

There are many types of optical scanners, but they all employ photoelectric devices to scan the characters being read. Reflected light patterns of the data are converted into electronic impulses that are then accepted as input into the computer system. Compact desktop scanners have become very popular due to their low cost and ease of use with personal computer systems. However, larger, more expensive *flatbed scanners* are faster and provide higher resolution color scanning. See Figure 13.16.

Another optical scanning technology is called **optical character recognition** (OCR). OCR scanners can read the OCR characters and codes on merchandise tags, product labels, credit card receipts, utility bills, insurance premiums, airline tickets, and other documents. OCR scanners are also used to automatically sort mail, score tests, and process a wide variety of forms in business and government.

Devices such as hand-held optical scanning **wands** are frequently used to read OCR coding on merchandise tags, product labels, and other media. Many business applications involve reading *bar coding*, a code that utilizes bars to represent characters. One common example is the Universal Product Code (UPC) bar coding that you see on product labels, product packaging, and merchandise tags. For example, the automated checkout scanners found in supermarkets read UPC bar coding. Supermarket scanners emit laser beams that are reflected off a UPC bar code. The reflected image is converted to electronic impulses that are sent to the in-store computer, where they are matched with pricing information. Pricing information is returned to the terminal, visually displayed, and printed on a receipt for the customer. See Figure 13.17.

FIGURE 13.17

Using an optical scanning wand to read bar coding of inventory data.

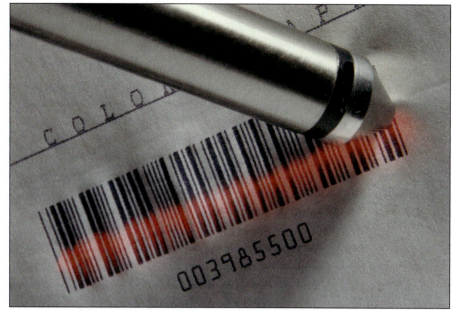

Source: Getty Images.

Other Input Technologies

Magnetic stripe technology is a familiar form of data entry that helps computers read credit cards. The iron oxide coating of the magnetic stripe on the back of such cards can hold about 200 bytes of information. Customer account numbers can be recorded on the mag stripe so it can be read by bank ATMs, credit card authorization terminals, and many other types of magnetic stripe readers.

Smart cards that embed a microprocessor chip and several kilobytes of memory into debit, credit, and other cards are popular in Europe, and becoming available in the United States. One example is Holland, where millions of smart debit cards have been issued by Dutch banks. Smart debit cards enable you to store a cash balance on the card and electronically transfer some of it to others to pay for small items and services. The balance on the card can be replenished in ATMs or other terminals.

The smart debit cards used in Holland feature a microprocessor and either 8 or 16 kilobytes of memory, plus the usual magnetic stripe. The smart cards are widely used to make payments in parking meters, vending machines, newsstands, pay telephones, and retail stores [9].

Digital cameras represent another fast-growing set of input technologies. Digital still cameras and digital video cameras (digital camcorders) enable you to shoot, store, and download still photos or full motion video with audio into your PC. Then you can use image-editing software to edit and enhance the digitized images and include them in newsletters, reports, multimedia presentations, and Web pages [8].

The computer systems of the banking industry can magnetically read checks and deposit slips using **magnetic ink character recognition** (MICR) technology. Computers can thus sort and post checks to the proper checking accounts. Such processing is possible because the identification numbers of the bank and the customer's account are preprinted on the bottom of the checks with an iron oxide–based ink. The first bank receiving a check after it has been written must encode the amount of the check in magnetic ink on the check's lower right-hand corner. The MICR system uses 14 characters (the 10 decimal digits and 4 special symbols) of a standardized design. Equipment known as *reader-sorters* read a check by first magnetizing the magnetic ink characters and then sensing the signal induced by each character as it passes a reading head. In this way, data are electronically captured by the bank's computer systems.

Output Technologies

Computers provide information to you in a variety of forms. Video displays and printed documents have been, and still are, the most common forms of output from computer systems. But other natural and attractive output technologies such as **voice response** systems and multimedia output are increasingly found along with video displays in business applications.

For example, you have probably experienced the voice and audio output generated by speech and audio microprocessors in a variety of consumer products. Voice messaging software enables PCs and servers in voice mail and messaging systems to interact with you through voice responses. And of course, multimedia output is common on the websites of the Internet and corporate intranets.

Video Output

Of all the peripherals you can purchase for your system, a [video] monitor is the one addition that can make the biggest difference. Forget about faster processors, bigger hard drives, and the like. The fact is, the monitor is the part of your system you spend the most time interacting with . . . Invest in a quality monitor, and you'll be thankful every time you turn on your computer [10].

Video displays are the most common type of computer output. Most desktop computers rely on **video monitors** that use a *cathode ray tube* (CRT) technology similar to the picture tubes used in home TV sets. Usually, the clarity of the video display depends on the type of video monitor you use and the graphics circuit board installed in your computer. These can provide a variety of graphics modes of increasing capability. A high-resolution, flicker-free monitor is especially important if you spend a lot of time viewing multimedia on CDs or the Web, or the complex graphical displays of many software packages.

The biggest use of **liquid crystal displays** (LCDs) is to provide a visual display capability for portable microcomputers and PDAs, though the use of "flat panel" LCD video monitors for desktop PC systems is growing rapidly as their cost becomes more affordable. LCD displays need significantly less electric current and provide a thin, flat display. Advances in technology such as *active matrix* and *dual scan* capabilities have improved the color and clarity of LCD displays. See Figure 13.18.

FIGURE 13.18
Using a flat panel LCD video monitor for a desktop PC system.

Source: Index Stock/Picture Quest.

FIGURE 13.19

This mobile inkjet printer produces high-quality color output.

Source: Courtesy of Hewlett-Packard.

Printed Output

Printing information on paper is still the most common form of output after video displays. Thus, most personal computer systems rely on an inkjet or laser printer to produce permanent (hard copy) output in high-quality printed form. Printed output is still a common form of business communications, and is frequently required for legal documentation. Thus, computers can produce printed reports and correspondence, documents such as sales invoices, payroll checks, bank statements, and printed versions of graphic displays.

Inkjet printers, which spray ink onto a page one line at a time, have become the most popular, low-cost printers for microcomputer systems. They are quiet, produce several pages per minute of high-quality output, and can print both black-and-white and high-quality color graphics. **Laser printers** use an electrostatic process similar to a photocopying machine to produce many pages per minute of high-quality black-and-white output. More expensive color laser printers and multifunction inkjet and laser models that print, fax, scan, and copy are other popular choices for business offices. See Figure 13.19.

Storage Trade-Offs

Data and information must be stored until needed using a variety of storage methods. For example, many people and organizations still rely on paper documents stored in filing cabinets as a major form of storage media. However, you and other computer users are more likely to depend on the memory circuits and secondary storage devices of computer systems to meet your storage requirements. Progress in very-large-scale integration (VLSI), which packs millions of memory circuit elements on tiny semiconductor memory chips, is responsible for continuing increases in the main-memory capacity of computers. Secondary storage capacities are also escalating into the billions and trillions of characters, due to advances in magnetic and optical media.

There are many types of storage media and devices. Figure 13.20 illustrates the speed, capacity, and cost relationships of several alternative primary and secondary storage media. Note the cost/speed/capacity trade-offs as one moves from semiconductor memories to magnetic disks, to optical disks, and to magnetic tape. High-speed storage media cost more per byte and provide lower capacities. Large-capacity storage media cost less per byte but are slower. This is why we have different kinds of storage media.

FIGURE 13.20

Storage media cost, speed, and capacity trade-offs. Note how cost increases with faster access speeds, but decreases with the increased capacity of storage media.

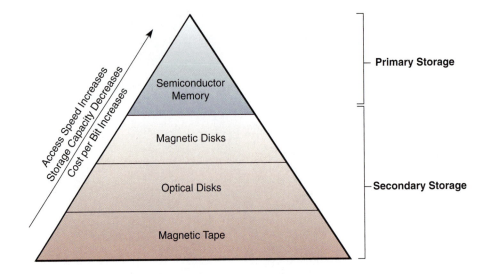

However, all storage media, especially memory chips and magnetic disks, continue to increase in speed and capacity and decrease in cost. Developments like automated high-speed cartridge assemblies have given faster access times to magnetic tape, and the speed of optical disk drives continues to increase.

Note in Figure 13.20 that semiconductor memories are used mainly for primary storage, though they are sometimes used as high-speed secondary storage devices. Magnetic disk and tape and optical disk devices, on the other hand, are used as secondary storage devices to greatly enlarge the storage capacity of computer systems. Also, since most primary storage circuits use RAM (random access memory) chips, which lose their contents when electrical power is interrupted, secondary storage devices provide a more permanent type of storage media.

Computer Storage Fundamentals

Data are processed and stored in a computer system through the presence or absence of electronic or magnetic signals in the computer's circuitry or in the media it uses. This is called a "two-state" or **binary representation** of data, since the computer and the media can exhibit only two possible states or conditions. For example, transistors and other semiconductor circuits are either in a conducting or nonconducting state. Media such as magnetic disks and tapes indicate these two states by having magnetized spots whose magnetic fields have one of two different directions, or polarities. This binary characteristic of computer circuitry and media is what makes the binary number system the basis for representing data in computers. Thus, for electronic circuits, the conducting (ON) state represents the number one, while the nonconducting (OFF) state represents the number zero. For magnetic media, the magnetic field of a magnetized spot in one direction represents a one, while magnetism in the other direction represents a zero.

The smallest element of data is called a **bit**, or binary digit, which can have a value of either zero or one. The capacity of memory chips is usually expressed in terms of bits. A **byte** is a basic grouping of bits that the computer operates as a single unit. Typically, it consists of eight bits and represents one character of data in most computer coding schemes. Thus, the capacity of a computer's memory and secondary storage devices is usually expressed in terms of bytes. Computer codes such as ASCII (American Standard Code for Information Interchange) use various arrangements of bits to form bytes that represent the numbers zero through nine, the letters of the alphabet, and many other characters. See Figure 13.21.

Storage capacities are frequently measured in **kilobytes** (KB), **megabytes** (MB), **gigabytes** (GB), or **terabytes** (TB). Although kilo means 1,000 in the metric system, the computer industry uses K to represent 1,024 (or 2^{10}) storage positions.

FIGURE 13.21

Examples of the ASCII computer code that computers use to represent numbers and the letters of the alphabet.

Character	ASCII Code	Character	ASCII Code	Character	ASCII Code
0	00110000	A	01000001	N	01001110
1	00110001	B	01000010	O	01001111
2	00110010	C	01000011	P	01010000
3	00110011	D	01000100	Q	01010001
4	00110100	E	01000101	R	01010010
5	00110101	F	01000110	S	01010011
6	00110110	G	01000111	T	01010100
7	00110111	H	01001000	U	01010101
8	00111000	I	01001001	V	01010110
9	00111001	J	01001010	W	01010111
		K	01001011	X	01011000
		L	01001100	Y	01011001
		M	01001101	Z	01011010

Therefore, a capacity of 10 megabytes, for example, is really 10,485,760 storage positions, rather than 10 million positions. However, such differences are frequently disregarded in order to simplify descriptions of storage capacity. Thus, a megabyte is roughly 1 million bytes of storage, a gigabyte is roughly 1 billion bytes and a terabyte represents about 1 trillion bytes, while a **petabyte** is over 1 quadrillion bytes!

Direct and Sequential Access

Primary storage media such as semiconductor memory chips are called **direct access** or random access memories (RAM). Magnetic disk devices are frequently called direct access storage devices (DASDs). On the other hand, media such as magnetic tape cartridges are known as **sequential access** devices.

The terms *direct access* and *random access* describe the same concept. They mean that an element of data or instructions (such as a byte or word) can be directly stored and retrieved by selecting and using any of the locations on the storage media. They also mean that each storage position (1) has a unique address and (2) can be individually accessed in approximately the same length of time without having to search through other storage positions. For example, each memory cell on a microelectronic semiconductor RAM chip can be individually sensed or changed in the same length of time. Also any data record stored on a magnetic or optical disk can be accessed directly in approximately the same time period. See Figure 13.22.

Sequential access storage media such as magnetic tape do not have unique storage addresses that can be directly addressed. Instead, data must be stored and retrieved using a sequential or serial process. Data are recorded one after another in a predetermined sequence (such as in numeric order) on a storage medium. Locating an individual item of data requires searching the recorded data on the tape until the desired item is located.

Semiconductor Memory

Memory is the coalman to the CPU's locomotive: For maximum PC performance, it must keep the processor constantly stoked with instructions. Faster CPUs call for larger and faster memories, both in the cache where data and instructions are stored temporarily, and in the main memory [10].

The primary storage (main memory) of your computer consists of microelectronic **semiconductor memory** chips. It provides you with the working storage your computer needs to process your applications. Plug-in memory circuit boards containing 32 megabytes or more of memory chips can be added to your PC to increase

FIGURE 13.22

Sequential versus direct access storage. Magnetic tape is a typical sequential access medium. Magnetic disks are typical direct access storage devices.

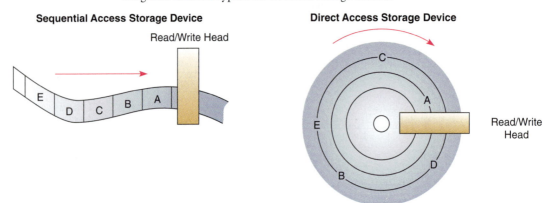

its memory capacity. Specialized memory can help improve your computer's performance. Examples include external cache memory of 512 kilobytes to help your microprocessor work faster, or a video graphics accelerator card with 16 megabytes of RAM for faster and clearer video performance. Removable credit-card-size and smaller "flash memory" RAM cards can also provide several megabytes of erasable direct access storage for PDAs or hand-held PCs.

Some of the major attractions of semiconductor memory are its small size, great speed, and shock and temperature resistance. One major disadvantage of most semiconductor memory is its **volatility.** Uninterrupted electric power must be supplied or the contents of memory will be lost. Therefore, emergency transfer to other devices or standby electrical power (through battery packs or emergency generators) is required if data are to be saved. Another alternative is to permanently "burn in" the contents of semiconductor devices so that they cannot be erased by a loss of power.

Thus, there are two basic types of semiconductor memory: random access memory (RAM) and read only memory (ROM).

● **RAM: random access memory.** These memory chips are the most widely used primary storage medium. Each memory position can be both sensed (read) and changed (written), so it is also called read/write memory. This is a volatile memory.

● **ROM: read only memory.** Nonvolatile random access memory chips are used for permanent storage. ROM can be read but not erased or overwritten. Frequently used control instructions in the control unit and programs in primary storage (such as parts of the operating system) can be permanently burned in to the storage cells during manufacture. This is sometimes called *firmware.* Variations include PROM (programmable read only memory) and EPROM (erasable programmable read only memory), which can be permanently or temporarily programmed after manufacture.

Magnetic Disk Storage

Multigigabyte magnetic disk drives aren't extravagant, considering that full-motion video files, sound tracks, and photo-quality images can consume colossal amounts of disk space in a blink [10].

Magnetic disks are the most common form of secondary storage for your computer system. That's because they provide fast access and high storage capacities at a reasonable cost. Magnetic disk drives contain metal disks that are coated on both sides with an iron oxide recording material. Several disks are mounted together on a vertical shaft, which typically rotates the disks at speeds of 3,600 to 7,600 revolutions

FIGURE 13.23   Magnetic disk media: A hard magnetic disk drive and a 3 1/2-inch floppy disk.

Source: Quantum.

Source: Corbis.

per minute (rpm). Electromagnetic read/write heads are positioned by access arms between the slightly separated disks to read and write data on concentric, circular tracks. Data are recorded on tracks in the form of tiny magnetized spots to form the binary digits of common computer codes. Thousands of bytes can be recorded on each track, and there are several hundred data tracks on each disk surface, thus providing you with billions of storage positions for your software and data. See Figure 13.23.

Types of Magnetic Disks

There are several types of magnetic disk arrangements, including removable disk cartridges as well as fixed disk units. Removable disk devices are popular because they are transportable and can be used to store backup copies of your data offline for convenience and security.

- **Floppy disks,** or magnetic diskettes, consist of polyester film disks covered with an iron oxide compound. A single disk is mounted and rotates freely inside a protective flexible or hard plastic jacket, which has access openings to accommodate the read/write head of a disk drive unit. The 3 1/2-inch floppy disk, with capacities of 1.44 megabytes, is the most widely used version, with a newer Superdisk technology offering 120 megabytes of storage.

- **Hard disk drives** combine magnetic disks, access arms, and read/write heads into a sealed module. This allows higher speeds, greater data recording densities, and closer tolerances within a sealed, more stable environment. Fixed or removable disk cartridge versions are available. Capacities of hard drives range from several hundred megabytes to many gigabytes of storage.

RAID Storage

RAID computer storage equipment—big, refrigerator-size boxes full of dozens of interlinked magnetic disk drives that can store the equivalent of 100 million tax returns—hardly gets the blood rushing. But it should. Just as speedy and reliable networking opened the floodgates to cyberspace and e-commerce, ever-more-turbocharged data storage is a key building block of the Internet [11].

Disk arrays of interconnected microcomputer hard disk drives have replaced large-capacity mainframe disk drives to provide many gigabytes of online storage. Known as **RAID** (redundant arrays of independent disks), they combine from 6 to more than 100 small hard disk drives and their control microprocessors into a single unit. RAID units provide large capacities with high access speeds since data are accessed in parallel over multiple paths from many disks. RAID units also provide a *fault tolerant* capacity, since their redundant design offers multiple copies of data on several disks. If one disk fails, data can be recovered from backup copies automatically stored on other disks. *Storage area networks* (SANs) are high-speed *fiber channel* local area networks that can interconnect many RAID units and thus share their combined capacity through network servers with many users.

Magnetic Tape Storage

Tape storage is moving beyond backup. Disk subsystems provide the fastest response time for mission-critical data. But the sheer amount of data users need to access these days as part of huge enterprise applications, such as data warehouses, requires affordable [magnetic tape] storage [16].

Magnetic tape is still being used as a secondary storage medium in business applications. The read/write heads of magnetic tape drives record data in the form of magnetized spots on the iron oxide coating of the plastic tape. Magnetic tape devices include tape reels and cartridges in mainframes and midrange systems, and small cassettes or cartridges for PCs. Magnetic tape cartridges have replaced tape reels in many applications and can hold over 200 megabytes.

One growing business application of magnetic tape involves the use of high-speed 36-track magnetic tape cartridges in robotic automated drive assemblies that can directly access hundreds of cartridges. These devices provide lower-cost storage to supplement magnetic disks to meet massive data warehouse and other online business storage requirements. Other major applications for magnetic tape include long-term *archival* storage and backup storage for PCs and other systems [16].

Optical Disk Storage

CD-ROM technology has become a necessity. Most software companies now distribute their elephantine programs on CD-ROMs. Many corporations are now rolling their own CDs to distribute product and corporate information that once filled bookshelves [10].

Optical disks are a fast-growing storage medium. One version for use with microcomputers is called **CD-ROM** (compact disk–read only memory). CD-ROM technology uses 12-centimeter (4.7 inch) compact disks (CDs) similar to those used in stereo music systems. Each disk can store more than 600 megabytes. That's the equivalent of over 400 1.44 megabyte floppy disks or more than 300,000 double-spaced pages of text. A laser records data by burning permanent microscopic pits in a spiral track on a master disk from which compact disks can be mass-produced. Then CD-ROM disk drives use a laser device to read the binary codes formed by those pits.

CD-R (compact disk–recordable) is a popular optical disk technology. CD-R drives or *CD burners* are commonly used to permanently record digital music tracks or digital photo images on CDs. The major limitation of CD-ROM and CD-R disks is that recorded data cannot be erased. However, **CD-RW** (CD-rewritable) drives have now become available that record and erase data by using a laser to heat a microscopic point on the disk's surface. In CD-RW versions using magneto-optical technology, a magnetic coil changes the spot's reflective properties from one direction to another, thus recording a binary one or zero. A laser device can then read the binary codes on the disk by sensing the direction of reflected light.

FIGURE 13.24

Optical disk storage includes CD and DVD technologies.

Source: PhotoDisc.

Optical disk capacities and capabilities have increased dramatically with the emergence of an optical disk technology called **DVD** (digital video disk or digital versatile disk). DVDs can hold from 3.0 to 8.5 gigabytes of multimedia data on each side of a compact disk. The large capacities and high-quality images and sound of DVD technology are expected to eventually replace CD-ROM and CD-RW technologies for data storage, and promise to accelerate the use of DVD drives for multimedia products that can be used in both computers and home entertainment systems. Thus, **DVD-ROM** is beginning to replace magnetic tape videocassettes for movies and other multimedia products, while **DVD-RAM** is being used for backup and archival storage of large data and multimedia files. See Figure 13.24.

Business Applications

One of the major uses of optical disks in mainframe and midrange systems is in **image processing,** where long-term archival storage of historical files of document images must be maintained. Mainframe and midrange computer versions of optical disks use 12-inch plastic disks with capacities of several gigabytes, with up to 20 disks held in jukebox drive units. Financial institutions, among others, are using optical scanners to capture digitized document images and store them on **WORM** (write once, read many) versions of such optical disks as an alternative to microfilm media.

One of the major business uses of CD-ROM disks for personal computers is to provide a publishing medium for fast access to reference materials in a convenient, compact form. This includes catalogs, directories, manuals, periodical abstracts, part listings, and statistical databases of business and economic activity. Interactive multimedia applications in business, education, and entertainment are another major use of CD-ROM and DVD disks. The large storage capacities of CD-ROM and DVD disks are a natural choice for computer video games, educational videos, multimedia encyclopedias, and advertising presentations.

Thus, optical disks have become a popular storage medium for image processing and multimedia business applications, and they appear to be a promising alternative to magnetic disks and tape for very large *mass storage* capabilities for enterprises' computing systems. However, rewritable optical technologies are still maturing, and most optical disk devices are significantly slower and more expensive (per byte of storage) than magnetic disk systems. Still, optical disk systems are slowly displacing magnetic disk technology in many business applications.

Summary

- **Computer Systems.** Major types of computer systems are summarized in Figure 13.2. A computer is a system of information processing components that perform input, processing, output, storage, and control functions. Its hardware components include input and output devices, a central processing unit (CPU), and primary and secondary storage devices. The major functions and hardware in a computer system are summarized in Figure 13.9.

- **Microcomputer Systems.** Microcomputers are used as personal computers, network computers, personal digital assistants, technical workstations, and information appliances. Like most computer systems today, microcomputers are interconnected in a variety of telecommunications networks. This typically includes local area networks, client/server networks, intranets and extranets, and the Internet.

- **Other Computer Systems.** Midrange computers are increasingly used as powerful network servers, and for many multiuser business data processing and scientific applications. Mainframe computers are larger and more powerful than most midsize computers. They are usually faster, have more memory capacity, and can support more network users and peripheral devices. They are designed to handle the information processing needs of large organizations with high volumes of transaction processing, or with complex computational problems. Supercomputers are a special category of extremely powerful mainframe computer systems designed for massive computational assignments.

- **Peripheral Devices.** Refer to Figures 13.12 and 13.20 to review the capabilities of peripheral devices for input, output, and storage discussed in this chapter.

Key Terms and Concepts

These are the key terms and concepts of this chapter. The page number of their first explanation is given in parentheses.

1. Binary representation (482)
2. Central processing unit (470)
3. Computer system (470)
4. Computer terminal (465)
5. Digital cameras (479)
6. Direct access (483)
7. Information appliance (465)
8. Laptop computer (463)
9. Liquid crystal displays (480)
10. Magnetic disk storage (484)
    - *a.* Floppy disk (485)
    - *b.* Hard disk (485)
    - *c.* RAID (486)
11. Magnetic ink character recognition (479)
12. Magnetic stripe (479)
13. Magnetic tape (486)
14. Mainframe computer (468)
15. Microcomputer (462)
16. Microprocessor (470)
17. Midrange computer (466)
18. Minicomputer (467)
19. Network computer (465)
20. Network server (463)

21. Network terminal (466)
22. Offline (474)
23. Online (474)
24. Optical character recognition (478)
25. Optical disk storage (486)
    - *a.* CD-ROM (486)
    - *b.* CD-R (486)
    - *c.* CD-RW (486)
    - *d.* DVD (487)
    - *e.* WORM disks (487)
26. Optical scanning (478)
27. Pen-based computing (476)
28. Peripheral devices (474)
29. Personal digital assistant (465)
30. Pointing devices (474)
    - *a.* Electronic mouse (475)
    - *b.* Pointing stick (475)
    - *c.* Touchpad (475)
    - *d.* Trackball (475)
31. Primary storage (471)
32. Printers (481)
33. Secondary storage (471)
34. Semiconductor memory (483)
    - *a.* RAM (484)
    - *b.* ROM (484)

35. Sequential access (483)
36. Smart cards (479)
37. Speech recognition (476)
38. Storage capacity elements (482)
    - *a.* Bit (482)
    - *b.* Byte (482)
    - *c.* Kilobyte (482)
    - *d.* Megabyte (482)
    - *e.* Gigabyte (482)
    - *f.* Terabyte (482)
39. Storage media trade-offs (481)
40. Supercomputer (469)
41. Time elements (471)
    - *a.* Millisecond (471)
    - *b.* Microsecond (471)
    - *c.* Nanosecond (471)
    - *d.* Picosecond (471)
42. Touch-sensitive screen (475)
43. Transaction terminals (466)
44. Video output (480)
45. Volatility (484)
46. Wand (478)
47. Workstation (463)

Review Quiz

Match one of the previous key terms and concepts with one of the following brief examples or definitions. Try to find the best fit for answers that seem to fit more than one term or concept. Defend your choices.

_____ 1. A computer is a combination of components that perform input, processing, output, storage, and control functions.

_____ 2. The main processing component of a computer system.

_____ 3. A small, portable PC.

_____ 4. Devices for consumers to access the Internet.

_____ 5. The memory of a computer.

_____ 6. Magnetic disks and tape and optical disks perform this function.

_____ 7. Input/output and secondary storage devices for a computer system.

_____ 8. Connected to and controlled by a CPU.

_____ 9. Separate from and not controlled by a CPU.

_____ 10. Results from the presence or absence or change in direction of electric current, magnetic fields, or light rays in computer circuits and media.

_____ 11. The central processing unit of a microcomputer.

_____ 12. Can be a desktop/laptop, or hand-held computer.

_____ 13. A computer category between microcomputers and mainframes.

_____ 14. A computer that can handle the information processing needs of large organizations.

_____ 15. Hand-held microcomputers for communications and personal information management.

_____ 16. Low-cost microcomputers for use with the Internet and corporate intranets.

_____ 17. Point-of-sale (POS) terminals in retail stores and bank ATMs are examples.

_____ 18. A terminal that depends on network servers for its software and processing power.

_____ 19. A computer that manages network communications and resources.

_____ 20. The most powerful type of computer.

_____ 21. A magnetic tape technology for credit cards.

_____ 22. One billionth of a second.

_____ 23. Roughly one billion characters of storage.

_____ 24. Includes electronic mouses, trackballs, pointing sticks, and touchpads.

_____ 25. You can write on the pressure-sensitive LCD screen of hand-held microcomputers with a pen.

_____ 26. Moving this along your desktop moves the cursor on the screen.

_____ 27. You can communicate with a computer by touching its display.

_____ 28. Produces hard copy output such as paper documents and reports.

_____ 29. Promises to be the easiest, most natural way to communicate with computers.

_____ 30. Capturing data by processing light reflected from images.

_____ 31. Optical scanning of bar codes and other characters.

_____ 32. Bank check processing uses this technology.

_____ 33. A debit card with an embedded microprocessor and memory is an example.

_____ 34. A device with a keyboard and a video display networked to a computer is a typical example.

_____ 35. Photos or video can be captured and downloaded to your PC for image processing.

_____ 36. A video output technology.

_____ 37. A hand-held device that reads bar coding.

_____ 38. Storage media cost, speed, and capacity differences.

_____ 39. You cannot erase the contents of these storage circuits.

_____ 40. The memory of most computers consists of these storage circuits.

_____ 41. The property that determines whether data are lost or retained when power fails.

_____ 42. Each position of storage can be accessed in approximately the same time.

_____ 43. Each position of storage can be accessed according to a predetermined order.

_____ 44. Microelectronic storage circuits on silicon chips.

_____ 45. Uses magnetic spots on metal or plastic disks.

_____ 46. Uses magnetic spots on plastic tape.

_____ 47. Uses a laser to read microscopic points on plastic disks.

_____ 48. Vastly increases the storage capacity and image and sound quality of optical disk technology.

Discussion Questions

1. Do you agree with the statement: "The network is the computer"? Why or why not?

2. What trends are occurring in the development and use of the major types of computer systems?

3. Refer to the Real World Case on the City of Richmond and Tim Beaty Builders in the chapter. Will the convergence of PDAs, sub-notebook PCs, and cell phones produce an information appliance that will make all of those categories obsolete? Why or why not?

4. Do you think that network computers (NCs) will replace personal computers (PCs) in business applications? Explain.

5. Are networks of PCs and servers making mainframe computers obsolete? Explain.

6. Refer to the Real World Case on United Technologies and Eastman Kodak in the chapter. Should a conglomerate like UTC with many diverse companies

standardize its PC hardware and software, and lock out downloads of other software? Why or why not?

7. What are several trends that are occurring in the development and use of peripheral devices? Why are these trends occurring?

8. When would you recommend the use of each of the following: (1) network computers, (2) network terminals, or (3) information appliances in business applications?

9. What processor, memory, magnetic disk storage, and video display capabilities would you require for a personal computer that you would use for business purposes? Explain your choices.

10. What other peripheral devices and capabilities would you want to have for your business PC? Explain your choices.

Application Exercises

1. Purchasing Computer Systems for Your Workgroup

SS You have been asked to get pricing information for a potential purchase of 5 PCs for the members of your workgroup. Go to the Internet to get prices for these units from at least two prominent PC suppliers.

The list below shows the specifications for the basic system you have been asked to price and potential upgrades to each feature. You will want to get a price for the basic system described below and a separate price for each of the upgrades shown.

	Basic Unit	Upgrade
CPU (gigahertz)	1.3	1.5
Hard Drive (gigabytes)	40	80
RAM (megabytes)	256	512
CD-ROM	48 speed	8 Speed DVD
Monitor (inches)	17	21

Network cards and modems will not be purchased with these systems. These features will be added from stock already owned by the company. Take the standard warranty and servicing coverage offered by each supplier, but be sure to note any differences in coverage.

a. Prepare a spreadsheet summarizing this pricing information and showing the cost, from each supplier, of the following options: **a.** 5 units with the basic configuration, **b.** 3 units with the basic configuration and 2 units with all of the upgrades, **c.** 3 units with the basic configuration plus the monitor upgrade and 2 units with all upgrades, and **d.** all 5 units fully upgraded.

b. Prepare a set of PowerPoint slides or similar presentation materials summarizing your results. Include a discussion of the warranty and servicing contract options available from each supplier.

2. Price and Performance Trends for Computer Hardware

SS The table below shows a set of price and capacity figures for common components of personal computers. Typical prices for Microprocessors, Random Access Memory (RAM), and Hard Disk storage prices are shown. The performance of typical components has increased substantially over time, so the speed (for the microprocessor) or the capacity (for the storage devices) is also listed. Although there have been improvements in these components that are not reflected in these capacity measures, it is interesting to examine trends in these measurable characteristics.

a. Create a spreadsheet based on the figures below and include a new column for each component showing the price per unit of capacity. (Cost per megahertz of speed for microprocessors, and cost per megabyte of storage for RAM and hard disk devices.)

b. Create a set of graphs highlighting your results and illustrating trends in price per unit of performance (speed) or capacity.

c. Write a short paper discussing the trends you found. How long do you expect these trends to continue? Why?

	1991	1993	1995	1997	1999	2001
Microprocessor						
Speed (Megahertz)	25	33	100	125	350	1,000
Cost	$180	$125	$275	$250	$300	$251
RAM Chip						
Megabytes per Chip	1	4	4	16	64	256
Cost	$55	$140	$120	$97	$125	$90
Hard Disk Device						
Megabytes per Disk	105	250	540	2,000	8,000	40,000
Cost	$480	$375	$220	$250	$220	$138

REAL WORLD CASE 3

Boscov's, Winnebago, and WPS Health: Moving to Linux on the Mainframe

When Joe Poole looks at his IBM zSeries mainframe, he doesn't just see a powerful system running traditional corporate workloads. He sees a distributed Linux applications environment that's starting to save his company big bucks. "Running Linux on the mainframe is inexpensive," says Poole, manager for technical support at mid-Atlantic retailer Boscov's Department Stores (www.boscovs.com). "We expect to see a two-year payback."

Those types of returns seem to be typical among the adventurous IBM mainframe users who have begun to shift applications from networked Intel-based servers to "virtual server" partitions in their data center mainframe workhorses. And analysts agree that for many companies, installing the Linux operating system to run applications on the mainframe can have a lower total cost of ownership (TCO) than supporting applications on hundreds or thousands of distributed servers. And for Poole, hardware and software savings translate to pocketing an extra $100,000 per year for Boscov's IT budget that would otherwise have been spent on Intel servers.

So far, Exton, Pennsylvania–based Boscov's is running its Web-based supply chain application and its Novell NetWare operations using Linux on the mainframe. The savings Boscov's achieves from not having to buy those Intel servers "means in two years, we'll pay for the $200,000 software license" for IBM's Virtual Machine and Integrated Facility for Linux software, which is necessary for loading Linux on zSeries mainframes, Poole says.

Winnebago Industries Inc. (www.winnebagoind.com) saw its Linux/mainframe savings come in part from lowering its software licensing fees. Dave Ennen, technical support manager at the Forest City, Iowa–based recreational vehicle manufacturer, says his company bought an e-mail application that runs on the company's mainframe Linux partition. Winnebago spent a third of what it would have spent for Microsoft Exchange on Intel servers.

Personnel costs are a much bigger area for savings with Linux on big iron, since it takes fewer support staffers to manage a single mainframe than it does to manage multiple Intel servers. Staffing to support Linux on a mainframe represents 37 to 40 percent of the TCO, say analysts. However, few mainframe administrators are versed in Linux today, and fewer Linux experts know IBM's z/OS mainframe operating system, thus creating a skills shortage. But David Mastrobattista, an analyst at Giga Information Group, says he isn't worried. "Linux is an enabling technology to get mainframes back in the politically correct spotlight," Mastrobattista says. He argues that Linux administrators who can be trained on mainframe systems will be attracted to the field and that Linux will be embraced by mainframe administrators seeking new career challenges.

The final TCO segment that IT managers need to review, analysts say, is facilities, which can be 37 to 43 percent of the total operating cost. With the new generation of smaller, air-cooled mainframes, Boscov's Poole says it's obvious that a network of servers with their attendant switches, routers, and hubs eat up much more space and consume far more power than a single mainframe. In fact, he estimates that the annual savings from lower electrical bills will pay for his company's annual IBM software maintenance fee. Running Linux on a mainframe "cut our electricity bill in half," he says.

"Server consolidation in Linux has reintroduced the mainframe to a whole new audience," says Peter McCaffrey, eServer director at IBM. "You can transform a single mainframe into hundreds of virtual servers." McCaffrey cautions that heavily used applications don't lend themselves well to consolidation. Thus, IBM suggests that organizations host databases on mainframes but run transaction-intensive applications on separate servers.

WPS Health Insurance (www.wpsic.com) in Madison, Wisconsin, is working on consolidating the applications now run on 40 Intel-based servers onto an IBM eServer z900 mainframe running Linux. So far, two small Linux systems have been migrated, six are in process, and five more are planned. WPS expects to transfer the applications of all 40 machines, including 15 Windows servers hosting e-mail, Web server, directory services, and health care applications.

WPS's health care claims processing system originally spanned multiple servers. Integration from servers to the mainframe has already improved efficiency on a system where claims have grown from $800 million to almost $5 billion in four years. "We now process 350,000 claims daily— 12 per second," says Randy Lengyel, senior vice president of MIS at WPS. Other advantages Lengyel cites include a 40 percent cost reduction per server, a threefold increase in performance, and a fivefold increase in reliability.

Case Study Questions

1. How can a mainframe run the equivalent of hundreds of Linux server applications at the same time?

2. Why can the total cost of ownership of running Linux applications on the mainframe be less than on Intel-based servers? What other IT and business benefits may be achieved?

3. What challenges or limitations can arise in moving business applications from servers to Linux on a mainframe?

Source: Adapted from Mark Hall, "TCO: Linux Delivers on Big Iron," *Computerworld*, May 13, 2002, p. 47; and Drew Robb, "Thinning the Server Ranks," *Computerworld*, February 4, 2002, pp. 24–25. Reprinted with permission from *Computerworld*.

La-Z-Boy and Corporate Express: The Business Benefits of Server Consolidation

The ascendancy of Intel-based servers running the Windows operating system, and the rise of the Internet and corporate e-mail over the past decade have generated an explosion in the number of servers IT must manage. At first, adding servers to accommodate growth seemed more attractive than a centralized mainframe-based computing model. But in some organizations, server proliferation has begun to spin out of control. "Our servers were multiplying like rabbits," says Jeff Smith, manager of corporate network services at La-Z-Boy Inc. (www.lazboy.com), a Monroe, Michigan–based residential furniture producer that just completed a Windows NT server consolidation project. "Our distributed environment was becoming more and more difficult to manage."

"It's quite common for organizations these days to be running hundreds of Windows or Unix servers, many of them simple-application boxes," says John Phelps, an analyst at Gartner Inc. He says many companies have no idea exactly how many servers they have. This proliferation of servers has proved far more costly than previously predicted. Though smaller scaled-out systems are less expensive than mainframes, IT departments need many more of them to support their companies' business operations. That translates into greater space requirements, more exposure to potential security breaches, and a greater management burden.

In response, a movement to consolidate servers has blossomed. Gartner says 70 percent of its enterprise clients are now trying to consolidate, compared with only 33 percent three years ago. But with so many servers running so many kinds of applications, where should IT managers start? Both vendors and users say infrastructure servers that handle tasks such as file and print, Web, e-mail, and perhaps some databases are a good first bet.

La-Z-Boy consolidated its servers onto three partitions on a Unisys ES7000 midrange system. It placed the infrastructure servers (such as imaging, file and print, e-mail, Web, and backup) on one partition, consolidated several Microsoft SQL Server databases on a second partition, and installed MetaFrame thin-client software from Citrix Systems in the third partition. Smith plans to add more partitions for Microsoft Exchange Server 2000 and a test environment.

But not everything fits the consolidation model. In the past year, Smith still added about a dozen Windows servers to handle Domain Name System and Windows Internet Naming Service functions. He says that because these machines were inexpensive and carry low administrative and maintenance costs, he saw no economic or performance benefits to adding them to the ES7000.

Even with an expanding workload and larger databases, the Unisys ES7000 runs at only 6 to 8 percent utilization. But companies can't just jam everything onto one server willy-nilly, says Jeff Vail, consolidation manager at Unisys.

Network capacity might limit the ability to consolidate Microsoft Exchange servers, for example, and peak traffic load and application conflicts are also potential problems, he says.

At Broomfield, Colorado–based Corporate Express Inc. (www.corporateexpress.com) the HP-UX Unix servers from Hewlett-Packard demand a different strategy. The big driver was space—the company's data center was full. The business-to-business office supply company migrated 43 servers onto two 26-processor Sun Microsystems Enterprise 10000 midrange servers running Solaris Unix. "This immediately freed up half the space in the data center," says Andy Miller, vice president of technical architecture. The result: a savings of $10,000 per day in operating expenses, 100 percent return on investment in nine months, a 10 percent decrease in total cost of ownership, 99.99 percent availability, and 100 percent faster processing. Miller says the move also helped IT accommodate a 157 percent increase in sales. "Without the Suns, we couldn't have supported the load and the data center would have imploded," he says.

The change from HP-UX to Solaris Unix required migrating to a new file system. Miller ran the systems in parallel for six weeks while the data migration proceeded. Though the applications ported to Solaris covered a wide range (enterprise resource planning, PeopleSoft financials, order processing, human resources, and a large data warehouse), Miller says he has had no serious problems hosting them on the Sun E10000 servers.

The secret? "Planning is the key," he says. "You have to test the applications to see which can co-exist at overall performance and traffic loads." As for saving space, Corporate Express's IT workload has grown, and added two more Sun E10000s, so the data center is once again full. Miller is now consolidating two of the Enterprise 10000s to one new Sun Fire 15000 midrange server. "That will again free up about 50 percent of my space, while reducing costs and increasing performance," he says.

Case Study Questions

1. What are the business and technical benefits of using multiple servers to run business applications for a company?

2. What are the business and technical challenges facing companies who depend on many distributed server systems?

3. What are the business and technical benefits of server consolidation initiatives? What are the limitations of such a strategy?

Source: Adapted from Drew Robb, "Thinning the Server Ranks," *Computerworld*, August 26, 2002, pp. 24–25. Reprinted with permission from *Computerworld*.

| REAL WORLD CASE 5 | Los Alamos National Laboratory and Others: The ROI of Blade Servers |

While total cost of ownership (TCO) and ROI issues are crucial to corporate IT managers, in the ivory tower world of supercomputing, most buyers of supercomputing power have paid little attention to the cost of power consumption, space, and environmental requirements, says Wu Feng, technical staff member and team leader of research and development for advanced network technology at Los Alamos National Laboratory in New Mexico. "In the next decade, size, power consumption, reliability, and ease of administration will be the key performance issues in supercomputing. Bigger and faster machines simply won't be good enough," he explains.

Feng's team has been testing RLX Technologies (www.rlxtechnologies.com) RLX ServerBlades in floating-point applications since late 2001 and has found several advantages to using blade servers for supercomputing. The blades from RLX were faster to deploy and are easier to manage than traditional server clusters. "We were able to build our RLX cluster and get our code running in less than three hours, an effort that normally takes several days," says Feng.

Meanwhile, the space savings of the RLX systems "is a factor of eight times that of our traditional clusters," Feng notes. And the price/performance of the RLX ServerBlades is also impressive, he adds. "We calculated the peak price/performance ratio of a 24-blade configuration of the RLX ServerBlades to be $1.81 per millions of operations per second, versus $6 to $9 per millions of operations per second for traditional supercomputers," Feng says.

Los Alamos National Laboratory and Washington-based e-learning software and application service provider (ASP) Blackboard Inc. (www.blackboard.com) are finding that blade servers cost 30 to 50 percent less than traditional rack-mounted servers, with the biggest savings derived from their smaller size, low power-consumption costs, and the reduced costs of cabling, power supply management, and integrated telecom switching. Dollar Rent A Car Inc. (www.dollar.com) began using HP blade servers in 2002 to help speed the deployment of new Unix-based Web and data center applications while keeping costs down, and will expand their use in 2003. Meanwhile, AOL (www.aol.com) began testing IBM BladeCenter servers running Linux in 2002, as part of their goal of reducing IT costs by 30 percent in 2003.

Freed of the physical bulk and componentry of traditional servers, blades slide into slots on racks. In most cases, blade servers consist of microcomputer processing and storage assemblies that fit into slots in a rack unit that provides a common backplane, cooling fan, cabling, and network and external storage connections, reducing both cabling and space requirements. Analysts say cost savings increase the longer these systems are used. "Blade servers take up less space, generate less heat, use less power, and don't need the environment requirements of air conditioning or raised flooring, as larger servers require," says Tom Manter, research director at Aberdeen Group. The primary caveat in trying to achieve quick ROI on blade servers largely rests on how well the processing, networking, and storage features are integrated. "Any cost savings can quickly be eaten away if maintaining blade servers becomes complex and time-consuming," says John Humphreys, an analyst at IDC.

Blade servers are a new technology. They became available in late 2000 from Egenera and RLX Technologies, in 2001 from HP and Compaq, and in 2002 from IBM with RLX, with Dell and Sun announcing availability in 2003. But despite their newness, blade server customers say that the savings potential is worth close examination.

Data Return Corp. (www.datareturn.com), an Irving, Texas–based e-commerce ASP for companies such as H&R Block Inc., BMW AG, and Match.com Inc., is beta-testing HP/Compaq blade servers to save space and lower power consumption costs, including thermal cooling costs, in its data centers. "If we can put 320 blade servers in the same space previously housing only 42 rack-mounted servers, we simply must give that option a try," says Stephen Johnson, group program manager of platform, network, and security technology at Data Return. A typical server rack takes up about 25 square feet, which costs customers about $300 per square foot on average.

Lower operational costs have also attracted Blackboard, which estimates that it will save more than 50 percent in maintenance and personnel costs this year using blade server technology from Egenera Inc. So Blackboard will strive to match increased demand for its e-learning tools and services by doubling its bladeserver farm from 300 to 600 by year's end, according to Greg Davies, the company's vice president of engineering.

Case Study Questions

1. What are the business and technical benefits of using blade servers versus rack-mounted or traditional servers?

2. What limitations or challenges might there be in the use of blade servers?

3. When should a company consider using blade servers? Visit the website of RLX Technologies to help you answer.

Source: Adapted from Barbara DePompa Reimers, "Blades Spin ROI Potential," *Computerworld*, February 11, 2002, p. 26, and Barbara Reimers, "Blades: Wait Till Next Year," *Computerworld*, November 18, 2002, pp. 42–44. Reprinted with permission from *Computerworld*.

CHAPTER 14

COMPUTER SOFTWARE

Chapter Highlights

Learning Objectives

After reading and studying this chapter, you should be able to:

1. Describe several important trends occurring in computer software.

2. Give examples of several major types of application and system software.

3. Explain the purpose of several popular software packages for end user productivity and collaborative computing.

4. Outline the functions of an operating system.

5. Describe the main uses of computer programming software, tools, and languages.

SECTION I   Application Software: End User Applications

Introduction to Software

This chapter presents an overview of the major types of software you depend on as you work with computers and access computer networks. It discusses their characteristics and purposes and gives examples of their uses. Before we begin, let's look at an example of the changing world of software in business.

Analyzing Intuit Inc.

Read the Real World Case on Intuit Inc. on the next page. We can learn a lot about the development and markets for consumer and small business software from this example. See Figure 14.1.

New CEO Stephen Bennett has brought profitability back to Intuit, the market leader in consumer finance and small-business software. He dropped several money-losing online finance businesses, and acquired several small-business software and services companies to strengthen Intuit's small-business offerings. Bennett has emphasized a more disciplined management approach for budgeting, planning, compensation, and quality processes. He also hired managers from his former executive post at General Electric to head Intuit's consumer and small-business divisions. Bennett's big thrust is to increase Intuit's small-business market share by expanding into the market segment of larger small businesses. It is there Intuit will have to learn to compete successfully with Microsoft's small-business offerings like Great Plains Software.

Types of Software

Let's begin our analysis of software by looking at an overview of the major types and functions of **application software** and **system software** available to computer users, shown in Figure 14.2. This figure summarizes the major categories of system and application software we will discuss in this chapter. Of course, this is a conceptual illustration. The types of software you will encounter depend primarily on the types of computers and networks you use, and on what specific tasks you want to accomplish. We will discuss application software in this section and the major types of system software in Section II.

FIGURE 14.1
Stephen Bennett is CEO of Intuit Inc. and leader of their drive to expand their success in the small-business software market.

Source: Robert Cardin.

| REAL WORLD CASE 1 | Intuit Inc.: Driving for Success in Small Business Software |

By most measures, November 29, 1999, was already a stellar day for Stephen M. Bennett. After 22 years at General Electric Co., he was promoted to executive vice president of GE Capital, a prize for boosting equipment-financing profits 150 percent and launching two GE Capital e-business units. But things would get even better. At home that night, a headhunter called. Software maker Intuit Inc. (www.intuit.com) needed a chief executive. Bennett didn't hesitate. At GE, he says, "I wondered how much of my success was GE, and how much was me."

Three years later, Bennett has his answer: A lot was him. After stagnating and stumbling during the dot-com boom, Intuit is hitting its stride in the tech bust. The 48-year-old GE vet has done a major reshuffle at the maker of Quick-Books small-business programs and TurboTax consumer software. Out went a raft of mostly money-losing online finance businesses. In came a half-dozen small software and online acquisitions in the past year, all to beef up Intuit's small-business offerings.

And up went the earnings: Net income went from an $82 million loss in fiscal 2001 to a profit of $140 million in fiscal 2002, which ended in July. Pro forma profits, excluding items such as the costs of acquisitions, are on track to jump 50 percent in 2002. Meanwhile, revenue, which shrank 1 percent in 1998, was up 18 percent in the last fiscal year, to $1.86 billion, and analysts predict it will grow more than 25 percent this year. Intuit's stock is up 13 percent in 2002, and 35 percent over the past 12 months, even as major indexes have lost 25 to 35 percent.

With numbers like that to his credit, Bennett is emerging as a management role model for Silicon Valley during the tech bust. Intuit was always innovative and its products were easy to use—but Bennett has made the company disciplined and results-focused, too. That's earning him admiring reviews even from competitors. "The keyword there is definitely discipline," says Ronald F. Verni, CEO of Best Software Inc., a maker of small-business software.

Much of what Bennett is doing comes directly from the GE playbook. He recruited former GE subordinates to run both of Intuit's major divisions and demanded better-thought-out budgets and clearer objectives from all of his managers. Like GE ex-CEO Jack Welch, he teaches management seminars to up-and-comers. And like Welch, he insists on sticking to businesses where Intuit can be No. 1 or No. 2. "The first part of strategic rigor is: Are you in a business where you can win?" Bennett says.

His major focus is small businesses. Intuit already has about 85 percent of the $280 million market for accounting software for companies with fewer than 20 employees. Now Bennett is targeting a much larger $4.8 billion market by churning out new versions of QuickBooks for companies with up to 250 employees, and by selling new software applications. He has spent almost $500 million on acquisitions—two firms that handle payrolls and automate computer help desks, and four whose software helps manage industries from construction companies to nonprofit agencies.

Will it work? Intuit will do best when it's selling to growing companies that step up from QuickBooks or similar products. But it will get a stiff fight when it tries to move up to companies with hundreds of employees. That's where Microsoft Corp. has staked out its ground. In the past two years, the software giant shelled out $2.5 billion to buy small-business software companies like Great Plains Software (www.greatplains.com), and it's just come out with new CRM software for managing relationships with customers. Analysts believe there's plenty of room for both companies' small-business units to grow at more than 20 percent for the next two years, but the competition will heat up after that.

For now, Bennett's biggest challenges are internal. He intends to make Intuit much more efficient. The goal is to deliver operating-profit margins of 24 percent this fiscal year, up from 14 percent the year before he arrived and 21 percent last year. Software's top performers deliver margins of more than 30 percent. To achieve that at Intuit, Bennett is working to improve discipline. To get employees focused on the bottom line, he adjusted pay incentives. Workers with top performance reviews get annual salary raises up to 10 percent, even when the average raise is 4 percent or less. "This was a consensus culture where rewards were spread like peanut butter," says Jim Grenier, Intuit's vice president for human resources.

Bennett also is pushing GE-like programs to boost quality and trim waste. One result: Error rates for Quicken personal finance software shipments fell to 2 percent during the release of the 2003 version from 22 percent for the 2002 edition. Intuit says its quality efforts have saved $10 million so far, with an additional $20 million due from projects under way. And Bennett wants more, as he and Microsoft go after the same small-business market.

Case Study Questions

1. Why has Intuit's success improved under Bennett's leadership? What are several things Intuit could do to successfully compete with Microsoft in the future?

2. Why does Intuit dominate its small-business software market segment? Visit its website and review its software products and services to help you answer.

3. What software products and services does Intuit have that might support Bennett's strategy to appeal to larger small businesses? Visit the Intuit and Great Plains websites to help you answer.

Source: Adapted from Timothy Mullaney, "The Wizard of Intuit," *BusinessWeek*, October 28, 2002, pp. 62–63.

FIGURE 14.2   An overview of computer software. Note the major types and examples of application and system software.

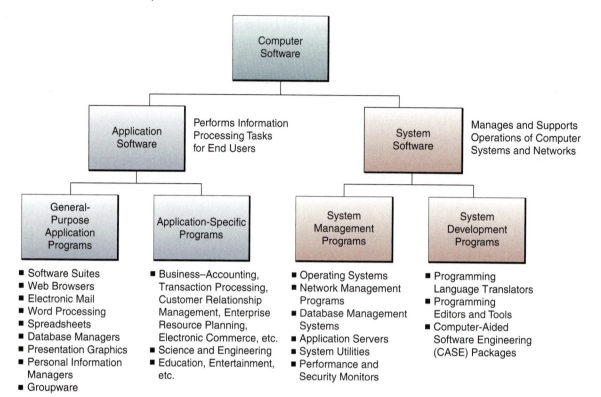

Application Software for End Users

Figure 14.2 shows that application software includes a variety of programs that can be subdivided into general-purpose and application-specific categories. Thousands of **application-specific** software packages are available to support specific applications of end users in business and other fields. For example, application-specific packages in business support managerial, professional, and business uses such as transaction processing, decision support, accounting, sales management, investment analysis, and electronic commerce. Application-specific software for science and engineering plays a major role in the research and development programs of industry and the design of efficient production processes for high-quality products. Other software packages help end users with personal finance and home management, or provide a wide variety of entertainment and educational products.

General-purpose application programs are programs that perform common information processing jobs for end users. For example, word processing programs, spreadsheet programs, database management programs, and graphics programs are popular with microcomputer users for home, education, business, scientific, and many other purposes. Because they significantly increase the productivity of end users, they are sometimes known as *productivity packages*. Other examples include Web browsers, electronic mail, and *groupware*, which help support communication and collaboration among workgroups and teams.

Software Suites and Integrated Packages

Let's begin our discussion of popular general-purpose application software by looking at **software suites**. That's because the most widely used productivity packages come bundled together as software suites such as Microsoft Office, Lotus SmartSuite, Corel WordPerfect Office, and Sun's StarOffice. Examining their components gives us an overview of the important software tools that you can use to increase your productivity.

FIGURE 14.3

The basic program components of the top four software suites. Other programs may be included, depending on the suite edition selected.

Programs	Microsoft Office	Lotus SmartSuite	Corel WordPerfect Office	Sun StarOffice
Word Processor	Word	WordPro	WordPerfect	StarWriter
Spreadsheet	Excel	1–2–3	Quattro Pro	StarCalc
Presentation Graphics	PowerPoint	Freelance	Presentations	StarImpress
Database Manager	Access	Approach	Paradox	StarBase
Personal Information Manager	Outlook	Organizer	Corel Central	StarSchedule

Figure 14.3 compares the basic programs that make up the top four software suites. Notice that each suite integrates software packages for word processing, spreadsheets, presentation graphics, database management, and personal information management. Microsoft, Lotus, Corel, and Sun bundle several other programs in each suite, depending on the version you select. Examples include programs for Internet access, e-mail, Web publishing, desktop publishing, voice recognition, financial management, electronic encyclopedias, and so on.

A software suite costs a lot less than the total cost of buying its individual packages separately. Another advantage is that all programs use a similar **graphical user interface** (GUI) of icons, tool and status bars, menus, and so on, which gives them the same look and feel, and makes them easier to learn and use. Software suites also share common tools such as spell checkers and help wizards to increase their efficiency. Another big advantage of suites is that their programs are designed to work together seamlessly and import each other's files easily, no matter which program you are using at the time. These capabilities make them more efficient and easier to use than using a variety of individual package versions.

Of course, putting so many programs and features together in one super-size package does have some disadvantages. Industry critics argue that many software suite features are never used by most end users. The suites take up a lot of disk space, from over 100 megabytes to over 150 megabytes, depending on which version or functions you install. So such software is sometimes derisively called *bloatware* by its critics. The cost of suites can vary from as low as $100 for a competitive upgrade to over $700 for a full version of some editions of the suites.

These drawbacks are one reason for the continued use of **integrated packages** like Microsoft Works, Lotus eSuite WorkPlace, AppleWorks, and so on. Integrated packages combine some of the functions of several programs—word processing, spreadsheets, presentation graphics, database management, and so on—into one software package.

Because Works programs leave out many features and functions that are in individual packages and software suites, they cannot do as much as those packages do. However, they use a lot less disk space (less than 10 megabytes), cost less than a hundred dollars, and are frequently pre-installed on many low-end microcomputer systems. So integrated packages have proven that they offer enough functions and features for many computer users, while providing some of the advantages of software suites in a smaller package.

Web Browsers and More

The most important software component for many computer users today is the once simple and limited, but now powerful and feature-rich, **Web browser.** A browser like Netscape Navigator or Microsoft Explorer is the key software interface you use

FIGURE 14.4
Using the Microsoft
Internet Explorer Web
browser to access the
pcworld.com website.

Source: Courtesy of PC World.

to point and click your way through the hyperlinked resources of the World Wide Web and the rest of the Internet, as well as corporate intranets and extranets. Once limited to surfing the Web, browsers are becoming the universal software platform on which end users launch into information searches, e-mail, multimedia file transfer, discussion groups, and many other Internet, intranet, and extranet applications. See Figure 14.4.

Industry experts are predicting that the Web browser will be the model for how most people will use networked computers in the future. So now, whether you want to watch a video, make a phone call, download some software, hold a videoconference, check your e-mail, or work on a spreadsheet of your team's business plan, you can use your browser to launch and host such applications. That's why browsers are being called the *universal client*, that is, the software component installed on all of the networked computing and communications devices of the clients (users) throughout an enterprise.

Electronic Mail and Instant Messaging

The first thing many people do at work all over the world is check their e-mail. **Electronic mail** has changed the way people work and communicate. Millions of end users now depend on e-mail software to communicate with each other by sending and receiving electronic messages and file attachments via the Internet or their organizations' intranets or extranets. E-mail is stored on network servers until you are ready. Whenever you want to, you can read your e-mail by displaying it on your workstations. So, with only a few minutes of effort (and a few microseconds or minutes of transmission time), a message to one or many individuals can be composed, sent, and received. See Figure 14.5.

As we mentioned earlier, e-mail software is now a component of top software suites and Web browsers. Free e-mail packages like Microsoft HotMail and Netscape WebMail are available to Internet users from online services and Internet service providers. Most e-mail software like Microsoft Outlook Express or Netscape Messenger can route messages to multiple end users based on predefined mailing lists and provide password security, automatic message forwarding, and remote user

FIGURE 14.5

Using the Microsoft
Outlook e-mail package.

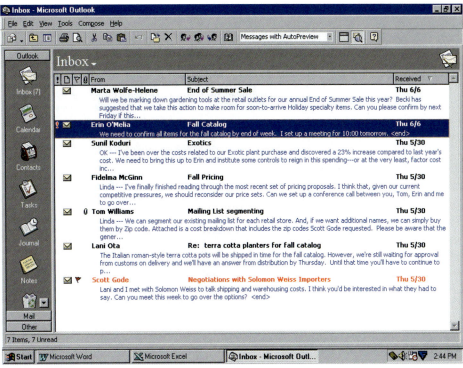

Source: Courtesy of Microsoft Corporation.

access. They also allow you to store messages in folders and make it easy to add document and Web file attachments to e-mail messages. E-mail packages also enable you to edit and send graphics and multimedia files as well as text, and provide computer conferencing capabilities. Finally, your e-mail software may automatically filter and sort incoming messages (even news items from online services) and route them to appropriate user mailboxes and folders.

Instant messaging (IM) is an e-mail/computer conferencing hybrid technology that has grown so rapidly that it has become a standard method of electronic messaging for millions of Internet users worldwide. By using instant messaging, groups of business professionals or friends and associates can send and receive electronic messages instantly, and thus communicate and collaborate in real time in a near-conversational mode. Messages pop up instantly in an IM window on the computer screens of everyone who is part of your business workgroup or circle of friends who are members of your IM "buddy list," if they are online, no matter what other tasks they are working on at that moment. Instant messaging software can be downloaded and IM services implemented by subscribing to many popular IM systems, including AOL's Instant Messenger and ICQ, MSN Messenger, and Yahoo Messenger.

Word Processing and Desktop Publishing

Software for **word processing** has transformed the process of writing. Word processing packages computerize the creation, editing, revision, and printing of *documents* (such as letters, memos, and reports) by electronically processing your *text data* (words, phrases, sentences, and paragraphs). Top word processing packages like Microsoft Word, Lotus WordPro, and Corel WordPerfect can provide a wide variety of attractively printed documents with their desktop publishing capabilities. These packages can also convert all documents to HTML format for publication as Web pages on corporate intranets or the World Wide Web.

Word processing packages also provide advanced features. For example, a spelling checker capability can identify and correct spelling errors, and a thesaurus feature helps you find a better choice of words to express ideas. You can also identify

FIGURE 14.6
Using the Microsoft Word
word processing package.
Note the insertion of a table
in the document.

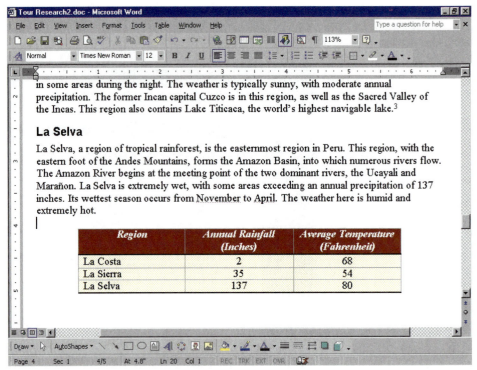

Source: Courtesy of Microsoft Corporation.

and correct grammar and punctuation errors, as well as suggest possible improvements in your writing style, with grammar and style checker functions. Another text productivity tool is an idea processor or outliner function. It helps you organize and outline your thoughts before you prepare a document or develop a presentation. Besides converting documents to HTML format, you can also use the top packages to design and create Web pages from scratch for an Internet or intranet website. See Figure 14.6.

End users and organizations can use **desktop publishing** (DTP) software to produce their own printed materials that look professionally published. That is, they can design and print their own newsletters, brochures, manuals, and books with several type styles, graphics, photos, and colors on each page. Word processing packages and desktop publishing packages like Adobe PageMaker and QuarkXPress are used to do desktop publishing. Typically, text material and graphics can be generated by word processing and graphics packages and imported as text and graphics files. Optical scanners may be used to input text and graphics from printed material. You can also use files of *clip art*, which are predrawn graphic illustrations provided by the software package or available from other sources.

The heart of desktop publishing is a page design process called *page makeup* or *page composition*. Your video screen becomes an electronic pasteup board with rulers, column guides, and other page design aids. Text material and illustrations are then merged into the page format you design. The software will automatically move excess text to another column or page and help size and place illustrations and headings. Most DTP packages provide WYSIWYG (What You See Is What You Get) displays so you can see exactly what the finished document will look like before it is printed.

Electronic Spreadsheets

Electronic spreadsheet packages like Lotus 1-2-3, Microsoft Excel, and Corel QuattroPro are used for business analysis, planning, and modeling. They help you develop an *electronic spreadsheet*, which is a worksheet of rows and columns that can be stored on your PC or a network server, or converted to HTML format and stored

FIGURE 14.7

Using an electronic spreadsheet package, Microsoft Excel. Note the use of graphics.

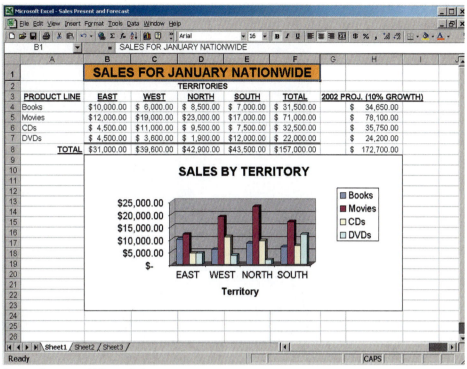

Source: Courtesy of Microsoft Corporation.

as a Web page or *websheet* on the World Wide Web. Developing a spreadsheet involves designing its format and developing the relationships (formulas) that will be used in the worksheet. In response to your input, the computer performs necessary calculations based on the formulas you defined in the spreadsheet, and displays results immediately, whether at your workstation or website. Most packages also help you develop graphic displays of spreadsheet results. See Figure 14.7.

For example, you could develop a spreadsheet to record and analyze past and present advertising performance for a business. You could also develop hyperlinks to a similar websheet at your marketing team's intranet website. Now you have a decision support tool to help you answer *what-if questions* you may have about advertising. For example, "What would happen to market share if advertising expense increased by 10 percent?" To answer this question, you would simply change the advertising expense formula on the advertising performance worksheet you developed. The computer would recalculate the affected figures, producing new market share figures and graphics. You would then have a better insight on the effect of advertising decisions on market share. Then you could share this insight with a note on the websheet at your team's intranet website.

Database Management

Microcomputer versions of **database management** programs have become so popular that they are now viewed as general-purpose application software packages like word processing and spreadsheet packages. Database management packages such as Microsoft Access, Lotus Approach, or Corel Paradox allow you to set up and manage databases on your PC, network server, or the World Wide Web. See Figure 14.8. Most database managers can perform several basic tasks, which we discussed in Chapter 3.

- **Database development.** Define and organize the content, relationships, and structure of the data needed to build a database, including any hyperlinks to data on Web pages.

FIGURE 14.8

Using a database management package. Note how Microsoft Access can organize a variety of database management tasks.

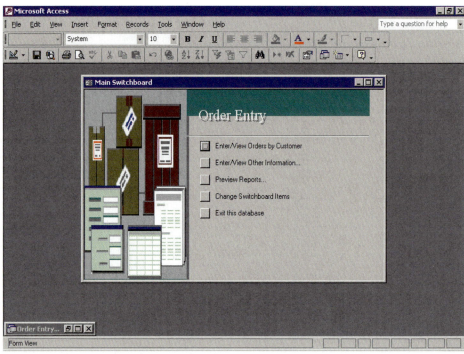

Source: Courtesy of Microsoft Corporation.

- **Database interrogation.** Access the data in a database to display information in a variety of formats. End users can selectively retrieve and display information and produce forms, reports, and other documents, including Web pages.
- **Database maintenance.** Add, delete, update, and correct the data in a database, including hyperlinked data on Web pages.
- **Application development.** Develop prototypes of Web pages, queries, forms, reports, and labels for a proposed business application. Use a built-in application generator to program the application.

Presentation Graphics

Which type of display would you rather see: columns or rows of numbers, or a graphics display of the same information? **Presentation graphics** packages help you convert numeric data into graphics displays such as line charts, bar graphs, pie charts, and many other types of graphics. Most of the top packages also help you prepare multimedia presentations of graphics, photos, animation, and video clips, including publishing to the World Wide Web. Not only are graphics and multimedia displays easier to comprehend and communicate than numeric data but multiple-color and multiple-media displays also can more easily emphasize key points, strategic differences, and important trends in the data. Presentation graphics has proved to be much more effective than tabular presentations of numeric data for reporting and communicating in advertising media, management reports, or other business presentations. See Figure 14.9.

Presentation graphics software packages like Microsoft PowerPoint, Lotus Freelance, or Corel Presentations give you many easy-to-use capabilities that encourage the use of graphics presentations. For example, most packages help you design and manage computer-generated and -orchestrated *slide shows* containing many integrated graphics and multimedia displays. Or you can select from a variety of predesigned *templates* of business presentations, prepare and edit the outline and notes for a presentation, and manage the use of multimedia files of graphics, photos,

FIGURE 14.9

Using the slide preview feature of a presentation graphics package, Microsoft PowerPoint.

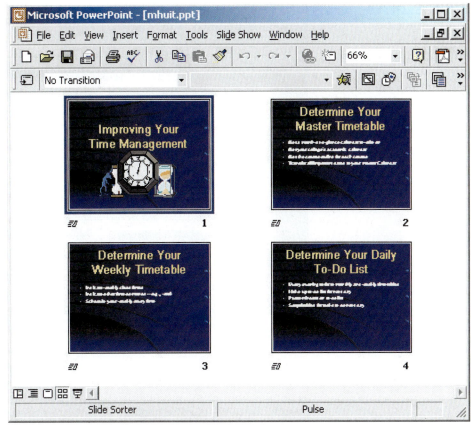

Source: Courtesy of Microsoft Corporation.

sounds, and video clips. And of course, the top packages help you tailor your graphics and multimedia presentation for transfer in HTML format to websites on corporate intranets or the World Wide Web.

Personal Information Managers

The **personal information manager** (PIM) is a popular software package for end user productivity and collaboration, and is a popular application for personal digital assistant (PDA) hand-held devices. PIMs such as Lotus Organizer and Microsoft Outlook help end users store, organize, and retrieve information about customers, clients, and prospects, or schedule and manage appointments, meetings, and tasks. The PIM package will organize data you enter and retrieve information in a variety of forms, depending on the style and structure of the PIM and the information you want. For example, information can be retrieved as an electronic calendar or list of appointments, meetings, or other things to do; the timetable for a project; or a display of key facts and financial data about customers, clients, or sales prospects. See Figure 14.10.

Personal information managers are sold as independent programs or are included in software suites, and vary widely in their style, structure, and features. For example, Lotus Organizer uses a notebook with tabs format, while Microsoft Outlook organizes data about people as a continuous A–to–Z list. Most PIMs emphasize the maintenance of *contact lists*, that is, customers, clients, or prospects. Scheduling appointments and meetings and task management are other top PIM applications. PIMs are now changing to include the ability to access the World Wide Web and provide e-mail capability. Also, some PIMs use Internet and e-mail features to support team collaboration by sharing information such as contact lists, task lists, and schedules with other networked PIM users.

FIGURE 14.10

Using a personal information manager (PIM): Microsoft Outlook.

Source: Courtesy of Microsoft Corporation.

Groupware

Groupware is *collaboration software*, that is, software that helps workgroups and teams work together to accomplish group assignments. Groupware is a fast-growing category of general-purpose application software that combines a variety of software features and functions to facilitate collaboration. For example, groupware products like Lotus Notes, Novell GroupWise, Microsoft Exchange, and Netscape Communicator support collaboration through electronic mail, discussion groups and databases, scheduling, task management, data, audio and videoconferencing, and so on. See Figure 14.11.

FIGURE 14.11

Lotus Notes is the leading corporate groupware package.

Source: Courtesy of IBM Lotus Software.

FIGURE 14.12

Some of the major application software categories used in business.

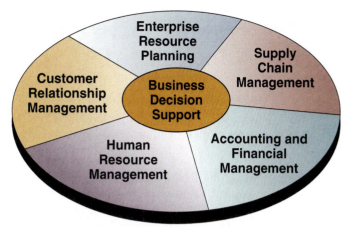

Source: Adapted from Ravi Kalakota and Marcia Robinson, *E-business: Roadmap for Success* (Reading, MA: Addison-Wesley, 2001), p. 243. © 2001 Addison-Wesley Publishing Company, Inc. Reprinted by permission of Addison-Wesley Longman Inc.

Groupware products are changing in several ways to meet the demand for better tools for collaboration. Groupware is now designed to use the Internet and corporate intranets and extranets to make collaboration possible on a global scale by *virtual teams* located anywhere in the world. For example, team members might use the Internet for global e-mail, project discussion forums, and joint Web page development. Or they might use corporate intranets to publish project news and progress reports, and work jointly on documents stored on Web servers.

Collaborative capabilities are also being added to other software to give them groupware features. For example, in the Microsoft Office software suite, Microsoft Word keeps track of who made revisions to each document, Excel tracks all changes made to a spreadsheet, and Outlook lets you keep track of tasks you delegate to other team members.

Other Business Software

As we mentioned earlier, there are many other types of application software used in business today. Application software packages support managerial and operational uses such as accounting, transaction processing, customer relationship management, enterprise resource planning, data warehousing and data mining, and electronic commerce, to name a few that are discussed in this text.

For example, data warehousing and data mining are discussed in Chapters 3 and 8; accounting, marketing, manufacturing, human resource management, and financial management applications are covered in Chapter 5; customer relationship management, enterprise resource planning, and supply chain management are the topics in Chapter 6; and electronic commerce is the focus of Chapter 7. Decision support and data analysis applications are explored in Chapter 8. Figure 14.12 illustrates some of these major application software categories.

SECTION II	# System Software: Computer System Management

System Software Overview

System software consists of programs that manage and support a computer system and its information processing activities. For example, operating systems and network management programs serve as a vital *software interface* between computer networks and hardware and the application programs of end users.

Analyzing Amazon, Orbitz, and Others

Read the Real World Case on Amazon, Orbitz, and Others on the next page. We can learn a lot about the business value of competitive developments in system software from this example. See Figure 14.13.

The business case for Linux is compelling. The companies in this case tell a powerful story of dramatic cuts in costs and gains in efficiency after switching to the Linux operating system running on generic Intel microprocessor servers. In some cases, like that of Amazon and E*Trade, the huge cost savings over their previous proprietary Sun/Unix systems has been a major factor in helping these companies move from operating losses to profitability. Other companies in the case also emphasize the big cost savings and gains in processing power and speed and ease of maintenance of switching from proprietary hardware and software to Linux on Intel-based systems.

Overview

Figure 14.14 shows that we can group system software into two major categories:

- **System management programs.** Programs that manage the hardware, software, network, and data resources of computer systems during the execution of the various information processing jobs of users. Examples of important system management programs are operating systems, network management programs, database management systems, and system utilities.

- **System development programs.** Programs that help users develop information system programs and procedures and prepare user programs for computer processing. Major software development programs are programming language translators and editors, and a variety of CASE (computer-aided software engineering) and other programming tools.

Operating Systems

The most important system software package for any computer is its operating system. An **operating system** is an integrated system of programs that manages the operations of the CPU, controls the input/output and storage resources and activities of the computer system, and provides various support services as the computer executes the application programs of users.

FIGURE 14.13

Mike Prince is CIO of Burlington Coat Factory, which has standardized on the Linux operating system for its IT operations.

Source: Andrew Kist.

REAL WORLD CASE 2

Amazon, Orbitz, and Others: The Business Case for Linux

When Amazon.com was considering converting to Linux early last year, says Jacob Levanon, Amazon's head systems engineer, "we had a lot of skeptics." Their concern: The company had built its business by giving customers a great purchasing experience, and here was a project that could blow that up overnight.

But Amazon (www.amazon.com) couldn't resist Linux's power as a money saver. "We didn't have a choice," Levanon says. "When we looked at our IT costs, we realized we couldn't sustain our growth with our existing infrastructure." Translation: If Amazon ever hoped to become profitable, it needed to convert. So in the space of 120 frenzied days in the summer of 2001, with its team's daily schedule broken down into one-minute increments, Amazon replaced 92 percent of its servers—about 2,000 Sun machines running Unix—with about the same number of Intel-based servers running the Linux operating system.

Levanon says the hardware and software savings are nice, but what has really made the conversion compelling is that his labor costs are down 10 to 20 percent. Linux has become the main operating system used in university computer science classes at places like Berkeley, Stanford, and Cornell. That means Linux programmers are more plentiful and cheaper to hire than ever. In all, technology costs at Amazon were down 16 percent, or $21.5 million, for the six months ending July 30, 2002.

The displacement of expensive proprietary systems with commodity hardware and software is not a new story in the computer business. But the big muscle corporate market has largely resisted the cut-rate model. That's because the computers that run the back ends of corporate networks—the websites, the databases, the e-mail, accounting, human resources, and production systems—must be not only fast but also as reliable as a telephone and as secure as a bank. Until recently it seemed that the only way to get all that was with specially tuned systems consisting of proprietary hardware and software. Such systems cost more, but corporations willingly paid the price because they had no alternative. Intel-based servers weren't fast enough, and the main operating system written for them, Microsoft Windows, wasn't reliable.

Today Intel machines are often faster than the proprietary systems from the three big vendors (HP, IBM, and Sun), and with Linux, the systems are just as reliable. "It's a sea change," says Bridget O'Connor, a top technology executive at Lehman Brothers (www.lehman.com) investment bankers. "Now I can play all the vendors off against each other to get the price I want. I never had that negotiating power when all my machines came from Sun." Mike Prince, the CIO at Burlington Coat Factory (www.burlingtoncoat.com) in Burlington, New Jersey, says he's been able to save so much money switching his systems to Linux—the software is free and the Intel-based hardware costs a fraction of what his old proprietary systems did—that he thinks he'll be able to cut his IT budget voluntarily in coming years.

Chicago-based Orbitz Inc. (www.orbitz.com) is also sold on the cost savings and enhanced processing power and speed afforded by the Linux/Intel combination. Now the transaction-intensive online travel reservation company is going a step further with Linux by replacing its 50 Sun Microsystems Java application servers running the Solaris Unix operating system. These heavy-lifting systems feed the company's 700 Web servers—already running Linux—which dish up the screens customers interact with when they make airline, hotel, and vacation reservations online.

Orbitz benchmarked several vendors' latest operations systems including Linux on Intel servers, and the results were compelling. "To maintain the same capacity in terms of the number of users on our site, we were able to move from the Unix servers to the Linux systems for about one-tenth the cost," says Roger Liew, vice president of technology development. "We also increased the speed in moving into a more efficient hardware and software environment," adds Liew, referring to the faster response times of the Intel environment. As for the Web servers, Liew especially appreciates Linux's ease of maintenance, which requires a single administrator for the 700 machines. "Everything is automated. It's probably one of the most reliable aspects of our system," he says.

For some companies, the gains from converting to Linux are so large that CIOs get giddy talking about it. Take E*Trade Financial (www.etrade.com). Three years ago it paid $12 million for 60 Sun machines to run its online trading website. CIO Josh Levine has just finished replacing those machines with 80 Intel-based servers running Linux for a mere $320,000. That has let E*Trade bring its tech budget down 30 percent, from $330 million in 2000 to $200 million in 2002—a big reason the company has stayed alive despite the carnage in its business. "It's remarkable," he says. "On top of all that, website response time has improved by 30 percent."

Case Study Questions

1. What are the business and technical benefits of switching from proprietary systems to Linux on Intel-based servers?

2. Why can Linux make a strategic difference in the profitability of some companies? Use companies from this case as examples.

3. What are the limitations of Linux for business use? Visit the Linux website (www.linux.com) for background information to help you answer.

Source: Adapted from Connie Winkler, "Zero Purchase Price, But . . . ," *Computerworld*, September 23, 2002, pp. 42–44. Reprinted with permission from *Computerworld*; Fred Vogelstein, "Servers with a Smile," *Fortune*, September 30, 2002, pp. 195–206; and "Finding Silver Linings in the Tech Bust," *Fortune*, October 14, 2002, pp. 151–154. © 2002 Time Inc. All rights reserved.

FIGURE 14.14

The system and application software interface between end users and computer hardware.

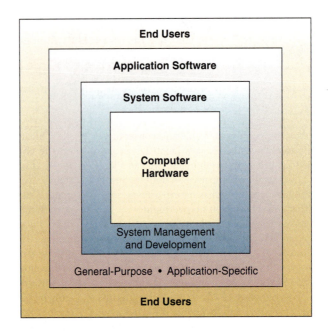

The primary purpose of an operating system is to maximize the productivity of a computer system by operating it in the most efficient manner. An operating system minimizes the amount of human intervention required during processing. It helps your application programs perform common operations such as accessing a network, entering data, saving and retrieving files, and printing or displaying output. If you have any hands-on experience on a computer, you know that the operating system must be loaded and activated before you can accomplish other tasks. This emphasizes the fact that operating systems are the most indispensable components of the software interface between users and the hardware of their computer systems.

Operating System Functions

An operating system performs five basic functions in the operation of a computer system: providing a user interface, resource management, task management, file management, and utilities and support services. See Figure 14.15.

The User Interface. The **user interface** is the part of the operating system that allows you to communicate with it so you can load programs, access files, and accomplish other tasks. Three main types of user interfaces are the *command-driven*, *menu-driven*, and *graphical user interfaces*. The trend in user interfaces for operating systems

FIGURE 14.15

The basic functions of an operating system include a user interface, resource management, task management, file management, and utilities and other functions.

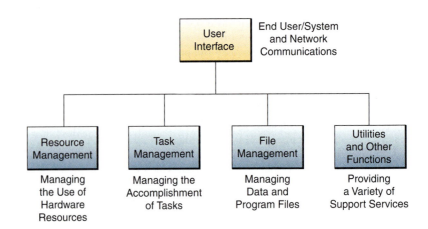

FIGURE 14.16

The graphical user interface of Microsoft's Windows XP operating system.

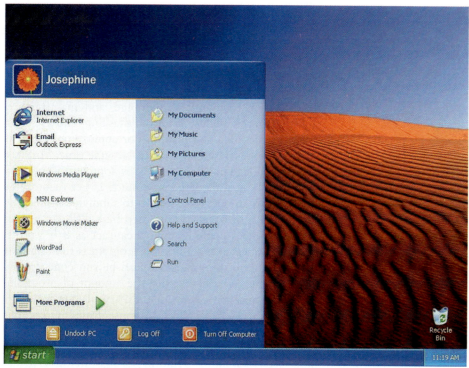

Source: Courtesy of Microsoft Corporation.

and other software is moving away from the entry of brief end user commands, or even the selection of choices from menus of options. Instead, most software provides an easy-to-use **graphical user interface** (GUI) that uses icons, bars, buttons, boxes, and other images. GUIs rely on pointing devices like the electronic mouse or touchpad to make selections that help you get things done. See Figure 14.16.

Resource Management. An operating system uses a variety of **resource management** programs to manage the hardware and networking resources of a computer system, including its CPU, memory, secondary storage devices, telecommunications processors, and input/output peripherals. For example, memory management programs keep track of where data and programs are stored. They may also subdivide memory into a number of sections and swap parts of programs and data between memory and magnetic disks or other secondary storage devices. This can provide a computer system with a **virtual memory** capability that is significantly larger than the real memory capacity of its primary storage circuits. So, a computer with a virtual memory capability can process large programs and greater amounts of data than the capacity of its memory chips would normally allow.

File Management. An operating system contains **file management** programs that control the creation, deletion, and access of files of data and programs. File management also involves keeping track of the physical location of files on magnetic disks and other secondary storage devices. So operating systems maintain directories of information about the location and characteristics of files stored on a computer system's secondary storage devices.

Task Management. The **task management** programs of an operating system manage the accomplishment of the computing tasks of end users. They give each task a slice of a CPU's time and interrupt the CPU operations to substitute other tasks. Task management may involve a **multitasking** capability where several computing tasks can occur at the same time. Multitasking may take the form of *multiprogramming*, where the CPU can process the tasks of several programs at the same time, or *timesharing*, where the computing tasks of several users can be processed at the same time. The efficiency of multitasking operations depends on the processing power of a CPU and the virtual memory and multitasking capabilities of the operating system it uses.

Most microcomputer, midrange, and mainframe operating systems provide a multitasking capability. With multitasking, end users can do two or more operations (e.g., keyboarding and printing) or applications (e.g., word processing and financial analysis) concurrently, that is, at the same time. Multitasking on microcomputers has also been made possible by the development of more powerful microprocessors and their ability to directly address much larger memory capacities (up to 4 gigabytes). This allows an operating system to subdivide primary storage into several large partitions, each of which can be used by a different application program.

In effect, a single computer can act as if it were several computers, or *virtual machines*, since each application program is running independently at the same time. The number of programs that can be run concurrently depends on the amount of memory that is available and the amount of processing each job demands. That's because a microprocessor (or CPU) can become overloaded with too many jobs and provide unacceptably slow response times. However, if memory and processing capacities are adequate, multitasking allows end users to easily switch from one application to another, share data files among applications, and process some applications in a *background* mode. Typically, background tasks include large printing jobs, extensive mathematical computation, or unattended telecommunications sessions.

Popular Operating Systems

Figure 14.17 compares four of the top operating systems today [3]. For many years, MS-DOS (Microsoft Disk Operating System) was the most widely used microcomputer operating system. It is a single-user, single-tasking operating system, but was given a graphical user interface and limited multitasking capabilities by combining it with Microsoft **Windows.** Microsoft began replacing its DOS/Windows combination in 1995 with the Windows 95 operating system, featuring a graphical user

FIGURE 14.17   A comparison of popular operating systems.

Windows 2000 *Microsoft*	Solaris 8 UNIX *Sun Microsystems*
Strengths. It is inexpensive. Used with servers based on Intel microprocessors, it's about one-third as expensive as UNIX-based combos from the likes of Sun.	**Strengths.** Solaris is the server operating system of choice for large websites. It's super-reliable and handles the most demanding tasks.
Weaknesses. Still not accepted for most powerful servers, since many computer systems administrators don't trust it for complex computing tasks.	**Weaknesses.** It is more expensive than Windows 2000 systems, though Sun is now offering Solaris free on low-end Sun servers.
Netware 5.1 *Novell*	Linux 6.1 *Red Hat Software*
Strengths. The directory software for keeping track of computers, programs, and people on a network has proved vital to companies such as Ford and Wal-Mart.	**Strengths.** Red Hat taps into tens of thousands of volunteer programmers who help out with improvements to the open-source Linux operating system. Plus, Red Hat's server package is nearly free: $149.
Weaknesses. NetWare is primarily a networking system—not able to run general applications such as databases or accounting.	**Weaknesses.** Linux is good for serving up Web pages and other tasks, but isn't as effective as Solaris at handling more complex jobs.

interface, true multitasking, networking, multimedia, and many other capabilities. Microsoft introduced an enhanced Windows 98 version during 1998, and a Windows ME (Millennium Edition) consumer PC system in 2000, with Windows XP consumer and professional versions released in 2001.

Microsoft introduced its Windows NT (New Technology) operating system in 1995. Windows NT is a powerful, multitasking, multiuser operating system that is installed on many network servers to manage client/server networks and on PCs with high-performance computing requirements. New Server and Workstation versions were introduced in 1997. Microsoft merged its Windows 98 and Windows NT products into the Windows 2000 operating system during the year 2000.

Windows 2000 has four versions, including:

- *Professional:* a full-featured operating system for PC desktops and laptops.
- *Server:* a multipurpose operating system for network servers and Web servers in smaller networks.
- *Advanced Server:* a network operating system to manage large networks and websites powered by *server farms* of many servers.
- *Datacenter Server:* a high-performance network operating system for large-scale business applications, such as online transaction processing and data warehousing.

Originally developed by AT&T, **UNIX** now is also offered by other vendors, including Solaris by Sun Microsystems and AIX by IBM. UNIX is a multitasking, multiuser, network-managing operating system whose portability allows it to run on mainframes, midrange computers, and microcomputers. UNIX is a popular choice for Web and other network servers.

Linux is a low-cost, powerful, and reliable UNIX-like operating system that is rapidly gaining market share as a high-performance operating system for network servers and Web servers in both small and large networks. Linux was developed as free or low-cost *shareware* or *open-source software* over the Internet in the 1990s by Linus Torvald of Finland and millions of programmers around the world. Linux is still being enhanced in this way, but is sold with extra features and support services by software vendors such as Red Hat, Caldera, and VA Linux. PC versions are also available, which support office software suites, Web browsers, and other application software.

The **Mac OS X** is the latest operating system from Apple for the iMac and other Macintosh microcomputers. The Mac OS X has a new graphical user interface as well as advanced multitasking and multimedia capabilities, along with a new suite of Internet services called iTools [9].

Network Management Programs

Today's information systems rely heavily on the Internet, intranets, extranets, local area networks, and other telecommunications networks to interconnect end user workstations, network servers, and other computer systems. This requires a variety of system software for **network management,** including **network operating systems,** network performance monitors, telecommunications monitors, and so on. These programs are used by network servers and other computers in a network to manage network performance. Network management programs perform such functions as automatically checking client PCs and video terminals for input/output activity, assigning priorities to data communications requests from clients and terminals, and detecting and correcting transmission errors and other network problems. In addition, some network management programs function as *middleware* to help diverse networks communicate with each other. See Figure 14.18.

Examples of network management programs include Novell NetWare, the most widely used network operating system for complex interconnected local area networks. Microsoft's Windows NT Server and its new Windows 2000 server versions are other popular network operating systems. IBM's telecommunications monitor

FIGURE 14.18
A display of a network
management program.

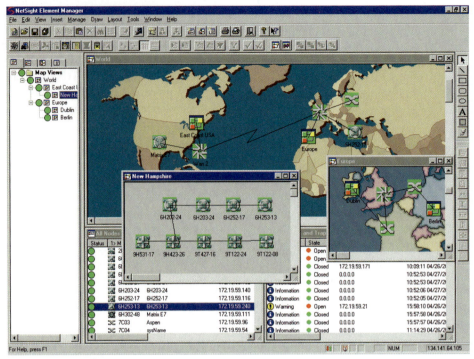

Source: Courtesy of Avnet.

CICS (Customer Identification and Control System) is an example of a widely used *telecommunications monitor* for mainframe-based wide area networks. IBM's NetView and Hewlett-Packard's OpenView are examples of network management programs for managing several mainframe-based or midrange-based computer networks.

Database Management Systems

In Section I, we discussed microcomputer database management programs like Microsoft Access, Lotus Approach, and Corel Paradox. In mainframe and midrange computer systems, a **database management system** (DBMS) is considered an important system software package that controls the development, use, and maintenance of the databases of computer-using organizations. A DBMS program helps organizations use their integrated collections of data records and files known as databases. It allows different user application programs to easily access the same database. For example, a DBMS makes it easy for an employee database to be accessed by payroll, employee benefits, and other human resource programs. A DBMS also simplifies the process of retrieving information from databases in the form of displays and reports. Instead of having to write computer programs to extract information, end users can ask simple questions in a *query language*. Thus, many DBMS packages provide *fourth-generation languages* (4GLs) and other application development features. Examples of popular mainframe and midrange packages are IBM's DB2 Universal Database and Oracle 11i by Oracle Corporation. We discussed such database management software in Chapter 3.

Other System Management Programs

Several other types of system management software are marketed as separate programs or are included as part of an operating system. Utility programs, or **utilities,** are an important example. Programs like Norton Utilities perform miscellaneous housekeeping and file conversion functions. Examples include data backup, data recovery, virus protection, data compression, and file defragmentation. Most operating systems also provide many utilities that perform a variety of helpful chores for computer users. See Figure 14.19.

FIGURE 14.19

Norton SystemWorks is a top suite of PC system utility programs.

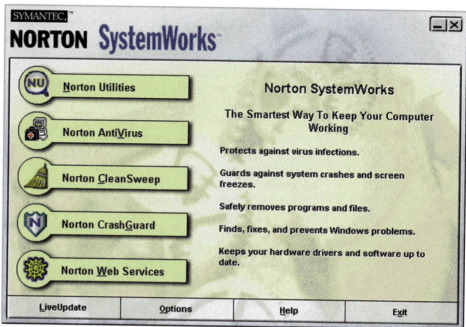

Source: Courtesy of Symantec.

Other examples of system support programs include performance monitors and security monitors. **Performance monitors** are programs that monitor and adjust the performance and usage of one or more computer systems to keep them running efficiently. **Security monitors** are packages that monitor and control the use of computer systems and provide warning messages and record evidence of unauthorized use of computer resources. A recent trend is to merge both types of programs into operating systems like Microsoft's Windows 2000 Datacenter Server, or into system management software like Computer Associates' CA-Unicenter, which can manage both mainframe systems and servers in a data center.

Another important software trend is the use of system software known as **application servers,** which provide a *middleware* interface between an operating system and the application programs of users. For example, application servers like BEA's WebLogic and IBM's WebSphere help Web-based e-business and e-commerce applications run much faster and more efficiently on computers using Windows, UNIX, and other operating systems.

| **TravelNow: Converting to an Application Server** | When Chris Kuhn became the chief information officer at TravelNow, he realized that the online travel agency's website was headed for expensive trouble. Hotel and airline bookings had been growing rapidly and showed no signs of slowing. He knew the site would start crashing if he didn't expand its capacity. Until recently that would have meant buying additional Web server hardware, networking those machines together, and hiring more employees to manage it all. But Kuhn decided to try another, potentially far less costly route: an application server, a software technology that promised to greatly expand the site's capacity—without buying any new machines or enlarging the staff—and add lots of flexibility in the bargain.

Application servers essentially make a website's important work—running search engines, verifying a user's credit-card number, serving up news articles, and so forth—much faster and more efficient. An application server amounts to a layer of software inserted between a server's operating system (Windows, Linux, Sun's |

Solaris, IBM's zOS, or another) and all those search engines and credit-card verifiers. It handles the heavy demands of serving up Web pages, accessing databases, and hooking into back-office servers. Think of it as a kind of automatic transmission for your e-business; a super agile intermediary between your website's applications and the raw power of the server's CPU and operating system.

Another nice thing about an application server is that it greatly simplifies the procedure for adding new functions to your website. Most application servers use Sun's Java programming language, and unlike older programs written for a specific set of hardware and software, Java programs can work unchanged on almost any system. So if you suddenly realize that your website needs a function that, say, allows customers to see their previous purchases, adding that function is a matter of simply dropping in a bit of code.

Off-the-shelf applications written in Java—content management software and personalization routines, for example—can easily be added to the collection of software on your application server. And most of these servers run on multiple hardware and software configurations, so moving from low-end Windows or Linux machines to higher powered Unix servers doesn't require a painful process of "porting," or rewriting, all of your code.

So it should come as no surprise that TravelNow's Kuhn eventually settled on BEA's WebLogic Server, which cost about $90,000 but allowed him to reduce his hardware from 22 servers to just three. There was a catch: It took almost six months to rewrite the site's applications in Java, with consulting fees of more than $500,000. But now that his programmers can add new functions and rewrite old ones much more easily than before, Kuhn doesn't expect to go through another rewrite anytime soon. He's glad he made the switch to an application server. "Our growth rate has been faster and harder than all the other years combined," he says. "There's no way the old system could have handled it" [12].

Programming Languages

To understand computer software, you need a basic knowledge of the role that programming languages play in the development of computer programs. A **programming language** allows a programmer to develop the sets of instructions that constitute a computer program. Many different programming languages have been developed, each with its own unique vocabulary, grammar, and uses.

Machine Languages

Machine languages (or *first-generation languages*) are the most basic level of programming languages. In the early stages of computer development, all program instructions had to be written using binary codes unique to each computer. This type of programming involves the difficult task of writing instructions in the form of strings of binary digits (ones and zeros) or other number systems. Programmers must have a detailed knowledge of the internal operations of the specific type of CPU they are using. They must write long series of detailed instructions to accomplish even simple processing tasks. Programming in machine language requires specifying the storage locations for every instruction and item of data used. Instructions must be included for every switch and indicator used by the program. These requirements make machine language programming a difficult and error-prone task. A machine language program to add two numbers together in the CPU of a specific computer and store the result might take the form shown in Figure 14.20.

Assembler Languages

Assembler languages (or *second-generation languages*) are the next level of programming languages. They were developed to reduce the difficulties in writing machine language programs. The use of assembler languages requires language translator programs called *assemblers* that allow a computer to convert the instructions

FIGURE 14.20

Examples of four levels of programming languages. These programming language instructions might be used to compute the sum of two numbers as expressed by the formula X = Y + Z.

Four Levels of Programming Languages	
● **Machine Languages:** Use binary coded instructions 1010 11001 1011 11010 1100 11011	● **High-Level Languages:** Use brief statements or arithmetic notations BASIC: X = Y + Z COBOL: COMPUTE X = Y + Z
● **Assembler Languages:** Use symbolic coded instructions LOD Y ADD Z STR X	● **Fourth-Generation Languages:** Use natural and nonprocedural statements SUM THE FOLLOWING NUMBERS

of such language into machine instructions. Assembler languages are frequently called symbolic languages because symbols are used to represent operation codes and storage locations. Convenient alphabetic abbreviations called *mnemonics* (memory aids) and other symbols represent operation codes, storage locations, and data elements. For example, the computation X = Y + Z in an assembler language might take the form shown in Figure 14.20.

Assembler languages are still used as a method of programming a computer in a machine-oriented language. Most computer manufacturers provide an assembler language that reflects the unique machine language instruction set of a particular line of computers. This feature is particularly desirable to *system programmers*, who program system software (as opposed to application programmers, who program application software), since it provides them with greater control and flexibility in designing a program for a particular computer. They can then produce more efficient software, that is, programs that require a minimum of instructions, storage, and CPU time to perform a specific processing assignment.

High-Level Languages

High-level languages (or *third-generation languages*) use instructions, which are called *statements*, that use brief statements or arithmetic expressions. Individual high-level language statements are actually *macroinstructions;* that is, each individual statement generates several machine instructions when translated into machine language by high-level language translator programs called *compilers* or *interpreters*. High-level language statements resemble the phrases or mathematical expressions required to express the problem or procedure being programmed. The *syntax* (vocabulary, punctuation, and grammatical rules) and the *semantics* (meanings) of such statements do not reflect the internal code of any particular computer. For example, the computation X = Y + Z would be programmed in the high-level languages of BASIC and COBOL as shown in Figure 14.20.

A high-level language is easier to learn and program than an assembler language, since it has less-rigid rules, forms, and syntaxes. However, high-level language programs are usually less efficient than assembler language programs and require a greater amount of computer time for translation into machine instructions. Since most high-level languages are machine independent, programs written in a high-level language do not have to be reprogrammed when a new computer is installed, and programmers do not have to learn a different language for each type of computer. Figure 14.21 highlights some of the major high-level languages still being used in some form today.

Fourth-Generation Languages

The term **fourth-generation language** describes a variety of programming languages that are more nonprocedural and conversational than prior languages. These languages are called fourth-generation languages (4GLs) to differentiate them from machine languages (first generation), assembler languages (second generation), and high-level languages (third generation).

FIGURE 14.21
Highlights of several important high-level languages.

High-Level Programming Languages
Ada: Named after Augusta Ada Byron, considered the world's first computer programmer. Developed for the U.S. Department of Defense as a standard "high-order language" to replace COBOL and FORTRAN.
BASIC: (Beginner's All-Purpose Symbolic Instruction Code). A simple procedure-oriented language designed for end user programming.
C: A mid-level structured language developed as part of the UNIX operating system. It resembles a machine-independent assembler language.
COBOL: (COmmon Business Oriented Language). An Englishlike language widely used for programming business applications.
FORTRAN: (FORmula TRANslation). A high-level language designed for scientific and engineering applications.
Pascal: Named after Blaise Pascal. Developed specifically to incorporate structured programming concepts.

Most fourth-generation languages are **nonprocedural languages** that encourage users and programmers to specify the results they want, while the computer determines the sequence of instructions that will accomplish those results. Thus, fourth-generation languages have helped simplify the programming process. **Natural languages** are 4GLs that are very close to English or other human languages. Research and development activity in artificial intelligence (AI) is developing programming languages that are as easy to use as ordinary conversation in one's native tongue. For example, INTELLECT, a natural language 4GL, would use a statement like, "What are the average exam scores in MIS 200?" to program a simple average exam score task.

The ease of use of 4GLs is gained at the expense of some loss in flexibility. It is frequently difficult to override some of the prespecified formats or procedures of 4GLs. Also, the machine language code generated by a program developed by a 4GL is frequently much less efficient (in terms of processing speed and amount of storage capacity needed) than a program written in a language like COBOL. Thus, some large transaction processing applications programmed in a 4GL have not provided reasonable response times when faced with a large amount of real-time transaction processing and end user inquiries. However, 4GLs have shown great success in business applications that do not have a high volume of transaction processing.

Object-Oriented Languages

Object-oriented programming (OOP) languages like Visual Basic, C++, and Java have become major tools of software development. Briefly, while most other programming languages separate data elements from the procedures or actions that will be performed upon them, OOP languages tie them together into **objects.** Thus, an object consists of data and the actions that can be performed on the data. For example, an object could be a set of data about a bank customer's savings account, and the operations (such as interest calculations) that might be performed upon the data. Or an object could be data in graphic form such as a video display window, plus the display actions that might be used upon it. See Figure 14.22.

In procedural languages, a program consists of procedures to perform actions on each data element. However, in object-oriented systems, objects tell other objects to perform actions on themselves. For example, to open a window on a computer video display, a beginning menu object could send a window object a message to open and a window will appear on the screen. That's because the window object contains the program code for opening itself.

FIGURE 14.22

An example of a bank savings account object. This object consists of data about a customer's account balance and the basic operations that can be performed on those data.

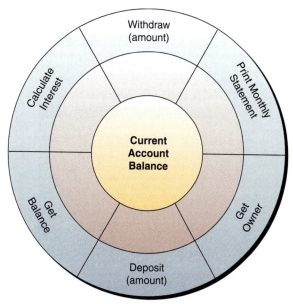

Savings Account Object

Object-oriented languages are easier to use and more efficient for programming the graphics-oriented user interfaces required by many applications. Also, once objects are programmed, they are reusable. Therefore, reusability of objects is a major benefit of object-oriented programming. For example, programmers can construct a user interface for a new program by assembling standard objects such as windows, bars, boxes, buttons, and icons. Therefore, most object-oriented programming packages provide a GUI that supports a "point and click," "drag and drop" visual assembly of objects known as *visual programming*. Figure 14.23 shows a display of the Visual Basic object-oriented programming environment. Object-oriented technology is discussed further in the coverage of object-oriented databases in Chapter 3.

HTML, XML, and Java

HTML, XML, and Java are three programming languages that are important tools for building multimedia Web pages, websites, and Web-based applications.

HTML (Hypertext Markup Language) is a page description language that creates hypertext or hypermedia documents. HTML inserts control codes within a document at points you can specify that create links *(hyperlinks)* to other parts of the document or to other documents anywhere on the World Wide Web. HTML embeds control codes in the ASCII text of a document that designate titles, headings, graphics, and multimedia components, as well as hyperlinks within the document.

As we mentioned earlier, several of the programs in the top software suites will automatically convert documents into HTML formats. These include Web browsers, word processing and spreadsheet programs, database managers, and presentation graphics packages. These and other specialized *Web publishing* programs like Microsoft FrontPage and Lotus FastSite provide a range of features to help you design and create multimedia Web pages without formal HTML programming.

XML (eXtensible Markup Language) is not a Web page format description language like HTML. Instead, XML describes the contents of Web pages by applying identifying tags or *contextual labels* to the data in Web documents. For example, a travel agency Web page with airline names and flight times would use hidden XML tags like "airline name" and "flight time" to categorize each of the airline flight times on that page. Or product inventory data available at a website could be labeled with tags like "brand," "price," and "size." By classifying data in this way, XML makes website information a lot more searchable, sortable, and easier to analyze.

FIGURE 14.23   The Visual Basic object-oriented programming environment.

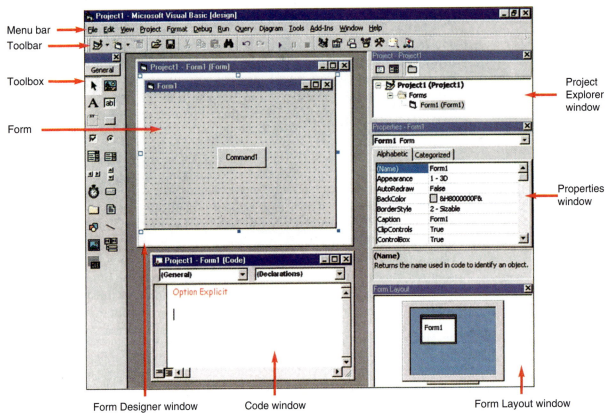

Menu bar
Toolbar
Toolbox
Form
Project Explorer window
Properties window
Form Designer window
Code window
Form Layout window

Source: Courtesy of Microsoft Corporation.

For example, XML-enabled search software could easily find the exact product you specify if the product data at a website had been labeled with identifying XML tags. And a website that used XML could more easily determine what Web page features its customers used and what products they investigated. Thus XML promises to make electronic commerce a lot easier and more efficient by supporting the automatic electronic exchange of business data between companies and their customers, suppliers, and other business partners [5].

Java is an object-oriented programming language created by Sun Microsystems that is revolutionizing the programming of applications for the World Wide Web and corporate intranets and extranets. Java is related to the C++ and Objective C programming languages, but is much simpler and secure, and is computing platform independent. Java is also specifically designed for real-time, interactive, Web-based network applications. So Java applications consisting of small application programs, called *applets*, can be executed by any computer and any operating system anywhere in a network.

The ease of creating Java applets and distributing them from network servers to client PCs and network computers is a major reason for Java's popularity. Applets can be small special-purpose application programs or small modules of larger application programs. Applets can reside at websites on a network server until needed by client systems, and are easy to distribute over the Internet or intranets and extranets. Applets are platform independent too—they can run on Windows, UNIX, and Macintosh systems without modification. Java continues to improve its speed of execution (which has been a major limitation), and thus is becoming the alternative to Microsoft's Active X language for many organizations intent on capitalizing on the business potential of the Internet, as well as their own intranets and extranets [11].

| Fidelity Investments: Converting to XML | Fidelity Investments completed a retrofit during October 2001 of its corporate data to an XML format in an effort that has already allowed it to eliminate a significant amount of hardware, proprietary databases, and Web and transactional protocols.

XML has become an important software development language as more and more companies, big and small, want to link both internal and external data sources and applications for use on their websites. These same companies will then need XML to help integrate the resulting data flows with their back office applications, says Payet Guillermo, president and CTO of the Ocean Group IT consulting firm in Santa Cruz, California.

But XML has a dark side, posing a new set of security vulnerabilities, which XML standards bodies and proponents like Microsoft and IBM are still working to solve. The powerful capabilities of XML data sets and dynamic links open up a whole new security can of worms because the code defined by XML could carry virtually any payload unchecked through a firewall. "Just as there are a bunch of hackers that use malformed HTML and Java to crash your browser or take control of your machine, we'll probably see the same types of attacks aimed at XML software engines and the applications using XML data," says Guillermo.

Two years ago, Fidelity started looking for a way to simplify communications between consumer Web applications and back-end systems. During the past decade, the Boston-based mutual funds giant had installed a plethora of proprietary messaging formats, remote procedure calls, interfaces, and commercial middleware applications, such as Sybase Enterprise Connect, to support its various e-commerce and e-business iniatives. By using XML as its core communications connection to translate data among its website, its UNIX and Windows NT servers, and its back-office mainframes, Fidelity was able to eliminate a glut of translation protocols and message buffers and 75 of its 85 midtier network servers.

Bill Stangel, XML team leader and an enterprise architect at Fidelity, said a common language has also allowed the company's IT managers to redeploy programmers who were tied up writing interfaces to work on more important business functions. The conversion should also improve time to market for applications, he said. "It's simplified our environment significantly," Stangel said. "Instead of us having to invent our own messaging, we can now use XML as the common language."

Getting the project off the ground was difficult, said Stangel, "but once the culture kicked in, we didn't have to explain why XML is a good thing. People picked up on it and realized if we can reduce the complexity of our systems, we can have a real competitive advantage [6]." |

Programming Software

A variety of software packages are available to help programmers develop computer programs. For example, *programming language translators* are programs that translate other programs into machine language instruction codes that computers can execute. Other software packages, such as programming language editors, are called *programming tools* because they help programmers write programs by providing a variety of program creation and editing capabilities. See Figure 14.24.

Language Translator Programs

Computer programs consist of sets of instructions written in programming languages that must be translated by a **language translator** into the computer's own machine language before they can be processed, or executed, by the CPU. Programming language translator programs (or *language processors*) are known by a variety of names. An **assembler** translates the symbolic instruction codes of programs written in an assembler language into machine language instructions, while a **compiler** translates high-level language statements.

FIGURE 14.24

Using the graphical programming interface of a Java programming tool, Forte for Java, by Sun Microsystems.

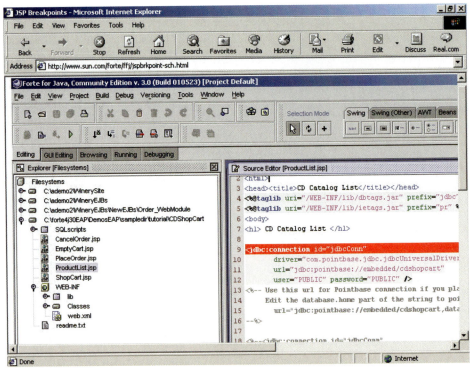

Source: Courtesy of Sun Microsystems.

An **interpreter** is a special type of compiler that translates and executes each statement in a program one at a time, instead of first producing a complete machine language program, as compilers and assemblers do. Java is an example of an interpreted language. Thus, the program instructions in Java applets are interpreted and executed *on-the-fly* as the applet is being executed by a client PC.

Programming Tools

Software development and the computer programming process have been enhanced by adding *graphical programming interfaces* and a variety of built-in development capabilities. Language translators have always provided some editing and diagnostic capabilities to identify programming errors or *bugs*. However, most software development programs now include powerful graphics-oriented *programming editors* and *debuggers*. These programmining tools help programmers identify and minimize errors while they are programming. Such programming tools provide a computer-aided programming *environment* or *workbench*. This decreases the drudgery of programming while increasing the efficiency and productivity of software developers. Other programming tools include diagramming packages, code generators, libraries of reusable objects and program code, and prototyping tools. Many of these tools may be part of the toolkit provided by *computer-aided software engineering* (CASE) packages.

Summary

- **Software.** Computer software consists of two major types of programs: (1) application software that directs the performance of a particular use, or application, of computers to meet the information processing needs of users, and (2) system software that controls and supports the operations of a computer system as it performs various information processing tasks. Refer to Figure 14.2 for an overview of the major types of software.

- **Application Software.** Application software includes a variety of programs that can be segregated into general-purpose and application-specific categories. General-purpose application programs perform common information processing jobs for end users. Examples are word processing, electronic spreadsheet, database management, telecommunications, and presentation graphics programs. Application-specific programs accomplish information processing tasks that support specific business functions or processes, scientific or engineering applications, and other computer applications in society.

- **System Software.** System software can be subdivided into system management programs and system development programs. System management programs manage the hardware, software, network, and data resources of a computer system during its execution of information processing jobs. Examples of system management programs are operating systems, network management programs, database management systems, system utilities, performance monitors, and security monitors. Network management programs support and manage telecommunications activities and network performance telecommunications networks. Database management systems control the development, integration, and maintenance of databases. Utilities are programs that

  perform routine computing functions, such as backing up data or copying files, as part of an operating system or as a separate package. System development programs help IS specialists and end users develop computer programs and information system procedures. Major development programs are language translators, programming editors, and other programming tools.

- **Operating Systems.** An operating system is an integrated system of programs that supervises the operation of the CPU, controls the input/output storage functions of the computer system, and provides various support services. An operating system performs five basic functions: (1) a user interface for system and network communications with users, (2) resource management for managing the hardware resources of a computer system, (3) file management for managing files of data and programs, (4) task management for managing the tasks a computer must accomplish, and (5) utilities and other functions that provide miscellaneous support services.

- **Programming Languages.** Programming languages are a major category of system software. They require the use of a variety of programming packages to help programmers develop computer programs, and language translator programs to convert programming language instructions into machine language instruction codes. The five major levels of programming languages are machine languages, assembler languages, high-level languages, fourth-generation languages, and object-oriented languages. Object-oriented languages like Java and special-purpose languages like HTML and XML are being widely used for Web-based business applications.

Key Terms and Concepts

These are the key terms and concepts of this chapter. The page number of their first explanation is given in parentheses.

1. Application server (515)
2. Application software (496)
3. Application-specific programs (498)
4. Assembler language (516)
5. Database management software (503)
6. Desktop publishing (502)
7. Electronic mail (500)
8. Electronic spreadsheet software (502)
9. File management (511)
10. Fourth-generation language (517)
11. General-purpose application programs (498)
12. Graphical user interface (499)
13. Groupware (506)
14. High-level language (517)
15. HTML (519)
16. Instant messaging (501)
17. Integrated package (499)
18. Java (520)
19. Language translator program (521)
20. Machine language (516)
21. Multitasking (511)
22. Natural language (518)
23. Network management programs (513)
24. Network operating systems (513)
25. Nonprocedural language (518)
26. Object-oriented language (518)
27. Operating system (508)
28. Personal information manager (505)

29. Presentation graphics software (504)

30. Programming tools (522)

31. Resource management (511)

32. Software suites (498)

33. System management programs (508)

34. System software (496)

35. Task management (511)

36. User interface (510)

37. Utility programs (514)

38. Virtual memory (511)

39. Web browser (499)

40. Word processing software (501)

Review Quiz

Match one of the previous key terms and concepts with one of the brief examples or definitions that follow. Try to find the best fit for answers that seem to fit more than one term or concept. Defend your choices.

_____ 1. Programs that manage and support the operations of computers.

_____ 2. Programs that direct the performance of a specific use of computers.

_____ 3. A system of programs that manages the operations of a computer system.

_____ 4. Managing the processing of tasks in a computer system.

_____ 5. Managing the use of CPU time, primary and secondary storage, telecommunications processors, and input/output devices.

_____ 6. Managing the input/output, storage, and retrieval of files.

_____ 7. The function that provides a means of communication between end users and an operating system.

_____ 8. The use of icons, bars, buttons, and other image displays to help you get things done.

_____ 9. Provides a greater memory capability than a computer's actual memory capacity.

_____ 10. Programs that manage and support the performance of networks.

_____ 11. Software that manages telecommunications in complex local area networks.

_____ 12. Manages and supports the maintenance and retrieval of data stored in databases.

_____ 13. Translates high-level instructions into machine language instructions.

_____ 14. Performs housekeeping chores for a computer system.

_____ 15. A category of application software that performs common information processing tasks for end users.

_____ 16. Software available for the specific applications of end users in business, science, and other fields.

_____ 17. Helps you surf the Web.

_____ 18. Use your networked computer to send and receive messages.

_____ 19. Creates and displays a worksheet for analysis.

_____ 20. Allows you to create and edit documents.

_____ 21. You can produce your own brochures and newsletters.

_____ 22. Helps you keep track of appointments and tasks.

_____ 23. A program that performs several general-purpose applications.

_____ 24. A combination of individual general-purpose application packages that work easily together.

_____ 25. Software to support the collaboration of teams and workgroups.

_____ 26. Uses instructions in the form of coded strings of ones and zeros.

_____ 27. Uses instructions consisting of symbols representing operation codes and storage locations.

_____ 28. Uses instructions in the form of brief statements or the standard notation of mathematics.

_____ 29. Might take the form of query languages and report generators.

_____ 30. Languages that tie together data and the actions that will be performed upon the data.

_____ 31. You don't have to tell the computer how to do something, just what result you want.

_____ 32. As easy to use as one's native tongue.

_____ 33. Includes programming editors, debuggers, and code generators.

_____ 34. Produces hyperlinked multimedia documents for the Web.

_____ 35. A popular object-oriented language for Web-based applications.

_____ 36. Middleware that helps Web-based application programs run faster and more efficiently.

_____ 37. Enables you to communicate and collaborate in real time with the online associates in your workgroup.

Discussion Questions

1. What major trends are occurring in software? What capabilities do you expect to see in future software packages?

2. How do the different roles of system software and application software affect you as a business end user? How do you see this changing in the future?

3. Refer to the Real World Case on Intuit Inc. in the chapter. Do you agree with CEO Bennett's strategy to have Intuit compete with Microsoft in the software market for larger small businesses? Why or why not?

4. Why is an operating system necessary? That is, why can't an end user just load an application program in a computer and start computing?

5. Should a Web browser be integrated into an operating system? Why or why not?

6. Refer to the Real World Case on Amazon, Orbitz, and Others in the chapter. Should most companies investigate the use of Linux for their businesses? Why or why not?

7. Are software suites, Web browsers, and groupware merging together? What are the implications for a business and its end users?

8. How are HTML, XML, and Java affecting business applications on the Web?

9. Do you think Windows 2000 and Linux will surpass Unix and Netware as operating systems for network and Web servers? Why or why not?

10. Which application software packages are the most important for a business end user to know how to use? Explain the reasons for your choices.

Application Exercises

Complete the following exercises as individual or group projects that apply chapter concepts to real world business situations.

1. **ABC Department Stores: Software Selection**
   ABC Department Stores would like to acquire software to do the following tasks. Identify what software packages they need.

   a. Surf the Web and their intranets and extranets.
   b. Send messages to each others' computer workstations.
   c. Help employees work together in teams.
   d. Use a group of productivity packages that work together easily.
   e. Help sales reps keep track of meetings and sales calls.
   f. Type correspondence and reports.
   g. Analyze rows and columns of sales figures.
   h. Develop a variety of graphical presentations.

2. **Evaluating Software Packages**
   Which of the software packages mentioned in this chapter have you used?

   a. Briefly describe the advantages and disadvantages of one of these packages.
   b. How would such a package help you in a present or future job situation?
   c. How would you improve the package you used?

3. **Tracking Project Work at AAA Systems**
   DB You are responsible for managing information systems development projects at AAA Systems. To better track progress in completing projects you have decided to maintain a simple database table to track the time your employees spend on various tasks and the projects with which they are associated. It will also allow you to keep track of employee billable hours each week. A sample set of data for this table is shown below.

   a. Build a database table to store the data shown below and enter the records shown as a set of sample data. (Note that this table has no natural unique

Project_Name	Task_Name	Employee_Id	Production_Week	Hours_worked
Fin-Goods-Inv	App. Devel.	456	21	40
Fin-Goods-Inv	DB Design	345	20	20
Fin-Goods-Inv	UI Design	234	20	16
HR	Analysis	234	21	24
HR	Analysis	456	20	48
HR	UI Design	123	20	8
HR	UI Design	123	21	40
HR	UI Design	234	21	32
Shipmt-Tracking	DB Design	345	20	24
Shipmt-Tracking	DB Design	345	21	16
Shipmt-Tracking	DB Development	345	21	20
Shipmt-Tracking	UI Design	123	20	32
Shipmt-Tracking	UI Design	234	20	24

identifier. A combination of the project name, task name, employee ID, and production week is required to uniquely identify a row in this table.

b. Create a query that will list the hours worked for all workers who worked more than 40 hours during production week 20.

c. Create a report grouped by project that will show the number of hours devoted to each task on the project and the total number of hours devoted to each project as well as a grand total of hours worked.

d. Create a report grouped by employee that will show their hours worked on each task and total hours worked. The user should be able to select a production week and have data for just that week presented.

4. Matching Training to Software Use

SS You have responsibility for managing software training for Sales, Accounting, and Operations Department workers in your organization. You have surveyed the workers to get a feel for the amount of time spent using various packages and the results are shown below. The values shown are the total number of workers in each department and the total weekly hours of use of each type of package. You have been asked to prepare a spreadsheet summarizing this data and comparing the use of the various packages across departments, and relating these data to the training data from the previous exercise.

a. Create a spreadsheet that will emphasize the average use and training per worker of each type of package and make it easy to compare the usage across departments. To do this you will first enter the data shown below. Next perform a query on the data of the previous application exercise to determine the total hours of training on each type of package for each department and add these results to your spreadsheet. Be sure to add overall use and training categories to show overall use and training across packages. Compute the average weekly use per worker by dividing hours by the number of workers in the department. Compute a similar figure for training hours by dividing by the number of workers and then dividing by 13 to convert the quarterly data to a weekly basis.

b. Create a set of graphs summarizing your results. Be sure to include a graph comparing training hours per package and usage hours per package in some way.

c. A committee has been formed to schedule future software training classes at your company. You have been asked to present the results of your analysis as a starting point for this committee's work. Using presentation software, produce a brief summary highlighting key results and including related spreadsheet pages and graphs needed to support your findings.

Department	Employees	Spreadsheet	Database	Presentation
Sales	225	410	1100	650
Operations	195	820	520	110
Accounting	235	1050	1225	190

Burlington Coat Factory and Others:
Evaluating Software Suite
Alternatives

Few IT managers knock the technology inside Microsoft's dominant Office suite, but quite a few are considering dumping it in light of recent licensing changes that in many cases increase their costs significantly. The question is, Are the alternatives to Office a good fit?

Products like Corel's WordPerfect Office and IBM's SmartSuite have long offered competitive upgrades. But the introduction of low-cost options such as gobeProductive ($124.95) from Gobe Software and StarOffice 6.0 ($75.95) from Sun Microsystems has some IT managers rethinking their office suite strategies. These cheaper alternatives have solved many of the compatibility issues that were once barriers to dropping Microsoft's core productivity programs: Word, Excel, and PowerPoint. And while technical hurdles remain between Microsoft Office and competing products, a growing number of IT managers have decided that the company's licensing and pricing policies, coupled with "good enough" application choices, make now as good a time as any to switch.

Tim Brennan, manager of store services at Burlington Coat Factory (www.burlingtoncoat.com) in Burlington, New Jersey, says the retailer has been running Sun's StarOffice 5.2 on 1,500 desktops throughout the company and is considering an upgrade to Version 6 to take advantage of its improved compatibility with Microsoft Office. Things have improved greatly in StarOffice 6.0, Brennan says. For example, you can open an Excel file, make changes, and save it by default as an Excel document, which isn't the case in 5.2.

Cam Scott, client support analyst for the city of Nanaimo (www.city.nanaimo.bc.ca) in British Columbia, Canada, is currently evaluating how to upgrade 400 desktops running Office 97. He says Microsoft's new licensing policies and the high costs of the software spurred him to look closely at StarOffice 6.0. The bottom line, Scott says, is that a StarOffice license costs about one-sixth the $579 costs of Microsoft Office Professional. But even that huge price gap doesn't make it an easy decision, because Microsoft Office's overwhelming control of the productivity software market makes the technical issues pervasive, if subtle.

Scott says StarOffice still lacks certain fundamentals. For example, StarOffice's StarBase can't handle the elaborate database applications the city has developed with Microsoft Access 2000. He says he's also disappointed that the software lacks a collaboration program such as Outlook. The latter issue can be handled by adding Evolution from Ximian Inc., says Scott. Evolution is an open-source software product that mimics Outlook's features. But using it means dealing with two companies when productivity software problems arise, Scott notes.

The real problem for the city of Nanaimo, according to Scott, is dealing with Microsoft Access. He says that about a dozen users require the Access-based applications and won't be able to migrate to StarOffice. That means he'll have to support two application suites. "Not an ideal situation, but workable considering the savings involved," he says.

Switching end users over to a new productivity suite also poses training problems. But it can have benefits, too, according to Dick From, IT manager at Puget Sound Financial Centers (www.psme.com). The Seattle-based financial services firm evaluated StarOffice as a replacement for Microsoft Office but found gobeProductive easier to set up and use. According to From, "The biggest negative is overcoming resistance to change, though this actually has a silver lining." That's because Puget Sound Financial used the swap as "an excellent opportunity to refresh word processing concepts, with many people learning new things they didn't know were possible irrespective of the word processing product," he says.

From adds that moving from Word to gobeProductive "may be even easier than going from one version of Word to another." However, the more proficient the user, the more difficult the training becomes. "The learning curve is steeper for people who create advanced spreadsheets, so the jury is still out on this," From says. So while he may need to support Excel for a handful of users, he says, "we're still money ahead."

But other factors may prompt users to switch from Office. For example, Brennan of Burlington Coat Factory says that what sold him on StarOffice was his company's multiplatform strategy. Burlington, which has Windows, Linux, and Solaris Unix installed on desktop PCs, has been saddled with using multiple Office suites. StarOffice 6.0, which runs on all three operating systems, will go a long way toward helping him manage the problem, Brennan says. "The big win for us is cross-platform support in StarOffice," Brennan says. "The cost savings were nice to have."

Case Study Questions

1. What is the business case for switching from Microsoft Office to alternatives like Sun StarOffice or gobeProductive?

2. What is the business case against such a switch?

3. What are several business or technical improvements the developers of Sun StarOffice or gobeProductive could make to better compete with Microsoft Office? Visit the www.sun.com/software/star and www.gobe.com websites of these products to help you answer.

Source: Adapted from Mark Hall, "Suite Deals," *Computerworld*, August 12, 2002, pp. 26–27. Reprinted with permission from *Computerworld*.

REAL WORLD CASE 4

Clark Retail and Others: Evaluating Operating System Upgrades

Consumers may be buying into Windows XP on new PCs, but they really don't have much choice—except of course for the Mac, most new PCs come with the latest version of Windows preinstalled inside. However, many corporate users are still putting off plans to migrate to Microsoft Corp.'s nearly one-year-old desktop operating system.

Even the early September 2002 release by Microsoft of the first "service pack" of bug fixes for XP—typically a signal for broader corporate adoption of Windows operating systems—was shrugged off by several IT managers. For example, a *Computerworld* poll of 25 Windows users in a wide range of industries found only four companies that are currently rolling out XP across their operations and four more that plan to start migrations in the coming months. Some users who are holding back on XP cited costs, the lack of a pressing business need, and recent Windows 2000 rollouts as factors in their decisions.

"We have not moved to XP, and we have no plans to. As far as I am concerned, this is an upgrade that offers nothing to a business customer," said Pat Enright, CIO at Clark Retail Enterprises Inc. (www.clarkretail.com), a convenience store chain in Oak Brook, Illinois. In particular, users that either have completed Windows 2000 projects or are now rolling it out said they see no reason to jump to Windows XP, which they view as an incremental release over Win 2K. "The cost is very high to upgrade, and there's not a lot of perceived value," said Rich Waugh, a technology architect at Telus Corp. (www.telus.com) in Burnaby, British Columbia.

Jim Cullinan, a lead product manager for Windows, said Microsoft is focusing on communicating the benefits of Windows XP to companies still running Windows NT, Windows 98, and Windows 95. Those benefits include improved stability and enhanced wireless and security management features, he said. "Most enterprise customers will have held to the tradition of waiting until Service Pack 1 to even look at it," Cullinan said. "IT spending has dried up, and it looks a little bit tighter. But IT spending should be on the rise in the coming months. We feel really good about where Windows XP is."

An April 2002 poll of 225 CIOs by Morgan Stanley showed that 60 percent of respondents had no plans to roll out Windows XP. That view has changed little since then, according to many of the IT pros interviewed recently by *Computerworld*. But Bill Lewkowski, CIO at Metropolitan Health Networks (www.metcare.com) in Grand Rapids, Michigan, saw a clear need for XP. Lewkowski said the vendors that make the applications his company runs will no longer be supporting Windows 95. "Since we held off on Windows 2000 for a while, we decided we might as well jump to the XP version," he said.

Navigant International Inc. (www.navigant.com), a travel services firm in Englewood, Colorado, is in the same boat. "Some of our critical software vendors skipped formal Windows 2000 support and leapfrogged with Windows 98 to Windows XP," said Navigant CIO Neville Teagarden. But more than half of the 25 companies surveyed recently said a majority of their end users still run Windows NT, Windows 98, or Windows 95. "We've been driven by what our vendors will support. So far, they will support Windows 98, so we stay with 98," said Bill Finefield, CIO at the Navy Exchange Service Command in Virginia Beach, Virginia.

Large companies face bigger obstacles to upgrading because of the sheer volume of PCs involved. For example, KeyCorp (www.key.com), a Cleveland-based financial services firm, has migrated 11,000 of its PC users to Windows 2000 with hopes of moving another 8,000 Windows NT 4.0 users and 1,500 Windows 95 users to Windows 2000 by the end of 2003. The company has no plans to change its decision to make Windows 2000 its corporate desktop standard, according to Jeff Glover, vice president and manager of Key-Corp's desktop systems group.

Andre Mendes, chief technology integration officer at Public Broadcasting Service (www.pbs.org) in Alexandria, Virginia, said he sees no need to move to XP, since Windows 2000 has been "unbelievably reliable" on his organization's 800 desktops. Its remote configuration and management features have also let him cut his help desk staff from five to two people, Mendes said.

Like other companies that have installed or are still rolling out Windows 2000 to their users, a move to Windows XP is a nonissue for PBS, given their satisfaction with the capabilities built into Windows 2000. The fact is, many corporate users bought Microsoft's sales pitch on the long-awaited, Windows NT-based, revolutionary improvements that would be built into Windows 2000. Now that they have installed or are still installing Windows 2000, they are in no mood to switch to what they view as marginal operating system improvements in Windows XP.

Case Study Questions

1. Why do many companies have no plans to switch to Windows XP?

2. What is a business case for switching to Windows XP?

3. What are several improvements you would like to see Microsoft make in the next version of Windows? Visit the Windows XP website at www.microsoft.com/windowsxp to help you answer.

Source: Adapted from Carol Sliwa, "Windows XP Slow to Gain Foothold," *Computerworld*, September 16, 2002, pp. 1, 65. Reprinted with permission from *Computerworld*.

Dollar Rent A Car and Imperial Sugar: Pioneering Web Services

Web services. The name alone is enough to induce fits of narcolepsy. But things get even worse when the experts try to explain what Web services actually do. Despite all the off-putting jargon and hype, however, Web services really are the future.

The term "Web services" is used to describe a collection of technologies—an alphabet soup of Web-based technical standards and communication protocols—such as XML, Universal Description Discovery and Integration (UDDI), and Simple Object Access Protocol (SOAP)—that link applications running on different computer platforms. Unlike present application integration approaches that require custom coding or expensive middleware to link individual applications, Web services aim to expose and link key functions within applications (such as the ability to see the balance in your checking account or to place an order from a factory) to other applications that need them to complete business processes.

Still confused? A few businesses have already started using Web services technology from BEA Systems, IBM, Microsoft, and others. Seeing it in action is probably the easiest way to understand what all this buzz is about.

Peter Osbourne, group manager of the advanced technology group at Dollar Rent A Car (www.dollar.com) in Tulsa, Oklahoma, is one of the first to successfully implement Web services using Microsoft's ".Net" technology. Osbourne built a system that lets travelers book car reservations with Dollar while buying tickets on the Southwest Airlines website. Instead of struggling to get Dollar's reservation system to share information with other companies' machines, Dollar used Microsoft's technology as an intermediary. Reservations from outside partners are translated into Web services protocols—which are then translated back into formats that Dollar's computers can understand.

The advantage of Web services is that they provide a standard way for Dollar's computers to talk to even more outsiders in the future. Osbourne has already used Microsoft's Web services to build direct machine-to-machine links to a small tour operator and a sprawling travel reservation system. He has also rolled out a wireless website for use on mobile phones and PDAs. Web services protocols are making all of this relatively easy to do, which in turn makes it more convenient for Dollar customers to reserve cars. "The potential for reuse was the real key for me," Osbourne says.

Imperial Sugar (www.imperialsugar.com), the largest sugar company in the United States, offers a more practical illustration of the path that many firms are likely to follow as they begin using Web services. In bankruptcy and forced to reduce IT spending, the Sugar Land, Texas, company wanted to streamline operations by providing customers with information about their orders over the Web. Imperial used Web services–compatible software from SilverStream to act as an "interpreter" between the Web and Imperial's enterprise computers. Imperial customers access a private website to request information about their orders, and the SilverStream

software translates those requests into commands that Imperial's aging order-management system can interpret. Responses from the system are then translated into XML and published on a Web page. This means that any customer with a browser can get real-time order information—data previously available only through Imperial customer service reps.

This is how most companies will start using Web services—not all at once, or under the best of circumstances, but by adopting Web services technologies one chunk at a time to get computer systems to share information. Imperial's Chief Information Officer George Muller taught his company's creaky old software to speak XML. Next he plans to make it easy for customers to enter orders via the Web. Before long he may also use Web services to exchange data more directly, so that information about sugar orders from Imperial can be transferred seamlessly into the manufacturing and logistics systems used by soda and candy makers.

Besides having to learn how to implement a complex new technology, security is the No. 1 factor keeping many IT managers from deploying Web services. The ease of integration provided by Web services also brings risks. When a Web service connects you to a business partner, you rely on that business partner to properly authenticate, or vouch for, the identity of users at their end of the transaction. That means an intruder who has gained access as a supplier, for example, could use that improper authentication to invade systems of the supplier's customers.

Security technologies that would solve such security concerns are still being developed. So for now, many IT managers are afraid to expose their Web services to the outside world until new security standards are firmly in place. These companies are deploying Web services only within their corporate firewalls. But other IT managers are now moving Web services beyond their firewalls, primarily to handle relatively low risk transactions, especially with trusted business partners.

Case Study Questions

1. What is the purpose and business value of Web services?

2. What is delaying the implementation of Web services at many companies?

3. What can companies do now to prepare to implement Web services? Visit the Web services websites of BEA (www.bea.com/products/webservices), IBM (www.ibm.com/solutions/webservices), and Microsoft (www.microsoft.com/webservices) to help you answer.

Source: Adapted from Brian Caulfield, "What the Heck Are Web Services?" *Business 2.0*, April 2002, pp. 106–108; Robert Scheier, "Safer Than You Think?" *Computerworld*, May 20, 2002, pp. 40–42; and Carol Sliwa, "IT Still Iffy on Web Services," *Computerworld*, November 11, 2002, pp. 1, 57.

APPENDIX

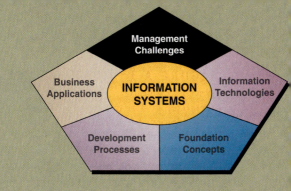

REAL WORLD CASE STUDIES

Introduction

This appendix contains the following five case studies:

- The Feld Group: Rescuing Failing IT Organizations
- Delta Airlines: From Failure to Success in Information Technology
- IBM Corporation: The Reinvention of an Information Technology Company
- Zara and Inditex: Using Information Technology for Competitive Advantage
- eBay Inc.: The Challenges of Online Marketplace Success

These real world cases describe the problems and opportunities in the business use of information technology confronted by a variety of business enterprises. They are based on real situations faced by actual organizations and are all designed to give you an opportunity to (1) integrate your knowledge of major information system concepts gained from reading and studying the text material, and (2) apply your knowledge to situations faced by real world business firms and other organizations.

Solving Case Studies

Several approaches can be used in analyzing cases. The simplest approach is to read the case and then try to find the answers to the questions at the end of each case study. This should give you a good exposure to the business and information system situations contained in the case. A more formal methodology is outlined in Figure A.1. Use this methodology to help you analyze a case study, develop an information system solution, and write up your results. Of course, you must first read the case, highlighting phrases or making notes that identify problems, opportunities, or other facts that may have a major bearing on your solution of the case.

Solution Constraints

The analysis you perform and the solution you develop with the methodology outlined in Figure A.1 will be limited by several major constraints. Being aware of these constraints will help you use this methodology more effectively. These constraints are:

- **Information.** The amount of data and information you can gather in a situation or find in case study material. Remember that in the real world, decisions usually have to be based on incomplete information.
- **Assumptions.** The number of assumptions you make or are allowed to make. Good, rational assumptions are a key ingredient in good solutions, since there is never enough information available in either real world situations or

FIGURE A.1

A systems solution methodology. Use this methodology to help you analyze an actual or case study situation, develop a solution, and write up your results.

A Systems Solution Methodology
1. Identification of problems, opportunities, and symptoms. Separate major problems or opportunities from their symptoms. Identify the major components of systems you feel are most involved in the problems or opportunities that you discover.
2. Statement of the problem. Briefly state the major problems or opportunities facing the organization.
3. Summary of alternative solutions. Briefly identify several alternative solutions to the problems you have identified.
4. Evaluation of alternative solutions. Evaluate the alternative solutions using evaluation criteria that reveal their advantages and disadvantages.
5. Rationale for the selected solution. Select the solution that best meets the evaluation criteria, and briefly explain the reasons for its selection.
6. Information system design proposal. Propose a design for any new or improved information systems required by the selected solution. Use one or more tools of analysis and design to illustrate your design proposal.
7. Implementation plan. Propose an implementation plan for the selected solution.

case studies. You should identify and explain the reasons for any major assumptions you make.

- **Knowledge.** The amount of knowledge about business and information systems you possess. Hopefully, this will increase as you cover more of this textbook and as you progress in your business education and career. For now, do the best you can with the knowledge you have.

- **Time.** The amount of time you spend on the analysis of the problem. Obviously, the more time you have, the more information you can gather, and the more analysis you can perform. Of course, time constraints are typical in the real world, so make judicious use of the time you have.

THE FELD GROUP:
RESCUING FAILING IT ORGANIZATIONS

Charlie, We Have a Problem

When Leo Mullin became CEO of Delta Air Lines (www.delta.com) in August 1997, he knew he had a technology problem, but he had no idea how bad it was. The company's IT department was in disarray. Delta was running 60 million lines of code across 30 technology platforms on more than 70 databases—all of which communicated as well as the Capulets and Montagues.

Mullin knew he had to act quickly, and he did. Today a quarter of the code and nearly half of the databases are gone, and every few weeks, yet another database disappears, folded into the Delta "nervous system." It manages a new flight every 39.3 seconds—about 2,200 flights a day—in real time: If there's a gate change, the news arrives simultaneously to gate agents, crews, baggage handlers, caterers, and even passengers via monitors or, in some cases, hand-held devices and phones. Ice-blue liquid-plasma screens hang over every Delta gate, continuously answering passengers' 20 most common questions about flight delays, standby and upgrade lists, and boarding status. Mullin looks like a hero.

And he may be one, but not because he figured out how to untangle Delta's out-of-control IT system. Mullin's smartest move was bringing in Charlie Feld—a high-tech smoke jumper.

The IT Smoke Jumper

Feld and his team, the Feld Group (www.feldgroup.com), are regularly called in to clean up tech disasters at some of America's biggest companies. Sometimes Feld becomes the interim chief information officer; sometimes he works alongside a CIO. He or a member of his group parachutes in with half a dozen experts who generally stay on-site for about two years. Their goal is to leave behind an overhauled tech infrastructure and a new management team that will keep the system running smoothly. "We're operations people, not consultants," says the 60-year-old Feld, who counts among his current clients Coca-Cola, Home Depot, and PricewaterhouseCoopers. See Figure A.2

Feld is the "CIO of CIOs," says Vivek Ranadive, CEO of Tibco Software, which makes applications that link corporate systems. "He has no agenda other than to do things right, to make technology strategic." That's hard. And the reason it's hard, Feld says, is that you have to keep it simple. "Technology hasn't been well led or well managed since 1964," Feld says. That's his way of saying it has *never* been well managed, ever since IBM's 360 series inaugurated the era of large-scale business computing 38 years ago.

Born in the Bronx in 1942, Feld studied economics at New York's City College. He then signed on at IBM, figuring himself for a salesman. After he aced a test for technical aptitude, however, IBM taught him systems engineering. By the 1970s, he was in Dallas, on the account of Frito-Lay, part of PepsiCo. As Feld tells it, "Every

FIGURE A.2
Charlie Feld leads the Feld Group team of IT turnaround specialists.

Source: Russell Monk.

couple of years, Frito-Lay would fire the CIO and ask me to take the job. Finally, in 1981, I said yes."

Fixing Frito-Lay

Company founder Herman Lay was 72 at the time. Though in bad health (he died the next year), Lay came to work a couple of half-days a week. Feld sat at the old man's feet, listening to his stories about selling potato chips out of his Model A Ford, about treating farmers right so they would return the favor by seeing that Lay always got spuds when they were scarce. In the early 1980s, critics mocked President Ronald Reagan's economic adviser, Michael Boskin, for saying that from an economic perspective there's no difference between potato chips and computer chips. Boskin never actually said that, but Feld says something like it: "Everything I learned about technology, I learned from Herman Lay. He was the e-man. He understood the new economy in the 1930s."

This is what Feld learned: "Herman said, 'The last time this business ran right was when I *was* the business—when I bought the potatoes, cooked the potatoes, delivered the chips, and collected the money. The physical running of the business was connected to the electronics of the business because it was all in my brain. I had perfect knowledge. I knew if I had cash, because I could feel it in my pocket. Over time the physical and the electronic moved so far apart that the people running this company don't know what's going on.'" Feld's job, Lay told him, was to wire them back together.

What followed became the stuff of legend—or, if not legend exactly, a stack of Harvard Business School case studies and a wall full of awards. Frito-Lay executives had PCs on their desks—in 1982. Feld equipped the 10,000-person field sales force with hand-held Fujitsu computers, which captured every sale in real time—in 1985.

The gadgetry wasn't the point, of course. The point was to reconnect muscle and mind. To this day most IT systems and departments operate on what Feld calls a service model: You ask, it answers. Ask CIOs for something and they'll buy or build it. Instead, Feld wants what he calls a publish-and-subscribe system, which continuously feeds real-time information to those who need it. And he likes IT management that behaves the same way, looking aggressively for opportunities instead of waiting for orders.

The results of that philosophy at Frito-Lay included a $40 million annual reduction in the amount of product the company had to take back because it went stale, a 40,000-hour drop in sales representatives' paperwork, and a revenue increase, between 1986 and 1989, from $3 billion to $4.2 billion. One piece at a time, Feld put together a system that he has been replicating and improving ever since.

By 1992, Frito-Lay was a three-star attraction on benchmarking tours. The PC revolution was in full swing. Reengineering was the rage. Companies were spending tens of millions of dollars to install huge enterprise resource planning (ERP) systems like those sold by SAP, hoping to integrate all their information needs on a single application. And history's greatest acquisition boom had begun, forcing incompatible systems to live under the same corporate roof. Coping with it all was a technologist's nightmare and an opportunity waiting to be grabbed. Feld hung out his shingle.

The Feld Group

At first the Feld Group consisted of Feld and a few PepsiCo colleagues. Now it's about 80 people, including support staff and code writers for proprietary products. At the center: two score seasoned execs operating in six or seven teams.

Diagnosing a company's technology problems is the easy part, Feld says. "We can spend a day and not say a word. We look at what's on desks, sit in a computer room for an hour, visit a store or a plant, and—like Poirot or Columbo—come back and tell you that you've got a service model, your apps are stovepiped, and your organization is locked in." Translation: If your business reorganizes anything, you'll seriously mess up your tech department.

Over the years, the group has been called to Coors Brewery, First Data Corp., Hewlett-Packard, Microsoft, and some companies associated with Feld's old haunts. Feld himself served as interim CIO of Burlington Northern Santa Fe Railway and presided over a number of other gigs, in addition to rewiring Delta. It hasn't always worked. Feld's ministrations couldn't save a food services company called AmeriServe from bankruptcy, for example. But his testimonials are legion and underscored by the fact that his old customers usually send him his new ones. See Figure A.3.

FIGURE A.3
The Feld Group has revitalized IT at many major corporations.

Company	A Portfolio of IT Turnarounds Problem
1. First Data Corp.	The biggest third-party processor of credit card transactions (317 million accounts) could no longer rely on its system built in the 1970s. The Feld Group converted it from batch-processing to online, real-time processing.
2. Burlington Northern Sante Fe Railway	When two of the biggest railroads in the United States merged in 1995, each of the companies had its own IT system. Feld migrated them to a new, combined system while keeping the trains running on time.
3. Delta	A failed joint venture left the airline with no IT department to speak of and systems that were convoluted, inefficient, and error-prone. Feld rebuilt the department and created a new system.
4. Westinghouse/CBS	Michael Jordan (Feld's boss at Frito-Lay) bought CBS and dismantled the old Westinghouse in the mid-1990s. Feld gave each piece a complete, viable information system.

The Five Dimensions Approach

The job of simplifying a company's information systems is almost always complex. Feld's team approaches the problem in five dimensions simultaneously.

The first dimension is understanding the company's business context—the strategic link between a business and its technology. That tie is often absent, because most business leaders can't talk tech and most tech leaders can't count except in base two. Feld calls it "the gap," and it drives him nuts. It explains why many companies with IT problems cry uncle and outsource the damn thing. To Feld, that's blaming the victim: "Usually it's the leadership that's the problem. Our model is to outsource the leadership."

Establishing a business context means drawing a picture (Feld's chalk talks are famous), showing executives how business and technology strategies connect. Mullin and the Delta team knew that they suffered from having too many different kinds of aircraft in their fleet. Feld showed them that they had the same problem in technology—and that it produced the same delays, costs, and inflexibility. When it was put that way, Delta's leaders got the picture.

Governance is another issue. Most of the time, Feld thinks, a decentralized IT operation is another form of abdication, like outsourcing. "You've got to stop letting everybody buy their own stuff," he insists. Otherwise, functional heads will overspend in fat years and underbuy in lean. Costs spin out of control; any long-range plan disappears. A big company needs just five or six major suppliers. One of the first things Feld did was put Delta's entire desktop business—46,000 computers—out to bid. Every three years, when the boxes have depreciated, Delta puts the contract up for bid again. Until then, it's one less headache.

The third and fourth pieces are the technology itself—applications software and the hardware it runs on. Failures of governance and context produce something every technology executive knows all too well—a Tower of Babel, full of fads and fossils. "This stuff doesn't go away unless you make it go away," Feld says. "You've got code from the '70s, '80s, and '90s. Vaxen [old Vax computers] are everywhere. And stuck in the middle of these busted pipes is a half-done ERP. It just runs HR and finance. You spent hundreds of millions of dollars and ended up with a new general ledger."

The Turnaround Project

You can't swing a wrecking ball at the tower, because you must operate the company while you fix it. The solution is enterprise application integration. Basically that's a technique for connecting different applications by building a layer of middleware that sends messages among them. Once the architecture is in place, you can go back and repair or replace junk. The turnaround trick is to get it built, and that requires finding a project big enough to engage the imagination of the tech organization, impress the CEO, and really affect customers.

At Burlington Northern Santa Fe, the business issue was a merger, the integration of two huge railroads. The company needed a single application to keep tabs on locomotives and cars as they moved from track that had been one company's to track that had been the other's. Only then could it use these assets more efficiently.

At Delta, where the problem was complexity run amok, the Trojan horse was a new gate-and-boarding application. "I wanted to force the issue with as many databases as I could," Feld says, and gate-and-boarding provided the opportunity. Sixty thousand employees see it. So do 100 million customers. It affects crews, baggage handlers, and maintenance staff, as well as gate agents, the reservation system, and the frequent-flier program. Before, each had its own data—"different versions of the truth," as Feld puts it. The gate-and-boarding application replaced them with a single set of data.

Turning around the IT Organization

The fifth and toughest job is improving the tech organization itself. Feld says, "My idea of a good time is to move people around." To do that he has to break managers of the idea that they "own" their people and help employees become comfortable moving around within large IT departments. Feld teaches them to recruit as a department; smart people are hired sometimes before there's a specific job for them and are placed only after the fact. Similarly, assessments and promotions involved the entire IT executive group. The goal is to identify and promote the best people while edging the worst toward the door. "We aren't Huns," he says.

But they are soldiers in a war that shows no signs of letting up. Tech problems plague companies more than ever, and there's a seemingly infinite supply of lousy leadership. Manufacturing executives bust their humps for minuscule productivity gains, while their tech departments are "operating at 70 percent of what they could be and not even caring about it," Feld says. "It's time this profession grew up." It all sounds so simple.

Case Study Questions

1. **The Feld Group's Mission**

   a. Why do large business organizations with large IT departments and many years of IT experience need the help of a company like the Feld Group?

   b. What is the goal of the Feld Group when called in to a company? Is this goal appropriate to the situations they usually face? Why or why not?

   c. Why can Charlie Feld say that diagnosing a company's IT problems is the easy part of his team's mission? Give several reasons this might be so.

2. **The Feld Group's Approach**

   a. Evaluate the Feld Group's five dimensions approach. Is it appropriate to the situations they usually face? Why or why not?

   b. What can be done about "the gap" that Feld sees in business/IT? Do you agree with him that outsourcing or decentralizing IT is not the way to solve the problem? Why or why not?

   c. Why do you think the Feld Group finds that many companies have a "Tower of Babel, full of fossils

and fads" in IT? What can be done to solve this problem in business?

3. **Turning around the IT Organization**

   a. Is the turnaround project used by the Feld Group a good turnaround device? Discuss its benefits and limitations.

   b. Why does Feld prefer a "publish and subscribe" model for IT in business, rather than the more usual "service model"? Discuss the issues involved and your position on Feld's view.

   c. Do you agree with how Feld likes to improve the IT organization in a company? Discuss its benefits and limitations.

   d. Feld says of IT: "Its time this profession grew up." Is this a fair assessment? Why or why not?

Source: Adapted from Thomas Stewart, "Techs Most Valued Temp," *Business 2.0*, August 2002, pp. 88–91. © 2002 Time Inc. All rights reserved.

DELTA AIRLINES:
FROM FAILURE TO SUCCESS IN INFORMATION TECHNOLOGY

The Airlines and IT

In a hangar next to the offices of Leo Mullin, chief executive of Delta Air Lines, Inc. (www.delta.com), there are two Delta planes that show the amazing progress that airplanes made between 1930 and 1940. From 1930, there is a five-passenger plane, with wicker seats, that closely resembles a cropduster. (The airline began as a cropdusting service in the Mississippi Delta, which is where it gets its name.) Close by, from 1940, is a huge, gleaming, silver bird, a DC 3 that is a recognizable member of the family of planes that are in service today.

In the interview that follows, Mullin demonstrates that the information systems used to operate airlines and the information technologies that power them are going through the same sort of fertile expansion that airplane technology experienced in the 1930s. The implications are important for passengers, employees, partners, and, of course, the airlines themselves, which must find ways to cut costs and innovate to survive the industry's hypercompetition and the steep fall in traffic caused by the weak economy and the terrorist attacks on September 11.

Mullin, who spent his career in banking and utilities before taking the top job at Delta almost five years ago, also describes how he used two "burning platforms" to change the airline from a technological laggard into a leader of its industry. See Figure A.4.

FIGURE A.4
CEO Leo Mullin has championed the strategic role of IT in the success of Delta.

Source: Ann States/SAPA/Corbis.

The Status of IT at Delta

Context: How did information technology become such a focus for innovation at Delta?

Leo Mullin: I joined Delta in August 1997, and I would say that I set technology as a priority within about two weeks. I went through a very fast educational process, not having come from the airline industry, so I was interviewing everybody who would speak to me, whether inside or outside the company. It became apparent that people felt Delta was a technology laggard.

The decision-making process for passengers had become highly oriented toward price. Airlines were no longer a "relationship" business, to use an old expression. Instead, airlines needed to be excellent in providing passengers with pricing options, which meant mastering technology. But Delta hadn't made the necessary investments.

The Role of Y2K

One of the best things that happened to Delta was that Y2K was on the horizon. To find out what our issues were regarding Y2K, I had a crucial meeting early on with Charlie Feld, who was a consultant at the time but soon became our chief information officer. Charlie told me, "You can't get there from here." Then he took me through the state of Delta technology. It was one of the worst reports on the status of a company's technology I've every heard.

Well, we had to get there from here; there was no way this airline was going to hit January 1, 2000, and not be able to fly. We had to transform this company technologically, and what we needed was a burning platform to get people to make the necessary leap. Y2K gave that to us.

I feel like if I had arrived in 1995, instead of the latter part of 1997, I wouldn't have been as effective in getting people to focus on technology because Y2K would have seemed too distant. But the timing was right.

The Role of Priceline

The other element that transformed us was Priceline.com Inc. Priceline was getting going during this period and needed a relationship with a major carrier to provide seats to sell. They got a cold shoulder from every other major carrier, but our marketing people talked to them because of our sense that online distribution was absolutely going to happen. There was a hot debate, which I participated in personally, about whether helping Priceline would reduce our higher-priced ticket sales and thereby actually reduce revenue. But we all made the determination to get on board.

Then our finance department did a terrific job of structuring a deal. We recognized that we were enabling Priceline to become a successful organization and, therefore, our compensation shouldn't be just in terms of ticket sales but also in equity in Priceline. The rest is history. We made an equity gain of nearly $1 billion from Priceline.

Even more than the financial success, the Priceline arrangement truly moved Delta to the forefront of the Internet world. To make Priceline go, we had to become educated about the Internet and be comfortable with it. All of a sudden, we were deeply in the game. We lucked out on the financial side, but we didn't just luck out in making the judgments that led to that deal, and that excited people. It really did. People thought, "We can do this stuff." Then everybody began to climb onto the bandwagon, and we had this very fertile intellectual environment, particularly where the Internet was concerned.

The Role of IT at Delta

As a result, the way we relate to customers is as good as it gets technologically. Now we generate roughly 20 percent of our passenger revenue from tickets sold online, which is far more efficient for us than other distribution channels. That percentage is growing dramatically. Even our interactions with travel agents are becoming much more effective because of technology. And we have designed products like the "Mind Your Own Business Travel" website (www.MYOBTravel.com), which offers professional travel-planning tools exclusively for small businesses that have not typically had the travel department or the technological expertise to relate to us.

Even in the current troubled economic times, we will spend approximately $600 million this year on information technology. I think Delta is as good as any airline now with respect to its technology. We've gone from being a technological laggard to a technological leader.

If an organization, in particular a large organization, is going to make a big change, such as our switch to being aggressive about technology, you have to have that burning platform, some message that really resonates and that will force change. We had two—Y2K and Priceline—and they both worked.

Context: You sound like as strong an advocate for information technology as any senior executive I've met in a long time.

Leo Mullin: When Jack Welch sat down with executives at General Electric, he might tell them they'd done a great job. But he'd spend five seconds on the congratulations. Then he'd say, "Because you've done such a great job, you get a chance to repeat your performance next year. How are you going to reduce your expenses by 5 percent and improve your competitive position by 5 percent at the same time?"

If you face a question like that—and lots of companies find themselves under that kind of pressure—you can't just tell your employees to work harder. In today's work, though, thank goodness, technology can let you make that sort of progress.

Delta Online

Context: You said that the online channels produce 20 percent of your sales. How big do you think that percentage can get over the next few years?

Leo Mullin: Our general feeling is around 40 percent, but it's tough to tell.

I'm a veteran of the automated teller machine wars because I ran retail banking at First Chicago NBD Corp. for 10 of my 15 years at the bank. There was a tremendous amount of discussion that began in the early 1980s and lasted seven or eight years about whether the machines would ever take off. The feeling was that the ceiling on usage would be 20 to 30 percent of customers. But then ATMs reached critical mass, and that percentage is probably somewhere between 70 and 80 percent today. Many people can't imagine life without ATMs.

So who knows whether 40 percent is the ceiling for online ticket purchases? In any case, we have a long distance to go and a lot of benefit to be gained.

IT and the Customer Experience

Context: Tell me more about how you're using technology to improve what customers experience.

Leo Mullin: Improving the travel experience for our customers is a constant focus. We know that passengers want fast, accurate information, especially during delays and cancellations. One of the basic things we are attempting to do is to contact customers very quickly when we have a problem. Our performance during Hurricane Floyd was a good example of this. Over a six-day span of difficult weather that affected 30 Delta cities and 25 percent of our operations, we contacted 78,000 affected passengers, and we let them know about changes an average of 12 hours in advance of their scheduled flight times.

In addition, we'll wake people up at 3 A.M. to tell them about delays on early morning flights. The phone calls probably scare the heck out of people, but they're glad to know that they have been rebooked on a flight departing at 9:30 A.M. and they don't have to hang around the airport because they arrived for the canceled 6:30 A.M. flight.

We're also trying to get much more information from our Operational Control Center into the hands of gate agents and passengers. Up until two years ago, there was no way to do that. Now, if you look at our Gate Information Display Screens, we provide a regular flow of information pertaining to flight status, current and forecasted weather in the destination city, and connecting flights. If there is a standby list, we show passengers where they rank and how many standby seats are available.

I like to tell this story:

I once got delayed on a Delta flight at LaGuardia Airport. The delay was initially two hours, then went to four, and ended up being seven hours. I went to the control tower to see what was going on and watched as the people there monitored the information flow concerning the weather, including extensive thunderstorms that were moving in jagged unpredictable patterns. Someone would say that they might be able to get flights going in half an hour, and then the storms would move in again.

In the gate area, you could see in the faces of the passengers on my flight that they didn't believe they were getting good information about what was going on. Well, there's no reason we can't put these weather delays on the screens at our gates, so people can see for themselves.

While I was at LaGuardia, I also observed how having authoritative information can make such a difference. A flight was unloading after passengers had been sitting on the plane for two hours, so I walked over to the gate to see how the situation was handled. You can imagine the looks on the passengers' faces as they gathered around the gate agents. The agents gave a pretty good explanation of what was going on. I'd rate their handling of the situation a B. Then something happened that changed the situation to an A. As the pilots walked off the plane, one of them stepped up to the microphone and said, "Ladies and gentlemen, we're really sorry that this has happened but let me tell you what's going on here." This pilot talked about what he, as a pilot, had to deal with and why the decision to unload the plane was completely appropriate and in their best interests. This pilot was so good that he transformed a negative situation into a positive one. People said, "We're really glad Delta is making decisions like this."

Overall, what passengers require is good information. Technology, along with personalized service, is an important tool in getting that information to the passengers.

IT and Delta's Employees

Context: How have your dealings with employees changed? In particular, what has been the effect of your decision to give every employee inexpensive access to a computer at home?

Leo Mullin: We have a large remote workforce. Approximately 9,500 pilots and 19,000 flight attendants never check into the office. There is no office. Yet they constantly have to get their assignments. They also need a way to get all of the basic employee and company information. So providing each employee with the opportunity to purchase a quality computer at an affordable price creates lots of benefits.

I also felt that, in terms of understanding the values of the Internet, people needed to experiment with it. If you don't have a computer, you're not going to use a computer.

The program has been a smashing success. We have a highly technologically educated workforce, and I think giving people access to computers enhanced our culture. We didn't start the program for this reason, but it was particularly beneficial for some folks in lower socioeconomic categories, who might not have had the money to buy a computer. I had a significant number of people come to me with tears in their eyes because their kids were going to be able to use a computer at home. Everyone has the same aspirations for their kids, and this program helped level the playing field.

Context: Do you feel this program contributed to the flight attendants' decision to remain nonunion?

Leo Mullin: Did the Wired Work Force program have anything to do with the fact that our flight attendants voted 71 to 29 percent to stay nonunion, in an industry that is totally unionized except for Delta? I don't know. But these things add up. People say we care about the employee, and I think technology has contributed to that feeling.

The Foundation for Success

Context: Has technology helped you work more efficiently with suppliers and partners?

Leo Mullin: It clearly has. For instance, we now share information automatically with our food-service vendors. You might think a long flight is going out with 50 passengers, but then a weather problem cancels the flight in front of it and all of a sudden your plane is jammed. You'd better have the right amount of food.

We're also using technology to do more competitive bidding and get the best price we can. We buy $7 billion of product every year, not including airplanes, so how we deal with suppliers is very important to the success of this airline.

Technology, more than anything else, is the foundation of future success for this industry. It's an extraordinarily competitive industry. With the existence of very strong discount carriers, we don't have a lot of pricing power. Yet employee costs have moved up dramatically. The margins have been squeezed, and this industry has been notoriously under-profitable. The crucial productivity improvements that are going to keep us moving ahead will rely on technology in every way—in relating to the customer, in relating to the employees, in relating to our suppliers.

Case Study Questions

1. **Changing IT at Delta**

   a. Why did Delta need something like Y2K to help change its IT operation?

   b. How did the investment in Priceline.com help change the state of IT at Delta?

   c. How do you rate Delta's leadership position in IT as claimed by CEO Leo Mullin after reading this case? Explain your evaluation.

2. **The Role of IT at Delta**

   a. Do you agree with Leo Mullin's position on the role of IT at Delta and for the airline industry? Why or why not?

   b. Visit the websites of Delta mentioned in this case. How do you rate them in terms of Delta's online performance? Explain your evaluation.

   c. How is IT helping to improve the customer experience at Delta? How do you rate their performance? Explain your evaluation.

3. **The Future of IT at Delta**

   a. Do you agree with the way Delta is using IT to improve its relationship with its employees? What else could they do? Explain your positions.

   b. How can Delta use IT to deal more efficiently with its suppliers and other business partners?

   c. How else could Delta use information technology to improve air travel for its customers? Explain the business and customer value of your proposals.

Source: Adapted from "Straightened Out and Flying Right," *Context*, April/May 2002, pp. 21–24.

IBM CORPORATION:
THE REINVENTION OF AN INFORMATION TECHNOLOGY COMPANY

Winning the eBay Bakeoff

It was one of the most high-profile technology deals to come up for grabs in years, and IBM (www.ibm.com) didn't seem to stand a chance. No way. In the summer of 2001, Web auctioneer eBay kicked off a ferocious bidding war for the contract to provide software to power the next version of its website. Microsoft already provided eBay with key technologies, and CEO Steve Ballmer was constantly on the phone to eBay boss Meg Whitman, pleading his company's case and dangling the possibility of free ads and promotions on Microsoft's MSN network. BEA Systems—the market leader in the Web application server software that eBay was looking for—was also in there pitching. BEA was teamed up with Sun Microsystems, another IBM rival with long-standing ties to eBay. Sun chief Scott McNealy was calling Whitman too. And IBM, for all its talk of e-business, didn't even count eBay as a customer.

But Big Blue had some heavy artillery of its own in Willy Chiu, a computer scientist who runs its high-volume website research lab and is routinely called in to sway important customers. "I have not met a single competitive situation where I have not won," he boasts. After a grueling four-month bakeoff in which the contestants had to meet eBay's strenuous performance requirements, IBM won: eBay went with IBM's WebSphere software. See Figure A.5.

FIGURE A.5
Willy Chiu is director of IBM's high-volume website research lab and also helps out in competitive situations involving major customers and prospects.

Source: Thomas Broening.

A13

Alfred Chuang, the CEO of BEA, still fumes over the loss, charging that the only reason IBM won was that it sweetened its bid with promises of co-marketing and other deals with eBay. "We don't pay our customers," he huffs. But the real key to IBM's victory was much more prosaic—and ultimately much more ominous for its rivals. eBay confirms that it was dazzled by IBM's expertise with the open-standard Java programming language and the power Java offered in a world of ever-increasing technological complexity. That's particularly telling given that BEA's partner, Sun, invented Java.

Changing the Business Model

Winning the contract, worth tens of millions of dollars in its initial phase, proved that IBM's e-business savvy extended beyond the captive data centers of its traditional corporate customers and gave IBM a big-time victory in the Silicon Valley backyard of its fiercest enemies. More fundamentally, it illuminated one of the most crucial and overlooked transformations wrought during the celebrated nine-year rescue of IBM by Louis Gerstner, who stepped down as CEO on March 1, 2002. In its long-ago heyday, IBM ruled the U.S. tech industry by creating a stubbornly closed, proprietary environment. But under Gerstner's rehabilitation, IBM changed its basic business model. Big Blue began building open-standards technologies like Java and the Linux operating system into everything it makes—and finding that customers like eBay are hungry for such technologies' capacity to simplify today's baroque, networked computing world.

In fact, open-standards technologies are powering many of the most remarked-upon aspects of IBM's resurgence under Gerstner. They fuel the explosion of IBM's services business by making it easier for IBM consultants to stitch together varied hardware and software systems. Last June, IBM's revenues from services such as systems integration, product support, consulting, and website hosting surpassed computer hardware revenues for the first time in the company's 91-year history. And while software—now almost entirely open-standards-compatible—accounted for just 15 percent of IBM's revenues in 2001, it contributed a third of gross profits. Not surprisingly, everyone from Hewlett-Packard to storage giant EMC is trying to copy IBM's services and software strategy. Indeed, that's what is behind HP's recent merger with Compaq.

But for all of its progress, IBM is still looking for the spark that will ignite companywide revenue growth. Profits grew faster than revenues under Gerstner because of some deft financial engineering. (Gerstner made the numbers with the help of an overfunded pension and massive share-buyback programs.) Last year, IBM's revenues fell 3 percent to $86 billion, while profits fell 5 percent—albeit during a year of double-digit declines for most of the company's competitors—to $7.7 billion. As shareholders become less forgiving of accounting acrobatics, new CEO Sam Palmisano will be under increasing pressure to deliver real top-line growth.

Luckily for Palmisano, he has inherited an organization that is poised to do just that. Whether it was prescient or providential, IBM has shifted toward software and services just as competition on the hardware side of the industry has smashed margins to almost nothing. At the same time, the complexity of running a networked business is driving chief information officers everywhere to seek the comforting hand of IT services providers such as IBM. Big Blue's strategy boils down to this: Instead of trying to lock in customers with proprietary technology, it now tries to lock them in with irreplaceable IT services. Open source technologies are the fountain that feeds that strategy, and they are leading IBM back to a position it enjoyed during its glory days: high-tech domination.

The Beaten IT Goliath

In one of the sleek, blond-wood conference rooms at IBM's Z-shaped headquarters in Armonk, New York, a slight, elfin man with curly gray hair is recounting how IBM discovered that open-standards fountain. "Once we decided we were embracing the Internet, and that our job was to help our customers integrate all their business processes and help them connect to all their employees, customers, and partners, how do you do that?" IBM technology strategist Irving Wladawsky-Berger asks. "You need an open platform."

It's difficult to overstate just how startling an admission that is, coming from a top executive at a company once famous for both a strict adherence to closed platforms and a towering "not-invented-here" arrogance, born of its long tradition of engineering breakthroughs. Historically, IBM software worked best with IBM hardware; that's how the company maintained its lock on customers. But in 1995, two years into Gerstner's tenure, IBM was a beaten company. The PC revolution in business it started in 1982 had been hijacked by more nimble competitors like Microsoft, Compaq, and Dell, and its mainframe technology seemed outmoded in an era of high-powered servers by Sun and client-server networks furnished by everybody else. IBM's fall from grace was spectacular—going from its most profitable year in 1990 to massive layoffs and a cumulative $16 billion in losses in the early 1990s. IBM seemed on the verge of dissolution into several smaller companies or gradual extinction.

Then Lou Gerstner was brought in from outside the industry in 1993, made CEO, and told to save the company. Still, all of its failures continued to weigh heavily on IBM in 1995. The Internet had exploded onto the scene, and customers were desperate to tie all their discordant computer systems together and link them to those at other companies. Something had to change.

Java to the Rescue

When Java came along that year, it seemed to be just what Big Blue needed. Java, a programming language, had the virtue of being able to create software that could run on any computer operating system. The official acceptance of Java and open standards triggered furious debates within the company. At the time, Java was seen as some TV set-top-box experiment (which is what it was originally designed for). "The reaction was that we were going to bet the business on something that does not exist," recalls Scott Hebner, WebSphere's marketing chief. In 1997, Wladawsky-Berger was part of an e-business strategy group that included Hebner, current hardware chief Bill Zeitler, and software chief Steve Mills; they observed that the railroad, automobile, and telecom industries really didn't take off until the various players agreed on underlying standards (such as what gauge railroad track to use or where to put the gearshift in a car).

Was the relatively young IT industry any different? In their view, the move to the Internet was the beginning of an industrywide effort to standardize on a common open platform. Java, with all its flexibility, would be crucial to that effort. "If the technology is right for the marketplace," Wladawsky-Berger notes, "companies that do not accept it become an asterisk of history." Hebner explains Java's importance in more concrete terms: "Why would I ever write my applications to a locked-in operating system when I can write to an open platform? Why would I try to create my own gauge?"

That thinking went into developing IBM's new WebSphere software, which was built completely around Java. Even though Java was originally oriented more toward devices such as PCs or set-top boxes, IBM helped make it the standard for enterprise and Web servers. In fact, last year was the first time an annual survey of 10,000 IBM customers found that those customers preferred working with systems centered on Java rather than Windows. As Hebner explains it, "There is a whole new market for building applications on the network, and to do that, you need software that is network-savvy." What IBM is trying to do, he says, is "build an operating system for the Internet."

Betting on Linux

That ambition goes well beyond Java. In the hardware arena every server and mainframe that IBM sells has been made compatible with the Linux open-source operating system since last year. Linux vastly expands certain capabilities of a mainframe; for instance, a single mainframe running on Linux can do the work of thousands of servers. IBM's $1 billion bet on Linux a couple of years ago is opening up a whole new market for the death-defying IBM mainframe, which, with new models, generated double-digit sales growth in 2001 for the first time in a decade. And this only a few years after the mainframe was considered a high-tech dinosaur and relegated to the scrap heap of IT history. The Linux/mainframe surge boosted sales of complementary products such as database software and storage systems. And IBM is also incorporating Web services, another set of hot open-source technologies, into its software.

Adopting open technologies has enabled IBM to advance its products much faster than if it had insisted on developing everything itself—because these technologies benefit from the input and talents of the larger software community. In turn, because of the company's formidable market clout, IBM's embrace of open systems has given a giant boost to the open-source movement. "They have legitimized Linux and open-source to the CIO/CEO buyer," says Matthew Szulik, CEO of Linux software firm Red Hat. Avery Lyford, CEO of Linuxcare, another Linux software company, likens IBM's adoption of open source to "a papal blessing."

The Trojan Horse Theory

Not everyone holds such charitable views. "I think IBM is the same as in the 1970s," says Shahin Khan, Sun's chief competitive officer. "A company basically interested in gaining control of information technology from its customers." He charges that Java and Linux are nothing more than Trojan Horses: "convenient vehicles for IBM to put together its disparate product lines."

But integrating those product lines, he maintains, is not simply a matter of dusting them with a little open-source code. It actually requires some reconfiguration of the underlying hardware. And since doing all of that is complicated, Khan says, "IBM's solution is to sell professional services. The only way to make sense of IBM's disparate products is to hire 200 people from IBM Global Services." As Oracle CEO Larry Ellison put it to an audience of software developers in December 2001, IBM's sales pitch is basically: "Hey, whatever you got, this morass, this briar patch of computing, we'll just take it over and we'll raise your prices."

The Attack-from-All-Angles Approach

Even Gerstner and Palmisano would agree that open systems have helped IBM's services business and, thus, the company's overall position in the tech universe. Open-source technologies allow IBM to tie together heterogeneous computer networks and offer that capability as a service. Indeed, IBM in effect seems to be transforming itself into a gigantic, diversified consulting company called IBM Global Services (which, incidentally, Palmisano helped create). The 150,000 Global Services consultants will furnish customers with whatever technology they want, even from competitors. But you can be sure they will push IBM products first. Today, 60 percent of IBM's sales to large customers include some bundling of hardware, software, and services.

"Today we bundle deals and bring everything IBM offers to the table, and in many cases leave our competitors in the wings with nothing to do," says IBM salesman Mark Edson. IBM also is doing an extremely good job of piggybacking on the sales efforts of other enterprise software companies, such as Siebel Systems and PeopleSoft. Last year such joint sales programs by IBM (with more than 9,000 business partners) brought in $3 billion in new revenues—a fourfold increase from the year before.

IBM's attack-from-all-angles approach, the company believes, is grinding down its rivals. Sitting in his office in Somers, New York, one recent morning, Lou D'Ambrosio, head of sales for IBM's software group, reads from an e-mail he received at 9:08 A.M. from a BEA sales executive. "Hello, Lou. Based on the success I am seeing IBM have in the marketplace, I would like to be part of the IBM team." D'Ambrosio says he's getting about 15 such pleas a month from rival salespeople. "Two years ago, I was lucky to get five," he says. IBM's momentum is also apparent in the latest market-share figures. IBM is closing in on Oracle in database software, on BEA in Web server applications software, on EMC in storage, and on Sun in Unix servers. Competitors dispute some of those figures, but it is clear that IBM is gaining ground on long-standing market leaders.

Obviously, all of IBM's sales efforts would be in vain if they were not backed by competitive technology. Here is where the $5 billion that IBM spends each year on research and development comes in handy. IBM scientists were the first to champion the company's moves to Java and Linux, and they continue to push into new areas such as advanced storage systems, self-healing networks, grid computing, and Web-mining software. In 2001, IBM filed a record 3,411 patent applications, making it the country's top patent filer for the ninth year in a row.

Sun's Khan says IBM can brag all it wants about its research, but software developers stitching together enterprise applications today really have only two choices for a development platform: the Sun-invented Java and Microsoft's .Net. "IBM does not have a party of its own," Khan says, so it is attending Sun's. Those are fighting words to Wladawsky-Berger, who clearly doesn't regard Sun as being in IBM's league—or in Microsoft's either. "For Sun to say when it comes to software you have two choices, Microsoft and Sun, is like saying when it comes to world powers you have two choices, the U.S. and Tajikistan." Then he pauses: "Maybe I am not being fair—the U.S. and Romania."

The Long-Term Danger

For all his dismissiveness, Wladawsky-Berger knows that IBM's open-source approach faces potential pitfalls. IBM still has a lot of work to do to get outside developers to rally around its products. For instance, there are many times more independent programmers who know how to work with Oracle databases than with IBM's competing DB2 software. IBM must also guard against fueling suspicions— which people like Khan are only too happy to fan—that it isn't an open-source purist. In one Web services standards body, for example, IBM has indicated it wants to be able to get royalties for any intellectual property it contributes. That runs counter to the open-source spirit, and if IBM is ever perceived to be trying to control the movement for its own commercial edge, the company will face trouble winning crucial support from developers.

There's a final long-term danger that IBM must be wary of. The endgame of all open-source technology is a world where tying together disparate hardware and software becomes much easier, almost automatic. With these technologies, says Steven Milunovich, head of Merrill Lynch's technology research team, "much of what now requires a complex IT services market becomes more open and easier to do. So you don't need IBM to do it for you." That day may be years away. For now, IBM's open-source strategy has positioned it to regain some of the dominance it enjoyed decades ago. This time, though, it must keep its pride in check. "You have to be very sensitive to the fact that the Internet is bigger than your own company," Wladawsky-Berger acknowledges. "Open-source is bigger than IBM."

Case Study Questions

1. Changing the Business Model

  a. How did IBM change its basic business model under CEO Louis Gerstner?

  b. Why did IBM change from closed proprietary systems to open-standards technologies?

  c. How has the change to open standards changed IBM's lines of business and business performance?

2. From Success to Failure to Success

  a. What was the basis for IBM's success before the 1990s?

  b. What were the reasons for IBM's dramatic failure in the early 1990s?

  c. What business and technology strategies and choices are the keys to IBM's current success? Explain why this is so.

3. The Future of IBM and the IT Industry

   a. How do IBM's competitors view its current business model? How does IBM view its new business strategies? What is your view on this controversy? Explain.

   b. How have IBM's competitors been affected by IBM's transformation? How should they compete with the new IBM business model?

   c. What are the challenges and dangers that could sabotage IBM's success in the future? What should they do to meet these challenges?

Source: Adapted from Erick Schonfeld, "This Is Your Father's IBM, Only Smarter," *Business 2.0*, May 2002, pp. 52–58. © 2002 Time Inc. All rights reserved; and Louis Gerstner, *Who Says Elephants Can't Dance? Inside IBM's Historic Turnaround*, New York, Harper Business, 2003.

ZARA AND INDITEX:
USING INFORMATION TECHNOLOGY
FOR COMPETITIVE ADVANTAGE

The Speed Merchants

It's half an hour before opening at Zara's flagship apparel store in downtown Madrid, and Esther Fernandez Gomez, clad in a black stretch dress with one bare shoulder, is taking stock. She scans the chrome racks holding the latest spring fashions, absorbing it all. Plenty of beige and white, but black, navy blue, and garnet are in short supply. Leather items—particularly the short skirts—are selling briskly; so are the tailored jeans, the black sequined shirts, and the red and blue gabardine blazers.

Fernandez spots a black dress hanging on a rack by itself. She grabs it and calculates aloud: On Monday she received four, and now just two days later, only one remains. "I've to make a bet on what we are going to sell next week," she says. "I'll probably order six to sell between Monday and Thursday." Thus decided, she pulls out a customized Cassiopeia Pocket PC and, with stylus in hand, taps in an order that's beamed over the Internet to Zara headquarters in the northwestern Spanish town of La Coruna.

There, in a bright and vast white room, some 200 designers and product managers are deciding what to create. Every day they gather suggestions from Fernandez and 518 other store managers worldwide—not just specific orders but ideas for cuts, fabrics, or even, say, a new line of men's knit vests. (Fernandez, for example, plans to pitch a proposal for making the hot-selling black dress in red and beige, perhaps with an asymmetrical cut exposing the left shoulder.)

After weighing the store managers' ideas, the team in La Coruna decides what to make. Designers draw up the latest ideas on their computers and send them over Zara's intranet to a smattering of its nearby factories. Within days, the cutting, dyeing, stitching, and pressing begin. And in just three weeks, the clothes will hang in over 500 Zara stores from Barcelona to Berlin to Beirut. Zara isn't just a bit faster than rivals such as Gap, whose lead time is nine months. It's 12 times faster.

The Networked Mega-Retailer

Little known in the United States, where it has just eight stores, Zara (www.zara.com) can lay a strong claim to owning the most impressive manufacturing and distribution process in the apparel industry. Although Zara is often called Europe's equivalent of Gap, the chain defies direct comparisons to American retailers. The bulk of its fashions, which appeal to dressier European tastes, are more Banana Republic than Gap. Its prices, however, are more Old Navy.

But what sets Zara apart is a network that ties the store floors to the design shops and in-house factories in the closest thing to real time that exists in retail. Its amazingly flexible factories can replace or redesign the shape of a pair of jeans almost as fast as a teenager can change her mind.

While recession and some merchandising missteps have forced Gap and comparable European stores like Sweden's H&M to retrench, Zara continues to expand. Profits at Zara's corporate parent, Inditex (www.inditex.com), more than tripled between 1995 and 2000 and climbed 31 percent in 2001—a year when many clothing chains saw sales and profits collapse. Zara's impact isn't confined to retail, however. For any company in any industry that cares about time to market, customer focus, and streamlining business processes, Zara is suddenly an organization to watch. "No one can replicate their model," says Elise Horowitz, an analyst with Lehman Bros. in London.

The Zara Business Model

The Zara model may be unique, but at its heart is a perfectly simple principle: In fashion, nothing is as important as time to market—not advertising (which Zara does just twice a year in newspapers), not sales promotions (which Zara does only sparingly), not even labor costs. For decades, apparel companies have farmed out their manufacturing to Third World countries in pursuit of lower costs. Zara decided against doing so. In the end, the company reasoned, the ability to respond quickly to shifts in consumer tastes would create far greater efficiencies than outsourcing to Third World sweatshops. "The fashion world is in constant flux and is driven not by supply but by customer demand," says Jose Maria Castellano, CEO of Inditex. "We need to give consumers what they want, and if I go to South America or Asia to make clothes, I simply can't move fast enough."

Once the company committed to having the world's most responsive supply chain, the pieces of its operating model fell logically into place. About half the items Zara sells are made in its own factories, rather than by the contract manufacturers who make virtually all other retailers' store-label apparel. Zara has a twice-a-week delivery schedule that not only restocks old styles but brings in entirely new designs; rival chains tend to receive new designs only once or twice a season. To make this possible, Zara's prolific design department cranks out more than 10,000 fresh items each year, far more than the competition does. "It's like you walk into a new store every two weeks," marvels Tracy Mullin, president and CEO of the National Retail Federation.

The advantages of their world-beating time to market, according to Zara, more than offset manufacturing costs that run 15 to 20 percent higher than those of its rivals. Responding so quickly to shifts in customer tastes means, for one thing, that Zara almost never needs to have across-the-board inventory write-offs to correct merchandising blunders. And the company maintains steady profit margins of 10 percent—in line with the best in the industry.

Since each store's merchandise changes so frequently, loyal customers come back often, without prodding, just to see what's new. The most important benefit of Zara's nimbleness, of course, is that customers are more likely to find stuff they want to buy on Zara's shelves. "They have clothes that are very hip, and the prices are great," gushes Barbara Santos, a 19-year-old student from Madrid, who admits to shopping at Zara about twice a month. On this sunny weekday afternoon, Santos snags a new winter coat for 48 euros ($42), a skirt for 16 euros ($14), and a leather change purse for 9.5 euros ($8.25). (Zara varies its prices from country to country using a formula that takes into account distribution costs and economic conditions.) "And if you can't find something in this Zara, you walk down the street to another one, and they'll have it."

How Zara Has Grown

The first Zara opened in La Coruna in 1975, the brainchild of a railroad worker's son named Amancio Ortega. Ortega got his start in the apparel industry running a gown and lingerie business out of his family's kitchen in 1963, but from the beginning, he understood the importance of building tight bonds with his customers. "The clothes he made were being sold through wholesalers who were simply not offering what customers wanted," Castellano says. So Ortega set out to build a company that would take control of every aspect of its business. The rest is one of the world's great retailing success stories.

Today the reclusive 66-year-old Ortega, who has never granted an interview and is rarely seen in public, is Spain's richest man, the world's richest fashion executive, ahead of Bernard Arnault of luxury goods empire LVMH and the Fisher family, which funded Gap. Inditex, the 3.25 billion euro ($2.8 billion) retail conglomerate that grew out of Zara, now includes five smaller chains: Bershka, Massimo Dutti, Pull & Bear, and Stradivarius, all of which carry styles ranging from upscale men's clothes to inexpensive teen fashions, and the recently launched Oysho, which sells lingerie. All told, Inditex has 1,315 stores in 40 countries.

Zara's 519 stores account for more than 75 percent of total sales. Although it has a sizable presence in the Americas and the Middle East, Zara is primarily European. And the company's executives still see plenty of room for expansion there. Even in Spain, Zara has only a 5 percent market share, compared with the 10 percent that H&M and Marks & Spencer have on their respective home turfs in Sweden and the United Kingdom. And in three of Europe's four biggest markets—Germany, Italy, and Great Britain—Zara is just getting started.

One of Zara's first international forays was to the United States, with the opening of a store in New York in 1989. Since then, the retailer's U.S. presence has grown slowly, with six stores in the New York area, two in Miami, and one in San Juan, Puerto Rico. "We get asked a lot what will happen with the U.S.," says Borja de la Cierva Alvarez de Sotomayer, Inditex's chief financial officer. "We are very happy with having a foothold there. It gives us visibility. We get to know the market. We get to build teams, and we make money." A full-scale onslaught in the United States would almost certainly require Zara to duplicate its manufacturing and distribution infrastructure nearby, perhaps in Mexico. Such an effort, de la Cierva says, just doesn't make sense when the company is still expanding in Germany and Italy. "For us," he says, "it is not a priority."

Zara's Logistics

To see what *is* Zara's priority, a good place to go is the imposing concrete and cinderblock fortress of a warehouse in La Coruna, across a two-lane highway from Inditex's headquarters. And a good person to talk to is Lorena Alba, Inditex's director of logistics, an intense woman with a rapid-fire delivery who made a model of efficiency out of the four-story, 5-million-square-foot building. (That's about nine times the size of Amazon.com's warehouse in Fernley, Nevada, or about 90 football fields.) See Figure A.6.

For Alba, the warehouse is not so much a place to store clothes as a place to move them. The cavernous building is connected to 14 Zara factories through a maze of tunnels, each equipped with a rail that hangs from its ceiling. Along the rails, cables carry merchandise on a system not unlike a ski gondola. At the factories, bunches of clothes on hangers or in suspended racks—10 pants here, a dozen jackets there—are latched onto the cables and whisked into the warehouse.

Each bundle is supported by a metal bar with a series of tabs that spell out a mechanical code—a sort of "address" that indicates where exactly in the warehouse the bundle must end up. The merchandise is selected, sorted, rerouted, and resorted—some of it automatically, some of it with the help of warehouse workers—until it gets to an area that Alba calls the "lungs" of the distribution center. Here every Zara store has its own staging area. It receives clothes on hangers from the upper two floors, folded items and an array of accessories from the lower two. As soon as a store's order is complete, it is carted directly to a loading dock. There it is packed along with other stores' shipments, in order of delivery, onto a truck for each European destination. (Shipments bound for places outside Europe are sent by plane, and the clothes go through a further packing stage.)

"The vast majority of the items are in here only a few hours," Alba says. To keep to that pressing schedule, Alba and her team of a dozen logistics specialists

FIGURE A.6
Lorena Alba is director of logistics for Inditex, the parent company of Zara.

Source: Dan Burn-Forti.

constantly tweak everything from the sequence and the size of deliveries to truck routes and rail configurations. In late January, for example, Alba was forced to revamp the entire distribution schedule. As the number of stores grew, shipping times had been lengthening—an unacceptable situation in a schedule that could be brought to halt by delays of only a few minutes. A truck would arrive in a city after a store opened and the staff would be too busy with customers to take the delivery. Or worse, a truck would arrive after the early morning and not be allowed into the city's commercial downtown to unload—stalling the delivery until the next morning.

Now, Alba schedules deliveries by time zones. In the early morning, while European store managers are still taking stock, Alba receives, packs, and ships orders to the Americas or Asia. In the afternoon, it's Europe's turn. "We are always fine-tuning things, always with the same objectives: flexibility and speed," Alba says. And growth. The company is building an entire new complex in Zaragoza, about 150 miles northeast of Madrid that should double its capacity.

The Secret of Their Success

Back at the flagship store on Gran Via in Madrid, the doors have opened and Fernandez is mingling with customers, asking what they like and don't like and, as always, making mental notes. She keeps an eye on her assistants, who walk the men's, women's, and kids' sections of the store, straightening a shirt here and a pantsuit there, tapping orders into their Cassiopeias.

Fernandez has her eye out for women's clothes that aren't selling well. When she finds an item that's not moving, she puts on her own hard sell—a trick she's learned in her 14 years with Zara. "I wear it," she says, "and everyone asks for it." Besides, as all of Fernandez's customers know, in two weeks there will be a whole new supply of fashions on Zara's shelves. Odds are that you won't have to wait long before you find something to your liking. No store on earth works faster to make that happen.

Case Study Questions

1. **Zara's Business Model**

   a. How does Zara's business model differ from other large apparel retailers?

   b. Is Zara's business model the key to their current success compared to their competitors in the retail apparel industry? Explain.

   c. Does Zara's use of information technology give them a competitive advantage in their business model? Why or why not?

   d. How important are store managers and their use of IT to the success of Zara's business model? Explain.

2. **Zara's Challenges**

   a. What business challenges might Zara face as it continues to expand in Europe and elsewhere?

   How could Zara use IT to help meet such challenges?

   b. Should other major apparel retailers in the U.S. market and other countries copy the Zara business model and use of IT? Why or why not?

   c. Visit the Zara and Inditex websites. Should Zara expand its present limited retail e-commerce presence or continue its emphasis on expanding its physical retail store locations? Explain your answer.

eBAY INC.:
THE CHALLENGES OF ONLINE MARKETPLACE SUCCESS

The World's Online Marketplace

After all these years, Lu Matis, a housewife in Flemington, New Jersey, has finally figured out how to "monetize eyeballs" on the Internet. Her secret? She sells them on eBay (www.ebay.com), which calls itself "the world's online marketplace." Glass eyeballs, that is, handblown and hand-painted by German artisans at the end of the 19th century and kept as a prosthetic inventory in doctors' offices. Matis got 700 of them a year and a half ago from a dealer for about $7 a pop, but on eBay they fetch anywhere from $20 for a brown eye to $40 for a blue, gray, or green one. "I pay my son's college this way," Matis says. "They are gory to look at, but once you realize the work involved, it is like having a piece of Tiffany glass." Her customers range from collectors to jewelry makers to a guy who glued them to his steering wheel. "Where else could you possibly sell these?" she asks.

Matis's ocular oddities are proof positive that eBay has come a long way on its quest, as CEO Meg Whitman explains it, "to build the world's largest online trading platform where practically anyone can trade practically anything." eBay has gone well beyond collectible Elvis prints and Beanie Babies—or glass eyeballs, for that matter. A motorcycle is sold on eBay every 18 minutes, a laptop every 30 seconds, and a book every 4 seconds. You can buy time-shares in Hawaii, restaurant equipment, gardening tools, or your pick of goods in 18,000 other categories. eBay traded $9 billion worth of goods in 2001—equivalent to roughly 20 percent of all consumer e-commerce that year. More than $1 billion of that total was estimated to come from autos alone, a category that did not even exist on eBay two years ago.

"If you had asked me in September 1998 (when eBay went public) if eBay would be in the used-car business, I would have said no," Whitman observes. Today, eBay is the largest online seller not just of autos and collectibles but also of computers, photo equipment and supplies, and sporting goods. To further promote the brand, it is developing with Sony a TV show profiling eBay users and the items they buy on the site. It is beginning to attract larger corporate sellers such as Disney, IBM, and Home Depot. And the company is expanding internationally, with operations in 18 countries.

In 1999, for instance, eBay Germany reached only 6 percent of the country's Internet users. Now one out of every four German Web surfers visits the site. Back when she was gearing up for the IPO, Whitman would tell investors that she was going after a $100 million slice of the U.S. collectibles market. Today she estimates the size of the markets that eBay addresses at $1.7 trillion. See Figure A.7.

FIGURE A.7
CEO Meg Whitman, head of U.S. operations Jeff Jordan (left), and CFO Rajiv Dutta are leading eBay into new business and global markets.

Source: Grant Delin.

Running on Social Capital

At one level, this success is easily explained; eBay has come closer than any other creation of the Internet boom to realizing the promise of the virtual corporation. With no inventory, no warehouses, and no sales force, eBay's electronic bazaar, run properly, is a profit-spewing machine.

Far less understood, however, is the invisible fuel that powers that machine: eBay's unique ability to attract vast amounts of what economists call social capital. The rest of us might call it trust, or goodwill, or credibility. Whatever you call this resource, eBay, in its vast community of buyers and sellers, deploys more of it than almost any company in memory. Social capital is what enables eBay to harness the creativity of the millions of entrepreneurs on its site striving to meet the most capricious demands of the even more numerous buyers who also congregate there. eBay's own customers do much of the company's work, bringing it countless new products and marketing techniques, picking up shipping costs, handling customer service. The high octane of eBay's social capital explains how, even in a down economy, with its dot-com brethren wounded and dying, eBay nearly doubled its profits in 2001 to $90 million. Revenues—bolstered by healthy online Christmas shopping—were $750 million, or equivalent to about 8 percent of the value of all the goods that were traded on its site. By 2005 the company expects to be raking in $3 billion in revenues and $1 billion in operating profits.

Inside the Money Machine

But getting there is far from a sure thing. To reach that goal, the company will have to more than triple the number of its registered buyers and sellers to 150 million. Yet some of the very steps eBay is taking to drive growth and keep its stock at a lofty price/earnings ratio of about 80 (on 2002 estimates) are straining the vital bonds between the company and its core customers. Out in the eBay community, it turns out, it's hard work to keep the social fabric from tearing.

As has been well chronicled, eBay takes advantage of the low communication and transaction costs of the Internet to bring its buyers and sellers together. The company takes a commission—typically 1 to 5 percent—on every trade on its electronic exchange; the rest of its revenues come from listing fees and other charges. eBay is considered the classic example of a company benefiting from so-called network effects. The more buyers who go to eBay, the more sellers they attract, who in turn draw even more buyers as the site becomes a larger source of supply with more competitive prices. This positive feedback loop magnifies the volume of trade on the site, and thus revenues to eBay, while making it increasingly difficult for other auction sites to survive.

But there is more to it than that. "eBay's business is so new that it's not well understood," says Rajiv Dutta, eBay's chief financial officer. "There is an enormous amount of subtlety and complexity underneath." eBay, according to Dutta and other eBay executives, is not so much a conventional company as a self-regulating, complex system. And indeed, eBay has few of the characteristics typical of traditional corporations—especially rival retailers such as Wal-Mart. "We have no real cost of goods, and customer acquisition is largely driven by word of mouth," Dutta says. Wal-Mart has nearly $15 billion in long-term debt; eBay has virtually none.

Free of many of the costs that almost every other corporation must bear, eBay's business throws off an increasing amount of cash, reflected in operating margins that have gone from slightly negative in 1999 to 19 percent in 2001. (Wal-Mart's operating margin is about 5 percent.) Dutta expects operating margins to hit 30 to 35 percent by 2005, which is how he gets to that $1 billion operating profit target.

Capitalizing on Social Capital

Such an achievement would be pretty spectacular, but it cannot be reached on the strengths of new-wave financials alone. Social capital is the crucial hidden asset that could make it possible. The forms of capital that most people are familiar with are physical (stores, factories, machinery), human (education, skills, expertise), and financial (cash, debt, equity). Social capital flows from social relationships—things like membership in old boys' networks, trust, reputation, and social norms that allow people to do more work (such as coffee breaks). eBay's network effects are an extremely valuable form of social capital, but there are others. What eBay has figured out how to do is tap into the social capital created on its site by the millions of people who trade there, and convert it into profits.

One source of eBay's social capital is its feedback system, whereby buyers and sellers can rate each other. People need such confidence-building mechanisms to buy stuff from faceless strangers. Negative feedback is posted very rarely (less than 1 percent of the time, according to a study by University of Michigan economist Paul Resnick), but sellers are afraid of getting any negative comments and go to great lengths to avoid them. It's not uncommon for sellers to be brutally honest about their wares, going so far as to describe every nick and scratch. "Every time you get a negative feedback, your sales go down," says Howard Getz, who does 600 auctions a week in collectibles such as Barbie dolls and *Star Wars* figures. Displaying a buyer's negative comment by a seller's name is like letting a disgruntled customer leave a sign in a store for all subsequent customers to see.

Like other kinds of capital, social capital earns a return. One of the unique ways it pays off at eBay is in the thousands of small pricing and product selection innovations its members make that keep eBay's merchandising always in tune with the whims of the economy. "No single company could react as quickly as our millions of users do," Whitman explains. MIT economist Erik Brynjolfsson concurs: "If you had a central purchasing department, you would not have all the creativity that the millions of people have who are posting on eBay trying to meet unmet needs and develop products that might otherwise have gone unnoticed." Glass eyeballs, unused vacation real estate, even packing supplies for other eBay sellers—eBay users create markets where none existed before. They then absorb expenses, such as inventory, marketing, and shipping that eBay itself would have to eat if it were a conventional company. Users even help out with customer support, as anyone who has ever visited an eBay discussion board knows. "Here you have people who are volunteering their time," notes Dan Ariely, a behavioral economist at MIT. "That is the amazing thing."

Managing the Marketplace

To keep the community of users happy Whitman and her lieutenants spend a lot of time listening to their customers and observing trends on the site. Every morning, for example, Whitman is handed a report excerpting comments posted on eBay discussion boards. And the company regularly conducts intense all-day focus groups, called Voices, with representative buyers and sellers.

The most important way that eBay manages its marketplace, however, is by organizing itself as a collection of start-ups. Each major category (books, collectibles, music, real estate, tickets) has its own manager. So does every country (eBay runs the number one auction sites in Australia, Britain, Canada, France, and Germany, among other nations). These managers are the stewards of the social capital on their turf. They must be experts in their particular markets and make sure nothing impedes trade there.

They are also responsible for the growth of their niches. When they notice that activity around certain items, such as tickets or automobiles, is growing organically, they signal up the chain that it's time to carve out a new category. "We decide to expand the trading platform based on where users want to go," Whitman explains.

Sometimes, that is away from auctions. So eBay is adding fixed-price components to its site as well, an unabashed challenge to Amazon.com's business. In 2000, eBay acquired Half-com, a fixed-price online store for discounted commodity goods that is being integrated into the regular eBay site. "Half-com is bringing the Amazon buyer into person-to-person trading," says Jeff Jordan, head of eBay's U.S. operations. And about 45 percent of all eBay auctions now have a "Buy It Now" button that lets the first bidder end the auction by agreeing to a preset price. All told, about 19 percent of sales on eBay are now fixed-price rather than auction.

Re-architecting the IT Platform

There's no surer way for eBay to burn up social capital than to inflict site crashes on the community. Three years ago, eBay infuriated users with a series of massive outages; that's when CEO Meg Whitman hired Maynard Webb, the former chief information officer at Gateway, to fix things. When he arrived, eBay was running its site with a single Sun server. Today, eBay's site is balanced across more than a dozen big servers. Webb boasts that the system has a 99.9 percent reliability rate and the technological muscle to support Whitman's expansionary ambitions. "We are able to scale infinitely now," Webb says.

But his work is far from done. To prepare for the increased flexibility required to serve so many new customers, categories, and countries, Webb is putting the site through yet another complete technological overhaul, known internally as V3 (or version3). After a bakeoff last summer, eBay decided to base its new architecture on IBM's WebSphere software, Sun servers, and Tibco back-end messaging software. Rolling it out in three phases—named Mercury, Gemini, and Apollo for the technological complexity involved—the complete conversion to V3 will take 18 months. Deutsche Bank analyst Jeetil Patel expects the project to cost about $40 million.

"Maynard is basically re-architecting everything they do around a more distributed, real-time platform that is very, very powerful and able to accommodate all kinds of new things," says Tibco CEO Vivek Ranadive. For instance, Tibco's database messaging software will allow eBay to shift information instantaneously from one database to another pending on demand. Tibco is also providing an integration pack for large corporate customers who want to hook in their own back-end inventory, supply chain management, and accounting systems to more easily take advantage of eBay as an alternative distribution channel.

But the real power of the platform will come from IBM's new WebSphere software, which processes transactions over the Web and keeps the site running. Chuck Geiger, eBay's VP for architecture and technology strategy, says WebSphere's use of Java makes it highly flexible; WebSphere, Geiger says, "will help us morph in the different directions we want to go as a business, deal better with mergers and acquisitions, and get our developers focused more on product differentiation and functionality than back-end maintenance."

Courting the Corporations

One of the most promising avenues for future growth hinges on eBay's ability to court a whole new class of customers: big corporations. Disney, IBM, and Home Depot, among others, are dipping their toes into eBay's market for discontinued goods, excess inventory, and returned items. Even Dell, which arguably does not need any help with online commerce, sells refurbished off-lease PCs on eBay. It's just another sales channel. Governments are getting into the act too. Seventeen state governments, up from zero in 1998, are using eBay to liquidate foreclosed assets.

The giant sellers are proceeding cautiously and so far account for less than 3 percent of eBay sales. But eBay is working on them—and urging them to expand their offerings to the types of fixed-price, in-season items that make up the bulk of the economy. In a pitch to the Gap clothing chain, for instance, eBay would say, "We have 10,000 Gap items on eBay right now, so whether you like it or not, we are a channel." Or, as eBay marketing VP Bill Cobb likes to tell reluctant corporate sellers, "We have the technology, the marketplace, and the buyers. Why are you going to do it on your own? Nobody visits your site."

Disney uses eBay to auction collector's items such as ride vehicles from its theme parks, animation cels, and movie props. Recently a statuette used by animators during the making of the film *Monsters, Inc.* went for $3,556. "We create archival items every time a park or a new movie opens," says George Grobar, the head of auctions for Disney's Internet group. Many of the objects used to end up in landfills, but by using eBay, Grobar says, Disney can sell them cost-effectively—and generate promotional buzz.

IBM has gone further. By selling mainly laptops that are reaching the end of their product cycle for about $1,000 each, Big Blue has become eBay's single largest seller (although it accounts for less than 0.1 percent of the site's total sales). The computer giant is finding that rather than stealing sales from IBM.com or their channels, eBay auctions are bringing new clients into the IBM tent. Some 70 percent of its eBay customers—half of which are small businesses—are new to IBM. "We see eBay as an incredible growth engine for us," says IBM.com auction manager Paul Canham. Indeed. Canham's sales on eBay are growing more than 40 percent per *month*.

Conflicts on the Level Playing Field

But the question remains: Will the forces pulling eBay in so many different directions undermine its social capital? After huge surges in 1999 and 2000, eBay's listings growth (a major contributor to revenues) has slowed dramatically. To meet its dramatic financial goals, eBay must continue to expand aggressively into new categories, geographies, formats, and customer types. But the faster eBay grows, the greater the risk to its social capital.

There are already signs that its expansionary strategies are beginning to alienate existing users. For instance, one of the basic principles that eBay has tried to maintain is neutrality. The company avoids taking sides between buyers and sellers whenever possible. That is what the feedback system is for. But the Switzerland stance increasingly does not wash with the people who are the source of all of eBay's revenues: the sellers. The most vocal are those who sell more than $2,000 a month on eBay, known as Powersellers.

Eric McKenna of Pittsburgh quit his sales job at a paging company about two years ago to sell guitars on eBay for $500 to $3,500 a piece. When he had a problem with a deadbeat buyer and wanted eBay to yank him from the site, customer service reps kept explaining to him that they could not do that, and that eBay was a social phenomenon where different rules applied. "I don't want any of your socialistic b.s.," McKenna would tell supervisor after supervisor. "You are a company. I am a Powerseller! I am paying you 1,000 bucks a month, and I want service." To eBay's credit, the deadbeat was finally barred from the site. But if McKenna wants preferential treatment from eBay for his BoogieStreet Guitars, imagine what IBM will want.

eBay insists that it will maintain a level playing field. "Our vision of eBay consists of a marketplace where your next-door neighbor can compete side by side with large corporations," Whitman says. Indeed, if you search for IBM laptops, you will see IBM's listings alongside auctions from other sellers. From the prominence of the listings, it's impossible to tell which are the next-door neighbors and which is the $86 billion corporation.

The level playing field approach, however, can create another problem. If customers stop benefiting from the relationships they make through eBay, all of the company's accumulated social capital goes out the window. In the original collectibles and antiques categories, for instance, eBay has created such an efficient market that average selling prices have declined 30 percent during the past year, according to the Internet Antique Shop. Gary Sohmers, an appraiser on *Antiques Road Show* and Boston radio host who has been selling pop culture collectibles online for years, is not happy about this trend. He says of dealers' feelings for eBay: "We all hate it. They leveled the playing field, but unfortunately they leveled it underwater."

The Checkout Controversy

Another uproar centered on the controversial checkout feature that eBay introduced last fall, which automatically exchanges information between the buyer and seller after an auction. eBay says it is meant to standardize the old procedure, in which buyers and sellers e-mailed one another after an auction to arrange delivery and payment. But many sellers despised the imposed feature, not only because they felt it was clumsy but also because they thought that eBay was trying to come between them and their customers—a violation of the social compact. "I was mad as a wet hen," says Frances Neale, a seller of used books on eBay.

eBay responded to sellers' concerns by making the feature optional, but Neale still sees the new checkout system as symptomatic of eBay's larger push to embrace corporate sellers and to further automate the interaction between customers. "I think they want to be the complete system for the large brick-and-mortar companies that want to be on the Web," she speculates.

eBay would be wise to quash that fear quickly. The company derives much of its social capital from the fact that its site is a place where people transact with people, not with large, impersonal corporations. The irony is that, so far, the corporations on eBay are typically the ones adjusting the way they do business. Buyers are just so much more demanding on eBay. Winning bidders expect an e-mail response the next day, not in six weeks, and shipping had better not cost half as much as the entire product.

The Virtual Dilemma

Some observers argue that eBay could afford to be at least a little less solicitous of its buyers and sellers (as a recent price hike demonstrates). After all, where else are they going to go? But the company knows deep down that its future hinges on figuring out how to continue to grow and appeal to multiple constituents without depleting its crucial social capital. At one recent Voices focus group attended by people who trade in autographs, car stereos, and Renaissance gowns, Jordan acknowledged that "the challenge is expanding eBay to car stereos and all the other things you sell without leaving behind the core."

Indeed, that's the dilemma of social capital in a virtual online marketplace. The difficulty of relying on a resource that does not appear on your balance sheet is that you won't know it is missing until it is already gone.

Case Study Questions

1. The World's Online Marketplace

a. Visit the eBay website and check out the many trading categories, specialty sites, international sites, and other features in their online marketplace. How well does eBay provide "the world's largest online trading platform, where practically anyone can trade practically anything"? Explain your evaluation.

b. Why do you think eBay has become the largest online market for certain products, such as autos, collectibles, computers, photo equipment, and sporting goods?

c. How do people make a living trading on eBay? Evaluate what it takes to be an eBay Powerseller, or to have someone sell for you. Explain your evaluation of the sell side of eBay.

2. The Business of eBay

a. Why has eBay become such a successful, growing marketplace?

b. How does eBay Inc. generate such large revenues and profits from its online global trading marketplace compared to other businesses?

c. How important is information technology to the success of eBay? Explain.

3. The Challenges of Social Capital

a. Why is the success of an online marketplace like eBay so dependent on its supply of social capital?

b. How has eBay succeeded in creating and managing its marketplace so it has been able to attract and retain substantial social capital?

c. What challenges does eBay now face in continuing to attract and retain the social capital it needs to succeed as an online marketplace?

4. Changing the Online Marketplace

a. Why is eBay developing fixed-priced selling and competing with Amazon.com? Is this a good business strategy? Why or why not?

b. Why is eBay encouraging large companies like Disney, Home Depot, and IBM to trade on its site? What are the business benefits and challenges of this strategy?

c. What can eBay do to "continue to expand aggressively into new categories, geographies, formats, and customer types" and still retain the social capital it needs to succeed as an online marketplace? Give and explain several suggestions.

Source: Adapted from Erick Schonfeld, "eBay's Secret Ingredient," *Business 2.0*, March 2002, pp. 53–58. © 2002 Time Inc. All rights reserved.

REVIEW QUIZ ANSWERS

Chapter 1

Foundations of Information Systems in Business

1. 21	7. 26c	13. 11	19. 4	25. 27a	31. 17d	37. 29
2. 22	8. 16	14. 28	20. 18	26. 27b	32. 17e	38. 20
3. 19	9. 1	15. 13	21. 14	27. 25	33. 30	39. 12
4. 26	10. 10	16. 2	22. 14a	28. 17a	34. 30c	40. 23a
5. 26a	11. 8	17. 3	23. 14b	29. 17b	35. 30b	41. 23
6. 26b	12. 9	18. 15	24. 27	30. 17c	36. 30a	42. 7

Chapter 2

Competing with Information Technology

1. 3	4. 11	7. 6	10. 14	13. 1	15. 15	17. 9
2. 4	5. 5	8. 17	11. 2	14. 18	16. 8	18. 7
3. 12	6. 13	9. 10	12. 16			

Chapter 3

Data Resource Management

1. 9	5. 1	9. 11d	13. 2	17. 14c	21. 11a	25. 6a
2. 12	6. 17	10. 18d	14. 4	18. 14d	22. 11e	26. 18e
3. 8	7. 10	11. 5	15. 3	19. 14e	23. 11b	27. 18a
4. 16	8. 18b	12. 7	16. 14b	20. 13	24. 6b	28. 18c

Chapter 4

Telecommunications and Networks

1. 35	7. 10	13. 11	19. 25	24. 28	29. 13	34. 16
2. 4	8. 32	14. 5	20. 39	25. 20a	30. 6	35. 1
3. 2	9. 37	15. 33	21. 24	26. 20b	31. 21	36. 29
4. 3	10. 17	16. 34	22. 36	27. 26	32. 27	37. 38
5. 12	11. 30	17. 18	23. 23	28. 14	33. 9	38. 22
6. 15	12. 31	18. 19				

Chapter 5

Introduction to e-Business Systems

1. 8	6. 21	11. 5	16. 23	21. 3	26. 24	31. 29
2. 7	7. 16	12. 11	17. 1	22. 2	27. 19	32. 25
3. 13	8. 30	13. 28	18. 22	23. 27	28. 31	
4. 9	9. 20	14. 18	19. 26	24. 14	29. 32	
5. 10	10. 6	15. 15	20. 17	25. 12	30. 4	

Chapter 6

Enterprise e-Business Systems

1. 1	4. 1*a*	7. 1*b*	10. 1*c*	13. 1*d*	15. 6*d*	17. 3
2. 4	5. 4*a*	8. 4*b*	11. 4*c*	14. 4*d*	16. 2	18. 5
3. 6	6. 6*a*	9. 6*b*	12. 6*c*			

Chapter 7

Electronic Commerce Systems

1. 6	5. 5	9. 8*d*	13. 9	17. 3*c*	20. 7	23. 1
2. 6*b*	6. 8	10. 8*i*	14. 3	18. 3*b*	21. 8*e*	24. 4
3. 6*a*	7. 8*a*	11. 8*f*	15. 3*d*	19. 2	22. 10	25. 11
4. 6*c*	8. 8*g*	12. 8*c*	16. 3*a*			

Chapter 8

Decision Support Systems

1. 8	7. 28	13. 1*c*	19. 10	24. 29	29. 13*b*	34. 21
2. 9	8. 7	14. 1*a*	20. 22	25. 30	30. 20	35. 26
3. 23	9. 6	15. 1*b*	21. 11	26. 17	31. 18	36. 15
4. 5	10. 25	16. 27	22. 2	27. 13	32. 14	37. 19
5. 12	11. 1	17. 3	23. 2*a*	28. 13*a*	33. 13*d*	38. 16
6. 24	12. 1*d*	18. 4				

Chapter 9

Developing Business/IT Strategies

1. 9	3. 8	5. 11	7. 12	9. 7	11. 4	13. 1
2. 3	4. 10	6. 3*a*	8. 6	10. 5	12. 2	14. 3*c*

Chapter 10

Developing Business/IT Solutions

1. 18	7. 27*b*	12. 4	17. 8	22. 23	27. 6*a*	32. 3
2. 26	8. 10*b*	13. 28	18. 19	23. 15	28. 6*c*	33. 23
3. 14	9. 20	14. 11	19. 29	24. 16	29. 6*b*	
4. 2	10. 22	15. 13	20. 24	25. 5	30. 1	
5. 27*b*	11. 7	16. 17	21. 21	26. 9	31. 25	
6. 10*b*						

Chapter 11

Security and Ethical Challenges

1. 26	6. 3	11. 16	16. 15*b*	21. 9	25. 27	29. 1
2. 21	7. 2	12. 6	17. 15*d*	22. 11	26. 22	30. 19
3. 29	8. 5	13. 28	18. 15*e*	23. 7	27. 20	31. 14
4. 17	9. 12	14. 15*a*	19. 8	24. 30	28. 10	32. 25
5. 18	10. 13	15. 15*c*	20. 24			

Chapter 12

Enterprise and Global Management of Information Technology

1. 13	6. 19	11. 7	16. 22	21. 25	26. 11*c*	31. 11*e*
2. 9	7. 2	12. 23	17. 3	22. 6	27. 11*d*	
3. 16	8. 1	13. 10	18. 8	23. 10	28. 15	
4. 18	9. 26	14. 4	19. 21	24. 11*a*	29. 24	
5. 17	10. 20	15. 5	20. 11	25. 11*b*	30. 14	

Chapter 13

Computer Hardware

1. 3	9. 22	17. 43	25. 27	33. 36	41. 45
2. 2	10. 1	18. 21	26. 30*a*	34. 4	42. 6
3. 8	11. 16	19. 20	27. 42	35. 5	43. 35
4. 7	12. 15	20. 40	28. 32	36. 9	44. 34
5. 31	13. 17	21. 12	29. 37	37. 46	45. 10
6. 33	14. 14	22. 41*c*	30. 26	38. 39	46. 13
7. 28	15. 29	23. 38*e*	31. 24	39. 34*b*	47. 25
8. 23	16. 19	24. 30	32. 11	40. 34*a*	48. 25*d*

Chapter 14

Computer Software

1. 34	7. 36	13. 19	18. 7	23. 17	28. 14	33. 30
2. 2	8. 12	14. 37	19. 8	24. 32	29. 10	34. 15
3. 27	9. 38	15. 11	20. 40	25. 13	30. 26	35. 18
4. 35	10. 23	16. 3	21. 6	26. 20	31. 25	36. 1
5. 31	11. 24	17. 39	22. 28	27. 4	32. 22	37. 16
6. 9	12. 5					

SELECTED REFERENCES

Preface

1. Sawhney, Mohan, and Jeff Zabin. *The Seven Steps to Nirvana: Strategic Insights into e-Business Transformation.* New York: McGraw-Hill, 2001.

Chapter 1—Foundations of Information Systems in Business

1. Emigh, Jacquiline. "E-Commerce Strategies." *Computerworld*, August 16, 1999.

2. Ewusi-Mensah, Kewku. "Critical Issues in Abandoned Information Systems Development Projects." *Communications of the ACM*, September 1997.

3. Fingar, Peter; Harsha Kumar; and Tarun Sharma. *Enterprise E-Commerce.* Tampa, FL: Meghan-Kiffer Press, 2000.

4. Haylock, Christina Ford, and Len Muscarella. *Net Success.* Holbrook, MA: Adams Media Corporation, 1999.

5. Hills, Mellanie. *Intranet Business Strategies.* New York: John Wiley & Sons, 1997.

6. Iansiti, Marco, and Alan MacCormick. "Developing Products on Internet Time." *Harvard Business Review*, September–October 1997.

7. Kalakota, Ravi, and Marcia Robinson. *E-Business: Roadmap for Success.* Reading, MA: Addison-Wesley, 1999.

8. Kalakota, Ravi, and Andrew Whinston. *Electronic Commerce: A Manager's Guide.* Reading, MA: Addison-Wesley, 1997.

9. Lee, Allen. "Inaugural Editor's Comments." *MIS Quarterly*, March 1999.

10. Leinfuss, Emily. "Making the Cut." *Computerworld*, September 20, 1999.

11. Marion, Larry. "Snap, Crackle, Pop, and Crash—Go the Income Statements." *Datamation* (www.datamation.com), February 1999.

12. Norris, Grant; James Hurley; Kenneth Hartley; John Dunleavy; and John Balls. *E-Business and ERP: Transforming the Enterprise.* New York: John Wiley & Sons, 2000.

13. Radcliff, Deborah. "Aligning Marriott." *Computerworld*, April 20, 2000.

14. Seybold, Patricia. *Customers.com: How to Create a Profitable Business Strategy for the Internet and Beyond.* New York: Times Business, 1998.

15. Shapiro, Carl, and Hal Varian. *Information Rules: A Strategic Guide to the New Economy.* Boston, MA: Harvard Business School Press, 1999.

16. Silver, Mark; M. Lynn Markus; and Cynthia Mathis Beath. "The Information Technology Interaction Model: A Foundation for the MBA Core Course." *MIS Quarterly*, September 1995.

17. Steadman, Craig. "ERP Pioneers." *Computerworld*, January 18, 1999.

18. Stewart, Thomas. "How Alcoa and Cisco Make Realtime Work." *Fortune*, May 29, 2000.

19. Wagner, Mitch. "Firms Spell Out Appropriate Internet Use for Employees." *Computerworld*, February 5, 1996.

Chapter 2—Competing with Information Technology

1. Applegate, Lynda; F. Warren McFarlan; and James McKenney. *Corporate Information Systems Management: Text and Cases.* Burr Ridge, IL: Irwin/McGraw-Hill, 1999.

2. Bowles, Jerry. "Best Practices for Global Competitiveness." Special Advertising Section. *Fortune*, November 24, 1997.

3. Caron, J. Raymond; Sirkka Jarvenpaa; and Donna Stoddard. "Business Reengineering at CIGNA Corporation: Experiences and Lessons from the First Five Years." *MIS Quarterly*, September 1994.

4. Cash, James I., Jr.; Robert G. Eccles; Nitin Nohria; and Richard L. Nolan. *Building the Information-Age Organization: Structure, Control, and Information Technologies.* Burr Ridge, IL: Richard D. Irwin, 1994.

5. Christensen, Clayton. *The Innovators Dilemma: When New Technologies Cause Great Firms to Fail.* Boston: Harvard Business School Press, 1997.

6. Clemons, Eric, and Michael Row. "Sustaining IT Advantage: The Role of Structural Differences." *MIS Quarterly*, September 1991.

7. Collett, Stacy. "Spun-Off Sabre to Sell Software to AMR Rivals." *Computerworld*, December 20, 1999.

8. Cronin, Mary. *Doing More Business on the Internet.* 2nd ed. New York: Van Nostrand Reinhold, 1995.

9. Cronin, Mary. *The Internet Strategy Handbook.* Boston: Harvard Business School Press, 1996.

10. Davenport, Thomas H. *Process Innovation: Reengineering Work through Information Technology.* Boston: Harvard Business School Press, 1993.

11. Deckmyn, Dominique. "Product Data Management Moves Toward Mainstream." *Computerworld,* November 8, 1999.

12. El Sawy, Omar, and Gene Bowles. "Redesigning the Customer Support Process for the Electronic Economy: Insights from Storage Dimensions." *MIS Quarterly,* December 1997.

13. El Sawy, Omar; Arvind Malhotra; Sanjay Gosain; and Kerry Young. "IT-Intensive Value Innovation in the Electronic Economy: Insights from Marshall Industries." *MIS Quarterly,* September 1999.

14. Emigh, Jacquiline. "E-Commerce Strategies." *Computerworld,* August 16, 1999.

15. Ewing, Jack. "Sharing the Wealth." *Business Week e-biz,* March 19, 2001.

16. Frye, Colleen. "Imaging Proves Catalyst for Reengineering." *Client/Server Computing,* November 1994.

17. Garner, Rochelle. "Please Don't Call IT Knowledge Management!" *Computerworld,* August 9, 1999.

18. Garvin, David. "Building a Learning Organization." *Harvard Business Review,* July–August 1995.

19. Goldman, Steven; Roger Nagel; and Kenneth Preis. *Agile Competitors and Virtual Organizations: Strategies for Enriching the Customer.* New York: Van Nostrand Reinhold, 1995.

20. Grover, Varun, and Pradipkumar Ramanlal. "Six Myths of Information and Markets: Information Technology Networks, Electronic Commerce, and the Battle for Consumer Surplus." *MIS Quarterly,* December 1999.

21. Hamm, Steve, and Marcia Stepaneck. "From Reengineering to E-Engineering." *Business Week e.biz,* March 22, 1999.

22. Hibbard, Justin. "Spreading Knowledge." *Computerworld,* April 7, 1997.

23. Kalakota, Ravi, and Marcia Robinson. *E-Business: Roadmap for Success.* Reading, MA: Addison-Wesley, 1999.

24. Kerwin, Kathleen; Marcia Stepanek; and David Welch. "At Ford, E-Commerce Is Job 1." *Business Week,* February 28, 2000.

25. Kettinger, William; Varun Grover; Subashish Guha; and Albert Segars. "Strategic Information Systems Revisited: A Study in Sustainability and Performance." *MIS Quarterly,* March 1994.

26. Kettinger, William; Varun Grover; and Albert Segars. "Do Strategic Systems Really Pay Off? An Analysis of Classic Strategic IT Cases." *Information Systems Management,* Winter 1995.

27. Kettinger, William; James Teng; and Subashish Guha. "Business Process Change: A Study of Methodologies, Techniques, and Tools." *MIS Quarterly,* March 1997.

28. Kover, Amy. "Schwab Makes a Grand Play for the Rich." *Fortune,* February 7, 2000.

29. Melymuka, Kathleen. "GE's Quality Gamble." *Computerworld,* June 8, 1998, p. 64.

30. Mooney, John; Vijay Gurbaxani; and Kenneth Kramer. "A Process Oriented Framework for Assessing the Business Value of Information Technology." *The Data Base for Advances in Information Systems,* Spring 1996.

31. Neumann, Seev. *Strategic Information Systems: Competition through Information Technologies.* New York: Macmillan College Publishing Co., 1994.

32. Nonaka, Ikujiro. "The Knowledge Creating Company." *Harvard Business Review,* November–December 1991.

33. Pegels, C. Carl. *Total Quality Management: A Survey of Its Important Aspects.* Danvers, MA: Boyd & Fraser Publishing Co., 1995.

34. Porter, Michael, and Victor Millar. "How Information Gives You Competitive Advantage." *Harvard Business Review,* July–August 1985.

35. Prokesch, Steven. "Unleashing the Power of Learning: An Interview with British Petroleum's John Browne." *Harvard Business Review,* September–October 1997.

36. Resnick, Rosalind. "The Virtual Corporation." *PC Today,* February 1995.

37. Seybold, Patricia. *Customers.com: How to Create a Profitable Business Strategy for the Internet and Beyond.* New York: Times Books, 1998.

38. Shapiro, Carl, and Hal Varian. *Information Rules: A Strategic Guide to the Network Economy.* Boston: Harvard Business School Press, 1999.

39. Siekman, Philip. "Why Infotech Loves Its Giant Job Shops." *Fortune,* May 12, 1997.

40. Weill, Peter, and Michael Vitale. *Place to Space: Migrating to E-Business Models.* Boston: Harvard Business School Press, 2001.

Chapter 3—Data Resource Management

1. Ahrens, Judith, and Chetan Sankar. "Tailoring Database Training for End Users." *MIS Quarterly,* December 1993.

2. Anthes, Gary. "Minding the Storage." *Computerworld.* March 22, 1999.

3. Atwood, Thomas. "Object Databases Come of Age." *OBJECT Magazine,* July 1996.

4. Baer, Tony. "Object Databases." *Computerworld,* January 18, 1999.

5. "Borders Knows No Bounds in E-Business." From www.software.ibm/eb/borders, March 1999.

6. Fayyad, Usama; Gregory Piatetsky-Shapiro; and Padraic Smith. "The KDD Process for Extracting Useful Knowledge from Volumes of Data." *Communications of the ACM*, November 1996.

7. Finkelstein, Richard. *Understanding the Need for On-Line Analytical Servers*. Ann Arbor, MI: Arbor Software Corporation, 1994.

8. Jacobsen, Ivar; Maria Ericsson; and Ageneta Jacobsen. *The Object Advantage: Business Process Reengineering with Object Technology*. New York: ACM Press, 1995.

9. IBM Corporation. "Credit Union Central Alberta Upgrades MIS Reporting with DB2." Success stories, ibm.com, July 19, 2002.

10. Kalakota, Ravi, and Marcia Robinson. *E-Business: Roadmap for Success*. Reading, MA: Addison-Wesley, 1999.

11. Morgan, Cynthia. "Data Is King." *Computerworld*, March 27, 2000.

12. Lorents, Alden, and James Morgan. *Database Systems: Concepts, Management and Applications*. Fort Worth: The Dryden Press, 1998.

13. Mannino, Michael. *Database Application Development and Design*. Burr Ridge, IL: McGraw-Hill Irwin, 2001.

14. Nance, Barry. "Managing Tons of Data." *Computerworld*, April 23, 2001.

15. Rosencrance, Linda. "Data Warehouse Gives Trimac Data for the Long Haul." *Computerworld*, July 30, 2001, p. 42.

16. Spiegler, Israel. "Toward a Unified View of Data: Bridging Data Structure and Content." *Information Systems Management*, Spring 1995.

17. Stedman, Craig. "Databases Grab Hold of Objects, Multimedia on the Web." *Computerworld*, October 21, 1996.

18. Storey, Veda, and Robert Goldstein. "Knowledge-Based Approaches to Database Design." *MIS Quarterly*, March 1993.

19. Ta Check, James. "IBM: Not by Databases Alone." *ZD Net*, February 3, 2000.

20. White, Colin. "Data Warehousing: Choosing the Right Tools." *Computerworld*, Special Advertising Supplement, March 2, 1998.

Chapter 4—Telecommunications and Networks

1. Anderson, Heidi. "The Rise of the Extranet." *PC Today*, February 1997.

2. Barksdale, Jim. "The Next Step: Extranets." *Netscape Columns: The Main Thing*, December 3, 1996.

3. Blum, Jonathan. "Peering into the Future." *Red Herring*, November 13, 2000.

4. Campbell, Ian. "The Intranet: Slashing the Cost of Doing Business." Research Report, International Data Corporation, 1996.

5. Cronin, Mary. *Doing More Business on the Internet*. New York: Van Nostrand Reinhold, 1995.

6. Cronin, Mary. *Global Advantage on the Internet*. New York: Van Nostrand Reinhold, 1996.

7. "Dialing for Data." In Technology Buyer's Guide, *Fortune*, Winter 2000.

8. Fernandez, Tony. "Beyond the Browser." *NetWorker*, March/April 1997.

9. Harler, Curt, and Donell Short. "Building Broadband Networks." Special advertising section, *Business Week*, July 12, 1999.

10. Housel, Thomas, and Eric Skopec. *Global Telecommunications Revolution: The Business Perspective*. New York: McGraw-Hill Irwin, 2001.

11. Kalakota, Ravi, and Marcia Robinson. *E-Business: Roadmap for Success*. Reading, MA: Addison-Wesley, 1999.

12. Lais, Sami. "Satellites Link Bob Evans Farms." *Computerworld*, July 2, 2001.

13. "Life on the Web." In Technology Buyer's Guide, *Fortune*, Winter 1999.

14. Martin, Chuck. *The Digital Estate: Strategies for Competing, Surviving, and Thriving in an Internetworked World*. New York: McGraw-Hill, 1997.

15. Messerschmitt, David. *Network Applications: A Guide to the New Computing Infrastructure*. San Francisco: Morgan Kaufmann Publishers, 1999.

16. Murphy, Kate. "Cruising the Net in Hyperdrive." *Business Week*, January 24, 2000.

17. Nee, Eric. "The Upstarts Are Rocking Telecom." *Fortune*, January 24, 2000.

18. O'Brien, Atiye. "Friday Intranet Focus." *Upside.com: Hot Private Companies*. Upside Publishing Company, 1996.

19. Papows, Jeff. "Endquotes." *NetReady Adviser*, Winter 1997.

20. "Phones to Go." In Technology Buyer's Guide, *Fortune*, Winter 1999.

21. Radding, Alan. "Leading the Way." *Computerworld ROI*, September/October 2001.

22. Rosenbush, Steve. "Charge of the Light Brigade." *Business Week*, January 31, 2000.

23. Stuart, Anne. "Cutting the Cord." *Inc. Tech*, 2001, No. 1.

24. Wallace, Bob. "Hotels See Service from Virtual Net." *Computerworld*, February 9, 1998.

Chapter 5—Introduction to e-Business Systems

1. Armor, Daniel. *The E-Business (R)Evolution: Living and Working in an Interconnected World.* Upper Saddle River, NJ: Prentice Hall, 2000.

2. Bylinsky, Gene. "The e-Factory Catches On." *Fortune,* August 13, 2001.

3. Caulfield, Brian. "Systems That Talk Together, Kick Butt Together." *eCompany,* January/February 2001.

4. "Communications Leader Becomes Customer-Focused E-Business." *Siebel.com,* March 12, 2001.

5. "Davenport, Thomas. *Process Innovation: Reengineering Work through Information Technology.* Boston: Harvard Business School Press, 1993.

6. Diese, Martin; Conrad Nowikow; Patrick King; and Amy Wright. *Executive's Guide to E-Business: From Tactics to Strategy.* New York: John Wiley & Sons, 2000.

7. DeMeyer, Desiree, and Don Steinberg. "The Smart Business 50—General Electric." *Smart Business,* September 2001.

8. El Sawy, Omar; Arvind Malhotra; Sanjay Gosain; and Kerry Young. "IT-Intensive Value Innovation in the Electronic Economy: Insights from Marshal Industries." *MIS Quarterly,* September 1999.

9. El Sawy, Omar. *Redesigning Enterprise Processes for E-Business.* New York: McGraw-Hill Irwin, 2001.

10. Essex, David. "Enterprise Application Integration." *Computerworld,* October 4, 1999.

11. Essex, David. "Get into Web Portals." *Computerworld,* March 15, 1999.

12. Fellenstein, Craig, and Ron Wood. *Exploring E-Commerce, Global E-Business, and E-Societies.* Upper Saddle River, NJ: Prentice Hall, 2000.

13. Gates, Bill. *Business @ the Speed of Thought.* New York: Warner Books, 1999.

14. Geoff, Leslie. "CRM: The Cutting Edge of Serving Customers." *Computerworld,* February 28, 2000.

15. Hamel, Gary, and Jeff Sandler. "The E-Corporation." *Fortune,* December 7, 1998.

16. Hamm, Steve, and Robert Hoff. "An Eagle Eye on Customers." *Business Week,* February 21, 2000.

17. Hoffman, Thomas. "Intranet Helps Workers Navigate Corporate Maze." *Computerworld,* June 4, 2001.

18. Johnson, Amy. "CRM Rises to the Top." *Computerworld,* August 16, 1999.

19. Kalakota, Ravi, and Marcia Robinson. *E-Business 2.0: Roadmap for Success.* Reading, MA: Addison-Wesley, 2001.

20. Keen, Peter, and Craigg Balance. *Online Profits: A Manager's Guide to Electronic Commerce.* Boston: Harvard Business School Press, 1997.

21. McCann, Stefanie. "Career Opportunities in Enterprise Resource Planning." *Computerworld,* February 7, 2000.

22. McCarthy, Vance. "ERP Gets Down to E-Business." *HP World,* January 2000.

23. Norris, Grant; James Hurley; Kenneth Hartley; John Dunleavy; and John Balls. *E-Business and ERP: Transforming the Enterprise.* New York: John Wiley & Sons, 2000.

24. Orenstein, David. "Enterprise Application Integration." *Computerworld,* October 4, 1999.

25. Perman, Stacy. "Automate or Die." *e-Company Now,* July 2001.

26. Robb, Drew. "Rediscovering Efficiency." *Computerworld,* July 16, 2001.

27. Salesforce.com. "Baker Tanks Leverages Salesforce.com's Wireless Access to Extend Range of Customer Service." Salesforce.com, 2002.

28. Sawhney, Mohan, and Jeff Zabin. *The Seven Steps to Nirvana: Strategic Insights into e-Business Transformation.* New York: McGraw-Hill, 2001.

29. Tapscott, Don; David Ticoll; and Alex Lowy. *Digital Capital: Harnessing the Power of Business Webs.* Boston: Harvard Business School Press, 2000.

30. Tucker, Jay. "The New Money: Transactions Pour across the Web." *Datamation,* April 1997.

31. "Your Body, Your Job." In Technology Buyer's Guide, *Fortune,* Winter 2000.

Chapter 6—Enterprise e-Business Systems

1. Betts, Mitch. "Kinks in the Chain." *Computerworld,* December 17, 2001.

2. Caulfield, Brian. "Facing Up to CRM." *Business 2.0,* August/September 2001.

3. Caulfield, Brian. "Toward a More Perfect (and Realistic) E-Business." *Business 2.0,* January 2002.

4. Engardio, Pete. "Why the Supply Chain Broke Down." *Business Week,* March 19, 2001.

5. Geoff, Leslie. "CRM: The Coming Edge of Serving Customers." *Computerworld,* February 28, 2000.

6. Hamm, Steve, and Robert Hoff. "An Eagle Eye on Customers." *Business Week,* February 21, 2000.

7. Johnsom, Amy. "CRM Rises to the Top." *Computerworld,* August 16, 1999.

8. Kalakota, Ravi, and Marcia Robinson. *E-Business 2.0: Roadmap for Success.* Reading, MA: Addison-Wesley, 2001.

9. Keenan, Faith. "Opening the Spigot." *Business Week e.Biz,* June 4, 2001.

10. Mello, Adrian. "ERP Fundamentals." *Tech Update,* ZDNet.com, February 7, 2002.

11. Mello, Adrian. "4 Trends Shaping ERP." *Tech Update,* ZDNet.com, February 7, 2002.

12. Merian, Lucas. "Supermarket Dumps $89 Million SAP Project." *Computerworld,* February 5, 2001.

13. Merian, Lucas. "Retailers Hit Installation Bumps with SAP Software." *Computerworld,* February 19, 2001.

14. Norris, Grant; James Hurley; Kenneth Hartley; John Dunleavy; and John Balls. *E-Business and ERP: Transforming the Enterprise.* New York: John Wiley & Sons, 2000.

15. Oliver, Keith; Anne Chung; and Nick Samanich. "Beyond Utopia: The Realists Guide to Supply Chain Management." *Strategy & Business,* Second Quarter 2001.

16. Oracle Corporation. "Visa to Save Millions a Year by Automating Back Office Processes with Oracle E-Business Suite." Customer Profile. Oracle.com, 2002.

17. Poirier, Charles, and Michael Bauer. *E-Supply Chain: Using the Internet to Revolutionize Your Business.* San Francisco: Brett-Koehler Publishers, 2000.

18. Rigby, Darrell; Frederich Reichheld; and Phil Schefter. "Avoid the Four Perils of CRM." *Harvard Business Review,* February 2002.

19. Sawhney, Mohan, and Jeff Zabin. *The Seven Steps to Nirvana: Strategic Insights into e-Business Transformation.* New York: McGraw-Hill, 2001.

20. Selden, Larry, and Geoffrey Colvin. "A Measure of His Success." *Business 2.0,* November 2001.

21. Senn, James. "Electronic Data Interchange: Elements of Implementation." *Information Systems Management,* Winter 1992.

22. Siebel Systems. "eBusiness: Managing the Demand Chain." White Paper. Siebel.com, 2002.

23. Siebel Systems. "Communications Leader Becomes Customer-Focused E-Business." Siebel.com, March 12, 2001.

24. Seybold, Patricia. *The Customer Revolution.* New York: Crown Business, 2001.

25. Sliwa, Carol. "Users Cling to EDI for Critical Transactions." *Computerworld,* March 15, 1999.

26. Songini, Marc. "Policing the Supply Chain." *Computerworld,* April 30, 2001.

27. SupplySolution Inc. "Modern Plastics Technology Derives Significant Process Improvements from Implementation of I-Supply Service." SupplySolution.com, 2002.

28. "Telifonica Servicios Avanzados De Informacio Leads Spain's Retail Industry into Global Electronic Commerce." Customer Profiles. Netscape.com, March 1999.

Chapter 7—Electronic Commerce Systems

1. Anthes, Gary. "Cha Aims Big with Micropayment Service." *Computerworld,* July 26, 1999.

2. Armor, Daniel. *The E-Business (R)Evolution: Living and Working in an Interconnected World.* Upper Saddle River, NJ: Prentice Hall, 2000.

3. "Click Here to Shop." In Technology Buyers Guide, *Fortune,* Winter 2000.

4. Collett, Stacy. "Sun, Newscape Develop Bill Payment Software." *Computerworld,* December 13, 1999.

5. Cross, Kim. "Need Options? Go Configure." *Business 2.0,* February 2000.

6. Davis, Jeffrey. "How IT Works." *Business 2.0,* February 2000.

7. Davis, Jeffrey. "Mall Rats." *Business 2.0,* January 1999.

8. Diese, Martin; Conrad Nowikow; Patrick King; and Amy Wright. *Executive's Guide to E-Business: From Tactics to Strategy.* New York: John Wiley & Sons, 2000.

9. El Sawy, Omar; Arvind Malhotra; Sanjay Gosain; and Kerry Young. "IT-Intensive Value Innovation in the Electronic Economy: Insights from Marshal Industries." *MIS Quarterly,* September 1999.

10. Fellenstein, Craig, and Ron Wood. *Exploring E-Commerce, Global E-Business, and E-Societies.* Upper Saddle River, NJ: Prentice Hall, 2000.

11. Fingar, Peter; Harsha Kumar; and Tarun Sharma. *Enterprise E-Commerce.* Tampa, FL: Meghan-Kiffer Press, 2000.

12. Georgia, Bonnie. "Give Your E-Store an Edge." *Smart Business,* October 2001.

13. Gulati, Ranjay, and Jason Garino. "Get the Right Mix of Clicks and Bricks." *Harvard Business Review,* May–June 2000.

14. Haylock, Christina, and Len Muscarella. *Net Success.* Holbrook, MA: Adams Media Corporation, 1999.

15. Hoque, Faisal. *E-Enterprise: Business Models, Architecture and Components.* Cambridge, UK: Cambridge University Press, 2000.

16. Kalakota, Ravi, and Marcia Robinson. *E-Business: Roadmap for Success.* Reading, MA: Addison-Wesley, 1999.

17. Kalakota, Ravi, and Andrew Whinston. *Electronic Commerce: A Manager's Guide.* Reading, MA: Addison-Wesley, 1997.

18. Kalakota, Ravi, and Andrew Whinston. *Frontiers of Electronic Commerce.* Reading, MA: Addison-Wesley, 1996.

19. Kastner, Peter, and Christopher Stevens. "Electronic Commerce: A True Challenge for IT Managers." In "Enterprise Solutions: Electronic Commerce." Special Advertising Supplement to *Computerworld,* January 13, 1997.

20. Keen, Peter, and Craigg Balance. *Online Profits: A Manager's Guide to Electronic Commerce.* Boston: Harvard Business School Press, 1997.

21. Keenan, Faith, and Timothy Mullaney. "Let's Get Back to Basics." *Business Week e.biz,* October 29, 2001.

22. Korper, Steffano, and Juanita Ellis. *The E-Commerce Book: Building the E-Empire.* San Diego: Academic Press, 2000.

23. Leon, Mark. "Trading Spaces." *Business 2.0,* February 2000.

24. Loshin, Peter. "The Electronic Marketplace." *PC Today,* July 1996.

25. Machlis, Sharon. "Portals Link Buyers, Sellers." *Computerworld,* January 25, 1999.

26. Machlis, Sharon. "Web Retailers Try to Keep Their Hits Up." *Computerworld,* February 8, 1999.

27. Martin, Chuck. *The Digital Estate: Strategies for Competing, Surviving, and Thriving in an Internetworked World.* New York: McGraw-Hill, 1997.

28. Morgan, Cynthia. "Dead Set against SET?" *Computerworld,* March 29, 1999.

29. Robinson, Edward. "Battle to the Bitter End(-to-End)." *Business 2.0,* July 25, 2000.

30. Rosenoer, Jonathan; Douglas Armstrong; and J. Russell Gates. *The Clickable Corporation: Successful Strategies for Capturing the Internet Advantage.* New York: The Free Press, 1999.

31. Schwartz, Evan. *Digital Darwinism.* New York: Broadway Books, 1999.

32. Schwartz, Evan. *Webonomics.* New York: Broadway Books, 1997.

33. Senn, James. "Electronic Data Interchange: Elements of Implementation." *Information Systems Management,* Winter 1992.

34. "Servers with a Smile." In Technology Buyers Guide, *Fortune,* Summer 2000.

35. Seybold, Patricia, with Ronnie Marshak. *Customers Com: How to Create a Profitable Business Strategy for the Internet and Beyond.* New York: Times Business, 1998.

36. Shapiro, Carl, and Hal Varian. *Information Rules: A Strategic Guide to the Network Economy.* Boston: Harvard Business School Press, 1999.

37. Sliwa, Carol. "Users Cling to EDI for Critical Transactions." *Computerworld,* March 15, 1999.

38. Tapscott, Don; David Ticoll; and Alex Lowy. *Digital Capital: Harnessing the Power of Business Webs.* Boston: Harvard Business School Press, 2000.

39. "Telefónica Servicios Avanzados De Informació Leads Spain's Retail Industry into Global Electronic Commerce." At www.netscape.com/solutions/business/profiles, March 1999.

40. Trombly, Marcia. "Electronic Billing Merger Should Benefit Billers, Banks." *Computerworld,* February 21, 2000.

41. Tully, Shawn. "The B2B Tool That Is Really Changing the World." *Fortune,* March 20, 2000.

Chapter 8—Decision Support Systems

1. Allen, Bradley. "Case-Based Reasoning: Business Applications." *Communications of the ACM,* March 1994.

2. Ashline, Peter, and Vincent Lai. "Virtual Reality: An Emerging User-Interface Technology." *Information Systems Management,* Winter 1995.

3. Begley, Sharon. "Software au Naturel." *Newsweek,* May 8, 1995.

4. Belcher, Lloyd, and Hugh Watson. "Assessing the Value of Conoco's EIS." *MIS Quarterly,* September 1993.

5. Blackburn, David; Rik Henderson; and Gary Welz. "VRML Evolution: State of the Art Advances." *Internet World,* December 1996.

6. Blattberg, Robert C.; Rashi Glazer; and John D. C. Little. *The Marketing Information Revolution.* Boston: The Harvard Business School Press, 1994.

7. Bose, Ranjit, and Vijayan Sugumaran. "Application of Intelligent Agent Technology for Managerial Data Analysis and Mining." *The Data Base for Advances in Information Systems,* Winter 1999.

8. Botchner, Ed. "Data Mining: Plumbing the Depths of Corporate Databases." Special Advertising Supplement. *Computerworld,* April 21, 1997.

9. Brown, Stuart. "Making Decisions in a Flood of Data." *Fortune,* August 13, 2001.

10. Bylinsky, Gene. "The e-Factory Catches On." *Fortune,* August 13, 2001.

11. Cox, Earl. "Relational Database Queries Using Fuzzy Logic." *AI Expert,* January 1995.

12. Cronin, Mary. "Using the Web to Push Key Data to Decision Makers." *Fortune,* September 29, 1997.

13. Darling, Charles. "Ease Implementation Woes with Packaged Datamarts." *Datamation,* March 1997.

14. "Dayton Hudson Knows What's in Store for Their Customers." Advertising Section. *Intelligent Enterprise,* January 5, 1999.

15. Deck, Stewart. "Data Visualization." *Computerworld,* October 11, 1999.

16. Deck, Stewart. "Data Warehouse Project Starts Simply." *Computerworld,* February 15, 1999.

17. Deck, Stewart. "Early Users Give Nod to Analysis Package." *Computerworld,* February 22, 1999.

18. Deck, Stewart. "Mining Your Business." *Computerworld,* May 17, 1999.

19. Egan, Richard. "The Expert Within." *PC Today,* January 1995.

20. Finkelstein, Richard. *Understanding the Need for Online Analytical Servers.* Ann Arbor, MI: Comshare, 1994.

21. Finkelstein, Richard. "When OLAP Does Not Relate." *Computerworld,* December 12, 1994.

22. Freeman, Eva. "Birth of a Terabyte Data Warehouse." *Datamation,* April 1997.

23. Freeman, Eva. "Desktop Reporting Tools." *Datamation,* June 1997.

24. Gantz, John. "The New World of Enterprise Reporting Is Here." *Computerworld,* February 1, 1999.

25. Gates, Bill. *Business @ the Speed of Thought.* New York: Warner Books, 1999.

26. Goldberg, David. "Genetic and Evolutionary Algorithms Come of Age." *Communications of the ACM,* March 1994.

27. Gorry, G. Anthony, and Michael Scott Morton. "A Framework for Management Information Systems." *Sloan Management Review,* Fall 1971; republished Spring 1989.

28. Hall, Mark. "Supercomputing: From R&D to P&L." *Computerworld,* December 13, 1999.

29. "Helping Customers Help Themselves."Advertising Section. *Intelligent Enterprise,* January 5, 1999.

30. Higgins, Kelly. "Your Agent Is Calling." *Communications Week,* August 5, 1996.

31. Jablonowski, Mark. "Fuzzy Risk Analysis: Using AI Systems." *AI Expert,* December 1994.

32. Kalakota, Ravi, and Marcia Robinson. *E-Business: Roadmap for Success.* Reading, MA: Addison-Wesley, 1999.

33. Kalakota, Ravi, and Andrew Whinston. *Electronic Commerce: A Manager's Guide.* Reading, MA: Addison-Wesley, 1997.

34. King, James. "Intelligent Agents: Bringing Good Things to Life." *AI Expert,* February 1995.

35. King, Julia. "Infomediaries." *Computerworld,* November 1, 1999.

36. King, Julia. "Sharing GIS Talent with the World." *Computerworld,* October 6, 1997.

37. Kurszweil, Raymond. *The Age of Intelligent Machines.* Cambridge, MA: The MIT Press, 1992.

38. Lais, Sami. "CA Advances Neural Network System." *Computerworld,* December 13, 1999.

39. Lundquist, Christopher. "Personalization in E-Commerce." *Computerworld,* March 22, 1999.

40. Machlis, Sharon. "Agent Technology." *Computerworld,* March 22, 1999.

41. Mailoux, Jacquiline. "New Menu at PepsiCo." *Computerworld,* May 6, 1996.

42. McNeill, F. Martin, and Ellen Thro. *Fuzzy Logic: A Practical Approach.* Boston: AP Professional, 1994.

43. Murray, Gerry. "Making Connections with Enterprise Knowledge Portals." White Paper. *Computerworld,* September 6, 1999.

44. Orenstein, David. "Corporate Portals." *Computerworld,* June 28, 1999.

45. Ouellette, Tim. "Opening Your Own Portal." *Computerworld,* August 9, 1999.

46. Pimentel, Ken, and Kevin Teixeira. *Virtual Reality through the New Looking Glass.* 2nd ed. New York: Intel/McGraw-Hill, 1995.

47. Plumtree Corporation. "Customer: Procter and Gamble." *Plumtree.com,* March 16, 2001.

48. Rosenberg, Marc. *e-Learning: Strategies for Delivering Knowledge in the Digital Age.* New York: McGraw-Hill, 2001.

49. Schier, Robert. "Finding Pearls in an Ocean of Data." *Computerworld,* July 23, 2001.

50. Turban, Efraim, and Jay Aronson. *Decision Support Systems and Intelligent Systems.* Upper Saddle River, NJ: Prentice Hall, 1998.

51. Vandenbosch, Betty, and Sid Huff. "Searching and Scanning: How Executives Obtain Information from Executive Information Systems." *MIS Quarterly,* March 1997.

52. Wagner, Mitch. "Engine Links Ads to Searches." *Computerworld,* June 2, 1997.

53. Wagner, Mitch. "Reality Check." *Computerworld,* February 26, 1997.

54. Watson, Hugh, and John Satzinger. "Guidelines for Designing EIS Interfaces." *Information Systems Management,* Fall 1994.

55. Watterson, Karen. "Parallel Tracks." *Datamation,* May 1997.

56. Winston, Patrick. "Rethinking Artificial Intelligence." Program Announcement, Massachusetts Institute of Technology, September 1997.

57. Wreden, Nick. "Enterprise Portals: Integrating Information to Drive Productivity." *Beyond Computing,* March 2000.

Chapter 9—Developing Business/IT Strategies

1. Afuah, Allan, and Christopher Tucci. *Internet Business Models and Strategies.* New York: McGraw-Hill/Irwin, 2001.

2. Clark, Charles; Nancy Cavanaugh; Carol Brown; and V. Sambamurthy. "Building Change-Readiness Capabilities in the IS Organization: Insights from the Bell Atlantic Experience." *MIS Quarterly,* December 1997.

3. Cole-Gomolski, Barb. "Users Loath to Share Their Know-How." *Computerworld,* November 17, 1997.

4. Collette, Stacy. "SWOT Analysis." *Computerworld*, July 19, 1999.

5. Cronin, Mary. *The Internet Strategy Handbook*. Boston: Harvard Business School Press, 1996.

6. Cross, John; Michael Earl; and Jeffrey Sampler. "Transformation of the IT Function at British Petroleum." *MIS Quarterly*, December 1997.

7. Das, Sidhartha; Shaker Zahra; and Merrill Warkentin. "Integrating the Content and Process of Strategic MIS Planning with Competitive Strategy." *Decision Sciences Journal*, November/December 1991.

8. De Geus, Arie. "Planning as Learning." *Harvard Business Review*, March–April 1988.

9. De Geus, Arie. "The Living Company." *Harvard Business Review*, March–April 1997.

10. Deise, Martin; Conrad Nowikow; Patrick King; and Amy Wright. *Executive's Guide to E-Business: From Tactics to Strategy*. New York: John Wiley & Sons, 2000.

11. Earl, Michael. "Experiences in Strategic Information Systems Planning." *MIS Quarterly*, March 1993.

12. El Sawy, Omar; Arvind Malhotra; Sanjay Gosain; and Kerry Young. "IT-Intensive Value Innovation in the Electronic Economy: Insights from Marshall Industries." *MIS Quarterly*, September 1999.

13. El Sawy, Omar, and Gene Bowles. "Redesigning the Customer Support Process for the Electronic Economy: Insights from Storage Dimensions." *MIS Quarterly*, December 1997.

14. Fingar, Peter; Harsha Kumar; and Tarun Sharma. *Enterprise E-Commerce: The Software Component Breakthrough for Business to Business Commerce*. Tampa, FL: Meghan-Kiffer Press, 2000.

15. Grover, Varun; James Teng; and Kirk Fiedler. "IS Investment Priorities in Contemporary Organizations." *Communications of the ACM*, February 1998.

16. Hawson, James, and Jesse Beeler. "Effects of User Participation in Systems Development: A Longitudinal Field Experiment." *MIS Quarterly*, December 1997.

17. Hills, Melanie. *Intranet Business Strategies*. New York: John Wiley & Sons, 1997.

18. Kalakota, Ravi, and Marcia Robinson. *E-Business: Roadmap for Success*. Reading, MA: Addison-Wesley, 1999.

19. Keen, Peter G. W. *Shaping the Future: Business Design through Information Technology*. Boston: Harvard Business School, 1991.

20. Kettinger, William; James Teng; and Subashish Guha. "Business Process Change: A Study of Methodologies, Techniques, and Tools." *MIS Quarterly*, March 1997.

21. Koudsi, Suzanne. "Actually, It Is Like Brain Surgery." *Fortune*, March 20, 2000.

22. Maglitta, Joseph. "Rocks in the Gears: Reengineering the Workplace." *Computerworld*, October 3, 1994.

23. Magretta, Joan. "Why Business Models Matter." *Harvard Business Review*, May 2002.

24. Norris, Grant; James Hurley; Kenneth Hartley; John Dunleavy; and John Balls. *E-Business and ERP: Transforming the Enterprise*. New York: John Wiley & Sons, 2000.

25. Prokesch, Steven. "Unleashing the Power of Learning: An Interview with British Petroleum's John Browne." *Harvard Business Review*, September–October 1997.

26. Senge, Peter. *The Fifth Discipline: The Art and Practice of the Learning Organization*. New York: Currency Doubleday, 1994.

Chapter 10—Developing Business/IT Solutions

1. Anthes, Gary. "The Quest for IT E-Quality." *Computerworld*, December 13, 1999.

2. Burden, Kevin. "IBM Waxes, Others Wane." *Computerworld*, March 15, 1999.

3. Clark, Charles; Nancy Cavanaugh; Carol Brown; and V. Sambamurthy. "Building Change-Readiness Capabilities in the IS Organization: Insights from the Bell Atlantic Experience." *MIS Quarterly*, December 1997.

4. Cole-Gomolski, Barbara. "Companies Turn to Web for ERP Training." *Computerworld*, February 8, 1999.

5. Cole-Gomolski, Barbara. "Users Loath to Share Their Know-How." *Computerworld*, November 17, 1997.

6. Cronin, Mary. *The Internet Strategy Handbook*. Boston: Harvard Business School Press, 1996.

7. Cross, John; Michael Earl; and Jeffrey Sampler. "Transformation of the IT Function at British Petroleum." *MIS Quarterly*, December 1997.

8. El Sawy, Omar, and Gene Bowles. "Redesigning the Customer Support Process for the Electronic Economy: Insights from Storage Dimensions." *MIS Quarterly*, December 1997.

9. El Sawy, Omar; Arvind Malhotra; Sanjay Gosain; and Kerry Young. "IT-Intensive Value Innovation in the Electronic Economy: Insights from Marshall Industries." *MIS Quarterly*, September 1999.

10. Fogarty, Kevin. "Net Manners Matter: How Top Sites Rank in Social Behavior." *Computerworld*, October 18, 1999.

11. Grover, Varun; James Teng; and Kirk Fiedler. "IS Investment Priorities in Contemporary Organizations." *Communications of the ACM*, February 1998.

12. Haskin, David. "If I Had a Cyberhammer." *Business Week Enterprise*, March 29, 1999.

13. Hawson, James, and Jesse Beeler. "Effects of User Participation in Systems Development: A Longitudinal Field Experiment." *MIS Quarterly*, December 1997.

14. Hills, Melanie. *Intranet Business Strategies.* New York: John Wiley & Sons, 1997.

15. Holtz, Shel. PCWeek: *The Intranet Advantage.* Emeryville, CA: Ziff-Davis Press, 1996.

16. Iansiti, Marco, and Alan MacCormack. "Developing Products on Internet Time." *Harvard Business Review,* September–October 1997.

17. Kalakota, Ravi, and Marcia Robinson. *E-Business: Roadmap for Success.* Reading, MA: Addison-Wesley, 1999.

18. Kettinger, William; James Teng; and Subashish Guha. "Business Process Change: A Study of Methodologies, Techniques, and Tools." *MIS Quarterly,* March 1997.

19. Koudsi, Suzanne. "Actually, It Is Like Brain Surgery." *Fortune,* March 20, 2000.

20. LaPlante, Alice. "Eyes on the Customer." *Computerworld,* March 15, 1999.

21. Machlis, Sharon. "Web Retailers Retool for Mainstream Users." *Computerworld,* March 22, 1999.

22. Maglitta, Joseph. "Rocks in the Gears: Reengineering the Workplace." *Computerworld,* October 3, 1994.

23. Millard, Elizabeth. "Big Company Weakened." *Business 2.0,* January 2000.

24. Morgan, James N. *Application Cases in MIS.* 4th ed. New York: Irwin/McGraw-Hill, 2002.

25. Neilsen, Jakob. "Better Data Brings Better Sales." *Business 2.0,* May 15, 2001.

26. Nielsen, Jakob. "Design for Process, Not for Products." *Business 2.0,* July 10, 2001.

27. Orenstein, David. "Software Is Too Hard to Use." *Computerworld,* August 23, 1999.

28. Ouellette, Tim. "Giving Users the Key to Their Web Content." *Computerworld,* July 26, 1999.

29. Ouellette, Tim. "Opening Your Own Portal." *Computerworld,* August 9, 1999.

30. Pereira, Rex Eugene. "Resource View of SAP as a Source of Competitive Advantage for Firms." *The Database for Advances in Information Systems,* Winter 1999.

31. Schwartz, Matthew. "Tweak This!" *Computerworld,* January 31, 2000.

32. Senge, Peter. *The Fifth Discipline: The Art and Practice of the Learning Organization.* New York: Currency Doubleday, 1994.

33. Sliwa, Carol. "E-Commerce Solutions: How Real?" *Computerworld,* February 28, 2000.

34. Songini, Marc. "To Customize or Not." *Computerworld,* September 3, 2001.

35. Whitten, Jeffrey, and Lonnie Bentley. *Systems Analysis and Design Methods.* 4th ed. New York: Irwin/McGraw-Hill, 1998.

36. Wreden, Nick. "Enterprise Portals: Integrating Information to Drive Productivity." *Beyond Computing,* March 2000.

Chapter 11—Security and Ethical Challenges

1. Anthes, Gary. "Biometrics." *Computerworld,* October 12, 1998.

2. Anthes, Gary. "When Five 9s Aren't Enough." *Computerworld,* October 8, 2001.

3. Bahar, Richard. "Who's Reading Your E-Mail?" *Fortune,* February 3, 1997.

4. Breen, Bill. "Bankers Hours." *Fast Company,* November 2001.

5. Cole-Gomolski, Barb. "Quick Fixes Are of Limited Use in Deterring Force Diet of Spam." *Computerworld,* October 20, 1997.

6. Collett, Stacy. "Net Managers Battle Online Trading Boom." *Computerworld,* July 5, 1999.

7. Culnane, Mary. "How Did They Get My Name? An Exploratory Investigation of Consumer Attitudes toward Secondary Information Use." *MIS Quarterly,* September 1993.

8. Deckmyn, Dominique. "More Managers Monitor E-Mail." *Computerworld,* October 18, 1999.

9. Dejoie, Roy; George Fowler; and David Paradice, eds. *Ethical Issues in Information Systems.* Boston: Boyd & Fraser, 1991.

10. Donaldson, Thomas. "Values in Tension: Ethics Away from Home." *Harvard Business Review,* September–October 1996.

11. Dunlop, Charles, and Rob Kling, eds. *Computerization and Controversy: Value Conflicts and Social Choices.* San Diego: Academic Press, 1991.

12. Duvall, Mel. "Protecting against Viruses." *Inter@ctive Week,* February 28, 2000.

13. Elias, Paul. "Paid Informant." *Red Herring,* January 16, 2001.

14. Ganesan, Ravi, and Ravi Sandhu, guest editors. "Security in Cyberspace." Special Section, *Communications of the ACM,* November 1994.

15. Harrison, Ann. "FBI Issues Software to Help Detect Web Attacks." *Computerworld,* February 14, 2000.

16. Harrison, Ann. "Internet Worm Destroys Data." *Computerworld,* June 14, 1999.

17. Harrison, Ann. "RealNetworks Slapped with Privacy Lawsuits." *Computerworld,* November 15, 1999.

18. Harrison, Ann. "Virus Scanning Moving to ISPs." *Computerworld,* September 20, 1999.

19. Joy, Bill. "Report from the Cyberfront." *Newsweek,* February 21, 2000.

20. Johnson, Deborah. "Ethics Online." *Communications of the ACM*, January 1997.

21. Kallman, Earnest, and John Grillo. *Ethical Decision Making and Information Technology: An Introduction with Cases.* New York: Mitchel McGraw-Hill, 1993.

22. Kover, Amy. "Who's Afraid of This Kid?" *Fortune*, March 20, 2000.

23. Lardner, James. "Why Should Anyone Believe You?" *Business 2.0*, March 2002.

24. Levy, Stephen, and Brad Stone. "Hunting the Hackers." *Newsweek*, February 21, 2000.

25. Martin, James. "You Are Being Watched." *PC World*, November 1997.

26. McCarthy, Michael. "Keystroke Cops." *The Wall Street Journal*, March 7, 2000.

27. McFarland, Michael. "Ethics and the Safety of Computer Systems." *Computer*, February 1991.

28. Nance, Barry. "Sending Firewalls Home." *Computerworld*, May 28, 2001.

29. Naughton, Keith. "CyberSlacking." *Newsweek*, November 29, 1999.

30. Neumann, Peter. *Computer-Related Risks.* New York: ACM Press, 1995.

31. Radcliff, Deborah. "Fighting the Flood." *Computerworld*, March 6, 2000.

32. Radcliff, Deborah. "Security Ambassadors." *Computerworld*, October 1, 2001.

33. Robinson, Lori. "How It Works: Viruses." *Smart Computing*, March 2000.

34. Rothfeder, Jeffrey. "Hacked! Are Your Company Files Safe?" *PC World*, November 1996.

35. Rothfeder, Jeffrey. "No Privacy on the Net." *PC World*, February 1997.

36. Sager, Ira; Steve Hamm; Neil Gross; John Carey; and Robert Hoff. "Cyber Crime." *Business Week*, February 21, 2000.

37. Sandberg, Jared. "Holes in the Net." *Newsweek*, February 21, 2000.

38. Smith, H. Jefferson, and John Hasnas. "Debating the Stakeholder Theory." *Beyond Computing*, March–April 1994.

39. Smith, H. Jefferson, and John Hasnas. "Establishing an Ethical Framework." *Beyond Computing*, January–February 1994.

40. Stark, Andrew. "What's the Matter with Business Ethics?" *Harvard Business Review*, May–June 1993.

41. Verton, Dan. "Insider Monitoring Seen as Next Wave in IT Security." *Computerworld*, March 19, 2001.

42. VanScoy, Kayte. "What Your Workers Are Really Up To." *Ziff Davis Smart Business*, September 2001.

43. Vijayan, Jaikumar. "Nimda Needs Harsh Disinfectant," *Computerworld*, September 24, 2001.

44. Willard, Nancy. *The Cyberethics Reader.* Burr Ridge, IL: Irwin/McGraw-Hill, 1997.

45. York, Thomas. "Invasion of Privacy? E-Mail Monitoring Is on the Rise." *Information Week Online*, February 21, 2000.

Chapter 12—Enterprise and Global Management of Information Technology

1. Alter, Allan. "Harmonic Convergence." In "The Premier 100." *Computerworld*, November 16, 1998.

2. Brandel, Mary. "Think Global, Act Local." *Computerworld Global Innovators*, Special Section, March 10, 1997.

3. Bryan, Lowell; Jane Fraser; Jeremy Oppenheim; and Wilhelm Rall. *Race for the World: Strategies to Build a Great Global Firm.* Boston: Harvard Business School Press, 1999.

4. Christensen, Clayton. *The Innovators Dilemma: When New Technologies Cause Great Firms to Fail.* Boston: Harvard Business School Press, 1997.

5. Corbett, Michael. "Outsourcing: Creating Competitive Advantage through Specialization, Alliances, and Innovation." *Fortune*, Special Advertising Section, October 14, 1996.

6. Cronin, Mary. *Global Advantage on the Internet.* New York: Van Nostrand Reinhold, 1996.

7. DeGeus, Arie. "The Living Company." *Harvard Business Review*, March–April 1997.

8. El Sawy, Omar; Arvind Malhotra; Sanjay Gosain; and Kerry Young. "IT-Intensive Value Innovation in the Electronic Economy: Insights from Marshall Industries." *MIS Quarterly*, September 1999.

9. El Sawy, Omar, and Gene Bowles. "Redesigning the Customer Support Process for the Electronic Economy: Insights from Storage Dimensions." *MIS Quarterly*, December 1997.

10. Fryer, Bronwyn. "Payroll Busters." *Computerworld*, March 6, 2000.

11. Gates, Bill. *Business @ the Speed of Thought.* New York: Warner Books, 1999.

12. Gilhooly, Kym. "The Staff That Never Sleeps." *Computerworld*, June 25, 2001.

13. Grover, Varun; James Teng; and Kirk Fiedler. "IS Investment Opportunities in Contemporary Organizations." *Communications of the ACM*, February 1998.

14. Hall, Mark. "Service Providers Give Users More IT Options." *Computerworld*, February 7, 2000.

15. Ives, Blake, and Sirkka Jarvenpaa. "Applications of Global Information Technology: Key Issues for Management." *MIS Quarterly*, March 1991.

16. Kalakota, Ravi, and Marcia Robinson. *E-Business: Roadmap for Success.* Reading, MA: Addison-Wesley, 1999.

17. Kalin, Sari. "The Importance of Being Multiculturally Correct." Global Innovators Series, *Computerworld*, October 6, 1997.

18. King, Julia. "Exporting Jobs Saves IT Money." *Computerworld*, March 15, 1999.

19. King, Julia. "Sun and Pay Lures Coders to Barbados Outsourcer." *Computerworld*, March 15, 1999.

20. King, Julia. "The Lure of Internet Spin-Offs." *Computerworld*, October 18, 1999.

21. Kirkpatrick, David. "Back to the Future with Centralized Computing." *Fortune*, November 10, 1997.

22. LaPlante, Alice. "Global Boundaries.com." Global Innovators Series, *Computerworld*, October 6, 1997.

23. Leinfuss, Emily. "Blend It, Mix It, Unify It." *Computerworld*, March 26, 2001.

24. McGrath, Dermot. "When 'E' Stands for Europe." *Computerworld*, September 6, 1999.

25. Melymuka, Kathleen. "Ford's Driving Force." *Computerworld*, August 30, 1999.

26. Mische, Michael. "Transnational Architecture: A Reengineering Approach." *Information Systems Management*, Winter 1995.

27. Morgan, Cynthia. "ASPs Speak the Corporate Language." *Computerworld*, October 25, 1999.

28. Palvia, Prashant; Shailendra Palvia; and Edward Roche, eds. *Global Information Technology and Systems Management.* Marietta, GA: Ivy League Publishing, 1996.

29. Neilson, Gary; Bruce Pasternack; and Albert Visco. "Up the E-Organization! A Seven-Dimensional Model of the Centerless Enterprise." *Strategy & Business*, First Quarter 2000.

30. Radcliff, Deborah. "Playing by Europe's Rules." *Computerworld*, July 9, 2001.

31. Songini, Marc. "PeopleSoft Project Ends Up in Court." *Computerworld*, September 10, 2001.

32. Thibodeau, Patrick. "Europe and U.S. Agree on Data Rules." *Computerworld*, March 20, 2000.

33. Taggart, Stewart. "Censor Census." *Business 2.0*, March 2000.

34. Vander Weyer, Martin. "The World Debates." *Strategy & Business*, First Quarter 2000.

35. Vitalari, Nicholas, and James Wetherbe. "Emerging Best Practices in Global Systems Development." In *Global Information Technology and Systems Management*, ed. Prashant Palvia et al. Marietta, GA: Ivy League Publishing, 1996.

36. West, Lawrence, and Walter Bogumil. "Immigration and the Global IT Workforce." *Communications of the ACM*, July 2001.

Chapter 13—Computer Hardware

1. *Computerworld*, *PC Week*, *PC Magazine*, and *PC World* are just a few examples of many good magazines for current information on computer systems hardware and its use in end user and enterprise applications.

2. The World Wide Web sites of computer manufacturers such as Apple Computer, Dell Computer, Gateway, IBM, Hewlett-Packard, Compaq, and Sun Microsystems are good sources of information on computer hardware developments.

3. Alexander, Steve. "Speech Recognition." *Computerworld*, November 8, 1999.

4. Collette, Stacy. "Thin Client Devices Shipments Soar." *Computerworld*, September 20, 1999.

5. "Computing in the New Millenium." In Technology Buyers Guide, *Fortune*, Winter 2000.

6. Crothers, Brooke. "IBM Wins Big on Supercomputer Deal." CNETNews.com, April 28, 1999.

7. DeJesus, Edmund. "Building PCs for the Enterprise." *Computerworld*, May 7, 2001.

8. "Desktop Power." In Technology Buyer's Guide, *Fortune*, Winter 1999.

9. Guyon, Janet. "Smart Plastic." *Fortune*, October 13, 1997.

10. "Hardware." In Technology Buyer's Guide, *Fortune*, Winter 1999.

11. Joch, Alan. "Fewer Servers, Better Service." *Computerworld*, June 4, 2001.

12. Kennedy, Ken, and others. "A Nationwide Parallel Computing Environment." *Communications of the ACM*, November 1997.

13. Messerschmitt, David. *Networked Applications: A Guide to the New Computing Infrastructure.* San Francisco: Morgan Kaufmann Publishers, 1999.

14. Morgan, Cynthia. "Speech Recognition." *Computerworld*, September 27, 1998.

15. Ouellette, Tim. "Goodbye to the Glass House." *Computerworld*, May 26, 1997.

16. Ouellette, Tim. "Tape Storage Put to New Enterprise Uses." *Computerworld*, November 10, 1997.

17. Simpson, David. "The Datamation 100." *Datamation*, July 1997.

18. San Diego Supercomputer Center (SDSC), Resources. "Blue Horizon: NPACI Teraflops IBM SP." www.sdsc.edu, October 17, 2001.

Chapter 14—Computer Software

1. Examples of many good magazines for current information and reviews of computer software for business applications can be found at ZD Net, the website for ZD Publications (www.zdnet.com), including *PC Magazine*, *PC Week*, *PC Computing*, *Macworld*, *Inter@ctive Week*, and *Computer Shopper*.

2. The World Wide Web sites of computer manufacturers and software companies like Microsoft, Sun Microsystems, Lotus, IBM, Apple Computer, Oracle, and Netscape Communications are good sources of information on computer software developments.

3. Hamm, Steve; Peter Burrows; and Andy Reinhardt. "Is Windows Ready to Run E-Business?" *Business Week*, January 24, 2000.

4. Jacobsen, Ivar; Maria Ericcson; and Ageneta Jacobsen. *The Object Advantage: Business Process Reengineering with Object Technology*. New York: ACM Press, 1995.

5. Johnson, Amy Helen. "XML Xtends Its Reach." *Computerworld*, October 18, 1999.

6. Mearian, Lucas. "Fidelity Makes Big XML Conversion." *Computerworld*, October 1, 2001.

7. Nance, Barry. "Linux in a 3-Piece Suit?" *Computerworld*, September 6, 1999.

8. Satran, Dick. "Sun's Shooting Star." *Business 2.0*, February 2000.

9. Schlender, Brent. "Steve Jobs' Apple Gets Way Cooler." *Fortune*, January 24, 2000.

10. "Suite Deals." In Technology Buyer's Guide, *Fortune*, Winter 2000.

11. Udell, John. "Java: The Actions on the Server." *Computerworld*, July 5, 1999.

12. Thomas, Owen. "Websites Made Easier." *eCompany*, March 2001.

Accounting Information Systems Information systems that record and report business transactions, the flow of funds through an organization, and produce financial statements. These provide information for the planning and control of business operations, as well as for legal and historical record-keeping.

Ad Hoc Inquiries Unique, unscheduled, situation-specific information requests.

Ada A programming language named after Augusta Ada Byron, considered the world's first computer programmer. Developed for the U.S. Department of Defense as a standard high-order language.

Agile Competition The ability of a company to profitably operate in a competitive environment of continual and unpredictable changes in customer preferences, market conditions, and business opportunities.

Algorithm A set of well-defined rules or processes for the solution of a problem in a finite number of steps.

Analog Computer A computer that operates on data by measuring changes in continuous physical variables such as voltage, resistance, and rotation. Contrast with Digital Computer.

Analytical Database A database of data extracted from operational and external databases to provide data tailored to online analytical processing, decision support, and executive information systems.

Analytical Modeling Interactive use of computer-based mathematical models to explore decision alternatives using what-if analysis, sensitivity analysis, goal-seeking analysis, and optimization analysis.

Applet A small limited-purpose application program, or small independent module of a larger application program.

Application Development See Systems Development.

Application Generator A software package that supports the development of an application through an interactive terminal dialogue, where the programmer/analyst defines screens, reports, computations, and data structures.

Application Portfolio A planning tool used to evaluate present and proposed information systems applications in terms of the amount of revenue or assets invested in information systems that support major business functions and processes.

Applications Architecture A conceptual planning framework in which business applications of information technology are designed as an integrated architecture of enterprise systems that support strategic business initiatives and cross-functional business processes.

Application Server System software that provides a middleware interface between an operating system and the application programs of users.

Application Software Programs that specify the information processing activities required for the completion of specific tasks of computer users. Examples are electronic spreadsheet and word processing programs or inventory or payroll programs.

Application-Specific Programs Application software packages that support specific applications of end users in business, science and engineering, and other areas.

Arithmetic-Logic Unit (ALU) The unit of a computing system containing the circuits that perform arithmetic and logical operations.

Artificial Intelligence (AI) A science and technology whose goal is to develop computers that can think, as well as see, hear, walk, talk, and feel. A major thrust is the development of computer functions normally associated with human intelligence, for example, reasoning, inference, learning, and problem solving.

ASCII: American Standard Code for Information Interchange A standard code used for information interchange among data processing systems, communication systems, and associated equipment.

Assembler A computer program that translates an assembler language into machine language.

Assembler Language A programming language that utilizes symbols to represent operation codes and storage locations.

Asynchronous Involving a sequence of operations without a regular or predictable time relationship. Thus operations do not happen at regular timed intervals, but an operation will begin only after a previous operation is completed. In data transmission, involves the use of start and stop bits with each character to indicate the beginning and end of the character being transmitted. Contrast with Synchronous.

Audit Trail The presence of media and procedures that allow a transaction to be traced through all stages of information processing, beginning with its appearance on a source document and ending with its transformation into information on a final output document.

Automated Teller Machine (ATM) A special-purpose transaction terminal used to provide remote banking services.

Back-End Processor Typically, a smaller general-purpose computer that is dedicated to database processing using a database management system (DBMS). Also called a database machine or server.

Background Processing The automatic execution of lower-priority computer programs when higher-priority programs are not using the resources of the computer system. Contrast with Foreground Processing.

Backward-Chaining An inference process that justifies a proposed conclusion by determining if it will result when rules are applied to the facts in a given situation.

Bandwidth The frequency range of a telecommunications channel, which determines its maximum transmission rate.

The speed and capacity of transmission rates are typically measured in bits per second (BPS). Bandwidth is a function of the telecommunications hardware, software, and media used by the telecommunications channel.

Bar Codes Vertical marks or bars placed on merchandise tags or packaging that can be sensed and read by optical character-reading devices. The width and combination of vertical lines are used to represent data.

Barriers to Entry Technological, financial, or legal requirements that deter firms from entering an industry.

BASIC: Beginner's All-Purpose Symbolic Instruction Code A programming language developed at Dartmouth College designed for programming by end users.

Batch Processing A category of data processing in which data are accumulated into batches and processed periodically. Contrast with Realtime Processing.

Baud A unit of measurement used to specify data transmission speeds. It is a unit of signaling speed equal to the number of discrete conditions or signal events per second. In many data communications applications it represents one bit per second.

Binary Pertaining to a characteristic or property involving a selection, choice, or condition in which there are two possibilities, or pertaining to the number system that utilizes a base of 2.

Biometric Controls Computer-based security methods that measure physical traits and characteristics such as fingerprints, voice prints, retina scans, and so on.

Bit A contraction of "binary digit." It can have the value of either 0 or 1.

Block A grouping of contiguous data records or other data elements that are handled as a unit.

Branch A transfer of control from one instruction to another in a computer program that is not part of the normal sequential execution of the instructions of the program.

Browser See Web Browser.

Buffer Temporary storage used when transmitting data from one device to another to compensate for a difference in rate of flow of data or time of occurrence of events.

Bug A mistake or malfunction.

Bulletin Board System (BBS) A service of online computer networks in which electronic messages, data files, or programs can be stored for other subscribers to read or copy.

Bundling The inclusion of software, maintenance, training, and other products or services in the price of a computer system.

Bus A set of conducting paths for movement of data and instructions that interconnects the various components of the CPU.

Business Ethics An area of philosophy concerned with developing ethical principles and promoting ethical behavior and practices in the accomplishment of business tasks and decision making.

Business Intelligence (BI) A term primarily used in industry that incorporates a range of analytical and decision support applications in business including data mining, decision support systems, knowledge management systems, and online analytical processing.

Business Process Reengineering (BPR) Restructuring and transforming a business process by a fundamental rethinking and redesign to achieve dramatic improvements in cost, quality, speed, and so on.

Byte A sequence of adjacent binary digits operated on as a unit and usually shorter than a computer word. In many computer systems, a byte is a grouping of eight bits that can represent one alphabetic or special character or can be packed with two decimal digits.

C A low-level structured programming language that resembles a machine-independent assembler language.

C++ An object-oriented version of C that is widely used for software package development.

Cache Memory A high-speed temporary storage area in the CPU for storing parts of a program or data during processing.

Capacity Management The use of planning and control methods to forecast and control information processing job loads, hardware and software usage, and other computer system resource requirements.

Case-Based Reasoning Representing knowledge in an expert system's knowledge base in the form of cases, that is, examples of past performance, occurrences, and experiences.

Cathode Ray Tube (CRT) An electronic vacuum tube (television picture tube) that displays the output of a computer system.

CD-ROM An optical disk technology for microcomputers featuring compact disks with a storage capacity of over 500 megabytes.

Cellular Phone Systems A radio communications technology that divides a metropolitan area into a honeycomb of cells to greatly increase the number of frequencies and thus the users that can take advantage of mobile phone service.

Central Processing Unit (CPU) The unit of a computer system that includes the circuits that control the interpretation and execution of instructions. In many computer systems, the CPU includes the arithmetic-logic unit, the control unit, and the primary storage unit.

Change Management Managing the process of implementing major changes in information technology, business processes, organizational structures, and job assignments to reduce the risks and costs of change, and optimize its benefits.

Channel (1) A path along which signals can be sent. (2) A small special-purpose processor that controls the movement of data between the CPU and input/output devices.

Chargeback Systems Methods of allocating costs to end user departments based on the information services rendered and information system resources utilized.

Chat Systems Software that enables two or more users at networked PCs to carry on online, real-time text conversations.

Check Bit A binary check digit; for example, a parity bit.

Check Digit A digit in a data field that is utilized to check for errors or loss of characters in the data field as a result of data transfer operations.

Checkpoint A place in a program where a check or a recording of data for restart purposes is performed.

Chief Information Officer A senior management position that oversees all information technology for a firm concentrating on long-range information system planning and strategy.

Client (1) An end user. (2) The end user's networked microcomputer in client/server networks. (3) The version of a software package designed to run on an end user's networked microcomputer, such as a Web browser client, a groupware client, and so on.

Client/Server Network A computer network where end user workstations (clients) are connected via telecommunications links to network servers and possibly to mainframe superservers.

Clock A device that generates periodic signals utilized to control the timing of a computer. Also, a register whose contents change at regular intervals in such a way as to measure time.

Coaxial Cable A sturdy copper or aluminum wire wrapped with spacers to insulate and protect it. Groups of coaxial cables may also be bundled together in a bigger cable for ease of installation.

COBOL: COmmon Business Oriented Language A widely used business data processing programming language.

Code Computer instructions.

Cognitive Science An area of artificial intelligence that focuses on researching how the human brain works and how humans think and learn, in order to apply such findings to the design of computer-based systems.

Cognitive Styles Basic patterns in how people handle information and confront problems.

Cognitive Theory Theories about how the human brain works and how humans think and learn.

Collaborative Work Management Tools Software that helps people accomplish or manage joint work activities.

Communications Satellite Earth satellites placed in stationary orbits above the equator that serve as relay stations for communications signals transmitted from earth stations.

Competitive Advantage Developing products, services, processes, or capabilities that give a company a superior business position relative to its competitors and other competitive forces.

Competitive Forces A firm must confront (1) rivalry of competitors within its industry, (2) threats of new entrants, (3) threats of substitutes, (4) the bargaining power of customers, and (5) the bargaining power of suppliers.

Competitive Strategies A firm can develop cost leadership, product differentiation, and business innovation strategies to confront its competitive forces.

Compiler A program that translates a high-level programming language into a machine-language program.

Computer A device that has the ability to accept data; internally store and execute a program of instructions; perform mathematical, logical, and manipulative operations on data; and report the results.

Computer-Aided Design (CAD) The use of computers and advanced graphics hardware and software to provide interactive design assistance for engineering and architectural design.

Computer-Aided Engineering (CAE) The use of computers to simulate, analyze, and evaluate models of product designs and production processes developed using computer-aided design methods.

Computer-Aided Manufacturing (CAM) The use of computers to automate the production process and operations of a manufacturing plant. Also called factory automation.

Computer-Aided Planning (CAP) The use of software packages as tools to support the planning process.

Computer-Aided Software Engineering (CASE) Same as Computer-Aided Systems Engineering, but emphasizing the importance of software development.

Computer-Aided Systems Engineering (CASE) Using software packages to accomplish and automate many of the activities of information systems development, including software development or programming.

Computer Application The use of a computer to solve a specific problem or to accomplish a particular job for an end user. For example, common business computer applications include sales order processing, inventory control, and payroll.

Computer-Assisted Instruction (CAI) The use of computers to provide drills, practice exercises, and tutorial sequences to students.

Computer-Based Information System An information system that uses computer hardware and software to perform its information processing activities.

Computer Crime Criminal actions accomplished through the use of computer systems, especially with intent to defraud, destroy, or make unauthorized use of computer system resources.

Computer Ethics A system of principles governing the legal, professional, social, and moral responsibilities of computer specialists and end users.

Computer Generations Major stages in the historical development of computing.

Computer Graphics Using computer-generated images to analyze and interpret data, present information, and do computer-aided design and art.

Computer Industry The industry composed of firms that supply computer hardware, software, and services.

Computer-Integrated Manufacturing (CIM) An overall concept that stresses that the goals of computer use in factory automation should be to simplify, automate, and integrate production processes and other aspects of manufacturing.

Computer Matching Using computers to screen and match data about individual characteristics provided by a variety of computer-based information systems and databases in order to identify individuals for business, government, or other purposes.

Computer Monitoring Using computers to monitor the behavior and productivity of workers on the job and in the workplace.

Computer Program A series of instructions or statements in a form acceptable to a computer, prepared in order to achieve a certain result.

Computer System Computer hardware as a system of input, processing, output, storage, and control components. Thus a computer system consists of input and output devices, primary and secondary storage devices, the central processing unit, the control unit within the CPU, and other peripheral devices.

Computer Terminal Any input/output device connected by telecommunications links to a computer.

Computer Virus or Worm Program code that copies its destructive program routines into the computer systems of anyone who accesses computer systems that have used the program, or anyone who uses copies of data or programs taken from such computers. This spreads the destruction of data and programs among many computer users. Technically, a virus will not run unaided, but must be inserted into another program, while a worm is a distinct program that can run unaided.

Concurrent Processing The generic term for the capability of computers to work on several tasks at the same time, that is, concurrently. This may involve specific capabilities such as overlapped processing, multiprocessing, multiprogramming, multitasking, parallel processing, and so on.

Connectivity The degree to which hardware, software, and databases can be easily linked together in a telecommunications network.

Control (1) The systems component that evaluates feedback to determine whether the system is moving toward the achievement of its goal and then makes any necessary adjustments to the input and processing components of the system to ensure that proper output is produced. (2) A management function that involves observing and measuring organizational performance and environmental activities and modifying the plans and activities of the organization when necessary.

Control Listing A detailed report that describes each transaction occurring during a period.

Control Totals Accumulating totals of data at multiple points in an information system to ensure correct information processing.

Control Unit A subunit of the central processing unit that controls and directs the operations of the computer system. The control unit retrieves computer instructions in proper sequence, interprets each instruction, and then directs the other parts of the computer system in their implementation.

Conversion The process in which the hardware, software, people, network, and data resources of an old information system must be converted to the requirements of a new information system. This usually involves a parallel, phased, pilot, or plunge conversion process from the old to the new system.

Cooperative Processing Information processing that allows the computers in a distributed processing network to share the processing of parts of an end user's application.

Cost/Benefit Analysis Identifying the advantages or benefits and the disadvantages or costs of a proposed solution.

Critical Success Factors A small number of key factors that executives consider critical to the success of the enterprise. These are key areas where successful performance will assure the success of the organization and attainment of its goals.

Cross-Functional Information Systems Information systems that are integrated combinations of business information systems, thus sharing information resources across the functional units of an organization.

Cursor A movable point of light displayed on most video display screens to assist the user in the input of data.

Customer Relationship Management (CRM) A cross-functional e-business application that integrates and automates many customer serving processes in sales, direct marketing, account and order management, and customer service and support.

Cybernetic System A system that uses feedback and control components to achieve a self-regulating capability.

Cylinder An imaginary vertical cylinder consisting of the vertical alignment of tracks on each surface of magnetic disks that are accessed simultaneously by the read/write heads of a disk drive.

Data Facts or observations about physical phenomena or business transactions. More specifically, data are objective measurements of the attributes (characteristics) of entities such as people, places, things, and events.

Data Administration A data resource management function that involves the establishment and enforcement of policies and procedures for managing data as a strategic corporate resource.

Database An integrated collection of logically related data elements. A database consolidates many records previously stored in separate files so that a common pool of data serves many applications.

Database Administration A data resource management function that includes responsibility for developing and maintaining the organization's data dictionary, designing and monitoring the performance of databases, and enforcing standards for database use and security.

Database Administrator A specialist responsible for maintaining standards for the development, maintenance, and security of an organization's databases.

Database Maintenance The activity of keeping a database up-to-date by adding, changing, or deleting data.

Database Management Approach An approach to the storage and processing of data in which independent files are consolidated into a common pool, or database, of records available to different application programs and end users for processing and data retrieval.

Database Management System (DBMS) A set of computer programs that controls the creation, maintenance, and utilization of the databases of an organization.

Database Processing Utilizing a database for data processing activities such as maintenance, information retrieval, or report generation.

Data Center An organizational unit that uses centralized computing resources to perform information processing activities for an organization. Also known as a computer center.

Data Conferencing Users at networked PCs can view, mark up, revise, and save changes to a shared whiteboard of drawings, documents, and other material.

Data Design The design of the logical structure of databases and files to be used by a proposed information system. This produces detailed descriptions of the entities, relationships, data elements, and integrity rules for system files and databases.

Data Dictionary A software module and database containing descriptions and definitions concerning the structure, data elements, interrelationships, and other characteristics of a database.

Data Entry The process of converting data into a form suitable for entry into a computer system. Also called data capture or input preparation.

Data Flow Diagram A graphic diagramming tool that uses a few simple symbols to illustrate the flow of data among external entities, processing activities, and data storage elements.

Data Management Control program functions that provide access to data sets, enforce data storage conventions, and regulate the use of input/output devices.

Data Mining Using special-purpose software to analyze data from a data warehouse to find hidden patterns and trends.

Data Model A conceptual framework that defines the logical relationships among the data elements needed to support a basic business or other process.

Data Modeling A process where the relationships between data elements are identified and defined to develop data models.

Data Planning A corporate planning and analysis function that focuses on data resource management. It includes the responsibility for developing an overall information policy and data architecture for the firm's data resources.

Data Processing The execution of a systematic sequence of operations performed upon data to transform it into information.

Data Resource Management A managerial activity that applies information systems technology and management tools to the task of managing an organization's data resources. Its three major components are database administration, data administration, and data planning.

Data Warehouse An integrated collection of data extracted from operational, historical, and external databases, and cleaned, transformed, and cataloged for retrieval and analysis (*data mining*), to provide business intelligence for business decision making.

Debug To detect, locate, and remove errors from a program or malfunctions from a computer.

Decision Support System (DSS) An information system that utilizes decision models, a database, and a decision maker's own insights in an ad hoc, interactive analytical modeling process to reach a specific decision by a specific decision maker.

Demand Reports and Responses Information provided whenever a manager or end user demands it.

Desktop Publishing The use of microcomputers, laser printers, and page-makeup software to produce a variety of printed materials that were formerly produced only by professional printers.

Desktop Videoconferencing The use of end user computer workstations to conduct two-way interactive video conferences.

Development Centers Systems development consultant groups formed to serve as consultants to the professional programmers and systems analysts of an organization to improve their application development efforts.

Digital Computer A computer that operates on digital data by performing arithmetic and logical operations on the data. Contrast with Analog Computer.

Digitizer A device that is used to convert drawings and other graphic images on paper or other materials into digital data that are entered into a computer system.

Direct Access A method of storage where each storage position has a unique address and can be individually accessed in approximately the same period of time without having to search through other storage positions. Same as Random Access. Contrast with Sequential Access.

Direct Access Storage Device (DASD) A storage device that can directly access data to be stored or retrieved, for example, a magnetic disk unit.

Direct Data Organization A method of data organization in which logical data elements are distributed randomly on or within the physical data medium. For example, logical data records distributed randomly on the surfaces of a magnetic disk file. Also called direct organization.

Direct Input/Output Methods such as keyboard entry, voice input/output, and video displays that allow data to be input into or output from a computer system without the use of machine-readable media.

Disaster Recovery Methods for ensuring that an organization recovers from natural and human-caused disasters that have affected its computer-based operations.

Discussion Forum An online network discussion platform to encourage and manage online text discussions over a period of time among members of special interest groups or project teams.

Distributed Databases The concept of distributing databases or portions of a database at remote sites where the data are most frequently referenced. Sharing of data is made possible through a network that interconnects the distributed databases.

Distributed Processing A form of decentralization of information processing made possible by a network of computers dispersed throughout an organization. Processing of user applications is accomplished by several computers interconnected by a telecommunications network, rather than relying on one large centralized computer facility or on the decentralized operation of several independent computers.

Document (1) A medium on which data have been recorded for human use, such as a report or invoice. (2) In word processing, a generic term for text material such as letters, memos, reports, and so on.

Documentation A collection of documents or information that describes a computer program, information system, or required data processing operations.

Downsizing Moving to smaller computing platforms, such as from mainframe systems to networks of personal computers and servers.

Downtime The time interval during which a device is malfunctioning or inoperative.

DSS Generator A software package for a decision support system that contains modules for database, model, and dialogue management.

Duplex In communications, pertains to a simultaneous two-way independent transmission in both directions.

EBCDIC: Extended Binary Coded Decimal Interchange Code An eight-bit code that is widely used by mainframe computers.

e-Business Decision Support The use of Web-enabled DSS software tools by managers, employees, customers, suppliers, and other business partners of an internetworked e-business enterprise for customer relationship management, supply chain management, and other e-business applications.

e-Business Enterprise A business that uses the Internet, intranets, extranets, and other computer networks to support electronic commerce and other electronic business processes, decision making, and team and workgroup collaboration within the enterprise and among its customers, suppliers, and other business partners.

e-Business Organization An e-business enterprise whose organizational structure and roles have been reengineered to help it become a flexible, agile, customer-focused, value-driven leader in e-commerce.

e-Business Planning The process of developing a company's e-business vision, strategies, and goals, and how they will be supported by the company's information technology architecture and implemented by its e-business application development process.

e-Business Technology Management Managing information technologies in an e-business enterprise by (1) the joint development and implementation of e-business and IT strategies by business and IT executives, (2) managing the research and implementation of new information technologies and the development of e-business applications, and (3) managing IT processes, professionals, and subunits within a company's IT organization and IS function.

Echo Check A method of checking the accuracy of transmission of data in which the received data are returned to the sending device for comparison with the original data.

e-Commerce Marketplaces Internet, intranet, and extranet websites and portals hosted by individual companies, consortiums of organizations, or third-party intermediaries providing electronic catalog, exchange, and auction markets to unite buyers and sellers to accomplish e-commerce transactions.

Economic Feasibility Whether expected cost savings, increased revenue, increased profits, and reductions in required investment exceed the costs of developing and operating a proposed system.

EDI: Electronic Data Interchange The automatic electronic exchange of business documents between the computers of different organizations.

Edit To modify the form or format of data. For example: to insert or delete characters such as page numbers or decimal points.

Edit Report A report that describes errors detected during processing.

EFT: Electronic Funds Transfer The development of banking and payment systems that transfer funds electronically instead of using cash or paper documents such as checks.

Electronic Business (e-Business) The use of Internet technologies to internetwork and empower business processes, electronic commerce, and enterprise communication and collaboration within a company and with its customers, suppliers, and other business stakeholders.

Electronic Commerce (e-Commerce) The buying and selling, marketing and servicing, and delivery and payment of products, services, and information over the Internet, intranets, extranets, and other networks, between an internetworked enterprise and its prospects, customers, suppliers, and other business partners. Includes business-to-consumer (B2C), business-to-business (B2B), and consumer-to-consumer (C2C) e-commerce.

Electronic Communications Tools Software that helps you communicate and collaborate with others by electronically sending messages, documents, and files in data, text, voice, or multimedia over the Internet, intranets, extranets, and other computer networks.

Electronic Conferencing Tools Software that helps networked computer users share information and collaborate while working together on joint assignments, no matter where they are located.

Electronic Data Processing (EDP) The use of electronic computers to process data automatically.

Electronic Document Management An image processing technology in which an electronic document may consist of digitized voice notes and electronic graphics images, as well as digitized images of traditional documents.

Electronic Mail Sending and receiving text messages between networked PCs over telecommunications networks. E-mail can also include data files, software, and multimedia messages and documents as attachments.

Electronic Meeting Systems (EMS) Using a meeting room with networked PCs, a large-screen projector, and EMS software to facilitate communication, collaboration, and group decision making in business meetings.

Electronic Payment Systems Alternative cash or credit payment methods using various electronic technologies to pay for products and services in electronic commerce.

Electronic Spreadsheet Package An application program used as a computerized tool for analysis, planning, and modeling that allows users to enter and manipulate data into an electronic worksheet of rows and columns.

Emulation To imitate one system with another so that the imitating system accepts the same data, executes the same programs, and achieves the same results as the imitated system.

Encryption To scramble data or convert it, prior to transmission, to a secret code that masks the meaning of the data to unauthorized recipients. Similar to enciphering.

End User Anyone who uses an information system or the information it produces.

End User Computing Systems Computer-based information systems that directly support both the operational and managerial applications of end users.

Enterprise Application Integration (EAI) A cross-functional e-business application that integrates front-office applications like customer relationship management with back-office applications like enterprise resource management.

Enterprise Collaboration Systems The use of groupware tools and the Internet, intranets, extranets, and other computer networks to support and enhance communication, coordination, collaboration, and resource sharing among teams and workgroups in an internetworked enterprise.

Enterprise Information Portal A customized and personalized Web-based interface for corporate intranets and extranets that gives qualified users access to a variety of internal and external e-business and e-commerce applications, databases, software tools, and information services.

Enterprise Knowledge Portal An enterprise information portal that serves as a knowledge management system by providing users with access to enterprise knowledge bases.

Enterprise Model A conceptual framework that defines the structures and relationships of business processes and data elements, as well as other planning structures, such as critical success factors, and organizational units.

Enterprise Resource Planning (ERP) Integrated cross-functional software that reengineers manufacturing, distribution, finance, human resources and other basic business processes of a company to improve its efficiency, agility, and profitability.

Entity Relationship Diagram (ERD) A data planning and systems development diagramming tool that models the relationships among the entities in a business process.

Entropy The tendency of a system to lose a relatively stable state of equilibrium.

Ergonomics The science and technology emphasizing the safety, comfort, and ease of use of human-operated machines such as computers. The goal of ergonomics is to produce systems that are user-friendly: safe, comfortable, and easy to use. Ergonomics is also called human factors engineering.

Exception Reports Reports produced only when exceptional conditions occur, or reports produced periodically that contain information only about exceptional conditions.

Executive Information Systems (EIS) An information system that provides strategic information tailored to the needs of executives and other decision makers.

Executive Support System (ESS) An executive information system with additional capabilities, including data analysis, decision support, electronic mail, and personal productivity tools.

Expert System (ES) A computer-based information system that uses its knowledge about a specific complex application area to act as an expert consultant to users. The system consists of a knowledge base and software modules that perform inferences on the knowledge and communicate answers to a user's questions.

Extranet A network that links selected resources of a company with its customers, suppliers, and other business partners, using the Internet or private networks to link the organizations' intranets.

Facilities Management The use of an external service organization to operate and manage the information processing facilities of an organization.

Fault Tolerant Systems Computers that have multiple central processors, peripherals, and system software and that are able to continue operations even if there is a major hardware or software failure.

Faxing (Facsimile) Transmitting and receiving images of documents over the telephone or computer networks using PCs or fax machines.

Feasibility Study A preliminary study that investigates the information needs of end users and the objectives, constraints, basic resource requirements, cost/benefits, and feasibility of proposed projects.

Feedback (1) Data or information concerning the components and operations of a system. (2) The use of part of the output of a system as input to the system.

Fiber Optics The technology that uses cables consisting of very thin filaments of glass fibers that can conduct the light generated by lasers for high-speed telecommunications.

Field A data element that consists of a grouping of characters that describe a particular attribute of an entity. For example: the name field or salary field of an employee.

Fifth Generation The next generation of computers. Major advances in parallel processing, user interfaces, and artificial intelligence may provide computers that will be able to see, hear, talk, and think.

File A collection of related data records treated as a unit. Sometimes called a data set.

File Management Controlling the creation, deletion, access, and use of files of data and programs.

Financial Management Systems Information systems that support financial managers in the financing of a business and the allocation and control of financial resources. These include cash and securities management, capital budgeting, financial forecasting, and financial planning.

Firewall Computer Computers, communications processors, and software that protect computer networks from intrusion by screening all network traffic and serving as a safe transfer point for access to and from other networks.

Firmware The use of microprogrammed read only memory circuits in place of hard-wired logic circuitry. See also Microprogramming.

Floating Point Pertaining to a number representation system in which each number is represented by two sets of digits. One set represents the significant digits or fixed-point "base" of the number, while the other set of digits represents the "exponent," which indicates the precision of the number.

Floppy Disk A small plastic disk coated with iron oxide that resembles a small phonograph record enclosed in a protective envelope. It is a widely used form of magnetic disk media that provides a direct access storage capability for microcomputer systems.

Flowchart A graphical representation in which symbols are used to represent operations, data, flow, logic, equipment, and so on. A program flowchart illustrates the structure and sequence of operations of a program, while a system flowchart illustrates the components and flows of information systems.

Foreground Processing The automatic execution of the computer programs that have been designed to preempt the use of computing facilities. Contrast with Background Processing.

Format The arrangement of data on a medium.

FORTRAN: FORmula TRANslation A high-level programming language widely utilized to develop computer programs that perform mathematical computations for scientific, engineering, and selected business applications.

Forward Chaining An inference strategy that reaches a conclusion by applying rules to facts to determine if any facts satisfy a rule's conditions in a particular situation.

Fourth-Generation Languages (4GL) Programming languages that are easier to use than high-level languages like BASIC, COBOL, or FORTRAN. They are also known as nonprocedural, natural, or very-high-level languages.

Frame A collection of knowledge about an entity or other concept consisting of a complex package of slots, that is, data values describing the characteristics or attributes of an entity.

Frame-Based Knowledge Knowledge represented in the form of a hierarchy or network of frames.

Front-End Processor Typically a smaller, general-purpose computer that is dedicated to handling data communications control functions in a communications network, thus relieving the host computer of these functions.

Functional Business Systems Information systems within a business organization that support one of the traditional functions of business such as marketing, finance, or production. Functional business systems can be either operations or management information systems.

Functional Requirements The information system capabilities required to meet the information needs of end users. Also called system requirements.

Fuzzy Logic Systems Computer-based systems that can process data that are incomplete or only partially correct, that is, fuzzy data. Such systems can solve unstructured problems with incomplete knowledge, as humans do.

General-Purpose Application Programs Programs that can perform information processing jobs for users from all application areas. For example, word processing programs, electronic spreadsheet programs, and graphics programs can be used by individuals for home, education, business, scientific, and many other purposes.

General-Purpose Computer A computer that is designed to handle a wide variety of problems. Contrast with Special-Purpose Computer.

Generate To produce a machine-language program for performing a specific data processing task based on parameters supplied by a programmer or user.

Genetic Algorithm An application of artificial intelligence software that uses Darwinian (survival of the fittest) randomizing and other functions to simulate an evolutionary process that can yield increasingly better solutions to a problem.

Gigabyte One billion bytes. More accurately, 2 to the 30th power, or 1,073,741,824 in decimal notation.

GIGO A contraction of "Garbage In, Garbage Out," which emphasizes that information systems will produce erroneous and invalid output when provided with erroneous and invalid input data or instructions.

Global Company A business that is driven by a global strategy so that all of its activities are planned and implemented in the context of a whole-world system.

Global e-Business Technology Management Managing information technologies in a global e-business enterprise, amid the cultural, political, and geoeconomic challenges involved in developing e-business/IT strategies, global e-business and e-commerce applications portfolios, Internet-based technology platforms, and global data resource management policies.

Global Information Technology The use of computer-based information systems and telecommunications networks using a variety of information technologies to support global business operations and management.

Globalization Becoming a global enterprise by expanding into global markets, using global production facilities, forming alliances with global partners, and so on.

Goal-Seeking Analysis Making repeated changes to selected variables until a chosen variable reaches a target value.

Graphical User Interface A software interface that relies on icons, bars, buttons, boxes, and other images to initiate computer-based tasks for users.

Graphics Pertaining to symbolic input or output from a computer system, such as lines, curves, and geometric shapes, using video display units or graphics plotters and printers.

Graphics Pen and Tablet A device that allows an end user to draw or write on a pressure-sensitive tablet and have the handwriting or graphics digitized by the computer and accepted as input.

Graphics Software A program that helps users generate graphics displays.

Group Decision Making Decisions made by groups of people coming to an agreement on a particular issue.

Group Decision Support System (GDSS) A decision support system that provides support for decision making by groups of people.

Group Support Systems (GSS) An information system that enhances communication, coordination, collaboration, decision making, and group work activities of teams and workgroups.

Groupware Software to support and enhance the communication, coordination, and collaboration among networked teams and workgroups, including software tools for electronic communications, electronic conferencing, and cooperative work management.

Hacking (1) Obsessive use of a computer. (2) The unauthorized access and use of computer systems.

Handshaking Exchange of predetermined signals when a connection is established between two communications terminals.

Hard Copy A data medium or data record that has a degree of permanence and that can be read by people or machines.

Hardware (1) Machines and media. (2) Physical equipment, as opposed to computer programs or methods of use. (3) Mechanical, magnetic, electrical, electronic, or optical devices. Contrast with Software.

Hash Total The sum of numbers in a data field that are not normally added, such as account numbers or other identification numbers. It is utilized as a control total, especially during input/output operations of batch processing systems.

Header Label A machine-readable record at the beginning of a file containing data for file identification and control.

Heuristic   Pertaining to exploratory methods of problem solving in which solutions are discovered by evaluation of the progress made toward the final result. It is an exploratory trial-and-error approach guided by rules of thumb. Opposite of algorithmic.

Hierarchical Data Structure   A logical data structure in which the relationships between records form a hierarchy or tree structure. The relationships among records are one to many, since each data element is related only to one element above it.

High-Level Language   A programming language that utilizes macro instructions and statements that closely resemble human language or mathematical notation to describe the problem to be solved or the procedure to be used. Also called a compiler language.

Homeostasis   A relatively stable state of equilibrium of a system.

Host Computer   Typically a larger central computer that performs the major data processing tasks in a computer network.

Human Factors   Hardware and software capabilities that can affect the comfort, safety, ease of use, and user customization of computer-based information systems.

Human Information Processing   A conceptual framework about the human cognitive process that uses an information processing context to explain how humans capture, process, and use information.

Human Resource Information Systems (HRIS)   Information systems that support human resource management activities such as recruitment, selection and hiring, job placement and performance appraisals, and training and development.

Hybrid AI Systems   Systems that integrate several AI technologies, such as expert systems and neural networks.

Hypermedia   Documents containing multiple forms of media, including text, graphics, video, and sound, that can be interactively searched, like Hypertext.

Hypertext   Text in electronic form that has been indexed and linked (hyperlinks) by software in a variety of ways so that it can be randomly and interactively searched by a user.

Hypertext Markup Language (HTML)   A popular page description language for creating hypertext and hypermedia documents for World Wide Web and intranet websites.

Icon   A small figure on a video display that looks like a familiar office or other device such as a file folder (for storing a file) or a wastebasket (for deleting a file).

Image Processing   A computer-based technology that allows end users to electronically capture, store, process, and retrieve images that may include numeric data, text, handwriting, graphics, documents, and photographs. Image processing makes heavy use of optical scanning and optical disk technologies.

Impact Printers   Printers that form images on paper through the pressing of a printing element and an inked ribbon or roller against the face of a sheet of paper.

Index   An ordered reference list of the contents of a file or document together with keys or reference notations for identification or location of those contents.

Index Sequential   A method of data organization in which records are organized in sequential order and also referenced by an index. When utilized with direct access file devices, it is known as index sequential access method, or ISAM.

Inference Engine   The software component of an expert system, which processes the rules and facts related to a specific problem and makes associations and inferences resulting in recommended courses of action.

Infomediaries   Third-party market-maker companies who serve as intermediaries to bring buyers and sellers together by developing and hosting electronic catalog, exchange, and auction markets to accomplish e-commerce transactions.

Information   Information is data placed in a meaningful and useful context for an end user.

Information Appliance   Small Web-enabled microcomputer devices with specialized functions, such as hand-held PDAs, TV set-top boxes, game consoles, cellular and PCS phones, wired telephone appliances, and other Web-enabled home appliances.

Information Architecture   A conceptual framework that defines the basic structure, content, and relationships of the organizational databases that provide the data needed to support the basic business processes of an organization.

Information Center   A support facility for the end users of an organization. It allows users to learn to develop their own application programs and to accomplish their own information processing tasks. End users are provided with hardware support, software support, and people support (trained user consultants).

Information Float   The time when a document is in transit between the sender and receiver, and thus unavailable for any action or response.

Information Processing   A concept that covers both the traditional concept of processing numeric and alphabetic data, and the processing of text, images, and voices. It emphasizes that the production of information products for users should be the focus of processing activities.

Information Quality   The degree to which information has content, form, and time characteristics that give it value to specific end users.

Information Resource Management (IRM)   A management concept that views data, information, and computer resources (computer hardware, software, networks, and personnel) as valuable organizational resources that should be efficiently, economically, and effectively managed for the benefit of the entire organization.

Information Retrieval   The methods and procedures for recovering specific information from stored data.

Information Superhighway   An advanced high-speed Internet-like network that connects individuals, households, businesses, government agencies, libraries, schools, universities, and other institutions with interactive voice, video, data, and multimedia communications.

Information System   (1) A set of people, procedures, and resources that collects, transforms, and disseminates information in an organization. (2) A system that accepts data resources as input and processes them into information products as output.

Information System Model   A conceptual framework that views an information system as a system that uses the resources of hardware (machines and media), software (programs and procedures), people (users and specialists), and networks (communications media and network support) to perform input, processing, output, storage, and control activities that transform data resources (databases and knowledge bases) into information products.

Information Systems Development   See Systems Development.

Information System Specialist   A person whose occupation is related to the providing of information system services. For example: a systems analyst, programmer, or computer operator.

Information Technology (IT)   Hardware, software, telecommunications, database management, and other information processing technologies used in computer-based information systems.

Information Technology Architecture   A conceptual blueprint that specifies the components and interrelationships of a company's technology infrastructure, data resources, applications architecture, and IT organization.

Information Theory   The branch of learning concerned with the likelihood of accurate transmission or communication of messages subject to transmission failure, distortion, and noise.

Input   Pertaining to a device, process, or channel involved in the insertion of data into a data processing system. Opposite of Output.

Input/Output (I/O)   Pertaining to either input or output, or both.

Input/Output Interface Hardware   Devices such as I/O ports, I/O buses, buffers, channels, and input/output control units, which assist the CPU in its input/output assignments. These devices make it possible for modern computer systems to perform input, output, and processing functions simultaneously.

Inquiry Processing   Computer processing that supports the real-time interrogation of online files and databases by end users.

Instruction   A grouping of characters that specifies the computer operation to be performed.

Intangible Benefits and Costs   The nonquantifiable benefits and costs of a proposed solution or system.

Integrated Circuit   A complex microelectronic circuit consisting of interconnected circuit elements that cannot be disassembled because they are placed on or within a "continuous substrate" such as a silicon chip.

Integrated Packages   Software that combines the ability to do several general-purpose applications (such as word processing, electronic spreadsheet, and graphics) into one program.

Intelligent Agent   A special-purpose knowledge-based system that serves as a software surrogate to accomplish specific tasks for end users.

Intelligent Terminal   A terminal with the capabilities of a microcomputer that can thus perform many data processing and other functions without accessing a larger computer.

Interactive Marketing   A dynamic collaborative process of creating, purchasing, and improving products and services that builds close relationships between a business and its customers, using a variety of services on the Internet, intranets, and extranets.

Interactive Processing   A type of real-time processing in which users can interact with a computer on a real-time basis.

Interactive Video   Computer-based systems that integrate image processing with text, audio, and video processing technologies, which makes interactive multimedia presentations possible.

Interface   A shared boundary, such as the boundary between two systems. For example, the boundary between a computer and its peripheral devices.

Internet   The Internet is a rapidly growing computer network of millions of business, educational, and governmental networks connecting hundreds of millions of computers and their users in over 200 countries.

Internetwork Processor   Communications processors used by local area networks to interconnect them with other local area and wide area networks. Examples include switches, routers, hubs, and gateways.

Internetworks   Interconnected local area and wide area networks.

Interoperability   Being able to accomplish end user applications using different types of computer systems, operating systems, and application software, interconnected by different types of local and wide area networks.

Interorganizational Information Systems   Information systems that interconnect an organization with other organizations, such as a business and its customers and suppliers.

Interpreter   A computer program that translates and executes each source language statement before translating and executing the next one.

Interrupt   A condition that causes an interruption in a processing operation during which another task is performed. At the conclusion of this new assignment, control may be transferred back to the point where the original processing operation was interrupted or to other tasks with a higher priority.

Intranet   An Internet-like network within an organization. Web browser software provides easy access to internal websites established by business units, teams, and individuals, and other network resources and applications.

Inverted File   A file that references entities by their attributes.

IT Architecture   A conceptual design for the implementation of information technology in an organization, including its hardware, software, and network technology platforms, data resources, application portfolio, and IS organization.

Iterative   Pertaining to the repeated execution of a series of steps.

Java   An object-oriented programming language designed for programming real-time, interactive, Web-based applications in the form of applets for use on clients and servers on the Internet, intranets, and extranets.

Job   A specified group of tasks prescribed as a unit of work for a computer.

Job Control Language (JCL)   A language for communicating with the operating system of a computer to identify a job and describe its requirements.

Joystick   A small lever set in a box used to move the cursor on the computer's display screen.

K An abbreviation for the prefix kilo-, which is 1,000 in decimal notation. When referring to storage capacity it is equivalent to 2 to the 10th power, or 1,024 in decimal notation.

Key One or more fields within a data record that are used to identify it or control its use.

Keyboarding Using the keyboard of a microcomputer or computer terminal.

Knowledge Base A computer-accessible collection of knowledge about a subject in a variety of forms, such as facts and rules of inference, frames, and objects.

Knowledge-Based Information System An information system that adds a knowledge base to the database and other components found in other types of computer-based information systems.

Knowledge Engineer A specialist who works with experts to capture the knowledge they possess in order to develop a knowledge base for expert systems and other knowledge-based systems.

Knowledge Management Organizing and sharing the diverse forms of business information created within an organization. Includes managing project and enterprise document libraries, discussion databases, intranet website databases, and other types of knowledge bases.

Knowledge Workers People whose primary work activities include creating, using, and distributing information.

Language Translator Program A program that converts the programming language instructions in a computer program into machine language code. Major types include assemblers, compilers, and interpreters.

Large-Scale Integration (LSI) A method of constructing electronic circuits in which thousands of circuits can be placed on a single semiconductor chip.

Legacy Systems The older, traditional mainframe-based business information systems of an organization.

Light Pen A photoelectronic device that allows data to be entered or altered on the face of a video display terminal.

Liquid Crystal Displays (LCDs) Electronic visual displays that form characters by applying an electrical charge to selected silicon crystals.

List Organization A method of data organization that uses indexes and pointers to allow for nonsequential retrieval.

List Processing A method of processing data in the form of lists.

Local Area Network (LAN) A communications network that typically connects computers, terminals, and other computerized devices within a limited physical area such as an office, building, manufacturing plant, or other work site.

Locking in Customers and Suppliers Building valuable relationships with customers and suppliers that deter them from abandoning a firm for its competitors or intimidating it into accepting less-profitable relationships.

Logical Data Elements Data elements that are independent of the physical data media on which they are recorded.

Logical System Design Developing general specifications for how basic information systems activities can meet end user requirements.

Loop A sequence of instructions in a computer program that is executed repeatedly until a terminal condition prevails.

Machine Cycle The timing of a basic CPU operation as determined by a fixed number of electrical pulses emitted by the CPU's timing circuitry or internal clock.

Machine Language A programming language where instructions are expressed in the binary code of the computer.

Macro Instruction An instruction in a source language that is equivalent to a specified sequence of machine instructions.

Magnetic Disk A flat circular plate with a magnetic surface on which data can be stored by selective magnetization of portions of the curved surface.

Magnetic Ink An ink that contains particles of iron oxide that can be magnetized and detected by magnetic sensors.

Magnetic Ink Character Recognition (MICR) The machine recognition of characters printed with magnetic ink. Primarily used for check processing by the banking industry.

Magnetic Tape A plastic tape with a magnetic surface on which data can be stored by selective magnetization of portions of the surface.

Mag Stripe Card A plastic wallet-size card with a strip of magnetic tape on one surface; widely used for credit/debit cards.

Mainframe A larger-size computer system, typically with a separate central processing unit, as distinguished from microcomputer and minicomputer systems.

Management Information System (MIS) A management support system that produces prespecified reports, displays, and responses on a periodic, exception, demand, or push reporting basis.

Management Support System (MSS) An information system that provides information to support managerial decision making. More specifically, an information-reporting system, executive information system, or decision support system.

Managerial End User A manager, entrepreneur, or managerial-level professional who personally uses information systems. Also, the manager of the department or other organizational unit that relies on information systems.

Managerial Roles Management as the performance of a variety of interpersonal, information, and decision roles.

Manual Data Processing Data processing that requires continual human operation and intervention and that utilizes simple data processing tools such as paper forms, pencils, and filing cabinets.

Manufacturing Information Systems Information systems that support the planning, control, and accomplishment of manufacturing processes. This includes concepts such as computer-integrated manufacturing (CIM) and technologies such as computer-aided manufacturing (CAM) or computer-aided design (CAD).

Marketing Information Systems Information systems that support the planning, control, and transaction processing required for the accomplishment of marketing activities, such as sales management, advertising, and promotion.

Mass Storage Secondary storage devices with extra-large storage capacities such as magnetic or optical disks.

Master File A data file containing relatively permanent information that is utilized as an authoritative reference and is usually updated periodically. Contrast with Transaction File.

Mathematical Model A mathematical representation of a process, device, or concept.

Media All tangible objects on which data are recorded.

Megabyte One million bytes. More accurately, 2 to the 20th power, or 1,048,576 in decimal notation.

Memory Same as Primary Storage.

Menu A displayed list of items (usually the names of alternative applications, files, or activities) from which an end user makes a selection.

Menu Driven A characteristic of interactive computing systems that provides menu displays and operator prompting to assist an end user in performing a particular job.

Metadata Data about data; data describing the structure, data elements, interrelationships, and other characteristics of a database.

Microcomputer A very small computer, ranging in size from a "computer on a chip" to hand-held, laptop, and desktop units, and servers.

Micrographics The use of microfilm, microfiche, and other microforms to record data in greatly reduced form.

Microprocessor A microcomputer central processing unit (CPU) on a chip. Without input/output or primary storage capabilities in most types.

Microprogram A small set of elementary control instructions called microinstructions or microcode.

Microprogramming The use of special software (microprograms) to perform the functions of special hardware (electronic control circuitry). Microprograms stored in a read-only storage module of the control unit interpret the machine language instructions of a computer program and decode them into elementary microinstructions, which are then executed.

Microsecond A millionth of a second.

Middleware Software that helps diverse networked computer systems work together, thus promoting their interoperability.

Midrange Computer A computer category between microcomputers and mainframes. Examples include minicomputers, network servers, and technical workstations.

Millisecond A thousandth of a second.

Minicomputer A type of midrange computer.

Model Base An organized software collection of conceptual, mathematical, and logical models that express business relationships, computational routines, or analytical techniques.

Modem (MOdulator-DEModulator) A device that converts the digital signals from input/output devices into appropriate frequencies at a transmission terminal and converts them back into digital signals at a receiving terminal.

Monitor Software or hardware that observes, supervises, controls, or verifies the operations of a system.

Mouse A small device that is electronically connected to a computer and is moved by hand on a flat surface in order to move the cursor on a video screen in the same direction. Buttons on the mouse allow users to issue commands and make responses or selections.

Multidimensional Structure A database model that uses multidimensional structures (such as cubes or cubes within cubes) to store data and relationships between data.

Multimedia Presentations Providing information using a variety of media, including text and graphics displays, voice and other audio, photographs, and video segments.

Multiplex To interleave or simultaneously transmit two or more messages on a single channel.

Multiplexer An electronic device that allows a single communications channel to carry simultaneous data transmissions from many terminals.

Multiprocessing Pertaining to the simultaneous execution of two or more instructions by a computer or computer network.

Multiprocessor Computer Systems Computer systems that use a multiprocessor architecture in the design of their central processing units. This includes the use of support microprocessors and multiple instruction processors, including parallel processor designs.

Multiprogramming Pertaining to the concurrent execution of two or more programs by a computer by interleaving their execution.

Multitasking The concurrent use of the same computer to accomplish several different information processing tasks. Each task may require the use of a different program, or the concurrent use of the same copy of a program by several users.

Nanosecond One billionth of a second.

Natural Language A programming language that is very close to human language. Also called very-high-level language.

Network An interconnected system of computers, terminals, and communications channels and devices.

Network Architecture A master plan designed to promote an open, simple, flexible, and efficient telecommunications environment through the use of standard protocols, standard communications hardware and software interfaces, and the design of a standard multilevel telecommunications interface between end users and computer systems.

Network Computer A low-cost networked microcomputer with no or minimal disk storage, which depends on Internet or intranet servers for its operating system and Web browser, Java-enabled application software, and data access and storage.

Network Computing A network-centric view of computing in which "the network is the computer," that is, the view that computer networks are the central computing resource of any computing environment.

Network Data Structure A logical data structure that allows many-to-many relationships among data records. It allows entry into a database at multiple points, because any data element or record can be related to many other data elements.

Neural Networks Computer processors or software whose architecture is based on the human brain's meshlike neuron structure. Neural networks can process many pieces of information simultaneously and can learn to recognize patterns and programs themselves to solve related problems on their own.

Node A terminal point in a communications network.

Nonprocedural Languages Programming languages that allow users and professional programmers to specify the results they want without specifying how to solve the problem.

Numerical Control Automatic control of a machine process by a computer that makes use of numerical data, generally introduced as the operation is in process. Also called machine control.

Object A data element that includes both data and the methods or processes that act on those data.

Object-Based Knowledge Knowledge represented as a network of objects.

Object-Oriented Language An object-oriented programming (OOP) language used to develop programs that create and use objects to perform information processing tasks.

Object Program A compiled or assembled program composed of executable machine instructions. Contrast with Source Program.

OEM: Original Equipment Manufacturer A firm that manufactures and sells computers by assembling components produced by other hardware manufacturers.

Office Automation (OA) The use of computer-based information systems that collect, process, store, and transmit electronic messages, documents, and other forms of office communications among individuals, workgroups, and organizations.

Offline Pertaining to equipment or devices not under control of the central processing unit.

Online Pertaining to equipment or devices under control of the central processing unit.

Online Analytical Processing (OLAP) A capability of some management, decision support, and executive information systems that supports interactive examination and manipulation of large amounts of data from many perspectives.

Online Transaction Processing (OLTP) A real-time transaction processing system.

Open Systems Information systems that use common standards for hardware, software, applications, and networking to create a computing environment that allows easy access by end users and their networked computer systems.

Operand That which is operated upon. That part of a computer instruction that is identified by the address part of the instruction.

Operating Environment Software packages or modules that add a graphics-based interface between end users, the operating system, and their application programs, and that may also provide a multitasking capability.

Operating System The main control program of a computer system. It is a system of programs that controls the execution of computer programs and may provide scheduling, debugging, input/output control, system accounting, compilation, storage assignment, data management, and related services.

Operation Code A code that represents specific operations to be performed upon the operands in a computer instruction.

Operational Feasibility The willingness and ability of management, employees, customers, and suppliers to operate, use, and support a proposed system.

Operations Support System (OSS) An information system that collects, processes, and stores data generated by the operations systems of an organization and produces data and information for input into a management information system or for the control of an operations system.

Operations System A basic subsystem of the business firm that constitutes its input, processing, and output components. Also called a physical system.

Optical Character Recognition (OCR) The machine identification of printed characters through the use of light-sensitive devices.

Optical Disks A secondary storage medium using CD (compact disk) and DVD (digital versatile disk) technologies to read tiny spots on plastic disks. The disks are currently capable of storing billions of characters of information.

Optical Scanner A device that optically scans characters or images and generates their digital representations.

Optimization Analysis Finding an optimum value for selected variables in a mathematical model, given certain constraints.

Organizational Feasibility How well a proposed information system supports the objectives of an organization's strategic plan for information systems.

Output Pertaining to a device, process, or channel involved with the transfer of data or information out of an information processing system. Opposite of Input.

Outsourcing Turning over all or part of an organization's information systems operation to outside contractors, known as systems integrators or service providers.

Packet A group of data and control information in a specified format that is transmitted as an entity.

Packet Switching A data transmission process that transmits addressed packets such that a channel is occupied only for the duration of transmission of the packet.

Page A segment of a program or data, usually of fixed length.

Paging A process that automatically and continually transfers pages of programs and data between primary storage and direct access storage devices. It provides computers with multiprogramming and virtual memory capabilities.

Parallel Processing Executing many instructions at the same time, that is, in parallel. Performed by advanced computers using many instruction processors organized in clusters or networks.

Parity Bit A check bit appended to an array of binary digits to make the sum of all the binary digits, including the check bit, always odd or always even.

Pascal A high-level, general-purpose, structured programming language named after Blaise Pascal. It was developed by Niklaus Wirth of Zurich in 1968.

Pattern Recognition The identification of shapes, forms, or configurations by automatic means.

PCM: Plug-Compatible Manufacturer A firm that manufactures computer equipment that can be plugged into existing computer systems without requiring additional hardware or software interfaces.

Peer-to-Peer Network (P2P) A computing environment where end user computers connect, communicate, and collaborate directly with each other via the Internet or other telecommunications network links.

Pen-Based Computers Tablet-style microcomputers that recognize handwriting and hand drawing done by a pen-shaped device on their pressure-sensitive display screens.

Performance Monitor A software package that monitors the processing of computer system jobs, helps develop a planned schedule of computer operations that can optimize computer system performance, and produces detailed statistics that are used for computer system capacity planning and control.

Periodic Reports Providing information to managers using a prespecified format designed to provide information on a regularly scheduled basis.

Peripheral Devices In a computer system, any unit of equipment, distinct from the central processing unit, that provides the system with input, output, or storage capabilities.

Personal Digital Assistant (PDA) Hand-held microcomputer devices that enable you to manage information such as appointments, to-do lists, and sales contacts, send and receive e-mail, access the Web, and exchange such information with your desktop PC or network server.

Personal Information Manager (PIM) A software package that helps end users store, organize, and retrieve text and numerical data in the form of notes, lists, memos, and a variety of other forms.

Physical System Design Design of the user interface methods and products, database structures, and processing and control procedures for a proposed information system, including hardware, software, and personnel specifications.

Picosecond One trillionth of a second.

Plasma Display Output devices that generate a visual display with electrically charged particles of gas trapped between glass plates.

Plotter A hard-copy output device that produces drawings and graphical displays on paper or other materials.

Pointer A data element associated with an index, a record, or other set of data that contains the address of a related record.

Pointing Devices Devices that allow end users to issue commands or make choices by moving a cursor on the display screen.

Pointing Stick A small buttonlike device on a keyboard that moves the cursor on the screen in the direction of the pressure placed upon it.

Point-of-Sale (POS) Terminal A computer terminal used in retail stores that serves the function of a cash register as well as collecting sales data and performing other data processing functions.

Port (1) Electronic circuitry that provides a connection point between the CPU and input/output devices. (2) A connection point for a communications line on a CPU or other front-end device.

Postimplementation Review Monitoring and evaluating the results of an implemented solution or system.

Presentation Graphics Using computer-generated graphics to enhance the information presented in reports and other types of presentations.

Prespecified Reports Reports whose format is specified in advance to provide managers with information periodically, on an exception basis, or on demand.

Private Branch Exchange (PBX) A switching device that serves as an interface between the many telephone lines within a work area and the local telephone company's main telephone lines or trunks. Computerized PBXs can handle the switching of both voice and data.

Procedure-Oriented Language A programming language designed for the convenient expression of procedures used in the solution of a wide class of problems.

Procedures Sets of instructions used by people to complete a task.

Process Control The use of a computer to control an ongoing physical process, such as petrochemical production.

Process Design The design of the programs and procedures needed by a proposed information system, including detailed program specifications and procedures.

Processor A hardware device or software system capable of performing operations upon data.

Program A set of instructions that cause a computer to perform a particular task.

Programmed Decision A decision that can be automated by basing it on a decision rule that outlines the steps to take when confronted with the need for a specific decision.

Programmer A person mainly involved in designing, writing, and testing computer programs.

Programming The design, writing, and testing of a program.

Programming Language A language used to develop the instructions in computer programs.

Programming Tools Software packages or modules that provide editing and diagnostic capabilities and other support facilities to assist the programming process.

Project Management Managing the accomplishment of an information system development project according to a specific project plan, in order that a project is completed on time, and within its budget, and meets its design objectives.

Prompt Messages that assist a user in performing a particular job. This would include error messages, correction suggestions, questions, and other messages that guide an end user.

Protocol A set of rules and procedures for the control of communications in a communications network.

Prototype A working model. In particular, a working model of an information system that includes tentative versions of user input and output, databases and files, control methods, and processing routines.

Prototyping The rapid development and testing of working models, or prototypes, of new information system applications in an interactive, iterative process involving both systems analysts and end users.

Pseudocode An informal design language of structured programming that expresses the processing logic of a program module in ordinary human language phrases.

Pull Marketing Marketing methods that rely on the use of Web browsers by end users to access marketing materials and resources at Internet, intranet, and extranet websites.

Push Marketing Marketing methods that rely on Web broadcasting software to push marketing information and other marketing materials to end users' computers.

Quality Assurance Methods for ensuring that information systems are free from errors and fraud and provide information products of high quality.

Query Language A high-level, humanlike language provided by a database management system that enables users to easily extract data and information from a database.

Queue (1) A waiting line formed by items in a system waiting for service. (2) To arrange in or form a queue.

RAID Redundant array of independent disks. Magnetic disk units that house many interconnected microcomputer hard disk drives, thus providing large, fault-tolerant storage capacities.

Random Access Same as Direct Access. Contrast with Sequential Access.

Random Access Memory (RAM) One of the basic types of semiconductor memory used for temporary storage of data or programs during processing. Each memory position can be directly sensed (read) or changed (write) in the same length of time, irrespective of its location on the storage medium.

Reach and Range Analysis A planning framework that contrasts a firm's ability to use its IT platform to reach its stakeholders, with the range of information products and services that can be provided or shared through IT.

Read Only Memory (ROM) A basic type of semiconductor memory used for permanent storage. Can only be read, not "written," that is, changed. Variations are Programmable Read Only Memory (PROM) and Erasable Programmable Read Only Memory (EPROM).

Real Time Pertaining to the performance of data processing during the actual time a business or physical process transpires, in order that results of the data processing can be used to support the completion of the process.

Real-Time Processing Data processing in which data are processed immediately rather than periodically. Also called online processing. Contrast with Batch Processing.

Record A collection of related data fields treated as a unit.

Reduced Instruction Set Computer (RISC) A CPU architecture that optimizes processing speed by the use of a smaller number of basic machine instructions than traditional CPU designs.

Redundancy In information processing, the repetition of part or all of a message to increase the chance that the correct information will be understood by the recipient.

Register A device capable of storing a specified amount of data such as one word.

Relational Data Structure A logical data structure in which all data elements within the database are viewed as being stored in the form of simple tables. DBMS packages based on the relational model can link data elements from various tables as long as the tables share common data elements.

Remote Access Pertaining to communication with the data processing facility by one or more stations that are distant from that facility.

Remote Job Entry (RJE) Entering jobs into a batch processing system from a remote facility.

Report Generator A feature of database management system packages that allows an end user to quickly specify a report format for the display of information retrieved from a database.

Reprographics Copying and duplicating technology and methods.

Resource Management An operating system function that controls the use of computer system resources such as primary storage, secondary storage, CPU processing time, and input/output devices by other system software and application software packages.

Robotics The technology of building machines (robots) with computer intelligence and humanlike physical capabilities.

Routine An ordered set of instructions that may have some general or frequent use.

RPG: Report Program Generator A problem-oriented language that utilizes a generator to construct programs that produce reports and perform other data processing tasks.

Rule Statements that typically take the form of a premise and a conclusion such as If-Then rules: If (condition), Then (conclusion).

Rule-Based Knowledge Knowledge represented in the form of rules and statements of fact.

Scalability The ability of hardware or software to handle the processing demands of a wide range of end users, transactions, queries, and other information processing requirements.

Scenario Approach A planning approach where managers, employees, and planners create scenarios of what an organization will be like three to five years or more into the future, and identify the role IT can play in those scenarios.

Schema An overall conceptual or logical view of the relationships between the data in a database.

Scientific Method An analytical methodology that involves (1) recognizing phenomena, (2) formulating a hypothesis about the causes or effects of the phenomena, (3) testing the hypothesis through experimentation, (4) evaluating the results of such experiments, and (5) drawing conclusions about the hypothesis.

Secondary Storage Storage that supplements the primary storage of a computer. Synonymous with Auxiliary Storage.

Sector A subdivision of a track on a magnetic disk surface.

Security Codes Passwords, identification codes, account codes, and other codes that limit the access and use of computer-based system resources to authorized users.

Security Management Protecting the accuracy, integrity, and safety of the processes and resources of an internetworked e-business enterprise against computer crime, accidental or malicious destruction, and natural disasters, using security measures such as encryption, fire walls, antivirus software, fault-tolerant computers, and security monitors.

Security Monitor A software package that monitors the use of a computer system and protects its resources from unauthorized use, fraud, and vandalism.

Semiconductor Memory Microelectronic storage circuitry etched on tiny chips of silicon or other semiconducting material. The primary storage of most modern computers consists of microelectronic semiconductor storage chips for random access memory (RAM) and read only memory (ROM).

Semistructured Decisions Decisions involving procedures that can be partially prespecified, but not enough to lead to a definite recommended decision.

Sensitivity Analysis Observing how repeated changes to a single variable affect other variables in a mathematical model.

Sequential Access A sequential method of storing and retrieving data from a file. Contrast with Random Access and Direct Access.

Sequential Data Organization Organizing logical data elements according to a prescribed sequence.

Serial Pertaining to the sequential or consecutive occurrence of two or more related activities in a single device or channel.

Server (1) A computer that supports applications and telecommunications in a network, as well as the sharing of peripheral devices, software, and databases among the workstations in the network. (2) Versions of software for installation on network servers designed to control and support applications on client microcomputers in client/server networks. Examples include multiuser network operating systems and specialized software for running Internet, intranet, and extranet Web applications, such as electronic commerce and enterprise collaboration.

Service Bureau A firm offering computer and data processing services. Also called a computer service center.

Smart Products Industrial and consumer products, with "intelligence" provided by built-in microcomputers or microprocessors that significantly improve the performance and capabilities of such products.

Software Computer programs and procedures concerned with the operation of an information system. Contrast with Hardware.

Software Package A computer program supplied by computer manufacturers, independent software companies, or other computer users. Also known as canned programs, proprietary software, or packaged programs.

Software Piracy Unauthorized copying of software.

Software Suites A combination of individual software packages that share a common graphical user interface and are designed for easy transfer of data between applications.

Solid State Pertaining to devices such as transistors and diodes whose operation depends on the control of electric or magnetic phenomena in solid materials.

Source Data Automation The use of automated methods of data entry that attempt to reduce or eliminate many of the activities, people, and data media required by traditional data entry methods.

Source Document A document that is the original formal record of a transaction, such as a purchase order or sales invoice.

Source Program A computer program written in a language that is subject to a translation process. Contrast with Object Program.

Special-Purpose Computer A computer designed to handle a restricted class of problems. Contrast with General-Purpose Computer.

Speech Recognition Direct conversion of spoken data into electronic form suitable for entry into a computer system. Also called voice data entry.

Spooling Simultaneous peripheral operation online. Storing input data from low-speed devices temporarily on high-speed secondary storage units, which can be quickly accessed by the CPU. Also, writing output data at high speeds onto magnetic tape or disk units from which it can be transferred to slow-speed devices such as a printer.

Stage Analysis A planning process in which the information system needs of an organization are based on an analysis of its current stage in the growth cycle of the organization and its use of information systems technology.

Standards Measures of performance developed to evaluate the progress of a system toward its objectives.

Storage Pertaining to a device into which data can be entered, in which they can be held, and from which they can be retrieved at a later time. Same as Memory.

Strategic Information Systems Information systems that provide a firm with competitive products and services that give it a strategic advantage over its competitors in the marketplace. Also, information systems that promote business innovation, improve business processes, and build strategic information resources for a firm.

Strategic Opportunities Matrix A planning framework that uses a matrix to help identify opportunities with strategic business potential, as well as a firm's ability to exploit such opportunities with IT.

Structure Chart A design and documentation technique to show the purpose and relationships of the various modules in a program.

Structured Decisions Decisions that are structured by the decision procedures or decision rules developed for them. They involve situations where the procedures to follow when a decision is needed can be specified in advance.

Structured Programming A programming methodology that uses a top-down program design and a limited number of control structures in a program to create highly structured modules of program code.

Structured Query Language (SQL) A query language that is becoming a standard for advanced database management system packages. A query's basic form is SELECT . . . FROM . . . WHERE.

Subroutine A routine that can be part of another program routine.

Subschema   A subset or transformation of the logical view of the database schema that is required by a particular user application program.

Subsystem   A system that is a component of a larger system.

Supercomputer   A special category of large computer systems that are the most powerful available. They are designed to solve massive computational problems.

Superconductor   Materials that can conduct electricity with almost no resistance. This allows the development of extremely fast and small electronic circuits. Formerly only possible at supercold temperatures near absolute zero. Recent developments promise superconducting materials near room temperature.

Supply Chain   The network of business processes and interrelationships among businesses that are needed to build, sell, and deliver a product to its final customer.

Supply Chain Management   Integrating management practices and information technology to optimize information and product flows among the processes and business partners within a supply chain.

Switch   (1) A device or programming technique for making a selection. (2) A computer that controls message switching among the computers and terminals in a telecommunications network.

Switching Costs   The costs in time, money, effort, and inconvenience that it would take a customer or supplier to switch its business to a firm's competitors.

Synchronous   A characteristic in which each event, or the performance of any basic operation, is constrained to start on, and usually to keep in step with, signals from a timing clock. Contrast with Asynchronous.

System   (1) A group of interrelated or interacting elements forming a unified whole. (2) A group of interrelated components working together toward a common goal by accepting inputs and producing outputs in an organized transformation process. (3) An assembly of methods, procedures, or techniques unified by regulated interaction to form an organized whole. (4) An organized collection of people, machines, and methods required to accomplish a set of specific functions.

System Flowchart   A graphic diagramming tool used to show the flow of information processing activities as data are processed by people and devices.

Systems Analysis   (1) Analyzing in detail the components and requirements of a system. (2) Analyzing in detail the information needs of an organization, the characteristics and components of presently utilized information systems, and the functional requirements of proposed information systems.

Systems Approach   A systematic process of problem solving that defines problems and opportunities in a systems context. Data are gathered describing the problem or opportunity, and alternative solutions are identified and evaluated. Then the best solution is selected and implemented, and its success evaluated.

Systems Design   Deciding how a proposed information system will meet the information needs of end users. Includes logical and physical design activities, and user interface, data, and process design activities that produce system specifications that satisfy the system requirements developed in the systems analysis stage.

Systems Development   (1) Conceiving, designing, and implementing a system. (2) Developing information systems by a process of investigation, analysis, design, implementation, and maintenance. Also called the systems development life cycle (SDLC), information systems development, or application development.

Systems Development Tools   Graphical, textual, and computer-aided tools and techniques used to help analyze, design, and document the development of an information system. Typically used to represent (1) the components and flows of a system, (2) the user interface, (3) data attributes and relationships, and (4) detailed system processes.

Systems Implementation   The stage of systems development in which hardware and software are acquired, developed, and installed; the system is tested and documented; people are trained to operate and use the system; and an organization converts to the use of a newly developed system.

Systems Investigation   The screening, selection, and preliminary study of a proposed information system solution to a business problem.

Systems Maintenance   The monitoring, evaluating, and modifying of a system to make desirable or necessary improvements.

System Software   Programs that control and support operations of a computer system. System software includes a variety of programs, such as operating systems, database management systems, communications control programs, service and utility programs, and programming language translators.

System Specifications   The product of the systems design stage. It consists of specifications for the hardware, software, facilities, personnel, databases, and the user interface of a proposed information system.

Systems Thinking   Recognizing systems, subsystems, components of systems, and system interrelationships in a situation. Also known as a systems context or a systemic view of a situation.

System Support Programs   Programs that support the operations, management, and users of a computer system by providing a variety of support services. Examples are system utilities and performance monitors.

Tangible Benefits and Costs   The quantifiable benefits and costs of a proposed solution or system.

Task and Project Management   Managing team and workgroup projects by scheduling, tracking, and charting the completion status of tasks within a project.

Task Management   A basic operating system function that manages the accomplishment of the computing tasks of users by a computer system.

TCP/IP   Transmission control protocol/Internet protocol. A suite of telecommunications network protocols used by the Internet, intranets, and extranets that has become a de facto network architecture standard for many companies.

Technical Feasibility   Whether reliable hardware and software capable of meeting the needs of a proposed system can be acquired or developed by an organization in the required time.

Technology Management The organizational responsibility to identify, introduce, and monitor the assimilation of new information system technologies into organizations.

Telecommunications Pertaining to the transmission of signals over long distances, including not only data communications but also the transmission of images and voices using radio, television, and other communications technologies.

Telecommunications Channel The part of a telecommunications network that connects the message source with the message receiver. It includes the hardware, software, and media used to connect one network location to another for the purpose of transmitting and receiving information.

Telecommunications Control Program A computer program that controls and supports the communications between the computers and terminals in a telecommunications network.

Telecommunications Controller A data communications interface device (frequently a special-purpose mini- or microcomputer) that can control a telecommunications network containing many terminals.

Telecommunications Monitors Computer programs that control and support the communications between the computers and terminals in a telecommunications network.

Telecommunications Processors Internetwork processors such as switches and routers, and other devices such as multiplexers and communications controllers that allow a communications channel to carry simultaneous data transmissions from many terminals. They may also perform error monitoring, diagnostics and correction, modulation-demodulation, data compression, data coding and decoding, message switching, port contention, and buffer storage.

Telecommuting The use of telecommunications to replace commuting to work from one's home.

Teleconferencing The use of video communications to allow business conferences to be held with participants who are scattered across a country, continent, or the world.

Telephone Tag The process that occurs when two people who wish to contact each other by telephone repeatedly miss each other's phone calls.

Teleprocessing Using telecommunications for computer-based information processing.

Terabyte One trillion bytes. More accurately, 2 to the 40th power, or 1,009,511,627,776 in decimal notation.

Text Data Words, phrases, sentences, and paragraphs used in documents and other forms of communication.

Throughput The total amount of useful work performed by a data processing system during a given period of time.

Time Sharing Providing computer services to many users simultaneously while providing rapid responses to each.

Total Quality Management Planning and implementing programs of continuous quality improvement, where quality is defined as meeting or exceeding the requirements and expectations of customers for a product or service.

Touch-Sensitive Screen An input device that accepts data input by the placement of a finger on or close to the CRT screen.

Track The portion of a moving storage medium, such as a drum, tape, or disk, that is accessible to a given reading head position.

Trackball A rollerball device set in a case used to move the cursor on a computer's display screen.

Transaction An event that occurs as part of doing business, such as a sale, purchase, deposit, withdrawal, refund, transfer, payment, and so on.

Transaction Document A document produced as part of a business transaction. For instance: a purchase order, paycheck, sales receipt, or customer invoice.

Transaction File A data file containing relatively transient data to be processed in combination with a master file. Contrast with Master File.

Transaction Processing Cycle A cycle of basic transaction processing activities including data entry, transaction processing, database maintenance, document and report generation, and inquiry processing.

Transaction Processing System (TPS) An information system that processes data arising from the occurrence of business transactions.

Transaction Terminals Terminals used in banks, retail stores, factories, and other work sites that are used to capture transaction data at their point of origin. Examples are point-of-sale (POS) terminals and automated teller machines (ATMs).

Transborder Data Flows (TDF) The flow of business data over telecommunications networks across international borders.

Transform Algorithm Performing an arithmetic computation on a record key and using the result of the calculation as an address for that record. Also known as key transformation or hashing.

Transnational Strategy A management approach in which an organization integrates its global business activities through close cooperation and interdependence among its headquarters, operations, and international subsidiaries, and its use of appropriate global information technologies.

Turnaround Document Output of a computer system (such as customer invoices and statements) that is designed to be returned to the organization as machine-readable input.

Turnaround Time The elapsed time between submission of a job to a computing center and the return of the results.

Turnkey Systems Computer systems where all of the hardware, software, and systems development needed by a user are provided.

Unbundling The separate pricing of hardware, software, and other related services.

Uniform Resource Locator (URL) An access code (such as http://www.sun.com) for identifying and locating hypermedia document files, databases, and other resources at websites and other locations on the Internet, intranets, and extranets.

Universal Product Code (UPC) A standard identification code using bar coding, printed on products that can be read by the optical supermarket scanners of the grocery industry.

Unstructured Decisions   Decisions that must be made in situations where it is not possible to specify in advance most of the decision procedures to follow.

User Friendly   A characteristic of human-operated equipment and systems that makes them safe, comfortable, and easy to use.

User Interface   That part of an operating system or other program that allows users to communicate with it to load programs, access files, and accomplish other computing tasks.

User Interface Design   Designing the interactions between end users and computer systems, including input/output methods and the conversion of data between human-readable and machine-readable forms.

Utility Program   A standard set of routines that assists in the operation of a computer system by performing some frequently required process such as copying, sorting, or merging.

Value-Added Carriers   Third-party vendors who lease telecommunications lines from common carriers and offer a variety of telecommunications services to customers.

Value-Added Resellers (VARs)   Companies that provide industry-specific software for use with the computer systems of selected manufacturers.

Value Chain   Viewing a firm as a series, chain, or network of basic activities that adds value to its products and services and thus adds a margin of value to the firm.

Videoconferencing   Real-time video and audio conferencing (1) among users at networked PCs (desktop videoconferencing), or (2) among participants in conference rooms or auditoriums in different locations (teleconferencing). Videoconferencing can also include whiteboarding and document sharing.

Virtual Communities   Groups of people with similar interests who meet and share ideas on the Internet and online services and develop a feeling of belonging to a community.

Virtual Company   A form of organization that uses telecommunications networks and other information technologies to link the people, assets, and ideas of a variety of business partners, no matter where they may be located, in order to exploit a business opportunity.

Virtual Machine   Pertaining to the simulation of one type of computer system by another computer system.

Virtual Mall   An online multimedia simulation of a shopping mall with many different interlinked retail websites.

Virtual Memory   The use of secondary storage devices as an extension of the primary storage of the computer, thus giving the appearance of a larger main memory than actually exists.

Virtual Private Network   A secure network that uses the Internet as its main backbone network to connect the intranets of a company's different locations, or to establish extranet links between a company and its customers, suppliers, or other business partners.

Virtual Reality   The use of multisensory human/computer interfaces that enable human users to experience computer-simulated objects, entities, spaces, and "worlds" as if they actually existed.

Virtual Storefront   An online multimedia simulation of a retail store shopping experience on the Web.

Virtual Team   A team whose members use the Internet, intranets, extranets, and other networks to communicate, coordinate, and collaborate with each other on tasks and projects, even though they may work in different geographic locations and for different organizations.

VLSI: Very-Large-Scale Integration   Semiconductor chips containing hundreds of thousands of circuits.

Voice Conferencing   Telephone conversations shared among several participants via speaker phones or networked PCs with Internet telephone software.

Voice Mail   Unanswered telephone messages are digitized, stored, and played back to the recipient by a voice messaging computer.

Volatile Memory   Memory (such as electronic semiconductor memory) that loses its contents when electrical power is interrupted.

Wand   A hand-held optical character recognition device used for data entry by many transaction terminals.

Web Browser   A software package that provides the user interface for accessing Internet, intranet, and extranet websites. Browsers are becoming multifunction universal clients for sending and receiving e-mail, downloading files, accessing Java applets, participating in discussion groups, developing Web pages, and other Internet, intranet, and extranet applications.

Web Publishing   Creating, converting, and storing hyperlinked documents and other material on Internet or intranet Web servers so they can easily be shared via Web browsers with teams, workgroups, or the enterprise.

Web Services   A collection of Web and object-oriented technologies for linking Web-based applications running on different hardware, software, database, or network platforms. For example, Web services could link key business functions within the applications a business shares with its customers, suppliers, and business partners.

What-If Analysis   Observing how changes to selected variables affect other variables in a mathematical model.

Whiteboarding   See Data Conferencing.

Wide Area Network (WAN)   A data communications network covering a large geographic area.

Window   One section of a computer's multiple-section display screen, each of which can have a different display.

Wireless LANs   Using radio or infrared transmissions to link devices in a local area network.

Wireless Technologies   Using radio wave, microwave, infrared, and laser technologies to transport digital communications without wires between communications devices. Examples include terrestrial microwave, communications satellites, cellular and PCS phone and pager systems, mobile data radio, and various wireless Internet technologies.

Word   (1) A string of characters considered as a unit. (2) An ordered set of bits (usually larger than a byte) handled as a unit by the central processing unit.

Word Processing The automation of the transformation of ideas and information into a readable form of communication. It involves the use of computers to manipulate text data in order to produce office communications in the form of documents.

Workgroup Computing Members of a networked workgroup may use groupware tools to communicate, coordinate, and collaborate, and to share hardware, software, and databases to accomplish group assignments.

Workstation (1) A computer system designed to support the work of one person. (2) A high-powered computer to support the work of professionals in engineering, science, and other areas that require extensive computing power and graphics capabilities.

World Wide Web (WWW) A global network of multimedia Internet sites for information, education, entertainment, e-business, and e-commerce.

XML (Extensible Markup Language) A Web document content description language that describes the content of Web pages by applying hidden identifying tags or contextual labels to the data in Web documents. By categorizing and classifying Web data this way, XML makes Web content easier to identify, search, analyze, and selectively exchange between computers.

INDEXES

Developing Business/IT Strategies

Security and Ethical Challenges

Developing Business/IT Solutions

Enterprise and Global Management of Information Technology